TO ALL PEOPLES

GO and make disciples of all nations,
baptizing them in the name of the Father and of the Son
and of the Holy Spirit, and
teaching them to obey everything I have commanded you.

And surely I will be with you always,
to the very end of the age.

Matthew 28:19-20

TO ALL PEOPLES

**Missions World Book of
The Christian and Missionary Alliance**

ROBERT L. NIKLAUS

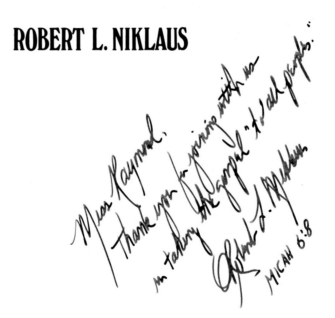

*Miss Raymond,
Thank you for joining with us
in taking the gospel "to all peoples."
Robert L. Niklaus
MICAH 6:8*

✝ **Christian Publications
Camp Hill, Pennsylvania**

All Scripture quotations are from
The New International Version.

ISBN 0-87509-432-5

LOC Catalog Card Number 90-81150

© The Christian and Missionary Alliance
Colorado Springs, Colorado.

Typeset in the United States of America.
Printed in the Republic of Singapore.

FOREWORD

THE UNSUNG HEROES of war are rear-echelon personnel who keep frontline troops supplied with everything from bullets to bandages. These supply soldiers do not get medals for battles won, but were it not for their unglamorous and often thankless duty, there would be no battles, no medals. Neither would there be victories.

The far-flung missionary lines of The Christian and Missionary Alliance also have their supply-line personnel. To some extent they are the unsung heroes of a remarkable advance being achieved by over 1,200 missionaries in fifty-one countries.

Who are these deserving but often unrecognized people?

Pastors and their wives who promote missions in the churches to the point of personal sacrifice. . . .

Professors who by their lives and lessons prepare students for the ministry. . . .

Women in the missionary prayer fellowships who give hours, even days, to pray for missionaries and provide their outfits. . . .

Men who forgo weekends of needed rest to hammer together crates for missionary equipment. . . .

Parents who joyfully release their children for overseas ministry, even though it means loneliness now and hardship later in their sunset years.

Louis L. King

The Alliance is widely recognized and respected for its work overseas. That reputation is well earned, for God has blessed our missionary force with some of the finest minds and noblest spirits to be found anywhere in the ministry. Yet these frontline soldiers are but a reflection of the many worthy people mentioned above, who helped them get where they are.

Our achievements together, however laudable, do not exempt us from further efforts. One of the inexorable pressures of our calling as a missionary people is the incessant cry for more — more workers, more funds, more converts.

This book is not the final record of the worldwide evangelistic work of the C&MA. The full scope of that work is too vast to be compressed into one volume. This book, at best, is but a preliminary word intended to awaken interest, stimulate serious consideration and elicit praise for the truly great things God has done and continues to do.

Therefore let us pause briefly to celebrate in the midst of challenge. The following pages record what God has graciously accomplished through the combined efforts of frontline missionaries and their indispensable support team at home.

Then let us return to the struggle with redoubled efforts, finding cause in our rejoicing to trust God for even greater advance together.

Louis L. King, President (1978–1987)
The Christian and Missionary Alliance

CANADA and the United States share the longest unfortified border in the world, an example of how two great and sovereign nations can live together in peace.

Christian and Missionary Alliance churches on both sides of the border do even better than just getting along without hassles. They work together in a spirit of harmony that pleases God and advances His work throughout the world to an extent neither one could achieve separately.

The Canadian churches opted for autonomy in 1980 not in a spirit of divisiveness, but in a desire to increase their effectiveness in reaching their countrymen in the Dominion. Yet they recognized the wisdom of continuing a cooperative overseas ministry that had worked well for over ninety years.

The joint effort has prospered in every respect. Look at it from any angle and the verdict comes up positive.

Representatives of the twin churches share in every step of the decision-making process, and then the carrying out of those decisions. The Division of Overseas Ministries even prepares for the two governing bodies an identical annual report.

The wisdom of working together overseas as one church

Melvin P. Sylvester

goes well beyond the logic of economics, logistics or convenience.

We share a message that is the same in detail both large and small. Our sons and daughters work shoulder to shoulder, often with total indifference to nationality—except, perhaps, playful spoofs at field conference time. And, on occasion, our workers have experienced together that ultimate sacrifice of life itself for the greater glory of God.

Our Canadian and American churches thus fall heir to a common heritage. More importantly, we anticipate together a future that will show the world as well as sister denominations how Christians can set aside national boundaries for a common cause demanding the best from all of us for Jesus' sake.

Melvin P. Sylvester, President
The Christian and Missionary Alliance of Canada

I am a recipient of God's marvelous saving grace through my Christian parents, who were directly influenced by Christian and Missionary Alliance missionaries.

I thank North American Alliance Christians for sustained missionary zeal and support, sending to our lands missionaries with the message of God's redeeming love. For almost a century now, missionaries have faithfully and lovingly labored among us. Because of their faith and example, literally thousands of believers today enjoy the blessings of God's grace.

The C&MA missionaries with whom I have personally served through the years have demonstrated divine love and humility of spirit. I am eternally indebted to them whose lives, exemplifying the very life of Christ, have been an inspiration and a challenge to me. They symbolize servanthood, leadership and world-wide evangelization. Their positive influence has left an indelible imprint in my life and ministry.

Benjamin P. De Jesus

I appreciate our great Christian heritage and feel privileged to be a part of a world-wide mission society. As a missionary movement, the Alliance exemplifies a passion for the lost. It is impossible to read the writings of its founder, Dr. A. B. Simpson, or sing his missionary songs, without catching the spirit of this man of God and the intensity with which he loved the peoples of the world. His commitment to world missions has greatly challenged us in our involvement in the Great Commission.

I therefore join the national church leaders and members of the fifty-four countries around the world, where the C&MA now serves, as they give God the glory and praise for raising up the Alliance, which the Holy Spirit has used tremendously to reach out to all peoples of the world with the Gospel.

Benjamin P. De Jesus
President
Alliance World Fellowship

ALLIANCE missions was born in the heart and vision of A. B. Simpson to disciple all the peoples. At the outset, missionaries evangelized; there were no churches. The few converts of the early years have now grown into fast-maturing national churches around the world, represented in The Alliance World Fellowship. It is this worldwide family of overseas churches that constitutes the greatest monument to 100 years of Alliance missions.

Men and women of the overseas churches are our partners in world evangelization. Yet to be written are their stories of heroes and commitment. They, too, have martyr graves. They have scars—external and internal—from persecutions for their faith and dedication to ministry. We learn from them as we work at their side.

Missionaries are weak, vulnerable, subject to failure. They leave the shores of their homeland to cross a tremendous bridge from where they are to where the people are, the ones to whom God sends them. There are difficult languages to learn, radically different cultures to penetrate, health hazards to endure. Missionaries undertake that impossible task with the objective of effectively communicating the Good News of Christ in life demonstration and verbal proclamation. They recognize that a missionary is an ordinary believer called to an extraordinary task by a very extraordinary God.

David H. Moore

Your missionaries, with national church pastors and laypersons, are evangelizing, planting churches, training leaders, translating the Scriptures, publishing literature, broadcasting the Good News, ministering to the sick, feeding the hungry. They are reaching out to people groups packed into cities and to those isolated in remote, rural areas.

In viewing the past, we lift our voices in praise to God: praise for the privilege of being His people; praise for enablement to follow our Lord to the earth's ends. Praise for the Spirit's ministry in opening the hearts of people to understand the Good News; praise for the Jaffrays, the Roseberrys, the New-berns, the Barnes, the Constances, the Mabel Francises, and a host of others who have been models of life-investors.

In peering into the future, we tremble. In 100 years, world population has almost tripled. Even as the overseas churches grow, numbers of the unreached grow more rapidly. There are the serious threats of nuclear destruction, ecological catastrophe, food famine. World religions are in resurgence. Political instability erupts in revolution and coup d'etat.

So gigantic is the task—and we are so small! It is in Him that we are able. His love embraces the convulsing world. His compassion wrings heart tears when viewing the unwon masses. His arms reach out to all the peoples. He touches the world through us. His love constrains, His power enables. His authority emboldens. His presence assures.

To all the peoples He sends us. Of those peoples who by faith commit themselves to Christ, He continues to build His Church.

David H. Moore
Vice President for Overseas Ministries

COMMENTS

THE Christian and Missionary Alliance is without doubt the leading missionary society of the 20th century. For many years less than 100 members of the C&MA sent out one missionary yearly. In most denominations it takes 6,000 to 10,000 members to send out one missionary.

The large number of countries in which missions are carried out; the considerable number of countries in which, notably Vietnam, Alliance churches by the middle 1960s numbered more than 100,000 members; the emphasis on missions in Alliance colleges in Canada and the United States—these factors and methods make the C&MA an outstanding force in Christian missions.

Donald McGavran
School of World Mission
Fuller Theological Seminary

FROM the earliest days of my ministry when as a young pastor I moved into a house adjacent to St. Paul Bible Institute, down through my years as a missionary in Japan and a professor at Trinity Evangelical Divinity School, I have been in rather close touch with Christian and Missionary Alliance missionary personnel and programs. It has always seemed to me that The Christian and Missionary Alliance is singularly blessed.

Its congregations are some of the most missionary-minded in North America. When it comes to preparing young people for service abroad, its schools are among the best. Its leaders have steered a straight course, avoiding the fads and extremes that sometimes characterize mission strategies. Its missionaries keep to New Testament priorities. And its national churches are some of the most indigenous and rapidly growing in the non-Western world.

David J. Hesselgrave
Professor of Mission
School of World Mission and Evangelism
Trinity Evangelical Divinity School

THE C&MA is a mission first and a church second. Since the days of A. B. Simpson, Alliance missionaries have moved out around the globe with a burning compassion to reach lost men and women with the Gospel. Congregations arose in the U. S. and Canada primarily to support missionaries. Now Alliance churches on other continents are in turn recruiting, training and sending their own missionaries. The C&MA has long been a model held up by missiologists for others to emulate. Leaders such as L. L. King, David Rambo and David Moore have been an inspiration to their colleagues in many lands and from many denominations. I salute the Alliance and their leaders and thank God for them.

C. Peter Wagner
Professor of Church Growth
School of World Mission
Fuller Theological Seminary

I AM enthusiastic about The Christian and Missionary Alliance. Indeed, no Scripture text is quite as appropriate as Psalm 126:2 when one reviews what Alliance missionaries have accomplished in the nearly fifty nations to which they have gone: "The Lord has done great things for them."

I have always admired the way the Alliance has refused to be merely a missionary society. Its theology of church is not separate from its theology of mission. It has no patience with a gospel that reduces the functioning local congregation to a pragmatic afterthought.

We could easily forget that it was the Alliance that pioneered the Bible school movement and wisely granted national church bodies freedom to decide their own form of church government and name. I cannot but believe that because of its past and present faithfulness to God, the Alliance has a glorious future in His missionary purpose.

Arthur G. Glasser
Dean Emeritus and Senior Professor
of Theology and East Asian Studies
Fuller Theological Seminary

SOME years ago I was visiting with a respected national church leader in one of the Alliance missions fields. Referring to a local Alliance missionary who had invested many years in loving and serving his people, he said, "She is the kind of missionary who, when she walks under the tree, the fruit falls." That is one of the finest commendations of missionary life and service that I have ever heard.

To me, Alliance missionaries have poured their lives unstintingly into the far corners of the globe, reaching people for Christ, training them in Christian life and godliness, and bringing them missionary vision as well. Statistically, it is impossible to total the impact that these missionaries have had on the unbelieving world. Suffice it to say, from my standpoint as a world missions observer, the Alliance churches and institutions have demonstrated a faithfulness, commitment, and a willingness to suffer for the cause of Christ and the Gospel around the world.

I have seen this not only in the lives of people like the missionary mentioned above, but also in the lives of national church leaders who are now serving Christ faithfully in their own spheres of ministry and opportunity.

James Reapsome
Executive Director
Evangelical Missions Information Service

FROM the time I was a boy in Canada, the world outreach of The Christian and Missionary Alliance has made a significant impact on my thinking. I remember young people from an Alliance church who greatly influenced me by their love for Christ, and pastors and missionaries from the Alliance who showed such a missionary passion. I remember early learning of the passion of A. B. Simpson and how he would pray in his study with his arms around a globe of the world.

The C&MA has been one of the significant missionary churches of this century. I believe that vision has been transmitted to other churches so that not only the direct missionary outreach of the Alliance, but also its indirect influence have been significant. May God keep that vision burning and the outreach growing as we move into the end of this century and beyond—and until the Lord returns.

Leighton Ford
Leighton Ford Ministries

DURING forty years of mission administration in North America and in the Philippines, I have had opportunity to be closely associated with most of the leaders of The Christian and Missionary Alliance Division of Overseas and a number of their missionaries and overseas leaders.

In evangelical mission executive circles the C&MA is well respected as one of the leading mission-minded denominations. It has made a major contribution to missions through participation in all of the major joint projects of the Evangelical Foreign Missions Association and the Interdenominational Foreign Mission Association.

Edwin L. (Jack) Frizen
Executive Director
Interdenominational Foreign Mission Association

CONTENTS

FOREWORD v

    Louis L. King v

    Melvin P. Sylvester vi

    Benjamin de Jesus vii

    David H. Moore viii

COMMENTS ix

INTRODUCTION Why Take on the World? xv

AFRICA A Christian Continent? 3

    Burkina Faso A Natural Resource: The Church 12

    Gabon Obstacles: Guideposts to Growth 18

    Guinea The Payoff of Indigenous Policy 26

    Ivory Coast (Cote d'Ivoire) Witness Befitting the Times 34

    Mali The Fruit of Farming 42

    Nigeria When Affiliating Makes Sense 50

    Zaire Missions Comes Full Cycle 54

ASIA MAINLAND Still the Greatest Challenge 63

    India A Conclusion Ordered and Orderly 74

    South Korea A Boost Toward Maturity 86

Thailand   Hairline Cracks in the Wall   92
Churches Under Communism   Color the East Red   104
Viet Nam   Protracted Struggle   105
  Cambodia (Kampuchea)   Preface to Greater Horror   108
  Laos   Peaceful *Putsch*   108
  China   War on the Church   109

LATIN AMERICA — Primacy of Politics   121

Argentina   The Lean Years First   130
Brazil   Spiritism: The Majority Choice   138
Chile   Supernatural Among the Surprises   144
Colombia   Evil Worked for Good   152
Costa Rica   Follow the Spirit's Working   162
Dominican Republic   Bypassed but not Abandoned   165
Ecuador   Church on the Grow   168
Guatemala   The Door Music Opened   176
Mexico   Too Close to Home?   182
Peru   A City Set Upon a Hill   186
Surinam   To the Chinese First   194
Venezuela   The Second Time Took   196

MIDDLE EAST/EUROPE — The Macedonian Call—Again   201

Israel   Connecting the Incompatibles   214
Arab Lands   Fortress Islam   222
  Jordan   Wary Hosts   225
  Syria   Beginning by Adoption   229
  Lebanon   Shattered Model   232
Europe   The Mission Connection   240
  France   Cosmopolitan Flair   240
  Germany   Reevangelizing Luther's Land   244
  Great Britain   A Fresh Start   248

Netherlands   Building Carefully   250
Spain   To the Hardest of Places   253

PACIFIC ISLANDS   Of Commerce, Creeds and Conquest   259

China (Taiwan)   Earning Respect the Hard Way   274
Hong Kong   The Many Faces of Fragrant Harbor   282
Indonesia   From Diversity to Unity   294
Japan   Still Unreached   330
Philippines   From Slow Starter to Pacesetter   340

ALLIANCE WORLD   The Support Network   361

EPILOGUE—DAVID L. RAMBO   Twenty-First Century Missions   378

APPENDICES   381

Acknowledgements   382
Notes   384
Bibliography   397
Index   402

COVER PHOTO CREDITS:

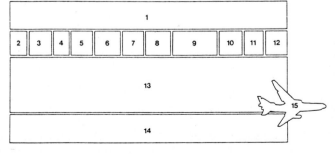

David C. Ritchie: 1, 4, 7, 8, 9, 10, 12, 14
Thomas H. White: 6, 11, 15
Debbie Storlie: 2, 3, 5
Weldon Trannies,
   Australia: 13

(See page 383 for all other photo
   credits.)

	MAPS	STATISTICS		MAPS	STATISTICS
AFRICA			**PACIFIC ISLANDS**		
Burkina Faso	13	17	China (Taiwan)	275	281
Gabon	19	25	Hong Kong	283	293
Guinea	27	33	Indonesia	295	329
Ivory Coast (Cote d'Ivoire)	35	41	Irian Jaya	313	
Mali	43	49	Japan	331	339
Nigeria	51	53	Philippines	341	359
Zaire	55	61			
ASIA MAINLAND					
India	75	85			
South Korea	87	91			
Thailand	93	103			
Churches Under Communism (Indo China)	105				
Kampuchea (Cambodia)		114			
Laos		118			
Vietnam		119			
LATIN AMERICA					
Argentina	131	137			
Brazil	139	143			
Chile	145	151			
Colombia	153	161			
Costa Rica	163	164			
Dominican Republic	165	167			
Ecuador	169	175			
Guatemala	177	181			
Mexico	183	185			
Peru	187	193			
Surinam	194	195			
Venezuela	197	199			
MIDDLE EAST/EUROPE					
Israel	215	221			
Arab Lands	223				
Jordan		227			
Syria		231			
Lebanon		234			
Europe	241				
France		244			
Germany		246			
Great Britain		250			
Netherlands		252			
Spain		257			

INTRODUCTION

Why Take on the World?

THE SUN never sets on The Christian and Missionary Alliance.

In less than a hundred years, the Alliance has penetrated every major continent except the extreme poles north and south. Directly or indirectly, missionaries have participated in the formation of a global church that is home for over 2.1 million people, praying to God in more languages than can be heard in the halls of the United Nations.

The following pages chronicle how that came about: by whom, when and where. But the impressive array of facts and photos gives rise to yet another question, basic to all: *Why?*

Why was the Alliance determined from the very beginning to take on the world? Why did men and women exchange the familiar security of their homeland for life-threatening hardships overseas — hardships that too often proved to be no empty threat? Why do their spiritual descendants today still insist that if you take "Missionary" out of their name, they are no longer "Alliance"?

The First Cause

Some people immediately respond with the obvious: "Albert B. Simpson is the answer. He was a missionary statesman. The world was his parish. He needed a missionary society to carry out his vision, so he started the Alliance."

The record does not agree. Simpson initiated two movements in 1887: the Christian Alliance and the Evangelical Missionary Alliance. He first organized the Christian Alliance, which he described as "the formation of a fraternal union of all who receive Christ in His fullness and look for His coming." The second organization, "designed to be purely missionary," appeared subsequently and subordinately to the first.

The same priority sequence appeared in the conventions and camp meetings that served somewhat like incubators to the fledgling movement. In 1886, at a campground in Old Orchard, Maine, Simpson conducted an eight-day series of meetings that would result in the formation of the two Alliances a year later. Six days were given to praise, prayer, healing and Bible teaching. Missions featured prominently only in the last two days.

Alliance missions cannot be explained simply as the vehicle of a man moved by the vision of multitudes without Christ. The question "Why?" remains unanswered.

Others attribute the emergence of the C&MA as a major missionary force to the total dedication of men and women to Jesus Christ. This comes closer to the thinking of Simpson, closer to answering the question "Why?"

In an 1891 editorial calling for a bold new missionary movement, Simpson noted, "It has pleased God in every age . . . to call forth humble and apparently insufficient instrumentalities to fulfill His most glorious purposes. He is calling a few in these days to a closer place of consecration and communion; . . . and may we not be tempted to hope that even we are being prepared to be the instruments of His mightiest work if we can but be humble enough, trustful enough and holy enough for Him to use us?"[1]

But just as personal consecration and communion with God are not self-centered in expression, neither are they in essence self-generated. The spiritual dynamics that empowered such a remarkable missionary expansion had to find their roots deeper than the resources of a movement, no matter how good, and their level higher than the leadership of a man, no matter how gifted.

If the answer to the question "Why Alliance missions?" lies not in Simpson the man, then in whom? If not in the movement, then in what?

"Jesus Only"

Louis L. King goes to the heart of the matter: "The genius of the Alliance is Jesus Christ Himself. We organize around Him. Our attachment to Him is the bond that holds us together and determines our relationship to each other. Our message to the world is 'Jesus only.' Our mission is to make Him known in His fullness everywhere."[2]

Simpson, poet of the movement as well as its founder, wrote:

> Once it was my working, His it hence shall be;
> Once I tried to use Him, Now He uses me;
> Once the power I wanted, Now the Mighty One;
> Once for self I labored, Now for Him alone.

As with faith itself, Christ is both Author and Perfecter of every missionary effort worthy of His name. The question "Why Alliance missions?" finds its ultimate answer in Him, the source and goal of all ministry, whether in the windswept cliff dwellings of Sangha or the soaring high rises of Lima.

Christ provides the motivation: "God so loved the world that he gave his one and only Son, that whoever believes in him shall not perish but have eternal life."

Missions is an essential expression of the very nature of God.

If Christians are those who have become "partakers of the divine nature," then it must follow that they reach out to those who need God's Son — and especially to those who lack any prior knowledge of Him.

Christ provides the model: "As you sent me into the world, I have sent them into the world."

If ever there was a cross-cultural, distance-spanning, foreign-involvement missionary effort, it took place between heaven and earth when the Son of God became the Son of Man. Heaven found nothing in common with earth except the image of God in man — and it had become so blurred by sin that it was barely recognizable. Jesus lived the missionary experience, and now He says, "Follow in My steps."

Christ provides the message: "I, when I am lifted up from the earth, will draw all men to myself."

Missionary enterprises of every description crisscross the world, but God has only committed Himself to prosper that work that exalts Jesus Christ in message and activity.

Once again it was Simpson who made this truth sing:

> Jesus only is our message,
> Jesus all our theme shall be;
> We will lift up Jesus ever,
> Jesus only will we see.

Christ provides the measure: "He died for all, that those who live should no longer live for themselves but for him who died for them and was raised again."

Quite simply, Christ gave everything for the sake of the people to whom He was sent; He can rightfully expect the same commitment from those who now stand in His stead.

Missionaries have reassuring comfort that they will never face a situation or experience He did not already meet while a citizen of heaven in the alien environment of Palestine. He asks of His servants a measure of commitment no greater than what He Himself has already given.

Christ provides the mandate: "Go into all the world and preach the good news to all creation."

While this is the final command He left to all His followers, not everyone can respond in the same literal sense of crossing an ocean or a cultural barrier. Yet the mandate stands as His last word on earth to His church, and it must be treated with the seriousness He obviously intended.

Some churchmen see in this mandate elements of conflict and competition between the church and the mission. Not Simpson. He wrote, "We ask our people to recognize the fact that the missionary interest is the chief business of every Christian, that the work of foreign missions is the one preeminent business of every minister, every congregation, and every Christian."[3]

Specialists in Missions

Simpson and subsequent leaders of the Alliance envisioned its having a special role in missions. In one of his messages, Simpson stated that in the providence and timing of God, the Alliance was born in "an age of specialists."

For example, "the Salvation Army is raised up by the great Head of the Church to emphasize the Gospel of Salvation for the poor and outcast," he said. Likewise, "the Alliance has its place and calling to lead the people of God farther into all the heights and depths of the life of Christ, and farther out into all the aggressive work which the children of God have so long neglected."[4]

This sense of special mission prompted the young movement to field over three hundred workers overseas in a five-year surge of missionary fervor. Yet Simpson cautioned his people that such achievements should not tempt them to look down on other denominations and groups with differing emphases.

"We must not think of any of these men or movements [including the Alliance] as having a monopoly of truth or grace or service," he preached. "We must learn to recognize Christ in all His providence and grace without becoming bigoted or narrow in our exclusive attachment to any single one.

"At the same time along with this larger charity, we need to know the standard under which we fight, recognize 'our own company,' and be true to the special trust which God has assigned to us," Simpson concluded.[5]

Specialists in missions, neither proud nor apologetic of their role, Alliance missionaries, pastors and laypeople have given expression to the indwelling Christ in a witness heard on almost every continent. That sums up why the Alliance has taken on the world.

The following pages celebrate what God has done, through a comparative handful of men and women, to bring eternal life to millions of people, just as Christ once fed thousands with a few loaves and fishes.

Thanksgiving and praise are in order, but not complacency. Some two thousand years ago, Christ said, "Go into all the world and preach the gospel." Today that world contains more people than ever before without the faintest idea who He is or that He ever lived. □

TO ALL PEOPLES

AFRICA

BURKINA FASO   12

GABON   18

GUINEA   26

IVORY COAST   34

MALI   42

NIGERIA   50

ZAIRE   54

AFRICA

A Christian Continent?

BLACK AFRICA, that vast expanse stretching from the arid underside of the Sahara Desert to the ocean-drenched tip of Cape Hope in South Africa, has always appealed to a romantic streak in the Western world. Mysterious jungles and sinister pythons, rolling savannahs and majestic lions, rustic villages and throbbing drums — it all has a curious attraction to those who live such totally dissimilar lives in completely different surroundings.

Church watchers have also been fascinated with Black Africa because of its explosive response to the Gospel, an acceptance unlike anything the world has ever witnessed.

One historian comments, "In no other continent during the last fifty years has Christianity shown so much growth and diversity, such a cheerful but perplexing flood of people confidently doing their own thing, often in seemingly strange and contradictory ways."[1]

The *World Christian Encyclopedia* attempts with some difficulty to quantify this flood of people into the churches of the sub-Sahara region. In 1900 an estimated 10 million Africans considered themselves Christians.[2] The total has now topped 236 million, and projections for A.D. 2000 reach as high as 393 million.[3] That would be nearly one out of every two Africans.

David Barrett, editor, observes, "For one hundred years now, the most massive influx into the churches in history has been taking place on the African continent."[4]

He and other researchers estimate that by the year 2000 Africa may become a Christian continent — Christian in the broadest term, embracing Roman Catholic, Protestant, Orthodox, independent church and other kinds of believers.

Missionaries have been as indispensable to this phenomenon as sun and rain are to harvest. These expatriate church workers of all persuasions may total as many as 40,000, but no one knows for sure. The *Mission Handbook* published by MARC estimates 7,700 North American Protestant missionaries, making Africa third in total missionary personnel after Latin America and Asia.[5]

Gospel Forerunner

What accounts for this surge toward the Cross, this spiritual movement unparalleled in Asia, Europe or the Americas?

Kenyan theologian John S. Mbiti believes that "the God described in the Bible is none other than the God who is already known in the framework of traditional African religiosity. The missionaries who introduced the Gospel to Africa in the past 200 years did not bring God to that continent. Instead, God brought them."[6]

A hunting tradition in Central Africa dramatizes this "African religiosity." Before the hunters set out in search of wild game, they knelt in a circle facing their leader. While he cast bits of food to the four winds, he intoned, "Almighty God, we do not know where You are, but help us in this hunt so we may gather food for our families."

Traditional religions in West Africa likewise reveal an amazing awareness of God. One oral tradition in Ghana describes how God once walked the earth and paid friendly visits to their villages. But on one occasion He leaned over to watch a woman pounding grain into flour. She raised her baton too high and hit Him in the face. Deeply offended, He stalked over the horizon,

never to be seen again. But the Africans know He is still around, because He growls at them in the thunder and spits at them in the rain.

The traditional religions of Africa enshrined an exalted sense of God, the Almighty Creator, but they could not show the people how to reach Him. That knowledge came only when the Africans learned of Jesus Christ, who said, "I am the way." And, in the beginning, only the missionaries could bring that good news.

Coattail Missions

The Africans must have questioned how good that news was, because it arrived on the coattails of adventurers, explorers and soldiers of fortune. Foremost among them in the fifteenth century was Prince Henry of Portugal. Though he never left his homeland, he was known as Henry the Navigator because he sent numerous expeditions to scout the coastline of Africa.

Prince Henry had mixed reasons for wanting to explore Africa. As member of a religious order founded to fight off the Muslims, he wanted to thwart their expansion in Africa. As member of the ruling clique in expansionist Portugal, he wanted to find a sea route to Asia. And as member of the Roman Catholic Church, he wanted to extend the spiritual domain of the Pope.[7]

The Roman Catholic Church had already begun missionary work in the Canary Islands in 1402.[8] Using the island ports as launching bases, profiteers and priests together probed the west coast of Africa, rounded the Horn and explored the east coast. They worked as a team with startling success at first. Throughout the fifteenth century they established commercial centers and religious missions along the coast.

A Portuguese mission in the Kingdom of the Kongo (now San Salvadore, Angola) converted both king and queen. Their grandson sailed off to Lisbon to enter the priesthood. Some twenty years later, in 1521, he was consecrated the first "Vicar Apostolic" for West Africa, a position more of symbol than substance since it is not certain he ever returned home to the kingdom.[9]

The crusader mentality of the missionaries in the Kongo neither encouraged cultural understanding nor generated patience in discipling converts. The Bible was not translated into the vernacular, and its precepts were not made relevant. Crusades of the era did not inspire sensitivity, they demanded submission.

By the middle of the sixteenth century the Portuguese mission in the Kingdom of the Kongo virtually disappeared, leaving behind little else but stone and iron crucifixes to be dug up later by women working the fields. Catholic missions elsewhere along the west and east coasts clung tenaciously to their beachheads with only marginal response. Africans had caught on to the fact that, in accepting the baptism of Rome, they were also acknowledging the sovereignty of Lisbon.[10]

A document dated 1751 reports that conversions in Mozambique were so uncertain that only a few slaves were permitted baptism while in the prime of life. Most adults were baptized only on their deathbeds, for fear they might later backslide.[11]

Stephen Neill points out why Catholic missions were so enfeebled: "No serious attempt seems anywhere to have been

efforts met with a response that continues to amaze onlookers. The early missionaries, however, confronted human needs and problems they could not ignore.

One was the total evil of slavery. Roman Catholic missionaries, the first to arrive, quickly saw the devastating consequences of the slave trade on their work. In 1537 Pope Paul III decreed excommunication of any Catholic who trafficked in human beings.[17]

The evangelical revival of the 1700s in England brought together churchmen like John Wesley and George Whitefield and humanitarians like William Wilberforce and Granville Sharpe. Their combined efforts brought about the abolition of slavery in England in 1807.[18]

The British navy extended enforcement of the Abolition Act to the coasts of Africa, but it remained for David Livingstone to arouse world opinion against the continuing trade on the continent. On his explorations he encountered too many smoldering villages, too many rotting corpses left along the trail by Arab slave hunters. His vivid accounts, along with protests from others, forced European powers into military and diplomatic action that brought a halt to the horrible hemorrhage of human life in Africa.

In this century many Africans came to view Christianity as the great deliverer from another type of bondage: colonialism. The implicit gospel message of the equal value of all human life — "Christ died for all" — and the explicit teaching of the Apostle Paul — "There is neither Jew nor Greek, slave nor free . . . for you are all one in Christ Jesus" — stirred dreams of freedom that would not be denied. One Rhodesian black nationalist called the church "the guardian angel of African nationalism."[19]

Missionaries encountered other human needs, painfully aware that, if they did nothing to help, no one would. They responded to the double evils of disease and ignorance with twin institutions of the church: schools and hospitals.

Emerging African nations realized they could neither match nor replace what churches had been doing in public education for many decades. So they either nationalized or subsidized the parochial school systems they inherited at independence time. At the All-Africa Ministers of Education Conference in Addis Ababa in 1961, it was estimated that 68 percent of the children in school were in church-related schools.[20]

Pioneer missionaries arriving in Africa had met with an appalling lack of medical services. Four out of five children died before age two, and the life expectancy of adults was among the lowest anywhere. The medicine box became a part of the basic outfit of each missionary, whether the owner had medical training or not.

Dispensaries and hospitals became as familiar a landmark on mission stations as chapels and classrooms. Before independence in Zaire in 1960, for example, Protestant missionary societies operated 171 hospitals and dispensaries, supported 56 doctors, 116 nurses and an African medical staff of nearly 1,100 workers.[21]

Rebellion and Imitation

Other aspects of missionary activity were not as easily understood by Africans. Sometimes this problem stirred rebellion; at other times, imitation.

Professor John S. Pobee of Ghana comments, "The partition of Africa [by European colonial powers] determined the denominational structure of West Africa in at least two ways. First it determined which missionary could go where. . . . A missionary society went where her home country exercised political control and was deemed an interested party. The partition of Africa, secondly, ensured that certain denominations predominated in some areas."[22]

Thus the Anglican Church and other British Protestant denominations were the major religious forces in colonies like Nigeria and Kenya. Roman Catholicism dominated in French colonies like Gabon and Ivory Coast and in Portuguese territories like Angola and Mozambique.

It was inevitable that in the heady decade of the 1960s, when many African colonies gained independence, these foreign missions so closely linked to the colonizing power should be viewed with suspicion, even hostility. To this day in some Black African countries, foreign missionary groups are still trying to convince the authorities of their loyalty to the new order.

The pervasiveness of animistic beliefs in every aspect of African life presented missionaries with another dilemma. What should they do with all the traditional art, music, dance and drama of the converts? In most cases the decision was to do away entirely with these aspects of culture.

But that policy caused problems. Bishop Stephen Neill observes, "At the start, the missionary was the sole and absolute authority; he alone had access to the sources and his word was accepted as infallible. The moment the African Christian could read the Bible and especially the Old Testament for himself, he found himself introduced to a world much more closely resembling his own than the world of the European. Inevitably he began to ask questions."[23]

Those questions led to rebellion and division. David Barrett estimates that between 1862 and 1968 some 5,000 groups separated from the parent mission or church in thirty-four nations. These independent church movements, ranging from ultraconservative to exotic distortions, had encompassed by 1967 more than seven million people in 290 different tribes. He estimates they are increasing annually by an average of ninety new groups and 100,000 new nominal adherents.[24]

"Unless other unforeseen circumstances enter the picture," Barrett predicts, "by the year 2000 the movement will have spread . . . to around 470 tribes, will have grown to well over double its present numerical strength, and will have become comparable in size, power and prestige to the entire Protestant and Catholic communities in many nations on the continent."[25]

Even within the established church community, lack of sound Bible teaching is encouraging a dangerous trend. Many nominal adherents are content with imitating Christian values and beliefs, rather than embracing them through conviction. The resulting mixture of theological principles and traditional practices is elevating ancestral beliefs to the role of redemption, which the Bible attributes alone to faith in Christ.

Before his untimely death, respected Nigerian theologian Byang H. Kato warned the church at large that unless drastic steps were taken to disciple the fast-multiplying multitudes of new believers, by the year 2000 the church may no longer be worthy of the name Christian.

Accelerating Pressures

The widely veering sentiments within the church toward rebellion or imitation prompted talk of a moratorium — or temporary suspension — of missionary activity several years ago. Church leaders at the All Africa Council of Churches, a regional affiliate of the World Council of Churches, called for a temporary halt to the sending of missionaries and overseas funds into Africa.

"The reasoning is that the large number of missionaries and the great amount of foreign money are a detriment to Christianity really taking root in Africa," explains Dr. Tite Tienou, an Alliance churchman from Burkina Faso and a theologian respected throughout Africa. "The purpose of the moratorium was to make Christianity fit into contemporary Africa."[26]

Dr. Tienou himself does not agree with calls for the suspension of missionary activity. But he believes that as long as Christianity is perceived as an imported religion, moratorium will continue to be an issue for many churches in Africa — as will the problem of independent church movements and the mixing of the Gospel with traditional beliefs and customs.

Given tranquillity and time, the African churches and their missionary colleagues might be able to work out most of these problems. But since 1960 Black Africa has experienced more than twelve wars, well over fifty coups, the assassination of thirteen heads of state, widespread refugee problems and famines that have killed millions and permanently deformed millions more by malnutrition.

Yet despite these devastations, by A.D. 2000 the population of Africa will have tripled since 1900.

Problem solving within the ranks of the church will have to be done on the run, while the church stretches to evangelize a radically changing, rapidly growing continent. ☐

BURKINA FASO

A National Resource: The Church

THE PRIMARY RESOURCE of any nation is its people. In land-locked Burkina Faso (formerly Upper Volta), people are just about the only resource.

Already one of the economically poorest nations in the world, Burkina Faso has been thrust reeling backward for fourteen continuous years (1972-1985) by two of the severest drought-induced famines in its history.

While such natural disasters come and go, they leave permanent scars on the land and its people. Encouraged by the droughts, the Sahara Desert has quickened its southward march, leveling the land with a scorched-earth policy that decimates herds, ruins farms and sends thousands fleeing into the cities and southern regions already struggling on a subsistence level.

The suffering of the determined but vulnerable people has produced at least one benefit: a more open attitude toward the Gospel. While animists sacrificed to their fetishes and watched their children grow silent and emaciated, while Muslims spoke of submission to Allah and hoarded grain stores for higher profits, Christians set up networks to distribute relief supplies to the neediest, regardless of religion or tribe.

The people watched — from the government official at the state post to the village farmer in his sun-baked mud hut — and began to believe there may be something to this Jesus Story.

It was not always so.

When the first Alliance missionaries arrived in western Burkina Faso in 1923, the spiritual terrain had long been divided between the millennia-long tyranny of animism (sacrificing to evil spirits symbolized by fetishes) and the centuries-old domination of Islam. Response to the Gospel, brought by foreigners stumbling in speech and strange in dress, was as bleak as the arid northern regions already overcome by the encroaching desert.

Bobo Beachhead

Alliance missionaries chose wisely when in 1923 they established their beachhead in Bobo Dioulasso. The town, already important by local standards, grew to become the nation's second largest city and its economic capital. Favored by unusual water sources, a moderate climate, good communications and a long history of trading between tribes, Bobo Dioulasso has attracted more than 230,000 inhabitants. Bobo people, on whose tribal turf the city grows, plus sizable communities from other parts of the country and Africa, have helped boost Bobo Dioulasso into the ranks of Black Africa's more important cities.

Both mission and national church maintain their headquarters in the city. Several organized churches and an outreach program eventually will embrace the whole city. Since 1972 a youth center has sponsored activities — ranging from sports to Bible studies — geared to the thousands of high school and college students drawn to the city's many schools.

"Voix de la Bible," Saturday-evening programs prepared locally and aired over Radio Bobo, proved exceptionally popular for a number of years. The broadcasts could probably have been heard without a break by someone walking from one end of the city to the other. Thousands more in outlying areas and as far away as Mali and Ivory Coast listened regularly to the programs presented in three languages on a rotating basis.

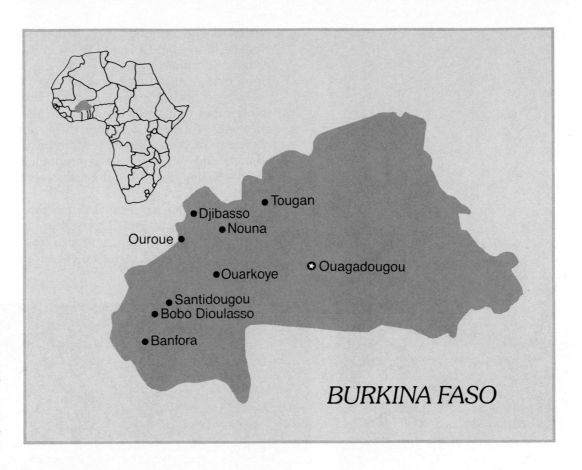

BURKINA FASO

A change in government policy forced a halt to the programs for several years. *"Voix de la Bible,"* however, proved its worth as an effective witness.

The French-language Maranatha Institute was founded jointly by church and mission in 1976. The school has an international mandate: to prepare men and women for ministry in the churches of Burkina Faso, Ivory Coast and Mali.

Short-term and regular Bible schools elsewhere in Burkina Faso and Mali offer training to church workers and lay leaders unable to follow more formal studies on campus. A French-language Bible school in Yamoussoukro, Ivory Coast, specializes in education on a high school level.

The preparation of pastors, teachers and evangelists holds the key to church growth, not only because of the need to nurture believers, but also because many areas lack Christian witness due to the shortage of workers. In Burkina Faso, only one-third of the churches have trained pastors.

Restrained Advance

Penetration by Alliance missionaries and national workers throughout the western regions of Burkina Faso has been restrained rather than rapid, reflecting a shortage of personnel and resources that simply adds to the country's already long list of needs.

The Dedougou district was entered in 1927, four years after the Alliance began work in the country. It took another three years before a mission station was built in the government post of Dedougou. The Santidougou station, some ten miles north of Bobo Dioulasso, began ministry in 1934. This was followed by entry into the Banfora district in 1937.

A lull in expansion then occurred until the end of World War II. Burkina Faso, like numerous other western African nations, formed part of the sprawling French West Africa Federation dating back to 1896. When France fell to Nazi occupation, development of every description came to a halt in her colonies. Missionary work was suspended until the war's end.

Missionary momentum picked up again with the opening of four stations in the 1950s: Ouarkoye (1951), a second station in the Dedougou district; Djibasso (1951) in the Nouna district; Tougan

(1958) in the northern part of western Burkina Faso; and Ouroue (1958) in the extreme northern region of the Black Bobo tribe near the Mali border.

During that decade of expansion when the number of stations doubled, a presence was established in each of the seven church districts of Alliance responsibility. Church and mission then concentrated on deepening their penetration of the regions.

Changes within the districts dictate flexibility in the placement of personnel. In 1971, for example, a family moved from a rural mission station near Banfora to the town itself because of its importance as a commercial center. The Banfora church, an active and growing congregation, has the potential for evangelizing much of the area's 200,000 population.

During the 1980s, missionaries took up residence among three additional tribes and in Ouagadougou, the capital.

Cautious Change

Change comes slowly to a nation where 95 percent of the population still farms the land in small family groups and scattered villages, where veneration of ancestral ways still predominates, where

(Above) *The youth center attracts many young people;* (right) *education will greatly affect his future;* (facing *page) the road to Santidougou has served generations of Africans.*

(Left) *Translating the New Testament into the Black Bobo language is of great importance to the church, but young people (below)* often prefer to read the Scriptures in French.

government has meager means to promote even necessary programs. But the African saying, "No situation is permanent," still applies.

Following World War II, the area now known as Burkina Faso was separated from the French West Africa Federation and made a territory in its own right. With self-determination given to individual territories, Burkina Faso became an autonomous republic in December, 1958, and moved to full independence in August of 1960.

Once colonial restrictions were relaxed, the national church was able to gain autonomy in 1960 instead of relying on the mission's charter. It took another nine years, however, before the government officially recognized the church as an entity separate from the mission.

The Mali and Burkina Faso Alliance churches were joined together like Siamese twins until 1971, when political realities forced a separation of the two churches. The mission followed suit in 1974.

These changes paved the way in 1976 for the first five-year working agreement between the Christian Alliance Church of Burkina Faso and the North American-based mission. Terms of the agreement defined both combined and separate areas of responsibilities between the two equal partners in ministry. Since then, two other agreements have been worked out, bringing church and mission even closer in their joint goal of evangelizing western Burkina Faso.

Exacting Agenda

The Alliance church and mission look back on a history with enough achievement and advance to encourage them for the greater demands that lie ahead.

The Bobo people, after years of exposure to the Gospel, continue unanswering. Less than one-tenth of 1 percent confess faith in Christ, and the churches among them register gains slowly. Only one in ten of the 200-plus villages of the Santidougou district have a Christian witness. Progress among people still concerned more about placating evil spirits than worshiping the Creator God is measured by individual conversions.

The Bwa people have responded to the Gospel in a totally different way.

From 1975 to 1984, the number of believers in the Dedougou district rose by 185 percent. Bwas make up more than 60 percent of the Alliance national church.

It is no coincidence that the Tougan district, hard hit by famine in 1973-1985 and greatly aided by Christian relief efforts, also contains significant numbers of Samogo people who have turned to the Lord. Many of the converts are former Muslims. In the government center of Tougan, local Christians joined with missionaries to build a church that seats 600 people, an expression of their faith in God's continued blessing.

How to nurture these believers? How to evangelize hundreds of villages still without resident believers? How to train capable leaders for the churches? How to win the youth, who form not only the largest segment of the population but also the nation's future?

The Alliance church and mission have their agenda for the future starkly defined in a courageous but struggling nation whose only resource in abundance is people — and all else is measured in terms of need. ☐

CHURCH AND MISSION

OFFICIAL NAME OF CHURCH:	Christian Alliance Church of Burkina Faso
ENTRY BY MISSIONARIES:	1923
NUMBER OF MISSIONARIES:	(1989) 40
ORGANIZED CHURCHES:	248
UNORGANIZED CHURCHES AND PREACHING POINTS:	519
BAPTIZED CHURCH MEMBERS:	10,690
INCLUSIVE MEMBERSHIP:	32,070
MEDICAL WORK:	4 dispensaries
EDUCATION:	Maranatha Bible Institute Poundou Bible School
RADIO BROADCASTS:	1
PAGES PRINTED:	270,305

COUNTRY

OFFICIAL NAME:	Burkina Faso
FORM OF GOVERNMENT:	Military
OFFICIAL LANGUAGE(S):	French
AREA:	105,869 sq. mi.
POPULATION:	6,900,000
CAPITAL:	Ouagadougou
PER CAPITA INCOME:	$150.00 (1983)
LITERACY:	8%
RELIGIOUS AFFILIATION:	Traditional religions 38%, Muslim 46%, Christian 16%

GABON

Obstacles: Guideposts to Growth

AMONG THE NUMEROUS crystal-clear streams intersecting the emerald rain forests like arteries of quicksilver, one waterway is favored above others by the Massangou people of southern Gabon. This particular stream flows to a precipice high in the jungle-matted mountains, tumbles in a wild, sheer drop of seventy-five feet to the base of the cliff, swirls in an agitated pool of confusion and then hurries on toward the ocean.

Mouyanama — or Wide Open — Falls, they call it, perhaps likening the reckless plunging stream to a diver from the high cliffs throwing away all caution.

As with many other unusual forms of nature, from oversize boulders to grotesque trees, graceful Mouyanama Falls is considered inhabited by spirits by the animistic Massangou people.

When the tribal elders learned that the land around the falls had been granted to Alliance missionaries for a new station, they gathered at the pool to appease the water spirits with offerings of food. Then they carried away the fetishes hidden in a small cave at the base of the cliff.

Wide Open Falls . . . fear of the spirits

. . . arrival of the Gospel . . . retreat of the fetishes: Mouyanama enacts a scenic parable of Alliance missions in Gabon.

Boomtown Prospects

Port Gentil, for instance, offers as many wide-open opportunities for the church as it does for commerce. Second in size only to the capital, but first in commercial development, Port Gentil has already earned a name for itself among other major cities along the west coast of Africa.

The port is built on a nineteen-mile peninsula jutting into the Atlantic Ocean on three sides and severed from the mainland by the immense Ogooue River. This geographical formation provides a natural harbor, a sheltered haven for ships. Small wonder the French named it "Gentle Harbor."

Port Gentil first came to prominence in the commercial world through the timber trade, especially the salmon-colored wood ideal for plywood. A factory reputed to be the world's third largest plywood factory employs some 2,500 workers.

The lumber industry, however, was surpassed when oil was discovered in the

bay shortly after Gabon's independence in 1960. The resulting exploitation of liquid black gold brought boomtown prosperity to the port and Gabon's entry into the OPEC oil cartel. Population mushroomed from 15,000 in 1963 to over 90,000 in 1984 — a 600 percent increase in twenty years.

Alliance entry into Port Gentil in 1984 paralleled somewhat the Apostle Paul's attempts to head eastward with the Gospel until he encountered a closed door and then turned westward in response to the Macedonian call. Missionaries tried unsuccessfully to enter the eastern Upper Ogooue Province, only to have the door slammed in their face. They then turned westward and found wide-open opportunities in Port Gentil.

Within weeks of moving to the coastal city, missionaries were conducting Sunday services attended by over one hundred people. They found more openings than they could respond to.

Port Gentil has five of the best college preparatory high schools and technical schools in Gabon. Some 4,000 teenage young people attend the different schools. Religious instruction classes are available

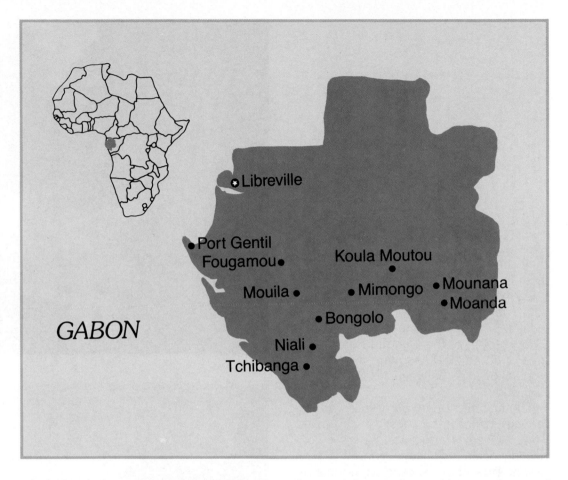

GABON

Libreville

Port Gentil
Fougamou

Koula Moutou

Mouila

Mimongo • Mounana
• Moanda

Bongolo

Niali

Tchibanga

to Protestant and Catholic students. The school ministry has particular significance because in 1980 a group of students from Alliance churches in the interior formed a prayer group to pray that Alliance missionaries would come work in the city.

Their prayer was amply answered when, in early 1987, a beautiful new church on a prominent boulevard became the center of active witness to the port city. As an added measure of blessing, a second congregation organized in another part of Port Gentil.

A hospital financed by oil revenues began serving Port Gentil in 1983. It was equipped with state-of-the-art equipment and staffed by several hundred medical people, including graduates of the nursing school at the Alliance church-sponsored hospital at Bongolo. The hospital has an open-door policy toward pastoral visitation and ministry among the hundreds of patients that come from all parts of the country.

A large English-speaking community of people hired by the numerous foreign companies represents witness in a totally different direction. Bible classes for children and Sunday evening services for the whole family have the potential of developing into an international church.

Full-Service Mission

Bongolo stands at the other end of the historical dateline of Alliance missions in Gabon. It is as rich in reflection as Port Gentil is in projection. Instead of a port city skyline pierced by high rises and dockside derricks, the mission station's horizon is broken only by uneven mountains and jutting trees. The morning calm at Bongolo surrenders not to impatient car horns and shrill lumber saws, but to the cacophony of squawking parrots and chattering children.

Bongolo stands at the source of Alliance ministry in Gabon. In 1932 missionaries from the Belgian Congo (now Zaire) reconnoitered the area south of the Ogooue River in then-called French Equatorial Africa. Concerned about the unevangelized area, they asked the Paris Evangelical Mission if it had plans to move southward from its already established work north of the Ogooue River.

The French mission replied that since the Alliance had an extensive area to

evangelize in French West Africa, perhaps they should refrain from entering Gabon for a few years. But later the Paris-based mission conceded it could not occupy the south country and permitted the Alliance to assume responsibility for nearly all of Gabon south of the Ogooue River — an area of about 60,000 square miles with a population of between 200,000 and 250,000.

The first missionary party followed waterways up from the coast for 250 miles. They arrived at a location where a connecting chain of hilltops offered a panoramic view of the forest-clad mountains. The spectacular Bongolo Falls on the Louetsi River won their hearts, and they settled at Bongolo in February, 1935.

The center developed into what might be termed a full-service mission center. The minicity contains residences for missionaries, the Gabonese pastor, schoolteachers and medical staff. In 1984, four schools operated at Bongolo: a primary and high school, a nursing school and a school for missionary children.

The Bongolo Evangelical Hospital, founded in 1977, has the distinction of being Gabon's only church-supported

(Top) *The falls at Bongolo;* (above) *the Bongolo Evangelical Hospital*

hospital. In one recent year the hospital reported 320 surgical cases, 1,152 inpatients, 10,015 outpatients and 23,605 consultations. Satellite dispensaries accounted for another 9,000 consultations and treatment for 4,050 people.

Obstacles to Openings

Wide-open opportunities brighten the horizon in Gabon. One major problem, however, is getting to them. Gabon, for example, has the richest, most important iron ore deposits in all of Africa, but they are tucked away in the mountains with few roads to reach them.

Like some other African countries, Gabon has largely bypassed the automobile era on its way from the laborious method of dugout canoes to the jet age. The only link to some parts of the country is by air, not by road.

Enterprising missionaries in search of unreached peoples have an even more difficult obstacle than the transportation problem facing commercial firms: language barriers. Although Gabonese belong to one of ten major language groups, the ten subdivide into forty-six smaller groups, each speaking a separate language or dialect.

Obstacles of travel and language help explain the missionaries' slow rate of penetration in mountainous southern Gabon. Although they spread out from Bongolo in every direction to evangelize whatever group they met, missionaries did not establish their second station, at Ileka, until 1943. Other stations gradually opened, until eventually the Alliance carried the Gospel into five of the ten major language groups.

Guevede illustrates the problem of penetrating interior Gabon. Some Mitsogo people went to live and work at Bongolo. Although their tribe was deeply involved in spirit worship as a part of their identity, a number of Mitsogos became Christians and returned to tell their people what they knew about God. Missionaries followed in 1948 and established a base at Guevede, from which they intended to evangelize the area.

Many of the Mitsogo villages, however, are buried deep in the mountains. They are accessible only by narrow footpaths that seem to clamber up one perpendicular side of the mountain and scramble straight down the other side — then disappear in marshland. One river in the area must be crossed and recrossed sixteen times in a single day's travel.

Koula Moutou presented a similar problem. To reach the area in 1948, missionaries traveled five hours by truck over mountain roads and then continued four more days on foot. But once there, response among the fifteen tribes proved worth the effort. Important chiefs, disappointed and disillusioned with other religions, welcomed the Gospel bearers and cooperated in many ways. In one area of Koula Moutou a Gabonese pastor baptized over 1,200 new converts between 1970 and 1976.

Sometimes the difficulty lay more with planning than anything else. A beautiful station was established in 1946 at scenic Mouyanama Falls in anticipation of a government road scheduled to be built nearby. But a change in plans shifted the road some miles away, leaving the station in splendid isolation atop a mountain.

The choice of Mouila proved more fortunate. The town developed into an important hub of education, commerce and travel. A general hospital, public

(Top) Itinerating requires the services of river ferries; (above) the Moanda Alliance Church.

(Far left) City of Libreville; (left) poster announcing the Howard Jones evangelistic crusade; (facing page) meetings were held in the city stadium.

schools, numerous commercial firms and government services attracted a large population to the Mouila environs. In 1949 the Alliance established a station that became headquarters for its mission activities in Gabon.

Capital Opening

The overall population density of Gabon is only five persons per square mile, and one city claims 250,000 residents — one-quarter of the entire population. It was therefore only a matter of time before Alliance mission and church leaders focused attention on that city. It happened in 1974, to Libreville, Gabon's modern capital on the Atlantic coast. Another mission had been working in the city for decades, but the population had outgrown its capabilities.

Within five years, drawing mainly on former members and adherents who had moved from the interior, the Alliance counted seventeen groups of believers meeting throughout the city. By 1982, with help from Alliance laymen from the United States, the church had built a 500-seat sanctuary on a choice site given as a gift by the city.

Seven major tribal groups, speaking ten languages, made up the congregation. Through radio and television programs the church reached into every part of Libreville. Theological Education by Extension and correspondence courses helped lay leaders equip themselves to lead others.

The multiple linguistic and cultural diversity of the Alliance community in Libreville prompted a three-layered meeting schedule for the church. The basic, largest level was the network of Bible-study/prayer cells. By 1984 some seventeen were reaching 750 people each week.

Homes were the most common meeting place, but variations included a police station for officers coming off duty, a construction site for steelworkers during lunch break, a rocky projection of seacoast for office workers on their way home after work.

The second level was the area group. Some twenty met during 1984, varying from fifteen to over one hundred people who share a common language and culture. The third level, the entire congregation, filled the new 500-seat sanctuary.

Off-limits to Opportunity

Every rule has its exception and every possibility its limitation. The wide-open attitude toward the Gospel common in much of Gabon does have its flaws. Franceville, for example.

This beautiful provincial capital of the Upper Ogooue Province had never hosted a resident missionary, though a Zairian pastor lived there from 1969 to 1971 and started a church. The government refused to renew his visa (missionaries from overseas were acceptable, but a black missionary from another African nation was something of an affront to national pride) and the group of believers dwindled in numbers and spirit.

A missionary couple was assigned to Franceville in 1983 to revitalize the work. They had begun renovating an unoccupied house belonging to the church when a most unusual communication was received from the president's office, prohibiting any Protestant church activity in the province. No reason was given, either then or later, though it appears that the spirit of Vatican II did not extend to interior Gabon. Respecting the ban on

(Left) *Attendance at the Libreville C&MA church jumped from 500 in 1986 to 1,300 one year later; (below) in many African congregations the men and women still sit separately.*

public services, Christians resorted to meeting quietly in several private homes.

Government rulings immobilize men, but not God.

Within a short while, an upper-echelon government official was transferred to Franceville. Perhaps the assignment would not have been made had his superiors known the man was a Christian who had studied Theological Education by Extension courses under an Alliance missionary. He opened his home to Bible studies that attracted other believers in the provincial capital.

Around the same time, an aviation mechanic moved to an air base outside Franceville. He was an irrepressible Christian whose employers knew better than to try to silence him. Instead, they requested Alliance church leaders to legitimize his activities by giving him credentials as a lay worker.

One missionary summarized the placement of these and other dedicated laymen in an officially closed city: God imported them, the church recognized them and the city received them.

The interdiction could eventually be lifted and Alliance pastors and missionaries may yet reenter the largely unevangelized province. Franceville, however, serves as a reminder that restrictions on Gabon's wide-open opportunities are only an official signature away.

But if opponents of the Gospel thought to win a victory, they proved too clever by half. Personnel and resources assigned to Franceville were redirected to Port Gentil, site of the most exciting church growth in Gabon.

The Lord has His own way of allowing the opposition to set itself up to be put down. □

CHURCH AND MISSION

OFFICIAL NAME OF CHURCH:	The Christian Alliance Church of Gabon
ENTRY BY MISSIONARIES:	1934
NUMBER OF MISSIONARIES:	(1989) 39
ORGANIZED CHURCHES:	171
UNORGANIZED CHURCHES AND PREACHING POINTS:	60
BAPTIZED CHURCH MEMBERS:	13,405
INCLUSIVE MEMBERSHIP:	40,215
MEDICAL WORK:	3 dispensaries, Bongolo Hospital
EDUCATION:	Bethel Bible School Libreville Bible Institute
RADIO BROADCASTS:	2
PAGES PRINTED:	276,000

COUNTRY

OFFICIAL NAME:	Gabon
FORM OF GOVERNMENT:	Republic
OFFICIAL LANGUAGE(S):	French
AREA:	103,346 sq. mi.
POPULATION:	820,000
CAPITAL:	Libreville
PER CAPITA INCOME:	$2,613.00
LITERACY:	30%
RELIGIOUS AFFILIATION:	Traditional religions 14%, Muslim 4%, Christian 82%

GUINEA

The Payoff of Indigenous Policy

THE PRESIDENTIAL DECREE of May 1, 1967, stunned the entire religious community of Guinea. Catholic and Protestant church leaders thought they had seen everything when in 1958 the former French colonial masters of Guinea left in a huff as President Sekou Toure started the new nation down a strangely mixed path of Marxism and Islam. But the president's action in mid-1967 left them in even greater shock: He decreed removal of all foreign missionaries from Guinean soil.

President Toure's avowed purpose was to speed total Africanization of the churches. His primary target was the Roman Catholic Church, which was controlled from abroad and yet heavily involved in national politics. To show impartiality, he included Protestant missions in the sweeping edict.

The Alliance mission and church, however, believed they had grounds for special consideration. In a meeting with President Sekou Toure, church and mission leaders pointed out that the Alliance mission had already granted autonomy to the African church. The mission could therefore be allowed to stay.

The record supported the C&MA appeal. In 1958, Guinean Alliance leaders had adopted a program whereby the churches would become self-supporting in three years. The plan stirred the African congregations to increased, cheerful giving, and the goal was achieved.

With self-support came self-government. In February, 1961, delegates from the various tribes gathered at N'Zerekore to establish a national church organization. A tentative constitution was later drawn up and adopted the following year. Government recognition confirmed the church's full autonomy — three years before President Toure's edict to accomplish the same objective.

Thus in 1967, Roman Catholic and other Protestant foreign missions hastily turned over properties and functions to their African churches and left the country. The Alliance mission was affected to some degree, but not as traumatically as the others.

Seven Alliance district stations were ceded to the national church and a number of missionary personnel reassigned to other countries. But the mission was permitted to consolidate its activities on three

stations and continue specialized ministries in which the national church was still deficient: Bible translation, medical work and leadership training. The school for missionary children continued until 1971.

This episode in Guinea dramatically underscored the wisdom of basic Alliance policy concerning mission-church relations overseas: The two must become equal and distinct partners as quickly as practical, each with clearly defined roles in their common goal of advancing God's kingdom on earth.

Beneficial Jolt

The partial expulsion of missionaries, though traumatic and painful, was not an unmitigated tragedy. Missions historian J. Herbert Kane noted, "It jolted the church leaders out of their complacency and forced them not only to assume responsibility, but also to provide leadership."

Accelerated growth of the church under national leadership was neither immediate nor universal. Among the Muslims in Guinea that growth has yet to be seen. Entrenched for centuries, Islam claims three-quarters of Guinea's population and four-fifths of its land area. All the major tribes — Fulas, Maninkas and Sousous — are almost completely Muslim and dominate the western, central and upper regions of the country.

The Guinean brand of Islam shuns fundamentalist fervor and settles for easy accommodation with ancient tribal rites and even contemporary doctrinaire Marxism. Even so, the grip of Islam on the vast majority of Guineans has thus far defied every attempt to loosen it.

Momentum Regained

After a transition period in which the national church accepted many of the mission's responsibilities and adjusted to the changes, the African believers turned their attention to evangelizing the areas where they lived. A pastors' retreat in 1973 spurred the districts to organize their own evangelistic teams. The results were gratifying: All the districts reported new churches opened that very year. The Kissidougou district team split into three parts, established three congregations and provided each with a full-time pastor.

In the providence of God, the resurgent spirit of evangelism in the church coincided with a government drive to collect

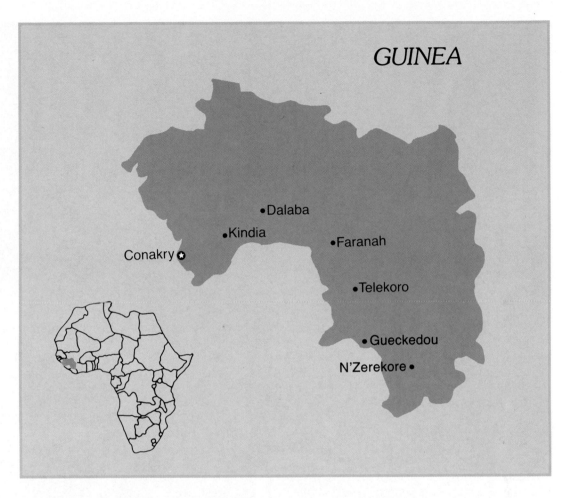

GUINEA

• Dalaba
• Kindia
Conakry ✪
• Faranah

• Telekoro

• Gueckedou

N'Zerekore •

and destroy fetishes used by spirit-worshiping people. In some areas, whole groups of Guineans deprived of their old religion went looking for a new one.

One such group lived in Dadazou, some ninety kilometers in the forest from Macenta, an important center with a strong Alliance church. A young man wrote to the Alliance church leaders, "Come and evangelize us."

The church lost no time in responding to this amazing invitation, engaging a large truck and Land Rover to transport

the evangelistic team. The road was so bad the four-wheel-powered Land Rover had to be towed half the distance — and the bumpy, rutted road was just the beginning of their problems.

The team arrived at Dadazou only to find the town already angry that a Muslim teacher was building a Koranic school against the peoples' wishes. Town officials turned hostile when they saw a big truck come rattling into town filled with enthusiasts of still another religion. Why further complicate matters by permitting these

(Facing *page) Workers harvest dryland rice;* (below) *pastors enjoy greater freedom in preaching than has been known for years.*

outsiders to hold a religious open-air meeting?

Then a newly arrived government official, a Christian from the Alliance church in Gueckedou, recognized the witness team as "our people" and vouched for them. Eighteen people responded to the evangelist's invitation at the close of the service. They were joined by a full one hundred converts during a second trip by the team. Dadazou soon had a church of 200 believers.

Capital Gains

Christians living out their faith under a revolutionary Marxist regime have problems, whether they are African, European or Asian. The tension is especially acute in a capital city, where they must live under the watchful eye of those in the center of political power. Yet the large Alliance church in Conakry, the capital of Guinea, not only survived under the intense scrutiny of the Russian- and East German-supported regime, it actually thrived.

In 1965 the Good News Bookstore opened in the capital. In 1967 a large new sanctuary and Christian education unit were dedicated. The new facility not

(Facing *page) A Telekoro Bible
Institute student enjoys conducting child
evangelism in a village, while adults
(below) hear the Word in a more
formal setting.*

only sheltered the large African congregation led by a Guinean pastor, it also gave
sanctuary to an English-speaking International Church.

Taking a page out of the communist
operations manual, the Conakry church
organized itself into nine cells citywide.
The decision solved a transportation
problem for the widely scattered congregation's midweek services. The cell system also helped believers relate to other
Christians in a deeper, more practical way
during their neighborhood weeknight
meetings.

Some openings for witness in the capital seemed little short of miraculous. In
1983 Christian students at the University
of Conakry persuaded school authorities
to approve the showing of *Suzanne,* an
evangelistic film with an all-African cast.
Over 500 curious but friendly students
and a dozen Russian professors attended
the meeting in the university auditorium.

The church youth choir sang, and a
young pastor gave a rousing message on
salvation before the showing. The audience reaction was so positive to the message and film that school officials
suggested a discussion period afterward.

Questions and answers flew back and forth for over two hours.

On the following Sunday, the Conakry church held a special afternoon meeting for interested university personnel. Only thirty attended, but six, including a professor of philosophy, professed faith in Christ.

All these activities in the capital of a Marxist-oriented country could only take place because the regime perceived the church as truly African. The Alliance policy of promoting church autonomy has proven to be the only way to go in Guinea and throughout Africa.

Foreign Investments

Alliance missionaries in Guinea, however, continue to make their own investment in the spiritual welfare of the people — sometimes unexpectedly so. In one instance a missionary arrived at the Conakry hospital while a Russian neurologist was treating a girl from the church. When the doctor finished, she beckoned the missionary into the corridor.

Expecting to hear an explanation of the girl's condition, he was totally unprepared for the Russian doctor's question: "Can you help me get a Bible?"

She had earlier purchased a Bible at the bookstore and then given it to a friend after returning to Russia on leave. She fully expected to buy another Bible when she got back to Conakry, but the bookstore had moved to a new location, and she did not know the address.

The doctor got a new Bible, just like hundreds of other Russians and eastern Europeans working in Guinea under contract with the Soviet Union. In one recent year, the Good News Bookstore in Conakry sold over 300 Bibles to specialists

Studies are serious business at the Telekoro Bible Institute.

and professionals from communist Europe.

Selective Service

Part of the agreement whereby Alliance missionaries were exempted from the presidential decree of May 1, 1967, specified that they continue only in functions the Guinean church workers were not yet ready to assume. That meant leadership training, translation and medical work.

All three of these missionary activities are centered in Telekoro, about 400 miles inland from Conakry, and all three are directly related to the Telekoro Bible Institute (TBI). The school, founded in 1945, has a faculty of both missionaries and Guineans, including the Guinean director. Its graduates thus far number over 180, most in full-time ministry. Student population has fluctuated between twenty and eighty, depending on the state of the church, the economy and prevailing politics.

TBI has shown remarkable flexibility in adjusting to the specific needs and conditions of Guinea. All students are self-supporting. This they accomplish by farming rice fields, using the harvest for food and barter for other needs. One innovative missionary designed a plow from discarded farm-equipment parts, increasing the crop yield and enriching the soil at the same time. Even government agricultural officials were interested in this aspect of TBI.

Classes and other activities are conducted in French, to make the school equally beneficial to all the language groups. Students must spend a year of supervised ministry between their second and third years of study. While still in school, students put their learning to immediate use in evangelistic teams.

In 1981, for example, the twenty-three team members of "Telekoro Workers for the Lord" secured government consent to hold youth rallies in Kissidougou. Over

2,000 high school and college students attended. The same group then turned its attention to two area villages, where more than 1,000 people gave them a hearing.

Unaltered Change

One of the longest lived African regimes ended in March, 1984, when President Toure died while undergoing surgery in a Cleveland, Ohio, hospital. Within days a bloodless military coup dismantled the 26-year regime which was often marred by oppressive policies and rocked by aborted coups and assassination attempts. A military committee assumed control of the government and almost immediately began to free thousands of political prisoners, abolish tyrannical measures and make overtures to Western nations.

Christians in Guinea took special delight in a change on the ministerial level. The Ministry of Islamic Affairs became the Ministry of Religious Affairs. The one-word change altered the entire religious landscape. Christianity was now recognized as a religion of the country. Religious toleration, if not freedom itself, was the winner.

But one of the changes made by the late Sekou Toure remains unaltered: Africanization of the church. Catholic and Protestant missions seeking to reenter Guinea must first demonstrate they are needed and will work to build the church, not control it.

Years ago the Alliance convinced the nation's Marxist-leaning Muslim president that church autonomy was the cornerstone of its overseas policy. Events in Guinea and throughout Africa have shown that such a policy is both sound theology and good politics. □

CHURCH AND MISSION

OFFICIAL NAME OF CHURCH:	The Evangelical Protestant Church in the Republic of Guinea
ENTRY BY MISSIONARIES:	1919
NUMBER OF MISSIONARIES:	(1989) 28
ORGANIZED CHURCHES:	134
UNORGANIZED CHURCHES AND PREACHING POINTS:	854
BAPTIZED CHURCH MEMBERS:	6,575
INCLUSIVE MEMBERSHIP:	19,725
MEDICAL WORK:	1 dispensary (for Telekoro Bible Institute)
EDUCATION:	Telekoro Bible Institute
RADIO BROADCASTS:	11
PAGES PRINTED:	0

COUNTRY

OFFICIAL NAME:	Republic of Guinea
FORM OF GOVERNMENT:	Republic under Military Committee
OFFICIAL LANGUAGE(S):	French
AREA:	94,964 sq. mi.
POPULATION:	6,100,000
CAPITAL:	Conakry
PER CAPITA INCOME:	$305.00 (1984)
LITERACY:	11%
RELIGIOUS AFFILIATION:	Muslim 85%, Christian 10%, Traditional religions 5%

IVORY COAST

Witness Befitting the Times

IVORY COAST PRESIDENT Felix Houphouet-Boigny attends the fiftieth anniversary celebration of Alliance ministry in his country and embraces Dr. Louis L. King, who receives the nation's second highest decoration. . . .

Evangelist Howard Jones is featured in an hour-long national telecast during an Alliance crusade in Abidjan. . . .

Baoule people, once clustered in the central region but now migrating to scattered areas, find a daily Alliance radio program a common bond. . . .

In seven months, the Deux Plateaux Alliance Church in Abidjan increases from twenty-two to 106, including two university professors, one school director, two chief engineers, two accountants, three high school teachers and three foreign embassy members. . . .

The first "Here's Life" evangelism campaign in French-speaking Africa is conducted by Alliance churches among Bouake's 350,000 residents. . . .

All these random glances of the Alliance at work in Ivory Coast lead to the same conclusion: The church is witnessing of Jesus Christ in a manner that fits the times and the nation.

Ivory Coast is the success story of black-and-white cooperation in Africa, a showcase well stocked to show the continent what can happen when a resource-rich African nation maintains harmonious relations with France.

Politics, however, in no way diminish the stature of Ivory Coast's President Houphouet-Boigny. A world statesman in his own right, the president opted for policies that have steered the nation clear of upheavals that scuttled the hopes and foreclosed the future of other equally promising African nations.

If Ivory Coast is a showcase of prosperity, then Abidjan is the centerpiece on display. A *New York Times* correspondent describes the capital: "Abidjan is a city with windows open on two worlds. The Western and African traditions fuse like light in a prism, producing something that is more than the sum of its parts."

One section of the city looks almost more European than Europe: glass-and-aluminum skyscrapers . . . fashion boutiques with a direct line to the salons of Paris . . . hotels stunning in service and furnishings . . .supermarkets stocked daily by air from France.

"But encircling and passing through the hub of westernization," continues the writer, "is an authentic African city whose people move to the rhythm of an African beat. A proud African mother sits amidst the skyscrapers breast-feeding her child and selling fried bananas to African businessmen dressed in three-piece western suits. Traditional African roots and herbs are being sold nearby by an old woman with a finely wrinkled face. A man rolls out his prayer rug and quietly makes his prayers toward Mecca, undisturbed by the din of traffic circulating around him."

Nation of Youth

The rapid modernization of Ivory Coast is all the more remarkable because 75 percent of the population is under twenty-five years of age. Beginning right at independence the government placed high priority on educating these young people. During the 1960-1970 decade, school population tripled, so that six of every ten children received primary education.

Quality did not fall victim to the crash school program. Bouake, one of the nation's leading education centers, became a prototype of educational methods des-

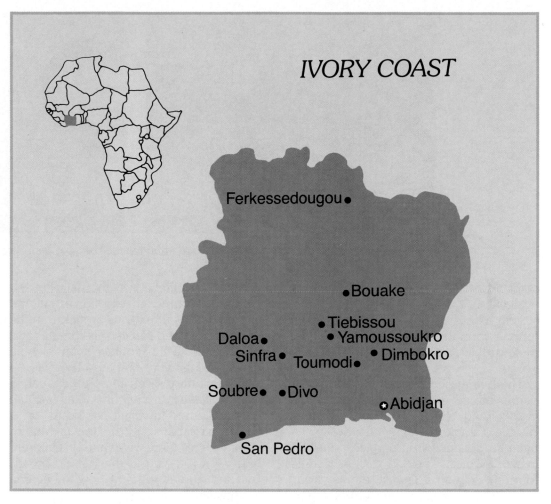

IVORY COAST

tined for the entire nation. A vast complex of television sets linked 4,500 classrooms to programs prepared specifically for various age levels. About half the primary school children were receiving televised classroom lessons before the experimental program ended.

God, in His prescient wisdom, led the first Alliance missionaries to establish their initial base in Bouake, the largest interior city of Ivory Coast in 1930. As Bouake grew in importance as a student center, so did Alliance youth work. The first Alliance youth complex was built in Bouake. Its schedule eventually assumed a twenty-four-hour daily ministry through Bible studies, sports, rallies and dormitory facilities.

The youth center enabled the church to impact on the city's large student population in a measure otherwise impossible. Young people, trained at the center in Bible teaching methods, spread out to teach their peers. In 1982 volunteer youth spread the Word in sixteen high schools and twenty-seven grade schools — to a total of 28,000 children. Of these, some 200 responded to the message of salvation.

Similar youth facilities opened in Dimbokro and Toumodi with the enthusiastic support of the church, and with good reason. Uprooted from ancestral lands and the security of tribal traditions, teenagers sent off to distant schools comprise the largest age group responsive to the ministry of the church.

Linked by Airwaves

People in Western nations can hardly imagine the importance of radio in developing countries. Government looks upon the broadcasting network as an intricate intercom system putting it in direct, immediate contact with every part of the nation. Thanks to cheap transistors and batteries, literally no corner of the land is beyond the voice of radio. Even the smallest, remotest village has its radio blaring nonstop, full volume — and usually in the village bar.

The government therefore does not hesitate to pay top-dollar value for the

Musical groups at Bouake enhance their singing with colorful dress.

most advanced broadcasting equipment available in Europe or Japan. It uses the system as a means not to inform, but to form — form the mentality of the masses, mold public opinion to accept official policy.

The Evangelical Protestant Church has demonstrated another use for radio: evangelizing the increasingly scattered Baoule people, which historically has been the Alliance's primary responsibility in Ivory Coast. The 1.8 million Baoules form the nation's largest ethnic group. Once found only in the central region, they have dispersed faster and farther throughout Ivory Coast than any other group.

The half-hour daily broadcast is prepared by Baoule speakers in the radio studio of the church in Bouake. A different format for each day — evangelistic messages, Bible teaching and reading, quizzes, questions and answers — gives the audience an unaccustomed variety of programming.

To the scattered Baoules, both Chris-tians and nonbelievers, the daily broad-cast has become an emotional, cultural link, as well as a religious program. In the most unexpected places, missionaries and pastors come in contact with people whose hearts were prepared by radio.

A missionary received an urgent call to visit a village no church worker had yet entered. After traveling for hours on a barely passable road, he met a Muslim who, with his three wives and six children, had been listening to the Baoule broad-cast and wanted to know how to become a Christian.

On another occasion some missionar-ies stopped at a market to ask directions. After answering their question, the villager inquired if they were, as he suspected, missionaries. He then told them he had been listening to the broadcasts and wanted to know how to accept Christ. Not only he, but his wife and brother also became believers.

Sometimes the broadcast even takes precedence over an individual bearing the same message. This happened to a missionary who, with a group of African workers, wanted to hold an open-air meeting in a new village.

"Yes, you can have a meeting," the chief replied, "but you must wait. It is almost time for our radio program. You can listen to that first and then talk to us."

Lure of the Cities

Religious broadcasts, however persua-sive and pervasive, have their limitations. You cannot get personal with an airwave. As the Baoule programs followed the migrating tribal people to fresh farmlands and budding cities, the church planters had to follow the radio results.

In a former era, this would have been impossible. The Baoules would have been restricted to ancestral lands, and the Alliance, by a gentleman's agreement, would have refrained from entering a region already occupied by another mis-sion.

Political independence and the loosen-ing of traditional bonds changed all that. People were suddenly free to travel and settle where they pleased, and they did. Missions that historically had specialized their work along ethnic lines in specific areas now found themselves being called to scattered areas to continue ministry among people who had left their ancestral lands but not their God or religious heritage.

Cities are the big winners in this unleashing of the ethnic groups, and so is the church. Urban migration doubles the population of most African cities in ten years or less. For the church, this means that people whom it might take years to reach in scattered villages are now crowded together in a few city blocks. Urban migration has speeded the evangelizing of Ivory Coast more than many other factors.

Soubre, for example, lies situated along the fast-flowing Sassandra River. Government planners decided the location would best suit the country's largest hydroelectric dam. The project was eventually suspended, but not before hundreds and eventually thousands of workers were drawn to the city. Anticipating the surge in growth, the Alliance mission and church assigned workers to the area in 1982. The decision brought immediate results, both among the Baoules who came in search of farmland and among other people in search of work.

Within a year of the center's being established in Soubre, some 400 people were baptized and thirty-five unaffiliated groups of believers asked to merge with the Alliance. By 1984 over sixty villages in the Soubre area had been visited and the congregation in the city itself had grown to 160, with double that number assured once the church was built.

Oftentimes in the village a single radio can draw a group of listeners.

(Above) *The Abidjan skyline projects Ivory Coast's image of the future, and so does the city's Yopopougon Alliance Church (left); (facing page) evangelist Howard Jones goes on national television with an Abidjan choir and a trio from Kinshasa.*

The biggest winner in the move toward the cities is Abidjan. Two million live in the capital, about half of whom are Ivorians from every group and corner of the country. The cultural diversity and sheer size of the urban population caused Abidjan and other cities to be declared "open cities" for religious work. No longer is a city the private preserve of the mission or church that got there first.

Those who choose to work in Abidjan face stiff competition. Nearly half the city's population is Muslim; four out of every remaining five people are Roman Catholics. Most of those who are now Muslims converted to Islam after coming to the city. Often alone and in need, newcomers accept with gratitude the food, lodging and jobs offered by Muslims. Accepting their benefactors' belief in Allah is an easy next step for the newcomers.

Some Jula-speaking Christians, numbering about one thousand in 1984, presented a beachhead for the Alliance in the tightly knit Muslim community of Abidjan, but their witnessing is like waving a target on the firing range. A favored Muslim technique for breaking up religious gatherings is to lob stones at the infidels.

Alliance church growth in the non-Muslim half of Abidjan has gone much better. Starting from zero in 1979, mission and church leaders set a goal of ten churches in ten years. Within six years the Alliance had nineteen church groups, eighty prayer cells and a combined membership of 4,000 believers.

Framework for Growth

Youth centers. Radio programs. Television coverage. Urban evangelism. These and other methods indicate that the Alliance speaks of Christ in the mainstream of life in Ivory Coast. More importantly, they constitute a framework for spectacular growth in a nation whose future beckons with unusual promise.

The church's keeping step with national progress received unusual recognition during the 50th anniversary celebration of Alliance work in Ivory Coast. President

The Alliance church's fiftieth anniversary was observed in Bouake.

Houphouet-Boigny sent word that he and numerous high government officials planned to attend the Sunday ceremony on December 12, 1982.

The announcement was all the more startling because the president had refused to visit Bouake for years, due to political friction. City officials went all out to welcome their distinguished guests: flags blossomed on lampposts, center-city buildings sported new coats of paint, freshly cleaned streets sparkled with fresh flowers and trimmed grass.

An estimated 300,000 people watched thousands of Christians commemorate the historical event in a daylong celebration of parading, preaching and praying. The jubilee made headline news and was carried on prime-time national television for several days.

All the public and official recognition of the Alliance ministry and witness in the nation seemed fitting. For just as Ivory Coast has become a showcase of prosperity and development, so the church of Jesus Christ — including The Christian and Missionary Alliance — is called to display to the Ivorians all the riches of God's forgiveness and blessing. □

CHURCH AND MISSION

OFFICIAL NAME OF CHURCH:	Evangelical Protestant Church of Cote d'Ivoire
ENTRY BY MISSIONARIES:	1930
NUMBER OF MISSIONARIES:	(1989) 60
ORGANIZED CHURCHES:	486
UNORGANIZED CHURCHES AND PREACHING POINTS:	709
BAPTIZED CHURCH MEMBERS:	52,367
INCLUSIVE MEMBERSHIP:	157,071
MEDICAL WORK:	0
EDUCATION:	Yamoussoukro Bible Institute
RADIO BROADCASTS:	7
PAGES PRINTED:	1,716,000

COUNTRY

OFFICIAL NAME:	Cote d'Ivoire
FORM OF GOVERNMENT:	Republic
OFFICIAL LANGUAGE(S):	French
AREA:	124,503 sq. mi.
POPULATION:	10,100,000
CAPITAL:	Abidjan
PER CAPITA INCOME:	$921.00 (1986)
LITERACY:	32%
RELIGIOUS AFFILIATION:	Traditional religions 40%, Muslim 25%, Christian 35%

MALI

The Fruit of Farming

TIMBUKTU, walled city of mystery. With its massive mud walls, cubical courtyards and labyrinth of narrow lanes, what secrets could this ancient crossroads of interior Africa reveal?

Camels carrying pouches of gold and, equally important, bars of salt, found fodder within its walls. Caravans of captives on their way to the slave markets of Europe trudged through it. Racing columns of mounted Tuareg warriors overran it. And fleets of war canoes from the vast Songhay empire beached on its sandy shores.

Timbuktu owed its fabled history to a strategic location high on the great bend of the Niger River bordering the furnace-like stretches of the Sahara Desert. For centuries the city served as a commercial junction for desert caravans and river flotillas. In the sixteenth century it became the southernmost beacon of Islam, site of a university and numerous mosques.

But over the course of the next two centuries Timbuktu shrunk to a dusty town, fiercely proud of its history, its religion and little else. It survives as a symbol of the Islamic and animistic West African empires in medieval times. Today it represents the continued domination of Islam throughout Mali and much of the Sahel region bordering the Sahara.

Dr. A. B. Simpson took up the challenge of Timbuktu in the 1890s and envisioned it as the interior anchor of a chain of mission stations strung along the Niger River. The first Alliance missionaries, however, did not reach the town until 1924. Timbuktu and its environs were so thoroughly Islamicized that the missionaries eventually moved to more responsive areas.

Muslim Shroud

The Muslim shroud drawn over much of the Malian population is almost impenetrable, but not totally. The government is secular, not Islamic, and Muslim domination in some areas is cultural, not religious.

However, messengers of Allah have shown increased aggressiveness in recent years, borrowing effectively from methods used by Christian missions. Regular radio broadcasts, cassette tapes and record players promote the cause of Allah and his prophet Muhammad. Evangelists go from village to village like salesmen, preaching the gospel of submission and the rewards of paradise for the faithful. Islam, they say, is the black man's religion, suited to his way of life.

Once converted, a Muslim faces many inducements and threats to stay faithful. Wealthy Muslims dominate the business community in the larger centers, exercising a virtual monopoly over who can and cannot buy or sell. Muslim landlords control much of the real estate, determining who can and cannot rent housing or buy land. Muslim village chiefs exercise authority over the community, choosing who wins or loses in disputes over land, livestock and property.

In such an environment, Christianity offers few incentives and many problems. Less than 1 percent of Mali's population dares to profess faith in Jesus Christ.

A closed system, however, does produce rebels.

One Dogon, born and raised a Muslim, attended the funeral of his father, who was a determined animist until he died. This act of family devotion stirred the disfavor of the local Muslim teachers because animists are considered pagans and

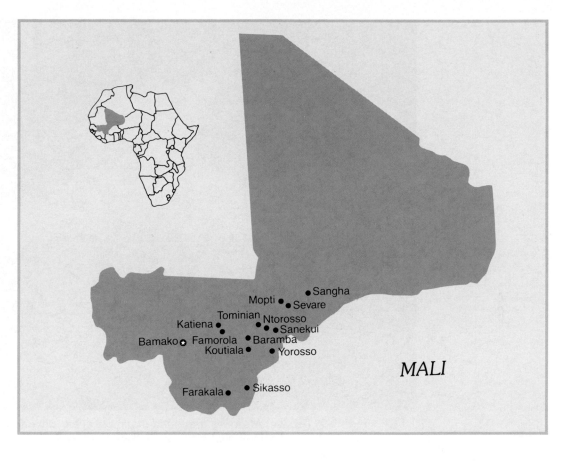

MALI

attending their ceremonies brings defilement. When one of the Dogon's wives died, the Muslims refused to bury her because he was considered defiled.

The bereaved and offended husband allowed the Catholics to inter his wife. He told his mother, "I don't want anything to do with the Muslims if that is the way they act. I will become a Catholic."

His mother advised him, "Before you change ways, go to your friend at the mission and talk to him."

The Dogon and his friend had played together as children when the white boy's parents were missionaries in Mali. The Dogon's boyhood friend had grown up, gone back to America for an education and then returned to carry on the work of his parents. Now, after forty years, the two friends became brothers as the Dogon put his trust in Jesus Christ. Eventually his family and widowed mother became Christians with him.

Famine Fruit

A two-step natural phenomenon is reshaping Mali as drastically as Islam did centuries ago: drought and famine. Advancing southward up to ten miles a year,

the Sahara has for centuries been waging a war called desertification, turning grazing and farmlands into an African version of an arid moonscape. Retreating southward before the desert's encroachment, nomads cut down more trees for firewood, farmers burn off and plow up more land for crops. Their actions upset the natural balance between land and sky, and prepare another swath of land for a desert takeover.

The combined assault of drought and famine on Mali and other West African nations has been catastrophic. During a 1973-1974 famine, perhaps a half-million

Africans starved to death and several millions more were permanently scarred by malnutrition. Another crisis in the 1980s prompted an alert by the United Nations that as many as 40 million Africans faced starvation and 150 million would be seriously affected.

The loss of herds and farms on which they depend for a living condemns survivors to a bleak future. One observer on a 5,000-mile journey noted, "Much of the Sahel has become a semi-desert of failed crops, lost herds and abandoned villages. At the dwindling number of water holes, tens of thousands of starving cattle jostle

(Above) *Mosques are found in almost every city and town;*
(facing *page*) *a Sangha village borders the desert.*

for a drink, along the roads lie the bleached bones and mummified corpses of thousands more."

During such crisis times almost every Alliance missionary in Mali is involved in some kind of relief aid. As one missionary put it, "How can you sit in your house and eat food when on your doorstep people are literally dying for lack of it?"

Whether it involves tons of grain donated by Alliance farmers in western Canada, or thousands of dollars in relief funds and supplies given by CAMA Services, or other aid from numerous agencies, the biggest problem in Mali and elsewhere is

funneling aid through an effective and honest distribution system. Massive shipments of supplies and six-digit bank drafts may ultimately depend on how far a bicycle or two-wheel cart can carry a sack of grain.

Alliance missionaries and Malian church leaders put together a delivery network of local church committees so efficient and fair they won praises all around. People called the bags of lifesaving food "Jesus grain."

One village had repeatedly rebuffed visits by gospel witness teams. But when famine stalked the village and Christians

brought aid with no strings attached, the Muslim headman invited them to speak of Jesus. A new church was born.

In 1984, it seemed that conditions could not get worse. In northern areas, 95 percent of the crops failed; elsewhere it was a 60 to 85 percent loss. But in that same year over $150,000 in relief supplies from Alliance sources were channeled by local church committees to the neediest ones. Added to this was aid supplied by four Christian relief agencies.

Overwhelmed by this demonstration of compassion, many grateful Malians spoke of 1984 as "The Year of the Protestants."

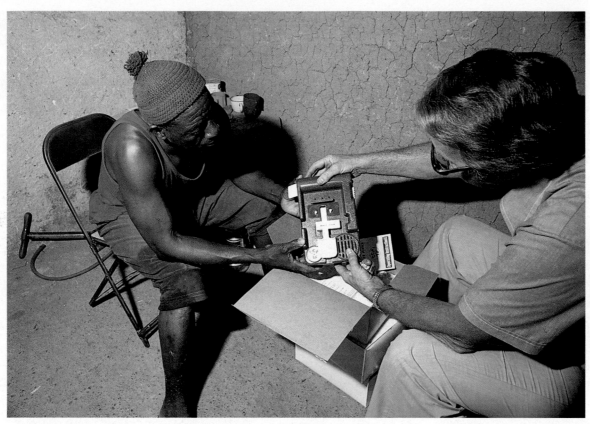

A local church leader inspects a battery-powered cassette player used to spread the Gospel.

While other forms of witness seemed to make little impact on the Muslim population, "Jesus grain," shared in fairness and sweetened by kindness, turned deeply ingrained Muslim indifference to thoughtfulness.

Somehow, in an almost unrelieved landscape of suffering, and with his hand outstretched in utter need, the amazing African has not lost his dignity or manners. One missionary recounts her struggles to refuse a chicken from an emaciated Fulani woman to whom she had given ten dollars the previous week. However politely she tried to return the gift, the African insisted on her keeping the chicken.

"If you come to visit in Dogon country, you would be welcomed as a fellow believer," she writes. "You would be served a meal even if it were the last bit of millet in the granary or the only chicken in the yard. It would be given to you and you would never be told that the family had nothing left to eat."

Why do those who live on the blunt edge of starvation give so generously? A Dogon pastor explains: "Giving is a part of our culture. We must share what little we have. Don't feel bad about taking gifts. We would feel shame if we couldn't give something in return for what is given to us."

Unhindered Growth — Almost

Despite opportunities of ministry it presents, famine does handicap progress. Church districts have to cancel Bible conferences and youth camps. Evangelistic teams cannot move into areas short of food and water. Students drop out of Bible school to find food for their families. Reduced income forces national leaders to postpone penetration of new areas.

But in spite of these drawbacks, the

Christian mothers appreciate the importance of God's Word in the home.

church grows. In one five-year period (1976-1981) the church increased by 64.5 percent. Church leaders became so concerned that converts be more than just Christian in name that they put great emphasis on baptism and discipleship. As a result, in 1982 the record showed more baptisms than conversions — a rare situation.

Part of the Mali Alliance church's pattern of growth is tied to its organizational structure. When pioneer missionaries viewed the diversity of groups, languages and cultures in Mali, and took into account the large areas involved, they de-

cided to develop church districts along tribal lines. Each of the ten church districts has its own administration, and the district superintendents compose the national executive committee.

The church's evangelism efforts are developed along parallel lines. The national evangelistic team unites outstanding evangelists from six different tribes and even more church districts. They are all ordained pastors, and most are graduates of the Ntorosso Bible School. The national team concentrates on the large population centers, running campaigns from two weeks to one month.

The national evangelists in turn train district evangelistic teams, which concentrate on market towns and administrative centers. Continuing the pyramid structure, several district teams develop local church groups, who move from village to village.

Bamako, the capital, received special attention from the national evangelists in 1982. The team conducted a two-week campaign in both the new and old sections of the city. An unusual fifth week featured a guest evangelist from the United States. Tent walls were removed to accommodate capacity crowds. Radio

Rocky terrain forces the cliff dwellers of Sangha to bury their dead under cliff ledges.

Mali carried public service announcements of the meetings, and the final service was a precedent-setting rally in the government-owned arena. Over 300 people responded to the altar call during the week-long series.

The Dogon Church District, which celebrated its 50th anniversary in 1980, decided it was not growing fast enough, so in 1983 the 10,000-member district subdivided into three. Already one of the strongest areas of Alliance work in Mali, the new districts almost immediately found their "divide to multiply" policy bearing fruit: In one baptismal service later in the year, over 275 converts were baptized.

Vision Renewed

Response to the Gospel in Mali comes almost entirely from non-Muslim people — spirit-worshiping, animal-sacrificing, fetish-believing people. Few among the large Muslim majority show any interest in the Bible. Islam arrived in Mali centuries before Christianity, and its grip on the people is almost unshakable.

When the first missionaries encountered stony silence among the Muslims at

Mopti on along the Niger River, they redirected their efforts to the more responsive animistic peoples. For years the Muslim population was ignored as a target group for evangelism. In the mid-1980s, that began to change.

A 1983 seminar on evangelizing Muslims stirred Dogon church leaders to reach out to the almost totally Muslim Fulanis. That decision in itself was a triumph of God's grace.

The Fulani people are referred to contemptuously as the "Jews of West Africa"

and are hated by the other groups. The Fulanis and Dogons fought each other with swords and spears in years gone by, and they continue that war through words and nastiness as they both try to wrest a living from the same scorched earth.

Mali has few Fulani Christians, and not a single church. The tribe stands as the largest unreached peoples group in the country.

The Dogon Church District added a Fulani-speaking evangelist to their district team and set as one of their goals an established church among their former antagonists. In concert with the church's awakened concern for Muslims, the mission appointed a new couple to language study and witness among the Fulanis.

One missionary backpacked across the dunes to a camp near the towering Sangha escarpment, home of the cliff-dwelling Dogons. He was warmly received and entertained by the Fulani chief. Through cassette tapes and discussion, he presented the Gospel to the nomadic Muslims.

The next day, as the missionary prepared to leave, the Fulani headman said, "You walked out to greet me. I'll not let you walk back." He loaned the missionary a beautiful black stallion for the trip home.

As other missionaries and church workers go out of their way to speak of Jesus Christ to Mali's millions of Muslims, they, too, may find a reception more friendly than they dared hope for. Even Timbuktu, that thick-walled Muslim citadel that barred its gates to the Gospel decades ago, may eventually welcome the outsiders now known as people of the "Jesus grain." ☐

CHURCH AND MISSION

OFFICIAL NAME OF CHURCH:	Evangelical Church of Mali
ENTRY BY MISSIONARIES:	1923
NUMBER OF MISSIONARIES:	(1989) 45
ORGANIZED CHURCHES:	597
UNORGANIZED CHURCHES AND PREACHING POINTS:	542
BAPTIZED CHURCH MEMBERS:	14,376
INCLUSIVE MEMBERSHIP:	43,128
MEDICAL WORK:	6 dispensaries
EDUCATION:	Bethel Bible School Baramba Bible School
RADIO BROADCASTS:	0
PAGES PRINTED:	534,326

COUNTRY

OFFICIAL NAME:	Republic of Mali
FORM OF GOVERNMENT:	Republic
OFFICIAL LANGUAGE(S):	French, Bambara
AREA:	478,764 sq. mi.
POPULATION:	7,700,000
CAPITAL:	Bamako
PER CAPITA INCOME:	$190.00 (1984)
LITERACY:	10% (1984)
RELIGIOUS AFFILIATION:	Muslim 81%, Traditional religions 17%, Christian 1.7%

NIGERIA

When Affiliating Makes Sense

THE INTERNATIONAL STATUS of the Alliance in North America acts as a magnet that attracts hundreds of independent churches overseas. These groups—large or small, indigenous or dissident, biblical or cultic—share a common characteristic: They want affiliation with a larger, respected fellowship of churches.

Beyond that desire to belong lie other reasons, often as diverse as the groups themselves.

How does the Alliance handle the continuous stream of applications from such churches? Why should the Alliance, accustomed to "starting from scratch," even consider any of them? What guidelines help determine the course of action?

The Division of Overseas Ministries set up three preconditions to an official tie between the applying group and the Alliance in North America.

First, the church must belong to The Alliance World Fellowship (AWF). Acceptance in the AWF depends in part on how the group originated—through vision or dissension—and on its statement of faith.

In addition, the church must achieve credibility and good relations with other evangelical groups in the country. The possibility of joining another evangelical mission already in the area must also be considered.

Finally, the kind of help requested of the North American Alliance must coincide with its commitment to encouraging strong indigenous churches.

Few independent overseas churches have successfully negotiated this three-part qualifying course, but those who did have gone on to enjoy a fruitful and respected partnership in mission with the North American Alliance.

The Saviour's Evangelical Church (SEC) of Nigeria shows how one independent group became part of the family.

Church Catalyst

Rev. Roland O. Onokalah, a promising young Igbo who was seminary trained and ordained by a leading evangelical denomination in Nigeria, wanted to minister among his own people. When this proved impractical within the denomination, he quietly withdrew and returned home to southeastern Nigeria. In 1975, he began pastoring two small congregations in the Umuahia area of Imo State.

Through Pastor Onokalah's ministry, the main congregation quickly grew to 800 attendees and the number of churches rose to fifteen. With the Umuahia pastor as their leader, and with a number of pastors having a background similar to his, the churches organized as the Saviour's Evangelical Church (SEC). With typical Igbo aggressiveness, their evangelistic vision included opening churches in major centers of southeastern Nigeria,and also in the future national capital of Abuja and other states.

Port Harcourt was one of the key cities that felt the impact of SEC's emphasis on evangelism in 1981. As in similar city crusades, Pastor Onokalah announced that the city, one of Nigeria's two major seaports, was the objective. He called for volunteers and then chose twenty-five people from the 200 responses. Some of the men had to leave their businesses for the entire week of ministry.

Campaign expenses ran high because of rental fees for just about everything: neon lights, vacant lot, generator with microphones and amplifiers, pickup truck and loudspeaker for publicizing the crusade, movie projector, operator and

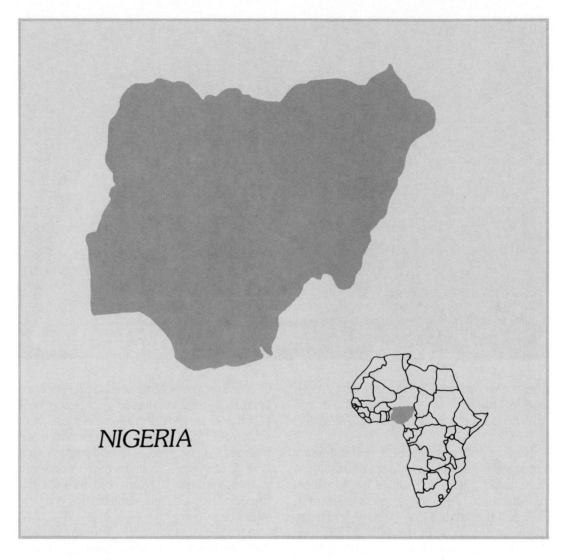

NIGERIA

rental films. A well-known evangelical singing group was engaged for the week at one hundred dollars per day. Supporting SEC churches underwrote crusade expenses.

On one typical crusade day, the pickup truck drove back and forth along the streets of Port Harcourt while the loudspeaker blared announcements of the evening meeting. Around 6:30 the singing group, plus joyous gospel songs and choruses accompanied by hand clapping, drums and guitars, got the meeting started.

Midway through the featured film, the screen fell silent and dark. It was intermission time: a forty-five-minute evangelistic sermon and altar call.

"First-timers" were separated from the fifty-plus respondents and subdivided into smaller groups led by SEC counselors. Each individual session concluded with an invitation to a Bible study the following morning.

The featured film resumed after the hour-long intermission. No one seemed to mind. Before the meeting concluded around eleven o'clock, Pastor Onokalah reminded the audience of what he had said repeatedly: SEC was not a hit-and-

run mission. They were in Port Harcourt to establish a church. Anyone seeking the Lord would have their full backing and an opportunity to meet with like-minded believers.

True to his word, when the week-long series concluded, Pastor Onokalah and other group leaders chose one of the twenty-five-member evangelistic team to

remain as pastor of the new church in Port Harcourt.

Unusual Alliance

One faithful visitor at the meetings had a special reason for coming. He was an Alliance missionary with instructions from the Division of Overseas Ministries in Nyack to observe and learn all he could

about the Saviour's Evangelical Church and its leaders.

Why would the Alliance be interested in SEC?

Part of the answer had to be Pastor Onokalah. After Igbo students studying in the United States first raised the question of affiliation, Alliance leaders met with Pastor Onokalah at a 1980 world missions conference in Pattaya, Thailand. That he was invited to the summit-level meeting of evangelical leaders already said much about the Nigerian churchman.

Pastor Onokalah's initial impression on Alliance delegates at the conference was positive. Numerous meetings with him and other missionaries over the next several years deepened the consensus that here was a man around whom, humanly speaking, a church could be developed.

Another part of the answer to Alliance interest in SEC related to encouragement by the evangelical denomination with which the Igbo church leaders had been formerly associated. "If you must work with foreigners," their former missionary mentors advised, "then call in the Alliance." They offered similar advice to the Alliance.

Another obvious part of the answer to Alliance interest in the Saviour's Evangelical Church lay in the growth potential of the African church if it could team up with an experienced mission such as the Alliance. "We would keep on growing and doing as we are now," Pastor Onokalah said, "only we would be doing it five times faster and better."

Dr. David L. Rambo, then vice-president of overseas ministries, recom-

mended that two missionary couples be assigned to Nigeria to assist in three priority areas of SEC activity: evangelism, church planting and ministry to women.

Dr. Rambo concluded with a statement that continues to express the attitude of the Alliance: "Our minimum assistance in Nigeria should help speed evangelism and represent a better use of personnel than if the two couples were sent to existing areas of ministry. I think a decision to enter Nigeria represents both good missionary strategy and use of resources."

Visits vs. Visas

The Saviour's Evangelical Church joined The Alliance World Fellowship in March, 1983. The Alliance officially entered Nigeria in September of the same year. The mission, however, was unable to establish a permanent base in Nigeria. The obstacle lay neither with the administration in Nyack nor with church leadership in Imo State. The central government's policy on permanent visas disrupted the long-term plans of more than one mission.

Meanwhile, veteran Alliance missionaries from surrounding African nations

(Left) *Rev. Rowland O. Onokalah is founder of The Saviour's Evangelical Church of Nigeria;* (far *left*) *The SEC is welcomed into The Alliance World Fellowship.*

made several short-term visits to southeastern Nigeria to conduct seminars, counsel church leaders and participate in church-planting evangelism, such as the crusade in Port Harcourt.

Basically, however, the rate and quality of growth within the Saviour's Evangelical Church in Nigeria depends not on the government's good graces nor on Alliance involvement, but on the Christians' closeness to the Lord of the Church.

One visiting missionary's vivid recollection shows how the Igbo believers, in their usual energetic way, are making use of already available resources for growth.

"I was informed that morning prayers began at 5:00 in a church about one mile away," he wrote. "When I awakened at 4:30 and looked out the window, I could see small lights piercing the darkness as people made their way to the church. I joined a number of old ladies and before we even entered the church they had joined the others in joyful song. Some sixty people were gathered for prayer."

Whatever their expectations of help from North America, the Igbo Christians have greater expectations from a higher source. □

CHURCH AND MISSION

OFFICIAL NAME OF CHURCH:	The Saviour's Evangelical Church of Nigeria
ENTRY BY MISSIONARIES:	1983
NUMBER OF MISSIONARIES:	0
ORGANIZED CHURCHES:	14
UNORGANIZED CHURCHES AND PREACHING POINTS:	8
BAPTIZED CHURCH MEMBERS:	4,150
INCLUSIVE MEMBERSHIP:	12,450
MEDICAL WORK:	0
EDUCATION:	0
RADIO BROADCASTS:	0
PAGES PRINTED:	0

COUNTRY

OFFICIAL NAME:	Republic of Nigeria
FORM OF GOVERNMENT:	Republic with strong presidential authority
OFFICIAL LANGUAGE(S):	English
AREA:	356,700 sq. mi.
POPULATION:	91,200,000
CAPITAL:	Lagos
PER CAPITA INCOME:	$760.00
LITERACY:	30%
RELIGIOUS AFFILIATION:	Muslim 36%, Traditional religions 15%, Christian 49%

ZAIRE

Missions Comes Full Cycle

BATEKE COUNTRY gives the impression of being left out of everything, and liking it that way. Bone-jarring rides in four-wheel-drive vehicles over dirt roads barely passable when dry, or backbreaking trips by canoe up a river whose swift current seems determined to turn intruders back, are the only ways to penetrate the isolation of Bateke Country. No wonder government officials, traders, educators and developers ignored the rolling plains some 100 miles up the Zaire River from the capital city of Kinshasa.

The Teke tribespeople, far more removed from Kinshasa in time than in distance, prefer their ancestral ways. They do not take kindly to outsiders trying to change their life-style. Would-be evangelists were threatened with death.

Perhaps that is why, along with government, commerce and education, the church, too, stayed away from the sparsely settled plateau. Protestant missions entered Zaire over a century ago and eventually divided the country into areas of ministry respected by a gentlemen's agreement known as mission comity. But in the assignment of territories, the Teke tribe was almost totally bypassed.

Isolation Breached

When the Gospel did finally breach the isolation of Bateke Country, it was not carried by one of the long-established churches or missions of the area.

An Alliance pastor had moved to Kinshasa in 1965 and challenged comity by asking, "Why not an Alliance church in the capital?" Years later, when he heard about the spiritual isolation of the Bateke, he again challenged the status quo: "Why not an Alliance pioneer work among the plateau people?"

Others were asking the same question. Consequently the Alliance church community and mission in Zaire took up the challenge of the unreached people of Bateke Country in 1983.

For the church it was pioneer evangelism in every sense of the word: The language differed from those used in Zairian Alliance churches; the culture, heavily laced with demon fear, isolation sentiment and willful backwardness, seemed foreign to the energetic big-city churches. Even the grassy, rolling savannahs contrasted sharply with the shimmering cement streets, kamikaze traffic and overpopulated shantytown sections of Kinshasa.

An evangelist assigned to the plateau region entered the small, riverside village of Enpumu. He quickly realized the chief held total control over the village. The headman's broad features, deeply furrowed and framed in sparse white hair from chin to crown, spoke of authority without a word uttered.

The chief listened gravely to the evangelist for several months and then resolved to break with his idols and trust God.

Some strange events followed. After burning the chief's charms and fetishes, the evangelist's right arm was inexplicably paralyzed for a day. The following night, the chief heard a loud crash in the room where he had stored his idols. The two outer walls had collapsed for no apparent reason. The night was calm and the walls, made of stone, had stood for years.

While the old chief of Enpumu began to wonder and worry crept into his heart, the chief of a neighboring village came to warn him: "You have been acting like a fool in allowing the gods of your ancestors to be burned. Just like the walls of your house collapsed, you, too, will soon collapse and die."

The old chief pondered his friend's offer to bring some of his idols to replace those destroyed. Then he replied, "I have served the idols all my life. They did not bring me peace. Now I have found the true and living God. I shall serve Him from now on. I forbid you to enter my house with any of your idols."

That night the headman of Enpumu slept well. He even dreamed that God came to him and said, "Don't be afraid. I will be with you all the days of your life."

The entire village followed the chief's example and became Christian. Other villages responded in similar fashion, either in part or in whole, to the message brought by evangelists. The isolation of Bateke Country was breached, the lengthy process of total evangelization begun.

Unlikely Patron

The unlikely patron of backward, superstition-riddled Bateke Country was brash, bustling Kinshasa, whose nearly

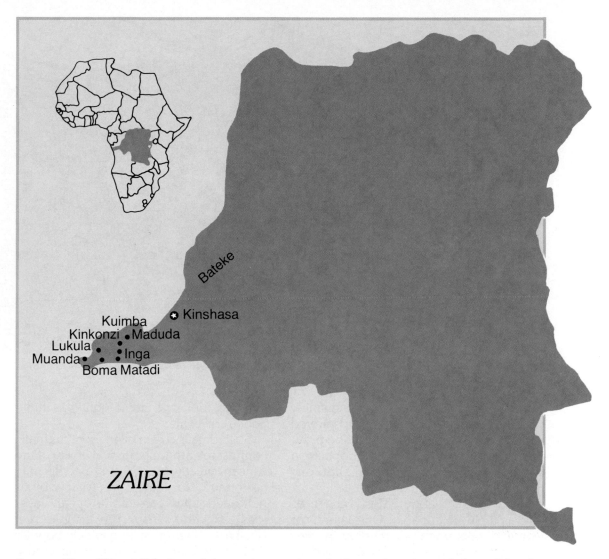

three million "Kinois" believed the entire nation — if not all of Africa — revolved around them.

There was a day when Kinshasa had been a prima donna. In the preindependence era of Belgian colonial rule, Kinshasa (then called Leopoldville) could have won first place in a beauty contest of Black African cities. The ultraefficient Bel-

gians laid out the city with broad boulevards, airy high rises, miniparks crammed with flowers. By controlling the city's population at 200,000, the Belgians managed to keep the capital sparkling with cleanliness and orderly municipal services.

Independence in 1960 brought swift and sweeping changes. The trauma of unsettled politics, army mutinies and civil

Bateke people worship in a temporary shelter.

wars severely curtailed city maintenance, while the capital simultaneously suffered a massive influx of people from the provinces. By the mid-1980s the population had swelled to three million, approximately one of every ten Zairians.

Hard statistics about Kinshasa are as rare as albino elephants. One figure, for example, puts unemployment at 30 percent of the work force. Another statistic indicates 30 percent of the work force employed. The latter may be more accurate, since on any given day the commercial zone and residential areas overflow with idle people, as if it were Sunday afternoon.

One observable fact tells much about the state of Kinshasa: In a city of three million people and an estimated 100,000

vehicles, not one traffic light has functioned for years.

Such details cast in even more dramatic contrast the amazing survival ability of the African city dweller. Young people may go hungry for days, yet wear clothes patterned after current European fashions. Poverty may run amok, yet Kinshasa-style music is so widely popular that other Black African nations accuse Zaire of cultural imperialism.

The Kinshasa Alliance churches reflect the city's incredible penchant for survival with a flair. Before 1965 not a single Alliance congregation existed in the city. By 1984 church leaders counted 82 churches, with a total attendance of over 12,000 on a Sunday morning. In addition, about 200 prayer groups, some

numbering as many as 250 people, met twice weekly. Out of these neighborhood groups would come even more churches.

Dr. Donald McGavran, noted church-growth specialist, stated: "An Alliance church of 20,000 [members in Kinshasa] by 1990 would not be an unrealistic goal. Kinshasa, more than any other city in the world, is ready for spiritual awakening."

The church-growth formula for Kinshasa seems straightforward: Put up a church, and it will fill up. One lively congregation envisioned a 300-seat sanctuary, but midcourse in construction they had to redesign it to handle 500 people. Another congregation built for 800, and when that space quickly filled, they built a 1,500-seat church around it and then dismantled the interior building.

(Clockwise beginning top right) Church-planting strategy session for Kinshasa pastors; evangelism center in Kinshasa; march offering; new church construction surrounding original meeting place

The Rifflart Church typifies how many Alliance churches get their start in Kinshasa.

Zairians moving from the provinces to the capital gravitate to areas where members of their tribe or region are already settled, making Kinshasa somewhat of a confederation of tribal communities. The Rifflart section attracted many people from the Mayombe, which contains the largest concentration of Alliance churches.

Mayombe Christians gathered for prayer and Bible study at the home of an Alliance pastor, who was teaching religion in Kinshasa schools. His full-time work made it possible for the group's offerings to go toward the construction of a chapel. The growing nucleus of believers outgrew the pastor's residence faster than the building could go up, so they met for months in the open air. Underfoot was a thick carpet of dusty sand and overhead an ineffectual lattice of palm branches that kept out neither sun nor rain.

Offerings purchased several sacks of cement at a time. Women carried water and sand, men pressed cement blocks and strung them out on the ground to harden. People who had work brought money; those without work donated labor. People with empty stomachs and bare hovels joined in a project bigger than themselves and found in it a source of pride and enthusiasm that somehow made more bearable their grim struggle to survive.

Cement walls gradually rose up around the increasing congregation, and all seemed well. Then, without warning, disaster. A violent rainstorm toppled two of the nearly completed walls on a Saturday afternoon.

On Sunday morning the pastor stood among the jagged bits of broken masonry and spoke to his disheartened people: "Tomorrow we start again." And they did.

Meanwhile, on an adjoining property, a bare blockhouse of classrooms also grew out of the dusty sand. It was a fact of life that if the church did not provide an education for its children, the Catholics would. Public school education was unavailable.

Eventually, approximately 500 children crowded in the blockhouse to learn from teachers supported by their parents' tuition until the government approved the school. The pastor, now fully supported by the church, supervised the school as well.

When the sanctuary walls once again stood tall, the mission provided tin roofing to cap the 500-seat building. To underscore the support by North American churches, the pastor painted on the underside of the roofing tins, visible for all to read: "Gift of the C&MA Mission."

Some ten years after the first small group of Mayombe Christians met in the pastor's crowded bungalow, the Rifflart Alliance Church stood completed. By then the pastor had already turned his energies to helping other congregations build.

It was he who first brought the spiritual plight of Bateke Country to the attention of the Kinshasa Alliance community.

The prospects of pioneer evangelism work within their region was not something the dynamic churches could pass up. They were true Alliance churches. Congregations already heavily engaged in their own building programs gave offerings for the evangelization of the plateau people. City pastors and missionaries

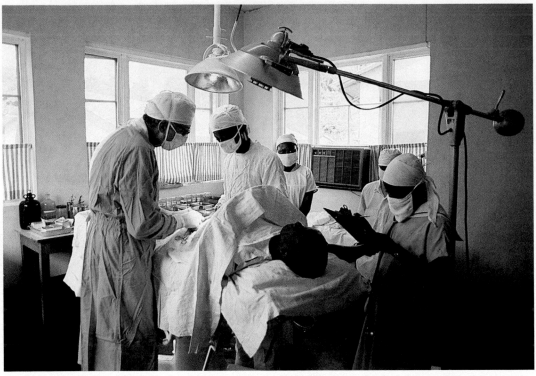

Missionary doctor performs surgery at the Kinkonzi hospital complex.

mapped strategy and made upriver trips to carry out their plans of evangelism.

Supporting a pioneer evangelism program while sacrificing to establish themselves in a city whose daily preoccupation was survival itself, showed the Kinshasa Alliance congregations to be capital-class churches.

Heritage Respected and Refined

If the cosmopolitan Kinshasa churches seemed the unlikely sponsors of evangelism among the Bateke, they themselves were the surprising offspring of a mother church born in another century amid the tangled green fastness of the tropical forest in Lower Zaire.

The Evangelical Alliance Community

of Zaire presents historians with a puzzle: an Alliance mission field established before there was a founding mission of The Christian and Missionary Alliance. Dr. A. B. Simpson, a man in a hurry for God, sent off his first missionary team to Zaire in 1884, three years before he and others got around to organizing the C&MA.

Had he lived another hundred years, Dr. Simpson would have been proud of the church growing out of Alliance missionary work. The Zaire church's vigorous and versatile activities would have excited his innovative mind, and the church's compulsion for outreach would have pleased his visionary spirit.

The first missionaries knew the church would only be as strong as the believers'

A patient is wheeled back to the ward after surgery.

knowledge of the Word. That meant turning the spoken language of Kikongo into written form, then translating the Bible and supporting material, and finally teaching the Africans to read and write so they could profit from the written Word.

The part-time bush school of the 1890s — bamboo benches, wood slates and charcoal sticks — evolved into an educational system unlike anything the Alliance does elsewhere: 25,700 pupils in elementary and high schools, whose education is financed by government funds in six-digit numbers. A Bible school and postsecondary theological school specialize in training church leaders.

The first missionaries knew that Africans wracked by fever and sapped by parasites would not make strong Christians. Therefore the medicine chest joined the chop box as essential supplies for their itineraries. The medicine chest pharmacy and backdoor dispensary developed into a 110-bed hospital in Kinkonzi and twelve district dispensaries treating over 30,000 patients in one year.

The Alliance church in Zaire was granted full autonomy in 1931, the first overseas C&MA church to become self-governing. More recently, the autonomous church added some activities of its own to those inherited from the missionaries. Fisheries in the Mayombe teach villagers how to increase their protein diet, thus showing the church's solidarity with the government's emphasis on de-

velopment. Savings-and-loan cooperatives in urban centers help families wracked by currency devaluations of as much as 500 percent at one time. Relief aid and supplies enable refugees along the border with troubled Angola to start a new life.

"Keep Going"

Perhaps the lesson most deeply etched on the church's mentality by early missionaries distills into one phrase: "Keep going."

The first mission superintendent covered as many as 1,000 miles on foot in his three-month treks. When early missionaries established one station, they immediately began scouting for the next site, deeper inland from the Zaire River, their entry point in the Lower Zaire.

That same compulsive spirit of advance pushed the Kinshasa churches into Bateke Country when they already had their hands full at home. It carried Alliance workers across the Zaire River boundary into the People's Republic of Congo, just as earlier the missionaries felt compelled to travel northward and open Gabon to Alliance ministry. It meant entering the

(Clockwise beginning top left) Dr. Kuvuna ku Konde Mwela, church president, looks over the enormous crowd celebrating the church centennial; church leaders sit together on one side; the women's choir dressed in special centennial cloth.

large port city of Matadi and starting four central churches and forty chapels in ten years.

"Keep going" also characterizes Rev. Kuvuna ku Konde Mwela, president of the Evangelical Alliance Community. Having already lived his fourscore years — over three score in the ministry — he was advised to scale down his extensive itineraries among the churches.

He smiled and recalled an early foot-soldier missionary. "He told me that if the time ever came when he had to sit and could no longer itinerate, he would die. He passed on to me that habit."

In mid-1985 Rev. Kuvuna was given an honorary doctorate by Nyack College. He was the third overseas church leader to be given that distinction, and rightly so. No other Alliance churchman had served in as many high places of leadership with distinction for as many years as he.

In his brief acceptance speech, however, Dr. Kuvuna said, "This honor is not mine alone. It belongs as well to your missionaries who brought the Gospel to my people, and to the remarkable church God raised up through their efforts."

Well spoken. □

CHURCH AND MISSION

OFFICIAL NAME OF CHURCH:	Evangelical Community of the Alliance in Zaire
ENTRY BY MISSIONARIES:	1884
NUMBER OF MISSIONARIES:	34
ORGANIZED CHURCHES:	481
UNORGANIZED CHURCHES AND PREACHING POINTS:	1,934
BAPTIZED CHURCH MEMBERS:	64,826
INCLUSIVE MEMBERSHIP:	194,478
MEDICAL WORK:	12 dispensaries Kinkonzi Hospital Maduda Hospital
EDUCATION:	Kinkonzi Bible Institute Kinshasa Bible Institute ISTEB (Boma Seminary)
PAGES PRINTED:	1,031,000

COUNTRY

OFFICIAL NAME:	Republic of Zaire
FORM OF GOVERNMENT:	Republic with strong presidential authority
OFFICIAL LANGUAGE(S):	French
AREA:	905,563 sq. mi.
POPULATION:	33,100,000
CAPITAL:	Kinshasa
PER CAPITA INCOME:	$160.00
LITERACY:	45%
RELIGIOUS AFFILIATION:	Traditional religions 8–12%, Muslim 1.4%, Christian 88–92%

ASIA MAINLAND

INDIA 74

SOUTH KOREA 86

THAILAND 92

CHURCHES UNDER COMMUNISM 104

ASIA MAINLAND

Still the Greatest Challenge

Although Asia has been a theater of evangelistic effort from the opening days of the New Testament Church, it remains the church's greatest missionary challenge. The East still ranks first in spiritual need after twenty centuries of the Christian era if for no other reason than its sheer mass of humanity.

Asia had a total of 2.7 billion people in 1985, more than the entire world population just thirty years earlier. Other statistics indicate that one of every two people alive was Asian;[1] one of every three lived either in India or China. The two giant countries will each have at least twenty cities with populations of twelve or more million by the year 2000.[2]

The mass of Asian peoples has not been totally neglected by the church. Donald E. Hoke estimated that in 1972 the total number of Christians in the East probably reached eighty-one million: over twenty-four million Protestants and fifty-seven million Roman Catholics.[3]

Startling developments in more recent years have significantly increased that figure. Mainland Chinese believers are now thought by some observers to number between forty and fifty-five million.[4]

In addition to the five thousand churches already registered with the Beijing regime in 1985, another three thousand awaited formal recognition. (Prerequisites for application included a membership list of at least three hundred Christians and a suitable number of pastors.) Many thousands of other meeting places served believers too suspicious of the Communist regime to seek official status. Dr. David B. Barrett, researcher and author on Christian world population, estimated

that in 1986 China had at least 81,600 worship centers (churches, congregations, house churches), making it the nation with the world's fastest growing church.[5]

A second remarkable development in Asia since Hoke's 1972 estimate has been church growth in South Korea.

The *World Christian Encyclopedia* reported over 11.4 million adherents in 1982, an unprecedented 30.5 percent of the Korean population.[6] During the mid-1980s, an average of six new churches were started each day.[7] The rate of growth will likely result in a Christian community of 21,609,000—better than four of every ten Koreans—in A.D. 2000.[8]

However, these glowing reports of remarkable church growth do not characterize response to the Gospel throughout all of Asia. In 1982, David Barrett ranked Asia third in numerical Christian growth, behind South America and Africa.[9]

The Christian community in India, for example, was 3.9 percent of the overall population in 1980. In Thailand, adherents to the Christian faith numbered only one in a hundred. Laos and Kampuchea (Cambodia) had even fewer Roman Catholics and Protestants: 1.8 percent and 0.6 percent respectively.[10]

Church of the Easterns

The relatively small Christian community in Asia today is hardly indicative of the sacrificial investment by the church since the earliest days of the apostolic era.

While the Apostle Paul turned westward to answer the Macedonian call and initiate the evangelization of Europe, other believers turned with equal fervor to win the East. In fact,

according to historian Gordon H. Chapman, "During the first few centuries of Christianity, the most extensive dissemination of the Gospel was not in the West but the East."[11]

Evangelism in Asia actually began on the Day of Pentecost, when "devout men from every nation under heaven" heard the Apostle Peter's dynamic preaching. Three thousand converts were added to the church in one day. Among the new believers were Jews and proselytes specifically mentioned as coming from Asia.[12] They formed the nucleus of the Eastern Church, sometimes called the Nestorian Church.

The ancient historian Eusebius reported that the twelve apostles divided among themselves missionary responsibility for the world.[13] Thomas accepted the Parthian Empire (now parts of Iran, Pakistan and Iraq) and India as his field of ministry; Bartholomew agreed to help evangelize India.

However, the church owed its rapid expansion eastward not to a few church leaders, but to a steady stream of Spirit-filled laymen who made it their business to evangelize wherever their travels took them.

One historian noted that Christian communities stretched from Near to Far East, possibly as early as the first century,[14] and this was due to "the involvement of a large percentage of the church's believers in missionary evangelism."[15]

The Christian community in Mesopotamia (now Iraq) played an especially significant role in outreach to the East. The city of Edessa (now Urfa) became the country's most important missionary center.

Edessa's monastic school, reported to have had eight hundred students, trained both laymen and clergy. Straddling trade arteries that crisscrossed within its walls from every direction, the city served as the starting point for these and other missionaries who gradually spread throughout Mesopotamia, Persia, Central Asia and China.[16]

Another missionary center gained prominence in Seleucia, along the Tigris River near Baghdad. By the latter half of the second century, itinerant missionaries, self-supporting as merchants and craftsmen, carried the Gospel from Seleucia to distant areas known today as Iran and Afghanistan, planting churches as they went.

Other Christians spread southward from Jerusalem to evangelize Arabia. Unlike the nomadic Bedouin who rejected anything new or foreign, townspeople were open to new ideas. Among them the Gospel found lodging. Christian communities began to appear all along the Arabian coast.

Thomas in India

Tradition, backed by some scholarly opinion, puts the Apostle Thomas in both north and south India during the latter part of the first century. In northwest India, he reportedly won many people to the Lord, including the Indo-Parthian king, Gundaphorus, who influenced the conversion of many people.

Moving to the Malabar coast of southern India, Thomas is credited with winning some seventeen thousand converts, including members from the four principal castes. Tradition and some ancient documents cite him as founder of the Mar Thoma Church, which bears his name.

The *Didache,* dating from the end of the first century, states: "India and all countries bordering it, even to the farthest seas

... received the Apostolic ordinances from Judas Thomas, who was guide and ruler in the church which he founded."[17]

Hoke regarded such claims with scepticism at first but, after researching available material, conceded a strong possibility that "the Mar Thoma Church of India is the world's oldest living church" and its founder was probably Thomas.[18]

However, evidence is fragmentary and inconclusive, according to historian Latourette. "We can neither demonstrate nor disprove the existence of Christians in India in the first three centuries," he decided.[19]

Tradition also maintains that Thomas reached China in his missionary travels. Upon returning to India, he was reportedly martyred by enraged class-conscious Brahmans, who feared his preaching would destabilize the caste system, India's basic social structure.[20]

Mounting Hostility

Thomas's reported successes culminating in martyrdom fits the pattern evident during the "golden age of early missions."[21]

Missionaries and dedicated laymen pushed eastward along the major trade routes, rapidly extending the Gospel message from Near to Far East. By A.D. 226, bishops oversaw churches in India, Afghanistan, Iran, Iraq, Tibet and perhaps even China.

As the church in Asia grew, so did resistance to it. Persecution became severe and widespread from the third century onward.

This increasing hostility resulted in part from Christianity's progress in the Roman Empire. As the church gained strength in the West, it became suspect in the East. And when Emperor Constantine signed the Edict of Milan in A.D. 313 and tilted the Roman Empire in favor of Christianity, historical enemies of Rome in Asia branded the church an enemy of their homelands.

Thus, "the comparatively meagre gains east of the Euphrates were the price which Christianity paid for its successes in the Roman Empire."[22] Despite accelerating resistance to the Gospel and persecution of believers, Asian Christianity continued to display remarkable strength.

Chapman wrote, "For at least twelve hundred years the Church of the Easterns was noted for its missionary zeal, its high degree of lay participation, its superior educational standards and cultural contributions, and its fortitude in the face of persecution."[23]

Entrenched Competition

The Gospel in Asia did not meet with response comparable to its success in Europe for several reasons—none of which suggests an inferior faith among the Easterns.

Perhaps the primary factor that held the church in Asia to a small minority status was competition from established indigenous religions.

Missionaries to the West met a Roman civilization already starting to crumble. Nowhere did they encounter a fully developed, vigorous religion that could mount stiff resistance.

In contrast, the Far East gave birth to several world-class religions that predated Christianity and were already firmly entrenched before the Gospel arrived. Among those great religions were Hinduism, Buddhism and Confucianism. Christendom's other chief rival, Islam, rose out of the Near East at a later date.

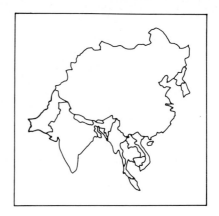

Because of their relatively small numbers and minority status, Christian communities under fire in the East tended to develop in tightly knit communities much like the Jewish ghettos of Europe. They clustered together, avoided integration with society in general, educated their own children, and patronized the buyers and sellers within their own ranks.

This isolationist attitude not only hampered growth and witness of the church, it made Christians easy targets for increased persecution from dominant religious groups, such as the following.

HINDUISM. When the Aryans invaded India around 1500 B.C., they brought a form of religion that became the region's dominant creed. Hinduism, called Brahmanism in earlier times, teaches that Brahman is the supreme world spirit whose attributes are similar to Israel's Jehovah: infinite, absolute, eternal and indescribable.

But unlike Jehovah, Brahman is an impersonal being. The ultimate goal of every Hindu, through death and rebirth, is union of his soul with Brahman, an absorption in the Absolute.

Hindus believe a soul pure enough to be united with Brahman cannot be achieved in one lifetime. It therefore passes through numerous reincarnations.

The law of Karma regulates the soul's progress through thousands of reincarnations into the invisible, formless world soul of Brahman. The doctrine of works specifies acts in this life that determine a person's form in the next state of transition, whether at a higher or lower rank. Dedication to good deeds, philosophic meditation, and devotion to one god are the surest ways to reach Brahman, according to Hindu law.

Hinduism also permits the worship of hundreds of gods as stepping-stones to understanding and achieving union with Brahman. It has therefore been termed not one religion, but a family of religions.

Writes one scholar, "They [Hindus] can be pantheists, polytheists, monotheists, agnostics, or even atheists; dualists, pluralists, or monists. They may follow different moral standards or they may choose instead a supramoral mysticism. They may live an active life or a contemplative one. . . .

"They may worship regularly at a temple or go not at all. Their only general obligation, whatever their divergences, is to abide by the rules and rituals of their caste and trust that by doing so their next birth will be a happier one."[24]

The caste system became a mandatory teaching of Hinduism and gradually formed the basis of India's social and religious life, permanently assigning individuals to one level in the multilayered structure of society.

Although Hinduism recognizes four great classes of caste—priests and teachers; rulers and warriors; traders, artisans and farmers; servants—India has many other castes and a great mass of "outcasts" or "untouchables."

Being a religion of religions, Hinduism lacked the dynamic impulsion to become a missionary movement. But it became deeply rooted in the social, religious, political and economic structure of India centuries before the birth of Christ. It checkmated the Early Church's missionary probes, preventing Christianity from gaining more than a foothold on the Indian subcontinent.

BUDDHISM. Despite Hinduism's lack of clear-cut dogma—

or perhaps because of the lack—it gave birth to other religions rejecting its teachings or practices. Of these rebel religions, the most important to emerge as a world religion was Buddhism.

It became the most influential non-Christian religion in Asia. Wherever Buddhism flourished, the Gospel failed to win a large following.

Buddhism began in the meditations of Gautama (563-483 B.C.), son of a rajah and member of the ruler-military caste in Nepal. Sickened by a life of luxury and laziness at age twenty-nine, Gautama became a wandering ascetic. After six years of aimless meandering in total poverty, he realized that such an existence was meaningless. He then assumed the more normal role of a holy man supported by the generosity of others.

Finally, in 528 B.C., Gautama sat down under a sacred fig tree and vowed not to leave until he became enlightened concerning the mystery of life. A certain clarity of vision came to him during his vigil and he remained under the tree for seven weeks, wrapped in little more than meditations and insights.

From that time on, Gautama became Buddha, "the enlightened one." The essence of his discovery through meditation was that "the cause of all human misery is desire, arising out of the will to possess."[25]

According to Buddha, progress toward the peace of Nirvana, a state of perfect absence of all desire, depended on recognizing this basic fact of human existence and dealing with it. In its plan of salvation, Buddhism steered a middle path between a total lack of discipline and morals and the total self-denial of asceticism.

"Four Noble Truths" identified the problem of human misery and its solution through a code of ethics and conduct known as the "Noble Eightfold Path," a lofty ethical code.

Buddhism abolished the Hindu caste system, rejected the Brahman priesthood's monopoly on spiritual leadership, and discarded Hindu concepts of deity and ritual order. The doctrine of Karma remained, as did belief in reincarnation and soul transmigration.

Although native to India, Buddhism was viciously attacked by Hinduism and almost entirely obliterated in its homeland. The movement took root elsewhere and gradually developed into two branches: the "little vehicle (Theravada)" and the "great vehicle (Mahayana)."

The "little vehicle" group appeared in the third century B.C., teaching that the ideal saint withdraws from the world and gives himself to attaining enlightenment and Nirvana through self-denial and reflection. This conservative form of Buddhism took root in Burma, Ceylon, Thailand, Laos and Kampuchea.

The "great vehicle" branch of Buddhism developed during the first century B.C. It maintained that followers of Buddha should strive to attain Nirvana not only for themselves, but also to save as many others as possible. This more liberal and aggressive movement took root in Tibet, China and Japan.

CONFUCIANISM. When Buddhism arrived in China around A.D. 67, it found Confucianism something of a state cult, but not the exclusive religion of the realm.

Confucianism actually began as a moral or ethical system. It was not intended to be a religion. Confucius (c. 551–479 B.C.) was a scholar who aspired to become a public official during a period of warfare, corruption and tyranny.

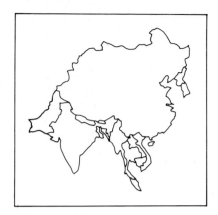

He advocated a new system based on peace, justice and good order in society. His teachings, recorded in the Five Classics, became the holy book of his followers.

At the heart of his precepts is a negative code in complete contrast to Jesus' positive admonition. It reads, "What you do not want done to yourself, do not unto others."[26]

The movement did not claim the status of religion, but gradually changed under the influence of other Chinese religions and eventually included ancestor worship in its teachings. After his death, Confucius himself was deified and became the object of state worship in 195 B.C.

ISLAM. Being born in the Middle East like Judaism and Christianity seemed to intensify the hostility of Islam toward its two neighboring religions.

Muhammad, founder of Islam, apparently did not harbor such negative feelings against Christians and Jews. He borrowed heavily from the Old Testament as he wrote the Quran (Koran), sacred book of Islam. Jesus was included among the prophets sent by Allah from time to time. Muhammad, however, claimed that in a series of revelations, an angel called him the last and greatest of the prophets.

The Muslim faith expounded by Muhammad and his successors contained relatively few teachings and principal practices. Most importantly, the Quran stresses the absolute unity of God, or Allah, and submission to Him. All forms of idolatry are forbidden.

Such teachings brought Islam into bitter conflict with Christianity's doctrine of a Triune God and of salvation through the redemptive death and resurrection of the Son of God.

Muslim Scourge

Following Muhammad's death in A.D. 632, a series of "caliphs," or successors, forged the warlike Bedouin tribes of the Arabian peninsula and other Muslims into an explosive religious and political force. Militant Islam burst upon both Western and Eastern civilizations like a scourge.

By the early seventh century, Islam had swept across the Fertile Crescent. Within its second century of conquest, it plunged deep into northern India and central Asia as far as China. Muslims threatened all of Europe until they were soundly beaten at the Battle of Tours in A.D. 732.

Christian communities under Islamic rule were not totally wiped out at first. Many survived hundreds of years, albeit under constant pressure and persecution. Muslims were forbidden under penalty of death to become Christians, while the church was expressly forbidden to evangelize.

Islam seized control of the great trade routes, both land and sea. This shut off vast regions of the East to the Gospel, forcing Christianity back into Europe from the first millennium to the modern era. While the Cross continued to make gains in Europe, the Crescent claimed almost all of Africa's northern tier, most of Asia Minor, Syria and Palestine, Persia and Central Asia.

Latourette summarized the times: "In the thousand years between A.D. 500 and 1500, Christianity was forced to surrender about as much territory and as many adherents as it gained."[27]

That the church disappeared in vast areas of the Near and Far East is not surprising. That Christian communities managed for almost one thousand years to confront a younger Islam promoted by aggressive, ruthless people politically in control is a heroic achievement Western Christianity has fortunately never had to equal.

Luminous Religion

No one is exactly sure when or where Christianity entered China and became known as the "Luminous Religion."

An ancient document of the Syrian Church of Malabar, India, mentions that "by means of St. Thomas the kingdom of heaven flew and entered into China."[28] If the claim is true, those first-century missionary efforts made no lasting impact. There exists little or no evidence of Christians in China before the seventh century.

Beginning with the T'ang era (A.D. 618–906), references to Christianity become numerous in Chinese documents. The remarkable "Nestorian Monument" still stands as dramatic proof of the church's existence in China by the mid-600s.

Erected in A.D. 781 near the city of Ch'angan (now Xian), the monument commemorates kind deeds of a local Christian merchant who used his wealth to help the poor and to build or restore churches and monasteries.

The inscriptions record valuable data concerning the "Luminous Religion." A doctrinal statement enumerates basic biblical beliefs. An historical account dates arrival of the first missionary to that region in A.D. 635. Another section of the monument lists over sixty names of Christian workers, including one bishop, twenty-eight presbyters, and thirty-eight monks.[29]

The Christian movement experienced highs and lows for about 250 years during the T'ang period. The government at times granted full freedom to worship. In other years, the church faced severe persecution, especially under the infamous Empress Dowager Wu (689–699), who was a zealous Buddhist.

Emperor Wu Tsung, an ardent Taoist, interdicted Buddhist and Christian activities in the ninth century, and the church declined to insignificance for four hundred years. It then soared to its peak when, in the thirteenth century, the Mongol Empire stretched from eastern Europe to the Pacific.

Genghis Khan (1167–1227), the great Mongol leader, drafted many Christians from the conquered provinces of Central Asia and the Middle East. He even married one of his sons to a Christian princess. She became the mother of Kublai Khan, the first Mongol emperor of China and founder of the Yuan dynasty (1213–1368).

Kublai Khan did not become a believer, but he encouraged growth of the church. A fourteenth-century report cited some thirty thousand Christians, although many seemed to be Westerners in government employ. The "Luminous Religion" grew to such stature that a special government bureau was established just to supervise Christian monasteries and churches.[30]

When the Yuan dynasty fell in 1368, so did state-favored Christianity. This sudden decline coincided with a resurgent Islam that was rapidly sweeping through the East.

Tamerlane (1336–1405), a bigoted Muslim of Mongol descent, waged an especially ruthless campaign against the church in the vast area of his conquest. Christians who refused to become Muslims were slaughtered; churches were destroyed and monasteries sacked.

In one generation, Christianity was virtually exterminated in

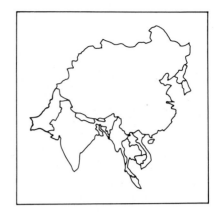

Asia. Only small remnants survived in Mesopotamia, Kurdistan, and in southwest India, where the Mar Thoma Church refused to die.

Dr. Samuel Zwemer summarized the fate of the church and its missionary movement: "The strength of the Nestorian [Eastern] Church was love and loyalty to Christ, emphasis on the Great Commission and heroism. Its weakness in the later periods was due to compromise in the face of persecution, which led to absorption by other faiths and final extermination in regions once Christian."[31]

Rome's Representatives

The Roman Catholic Church was introduced to the East by laymen, not priests.

Many European merchants who came to Kublai Khan's China during the thirteenth century were Catholics by persuasion. Through them the emperor learned of Rome and requested the Pope to send teachers of science and religion.

The first Roman Catholic missionary probably reached China around 1294. His successes encouraged the Papal See to send more priests. Collapse of the Mongol Empire and hostility of subsequent regimes in China, however, brought the Catholic community to the same "final solution" inflicted on the Nestorian Church.

India, the other great concentration of Asian people, received hardly a glance from Rome in the thirteenth and fourteenth centuries. Some missionaries on their way to China stopped off in India to win a few converts. Only a few remained to establish the church, and their results died with them.

The next era of Roman Catholic missions in Asia was largely sparked by one of the most famous missionaries of all time: Francis Xavier (1506–1552). He was assigned to India, but his heart encompassed all of Asia.

Other missionaries had arrived in India with Portuguese naval fleets reopening trade routes cut by Muslims. But none of Rome's other emissaries could match the panoramic sweep of Xavier's vision, none could equal his zeal or results.

"His was the vision and the task of the explorer and the pioneer, to blaze new trails, to open doors, and to lay foundations," wrote Latourette.

"He had only slightly more than ten years in the East, but in that brief span of time he ranged over parts of India and Ceylon, to Malacca, and to the East Indies; he began Roman Catholic missions in Japan, and he died, towards the end of the year 1552, off the coast of China while endeavoring to gain entrance to that vast empire."[32]

In Japan alone, Xavier's two years of aggressive evangelism resulted in a church that burgeoned until membership may have reached two hundred thousand within 150 years. Vicious persecution then obliterated the visible church for almost two hundred years.[33]

Roman Catholicism on mainland Asia had its tense times and suffered reverses, but never shared the tragic fate of the church in Japan. Despite successive waves of persecution, a series of hostile regimes, and diminishing support from Europe as Spain and Portugal declined in power, the church hung on and in some places actually grew.

By the close of the eighteenth century, the Catholic community in China was estimated between 200,000 and 300,000;[34] in India, between 475,000 and 1,200,000;[35] and in Indo-China, over 150,000.[36]

Protestants' Great Century

If the previous centuries in Asia belonged to the Church of the Easterns and the Church of Rome, the nineteenth century belonged to the Protestants. Some historians call it "the great century of Christian missions."

Commented Latourette: "Never in the preceding eighteen centuries of its history had the Christian message been so widely proclaimed by word and life in the continent of its origin. Never, indeed, had any religion been so extensively propagated in Asia."[37]

The wave of Protestant missions that swept over not only Asia, but Africa and Latin America as well, grew out of great revivals, faith missions, Bible schools and other spiritual movements that mobilized evangelicals in Britain and North America.

The total number of new Asian believers for the entire period from 1800 to 1914 probably numbered less than ten million Catholics and Protestants, with the latter growing faster, percentage-wise.[38] The number was miniscule when compared with Asia's massive population.

The growth, however, was achieved in the face of seemingly overwhelming odds. Firmly entrenched religions, such as Hinduism and Buddhism, contested every inch of advance. Christians faced terrible persecution as late as 1866 in Korea and repressive edicts in Japan during the 1870s. Repression of Christians in China raged throughout the late 1800s and revived again in the 1920s. Yet millions were converted by a relatively small missionary force of less than thirty thousand by 1914.[39]

The high standards required for Protestant church membership kept the official total of Christians low, but tended to insure a higher quality of faith and commitment within the church. Training and support of qualified national workers also figured significantly during the "great century of missions."

One aspect of missions during the 1800s is seldom acknowledged: the relationship between missions and colonial powers. Roman Catholicism and temporal powers had long worked together closely. For Protestants in the nineteenth century, it was a relatively new and, at times, uncomfortable alliance.

"While it is common to curse European colonialism, the facts are that the church in Asia has been most firmly planted where the European nations ruled," observed Hoke.[40] "It is incontrovertible that colonialism, however it might be politically assessed, was an instrument in the hands of the sovereign God to open doors for the penetration of the Gospel in those lands."[41]

William Carey, who spearheaded the modern era of Protestant missions, was only the first of many remarkable missionaries who followed the great trade routes taken over by European powers. Among the early greats: Henry Martyn in India; Robert Morrison and Hudson Taylor in China; Adoniram Judson in Burma; and at a later date, Robert Jaffray in South China, Indo-China and Indonesia.

These heroic pioneers and thousands of like-spirited colleagues laid the foundation for a church that in the twentieth century would regain some of the dynamic spirit that propelled

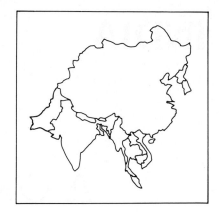

the Church of the Easterns to evangelize much of Asia in the first centuries.

By the mid-nineteenth century, the numbers of Christians doubled in some Eastern countries. In others, they impacted on society to a degree far greater than their numerical size. And they infiltrated closed nations to plant churches even the most determined efforts of hostile regimes could not suppress.

Third World Missions

By its sheer size in numbers and area, Asia defies evangelization by Western missions alone. In 1979, North American Protestant agencies fielded over 10,600 overseas workers among Asia's hundreds of millions. Their small number prompts a question once voiced by Jesus' disciples concerning a little lunch of loaves and fishes: "What are these among so many?"

Fortunately, they are not alone in their task.

One phenomenon of twentieth century evangelicalism is the emerging missionary force of Third World countries. Worldwide, cross-cultural missionaries from non-Western nations numbered 20,000 in 1985. During the decade beginning 1972, these missions increased by 448 percent. They are projected to support as many as 100,000 missionaries by the year 2000.[42]

The All Asia Missions Consultation in 1972 called on Asian churches to send out 10,000 new missionaries by the end of this century. In related moves, it proposed establishing a center for missionary research and development and an All-Asia missions training center.[43]

Some Eastern churches have started to put those plans into action.

India's churches ranked first in 1985 among non-Western, missionary-sending agencies: some 4,200 workers carried on cross-cultural ministries.[44]

Christians in Singapore have one of the best missionary-to-member ratios in the world. Their churches supported about 400 missionaries in the mid-1980s—approximately one missionary for every 522 church members.[45]

Despite these encouraging signs, churches in the East will need the involvement of large numbers of committed laymen, just as happened in the opening years of the Christian era, if Asia is to have an adequate witness.

Someone calculated in 1975 that evangelizing Asia would require twenty million Christians, each one witnessing effectively to at least ten persons per year for twelve years—and then continue for another eight years in order to cover population growth in that period of time.[46]

The biblical phrase, "The first shall be last," could well apply to the East. Asia, which first heard the Gospel in apostolic times, still remains the church's last and greatest missionary challenge twenty centuries later. ☐

INDIA

A Conclusion Ordered and Orderly

Explaining his government's restrictions on foreign missionaries, India's Prime Minister Nehru wrote to a Lutheran Church of Sweden official: "As far as possible, the Indian Church should be independent.

"We have in India the Syrian Church, which has been here for 1800 years and more. We have had various churches of the Protestant persuasion for the last 100 to 150 years. These periods are long enough to build up an indigenous church which need not rely too much upon external assistance for its existence."[1]

The long-standing Indian policy of denying visas to missionaries is slowly and effectively rendering Western church workers a vanishing breed. From 1960 to 1975, the total missionary force in India shrank 40 percent; it continues to drop today.[2] The *Mission Handbook* listed 614 North American Protestant personnel in India in 1985.[3]

The Alliance mission, known officially as Alliance Ministries, faces a dilemma common to other Western church agencies in India. Unless the government reverses its policy and grants visas to new missionaries—an unlikely development—

the remaining Alliance foreign workers will be eligible to retire by 1992.

Should that happen, the mission will have transferred all its properties and responsibilities to The Christian and Missionary Alliance of India.

If the nation one day is closed to Christian missions, it will not mark a government triumph over the church, but just one more event permitted by God in His ongoing sovereign purpose for His people. Church history has often recorded that when the parent mission is forced to withdraw, the national church experiences unprecedented growth. Nor can it be assumed that, if a Western mission can no longer work in a country, the church is shut off from all help. History has also recorded that churches from other Third World nations can still render invaluable assistance.

Hindu Nationalism

The government of India has its own reasons for locking out Western missionaries. "The government is promoting the indigenization of all foreign-related organizations, especially the churches," explains Theodore Williams, a leading

Indian evangelist and chairman of the World Evangelical Fellowship theological commission.[4]

Only missionaries with skills lacking in the Christian community have a chance of getting in—even they are expected to train Indians in their skills and then move on. Anyone else trying to enter India is wasting time, Williams warns.

Official Indian policy reflects some resentment against foreign missions that formerly tried to take advantage of India's difficulties by "buying" converts among the suffering, impoverished masses. In more recent times, Muslim religious leaders have won many followers with inducements financed by oil-rich Islamic nations.

At the heart of the government's anti-missionary attitude lies a motive that is equally religious and political: Hindu nationalism.

The nation's leaders and the overwhelming majority of its citizens believe that India is Hinduism. This great world religion, with its made-in-India label, mingles national identity and religious belief so completely that the two are one.

To be other than Hindu is unpatriotic, argue politicians. To reject Hinduism and

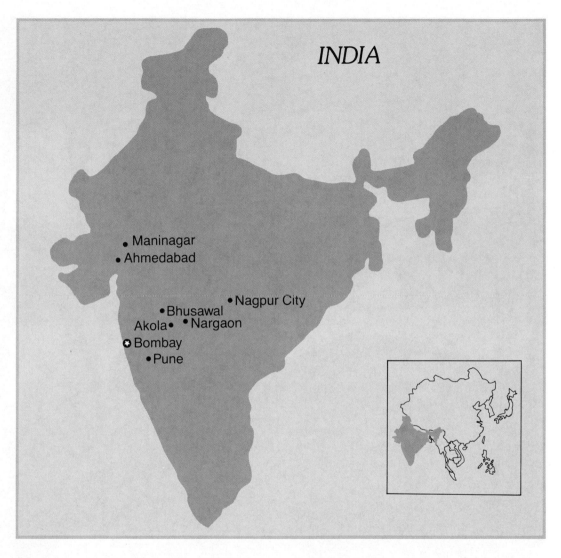

INDIA

embrace another religion is an act of treason, claim religious leaders. Christian evangelism is viewed as an attack on the social structure and value system that hold the widely diverse nation together.

This kind of reasoning prompted various states at different times to outlaw attempts to convert Hindus. The Indian Supreme Court has struck down these laws on the basis that India is a secular state. However, fundamentalist politicians and religious leaders push on with their efforts to make India a Hindu state.

Mission Incomplete

Facing an eventual government-imposed withdrawal, Christian missions must consider their work incomplete. Part of the problem lies in the enormous number of people who live in India. Its 767,650,000 inhabitants by mid-1980 equalled the combined populations of North and South America, with Australia added as well. Already containing one-sixth of the world's population, India is exploding toward the billion mark by century's end and could eventually have more people than China.

The 1971 census showed Christianity emerging as the country's fastest growing religion, with a 32.6 percent increase. During the sixties, churches claimed three million new adherents. That still left Roman Catholics, Protestants and related cult groups with only 2.6 percent of the total Indian population. Hinduism dipped almost 1 percent, but nearly 83 percent of all Indians remain Hindus.[5]

The relatively small Christian community belies the great length of time during which churches have been present in India. The Mar Thoma Church in South India claims one of the original apostles, "Doubting" Thomas, as its founder (*see* Asia Mainland). This would have placed the Gospel in India earlier than in most parts of Europe.

Why has the Gospel fared so poorly? Indian evangelist Theodore Williams comments, "One of the weaknesses of the church in India is the lack of lay witness. Evangelism still remains the responsibility of the full-time worker."[6]

Based on 1975 statistics, this means a ratio of one church worker for every 111,600 individuals, he points out, or one pastor for eight churches and 400 villages. In some places, a pastor may be actually responsible for 180 to 200 churches.[7]

Williams cites another reason for the small number of Christians after centuries of work: nominalism in the church. Instead of born-again believers, many church members are "caste" Christians, born into the membership of their parents' church.

"To a great extent," Williams explains, "this is the result of the mass movements of earlier periods. A vast majority of professed Christians have no personal knowledge of Christ. Petty rivalries and divisions, plus strife based on caste, language, and region, mar the witness of these churches. Litigation among believers is a common evil. Evangelistic zeal and missionary vision are sadly lacking in the larger part of the church."[8]

Western missions must share responsibility for this state of affairs in the Indian Christian community.

Third World churches are the offspring of their founding missions, and often bear a striking resemblance to them. Although British colonialism helped the Gospel to enter India, close relations between the largely Protestant colonial administration and Protestant missions did not greatly advance spiritual maturity in the Indian church.

Still another factor limiting church growth is opposition to the Gospel by rival religions. "India has ever been the home of religions," writes Sherwood Eddy, "a vast religious area where the world's great faiths are on trial."[9]

Buddhism, Jainism, Brahmanism, Sikhism are all home grown faiths that fight Christianity with the hostility of native sons opposing a foreign intruder.

Islam also contends for the hearts of the masses. Although the majority of Muslims moved to Pakistan during the 1947-1948 massive exodus when India was partitioned, Islam's thirty-eight million followers still make it India's second largest religion.

Hinduism, however, towers above all other rivals as Christianity's chief antagonist. The struggle not only involves vast numbers of people (approximately 660,205,000 Hindus in 1985), but also totally opposite sets of beliefs.

Christians stake everything on the truth of the Bible that declares the only way to God and eternal life is through Jesus Christ, the Son of God. Hinduism vaunts itself as a religion of religions, embracing the best of all beliefs, yet retaining its basic character.

In reality, however, Hinduism is far from tolerant. Although Buddhism was born in India, it had to flee elsewhere to survive, hounded out of India by hostile Hindus. Only a small group of Buddhists remain in their spiritual homeland. Hinduism likewise attacks Christianity, insisting that since it already incorporates the best of Christian beliefs, there is no further need for that foreign religion to remain.

Mission Legacy

Should Alliance Ministries indeed conclude its work, what legacy would it leave the church in India? The following survey indicates what the missionaries and Indian pastors have accomplished together and what the church could continue doing.

The Scriptures remain. The missionaries and Indian believers have impacted India to an extent far greater than their relatively few numbers imply.

Large areas and vast numbers of people have at least an awareness of the Gospel in Marathi and Gujarati, two major languages of the people. Radio programs, correspondence courses and other literature have circulated widely. Over a thirty-year period, for example, more than 400,000 Gospels of John and introductory lesson series went out to individuals responding to radio programs and literature distribution efforts.

The organized church remains. Autonomous since 1931, The Christian and Missionary Alliance of India provides an infrastructure of fellowship for believers in two major states and some of the largest cities.

The Gujarat and Maharashtra Synods, organized for many years, were joined recently by a third, the Urban Church Synod, which consists of congregations in

metropolitan centers that have more in common with one another than with neighboring rural churches in Maharashtra.

Alliance pastors from all three groups met together for the first time in a combined spiritual retreat in 1983. Dr. Ravi Zacharias, an Indian-born North American evangelist, ministered during the ten-day session. A spirit of openness, even brokenness, among the twenty-eight pastors gave promise that the three diverse groups could become a unified fellowship in the Gospel.

The witness remains. Established churches dot rural areas and some key cities of Gujarat and Maharashtra.

Urban congregations show the most

(Left) *Bombay's modern and stylistic architecture announces that the future is already here,* (facing page) *while the church's buildings, such as this portable chapel financed by Women's Missionary Prayer Fellowships in the United States, serve to remind the nation of another world yet to come.*

initiative in evangelism and represent the church's best potential for growth. Churches in Bombay, Nagpur and Pune set a goal in 1985 to double within two years, to six hundred baptized members and sixteen organized and unorganized churches. The target may have been set too high, but it did indicate a growth mood among the believers.

Bombay, the larger of India's two major seaports, offers unbounded opportunities for evangelism. Burgeoning from 4.1 million in 1961 to over eight million within two decades, Bombay is a congested microcosm of the entire nation.

Fourteen major language groups are resident in large numbers, as well as most of the religions. Protestants claimed 2 percent of Bombay's people in 1981, but most of the 180 congregations met in homes and few were evangelical.

The Alliance began the first in a series of church-planting projects in 1970. Ten years later, four missionary couples and several pastors counted 271 members in five churches, three of which were self-supporting.

The New Bombay Church, founded in 1974, encountered some obstacles to

growth familiar to other Alliance groups in the great city. The congregation chose English as their language of worship because they belonged to seven different linguistic groups.

First they met in two homes, outgrowing each one. Then they moved to a 125-seat portable chapel provided by the Women's Missionary Prayer Fellowships of North America.

The growing congregation made plans to build a 400-seat sanctuary in 1983, but bureaucratic delays and supply shortages pushed construction costs to $130,000—triple the original estimate. A grant from the ''Good News for Great Cities'' fund in North America enabled the congregation to dedicate the new sanctuary in 1984.

Pastoral training schools remain. The lack of trained pastors handicaps church growth, but the problem lies in a shortage of students, not facilities.

The Marathi Bible College, located in Nargaon, began in 1908 as a training school for Alliance workers. For over seventy years it has served not only the Alliance but other denominations in Maharashtra State.

The Alliance mission and church joined with several other evangelical groups to form Union Biblical Seminary at Yeotmal in September of 1953. They realized that only a seminary-level training program could prepare young men and women for city pastorates.

Growth of the student body and ex-panded programs of study forced the seminary to relocate in 1983 to Pune, a city considered a Hindu stronghold and an important educational center in Maharashtra.

By 1986, the seminary had grown to 215 students from all the states of India and nine other countries. The student body, including some ten Alliance students, represented thirty denominations. Another 200 students were enrolled in the seminary extension program.

Nearly 1,000 alumni were serving churches across India, in Asia and Africa, by 1986. The C&MA of India especially depends on the seminary to supply pastors for its urban ministries.

The Women's Bible Training School in Khamgaon merged with the Marathi Bible College in 1971, making it coeducational. Another major change came in 1983, when the college reorganized as a union school sponsored by the seven different churches and missions that had used the school for years. Sixteen of the thirty-three students in 1985 came from Alliance churches.

Media operations remain. As personnel decreased in number, missionaries made increasing and effective use of mass media to make the Gospel known.

At the same time, the illiterate population rose rapidly, despite strenuous government efforts to promote literacy. Though they could not read, they had no problem listening. Portable radios proliferated among these people, who number in the tens of millions, and created a vast new audience for the Gospel.

Missionaries and Indian colleagues began Gujarati-language programs in 1966. At first, the programs—broadcast from Trans World Radio's shortwave transmitters—scored only passing success. Then in August of 1978, TWR opened a new medium-wave station in Sri Lanka.

Letters began pouring into the station from Gujaratis, sometimes over two thousand a month. The radio staff termed Gujarat State the most responsive of all regions in India. Encouraged by the response, Alliance broadcasters increased their output to five thirty-minute programs a week.

An indigenous missionary society in southern Gujarat reported that some 3,000 people converted through the broadcasts had been organized into

(Above) *An Alliance pastor preaches to a congregation* (facing page) *composed in part of women, whose saris brighten the meeting.*

churches. In another region, there were enough program listeners to form six or eight house churches.

In 1984, over 15,400 "Light of Life" introductory correspondence courses went out to listeners who wrote in. One in every three of the 3,086 who signed up for the series completed the lessons.

Marathi-language broadcasts began in 1979 from Sri Lanka. Despite limited backing, the fifteen-minute programs steadily drew listener response. By the mid-1980s, an average of nine hundred letters arrived each month at the radio office.

Christian literature does not cover as wide an audience because of India's literacy rate. Though literacy climbed steadily to 36 percent by 1981, the market for such material is limited. Alliance publishers in both Gujarat and Maharashtra produce a variety of material for the churches.

The Gujarati bookstore, Treasury of Living Literature, operates in Ahmedabad's central commercial district. It is the only Christian literature outlet for the city of nearly two million people. Even some Roman Catholics in Gujarat use Sunday school and vacation Bible school lessons prepared by the Ahmedabad-based editorial office.

Marathi translations of A. W. Tozer's writings hold first place among Alliance publications in Maharashtra. The paperback editions distributed by Alliance Publications in Akola also sell well elsewhere in India.

Correspondence courses offered to radio listeners exemplify how print and broadcast media can work together. By 1982, an overall total of almost 55,000 certificates had been awarded to individuals completing one or more courses in Gujarati.

The mass media programs—literature,

correspondence courses, radio broadcasts—along with established churches, pastoral training centers and overall organization represent a legacy of the mission to the Alliance Church of India. Should the North American staff leave, these ministries would enable the church to continue its witness along many lines.

Ramabai Mukti Mission

The anticipated retirement of Alliance missionaries in 1992 would directly affect the operations of a famous indigenous mission: Ramabai Mukti Mission in Kedgaon, Maharashtra. The close relationship between the two agencies resulted from the express wish of the great lady who founded the mission, Pandita Ramabai.

The life of this remarkable woman shows that good deeds truly outlive the doer. The faith she exercised in Christ's name has expanded to bless succeeding generations, just as concentric rings in a pool spread outward in every direction.

Born to high-caste Hindu parents, Pandita had every opportunity to study the philosophy of her parents' religion. She also saw it devoutly practiced by them in the finest manner. Yet she found Hinduism tragically inadequate when compared to the Gospel and to the example of godly men and women who providentially crossed her path.

The Lord transformed her life into an instrument of unusual blessing. The in-

Indian Christians highly regard literature that relates to their faith.

caste girls. Kedgaon sheltered six hundred girls and Gulbarga an additional seventy.

In her will, Pandita requested the Alliance to assume responsibility for the mission and insure that it continue in the purpose and principles to which she had committed her life and work.

Why the Alliance?

The field report concerning her request noted, "It is not generally known that although converted in connection with the English Church, Ramabai received much of her light on deeper spiritual things from Mrs. Jennie Fuller, and that throughout the last twenty-five years she has lived and worked in closest harmony with the Alliance truth and testimony."[10]

The C&MA accepted responsibility as guardian and provided encouragement and counsel to the Mukti mission and its autonomous board of governors through the years. Should the North American mission withdraw from India, it will seek another compatible agency to continue assisting this remarkable mission with its approximately five hundred residents and staff.

Beginning Years

When Pandita Ramabai started her mission in 1896, the Alliance had already been at work in India for years. Jennie Fuller, mentioned as a spiritual mentor of Pandita, had begun ministry with her husband in 1882. Other events linked to Alliance Ministries dated back to even earlier years.

A godly British colonial official and his wife, stationed in Berar, became so bur-

tense suffering and inferior status of women in Hindu society motivated her in 1896 to establish a home for ill-treated child widows and abandoned orphans.

Her work in Kedgaon became famous as Ramabai Mukti Mission. In a striking parallel to George Mueller's orphan work in England, she trusted God for the needs of as many as 2,000 girls at one time. She never found Him to fail.

By the time of her death in 1922, the mission at Kedgaon had expanded to include a widows' home, an orphanage, and a rescue home for prostitutes. Schools included primary, middle and secondary levels. A printing press and a fertile 116-acre farm completed the inventory of mission activities.

In addition, a ten-acre branch mission at Gulbarga operated a school for high-

dened for the province's 2.5 million people that they spent New Year's Day of 1874 in fasting instead of feasting. Their prayers set in motion events that culminated in the North Berar Faith Mission founded by Rev. and Mrs. M. B. Fuller in 1882.

Dr. A. B. Simpson's newly organized International Missionary Alliance sent four missionaries to India—one single lady each year—from 1887 to 1890. Helen Dawley sailed first and was joined a year later by Carrie Bates, and then by the others.

All four women associated themselves with the Fullers. In 1892, the North Berar Faith Mission merged with Dr. Simpson's missionary movement and its property in Akola became mission headquarters.

A larger contingent of seventeen new workers arrived in 1892 and enabled the mission to open twelve additional stations. During the next five years, the North American movement heavily committed itself to India with seventy-seven more workers. By 1897, the Alliance had established a string of mission stations so strategically located that they substantially represent the present-day area of responsibility.

A terrible famine broke out in 1900 and presented missionaries with a dramatic opportunity to show what God's love could accomplish.

They gave themselves unstintingly and reaped the rewards. Baptized members increased to 1,300 that year. They also paid the price: Six missionaries, including Jennie Fuller, and four children died in

The Gospel has an attraction for children as well as adults.

1900. Others had to return home, broken in health.

When the famine receded four years later, missionaries had taken in 1,185 orphans. The children may have seemed, at times, a blessing too well disguised, but out of that group emerged a whole generation of trained and dedicated workers for the church.

Some were still in active ministry in 1931, when The Christian and Missionary Alliance of India became an autonomous church. It was among the first religious organizations to become incorporated as a purely Indian entity.

As with any organization composed of widely divergent individuals, the passage of time generated increasing opportunities for tension and problems within the Alliance community.

Churches filed litigation suits against churches; pastors were pitted against each other and laymen. Missionaries became involved. Growth slowed, evangelistic zeal waned, and superficial beliefs crept in. There was enough blame for the church's disarray to be shared equally by pastors, congregations and missionaries.

Signs of renewed momentum in recent years give hope that a new era of growth is dawning for the church. The sobering reality that the church may soon be on its own could also strengthen the trend back to the basics of evangelism and church growth.

An event in 1984 suggests another way to revive interest in witnessing and discipling. Four key leaders from the Filipino Alliance church (CAMACOP) toured the Indian churches for nearly three weeks. Then, led by Filipino church president Dr. Benjamin DeJesus, the delegation conducted a three-day seminar for pastors and key laymen from both Gujarat and Maharashtra.

Reports of the dramatic increase in new converts and congregations by a sister Asian Alliance church made a deep impression on the attentive Indian pastors. Some went home and immediately instituted their own growth programs and methods.

Transfer Timetable

If indeed the government is determined to phase out Western missions, it has nonetheless permitted them an advantage not granted by other unsympathetic Asian nations: time to carry out an orderly withdrawal. Mission agencies have time to finalize their operations in a manner that provides continuity and stability.

By the mid-1980s, Alliance Ministries was already well advanced in the transfer of properties to the national church. Some buildings no longer needed by either the church or mission were sold. Proceeds went into an account to be administered by a special committee known as the Alliance Church Association (ACA).

The ACA, composed of representatives from all three synods and a disinterested third party, organized in 1981. It is legally empowered to hold properties and administer funds according to stipulations by the donor. The mission specified that a large part of income from property sales be used for evangelistic and church-planting projects.

The transfer of responsibility for ministries was seen as taking longer than financial matters because it involved adequate training of Indian replacements. The management of radio, literature and other specialized activities require expertise gained only by training and supervision over an extended period. This training phase has already begun.

In the critical area of pastoral training, both the mission and church moved to strengthen Maharashtra Bible College and Union Biblical Seminary. These schools are already under Indian supervision.

What of future participation by North American churches with the Alliance in India? Insights gained by experience with other Asian churches in countries now closed to Western missions suggest several possibilities:

1. *Share in costs of paid radio time to beam gospel programs into India.* The marked success of Gujarati and Marathi programs makes this prospect attractive.

2. *Make possible short-term visits and tours.* The successful 1984 tour by Filipino church leaders could be repeated. Promoting interaction with growing Alliance churches in neighboring countries is imperative.

The sacred status of cows cloaks them with the right-of-way even in heavy downtown traffic.

3. Enable church leaders to take advanced studies. Whether through scholarships to graduate school in India or abroad, the preparation of key workers for important roles would constitute a major investment in the church's future.

Probability Factors

All these options are already under study and discussion between mission and church leaders as they face the potential phasing out of missionary activity due to government policy. Future plans depend not only on agreement between the mission and church, but also with the government of India.

Will the administration in power, with its strong bias toward Hindu nationalism, ease its pressure on the churches after their association with foreign agencies has ended?

Will Christians no longer be under suspicion as tools of foreign interests and be allowed to carry on their evangelistic efforts as biblical churches are admonished to do?

Or will hostile pressure on churches intensify once the foreigners are gone and can no longer complain to their embassies or arouse public opinion back home?

No one truly knows—save the sovereign Lord, who not only opens and closes doors according to His good pleasure, but also rules over the policies of governments, making them servants to accomplish His good purposes.

History has shown, however, that when government action forces the national church to stand alone, that church grows in a manner not previously known. History also shows that many countries closed to the Gospel eventually reopen to ministry by churches in other nations. □

CHURCH AND MISSION

OFFICIAL NAME OF CHURCH:	The Christian & Missionary Alliance of India
ENTRY BY MISSIONARIES:	1887
CHURCH AUTONOMY:	1931
NUMBER OF MISSIONARIES:	12
NATIONAL MINISTERS:	57
ORGANIZED CHURCHES:	70
UNORGANIZED CHURCHES AND PREACHING POINTS:	62
BAPTIZED CHURCH MEMBERS:	7,080
INCLUSIVE MEMBERSHIP:	21,240
EDUCATION:	Maharashtra Bible College, 2 elementary schools
RADIO BROADCASTS:	19 per week
PAGES PRINTED:	1,959,000

COUNTRY

OFFICIAL NAME:	Lao People's Democratic Republic
FORM OF GOVERNMENT:	Communist
OFFICIAL LANGUAGE(S):	Lao
AREA:	91,428 sq. mi., slightly larger than Utah
POPULATION:	3,605,000 (1985 est.)
CAPITAL:	Vientiane
PER CAPITA INCOME:	$85
LITERACY:	50%
RELIGIOUS AFFILIATION:	Non-religious 6%, Animist 33%, Muslim 1%, Buddhist 58%, Christians 2% (R.C.,.8%/Protestants, 1.2%)

SOUTH KOREA

A Boost Toward Maturity

Presbyterianism began in Scotland, but its largest church is in South Korea.

Methodists got their start in England, but their largest congregation is in South Korea.

The Assemblies of God originated in the United States, but their largest assembly is in South Korea.

Dr. Samuel Hugh Moffett, son of a pioneer missionary to Korea and author of two books on the country, supports this generalization: "Christianity came late to the ancient country of Korea, but it has found in the Korean heart an openness and receptivity almost unmatched in the history of modern missions."[1]

With an estimated 30 percent of the country's forty million people belonging to one denomination or another, Korea has the largest Christian community in Asia.

Seoul, the national capital, has been described as a city of churches. Spires and steeples pierce the skyline in all directions. Some six thousand churches congregated in the city by 1980. Korea has the largest Methodist, Presbyterian and Pentecostal congregations in the

world. The largest of these is the Full Gospel Central Church with 550,000 members and about 5,000 new members each month.[2]

The full account of South Korea's Christian population is yet to be told because it is still growing at an average of 10 percent annually. At its current rate, Korea could conceivably become a Christian nation.

Response to the Gospel in the nation's large standing army ranks even higher than the national average. In one mass service in April of 1973, over 3,475 officers and troops were baptized.[3] The number of professing believers rose from 16 percent in 1965 to 25 percent of the armed forces personnel just seven years later.

How does Korea's response to the Gospel compare to its reception of other religions?

Preempted Asian Religions

Eastern religions got off the mark in Korea much faster than Christianity.

Buddhism arrived in the fourth century and made considerable progress among the people. Later, however, its leaders

meddled in local politics and incurred the government's wrath. Authorities banned the religion and destroyed many of its temples.

Confucianism came to "The Land of Morning Calm" in the seventh century. Its concepts are still evident in Korean society: ancestor worship, strong family ties and a high priority on education.

The most active indigenous religion is the oldest: Shamanism. Brought by the original ethnic tribes, probably from Mongolia several millennia before Christ, it still controls the hearts and minds of millions. Over 27,000 shamanist sorcerers were registered practitioners in 1975, and their numbers were growing.

Generally unorganized but answering to felt needs of the people, Shamanism involves demon worship, veneration of ancestors and related activities such as fortune-telling and folk healing. A persistent survivor, it infiltrated both Buddhism and Confucianism and has influenced numerous sects related to the Christian faith.

"The old religions are not, at least on the surface, a significant factor in Korea today," believes Dr. Moffett. "Most of modern Koreans profess no religious faith, and the largest organized religion . . . may well be Christianity.''[4]

Strong Indigenous Start

Several factors explain why the Gospel has flourished where ancient Eastern religions failed.

The first major factor was a strong indigenous start. Both Roman Catholic and Protestant faiths were accepted and propagated by Koreans themselves before the arrival of missionaries.

Roman Catholic literature had been filtering into Korea from China since 1631. A young Korean went to Beijing to seek more information about the strange doctrine. Impressed by what he learned, he embraced Catholicism and returned home to tell his friends what had happened.

When the first Catholic missionary, a Chinese priest, entered Korea ten years later, he was amazed to find some 4,000 Catholics. The first Western missionary priest did not arrive until 1835. He was just in time to be martyred in the middle of four severe persecutions that decimated but did not destroy the church.

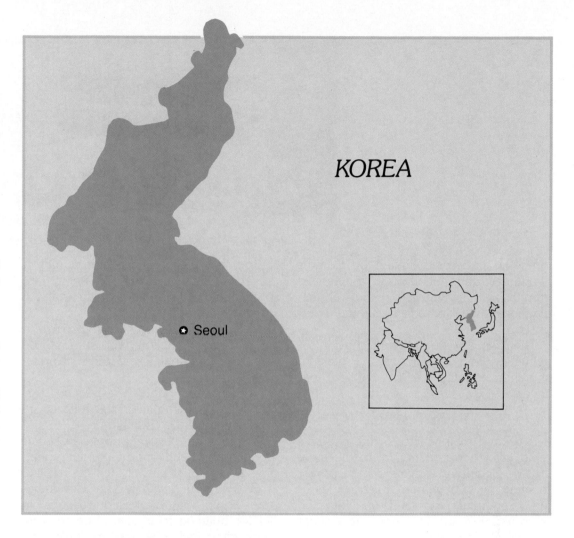

KOREA

Seoul

The Protestant community began in a similar indigenous fashion. Two Scottish missionaries in Manchuria baptized the first Protestant convert in 1876. The new believer, So Sang Yun, stayed long enough to help them translate the New Testament into Korean.

So Sang Yun then returned home in 1883 to evangelize his people. When Dr. Horace N. Allen, a Presbyterian medical missionary, arrived in 1884, he encoun-tered a Protestant congregation of over one hundred believers won by Korea's first Protestant believer.

The first Methodist missionary began work in Korea on Easter Sunday of 1885. His chief interest lay in establishing a school, while the first ordained Presbyterian missionary, who also arrived the same year, immediately concentrated on planting a church.

Their different concerns symbolized

Dongdae-Mun Gate in Seoul, the nation's capital

emerging patterns followed by Korea's two largest denominations. Presbyterians emphasized evangelism and church planting, while Methodists majored in education.

The two programs worked well together. Within fifteen years, Protestant churches counted 18,000 baptized believers.

Faith Tested

A second major factor in the church's rapid growth was a revival in the early 1900s. Beginning privately in a prayer meeting by two women missionaries in 1903, spiritual renewal broke into the open in 1907 and for three years swept through the churches.

Protestants profited most from the movement. They reported a 900 percent increase in adherents—almost 150,000 new believers between 1900 and 1910. Roman Catholics reported only a 25 percent growth, from 60,000 to 75,000.[5]

The increase in numbers did not dilute the quality of faith.

John Caldwell Thiessen writes, "Quite certainly [the Korean Church] has had its weaknesses, but never in modern church history has there been a community of believers anywhere that so nearly approached those standards of life and faith to which Christians aspire."[6]

Thiessen then cites a Presbyterian author, C. Darby Fulton, who summarized the qualities that characterize Korean believers:[7]

1. *They are Sabbath-respecting people.* Members who fail in this respect are disciplined by the church.

2. *They are praying people.* Believers congregate in early morning prayer meetings as a regular part of their church life.

3. *They are giving people.* Congregations accept without question responsibility for building their own churches and supporting their own pastors. From the very beginning, Presbyterian missionaries built the church on the bases of self-support and self-propagation.

4. *They are missions-minded people.* The first Presbyterian missionaries set the standard by organizing a missionary society among the Koreans at the same time they organized the denomination. "The true church is a missionary church," they insisted.

5. *They are Bible-studying people.* An early decision by missionaries to use the simplified *eunmum* script for translation put the Bible within reach of the masses. (The literary elite despised the *eunmum* because it was "so easy that a woman could learn it.")

As often happens, revival was prelude to persecution. Korea became a Japanese colony in 1910. The church was viewed with distrust and distaste by the new regime.

That hostility broke into open violence during the 1930s. About 3,000 Christians were imprisoned; fifty of them were executed. All the denominations were compelled to join the government-controlled Korean Christian Church of Japanese Christianity.

Peace in 1945 did not extend to Christians in North Korea, where churches had been the largest and strongest. The Communist government moved against the churches in an outright campaign of extermination. Over four hundred Protestant ministers and one hundred Catholic priests were murdered. The number of lay believers killed will probably never be known.[8]

Only a few Christians survived the on-

Children must dress warmly in the cold winter season.

slaught until the Korean War in 1950. They joined in the mass flight of 4.5 million North Koreans to freedom below the thirty-eighth parallel. Today there are no known churches in North Korea, but reports suggest that several thousand believers still meet in secret to worship and pray.

Division and Multiplication

The conclusion of World War II marked the emergence of divisions within the Protestant community. Prior to 1940, only six nationally recognized denominations worked in Korea. Ninety percent of the churches belonged to the National Council of Churches.

Twenty years later, the total number of denominations had multiplied to fifty-seven; only six belonged to the church council.

The realignment of churches resulted from both organizational and doctrinal causes. Many of the new mission agencies were either nondenominational faith missions or independent church groups.

At the same time, the Korean Council of Churches was drawing closer to the World Council of Churches, which was strongly ecumenical and perceived as increasingly anti-evangelical in character.

These new developments profoundly affected the Korean Christian community and gave rise to divisions in church groups and denominations. One group that eventually emerged from this situation was the Jesus Korea Holiness Church (JKHC).

The JKHC claimed a rich spiritual heritage from the Oriental Missionary Society (OMS), which had organized the church earlier in the century. Rev. and Mrs. Charles E. Cowman, founders of the mission, were motivated to become missionaries while attending Dr. Simpson's missionary conventions. Deeply influenced by his teachings known as the Four-fold Gospel, they propagated this message in Korea.

Later, during the Japanese occupation of Korea, all Korean churches were compelled to sever relations with their parent missions. The Christians then faced intense opposition and persecution until the war ended.

Theological tensions forced a group to break away from the National Council of Churches after the Korean War. The group split again in 1973 for the same reason. One of the resulting denominations became known as the JKHC.

Church leaders nonetheless recognized the need to associate with a larger Christian fellowship having the experience and personnel to help them grow. The Christian and Missionary Alliance came increasingly to mind because of prior contact.

The church had already benefited richly from the translated writings of Dr. A. B. Simpson. In fact, the Four-fold Gospel of Dr. Simpson held a central place in the church's teaching.

A report on graduates of the JKHC seminary indicated that students often considered Dr. Simpson's writings more helpful than others. "The graduates expressed this thought," noted the report: "The Four-fold Gospel we preach is more biblical, more practical and more relevant to experience than any other doctrine of any other denomination. We feel a sense of satisfaction that ours is a glorious Gospel that supplies all the deep needs of the human heart."[9]

Church leaders came into direct contact with the Alliance through Korean pastors

Village combines the past and present

Male and female Buddhas sculptured in stone

Autumn's vivid colors

ministering to their countrymen in the United States. Three years of visits, discussions and deliberations followed.

New Year's Day of 1980 marked the beginning of a formal agreement between the Alliance of North America and the Korean church, which now took the name Jesus Korea Alliance Holiness Church (JKAHC).

Only rarely does the Alliance in North America establish a formal working relationship with an overseas church not originating from its own missionary work (see Nigeria). Concerning the South Korean church, however, it seemed the right thing to do. The church needed help in establishing a missionary program and in conducting a pastoral training program that emphasized the Four-fold Gospel as enunciated by Dr. Simpson himself.

Working with the JKAHC, especially in these two areas, helped the Alliance fulfill its own historical role of promoting deeper life truths and missions.

Problems and Progress

Helping the Korean church's seminary to firm footing was a major need. A denomination without an adequate seminary is not taken seriously by Koreans, who place a high priority on education. This was certainly true in Seoul, where the JKAHC had forty of its ninety churches in 1982.

The need of adequate preparation for leadership became evident from another direction as well. Baptized membership numbered 4,000, but inclusive membership reached 23,000, representing thousands of individuals who needed to be converted from onlookers to committed disciples.

When the Alliance entered Korea with three missionary couples, the government was already shutting down over one hundred so-called seminaries that did not academically measure up to the name. The JKAHC seminary in Seoul was one such institution.

Church leaders reorganized the school as a theological institute and reapplied for seminary status. Meanwhile, the missionaries continued their teaching ministry in the classroom and in small, private gatherings.

Graduates of the pastoral training program face a requirement for ordination quite apart from academic preparation: a candidate is expected to start a new church—and make sure it keeps going.

Temporary facilities are tolerated at first, but each congregation is expected to construct or finance its own permanent worship place.

Rev. Clement Dreger, the first resident Alliance missionary, observes in one of his evaluation reports: "These pastors live sacrificially and work diligently. They work at it wholeheartedly!"[10]

JKAHC's problems did not end when it associated with the Alliance and joined The Alliance World Fellowship.

Numerous churches in 1985 decided to return to their previous denomination. In addition, the application for seminary status was put on hold by the government for unspecified reasons. Another problem became evident when the government imposed stricter visa requirements for foreigners working in Korea.

Yet the young church continued to grow. The Mahn Min congregation in Seoul, for example, began in 1982 with a student pastor. Fourteen people attended the first service. In four years, the congregation grew to six hundred people meeting in three services on Sunday morning.

The Honam Church in Cheonju, a rapidly growing city in central South Korea, began meeting in rented quarters in 1978. Fifty people attended a 1983 ground-breaking ceremony for a church building. As the building went up, so did the attendance. By 1986, nearly two hundred people worshiped in Honam Church.

Missionary vision increased as the church grew. One young man was especially interested in missions. Although graduated from a top university and already successful in business, he attended the theological institute and then served as an assistant pastor. His next move was

CHURCH AND MISSION

OFFICIAL NAME OF CHURCH:	Jesus Korea Holiness Church
ENTRY BY MISSIONARIES:	1980
NUMBER OF MISSIONARIES:	
ORGANIZED CHURCHES:	
UNORGANIZED CHURCHES AND PREACHING POINTS:	
BAPTIZED CHURCH MEMBERS:	81,084
INCLUSIVE MEMBERSHIP:	318,277

COUNTRY

OFFICIAL NAME:	Republic of Korea
FORM OF GOVERNMENT:	Republic (with power centralized in a strong executive)
OFFICIAL LANGUAGE(S):	Korean
AREA:	38,025 sq. mi.
POPULATION:	(1989 est.) 45,243,000
CAPITAL:	Seoul
PER CAPITA INCOME:	(1984) $2,180
LITERACY:	92%
RELIGIOUS AFFILIATION:	Buddhism, 33% Confucianism, 12% Christian 30%

to the Alliance Bible Seminary in the Philippines. His goal: to return after graduation and teach missiology in a Korean seminary.

Not all the churches will match Mahn Min's record, and not all pastors will go on to graduate studies. Even so, the solid character of Korean faith will surely win a larger and larger place of ministry for the Jesus Korea Alliance Holiness Church.

Whatever the Alliance in North America can do to help this promising church toward maturity promises rich returns on its investment. ☐

THAILAND

Hairline Cracks in the Wall

P.S. Can a man be bireligious as a person can be bilingual?"

The question was jotted down as an afterthought to a letter written by a retired Thai army general to a missionary.

He had written, "During the thirty-plus years of our friendship, I have not been a Christian as you have wanted me to be. Now I want to be one, in spite of my Buddhism. What must I do to be a real Christian?"

And then, in a retreat to caution, the postscript: "Can a man be bireligious as a person can be bilingual?"[1]

The general's ambivalent attitude toward Christ reflects the mood of many people in Thailand. Although adherents of Buddhism, they wonder if perhaps their faith should be in Christ—and yet they hesitate at the point of decision.

Primacy of Buddhism

Even ambivalence about Buddhism and some serious thought about Christ indicates a significant shift in Thailand's religious attitude.

The nation is solidly Buddhist: over 94 percent of the population. According to David Barrett, in 1982 it had one of the smallest Christian communities in all Asia—1.1 percent of the population was Christian, of which 0.2 percent was Protestant.[2]

The tenets of Buddhism permeate every aspect of Thai life. John Caldwell Thiessen notes that "the majority of men spend at least a few years in the priesthood and there is scarcely a family which is not personally represented in it."[3]

Its pervasive influence is not surprising. The Indian-born religion has been working its way into every nook and cranny of the social structure since the seventh century, when immigrants from India brought along their Hindu and Buddhist beliefs.

Another powerful factor in Buddhism's favor has been the absence of foreign domination. Unlike every other nation in mainland Asia, Thailand has never been under colonial rule by an European nation.

Spared the trauma of national defeat, the Thai had no reason to question the adequacy of their religion. Even natural disasters such as floods and earthquakes seemed to avoid the favored nation throughout the twentieth century.

Buddhism's apparent success, however, did not stop the Thai from giving it a distinctive local character. Perhaps more than other Eastern religions, Buddhism is syncretic in nature: It absorbs other religious beliefs while retaining its basic identity.

In Thailand, the conservative Theravada form of Buddhism prevailed, but it absorbed large amounts of animism, or spirit worship. No matter how high they may rank Buddha in worship, most citizens spend most of their time trying to manipulate the spirit world.

One analyst of Thai culture observes, "Popular opinion has it that human beings in Thailand are greatly outnumbered by the evil spirit population, who are believed to spend their time generally messing up human activities. . . .

"Since they can be bribed, coerced, and deceived, these evil spirits must be propitiated with suitable gifts, because their help in an emergency can be invaluable, and their hostility can be ruinous."[4]

Hairline Cracks

Despite the centuries-old primacy of Buddhism, hairline cracks have appeared

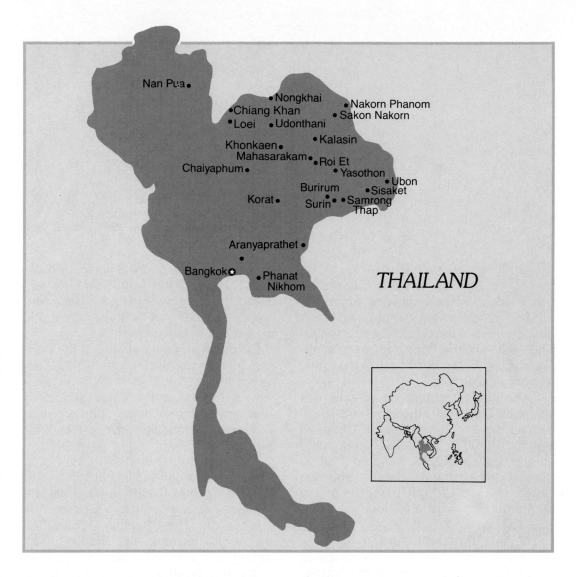

THAILAND

in its impregnable wall around Thailand. It has begun to show the strain of modern life.

Donald E. Hoke, drawing upon twenty-one years of experience in Asia, states in general: "I feel that particularly in the growing urban centers we are witnessing the spread of a great, gray, materialistic, secular uniculture across the entire continent.

"Jet down into any city of Asia and the sights are the same: glaring neon advertisements (usually of Japanese products); movies from every country of the world (many of them pornographic); standard-looking taxis, clothing, recreation, and central shops.

"If it be complained that these are superficial similarities, then I answer that under the surface lies the same existential meaninglessness, the same search for pleasure, the same indifference to old religions (except for marriage and death ceremonies), the same agnosticism, and the same openness toward Western 'improvements.' This is the real Asia of today."[5]

Dr. Timothy Jeng notes one positive result of this strain on Thai Buddhism: "In the past ten years [since 1972] I have seen a new openness in Thailand. People are more and more responsive to the Gospel."[6]

In addition to social and cultural causes, Jeng cites political uneasiness arising from the fall of Indo-China to Communism. All these tensions have generated an interest in the Gospel with positive results: "People are beginning to understand what Christianity actually is," Jeng says.[7]

This openness—even if only a question of "bireligious"—assumes greater importance when we realize there has not been a large-scale movement toward Christ in over 475 years of missionary activity in Thailand.

In 1511, Roman Catholic missionaries

(Left) *A multi-level department store and* (facing page) *city traffic flowing around a monument support Bangkok's claim as the leading city of Thailand.*

accompanied a Portuguese delegation visiting Thailand (then called Siam). The first resident missionary priest arrived in 1555. French clergy established their headquarters in the capital a century later. Their mission, the Paris Foreign Missionary Society, has worked from then to now without interruption.

Concentrating mainly on schools and convents, Roman Catholicism at first advanced slowly. The number of Catholics reached 2,500 in 1803. The community grew by only about five hundred through the rest of the century. But by 1963, the church claimed 116,000 members and in another ten years the total reached 167,000.[8]

The first Protestant known to show concern for the Thai bore an illustrious name. Anne Judson, wife of the famous missionary to Burma, came in contact with some Thai prisoners in 1819, when Burma and Thailand were at war. She studied their language for eighteen months and then attempted to translate a catechism and the Gospel of Matthew.

The first Protestant missionaries set foot in Thailand in 1828. Dr. Carl F. A. Gutzlaff, a self-supporting volunteer with the Netherlands Missionary Society, and Jacob Tomlin of the London Missionary Society, began translating the Bible and preparing a bilingual dictionary after only six months of language study.

Gutzlaff married a member of the London Missionary Society in Burma. Together they accomplished the prodigious task of translating the entire Bible into Thai, and even Scripture portions into Lao and Cambodian—all within four years.

Their exhausting work no doubt contributed to Gutzlaff's failing health and to his wife's death. During those years, he baptized just one convert, a Chinese.

American Presbyterians established and expanded the first lasting work among the Thai from the mid to late nineteenth century. They pioneered in evangelism, church planting and medical work.

The first Alliance missionaries arrived on New Year's Day, 1929. While working in Cambodia, Rev. and Mrs. Paul Gunther experienced a special concern for Thailand. They established their base in Ubon, the most populous province outside Bangkok. Rev. and Mrs. Peter A.

Voth settled in Khon Kaen that same year.

Although by this time Protestant missions had been at work in the country for about one hundred years, the whole northeastern region, including Ubon, lacked gospel witness. The Alliance eventually accepted responsibility for all seventeen provinces of northeast Thailand.

If the early missionaries expected an enthusiastic response, they were painfully disappointed. They could only count eighty-five converts after twelve years of witness. Their strategy for years was to place a missionary in each province, instead of among population centers and responsive groups. This no doubt contributed to slow growth of the work prior to World War II.

War's Aftermath

Although never officially at war with Thailand, Japanese forces occupied the country until the war ended. Western missionaries were interned and then repatriated in exchange for Japanese citizens. All mission work halted. The small Thai church struggled through the war years alone and harassed.

The war's aftermath seemed to bring little change in church growth, but help was coming. An advance party of nine Alliance missionaries and ten children boarded ship on Christmas Eve Day, 1946, Thailand-bound to resume ministry. Over the next two decades, the Alliance mission and the Gospel Church (CMA) of Thailand continued to struggle against seemingly superior odds with little success, as did other groups.

The apparent unsuitability of large-scale evangelism in a Buddhist culture left Alliance workers with no alternative but to slowly, painstakingly win converts one by one.

Many Thai considered the Alliance a rural-based mission and small church with poorly trained leaders and many leprosy-inflicted members. This general attitude did not help church growth.

The church did experience hard-won growth and in percentages it looked impressive. The prewar total of eight-five baptized members rose to 1,446 by 1964. This represented an incredible 1,700 percent increase in twenty-three years, despite the interval of a costly war.

But in comparison to an estimated nine million people in northeast Thailand in 1964, believers constituted only .016 percent of the population.

Several events stood out during those difficult years from 1946 to 1970.

The Gospel Church of Thailand was organized with a provisional constitution in 1950. The church achieved permanent and official autonomy four years later, becoming an equal partner with the mission in evangelizing the nation.

In 1950 also, the Alliance began broadcasting the Gospel over medium-wave radio. Realizing their work could be more effective by teaming up with the Far East Broadcasting Company (FEBC), the Alliance programmers entered a cooperative effort with the Manila-based radio mission in the late 1960s.

In 1951, the Alliance initiated a special ministry to people suffering from leprosy, outcasts victimized not only by a dread disease but also by widespread ignorance within society. Response to this proffered medical help, at first wary and then enthusiastic, grew swiftly. In 1953, the Maranatha Bible School was founded to train patients how to minister spiritually to others in similar straits.

One event in 1952 dramatized the fact

that missionary work is often one breath away from martyrdom. Paul and Priscilla Johnson were conducting an evening church service when bandits entered the small village chapel and fatally wounded them. The Johnsons became the first Alliance missionaries in Thai history to give their lives for their work.

Spiritual Stirrings

The first Thai Congress on Evangelism opened in January of 1970 with the prophetic motto, "The Hour Has Come."

The conveners had no idea how many

(Facing page) *An ornate Buddhist temple contrasts sharply with (above) the Evangelical Church of Bangkok, used by the International Church congregation and the Mahapawn Sukumit (Thai) congregation. (Left) A Chinese pastor from Hong Kong is one of several missionaries supported in Thailand by overseas Alliance churches.*

Students study in the Bangkok Bible College, a school approved by the C&MA and supported with faculty.

would attend, but before the congress ended, they began to hope that a new hour had indeed come for their country. From nearly every denomination and Christian organization came 250 representatives. The sense of unity in purpose and fellowship touched the participants deeply.[9]

At least 125 prayer cells formed after the congress, and unusual events began happening in scattered parts of the country: revival broke out among nominal Christian youth at a church high school; churches reported healings and miracles; evangelistic cells appeared in congregations once spiritually dormant.

The Alliance saw a surge in correspondence courses as people showed increased interest in Christian literature. One particular course attracted five thousand students in 1970, and better than eight out of ten completed the lessons.

The executive secretary of the Church of Christ in Thailand (largely Presbyterian) reported that conversions that year had doubled.[10]

One event took place in the early seventies that promised to aid in the spiritual awakening of Thailand. The Bangkok Bible College, sponsored by the Overseas Missionary Fellowship with help from some C&MA missionaries, opened in 1971. The missions seconded personnel to the faculty, while Thai Christians contributed to the support of students.

Within ten years, the school graduated fifty students, who, with few exceptions, found their way into church ministry. Graduates assumed roles of leadership in organizations and institutions throughout the nation, helping the Christian community to its best decade ever.

Ups and Downs

Bad news and good launched the 1980s to an uncertain future for the Alliance.

The Department of Religion called for a meeting with mission leaders in February, 1981. The director informed them that effective immediately, the current number of missionaries in the country would be frozen for each mission.

There was more. The director said that

after three years, during which replacements could be brought in, the agencies were expected to begin reducing their staff by 10 percent yearly until they were all withdrawn. This part of the program was not enforced, but missions were required to limit the size of their staffs.

The decision could not have come at a more inopportune time for the Alliance. Mission staffing had shrunk from a high of seventy-four to a low of thirty-six; thirteen of the seventeen northeastern provinces had no resident missionary.

The Gospel Church of Thailand had not yet found itself; its 125 churches and 2,112 members lacked a concerted sense of direction in evangelism and extension. The Central Bible School mustered only eighteen students in its full-time curriculum.

At that low point, Alliance mission and church leaders showed something of the spirit that animated a great French general in World War I: "My center is giving way, my right retreats, situation excellent, I am attacking!"

The Thai and North Americans attacked their problems together.

Over a short period of time they formed joint evangelistic teams that targeted populous cities for church planting, rather than vast, sparsely settled provincial areas. Together they adopted a doubling formula for growth: Harvest 5000/87: five thousand baptized believers by centennial 1987.

The goal, though perhaps not realistic, signified that the Alliance church in Thailand had finally focused on a strategy of growth.

Realizing that churches would start moving only if their pastors and lay workers were challenged, church leaders started visiting local congregations more often. The church president relinquished his teaching post at the Central Bible School in order to devote all of his time to church leadership.

Another needy area received some realistic but drastic action: pastoral training.

The Central Bible School at Khon Kaen raised its entrance requirements, thus reducing the number of students and classes. This permitted the faculty and staff to upgrade their own education. The Bangkok Bible College inaugurated a program to enable both students and faculty of the Bible college to continue their education.

Graduate schools overseas, such as the Manila-based Alliance Biblical Seminary and Fuller's School of World Mission in California, were approved for top-level education of the most promising students.

Full Circle

One great strength of an international community such as The Alliance World Fellowship is the availability of diverse resources God can call upon at will. Realizing the spiritual needs of Thailand, Alliance churches in other Asian nations sent missionaries to work with the church where needed.

The first missionary from another Third World Alliance church came from Hong Kong in 1977. Vaneda Suwatchalapinum set a high standard for those who followed. A graduate of the Alliance Bible Seminary in Hong Kong who held a master's degree in religious education from an American seminary, she spoke fluently in two Chinese dialects, English, and Thai.[11]

By 1981, the C&MA Church Union Hong Kong, Ltd. had placed five workers. Within five years, the number of Third World missionaries grew to twelve: two couples from Japan, two couples and two ladies from Hong Kong, and two single ladies from the Philippines. All but the two Japanese couples were sent by Alliance churches.

Thai Christians play a key role in church leadership training.

They lost no time in setting to work. One Filipina missionary arrived already conversant in five languages. After two weeks with a Thai teacher, she could speak Thai well enough to be understood.

A Western missionary with twenty-eight years experience marveled at her progress in language skills: "It had taken some of us nearly two years!"[12]

A ceremony in May of 1980 demonstrated what Asian missionaries and their supporting churches could do. On that date, the first Chinese church in northeast Thailand was dedicated, debtfree. Gifts from Christians in Hong Kong, Taiwan, U.S. and Canada provided more than enough for the $45,000 needed for land and building.

Miss Suwatchalapinum had begun holding services for Chinese in Khon Kaen while she served on the Central Bible School faculty. A couple from Hong Kong arrived later to help organize and then pastor the new church.

Some of the Chinese Christians had previously attended the Thai Alliance church, which was experiencing its own excitement of growth and blessing.

The Khon Kaen church had begun holding services in the Bible school chapel prior to World War II, but seemed to do little more than exist. Even moving to a church building of its own in 1971 failed to improve the membership, which fluctuated between twenty and forty. Pastors generally stayed only a year or two and then moved on.

Perhaps stirred by spiritual movement elsewhere during the early 1970s, some of the congregation started early morning prayer meetings. Prayer led to increased concern for non-Christian relatives and friends. That, in turn, prompted the forming of witness teams to visit the villages and homes of those prayed for.

Students add a new chorus to their repertoire.

The Khon Kaen church itself began to grow. Shedding its exclusive campus image and to some extent its denominational identity, the church reached out to the surrounding community. Prayer-and-share groups formed throughout the city. Members of the middle class—doctors, businessmen, university professors and students—joined the church and helped it grow.

Equally important, the congregation finally found a pastor willing to stay and build up the work instead of leaving like his predecessors. He did have to face one serious problem: The church was over-flowing its facilities by 1983. What should be done? It was probably the most welcome problem he ever faced.

Setback and Push Forward

Blessing was coming too easily in some areas of the field. Something bad had to happen, and it did.

The Thai mission suffered a severe setback where it could ill afford to lose: finances.

A clever bookkeeper employed by the mission office first won the confidence of her associates and then swindled the accounts of many thousands of dollars. She fled the country, leaving behind legal problems that took months to solve, financial losses requiring months to cover, and a missionary under arrest.

Significantly, the same year of 1984 that saw the mission in such financial difficulties also witnessed initiatives that carried a strong message: "We will not stop!"

Bangkok Bible College signaled this determination when it broke ground for a four-story building that would increase its capacity for students and its effectiveness in operations.

The mission expressed the same inten-

Bible stories are attention-getters the world over.

One of Thailand's many Venice-like canals

tion by moving its headquarters from the interior city of Korat to the capital city of Bangkok in 1986. The move reaped several advantages:

—Bangkok provided better communications links, both within the country and internationally.

—The move improved management of mission business, including finances.

—The mission could more effectively encourage an unprecedented program of church-planting in the city.

Bangkok, with over five million inhabitants, ranked among the key cities of Alliance overseas ministries. It was therefore included in an urban church growth plan entitled "Good News for Great Cities."

The Mahapawn Saphan Kwai congregation, one church to be helped by the plan, had already been in existence for several years. By 1984 it was overflowing its meeting place on the mission guest house property. That same year, two more congregations were formed in the city.

One small group of believers began meeting in Rachada, a new middle-class section of Bangkok. One of the two missionary couples from Japan agreed to organize the promising congregation. The second new group had its start in facilities loaned by the Evangelical Church of Bangkok, an English-speaking international congregation composed mainly of foreigners working in the capital.

Under Alliance pastoral leadership, the English-speaking Evangelical Church of Bangkok became a spiritual force in the city, reaching into the foreign diplomatic and business communities. Sunday morning worship attendance by the end of 1986 topped the 300 mark. In addition to the regular schedule of public meetings, the church added innovative ministries such as providing counseling staff for the Community Services of Bangkok.

All three Thai churches made noticeable progress within two years. The Mahapawn congregation at Saphan Kwai, with an attendance of 160, was already worshiping in its new sanctuary. The two newer groups doubled in size and could look back upon separate Christmas programs that had attracted a combined total of seven hundred people—unheard-of figures just a few years before.

Sharpened Focus

Meanwhile, the national leaders sharpened their focus on church growth in what appeared to be an emerging nationwide openness to the Gospel.

The transfer of mission headquarters to Bangkok placed on church leadership an increased responsibility for evangelizing the provinces. The Gospel Church of Thailand relocated its central office to the administration building of the Khon Kaen-based Central Bible School. The decision enabled church leaders to coordinate the various training programs more closely with evangelism and extension.

At the same time, church and mission officials enlarged their cooperative efforts. A church development team composed of pastors and missionaries scheduled two series of meetings per month, and stuck to it. The two executive committees met twice annually to strengthen their relations and improve joint efforts.

The Harvest 5000/87 campaign (five thousand baptized members by 1987) gained momentum as local churches got involved. Media evangelism did its part as well. In one instance, a provincial governor accepted a video cassette version of the film "Jesus" for a private showing at his residence.

Evangelism efforts of necessity included the young because six of every ten

CHURCH AND MISSION

OFFICIAL NAME OF CHURCH:	The Gospel Church of Thailand
ENTRY BY MISSIONARIES:	1929
NUMBER OF MISSIONARIES:	47
ORGANIZED CHURCHES:	70
UNORGANIZED CHURCHES AND PREACHING POINTS:	95
BAPTIZED CHURCH MEMBERS:	2,868
INCLUSIVE MEMBERSHIP:	1,160
MEDICAL WORK:	0
EDUCATION:	Central Bible School, TEE
RADIO BROADCASTS:	68
PAGES PRINTED:	4,759,633

COUNTRY

OFFICIAL NAME:	Kingdom of Thailand
FORM OF GOVERNMENT:	Constitutional Monarchy
OFFICIAL LANGUAGE(S):	Thai
AREA:	198,456 sq. mi., size of Texas
POPULATION:	55,017,000
CAPITAL:	Bangkok
PER CAPITA INCOME:	$771.00 (1986)
LITERACY:	89% (1988)
RELIGIOUS AFFILIATION:	Buddhist 95%, Muslim 4% Christian 1%

Thai are age twenty-five or younger. Youth camps were not welcomed in the country's adult-oriented society as late as 1958, when the first such camp attracted thirty teenagers. Twenty-seven years later, the summer camp program reached one thousand young people.

Church and mission leaders recognized the necessity of improving the quality of ministry in local churches if the Alliance were to respond to stirrings of spiritual awakening in the country. Thus, in 1985, consultations with local workers took place regularly in thirteen of the seventeen provinces in the northeast.

That same year, two Filipino Alliance pastors, successful church-planters, conducted an inspiring seminar on the basics of church growth. Missionaries and church leaders attended a seminar on more effective communication of the Gospel.

No one can predict if the hairline cracks in the wall of Buddhist resistance will multiply and widen. But as opportunities increase, Alliance missionaries and Thai Christians will do then as they do now: Make clear there can be no "bireligious" person in the Kingdom of God.

Christ alone is Lord. ☐

CHURCHES UNDER COMMUNISM

Color the East Red

World War II officially ended September 2, 1945, on the battleship *Missouri* in Tokyo Bay. Western allies could stack their arms and turn to peace.

Not so the East. V-J Day, formalizing victory over Japan, offered Asian combatants only a pause long enough to retrain their sights on new enemies and continue a deadly struggle.

India confronted England. Indo-China resisted France. The East Indies rebelled against Holland. Chinese Communists and Nationalists resumed their civil war. Korean communism tried to overpower Korean democracy.

Colonialism, nationalism, communism and democracy battled one another in a melee of shifting alliances, deceptive fronts and broken promises that allowed no middle ground, only victory or defeat.

And while the armies battled in the fields, the masses of people longed for an end to it all. They had no real preference for communism, democracy or any other political system. They just hoped the winners would be able to provide them with rice and otherwise leave them alone with their traditional ways.

Except for India, the struggle on mainland Asia sooner or later narrowed to a war of freedom versus domination as communism fought to fulfill its battle hymn, "The East Is Red." England and India worked out their differences fairly peacefully, with democracy the winner.

China: Top Prize

Communist strategists seeking to dominate Asia targeted the biggest prize of all: China.

Struggle for mastery of the world's most populous nation had actually begun years before World War II. Nationalists (Guomindong) and Communists (Gongchandong) cooperated during the 1920s as uneasy partners in the National Revolution.

Their aim: to unify China, throw off foreign interference, and institute reforms, especially the redistribution of land.

The united front collapsed in 1928, and for the next decade, the tide of victory flowed with the Nationalists under Jiang (Chiang) Kaishek. The battered Communist forces under Mao Zedong (Tse-tung) retreated on "The Long March" across China to mountains and

caves in the northwest. There they reorganized their military forces and their political apparatus.

World War II forced the two rival camps to suspend hostilities and concentrate on a common foe, the invading armies of Imperial Japan. The Communists emerged from the conflict tactically and militarily stronger than the Nationalists. The tide of victory swung in their favor.

Under the guise of retiring, Jiang Kaishek abandoned the mainland struggle in January of 1949 and settled on Taiwan, turning it into a bastion of last resort. By the end of that year Mao Zedong's armies completed their sweep of mainland China.

Korea: Blocked Grab

Russia had moved into North Korea in the waning days of World War II and then was forced to halt at the thirty-eighth parallel because American forces had set up camp in South Korea to guarantee its freedom.

North Korean forces took up where the Russians left off. They surged across the border in 1950 in an attempt to overrun the South before help from the West could arrive. The *blitzkrieg* failed, the United Nations and China collided in conflict, and a punishing land war see-sawed across the peninsula's midsection.

An armistice in 1953 stopped the fighting, leaving the two Koreas roughly where the struggle had begun three years before. The church in South Korea was kept free to experience the most remarkable record of church growth in Asia.

Viet Nam: Protracted Struggle

Various Vietnamese resistance groups opposed French colonial occupation that had controlled Indo-China since the 1880s. One clandestine movement was the Indochinese Communist Party. Founded in 1930 under the leadership of Ho Chi Minh, the party took orders from the Comintern, Russia's command center for the spread of international communism.

This obedience carried rewards of support that gave Ho Chi Minh's forces the edge over other resistance movements. They emerged from World War II with the best trained and equipped cadres.

France tried to reimpose colonial rule in Viet Nam, but the people refused to

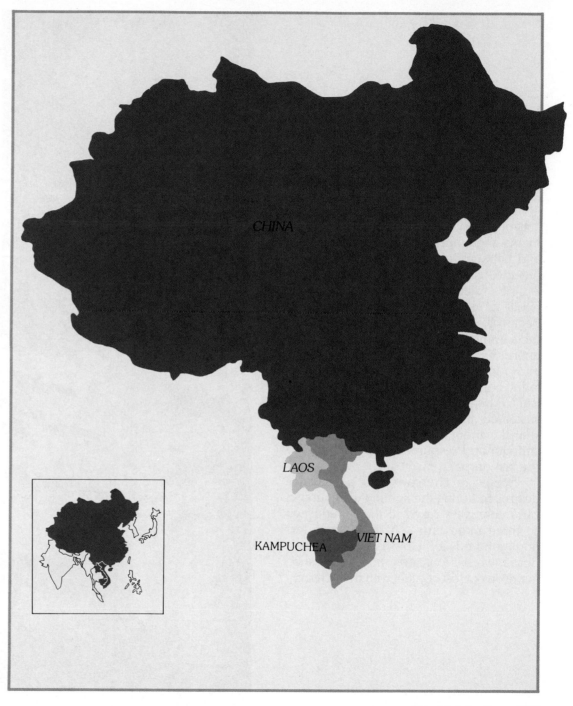

CHINA

LAOS

KAMPUCHEA   VIET NAM

accept a new era of domination. Movements and counter-movements, intrigues and betrayals convulsed the land in furious confusion.

One Vietnamese church historian wrote of this period: "While the world began to enjoy peace and prosperity after the surrender of Germany and Japan, the entire Vietnamese nation was plunged into a long and most vicious and devastating colonial war. The ECVN [Evangelical Church of Viet Nam], which had well sustained the adverse effects of World War II without the mission's help, saw its strength and resources sapped almost to the last drop.

"Scores of churches and parsonages destroyed during the fighting were rebuilt, but many were razed to the ground two or three more times. A dozen ministers and hundreds of Christians were murdered, while thousands more languished in prisons or lost contact with their church.

Tin Lanh congregations of the Evangelical Church of Viet Nam (C&MA) show their love of the Lord in a rich variety of church buildings, some of which have been closed or taken over by the government.

"Deaths, serious illnesses and civilian casualties indirectly caused by the war all combined to shake the indigenous church structure to its foundation. . . . Although between 400 and 1,000 persons were baptized each year during this period, the losses during the war were so staggering that the ECVN did not recover its antebellum numerical strength until 1952."[1]

The smoke of battle cleared long enough at Dien Bien Phu on May 7, 1954, to establish two realities: France was finished in Indo-China, and the new master was communism. On that day, the French forces, badly mauled and beaten on their own terms, surrendered to the besieging battalions of Ho Chi Minh's military strategist, Vo Nguyen Giap.

Peace terms at Geneva in 1954 gave communism only half of Viet Nam, from the seventeenth parallel northward. Now only the United States stood in the way of uniting the entire nation under Hanoi.

It took another twenty years to finally rid South Viet Nam of the Americans—and even then it was not accomplished on the brutal field of battle, but in the poll-sensitive halls of Congress.

The Paris Agreements in 1973 were regarded by Ho Chi Minh as nothing more than a piece of paper, an exit visa for the Americans, enabling him to get on with the job of conquering South Viet Nam. In the first year of the so-called cease-fire, another 60,000 soldiers died in battle as the Saigon government fought on alone, crippled by the sudden loss of its most trusted ally.

Hanoi's persistence had its ultimate reward on April 30, 1975, when South Viet Nam surrendered unconditionally and North Vietnamese tanks punched through the wrought-iron gates of Saigon's presidential palace.

Hmong singers, wearing traditional garb as they sing, show that the Gospel has not robbed them of a rich cultural heritage.

Kampuchea: Preface to Greater Horror

Anticommunist regimes in Kampuchea (Cambodia) and Laos, the other nations of Indo-China, quickly toppled after the fall of South Viet Nam because their fates were intertwined.

With tacit approval of Norodom Sihanouk, the Kampuchean head of state, North Vietnam had turned the eastern region bordering South Viet Nam into a honeycomb of tunnels and depots during the 1960s. The region became a staging and supply district for the Viet Cong, Communists of South Viet Nam.

Pro-Western Marshal Lon Nol deposed Sihanouk in 1970 and appealed to the Americans to destroy the Viet Cong supply network. American forces largely achieved that objective during a sixty-day foray in Kampuchea, but the campaign brought Communist insurgency to an open blaze.

By 1973, the Red Khmer led by Pol Pot controlled 80 percent of the land and one-quarter of the population. The fall of Saigon two years later precipitated the collapse of Lon Nol's regime. Communist columns filed into Phnom Penh, the capital, like the opening lines of a horror story that would take many bizarre twists and stun the civilized world.

Laos: Peaceful *Putsch*

Even more than Kampuchea, Laos was a client state of North Viet Nam. The Communist Pathet Lao, financed and directed from Hanoi, shared in a tripartite power agreement after the French Indo-China war in 1954. But it withdrew from the coalition and began carving out territory of its own.

By 1975, Pathet Lao cadres already controlled a third of Laos and one of every four Laotians. Another coalition of conservatives and neutralists led by Prince Souvanna Phouma tried to hold the nation together, but watched helplessly as Communist armor rolled into Vientiane, the capital. The Pathet Lao eventually abolished both the coalition and the monarchy, then in December of 1975 proclaimed the Lao People's Democratic Republic.

China: War on the Church

Communism in Asia and elsewhere indulges in a curious contradiction. It ridicules religion as "the opiate of the people," a sterile collection of superstitions unworthy of notice and forfeit of any future. Yet Marxist regimes devote personnel, funds and programs on a total-war scale to combat this so-called dead dog.

The People's Republic of China set the pace for treatment of Asian Christians under communism.

Christian missions and churches in China had rebounded sharply at the close of World War II. The Protestant missionary force increased rapidly to more than three thousand by 1948. Roman Catholicism claimed 3,266,000 baptized members and another 1,502,000 communicant members. Various Protestant groups counted 700,000 baptized members and a total community of approximately 1,500,000,[2] or even higher.

"The widespread distribution of Christians was also impressive," comments Arthur F. Glasser. "One could draw a line across China in any direction and on an average of every twenty-five miles come upon a Christian congregation."[3] This

estimate based on averages, however, fails to indicate that vast areas of postwar China had no witness at all.

Beijing (Peking) lost little time in 1949 in altering that distribution. Premier Chou En-lai summoned representatives of major religious groups to draw up a "Christian Manifesto" that condemned "all imperialism and aggressive designs in China." It pledged their "patriotic support of the Common Program" and set before them "the goal of self-support in the near future."[4]

Within months, mission agencies began withdrawing their personnel—all told, approximately 5,500 Roman Catholic and 4,500 Protestant workers by 1949. The remaining Catholic and Protestant missionaries were withdrawn by 1951.

The "Three-Self Patriotic Movement" era began immediately. Committed to

Vietnamese orphans from a C&MA orphanage sang at the opening of the Nhatrang Bible School years ago during the North/South war.

self-support, self-propagation and self-government, the state-sponsored church moved to isolate all Christian churches and organizations from foreign contacts and bring them into line with government policy.

In so doing, the movement became servile to the point of losing its own soul. Its message eventually became, "Turn your hearts over to the party."[5]

The Three-Self Patriotic Movement added something new to the church's liturgy: "denunciation meetings." Congregations were obligated to convene special meetings in which members accused and denounced one another of "imperialist and reactionary acts." Churches learned they could receive tax-exempt status only if they could prove they had held "a successful accusation meeting against at least four of their own members."[6]

If Three-Self leaders thought that by turning Christians against one another they could themselves escape suffering, they were tragically mistaken.

Mao Zedong launched the "Great Proletarian Cultural Revolution" in 1966 with zealous support from millions of teenagers. Incited to destroy the "four olds" (old ideology, old culture, old customs, and old habits), the youthful Red Guards assaulted Three-Self leaders along with the followers of Buddhism, Confucianism, Islam and Taoism. Nearly every vestige of organized Christianity was destroyed during the scourge of revolutionary zeal that lasted until 1976.

Rehabilitation and Resurgence

The Cultural Revolution proved to be the "Great Leap Backward." It dissipated decades of progress and virtually an entire generation of school-age youth.

After Mao's death, the "Gang of Four" felt the other side of retribution's two-edged sword. The four, including Mao's wife, were jailed for crimes against the people. Their place was taken by the "four modernizations," a campaign to revitalize the traumatized sectors of agriculture, industry, science and technology, and defense.

The new rulers sought help from everyone, even the formerly despised religionists. One Three-Self official said the government of Deng Xiaoping wanted to promote a united front involving all groups, secular and religious. "The government no longer views the Christian faith as a threat," he said, "and it realizes that Christians are honest workers."[7]

The state-sanctioned church leader added that the revised 1979 constitution changed the government's priorities, de-emphasizing the propagation of atheism and insuring religious freedom for those who chose to believe.[8] He did not mention, however, that churches were still denied the right to evangelize outside church walls.

Assurances of religious freedom precipitated an amazing development that must have disconcerted party leaders who had considered Christianity a dead issue.

During the "golden years" of 1979 to 1983, Christians surfaced and multiplied in numbers alarming to government leaders. Leslie Lyall, China watcher and former missionary, estimated that as many as 27,000 individuals daily were becoming believers.[9] The sudden emergence of twenty to twenty-five million Christians threw the charge of "decadent religion" back in the faces of its framers.[10]

(Above) *Bicycles remain the chief mode of transportation in the People's Republic of China for the present,* (facing page) *while the nation's fabled Great Wall serves as a reminder of what can be accomplished through united effort.*

The new religious climate included a revitalized Three-Self Patriotic Movement. Reappearance of the official Protestant church did not signal rejoicing among many believers. They remembered too well arrests and persecutions prompted by accusations from local Three-Self leaders.

Creation of Amity Foundation in 1985 indicated how far Beijing was willing to go in its policy of pragmatism. The agency presented itself as the official channel for contributions from overseas religious organizations. "Gifts of personnel and money are invited," was the unabashed official word, "to make Christian participation and witness in society more widely known to the Chinese people."[11]

Amity Foundation's first major success was agreement on a multimillion-dollar printing plant. Funded primarily by the United Bible Societies, the facility would publish the Scriptures, hymnbooks and some social materials for the betterment of society.

Leaders of the foundation denied that its fund raising and recruiting activities ran counter to the official church's policy of self-support. The organization is neither a religious organization nor a division of the church, officials explained.

By the mid-1980s, despite fluctuations of government attitudes, more than five thousand Three-Self churches reopened and continued to grow at the rate of one a day. In addition, more than thirty thousand officially sanctioned meeting points operated under lay leadership.

Christianity's most amazing resurgence of faith, however, was taking place in secret or semipublic house churches. These unregistered groups, loose in structure with no fixed time or place for meet-

China's billions constitute for the church the greatest challenge of evangelism in the world.

ing, numbered 100,000–300,000 by 1986.[12]

Wary of the government's intentions and doubly suspicious of the state-supported Protestant church, house church Christians probably make up the majority of China's Christians.

Obliterated Past

Virtually nothing remains as a physical reminder of the missions era, when Western churches poured thousands of missionaries and millions of dollars into China.

The Christian and Missionary Alliance entered China in 1888 and for over sixty years maintained a high level of commitment to the Chinese people, including an overall total of nearly 550 missionaries. In the years prior to Communist domination, the Alliance worked in Shanghai and seven interior provinces.

Active forces during those years averaged eighty-five missionaries and 225 Chinese church workers. By 1949, the church numbered 8,000 baptized believers and many more adherents.

Despite the immensity of their responsibility, Alliance missionaries in Gansu (Kansu) Province tried to penetrate Tibet, which was closed to the Gospel. Historian Kenneth Latourette writes of those years: "The prolonged effort to penetrate Tibet by way of Kansu was made in the face of almost continuous danger and entailed great heroism."[13]

Not only have those early vestiges of missionary presence disappeared, but also all denominational distinctives. Contemporary China has no Baptists or Methodists or Alliance Christians, though Roman Catholic and Protestant differences continue because each has its own government-approved church. Otherwise, the followers of Christ are simply known as Christians—perhaps an unwitting favor to the church by the Beijing regime.

However, an Alliance missions professor and former missionary touring Guangxi (Kwangsi) Province in 1985 was able to identify several pastors with Alliance backgrounds.

He writes, "At present there are six former C&MA pastors working in Guangxi (we know of a total of twelve throughout China). . . .The Liuzhou Church is the largest in the province.

They had been meeting in one of the former C&MA buildings, but that is being demolished to build a new road. The other C&MA building as well as another piece of Alliance property have also been torn down for road construction. But a new church building, adequate for the congregation of 800, is nearly completed.

"The Nanning Church is not the largest but appears to be the most influential. It conducts a prayer meeting every morning of the week. There is also a Wednesday evening prayer meeting. . . . The Sunday service is full with more than 200 worshippers."[14]

A research center in Hong Kong estimated in 1986 that Protestants comprised nearly 5 percent of the total population, somewhere between thirty-five and fifty million Protestants. That estimate rose from only 1.8 million in 1948, an astonishing 3,000 to 4,000 percent growth in forty-five years.[15]

How many of those believers have an Alliance heritage will never be known this side of heaven, but given the vitality of the church when missions were forced out, their numbers may well reach into the tens of thousands.

Buddhist temples in Kampuchea silhouette the horizon.

Viewing his crowded church on Christmas Day, a Protestant pastor in Beijing said, "Never in thirty-five years has there been a better time."[16]

But a *New York Times* correspondent noted in his conversations with pastors that "there is an edge of wariness about their exchanges with visitors, as though nobody is quite sure how long it will last."[17]

That wariness probably exists on both sides. Certainly Christians have every right not to trust a Communist regime at whose hands they have suffered so terribly for doctrinal reasons that still remain. The Beijing government, however, must in turn be viewing with grudging respect and some confusion a religion once thought dead.

Red Khmer's Final Solution

Kampuchea tried to impose on the churches a Nazi-style final solution. As a result, the landscape offers no sign of a visible church. Believers who survived a decade of unspeakable horrors meet quietly and secretly in small groups to pray and worship.

Evangelical Christianity was never strong in Kampuchea. The Christian and Missionary Alliance entered the country in 1923, when it still carried the name of Cambodia and was a French colony.

Resistance from Buddhist leaders, who claimed about 98 percent of the people, and hostility by French colonial adminis-

CHURCH AND MISSION

OFFICIAL NAME OF CHURCH:	Evangelical Church of Kampuchea
ENTRY BY MISSIONARIES:	1923
BAPTIZED CHURCH MEMBERS:	2,198
RADIO BROADCASTS:	16 per week

COUNTRY

OFFICIAL NAME:	State of Cambodia
FORM OF GOVERNMENT:	Communist
OFFICIAL LANGUAGE(S):	Khmer, French
AREA:	69,898 sq. mi.
POPULATION:	(1989 est.) 6,855,000
CAPITAL:	Phnom Penh
PER CAPITA INCOME:	$100.00
LITERACY:	48%
RELIGIOUS AFFILIATION:	Buddhist 85%, Non-religious 9%, Animist 3%, Christian .07%,

trators generally Roman Catholic and anti-American, hampered Alliance missionaries at every turn. No other mission came to help evangelize the country.

Three decades of witness yielded only a handful of believers and a struggling Bible school. When leftist-leaning Norodom Sihanouk, the chief of state, expelled Alliance missionaries in 1965, the church numbered only about six hundred members led by less than a dozen ordained ministers. Through harassment and ar-

rests, Sihanouk tried to keep it that way.

A remarkable spiritual awakening came to Phnom Penh, the capital, after Marshal Lon Nol deposed Sihanouk in 1970 and permitted missionaries and relief workers to return.

Church membership doubled in size by 1973, tripled a year later. Over one hundred people were turning to the Lord every week—an unheard-of phenomenon in Buddhist Cambodia. Churches in the city mushroomed from one to twenty-

seven. One church attracted three hundred people to its Sunday morning services.

The Christian community expanded rapidly to 5,000, including outstanding laymen such as the president of the Supreme Court, a police commissioner and prominent businessmen.[18]

Songs of rejoicing were suddenly silenced when Kampuchea fell to Pol Pot's forces. What happened next has seldom been equalled in the horror stories of history.

Over two million Kampucheans were forced to evacuate the city at a moment's notice. Even hospital patients were prodded from their beds to join the exodus of misery. Many of the elderly and infant children never got to the city outskirts. They died where they dropped.

Phnom Penh was just the beginning. Through terror and brutality, the Pol Pot regime "commanded sufficient loyalty among the armed forces and cadres to keep the entire nation at work, without pay or material incentives, on what was often a starvation diet for three and a half years."[19]

Congregations were scattered, services

prohibited, church leaders killed. The visible church ceased to exist. Hundreds of thousands of Kampucheans of all social classes and religions had their families exterminated by clubs, bayonets and live burials—human life was not even worth a bullet.

Viet Nam invaded Kampuchea in December of 1978, but the objective was to conquer, not to end killing or ease suffering. The puppet regime did not lift the interdiction on the church's right to exist.

Did surviving believers go underground to preserve their faith in house churches, as in China? Will time soften official hostility toward the church? To these and other questions, Kampuchea remains as inscrutable and silent as its neglected stone Buddhas.

Laotian Benign Indifference

The Lao People's Democratic Republic began in December of 1975 with a grudge against Christians. It closed down churches, demolished buildings and hustled Christian leaders off to reeducation camps. The church president spent forty months in one such camp.

The situation resembled communism's

War and governments come and go, with barely a ripple of change reaching the traditional Loatian village.

typical total war against the church. But hostility gradually diminished and tolerance took over. Pathet Lao forces had apparently assaulted the church more for its former association with an American mission, the Alliance, than for its beliefs.

A 1978 edict granted freedom of religion, which added stature to Christianity, since Laos had formerly been a Buddhist state. Buddhism, in fact, played a moderating role in the new government's attitude.

Sihanouk, leader of Buddhist Kampuchea in prewar days, could well have spoken for Laos when he wrote, "Buddhism, contrary to certain other religions, does not make its followers aggressive in respect to others. On the contrary, it does not extol proselytism but perfect respect for the beliefs of others. That is why our state, of which the religion is Buddhism, protects just as steadfastly the other religions."[20]

Communist leaders in Laos played

down Marxist insistence on atheism, preferring to develop their own pragmatic brand of socialism. Thus the director of religious affairs could state, "Religion is something we must all partake of, even as we must eat and drink. No matter what kind of regime there is, religion is important."[21]

Tolerance toward Laotian Christians did not extend to ethnic tribes such as the Hmong in the jungles and hills.

Whereas Laotian plains people tended with Buddhistic passiveness to accept whatever government prevailed, animistic Hmongs, hardened to life in the jungle, made excellent fighters.

American CIA operatives trained and equipped tough fighting units of tribal guerrillas, then used them effectively against North Vietnamese and Pathet Lao supply routes. The Communists did not forgive or forget.

After the Americans left in 1973, North Vietnamese planes bombed and strafed Hmong villages. Worse yet, they showered yellow, red and black rain on the jungle, wiping out whole villages with chemical warfare. Pathet Lao ground units pursued the surviving Hmongs as they fled toward sanctuary in Thailand.

Flight of the Hmongs created serious problems for the Evangelical Church (C&MA) of Laos. Only 2 percent of the baptized membership were Laotians from the towns and plains. Most of the 5,000 Alliance members and their leaders in 1975 were tribespeople from the jungle.

The church's ethnic imbalance was rooted in history. The first resident Alliance missionary arrived in the royal city of Luang Prabang in 1929. Work among the Buddhist Lao progressed very slowly for years.

Then in 1950, a people's movement sprang up among the Hmongs. One thousand tribespeople became believers in eight weeks. Thousands more joined the movement over the next few years until the Laotian Alliance was almost totally composed of former animistic tribespeople. Only a few members were urban believers converted out of Buddhism.

The few Laotian Alliance pastors who remained after the Pathet Lao took over in 1975 worked hard to fill the vacuum of leadership. They conducted quarterly leadership seminars and slowly built a new generation of church workers.

Meanwhile, churches continued to grow. The Evangelical Church of Laos numbered nearly 7,400 baptized believers in approximately eighty congregations by 1986. Even if only within church walls, these believers spread their witness to ten of Laos' seventeen provinces.

If the Laotian government thinks that by tolerantly ignoring the church it will someday disappear, it will need the patience of Buddha in great measure.

Vietnamese Strategy of Deceit

Each Communist regime in Asia seemed to implement a different strategy to solve the religious problem. China used the puppet church. Kampuchea pursued outright extermination. Laos tried benign indifference. Viet Nam used some of all three.

Following the collapse of South Viet Nam, a lull settled down over the battered country, exhausted after thirty years of continuous warfare. Would Hanoi carry out its pledge of reconciliation? Would the Communists honor their promise that once united, Viet Nam would know an end to suffering and strife?

(Above) *Before South Viet Nam fell to communism, the Bible school at Nhatrang prepared many leaders for the church, (facing page) but following the war the campus was requisitioned by the government.*

So it seemed at first. No massacres were carried out, no rape of the population, no mass executions, no seizure of South Vietnamese assets to enrich the bomb-battered North. Tolerance seemed to prevail.

It appeared that the thousands who had fled the country in panic should have stayed home, and that the United States had protected South Viet Nam from non-existent danger.

Communist leaders promised religious liberty with apparent benign indifference. The Evangelical Church of Viet Nam, largest Protestant denomination in the South, was not singled out for special punishment because of its origin in an American mission, The Christian and Missionary Alliance.

Known commonly as Tin Lanh, the denomination continued its normal activities with 500 pastors and 53,000 baptized believers. Christians moved about freely in Saigon, the Communists' showcase city renamed in honor of Ho Chi Minh.

Showcase status, however, did not extend to the Central Highlands. Word filtered out from the sealed-off region that Tin Lanh pastors were arrested, their families left destitute, their churches destroyed and their congregations scattered. The once thriving church in the highlands disappeared from view.

Then on June 10, 1975, the new regime announced a plan of reeducation for all military officers, policemen, civil

CHURCH AND MISSION

OFFICIAL NAME OF CHURCH:	Evangelical Church of Laos
ENTRY BY MISSIONARIES:	1929
BAPTIZED CHURCH MEMBERS:	1,813 (est.)
INCLUSIVE MEMBERSHIP:	7,500
RADIO BROADCASTS:	8 per week

COUNTRY

OFFICIAL NAME:	Laos People's Democratic Republic
FORM OF GOVERNMENT:	Communist
OFFICIAL LANGUAGE(S):	Lao
AREA:	91,428 sq. mi.
POPULATION:	(1989 est.) 3,923,000
CAPITAL:	Vientiane
PER CAPITA INCOME:	(1989 est.) $500.00
LITERACY:	41%
RELIGIOUS AFFILIATION:	Buddhists 50%, Tribal 50%

servants and community leaders, including many religious workers.

Over the next three years, an estimated 1,340,000 people passed through reeducation camps.[22] Between 100,000 and 300,000 were detained over a long period of time for brainwashing and hard labor in conditions best described as concentration camps.[23]

Revival and Repression

The Tran Cao Van Church in Ho Chi Minh City (Saigon) illustrated what happened in the postwar era.

Before the "Liberation," the sanctuary had been used by the Alliance for an English-speaking international congregation. It was transferred to the Tin Lanh Church when the missionaries left in 1975.

Attendance temporarily dropped to seventy after the fall of Saigon, but by 1982 the congregation swelled to over seven hundred. Revival came and attendance grew to one thousand, requiring two Sunday morning services.

A group of people were praying in the sanctuary on Saturday morning, December 10, 1982, when security police surrounded the church and arrested Pastor Ho Hien Ha. Police evicted his family from the parsonage and seized their possessions.

People arriving for services on Sunday found the gates locked. Hundreds stayed to weep and pray until security forces again surrounded the area and scattered them. The handsome, large church building was later appropriated for a government youth center.

The government could have pointed out that Pastor Ha did not have a resident permit and the church was situated in an area zoned for diplomatic residences. But in reality, the police did not move against the church until revival stung the authorities into action.

When Pastor Ha and three other ministers were brought to a courthouse in Ho Chi Minh City almost two years later for a "trial," he found over five hundred Christians crowding the courtroom and outside courtyard. Finding it impossible to proceed, the presiding officials ordered the prisoners back to prison.

Pastor Ha encouraged his people with a reminder, "Remember: no cross, no crown!"

Progressive Spirit

Communist authorities criticized the Tin Lanh Church in the mid-1980s for a lack of "progressive spirit."

Roman Catholics and Buddhists in North and South Viet Nam were reunited, but Tin Lanh leaders resisted merging with the Evangelical Church of North Viet Nam, formerly Alliance and now government approved. They also showed a further lack of progressive spirit by failing to cooperate with authorities in "political activism."

But perhaps Tin Lanh Christians do display a "progressive spirit," if viewed from another angle.

By 1985, 40 percent of South Vietnam's evangelical churches were closed—but 60 percent still carried on. Tin Lanh's seminary and Bible schools were all closed—but a network of "pocket seminaries" continued to train workers. Nineteen evangelical pastors were still detained in reeducation camps—but they evangelized their fellow prisoners.

One imprisoned pastor baptized seven converts in a well during a work detail. When questioned, he replied: "In Viet Nam, buffaloes pull plows, dogs guard houses, and evangelical preachers witness. That's just the way it is."[24]

Help Limited and Unlimited

Alliance churches in North America are severely limited in what they can do to help their sister churches under communism in Asia.

Radio ministry does penetrate the bamboo curtain to bring encouragement and Bible teaching not otherwise available. Listener response is understandably sparse, but information from various sources indicate that the programs are well and widely received.

Christians in free countries, however, can help their Asian brothers and sisters in a manner no border guard or barbed wire can hinder. A Vietnamese pastor showed the way in a hurried whisper to a relief worker: "Tell them we are living by faith day by day. Pray for us."□

CHURCH AND MISSION

OFFICIAL NAME OF CHURCH:	The Evangelical Church of Vietnam
ENTRY BY MISSIONARIES:	1911
BAPTIZED CHURCH MEMBERS:	53,428
INCLUSIVE MEMBERSHIP:	250,000
RADIO BROADCASTS:	23 per week

COUNTRY

OFFICIAL NAME:	Socialist Republic of Vietnam
FORM OF GOVERNMENT:	Communist People's Republic
OFFICIAL LANGUAGE(S):	Vietnamese
AREA:	128,401 sq. mi.
POPULATION:	(1989 est.) 66,708,000
CAPITAL:	Hanoi
PER CAPITA INCOME:	$180.00 (1987)
LITERACY:	94% (1983)
RELIGIOUS AFFILIATION:	Non-religious/Atheist 22.5%, Buddhist 54%, Animist 4%, Muslim 1%, Hoa Hao/Cao Daij 11%, Christian 7.5%

LATIN AMERICA

ARGENTINA	130
BRAZIL	138
CHILE	144
COLOMBIA	152
COSTA RICA	162
DOMINICAN REPUBLIC	165
ECUADOR	168
GUATEMALA	176
MEXICO	182
PERU	186
SURINAM	194
VENEZUELA	196

LATIN AMERICA

Primacy of Politics

THE RIO GRANDE RIVER does more than simply provide a meandering boundary between the United States and Mexico. It separates two vastly different halves of the Western Hemisphere, ranging from Canada to Argentina.

Latin and North America do share some striking but superficial similarities.

Massive, snowcapped mountain ranges run like a jagged, frosted spinal column along the western flank from north to south. Both Americas have rolling plains and wide rivers across their midsection. The coastlines of each are lined with tall-standing cities and washed by the same great bodies of water.

The two Americas also claim similar backgrounds.

They were largely inhabited by Indians and eventually conquered by European invaders. Nationalistic descendants of the colonizers threw off Old World domination by force of arms, but retained much of its cultural heritage. Later immigrants from Europe strengthened those ties to the "old country."

Superficial similarities on both sides of the Rio Grande, however, cannot hide deep and serious differences. In matters of economy, language, politics, culture and religion, south differs from north almost as much as east from west.

Why the sharp cleavage?

More than any other combination of factors, politics and religion forced the two Americas apart—and continue to do so.

Conquistadores and Clergy

Absolute monarchs, in close alliance with the Roman Catholic Church, ruled Spain and Portugal, the two major colonial powers in Latin America. Both countries had experienced the Inquisition, but not the Reformation. Especially in Spain, the Pope had virtually ceded to the king internal control of the church, in return for the monarch's support of the Pope's larger designs for Europe.[1] This arrangement thoroughly politicized the Spanish church.

Military expeditions to Latin America sailed under royal orders to conquer, annex and despoil for the enrichment of the crown. Papal emissaries sailed with the armadas to complete the conquest by enlightening heathen mentality through Catholic dogma and supplanting primitive customs with European culture.[2]

The lusty conquistador and zealous priest made a strangely contradictory but complementary team.

"Neither, when he was most himself, could understand or forgive the other," wrote one historian. "Yet they were inseparably yoked, sent together into a new world, and together they were responsible for the action and achievement of the Old World in the New."[3]

In a mere fifteen years, Hernan Cortes conquered the Aztecs in Mexico with 600 men. Francisco Pizarro overran the Inca empire in Peru with less than 200. Thus from 1519 to 1534, a handful of Spaniards destroyed the two most advanced civilizations in the Western Hemisphere and began a 300-year empire that was to be Spanish in character and Catholic in creed.

The Portuguese occupied Brazil with little fanfare or warfare, but their intentions were just as long-term as Spain's.

From that point onward, Latin America started on a separate

course totally different from that of its neighbors above the Rio Grande River.

The New Order

Latin America actually began its new era in a more advanced state than North America. Mayan, Aztec and Inca civilizations had built fabled cities and developed arts and sciences to an amazing level.

When Cortes saw Tenochtitlan, the Aztec capital, with its temples and flower gardens, lakes and causeways, he said it rivaled anything Europe had produced.

But the New Order decreed that everything must go, and on its ashes and debris would arise a new and superior civilization. The conquistadores plundered in the name of greed. The emissaries of Rome burned manuscripts and records, smashed art treasures and demolished temples in the name of God.

"The Spaniards believed that the Christian Church could stand only on the ruins of pagan temples," wrote historian German Arciniegas.[4] In Mexico alone, they destroyed 500 temples and 20,000 idols.

In some instances, priests discovered similarities to their own beliefs in Indian religions. The Mayans of Central America, for instance, believed in a god who came in human form to save his people; they also practiced baptism and believed in life after death. Congregations of monks and nuns under special vows performed Mayan religious rites.[5]

Missionaries incorporated some of these beliefs into church rites and even liturgy, leaving many Indians with the impression they could continue in their old ways while accepting the new.

Priests further confused them by naming local deities after Catholic saints and encouraging people to invoke their aid.

Added to this curious mix of religions, and further complicating it, was poor communication. Pioneer missionaries, unfamiliar with Indian languages, hired local translators almost as inept in Spanish or Portuguese. Confusion and distortions inevitably followed.

One early report noted that when a priest tried to explain the Holy Trinity as "Three in One," his translator added them together and told the people the new religion believed in four gods.[6] Latin America's dimly perceived conversion to Catholicism resulted in a part-Catholic, part-pagan faith that would endure for centuries.

For Spanish author Victor Alba, road shrines summed up the syncretic religion of Latin American Catholicism. "In recent years," he observed, "when it has been necessary to move the Spanish wayside crucifixes to make way for modern highways, the engineers have often found clay images of ancient idols buried in the base of the pedestals."[7]

Diminishing Zeal

One of the first conquistadores, Bernal Diaz del Castillo, explained why they invaded Mexico: "We came in order to serve God and His Majesty, to give light to those that were in darkness, and also to become rich, which we all commonly came in order to seek."[8]

Castillo may well have spoken for Rome as well as Spain—including the part about getting rich. From the first day of conquest, the church laid claim to houses and lands. Each ecclesiastical unit eventually had its own properties and Indian workers.

Missionary zeal had almost vanished by the seventeenth century, as the church looked after its vast holdings. A century later, some bishops as well as colonial administrators were warning that, unless stopped, the church would eventually own everything.

By then, one-fifth of all Spanish lands belonged to Rome. The church claimed four-fifths of Mexico. Lima, typical of many other cities, had one-third of all its buildings owned by the church.[9]

To protect its vast interests, the church played politics .

"In the capitals of the viceroyalties," wrote Alba, "the church was the ally of the royal authorities; in provincial towns and pueblos, it was the ally of the Creoles [American-born Spaniards]; in the hamlets, the parish priest was the real authority."[10]

Morality among the clergy declined as riches increased.

Two Spanish naval officers investigating Peruvian clergy reported on "the perverted customs of their disordered lives."[11] They noted that in many Peruvian parishes, the priest openly kept a woman, and monasteries were little more than "public brothels." Monasteries in larger cities frequently became a "theatre for unheard of abominations and execrable vices."[12]

The Catholic church's record in Latin America was not totally without merit. Sincere priests protested the excesses of their colleagues and some were martyred for their defense of the Indians against exploitation.

And, to its credit, the church used some of its wealth for social services.

Catholicism provided the first hospitals and founded the first universities in the New World. The Dominican-funded University of St. Thomas Aquinas in Santo Domingo led all others by opening its doors in 1538. The first secondary school had already been founded in 1505.

But overall, early patterns of partial conversions among the people, wholesale politics and widespread corruption among the clergy resulted in a Roman Catholicism that, despite deep roots and often fervent faith, would be spiritually anemic and passive.

Protestant Stirrings

Initial scattered and feeble attempts by Protestants to penetrate Catholic America met with predictable failure. Strongly entrenched Spanish and Portuguese authorities found their presence intolerable and made sure the newcomers felt the same way about them.

French Huguenots sought a haven from persecution during the 1500s in Brazil, but the Portuguese quickly drove them out. Dutch Protestants tried in 1661, but they, too, were repulsed.

The Spanish Inquisition cast its long shadow over native-born American or European settlers who considered converting to the Protestant faith. Church tribunals in Latin America tried approximately 6,000 cases before they were suppressed.

The closure came too late for some one hundred victims burned at the stake. Hundreds more died in prison or under torture.[13]

The only footholds Protestants could gain on the continent into the 1700s were through Dutch, English and French colo-

nies—some of them pirate settlements. Moravian missionaries began working in the Guiana colonies controlled by the British and Dutch around 1738. Congregational and Methodist missions joined them in the early 1900s.

Even in 1900, the heaviest concentration of Protestants in all of Latin America centered in the two tiny Guiana colonies of the Netherlands and Great Britain. Together they claimed 14,376 communicants.

Brazil listed 11,376 Protestants, thanks to a more lenient attitude than had prevailed in earlier centuries. In all the rest of Latin America in 1900, only 5,246 people admitted to belonging to a Protestant church.[14]

Prospects for an expanded Protestant witness brightened after Simon Bolivar and Jose de San Martin swept Spain from much of South America by 1830. Country after country gained freedom from Spain, and Brazil followed after.

The new governments altered the status of Protestantism by changing one word in their existing constitutions. "Permits" replaced "prohibits," thus putting the governments on record that they "permit the public exercise of other religions."

That key constitutional change put religious freedom on the books, but getting it into the streets was another matter.

After independence came to the Latin American countries, Catholicism retained a privileged status in every one. Even if the church was not named the official religion, it enjoyed a special relationship, while Protestants were considered cultural, as well as religious, aliens.

Latin American bishops were summoned to Rome as the colonial era dimmed and died. They formulated a strategy designed to check any advance by Protestant missionaries. Numerous waves of persecution for non-Catholics resulted from the bishops' meeting, and largely achieved their purposes for a time.[15]

One historian wrote, "The shadow of the Inquisition lay heavy on Latin America: even when the law permitted Protestantism, local public opinion did not, and the church often pressed persecution long after the legislation abolished it."[16]

The newly independent nations may not have wanted Protestants, but they did encourage Europeans—whatever their religion—to settle within their borders. Argentina, Chile, Uruguay and Brazil offered settlers from the Old World free transportation and rich lands for as little as a dollar an acre.

Among others, many German Lutherans responded to the offer to settle in Latin America. By 1903, over 200,000 German immigrants organized thirty-nine churches in southern Brazil. They set up the Rio Grande Synod and in twenty years counted 281 congregations and a community of 123,616 Lutherans.[17]

Bible Forerunner

Although immigration boosted the Protestant population, newcomers did not spill over ethnic boundaries to evangelize the local people. Bible colporteurs did much more than immigrants in unlocking the doors of Roman Catholic America.

For almost three centuries, Rome succeeded in keeping the Bible from the people. Its distribution was forbidden by both Pope and king. "The Roman Catholic Church intended to keep Latin America free from the 'poison' of the Reformation and the Inquisition backed up its intent," added one historian.[18]

As nations gained independence, however, Bibles began to filter through cracks in the papal wall. The American and British Bible Societies shipped Bibles to merchants in towns along the Atlantic and Pacific coasts. God's Word gradually worked its way into the continent.

James Thompson, a Scot who ostensibly came to South America to promote public education, became a highly successful colporteur. With a Bible under one arm and a blueprint for elementary education under the other, he organized hundreds of schools and championed circulation of the Bible. Argentina, Chile and Peru made him an honorary citizen.

By 1828, Thompson founded the National Bible Society of Colombia. Later, in Mexico, he distributed an edition of the Scriptures without notes, with the cooperation of Roman Catholic clergy.

Bible distribution began slowly to accelerate as capable and brave men and women devoted themselves to colportage work. They faced the fury of mobs incited by hostile priests, and suffered beatings and imprisonment, but in their wake, they left hearts prepared for the Gospel.

A pattern of church growth emerged: first a Bible, then a convert, then a church.[19]

One colporteur in Brazil observed: "In dozens of places where I sold the first copies of the Scriptures the people ever saw, there are now strong evangelical churches today. . . . I cannot recall a single case where the Bible came second. Speaking from personal experience, I should therefore say, that if you want to open up a new area, the first thing to do is to send in someone with a Bible."[20]

Awakened Commitment

Protestant missions almost canceled their future in Latin America around 1825. The American Board of Commissioners for Foreign Missions sent two young men to explore the possibilities of missionary work. One of the two reported back that the time was not right.

Fortunately, others ignored this pessimistic assessment. Allen Francis Gardiner, a former British naval officer, determined to evangelize an area yet untouched by the Gospel. On some bleak and barren islands off the tip of South America, he found inhabitants as inhospitable as the elements.

Gardiner and his small band of missionaries died of exposure and starvation on Tierra del Fuego in 1851, when their supply ship failed to arrive on time. News of their commitment to the Lord and manner of their death stirred others in Britain to take their place.

From the United States, however, came the most extensive missionary efforts. Perhaps because North and South America are linked together on the same continent by Central America, both Protestants and Catholics in the United States sensed a special debt to evangelize their neighboring southern nations. By the beginning of the twentieth century, Protestant missions had work in all Latin American countries.[21]

In 1900, three-quarters of the population from Mexico southward were illiterate. Some Protestant missions envisioned education as a sure way to remove prejudice and win a hearing for the Gospel. "The time has come to fortify, and to build colleges is to effect fortification," suggested one leading churchman. "A church is no stronger than its institutions of learning."[22]

Around 1925, denominational strategists turned the responsibility of direct evangelism over to small and struggling national churches, while they gave top priority to the indirect method of persuasion through education.

Though their schools could not match the Catholic parochial system in size or scope, Protestant educators did a good job, and their schools enjoyed a standing far exceeding their numbers.

But financing and staffing the mission schools claimed a constantly increasing share of mission resources. Tensions mounted year after year at annual conference time, as educators and missionaries in other ministries debated the allocation of personnel and funds.

Institutional-oriented missions fell further and further behind in evangelism efforts as national population growth outstripped their efforts. Unfortunately, this failing did not become obvious for years.

Meanwhile, other missions with a single-minded evangelistic approach began moving into Latin America around 1900. The Bible school movement, the rise of independent churches and a certain antidenominational spirit in North America sparked an increase in faith missions. Their numbers became significant around 1930 and again after World War II.

Limited resources and, in some cases, institutional strategy of Protestant missions had an unexpected but salutary effect on the young national churches.

One church-growth specialist noted, "Heavy responsibilities were placed immediately upon willing, able and enthusiastic converts, encouraging the emergence of national leadership."[23]

The number of native-born church workers rose from 342 in 1911 to 1,540 by 1936. Increased participation by Latin American believers undoubtedly contributed to the growth of Protestantism from 139,000 to over 424,000 in that same twenty-five-year period.[24]

The Pentecostal movement originated about the same time and quickly became a major force in Catholic America. Luis Francescon, for example, had a Pentecostal experience in Chicago before going to Brazil in 1909. He established the *Congregacao Crista*, which became the second largest Protestant church in Brazil.

Protestant Expansion

Latin Americans began to realize that Protestant missionaries were not devils in broadcloth and that leaving the Catholic church did not mean denying their rich cultural heritage. They experienced in growing numbers that the Gospel provided a deep, personally satisfying response to their passionate longing for spiritual reality.

Catholicism in Latin America held aloft "the Christ of the crucifix—made of stone, distant and cold, powerless to transform—who could not satisfy the spiritual longings of the Latins," observed one historian.[25]

Once past barriers of distrust and fear, Latin Americans could find in the evangelical faith an avenue of spiritual expression that had long been denied them.

The era of Protestant expansion began in peculiar circumstances. Some mission leaders at the 1910 World Missionary Conference in Edinburgh refused to allow consideration of

Latin America. The meetings were to focus on "pagan" countries, some argued. Latin America, at least nominally Roman Catholic, did not fit into that category.

Before the conference ended, North American delegates had decided on a special meeting to deal specifically with Latin America.

The resulting Panama Congress in 1916 brought together 304 delegates from fifty mission boards—forty-four from the United States—for an unprecedented study and strategy effort.

"Many missionary leaders divide the period of the evangelical enterprise in Latin America into the 'pre-' and 'post-' Panama Congress eras. This conference proved to be a watershed for the evangelical movement in Latin America."[26]

The impact of that gathering was dramatically reflected in a similar congress ten years later. Latin Americans comprised one-half the total attendance, while ten years earlier they had represented less than 10 percent of the participants. Spanish, not English, was the conference language, and a Brazilian, not a North American, presided at the sessions.[27]

Most Latin American countries sat on the sidelines during the two world wars, but both Protestant and Catholic mission work profited directly from the conflicts: Missionaries who could no longer work in Africa or the Orient were transferred to Latin America.

The aftermath of World War II registered enormous changes in Central and South America. One historian wrote, "Industrialization, urbanization, mechanization, education, migration and revolution turned more and more of the common people responsive to new ideas — and to the evangelical position."[28]

This new openness to the Gospel coincided with such a surge of missionary activity that by 1958, fully one-quarter of all missionaries at work in the world ministered in Latin America.[29] Sixty percent of those 5,431 missionaries belonged to two evangelical agencies: International Foreign Mission Association (IFMA) and Evangelical Foreign Missions Association (EFMA).

Twenty years later, the number of North American Protestant personnel climbed to 11,535, or one-third of the worldwide missionary force. Brazil, with 1,995 foreign church workers, hosted a larger mission presence than any other country.[30]

Ferment of Change

Religious history in Latin America seemed to have reversed itself by the twentieth century: Now Protestantism flourishes, while Catholicism struggles.

Rome's extensive land holdings and its policy of supporting entrenched regimes that were too often oppressive and corrupt, brought Catholicism to hard times. Not only is the hierarchy often in conflict with reformers and revolutionaries, it is at odds with a growing number of its own foot soldiers, the priests and nuns. Some clerics actually join armed rebel bands, while others openly criticize church policies and leadership.

A new wave of thought called Liberation Theology has gained wide acceptance among the clergy and lay leaders of the Catholic church in Latin America.

Couched in radical terms, the new doctrine portrays Christ as the Great Revolutionary who endorses violence to overturn regimes that prey on the people. Liberation Theology equates

revolution with redemption. Salvation means liberation from oppression, and the kingdom of God is likened to a new political structure installed through civil war.

Latin American bishops met in Medellin, Colombia, in 1968 to study the church's stance relating to rapidly changing social conditions. They met again in Puebla, Mexico, a decade later, still grappling with the basic issue of the church's response to pervasive injustice, poverty and violence on the continent.

Pope John Paul II roundly rejected the violent implications of Liberation Theology, while committing the church to the kinds of reform it demanded. This has turned the church into an opposition party against governments it had long supported, bringing it into conflict with the political right as well as the left.

"Religion and politics have depended on and influenced one another since the origin of what we know as Latin America," comments historian Daniel H. Levine.[31]

Through the centuries, though, politics have manifestly had the upper hand. By rendering unto Caesar what was God's, the Catholic church lost its primacy in religion. By mid-twentieth century, only one in ten professing Catholics actually practiced his faith.[32]

In more recent decades, Roman Catholicism underwent some changes that have improved its position in Latin America. Since Vatican II, for example, violent opposition to Protestant witness changed in many areas to passive rejection, and in some places even cooperation.

Related to this change of attitude toward Protestants has been the charismatic movement within the Catholic church.

What began as a Pentecostal experience in some Protestant missions leaped over the confessional gap like a forest fire across man-made barriers. This spiritual awakening, ignited in part by greater access to the Bible, brought many devout Catholics face to face with Christ.

W. Dayton Roberts, a knowledgeable missions leader, believes the number of such people runs high: "The renewal movement within Latin America's Catholic Church has resulted in a body of 'charismatic' Catholic Christians perhaps comparable in numbers to the evangelical Christian community."[33]

In seven trips to the continent between 1979 and 1987, however, conservative-minded Pope John Paul II reinforced papal control over direction of the Latin American church. "Both the charismatic renewal and the theology of liberation leveled off," believes Roberts. The pope "was firmly in the saddle, and theological innovation was discouraged."[34]

Samuel Escobar, one of Latin America's top evangelical theologians, thinks that behind conservative reaction to movements of change lies more than a concern for orthodoxy. "Rather, there is an effort to protect the centuries-old association between church and political power," he writes.[35]

Meanwhile, Protestantism continues to grow rapidly in numbers. Although researchers are only beginning to compile data, Protestants and various sects already claim an estimated 10 percent of Latin America's 310 million population. Churches claim an even higher percentage in some countries, and are growing at an annual rate of 15 percent or better.[36]

While the Catholic church seems locked into its centuries-old pattern of politics and religion, Protestants in general, and evangelicals in particular, have embarked on a new day which has yet to see its high noon of ministry in Latin America. ☐

ARGENTINA

The Lean Years First

NOSOTROS *somos Europeos!* "We are Europeans!" The proud assertion of many Argentines is reflected in ornately gilded chambers of government, enacted constantly along bustling boulevards of raucous traffic and jostling pedestrians, echoed repeatedly between gleaming glass and steel towers of commerce.[1]

Ninety-seven percent of the population do indeed claim Old World connections. They speak the language of Spain (accented with Italian), wear the fashions of France and prefer the products of Germany. Buenos Aires, their capital, considers itself the Paris of Latin America—perhaps a tacit recognition that though they dress and talk like Europeans, their feet are rooted in Latin America.

Three of every four Argentines live in a city. As a nation, they form the most literate population in the southern half of the hemisphere. Buenos Aires alone supports sixty newspapers.

Argentina resembles Europe in another way: disinterest in religion.

Ninety-six percent of the population are Roman Catholic by infant baptism, but only two of every ten actually attend mass. In some urban dioceses, the number of practicing members falls as low as 2.3 percent. Understaffed clergy average one priest for approximately every 4,350 communicants.[2]

Protestantism has fared little better among the Argentines. From the early years of the nineteenth century to the present, the Protestant community has comprised only about 4 percent of the population. Estimates vary between 675,000 and 932,000 believers.

The Alliance portion of that community totals approximately 6,000 inclusive members, of which 3,500 are baptized. These Christians attended sixty-seven organized and unorganized churches during 1986.

Limited Efforts

The first Alliance missionaries entered Argentina via Brazil in 1897. Their early activities in the Province of Buenos Aires, though ennobled with sacrifice and heroism, seemed to set an uneven pattern of ebb and flow in Alliance commitment to the country for years to come.

The church they started in La Plata, and other groups of believers as well, passed into the care of other missions as the Alliance experienced difficulties in staffing and funding.

The next high-water mark came in 1925, when eighteen missionaries worked in the Province of Buenos Aires, especially Azul. They founded a Bible institute in the capital and moved throughout the province with a large tent and an evangelistic program.

The Alliance mission was then caught between a juggernaut of rising nationalism in Argentina and a diminishing level of support from North America during the Depression. The dilemma brought the mission's activity to a virtual standstill from the 1930s until the end of World War II.

One missionary couple, Rev. and Mrs. Samuel G. Barnes, refused to give up on the proud, Gospel-resistant Argentines. They kept the field open almost single-handedly, until reawakened interest in North America brought reinforcements and funds.

Following World War II, the Alliance began slowly, very slowly, to rebuild its ministry in Argentina. From 1950 to 1975, the staff increased by only one new couple every five years. However, over the next five-year period, four couples and three single persons joined the Argentine Alliance Mission.

Rejection Discarded

The unusual increase in personnel reflected a change in Argentina itself. Openness to the Gospel had begun to replace haughty rejection; resistance was turning to response.

The change in attitude seemed linked to two nationwide problems: violent politics and rampant inflation.

Human rights fell victim in the streets during the seventies, as many innocent civilians were caught in the cross fire between government troops and leftist rebels.

The Mothers of Plaza de Mayo symbolized the tragedy of that conflict. Wearing white scarves and carrying rosaries or placards, the women gathered every Friday at the cathedral and marched silently to La Casa Rosada, the government palace. They were protesting the disappearance of family members arrested by the government and never again seen.

Desaparecidos, they called their miss-

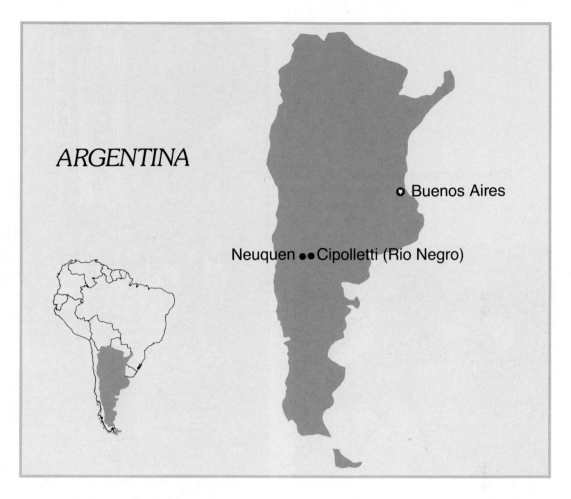

ARGENTINA

◉ Buenos Aires

Neuquen ●●Cipolletti (Rio Negro)

ing loved ones. "The disappeared ones" totaled over eight thousand.

The government later conceded that "mistakes were made," but such things could be expected "in a war of such peculiar circumstances as this one, where the enemy did not use uniforms."[3]

Rampant inflation, reaching 1,000 percent annually by 1983, was the second nationwide problem that helped crack the stony facade of indifference to the Gospel.

Argentina had enjoyed perhaps the highest living standard in Latin America for many years. It had long led the world in beef exports. Only Australia surpassed it in selling wool abroad. It was the world's second largest exporter of wheat. It was nearly self-sufficient in oil.

Then an imbalance of trade, falling world prices and rising costs at home started Argentina on an economic spiral. Economic hard times rudely awakened many people to the impermanence of possessions and the reality of the spiritual.

With these factors at work, the decade

(Below) *European influence is seen in polo matches and* (right) *downtown Buenos Aires.*

of the 1970s recorded numerous events of far-reaching importance for the Alliance church and mission.

1971: The Argentina Alliance received government recognition of its status as an incorporated, autonomous church body.

1976: The national church and foreign mission adopted their first five-year working agreement. In addition to recognizing each other's separate functions and pledging to support each other's minis-

tries, they agreed to carry out combined ministries. They formed a church/mission evangelism commission and a joint board of directors for the Buenos Aires Bible Institute.

1977: Mission and church leaders set up a Theological Education by Extension (TEE) program to upgrade the level of training and education of the pastors and lay leaders.

1979: An accelerated pace of evange-

lism and an enlarged cadre of missionaries and Argentine church workers showed encouraging results. During the 1970s, church membership doubled, to 2,218 baptized believers.

Queen City

Buenos Aires may not be the sum total of Argentina, but were it removed, the country would be greatly diminished. Already home to over 11 million people and growing by 1.5 million every decade, greater Buenos Aires claims one-third of the nation's population.

The Alliance has ministered in the city for many years, both through the Bible institute and through city churches. The Gospel, however, did not rank high in priority among the pragmatic, industrious city dwellers until problems emerged in the seventies. As violence and inflation escalated, so did interest in spiritual matters.

Then in 1980, several pastors visited Lima to study the highly successful "Encounter with God" evangelism program (see Peru). They returned home changed men.

Inspired to see what God could do in their city, the pastors launched intensive evangelism efforts in their churches. One pastor conducted a three-day campaign and was amazed to see fifteen converts— an unheard-of response.

A team of missionaries and pastors initiated a mass evangelism program the following year. Buenas Nuevas Buenos Aires ("Good News Buenos Aires" later became "Buenos Aires Encounter with God") began laying plans to eventually reach the entire city. Most of the thirteen organized and five unorganized churches reported growth in numbers.

The Coghlan and Urquiza congregations did something else unusual: They combined forces and finances in 1984, to relocate on a main street and pursue an aggressive campaign of outreach. [4]

Under their new name, Saavedra, the church alternated evangelistic campaigns with discipling sessions for new converts. Not content with just one program, the church also began using Evangelism Explosion and network evangelism techniques. Another team of missionaries and an Argentine pastor started a second church on a major boulevard of the city in 1985. Following the Encounter plan, it soon showed a pattern of strong growth.

The Argentine Alliance's popular Mar del Plata Trio, one of the few evangelical singing groups in full-time ministry, participated in some of the campaigns as their own ministry expanded throughout Latin America. They attracted people who would not otherwise have come to the services.

"Buenos Aires Encounter with God" received a big boost when The Christian and Missionary Alliance of Canada made Buenos Aires part of its strategy of special support for evangelism and church growth in key cities overseas. [5]

With a generous Canadian grant, the Saavedra congregation secured a choice site and designed a four-story evangelistic center, from which groups would spread out to start new churches. The soaring inflation rate of 700 percent forced building plans to be scaled down, but in 1984 the church dedicated a 400-seat sanctuary and continued its outreach campaign.

Meanwhile, other churches in the city were experiencing growth, even though they were not part of the "Buenos Aires Encounter with God" effort. The Liniers, Suarez and Belgrano churches grew weekly through conversions. The Liniers church prayer meeting increased from ten to 140 attendees in two years.

Teaching and Training

The highly literate, culture-conscious Argentines place great emphasis on education. Sensitive to the need for well-trained pastoral leadership, the Alliance

Thirty-year-old subway system in Buenos Aires still gleams like a showpiece.

made schooling an important part of their work from the very beginning.

The first missionaries in the 1890s opened a short-lived training school in La Plata. When the mission later established its headquarters in Azul, it added a night school, while opening a similar day school in Olavarria. Both schools had the single purpose of preparing students for church ministry.

The 1921 annual field conference authorized a permanent Bible institute. This took place the following year, with fourteen students in the first class. Three men and one woman from the group formed the first graduating class three years later.

By this time, Argentine support for the school had become a major factor: 71 percent of funds paid or pledged came from local sources, not from the mission.

The school, now named the Buenos Aires Bible Institute, grew steadily. By the mid-1960s, its curriculum increased to four years of study leading to a bachelor's degree in theology. Its student body grew to about thirty students from eleven different denominations and groups.

The institute moved in 1966 to a commodious building in the prosperous residential Belgrano district of the capital. The new quarters also provided dormitory quarters for forty students, four apartments for faculty and staff, and headquarters space for the mission.

An important transition took place in 1979. The cost of living, increasing that year alone by 698 percent, forced the school to begin switching all its classes to evening hours. This enabled students to earn a living by day and pay the costs of their education. The switch to an evening schedule resulted in a peak enrollment: 202 students. Four different study programs were conducted by sixteen professors, with the help of four staff members.[6]

The changeover to evening courses lengthened the time needed for students to graduate, but enrollment continued high, reaching 334 by 1986. Both students and faculty determined not to allow economic or political difficulties to deter the school from adequate preparation for ministry.

They all knew that beyond graduation awaited a people who expect much from their leaders.

End of the Lean Years

The long, thin line of Alliance churches stretches almost 2,000 miles, from tropi-

(Below) *An evening Bible class in the capital meets under the direction* (right) *of a missionary.*

cal Asuncion in Paraguay to blustery, cold Rio Gallegos in Patagonia. Trying to administer churches scattered over such a vast area proved too difficult for the Argentine Alliance church leaders.

Consequently, church growth was an individual matter, depending on the quality of leadership in each congregation. While some churches became stalemated, others flourished.[7]

The General Pico congregation in Buenos Aires Province, for example, numbered between 400 and 500 each Sunday in the 1980s. The Curuzu Cuatia church outgrew its new facilities before they were completed in 1982. On the other hand, some struggling churches in the provinces could not even afford a full-time pastor after years of trying.

Recognizing the problem caused by distance, the national church reorganized the churches into eight districts in 1979. Grouped in smaller areas, the churches related more closely to one another and combined their efforts in church-planting projects.

The relatively large staff of about twenty missionaries during the 1980s enabled them to work more closely with churches in the interior provinces.

Ministry among Chilean immigrants proved especially fruitful over the years. Clustered near Argentina's border with Chile in the south, many of the newcomers were already Alliance church members. Other immigrants listened more readily to the gospel witness than the long-entrenched Argentines of the same area.

In the Patagonian city of Comodoro Rivadavia, a new pastor successfully brought together two congregations who were long at odds with each other. Church attendance rose to 300, and the

reunited believers sponsored ten preaching points in the city.

Church statistics indicated in 1985 that 542 new believers were baptized, the highest number in many years. The Alliance in Argentina had good reason to hope that the many lean years had ended and that the long-awaited spiritual awakening had finally come.

Mission Uruguay

To the eternal credit of the Argentine Alliance, it did not wait for the fruitful years before launching its own missionary outreach. During the 1960s, with many churches small and struggling and the mission understaffed, Argentine believers

(Top) *The Mar del Plata Trio is popular throughout Latin America;* (above) *two congregations merged to form the Saavedra Church and relocated on a main street.*

turned to their "Samaria" in an enlarging circle of witness.

Across their northeastern border lay Uruguay, the smallest country in South America.

Almost totally European in background (Spanish, Italian and French), distinguished by a high literacy rate (91 percent) and a large middle class, the nation seemed to have much going for it—except for a widespread ignorance of Christ as found in the Gospels.

Catholicism claimed a large majority of Uruguayans, but would be hard pressed to find more than 10 percent in church on Sunday. In a government census, fully 30 percent identified themselves as atheists. Protestant and Jewish communities could point to even less success: 2 percent of the population.

Pastor Carmelo Terranova entered Paso de los Libres in 1958. Two years later, Pastor Francisco Perez found an opening for ministry in Rivera, a border city divided from its Brazilian twin city, Livramento, by a mere street. Perez encountered little opposition or welcome among the people, at first. A daily program broadcasted over local radio gradually opened hearts and doors in Rivera.

Perez did not wait for the people to come to him. He rented a large hall and began an intense campaign of evangelism. Within eight years, the congregation had purchased land, built a chapel seating 200 people, added a parsonage, library and guest room. The property was debt free by 1972.

The pastor and congregation achieved this through a seemingly endless and tireless variety of ways. One missionary described Perez as "the nearest thing to

Pastors stop for mate (tea) *by the harbor of Montevideo, Uruguay.*

perpetual motion I have seen in a long time."[8]

Evangelistic campaigns in a tent or on a plaza, literature distribution and neighborhood visitation, banquets for men only, short-term Bible schools—the pastor seemed to have an inexhaustible source of techniques to keep the church alert and active.

The Uruguay Alliance grew and reached out to other towns, even to Montevideo, the capital city that was home to half the country's 3 million people. The church gained recognition by the government by 1968.

Thirteen years later, it was fully autonomous and self-supporting. In the mid-1980s, the denomination numbered seven churches and over 400 members.

Paraguay Next

Confident by 1966 that the Uruguayan mission was well launched and growing, the Argentine Alliance looked to the spiritual needs of another neighboring nation: Paraguay.

This time, Rev. Myron Voth, of the mission, and Rev. Carmelo Terranova, of the church, made the survey trip. After surveying the cities and talking with other evangelicals already at work in Paraguay, they concluded that Asuncion, the nation's capital and largest city, should be the target.

Asuncion has a population of only a half-million, but the vast majority of the nation's 3.1 million people live within a hundred-mile radius of the capital. Ethnically, culturally and socially, Paraguayans are more like one another than the population of any other South American country.[9] *Mestizos* (people of mixed Spanish and Indian descent) comprise about 95 percent of the population.

The obvious strategy of evangelism by the Argentine Alliance called for establishing a strong central church in the principal city and then spreading out from the center, to start churches in heavily populated areas surrounding Asuncion.

Pastor Terranova and his family rented a house, turning half into a meeting hall and half into a parsonage. Strong biblical teaching and tireless visitation produced a congregation within one year.

His successor gave up the rented building in 1971 and moved into a borrowed house. This sacrificial move meant rent money could be used for purchasing land and constructing the congregation's own building. The people sacrificed, as well: For over six months, they moved from one member's house to another for their services.

In December of 1971, just five years after the Argentine Alliance entered Paraguay, the congregation dedicated its own house of worship in Asuncion. A second church was opened in 1986 by an Argentine missionary-pastor.

Alliance churches in Uruguay and Paraguay represent more than just additions to The Alliance World Fellowship. They demonstrate convincingly that Third World churches need not wait until they are strong and prosperous at home before becoming missionary churches.

Indeed, overseas pastors who have learned how to triumph in faith through suffering and sacrifice have already grasped the essentials necessary to be an effective missionary. ☐

CHURCH AND MISSION

OFFICIAL NAME OF CHURCH:	The Argentine Christian and And Missionary Alliance
ENTRY BY MISSIONARIES:	1897
NUMBER OF MISSIONARIES:	27
ORGANIZED CHURCHES:	41
UNORGANIZED CHURCHES AND PREACHING POINTS:	27
BAPTIZED CHURCH MEMBERS:	4,135
INCLUSIVE MEMBERSHIP:	11,780
MEDICAL WORK:	0
EDUCATION:	Buenos Aires Bible Institute 2 TEE Centers
RADIO BROADCASTS:	5
PAGES PRINTED:	37,000

COUNTRY

OFFICIAL NAME:	Argentine Republic
FORM OF GOVERNMENT:	Republic
OFFICIAL LANGUAGE(S):	Spanish
AREA:	1,065,189 sq. mi.
POPULATION:	32,617,000
CAPITAL:	Buenos Aires
PER CAPITA INCOME:	$2,331.00
LITERACY:	93%
RELIGIOUS AFFILIATION:	Roman Catholic 86.5% Protestant 5.5%

BRAZIL

Spiritism: The Majority Choice

A MAJOR business deal is pending, so the Sao Paulo banker flies with six associates to the Amazon River; they drop six bowls of yellow manioc flour into the muddy waters. . . .

Trying to beat the competition, a Rio de Janeiro entrepreneur and his wife bury themselves in the sand, with only a handkerchief over their faces to prevent suffocation. . . .

In a hillside slum area of Salvador, a man walks away from bodies of dead chickens littering the floor; the head of a freshly killed goat dangles from his clenched teeth.

All these Brazilians are practicing, in one form or another, rituals of cults collectively known as *macumba*. Adapted from African religions ranging from voodoo and spiritism to sorcery, these cults claim more than 30 million people—one-quarter the total population—and are growing fast.

Sao Paulo, the country's business and industrial capital, had 90,000 *macumba* centers by the mid-1980s; Rio de Janeiro, the nation's cultural hub, counted 60,000 such congregations. Salvador supported 365 churches and nearly four times as many spiritist groups.[1]

Macumba involves much more than attending seances to catch a glimpse of the future. It is a way of life based on the belief that a person can contact the spirits and influence them to act in his behalf. *Macumba* has permeated the nation at all levels of society, from banker to slum dweller.

The cults originated with African slaves brought to Brazil by Portuguese landowners to work their plantations. The slaves appeared to embrace Catholicism in order to preserve their ancestral beliefs. The priests thought they were praying to the saints of the church, but they were, in fact, appealing to the more familiar spirits of their African heritage.[2]

The mixture of beliefs still prevails. Ninety percent of the population claims to be Roman Catholic, making Brazil the world's largest Catholic country. Yet only 9 percent actually practice their beliefs, while church officials suspect that fully one-half of their people follow spiritism to one degree or another.

Protestants, about 10 million in number, seem to have fewer problems with their people mixing spiritism with biblical spirituality. Protestant doctrine has no place for saints acting as mediators between God and man, nor does it have the flexibility that permitted slaves to adopt Catholicism without relinquishing their ancestral practices.

Macumba operates on various levels. The Afro-Brazilian cults, as practiced by the masses, involve one main deity and many secondary deities. Through fetishes and offerings, these lesser gods or spirits are manipulated to better the fortunes of the supplicant.

Kardecism, perhaps the highest form of spiritism, deals more on a metaphysical level, which attracts doctors, lawyers and other intellectuals. It was formulated by Allan Kardec, a professor of science and mathematics who considered himself the reincarnation of a Druid poet.[3]

This higher level of spiritism incorporates the idea of reincarnation and emphasizes doing good deeds to make up for the evil done in previous existences. Acts of charity, counseling and healing relate spiritism to everyday life in a manner that wins praise and gratitude from society.

Thus spiritism has gained respectability and goodwill among the Brazilians to a degree seen nowhere else in Latin America, though it is spreading to other areas.

Initial Probes

Macumba was perhaps already a struggling underground form of religion practiced by slaves on Portuguese plantations when French Huguenots tried to establish a Protestant outpost on an island off the Brazilian coast in 1555. The venture was quickly repulsed by ultra-Catholic Portugal.

The huge colony, making up more than half the continent of South America, remained off-limits to Protestant missions for over three hundred years.

American Methodists tried unsuccessfully in 1835, then returned to stay in 1887. By that time, Presbyterians had been at work almost thirty years—and the first formally organized spiritist society was already fifteen years old.

The Alliance saw its early efforts fail in the 1890s and 1920s. The first permanent Alliance mission venture in Brazil originated not in North America, but in a daughter church: the Japanese Alliance.[4]

The Brazilian government had made a bold bid to open up the interior by building Brasilia, a gleaming new national capital a thousand miles inland. The government's offer of land to immigrant settlers attracted many Japanese. Concerned for their spiritual welfare, the Alliance church in Japan decided to follow their countrymen with the Gospel.

A diminutive but plucky young woman, Miss Mutsuko Ninomiya, arrived in 1959 to work among the Japanese in Gama, a satellite city of Brasilia. Her ministry made slow headway at first.

The addition of a young couple five years later helped, but it was almost ten years before a church began to flourish among the Japanese immigrants. The Japanese Alliance mission added a Portuguese-language ministry in 1982.

The North American Alliance opened its work in Goiania, a city south of the futuristic capital. Samuel and Vera Barnes, forty-year veterans in Argentina, had for years looked longingly into Brazil from across the border. They finally had their chance in 1962.

Progress of the work—or lack of it—in Goiania seemed to set the pattern for Alliance missions in Brazil for years to come.

Despite house-to-house visitation, evangelistic services, and even radio broadcasts six times weekly, the city's

(Right) The Porto Alegre Alliance Church uses various methods of evangelism, (facing page) including a Muppet's version of Noah's Ark that has drawn parents as well as children.

middle class seemed spiritually impenetrable to all efforts. After six years of hard work and minimal results, the Alliance effort ended.

Missionaries in Brasilia and Taguatinga met with a similar lack of success, perhaps because their target group was also the middle class. In Brazil as elsewhere, the more people succeed financially, the less they often have to do with God.

Eventual Encouragement

Curitiba in the south provided welcome encouragement for the hardworking but sorely pressed missionaries, who must have been wondering what was wrong with them—or even with their message.

A 100-day evangelistic tent campaign during 1968 in Curitiba attracted scores of people to faith in Christ. The tent turned into a chapel as a group of new believers took on the character of a congregation. Within a year, the church moved to a building and began looking for a permanent location.

After careful searching, the strategic suburb of Capao da Imbuia seemed the most likely area. A prefabricated twenty-one-foot A-frame tabernacle popped up

almost overnight on one of the choice corner lots.

Extensive advertising, fervent prayer and other preparations focused on the opening services in October of 1969. During the first week alone, over 3,000 people attended the services, and crowds extended well into the streets on the weekend.

A permanent building replaced the portable chapel within two years, and an Alliance church was born. Increased attendance and financial stability enabled the church to support its own Brazilian pastor by 1973, just four years after locating in Curitiba.

Like the Israelite tabernacle in the wilderness, the portable chapel was on the

move again in 1971. It came to rest in Colombo, on the outskirts of Curitiba. Evangelistic services soon produced a nucleus of believers. Attendance averaged sixty by the end of the year, and in 1973, with nineteen charter members, the Colombo congregation organized.

The following year, still another group formed in the downtown area of Curitiba. Missionaries started a small Bible institute program to train Brazilian pastors for the growing work in the city and elsewhere.

Review and Reorganization

Rewarding though these and some other ventures proved, overall results did not give evidence of great openness throughout the nation. After two decades

(Far *left*) Sao Paulo could be the world's second largest city by A.D. 2000; (left) Brazilia's modern congressional building represents Brazil's determination to join the world's foremost nations.

of diligent and sacrificial ministry, the Brazil Alliance could count no more than thirteen churches and 317 members.

The frustration felt by mission and church workers alike did nothing to promote harmony in ministry. The work appeared stalemated.

A study team of Latin and North American Alliance leaders experienced in church growth spent two weeks touring Brazil in late 1983. They visited areas of activity and interviewed each missionary and local pastor. They also spoke with other evangelical groups working in the same localities.

Pooling their observations and interviews, the five-man team concluded that basically the work suffered from an overall lack of leadership and planning.[5]

Their recommendations, later approved, involved reorganizing mission structure and concentrating resources on strategic growth. Study seminars and spiritual retreats conducted jointly by mission and church dealt with harmony of goals and relationships among workers.

The study team noted that the fastest growing denominations in Brazil mounted a major effort to establish a large and strong central church in a city. Then, operating as a growth center, the congregation trained new workers and branched out to open satellite churches.[6]

The Brazil Alliance applied this principle in its redirected efforts. Work would be maintained in existing church areas, but mission and church committed themselves to establishing strong mother churches in the two key cities of Porto Alegre and Sao Paulo. A 1984 Church-Mission Working Agreement between church and mission ratified these plans.

Porto Alegre, a state capital with 1.5 million people, had already been entered by Alliance missionaries before the study commission met. In 1981, two missionary couples had targeted the Santa Fe district of the city for multimethod evangelism.

Their methods included mass distribution of Scripture, door-to-door visitation and open-air meetings. Street evangelism enjoyed the help of an unusual ally: "Noah's Ark." This mobile puppet theater proved extremely effective not only in attracting children, but in breaking down adult prejudice as well.[7]

Over a period of months, scores of conversions and hundreds of inquiries resulted from the multiple approach. During one special celebration, over 800 people milled around the puppet theater to hear the Gospel from the Noah's Ark version of the Muppets.

The Parque dos Maias congregation outgrew its sixty-person capacity in 1984. That same year, the Dona Leopoldinha congregation was started through evangelistic services on rented property only 200 feet from the site of their proposed sanctuary.

Church growth depends a great deal on momentum, and the Porto Alegre churches had it.

Alliance growth in Sao Paulo had to be measured in terms of future potential rather than present reality: it was rich in projections.

Demographers estimate that by the year 2000, Sao Paulo could be the second largest city in the world. With a 12-million population in 1985, it already ranked as Brazil's largest city.[8]

Over three hundred Protestant missionaries worked in the city during the mid-eighties, but spiritist centers numbered in the thousands. Millions more of Sao Paulo's dwellers totally ignored religion by any name.

The spiritist centers in Sao Paulo and elsewhere throughout Brazil pointed the 1983 study commission toward another suggestion in its final report.

Noting that missionaries and church leaders should be more aware of the full dimension of spiritual warfare that confronted them, the commission recommended seminars on how to combat spiritism and neutralize satanic opposition.

Attention to that problem would provide one of the best long-term means of achieving significant Alliance church growth in Brazil. ☐

CHURCH AND MISSION

OFFICIAL NAME OF CHURCH:	The Brazilian Christian and Missionary Alliance
ENTRY BY MISSIONARIES:	1962
NUMBER OF MISSIONARIES:	32
ORGANIZED CHURCHES:	9
UNORGANIZED CHURCHES AND PREACHING POINTS:	11
BAPTIZED CHURCH MEMBERS:	540
INCLUSIVE MEMBERSHIP:	1,539
MEDICAL WORK:	0
EDUCATION:	Cutitiba Bible Institute 1 TEE Center
RADIO BROADCASTS:	0
PAGES PRINTED:	650,000

COUNTRY

OFFICIAL NAME:	Federative Republic of Brazil
FORM OF GOVERNMENT:	Federative Republic
OFFICIAL LANGUAGE(S):	Portuguese
AREA:	3,286,470
POPULATION:	153,992,000
CAPITAL:	Brasilia
PER CAPITA INCOME:	$1,523.00
LITERACY:	76%
RELIGIOUS AFFILIATION:	Roman Catholic 73%, Protestant 17.4%

CHILE

Supernatural Among the Surprises

APPEARANCES can deceive, especially in Chile.

When the Spanish explorer and colonizer Pedro de Valdivia came upon a valley crowded with luxuriant greens watered by a serene river, he exclaimed: "The Valley of Paradise!"

He probably had second thoughts when, according to tradition, fierce Araucanian warriors seized and executed him by forcing molten gold down his throat.[1]

Afflicted with what one writer calls "a crazy geography," Chile looks like a wrinkled string bean 2,600 miles long and only an average 110 miles wide. Misled by its odd appearance, the casual observer could miss features of the land fully as remarkable as its shape.

Rain has not fallen in the northern desert regions for over two centuries, while in the south, rainfall averages 110 inches annually and seems never to stop.

The jagged, snowcapped Andes on the eastern border turn all of Chile into a lopsided valley whose western limits rise only as high as the waves that wash the full length of its coastline.

The religious landscape holds surprises as intriguing as the geography.

An Alliance missionary, for example, pastors a church that is not only the oldest Protestant church on South America's Pacific coast, but one that predates the Alliance by more than three decades.

The Chilean Alliance maintains three churches in the southernmost city of the whole world.

Perhaps most unusual, Alliance missionaries operated in the country for more than fifty years before the Chile Alliance Mission was formally organized.

Churches Oldest and Remotest

The Alliance concentrated on the southern region when it began supporting some independent missionaries in 1897. Later the radius of ministry expanded until it reached into all of Chile, from the northernmost to the southernmost cities. Many churches have a distinct character molded by their beginnings and surroundings.

Union Church, in Vina del Mar, has a longer history than any other Protestant church in the country, and it still makes news.

The church began in 1847. Rev. David Trumbull, a Presbyterian pastor, had al-ready been at work for two years among the many British and American sailors in the port city of Valparaiso. He founded the church as a witness to the sailors and other English-speaking people in the Valparaiso-Vina del Mar area.

Trumbull was also burdened for the Chileans. The Roman Catholic Church, however, hampered his efforts so effectively that it took him twenty years to break through to the Chilean people. His persistence paid off, and in time he was credited as the father of evangelical missions in Chile.[2]

By 1981, Trumbull was long gone. So, apparently, was interest in Union Church by its sponsoring denomination. On the verge of being abandoned, the church requested the Alliance to supply a missionary to pastor the congregation, still primarily drawn from the English-speaking, economically upper-class community of the resort area.

Within two years, the church started an unheard-of activity: a midweek Bible study. Something even more amazing happened in the highly traditional congregation: Eleven people made a public commitment to Christ during a series of meetings. Another innovation took the form of a Union Church Spanish congregation in 1985.

Punta Arenas qualifies as fulfillment of the biblical command to take the Gospel to the ends of earth. Although smaller towns and settlements can be found closer to Antarctica, Punta Arenas is the world's southernmost city.

With 100,000 inhabitants situated on the Straits of Magellan, the city responded to the Gospel with a warmth quite unlike its constantly windswept, chilly and damp terrain.

An Alliance missionary couple and several Chilean C&MA families moved to the city and started a church in 1959. Within three years, the congregation had grown enough to organize, and by 1963 had matured enough to call a pastor. It was the first of three churches that in the 1980s were bringing gospel joy and love to a remarkable city in harsh surroundings.

Contested Beginnings

Alliance pioneers Rev. and Mrs. Henry Weiss obviously chose Valdivia for their first evangelistic effort because of its stra-

tegic value, not its openness to the Gospel in the late 1890s. Deeply entrenched Roman Catholicism had taken up residence on the first day of the city's 400-year history.

Local priests sent agitators to break up the Protestant meetings and then instigated street fights when people fled the building. Citizens of Valdivia who became believers hesitated to go public with their testimony for a year. Freedom of religion guaranteed by the constitution had little meaning in the city's ancient streets.

Missionaries and Valdivians persisted, however, and together they scored a series of firsts: in 1901, the first annual conference; in 1902, the first Alliance church built on the west coast of Latin America; that same year, installation of the first Alliance Chilean pastor.[3]

The believers did not stop there. For many years, the Valdivia Alliance Church was the largest in Chile. Not even the 1960 earthquake that leveled their building could deter them. They constructed a large frame sanctuary in a more strategic location of the city.

Temuco was for many years the center of operations for the Alliance in Chile.

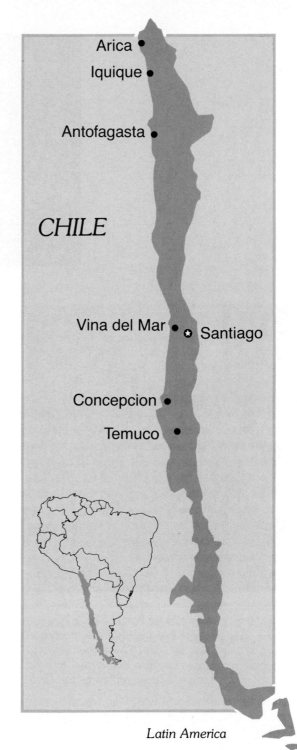

Latin America

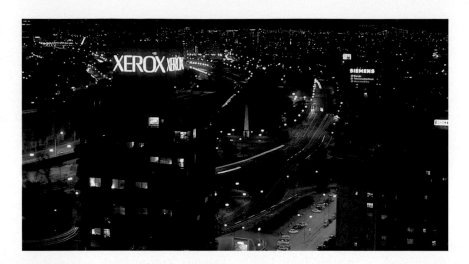

(Top) *The First Alliance Church and Metro Bible Institute are located in this section of Santiago;* (above) *family residences climb a Valparaiso hillside;* (right) *many Chileans still farm the land.*

The field chairman's office, press and publications operations, and the Temuco Theological Institute all called Temuco home. (The mission administrative office moved to Santiago, the capital city, in 1981.)

Eleven congregations carried an evangelical witness throughout Temuco and its environs during the 1980s. Having had Bible-school students in the city for over sixty years did help, but the churches possessed a dynamic of their own.

Fire destroyed the Second Alliance Church's 800-seat sanctuary in 1986. The congregation had remodeled and enlarged their church just seven years before, but they determined to rebuild within a year—only this time, the church was designed to seat 1,200 people.

Church/mission cooperation in Temuco produced an historic first in religious communications: The nation's first Christian radio station.

Through something of a miracle, Radio Esperanza (Hope) received government permission to broadcast only seven months after application. Commercial stations usually wait for two years to be licensed. Beginning in September of 1985, Christian music and messages on a clear FM signal flooded the city streets and delighted many listeners, whether they attended church or not.

Capital Campaign

An evangelistic-minded church must go where people are. This meant that the Alliance was drawn eventually and inevitably to Santiago, the nation's capital, with its 5.1 million residents.

Already realizing the importance of Santiago in 1910, Dr. Simpson had suggested that missionaries should begin work in the capital. After an initial unsuccessful effort, the mission withdrew until 1939, when a missionary couple lived for a brief period in the city.

Lay people organized the first Alliance church two years later, with twenty-eight members. It grew slowly in size and witness, but could not begin to cope with the massive spiritual needs of a city that sheltered one-third of Chile's entire population.

The second Alliance church began in a remarkable fashion. For many years a domestic servant who loved the Lord had put aside money from her meager income. She converted her savings into gold coins that ultimately totaled twenty.

Like the woman whom the Lord commended for putting all she had in the offering, in 1965, this housemaid gave her twenty gold coins to help purchase land in a growing middle-class section of the city.

The pace of Alliance penetration in Santiago quickened, until by the 1980s twelve churches spread throughout the city. Long-range strategy called for at least one church in each of the capital's sixteen municipalities.

A decisive turning point in evangelism followed the visit of six pastors and the mission chairman to Lima, Peru, in 1980. They attended church-growth seminars and saw what an all-out evangelism effort could accomplish. Other pastors attended a workshop on church growth conducted by Dr. Vergil Gerber in Chile that same year.

Dr. Alfredo Smith, pastor of the main Lima church and a key participant in that city's *Encuentro con Dios* ("Encounter With God") campaign, put spark to the tinder. He spent a week with the Villa Frei church in Santiago, explaining the Encounter plan and inspiring the church to get moving.

Two nine-day pilot campaigns proved so effective that the church committed itself to an evangelistic effort with a goal of 500 members within two years. Churches in Santiago and other cities initiated their own Encounter campaigns. They set a goal of doubling in membership by 1987.

The Santiago churches discovered different ways of doing evangelism. Pastors united in a sustained radio program, "Power From on High," five nights weekly. Alliance Men joined local churches in conducting tent campaigns that drew over 8,500 people to the services. Others literally took the Gospel to the streets with sidewalk evangelism. Pastors attended Evangelism Explosion courses and led their people in house visitation.

By 1983, almost all the Santiago churches reported capacity attendance and the need to open new preaching centers. Three churches joined efforts in their campaign during 1985 and talked of merging to form a strong central church capable of ministering to a thousand people. Urgent requests for assistance in building programs related to Encounter-type campaigns in Chile and elsewhere in Latin America totaled 1.5 million dollars.

The regional director commented, "Our blessings are coming back to hit us like boomerangs."

Missing: Converts

Growth, however, did have its problems. Increase in church membership at

Tent campaigns prove very successful.

The C&MA sponsors a primary school in Antofagasta.

times resembled a trickle, when it should have been a flood.

One 1986 report summarized the problems in a word: retention.

"In the last four years there have been 15,473 registered decisions and 3,721 baptisms," the report noted, "but an increase in baptized membership of only 1,953. Only 24 percent of those making decisions were baptized and only half of those baptized remain in the church."[4]

Churches involved in the Encounter program alternated evangelistic series with weeks of evening Bible classes for new converts. A theological institute was organized in Santiago to help church workers become more effective in ministry. These and other measures helped resolve the problem, but the question of retention remains a troubling one.

Elsewhere in Chile, the Alliance pursued an evangelistic ministry by various means. For several years, a motor launch linked churches on the offshore Islands of Chiloe with the mainland. An evangelistic film program drew a total audience of over 20,000 and was even successful in taking the Gospel message into public schools.

An orphanage for girls at La Pintana and another for boys at Linares nurtured neglected children in an environment of Christian love.

Only one of several, the church in the northern desert city of Antofagasta sponsored a Christian grade school that in the mid-1980s registered over four hundred children.

Support Systems

The Alliance church and mission in Chile cooperate in numerous ways, not only to disciple new believers, but to help older Christians and church workers better serve the Lord.

Bible correspondence courses start on the most popular level; these studies enrolled over two thousand students in 1986. Theological Education by Extension (TEE) added skills to 306 church workers in twenty-three locations during the same year.

The *Imprenta Alianza*, or Alliance Publishing House, in Temuco publishes material for the Alliance in Chile, and has served churches throughout Latin America, as well. Through the years, it has produced over fifty book titles, more than 50,000 Alliance hymnals and several magazines including *Salud y Vida* (*Salvation and Life*), a monthly magazine with sixty years of continuous publication.

Contested Beachhead

The publishing house and mission are closely intertwined because they both were begun about the same time by the same man.

Henry Weiss and his wife felt called of God to be missionaries in a Roman Catholic country. They applied for ministry with the Alliance, but the fledgling move-

Printing press at the Alliance publishing house, Temuco

Alliance literature used throughout Latin America.

(Left) *The Bible institute in Temuco,* (below) *where students do library research.*

ment in the 1890s had no such opening.

Undaunted, the Weiss couple and Albert E. Dawson, a Canadian Methodist, teamed up to enter Chile in 1897 as independent missionaries. A delegation from the large German colony in Chile visited Henry Weiss almost immediately and urged him to work among them.

Born and raised in a German-speaking Mennonite family, Weiss had no difficulty in effectively ministering among the colonists. Converts were numerous, and churches quickly formed.

Dr. Simpson recognized the value of Weiss's work and saw to it that all three were duly appointed Alliance missionaries with full support in 1898.

Meanwhile, Weiss continued his study of Spanish and, accompanied by a translator, preached the Gospel from town to

town. He felt led of the Lord to take a stand in Valdivia. He, his wife and Dawson settled there in 1899 and organized the first Alliance church on the west coast of Latin America, despite heavy opposition. The rest is history.

Weiss, a printer by training, began a publications program almost immediately. He financed from his own pocket the purchase of equipment and material. The first book off the press, a hymnal with 100 selections, sold out the first edition of 800 copies. He then added a magazine and a variety of tracts.

The resident priest in Valdivia provided competition by setting up his own press and vilifying Protestants with contemptuous names like "black hands" and "poisonous Protestants" in articles of his own magazine.[5]

The ensuing battle of ink on paper probably furnished a grateful community with evening table talk in an era without radio or television. Catholic denunciations certainly whetted the interest of many people to read the Protestant publications, and helped the Alliance Press become an established institution.

Firming the Foundation

Legal restrictions concerning foreign religious groups forced missionaries and Chileans to work together within the church from the start. "Missionaries were pastors and pastors were missionaries," one writer noted. Intermingling their efforts, they started churches throughout the southern region of Chile.

This integration did not keep the church from receiving legal recognition by the government in 1920 or from becoming an autonomous church, free of mission control, in 1927. However, pastors and missionaries continued working side by side. Not until 1956 did the mission have its own organization, and in 1986 it received legal recognition as an entity separate from the church.

One of the areas of closest cooperation between church and mission is pastoral training.

The first formal effort to prepare workers for the ministry began in 1910, with the Bible Convention program. Two week-long teaching and training conventions were held annually for the next twenty years.

Recognizing the need for more instruction, the annual field conference tried a "roving institute" in 1921. Carrying a collapsible desk and a box of books, the missionary instructor conducted classes in one area five days a week for ten weeks and then moved to another location and repeated the curriculum.

The inadequacy of this system quickly became apparent. Within two years, the roving institute settled with a sigh of relief in a permanent location in Temuco. There it developed and grew into a fullscale, four-year theological institute with both day and evening classes. Another institute began holding evening classes in Santiago in 1984.

Both institutes offer extensive training and teaching for the church's future leaders.

Innovations and adaptations in the early days made Chile a mission field of surprises and unusual features. Willingness to continue customizing ministry to the nature of need will keep the church growing in true Chilean character. □

CHURCH AND MISSION

OFFICIAL NAME OF CHURCH:	The Christian and Missionary Alliance of Chile
ENTRY BY MISSIONARIES:	1897
NUMBER OF MISSIONARIES:	27
ORGANIZED CHURCHES:	101
UNORGANIZED CHURCHES AND PREACHING POINTS:	18
BAPTIZED CHURCH MEMBERS:	10,903
INCLUSIVE MEMBERSHIP:	31,074
EDUCATION:	Theological Institute of Temuco Metropolitan Theological Institute (Santiago) 39 TEE Centers
RADIO BROADCASTS:	5
PAGES PRINTED:	3,352,042

COUNTRY

OFFICIAL NAME:	Republic of Chile
FORM OF GOVERNMENT:	Republic
OFFICIAL LANGUAGE(S):	Spanish
AREA:	292,257 sq. mi.
POPULATION:	12,866,000
CAPITAL:	Santiago
PER CAPITA INCOME:	$1,950.00
LITERACY	91%
RELIGIOUS AFFILIATION:	Roman Catholic 63.8%, Protestant 22.5%

COLOMBIA

Evil Worked for Good

ALLIANCE MISSIONARIES first entered southern Colombia in 1923, while temporarily leaving Ecuador in the face of persecution. Had they known what awaited them across the border, they might have preferred to stay where they were, because they were jumping from the frying pan into the fire.

Colombia responded to the Gospel with opposition unparalleled elsewhere in Latin America. During a certain period of Colombian history, that opposition turned violent as a part of state policy.

The missionaries should not have been surprised by their less-than-cordial reception. James Thompson, the remarkable educator and representative of the British and Foreign Bible Society, had encountered hostility back in 1825, when he tried to promote reading and distribution of the Bible.

American Presbyterians launched the first missionary effort in 1856 and for twenty years could barely hold their own against the combined opposition of church and state. The arrival of other missions was equally contested.

In all of Colombia, the most adamant resistance to the Gospel centered in the southern region entered by the Alliance. Southern Colombia was less economically developed than other areas. Poor road conditions also put much of the region beyond direct control of the central government. Southern Colombia was populated by small towns and villages, where everybody knew everyone else's business and the village priest ruled over all.

Alliance missionaries who crossed the border from Ecuador and settled in Ipiales immediately began to witness among the Colombians. Just as quickly, they met with resistance from the local parish priest. Opposition erupted into the open in 1926, when an organized mob of about 5,000 people attacked the mission residence with stones and heavy poles, breaking windows and doors.

The mayor and local police urged the missionaries to cross back into Ecuador for about two weeks. Then they returned to Ipiales, where for another month the military protected them until passions among the local people cooled to flinging curses instead of stones.[1]

The same pattern of organized violence followed efforts to establish churches elsewhere. Popayan, Silvia, La Plata, Campohermoso—these and other cities and towns flared with conflict as religious authorities challenged every step of advance by the Alliance.

Why would these foreigners and their Colombian colleagues deliberately move into areas where they were sure to encounter hostility, hatred and even violence in the very name of the Christ they preached?

Why would they persist in exposing themselves to rejection, resistance and perhaps death when, humanly speaking, there was nothing in it for them?

The answer must lie in matters of the spirit. Missionaries and Colombians were possessed of a love stronger than the hatred of their opponents. They were convinced of a message greater than the harangues of mob-organizing clerics.

In retrospect, it seems as if those difficult early years were but a conditioning process for the church and its leaders. The example set and the message imparted to the growing number of Colombian believers helped prepare them for an even more harsh era of testing.

The Violent Years

La Violencia, they called it. From 1946 to 1962, the nation was torn by undeclared civil war. Conservative and liberal party members battled each other for political supremacy, even if it meant crippling their nation.

The exact toll in human lives cannot be determined, but estimates run between 200,000 and 400,000 deaths. Much of the violence occurred in the hinterland, where information was buried with the dead and investigators found the living just as unhelpful.[2]

Fanatical elements within the Roman Catholic Church turned the civil upheaval into a weapon against the Protestants.

Dr. Karl-Wilhelm Westmeier, a student of Colombian church history recorded 3,456 documented acts of nonviolent persecution.[3] This included Protestants being turned away at the hospital and the municipal cemetery, denied police protection, boycotted in business and kicked out of their hometowns.

Furthermore, Protestants were harassed in over 1,460 incidents, such as disruption of meetings, fines for conducting school for their children, Catholic

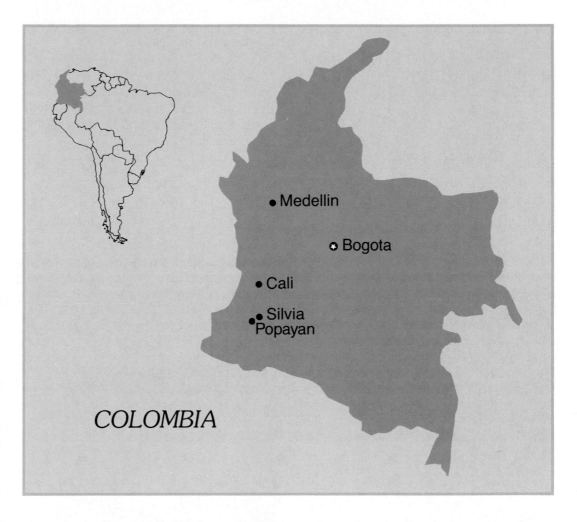

COLOMBIA

shrines built near Protestant homes and churches, and forced compliance with Catholic rites.

Records document over 2,400 violent acts against Protestants. They were jailed, tortured, beaten and murdered. Their homes, churches and schools were destroyed.

The Alliance suffered some of the severest losses in *La Violencia*. The toll reads like a bulletin from the War Depart-

ment: New station at Samaniego dynamited and missionaries withdrawn from the area . . . Puerto Leguizamo mission station burned down and missionaries withdrawn from the area . . . Alfred Lopez, first ordained Colombian pastor and former church president, shot in the street by fanatical Catholic policemen . . . Two Paez Indians martyred, the house they were in, their funeral pyre.

Why were Protestants so severely

mauled in a struggle that was basically political?

Dr. Westmeier, aided by years of ministry in Colombia, lists several reasons why Protestantism was caught in the cross fire. These same reasons also explain, to a greater or lesser extent, why Protestants in other Roman Catholic-dominated countries have a difficult time exercising their faith.[4]

1. Colombia's laws "portray an almost complete integration of politics and religion." Therefore, people who promoted a non-Catholic religion were actually in conflict with the state.

2. Catholic teaching constituted the conscience of Colombian society. The contrary teaching of Protestantism was therefore seen as an attack on the nation's basic value system and a destabilizing influence on society.

3. Dating back to colonial times and beyond, violence was used as a tool of power in Colombia. It was historically exercised to achieve dominance over the opposition. Over the course of centuries, this mentality reached down to society's grass roots; violence against Protestants became a legitimate means of overcoming a foreign religion that was trying to subvert Colombians from their national heritage.

In the short term, it appeared that Roman Catholic authorities successfully manipulated *La Violencia* to strike a staggering blow to Protestantism. But in reality, the fanatical faction overplayed its hand and has had to live with the consequences of their miscalculation.[5]

A combined missionary and national team visit coastal towns.

For one thing, violence in the towns and villages sent Christians streaming to larger cities and centers for protection. This helped urban churches grow in size and strength, thus preparing them for an outreach and response that only strong churches could accomplish.

La Violencia backfired in another way: It disgusted many decent Colombians. When they saw priests inciting mobs to burn and kill, their disenchantment with the church deepened.

Furthermore, tirades against Protestantism stirred people's interest in learning what the so-called heretics really believed. Free advertising for Protestants was not what the hierarchy had in mind, but it happened.

Perhaps most damaging, the violent political struggle between conservatives and liberals disrupted many of the Catholic-dominated society's checks and balances.

One historian noted, "The national anguish uprooted thousands of people, cut traditional family ties, and effected serious changes in the social classes, public and private institutions, political affairs, and the customs and cultures of the Colombians."[6]

Shaken free of cultural and religious restraints, many people were open to new ideas and beliefs. That helps explain why the total number of Protestant communicants for 1967 was over 70,000— seven times the total for 1950.

Initiative Regained

At first, the Alliance did not experience the accelerated growth of other evangelical groups. Its 1945 level of membership on the eve of the violence was not regained until 1959.

This slowness in recovery resulted in

A joyful welcome awaits the team.

part from continued attacks on the church after hostilities had died down in other areas. Again, remoteness of small towns in the south, and control of Catholicism over less-developed areas, worked against Alliance congregations.

As late as 1983, of the 101 organized C&MA churches, seventy-eight were in rural or small-town areas. Of the 106 unorganized groups, all but two were in remote settings, where the conciliatory spirit of Vatican II did not always prevail.

In the 1960s, for example, Roman Catholics resisted efforts of Colombian believers who tried to start an Alliance church in Medellin. The local priest visited all the families they had contacted and pressured them to stay away from the Protestant services.[7]

Another reason for slow church growth became apparent in the years following *La Violencia*. Almost the entire mission staff was committed to support ministries. Working with existing churches and heavily involved in education, they were unable to fulfill a basic role as pacesetters in evangelism and church planting.

The field chairman in his 1979 report noted that over the previous seven years, missionaries had started only two churches.

Concerned with rapid growth of the cities and depopulation of the rural areas, mission and church leaders became more urban conscious in their planning. Amazing results in Lima's Encounter with God campaigns spurred them to try the same in Colombia.

(Below) *Ricardo Diaz sold his insurance business to serve the Lord full time in Bogota's Encounter program, including Bible study classes (right).*

The year 1981 stands out as a turning point for Alliance missions in Colombia, but it did not begin well. Disheartening events followed hard on the heels of one another.

Local newspapers linked the mass suicide of Jim Jones's followers in Jonestown, Guyana, to Protestants in their country. A Wycliffe Bible translator was kidnapped and killed by guerrillas trying to force the group out of the country. Three key Alliance Paez Indian laymen were killed by guerrillas for refusing to cooperate with their movement.

That same year, mission headquarters moved from Cali to Bogota. The field chairman called it a "giant" move, and in fact it was. The transfer was the mission's declaration to all concerned: We must get on with the business of evangelizing cities and opening churches.

The nature of mission activities changed dramatically by 1982, from 95 percent of personnel in support roles to 60 percent in frontline duty. Missionary personnel in Bogota jumped from zero in 1981 to thirteen in 1982.[8]

The national church was in full accord with the new initiative. While the missionaries concentrated primarily on Bogota with help from the church, the Colombian Alliance mounted a similar campaign in Cali, with help from the mission.

Bogota's Encounter

Bogota, the hub of government, is also home to 6 million people—one in every three Colombians. While becoming a modern city for the sake of progress, the capital preserves whole sections of its historic past. Villas, shops, and even the pace of life, reflect an era of Spanish occupation embellished by the human trait to idealize the past.

The capital's religious life contains a similar dichotomy between the functional present and the bygone days when Catholicism commanded a widespread following.

Approximately 95 percent of all Colombians claim to be Roman Catholics. Perhaps only 10 percent nationwide, and even fewer in the cities, actually follow the prescribed rites and rules.

Most middle- and upper-class residents of Bogota consider religion a minor part of their lives. That explains in part why in

(Left) *A father and child participate in an Encounter meeting led by Mrs. Gloria Diaz* (below), *who resigned as bank manager to minister with her husband Ricardo.*

1979 the more affluent northern section had far fewer churches than the less prosperous but more populous southern part.

A study team surveyed one section of northern Bogota that was noticeable for its lack of evangelical witness. The team also interviewed some key people in the area. Then, in 1981, two missionary couples launched the first Alliance church-planting effort specifically among middle- and upper-class Colombians.

Meanwhile, evangelistic campaigns began in cooperation with the four other Alliance churches of south Bogota. One campaign resulted in 410 decisions and spurred the churches to find more ways to unite and intensify their efforts.

Bogota al Encuentro con Cristo was underway.

Home Bible studies were tried during 1981 in the northern section, but did not accomplish much. Missionaries started over again, using a varied program that included books, films, counseling, Ping-Pong and weekend services. In 1983, the mission chairman reported that the group had grown from zero to 140 in just sixteen months.

In addition, the new congregation had elected its own board, become the highest-giving Alliance church in Colombia and was looking for a lot to build a 1,000-seat sanctuary. Appropriately, the new congregation named itself *Iglesia El Encuentro*, The Encounter Church.

By 1986, The Encounter Church was building its own facilities on an important thoroughfare. The first unit, a 550-seat

auditorium, was already completed and being used by an average of 500 worshipers in two Sunday-morning services. All the other churches in Bogota were crowded, as well, some having to conduct two services on Sunday to accommodate everyone.

Cali's Encounter

Evangelistic efforts sponsored by the churches in Cali proved equally rewarding.

The outreach campaign had begun in 1979. Perhaps its biggest achievement was an awakened spirit of enthusiasm among Cali Alliance churches for what could be accomplished. Such an attitude could not long be denied.

Five back-to-back campaigns by two

churches brought encouraging results in 1980. The central church, San Bosco, had targeted an attendance of 250 for the year, but the goal was reached early in 1980 and had to be revised upward to 300, which was also reached.

Several Cali pastors attended a church-growth seminar in Lima the following year and returned home determined to unite their churches for an Encounter campaign that would blanket the city of 1.2 million people. Three congregations merged in 1983, forming one church with greater impact than the smaller, scattered ones. Sixty cell groups throughout the city not only trained believers to witness, but attracted a number of individuals seeking the Lord.

The work continued to expand in 1985. Street meetings, where over one thousand people publicly declared their faith in Christ, were especially effective. Chartered bus loads of enthusiastic young people helped make it happen. San Bosco Church attendance topped the 700 mark.

Decentralized for Growth

Evangelism gains in Bogota and Cali could be preserved and used as springboards for more growth only if trained, capable leaders showed the way. This necessitated an evening training school in the two cities, to prepare workers for urban ministries.

(Clockwise *beginning bottom left*) *Student in outdoor evangelism; the institute library; student witnessing; letters from* Alianza en Marcha *radio program listeners.*

tions. Property taxes in Armenia had doubled, utility bills had tripled, and other expenses made tuition costs prohibitive for students. Soaring costs contrasted sharply with dwindling enrollment. The school decided to decentralize and transfer students to seminary night classes in either Bogota or Cali.

The decision, painful as it was unavoidable, did not cripple the seminary-level preparation of Alliance workers. By adapting to changes and adjusting to needs, the seminary program saw enrollment climb to 150 by 1985.

Neither did the quality of education suffer. Courses were now integrated with highly successful Encounter evangelism and church-planting programs. This enabled the seminarians to apply what they studied in class immediately in local congregations.

And happily, the school in Armenia did not close. It continued with a short-term educational program and extension courses more closely suited to the needs of rural Alliance churches in southern Colombia.

Alianza en Marcha

Political and social factors may mean that evangelism and church planting will always be contested in Colombia. Yet the Gospel has managed to breach every wall of opposition, sometimes by unexpected means.

That happened in Sonson. Although only a small city, its three Roman Catholic seminaries made Sonson a key center for preparing priests and defending the church. Every attempt by evangelicals to establish a witness in the city was repelled for many years—often violently.

Radio waves, however, with their quiet

A team of missionaries and pastors in Bogota moved to prevent a leadership gap. With both mission and church backing, they organized the university-level Alliance Bible Seminary of Bogota in early 1983 with seven students. Attendance the second semester jumped to twenty-two students.

That same semester, the struggling Alliance Bible Seminary in Armenia closed with an enrollment of thirteen, of which only three were Alliance students.

Change had caught up with the fifty-year-old school that had trained with distinction over one thousand pastors for the Alliance and many other denomina-

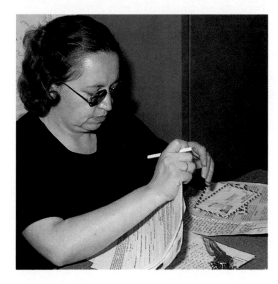

(Left) *Class for Paez Indians is joined by Colombian church leader Porfirio, Ocana; (above)* young Paez students prepare for the ministry.

penetration and invisible form, accomplished what people could not: They started a church.

Alianza en Marcha broadcasts singled out individuals hungering for God in Sonson and brought them together in a fellowship of the Gospel that no amount of persecution or internal problems could undo.

Alianza en Marcha, radio voice of the Alliance, went on the air in 1964. The first programs were broadcast by Trans World Radio in the Caribbean and later by HCJB, Ecuador, and TGNA, Guatemala, and other stations in Latin America. A correspondence and literature office in Cali followed up literature response, while Dr. Manuel Lecaro, of Guayaquil, Ecua-

dor, became the radio pastor known throughout much of Latin America.

Alianza programs open remote towns and jungle villages never visited by a missionary or national evangelist. They enter cities that seem to have everything but the Gospel. At times, the broadcast turns listeners into believers, and believers into congregations.

Bucaramanga, with its half-million residents near the Venezuela border, has reason to remember *Alianza en Marcha*. A group of listeners asked for spiritual help, and got it from a missionary sent to the city. The new believers organized a church in 1971 and kept growing. Five years later, they were worshiping in a new sanctuary with room for 300 people.

Familiar Struggle

Opposition to the Gospel took on a new and ominous identity in recent years: the M-19 Movement. The objective of this communist insurgency force is to overthrow the government and install a Marxist regime.

The guerrillas are especially active in areas of southern Colombia, where the Alliance has a growing ministry among the Indians, proud descendents of an ancient kingdom in the Andes.

This work began in 1941, when missionaries settled in Silvia, a center of about seventy thousand Paez and six thousand Guambiano Indians. Despite fanatical Roman Catholic opposition, congregations formed and flourished on both sides of the central mountain range. The Indian work eventually developed into autonomous Paez and Guambiano churches, so they could grow more freely within their cultural context. The autonomy decision proved a wise one.

Indian church leaders surprised missionaries and Colombian church leaders in 1985, when they reported 3,000 baptized members among the Paez and 500 among the Guambianos. This represented a 100-percent increase within two or three years. The Indian pastors then announced a five-year goal of 15,000 baptized members.

Their growth and goal became even more amazing when viewed in the context of intense guerrilla activity. At times, the church leaders themselves were hunted men. By direct and indirect tactics, the communists attempted to control the churches.

Pastoral training had to be done in disguise. Believers in some areas were forced to worship alone in their houses because guerrillas closed the churches at sunset. Christians were threatened with death if they did not join the communists.

Yet when the believers gathered to worship, they found their numbers increased. Evangelistic campaigns conducted by some churches had to be held outdoors because crowds numbered over one thousand. Some guerrillas who attended, either from curiosity or to spy, found themselves on their knees, praying to God.

The Indian Christians, like other Colombian believers present and past, have found the words of Joseph to his brothers a hard saying, but wonderfully true: "You meant it for evil, but God meant it for good." ☐

CHURCH AND MISSION

OFFICIAL NAME OF CHURCH:	The Colombian Christian Alliance The Guambiano Christian Alliance Community The Paez Christian Alliance Community
ENTRY BY MISSIONARIES:	1923
NUMBER OF MISSIONARIES:	37
ORGANIZED CHURCHES:	172
UNORGANIZED CHURCHES AND PREACHING POINTS:	340
BAPTIZED CHURCH MEMBERS:	14,734
INCLUSIVE MEMBERSHIP:	41,992
EDUCATION:	12 TEE Centers Bible Seminaries in Bogota and Cali, Ambachico Bible Institute
RADIO BROADCASTS:	2
PAGES PRINTED:	1,530,000

COUNTRY

OFFICIAL NAME:	Republic of Colombia
FORM OF GOVERNMENT:	Republic
OFFICIAL LANGUAGE(S):	Spanish
AREA:	439,735 sq. mi.
POPULATION:	31,821,000
CAPITAL:	Bogota
PER CAPITA INCOME:	$1,112.00
LITERACY:	84%
RELIGIOUS AFFILIATION:	Roman Catholic 93%, Protestant 3.1%

COSTA RICA

Follow the Spirit's Working

"TODAY THERE IS hardly a city or town of any consequence without one or more evangelical congregations."

So said the rector of San Jose-based *Seminario Biblico Latinoamericano* in a dissertation written decades ago concerning Costa Rica.[1]

Why, then, did The Christian and Missionary Alliance enter Costa Rica in 1975?

Committees can plan, specialists strategize and councils mandate, but a basic principle of missions will always take precedence: Follow the working of God's Spirit.

Soon after her arrival in New York City, a young Costa Rican found new life in Christ through the ministry of an Hispanic Alliance pastor. Nidia Quiroz experienced the kind of conversion that must be shared.

She returned to her family in San Jose, capital of Costa Rica, and told them what had happened. In six months, she had a congregation of fifty people, twelve of whom were ready for baptism.

Miss Quiroz invited her former pastor in New York to conduct the baptismal service. He brought with him the director of Specialized Ministries for the Alliance and helped the congregation associate with the C&MA.[2]

Quiroz's enthusiasm for the Gospel had a contagious quality. By 1982, seven congregations and 400 baptized believers were meeting in San Jose, each with a Costa Rican pastor or lay leader. Mission leaders called for a respite from expansion, in order to consolidate the gains.

Missed Opportunity

This kind of growth did not happen for long years in Central America's smallest nation.

The San Francisco Church has educational facilities behind the sanctuary.

COSTA RICA

Catholic priests arrived with Columbus in 1502 and established a religious monopoly that endured uncontested for nearly 400 years. An anticlerical government came to power in 1890 for several decades and liberalized laws that had closed Costa Rica's borders to Protestant workers.

Missions hardly distinguished themselves by their enthusiasm in responding to the newly opened door.

Rev. Francisco G. Penzotti entered the country in 1892 as a representative of the American Bible Society. He also helped the American Methodist Church get started, but the mission did not formally organize for another twenty-five years.

The Central American Mission also arrived in 1892, the first of its several fields. Missionaries evangelized widely, but established few churches. They could claim only 300 baptized believers after forty-five years of operations. The Latin American Mission made Costa Rica one of their most important fields.

By 1930, these three missions had a combined membership of fewer than 500.

One seminary educator listed several reasons why Protestant missions got off to a slow start in Costa Rica:[3]

1. Central America was the most neglected area of all Spanish America.

2. The early Protestant movement suffered heavy attacks from Roman Catholic clergy; except for a brief span of time, Catholicism has always dominated the religious scene.

3. Evangelism was not linked to church planting.

4. Inadequate understanding of the church led to little emphasis on the visible assembly of believers and too much on the invisible church.

Around 1950, some of the twelve missions working in Costa Rica realized the importance of establishing churches. The evangelical community then began to grow.

Regroup to Restart

The Costa Rican Christian and Missionary Alliance organized in 1982. George Scranton, a retired American businessman living in the country and very active in getting the work started, was elected president.

Of the seven congregations in San Jose, only one owned the building it met in. Five of the seven groups congregated in tin shacks that did nothing to commend

CHURCH AND MISSION

OFFICIAL NAME OF CHURCH:	Association of Christian and Missionary Alliance Churches of Costa Rica
ENTRY BY MISSIONARIES:	1975
NUMBER OF MISSIONARIES:	5
ORGANIZED CHURCHES:	5
UNORGANIZED CHURCHES AND PREACHING POINTS:	2
BAPTIZED CHURCH MEMBERS:	406
INCLUSIVE MEMBERSHIP:	845
MEDICAL WORK:	0
EDUCATION:	4 TEE Centers
RADIO BROADCASTS:	0
PAGES PRINTED:	0

COUNTRY

OFFICIAL NAME:	Republic of Costa Rica
FORM OF GOVERNMENT:	Democratic Republic
OFFICIAL LANGUAGE(S):	Spanish
AREA:	19,575 sq. mi.
POPULATION:	2,922,000
CAPITAL:	San Jose
PER CAPITA INCOME:	$1,584.00
LITERACY:	90%
RELIGIOUS AFFILIATION:	Roman Catholic 87%, Protestant 7.7%

the church to outsiders, especially those in the economic middle class. Only two of the pastors had formal training or instruction for ministry.

Two apparent needs were highlighted by the survey: church workers needed training, and church groups needed help to finance suitable meeting places.

Until church workers could pursue formal full-time schooling, on-the-job training would have to do. Theological Education by Extension (TEE) drew seventy students to eight study centers. Most of them completed the study cycle.

The 1982 General Council offering helped the Colima congregation to construct a 350-seat sanctuary. The San Francisco church used its portion of the council offering to purchase property on a busy avenue. The attractive building, able to accommodate 300, went up in just over four months and was nearly filled for the dedication service.

The church also became something of a big brother to several smaller groups. It gave haven to believers of one church that closed and helped support the leader of another struggling congregation.

Given Costa Rica's background of opposition to evangelicals, it will not yield easily to those dedicated to its being evangelized. Events in the mid-eighties meant the loss of sorely needed pastors to other responsibilities, while some loss in church growth momentum caused a reduction in students taking TEE courses.

At such a juncture, the churches and missionaries who work with them do well to remember that the Costa Rican Alliance came into being not by human planning, but by God's moving. Implicit in that fact lies the promise of His blessing, available for now and for the future. ☐

DOMINICAN REPUBLIC

Bypassed but not Abandoned

CHRISTOPHER COLUMBUS had seen countless and strange wonders, but it was love at first sight in 1492 when he discovered a Caribbean Island he named *La Isla Espanola*. It reminded him of Spain.

"There is no more beautiful land in the world!" he exclaimed. The profusely forested island, outlined with sun-dazzled beaches and azure-tinted water, appeared like an emerald set in sparkling diamonds on a field of blue velvet.

His love affair with Hispaniola, as it became known, never ended. On it he founded La Isabela, the first permanent European settlement in the New World. From it he launched expeditions to explore a new continent and search for the way to China. To it he brought his brother Bartholomew, to found Santo Domingo, and his son Diego, whom he made promise to bury his remains on the island.[1]

Hispaniola became the center of Spain's operations in the New World—at least until colonies in Cuba, Peru and Mexico proved more profitable and exciting. By the mid-sixteenth century, Hispaniola had reached its zenith of prosperity and begun a decline that seemed never to end. A third of the island eventually fell to France and became known as Haiti. The remaining two-thirds won independence from Spain in 1844 and took the name of Dominican Republic.

In more recent times, cynical brokers of world power and wealth added the small island republic to their list of nations they judged could disappear overnight and never be missed.

But to those born there, the island had a never-to-be-forgotten quality. Bypassed by a world of computer programs and balance sheets, it would never be aban-

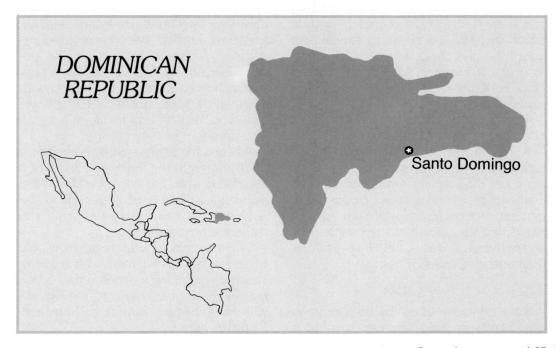

doned by its sons and daughters, no matter how far abroad the pursuit of a better life made them travel.

Homeland Remembered

Alfredo S. Braudy was one of those sons whose dreams drew him to New York, where he played accordion in a jazz band. He found something totally unexpected in the brash metropolis: evangelical faith that transformed him from entertainer to evangelist.

Braudy could not forget the people of his island home. Sensing a call from God, he sought support from several Hispanic Alliance churches and returned to the Dominican Republic in 1968.

He settled the family in San Pedro de Marcoris and began to travel with his accordion and Bible, an effective combination enabling him to form seven small groups of believers in a year or so.

Perhaps realizing the work was growing faster than he could handle, Braudy asked the Alliance in North America to adopt the churches. Because of his previous link to Hispanic Alliance churches in New York, the Office of Specialized Ministries offered to help.[2]

The fledgling Alliance movement faced odds reminiscent of David and Goliath.

A handful of small churches, mostly rural and all with untrained leaders, faced a nation that legally embraced Roman Catholicism as its religion. Some thirty mission groups already worked on the island, but 98 percent of the people considered themselves Catholics—whether they attended mass or not.[3]

Key Cities

Two principal cities, Santo Domingo and Santiago, held the key to church

The Santo Domingo Alliance Church sponsors a grade school (left) *with 200 students.*

growth. Strong churches established in these centers could provide leadership and support to small, struggling congregations in rural areas.

Braudy had established his first group of Christians in Santo Domingo in 1969. He found a former businessman who felt called of God to the ministry and had prepared himself with correspondence courses. Although unaffiliated, he had been listening to *Alianza en Marcha* and readily agreed to pastor the new church. Attendance soon grew to 100 people, including the wife and family of a former vice-president of the country.

Alliance ministry in Santiago began in 1971 through the intense efforts of a talented couple. He was a builder as well as evangelist and used both skills to start a church in a new development area without a gospel witness.

While forming a congregation of new believers, he built a church with adjoining classrooms. His wife began a day school that in three years grew to nine grades with 300 children, almost all from non-Christian homes.

The pastor initiated an effective outreach program several years later. He selected twelve men, instructed them, and then sent them out to small preaching points in Santiago. On Wednesday evenings, the church divided into twelve similar groups and spread across the city for evangelistic Bible study groups.

Aiming Higher

As the number of churches and members increased, the Dominician Alliance formally organized in 1975. A three-year program of evangelism that anticipated 120 campaigns and should have climaxed in 1979 was disrupted by a hurricane that put thirteen churches out of commission.

Events made 1982 and 1983 pivotal years for the work. In Nyack, responsibility for helping the Dominican Alliance was transferred from Specialized Ministries to the Division of Overseas Ministries. The Dominican national committee approved a plan that regrouped the churches into four districts, each responsible for its own activities, such as youth work and extension.

The national committee agreed on a set of bylaws for organized churches. Each must have twenty members, a functioning secretarial office and good financial controls. Sixteen of the thirty-eight churches met the standard that year.

Dominican Alliance leaders also set goals for growth. For the short term, they optimistically decided to go for 100 churches, nearly tripling their 1983 total of thirty-five. For the longer-range ten-year plan, they set their sights for a 10,000-member denomination, a national radio broadcast, twenty churches in the capital, and many other goals.

Over sixty students enrolled in Theological Education by Extension courses, while church leaders sought ways to raise pastoral training a notch higher, to the Bible institute level.

The national committee requested the North American Alliance to send them an experienced missionary couple to help train workers and counsel leaders. Rev. and Mrs. Kenn Opperman, who had played a key role in launching Lima's Encounter program (*see* Peru), moved to Santo Domingo in 1984.

Several outstanding Alliance church leaders from South America visited the Dominican Republic the following year, to offer suggestions and encouragement. Both Alliance leaders and believers on the island began to realize they were part of a larger team, an international fellowship that deeply cared for their well-being and growth.

Bypassed, but not abandoned. The rich and powerful may ignore their island home, but Dominican Alliance people know they have support where it counts: from fellow believers in the Lord Jesus Christ. ☐

CHURCH AND MISSION

OFFICIAL NAME OF CHURCH:	The Christian and Missionary Alliance of Dominican Republic
ENTRY BY MISSIONARIES:	1969
NUMBER OF MISSIONARIES:	8
ORGANIZED CHURCHES:	19
UNORGANIZED CHURCHES AND PREACHING POINTS:	34
BAPTIZED CHURCH MEMBERS:	1,375
INCLUSIVE MEMBERSHIP:	2,750
MEDICAL WORK:	0
EDUCATION:	12 TEE Centers
RADIO BROADCASTS:	3
PAGES PRINTED:	0

COUNTRY

OFFICIAL NAME:	Dominican Republic
FORM OF GOVERNMENT:	Representative Democracy
OFFICIAL LANGUAGE(S):	Spanish
AREA:	18,815 sq. mi.
POPULATION:	7,307,000
CAPITAL:	Santo Domingo
PER CAPITA INCOME:	$1,221.00
LITERACY:	72%
RELIGIOUS AFFILIATION:	Roman Catholic 77%, Protestant 6.4%

ECUADOR

Church on the Grow

WITH DAZZLING snowcapped ranges soaring from a tufted carpet of jungle green, Ecuador adorns Latin America like a prized crown jewel.

Those who seek the uniqueness of Latin America need travel no farther. Ecuador blends centuries-old architecture and ancient ruins with high rises, passionate nature with pragmatic ways, jeans and sound boxes with Old World Spanish culture and proud Indian customs predating the conquistadors.

The nation naturally divides into three geographical regions representing different sectors of society. Each part of the country—mountainous plateaus, coastal plains and inland jungles—bears evidence that the Gospel is literally working wonders.

Over half the nation's 8.5 million people live on a high-altitude plateau hung like a hammock between two massive Andean ranges. Quito, already an ancient city before the Incas claimed it, reigns not only as queen of the highlands, but also as capital of the nation.

In the mid-1980s, seven Alliance churches in Quito recorded either capac-

ity or crowded attendance. Citywide and local church evangelistic campaigns continually added to their numbers.

Guayaquil, Ecuador's largest city, dominates the coastal strip between the Pacific Ocean and the Andes, where 47 percent of the population lives. While history-conscious Quito preserves traditional ways, Guayaquil enjoys the more open society of a seaport's intermingled cultures and peoples of the world.

In keeping with its rank as *numero uno* in population, Guayaquil contains the largest, in size and number, of Christian and Missionary Alliance churches in Ecuador. On any day of the month, at least one congregation is conducting an evangelistic campaign somewhere among the city's 1.5 million residents.

Ranging from the low-lying, steamy jungles of the interior to the jagged and windy heights of the Andes, the remaining 2 percent of the people live in scattered clusters. Many of them are Indians who, with their urban relatives, represent four of every ten Ecuadorians.

These Indian groups trace their ancestry back to preconquest times, as citizens or slaves of the fabled Inca Empire. Te-

naciously protecting their ancient spirit worship with a veneer of Roman Catholicism, they have proven most resistant to the Gospel. Yet over 500 Indian church leaders, including many Alliance workers, met for six days in late 1986 to learn how better to evangelize their people.

The Ecuadorian Alliance, the nation's largest and most active evangelical denomination (especially among the Spanish-speaking people), reached its five-year goal of 260 churches by 1986—and promptly raised the goal to 320 churches over the next five years.

Late Start

The tableau of a church on the grow did not always represent Protestantism in this Andean country. Ecuador, in fact, was the last South American country to allow Protestant missionaries within its borders.

For centuries, the landed aristocracy had held the Indian population in virtual economic bondage on their haciendas. They determined to keep out Bible-spouting missionaries, who might destabilize their feudal system.

Roman Catholic priests in the popula-

ECUADOR

tion centers firmly controlled the whites and mestizos (mixed Spanish and Indian background). They, too, vowed to keep their parishes free of Protestant pollution. Joined with the aristocracy in an alliance of religious, economic and political power, they stonewalled Protestant penetration longer than any other South American country.[1]

Openness to religious change of any kind in Ecuador lagged behind developments elsewhere. James Thompson, the colporteur who had successfully set up Bible societies in other countries, managed to sell only 700 Bibles in 1824, before he was pressed to move on.

The coalition of Catholic church and landed aristocracy then managed to keep their monopoly free of Protestant interference for another seventy-two years.

Francisco Penzotti, representing the American Bible Society, tried to bring a shipment of Bibles into Guayaquil in 1888. He was confronted by a stern customs agent, who informed him, "The Bible will not enter Ecuador as long as Chimborazo stands."[2]

Today the towering Chimborazo of the Andes still stands 21,000 feet tall, the

Bible circulates freely in Ecuador, and the unsympathetic customs official is long gone.

Liberal Opening

Eight young men, organized in two groups supported by the Gospel Missionary Union (GMU), started for Ecuador in 1896. They had plenty of enthusiasm, but no visas for their destination, which was a Roman Catholic country by law, "to the exclusion of all other religions."

But while still en route, the young men

learned that the conservative government of Ecuador had been toppled. The new regime, liberal in politics, guaranteed religious freedom. So hardly had the door opened a crack in 1896 before the first group of GMU missionaries arrived in Guayaquil.[3]

The pioneer Alliance team reached Guayaquil the following year. Mr. and Mrs. Edward E. Tarbox moved on to Quito, while Mr. W. G. Fritz remained in the port city.

Guayaquil, like all port cities, had a

A retired army general, and Alliance layman, is president of the Christian Military Movement; (right) Templo Alianza is situated in downtown Guayaquil.

certain tolerant attitude toward life, including religion. Fritz and other evangelical missionaries soon met with success.

Quito, however, was another story.

The ancient city had been "modernized" by the Spaniards in 1543—eighty-one years before the Pilgrims landed on Plymouth Rock—making it the oldest capital in the New World. Fiercely protective of its heritage, a proud mixture of religion and culture, Quito did not embrace foreigners promoting a creed that called theirs into question. The government repeatedly had to dispatch police or army units to protect the *gringos* from priest-incited mobs.

Public meetings drew opposition like lightning rods attract thunderbolts. In a way, this was fortunate, because it forced

missionaries to concentrate on one-to-one evangelism and low-keyed home gatherings. Although not attractive information for press releases, the individual approach quietly and effectively brought into being a church of handpicked believers.[4]

The first twenty years of ministry produced hardly any converts. Another ten years brought the total to twenty-five baptized believers.

A little-noticed event in 1903 would have long-term benefits for the Alliance. GMU missionaries Homer and Leticia Crisman joined the C&MA after their original team had gone home.

"We were the only [GMU] missionaries in the country at the time," Crisman explained, "and we became lonely and

despondent as there was no one to share with."[5]

Lonely and despondent they may have been, but not vacillating.

After six years in Manabi Province, they could report only four converts, but the Crismans persisted until the church was formed. They served with the Alliance for forty years in Ecuador and Colombia, until Mrs. Crisman's ill health forced them home.

After her death in 1950, he returned to Ecuador, married a coworker and completed a record-setting seventy-one years of ministry. Crisman finally retired at age ninety-three.

Scattered Progress

Ecuador was destined to inching growth because of deep-rooted opposition and indifference—or so it seemed.

The first C&MA chapel, built in Junin, was not dedicated until 1913. Alliance missionaries started construction of Quito's first Protestant church in 1919, but took three years to complete the building because frequent night raids demolished the previous day's work.

The contested construction, two steps forward and one step backward, may explain why the 1922 Central Church remained the only Protestant edifice in Quito until 1948.

Progress elsewhere seemed spotty, at best. A beachhead among the Quechua Indians in 1902 was evacuated after thirteen years of fruitless labor. Missionaries managed to open a station among the Otavalo Indians in 1916, but the move triggered fierce opposition that stalled growth.

By 1925, after twenty-eight years of sacrifice and hard work, Alliance missionaries could only name 150 baptized believers in the whole country. Eleven of Ecuador's twenty provinces still lacked a resident gospel witness.

Guayaquil provided one bright spot in this era of spotty growth. An aggressive church, pastored by former GMU missionary W. E. Reed, merged with the Alliance in 1922. The renamed *Templo Alianza* showed the way to self-support and outreach under the dynamic leadership of Dr. Manuel Lecaro.

Reed believed the Gospel would penetrate Ecuador "through the kitchen rather than the parlor," i.e., working-class believers would be the means of evangelizing society from the bottom up.[6]

With this in mind, teams of Christians from *Templo Alianza* spread out through the city to distribute literature. On some Sundays, they distributed up to 6,000 tracts. And the church grew.

Templo Alianza inaugurated a Bible-study course in 1925 and enrolled sixteen young Christians eager to study God's Word. It may have seemed insignificant at the time, but the Bible class grew until it reached the stature of a fully organized school in 1928. The school continued to grow, until it became the Alliance Bible Seminary in 1952 with an international student body.

A different milestone was reached in 1931, when World Radio Missionary Fellowship began gospel broadcasting over Radio HCJB, Quito.

The arrival of missionary radio meant that middle- and upper-class people, who abhorred or feared street meetings, could now hear the Gospel in the security of their homes. HCJB quickly expanded the horizons of potential ministry for the Ecuadorian church.

Autonomy laid the groundwork for a church that could hold its own and grow on its own in Latin American society. The Ecuadorian Evangelical Church of the C&MA organized in 1945, with eleven pastors and fourteen churches. Full self-support came in 1960, after a decade of diminishing subsidies from North America.

The mixed gains and losses in spotty growth, however, continued into the 1960s, as the Alliance faced opposition and indifference to the Gospel. In this they were not alone. Even as late as 1967, the ratio of all evangelical missionaries to baptized believers stood at one to thirty-four.

One church-growth analyst noted in 1969: "No other country in Latin America has such a concentration of missionaries for such a small evangelical fellowship— or such large resources for so little church growth."[7]

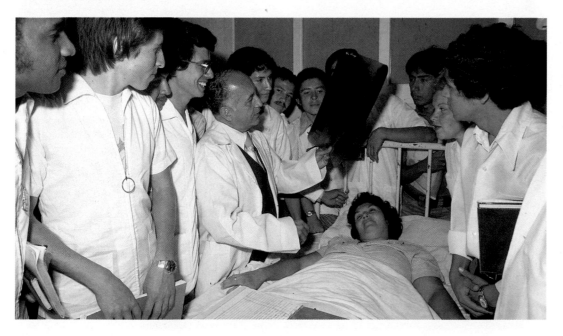

(Left) *A medical doctor, and active layman, conducts a medical seminar for his students;* (right) *Ecuadorian secular television is a communication medium of growing importance.*

Dr. Alfredo Smith carried his experience in the eminently successful Encounter strategy in Lima to his next pastorate in Quito.

Turning Point

Evangelicals got a preview of possibilities for the future when Evangelism-In-Depth (EID) conducted a campaign of mass evangelization from July of 1969 to August of 1970.

EID usually followed a pattern of beginning locally and building to a massive nationwide rally. The Ecuadorian effort followed a totally opposite strategy.

Large regional rallies opened the campaign in Quito, Guayaquil and Cuenca. Action then moved to subregions and finally to a climax in local churches. Campaign organizers decided on this strategy to emphasize that ultimate responsibility for evangelism lies with the local church.

Efforts in Alliance areas claimed an amazing 6,000 decisions for Christ. Nevertheless, actual growth totaled only 1,160 new members, fewer than two for every ten public commitments.[8]

EID had obvious shortcomings, but if nothing else, it demolished a pervasive impression that Ecuador had a closed mind toward the Gospel. This realization,

plus the training of thousands of campaign volunteers in outreach methods, marked a turning point for all evangelical groups, including the Alliance.

The Ecuadorian C&MA seemed poised for an era of growth, but before that could happen, their leaders needed to take a long, hard look at past strategy.

What were the true causes of the minimal growth that had shackled advance? Were outside opposition and indifference the only obstacles? Or were church and mission partly to blame through inadequate planning?

The regional director for Latin America prepared a fifteen-year analysis that cited stumbling blocks. He then listed action steps that he, church leaders and missionaries saw as essential to growth.[9]

They concluded that church and mission should concentrate their resources in areas of response, instead of trying to cover the whole field. Missionaries, most of whom were in church support ministries, should be transferred to the frontline activity of evangelism and church planting.

The training of pastors and lay leaders in theological studies and church-growth methods needed upgrading. And together they needed to find improved methods of quickly incorporating new converts into local churches.

These and other points became part of a five-year plan adopted by church and mission. The stage was now set for ex-

People crowd into the Alliance church of El Batan.

pansion unlike anything the Alliance had previously seen in Ecuador.

Quito Encounter

Once again, Lima's *Encuentro con Dios* served as a catalyst (*see* Peru). Inspired by what they saw happening in Peru, missionaries and church workers in Quito conducted a week-long pilot campaign in late 1978.

Attendance rose from 500 to 1,000 as the week progressed. Ninety-seven individuals professed faith in Christ. From then on, the Encounter campaigns became the mainstay of Alliance evangelism in the capital city.

Quito gave another indication of its changed attitude toward the Gospel in 1978. For the first time in its nearly 460-year history, the city donated land for an evangelical church.

The choice location went to the Batan Church, a six-year-old congregation that took the lead in evangelizing Quito. Begun through the initiative of Manuel Contag, a city businessman, the church attracted middle- and upper-class people who considered vision, growth and initiative as essentials of life.

The city's Alliance churches joined in annual citywide campaigns and then continued with local efforts throughout the year. Evangelism soon brought rewards. Each of the churches was filled to capacity by 1984, needing either to build larger facilities or to begin daughter churches.

Dr. Alfredo Smith, who for eleven years played a key role in Lima's Encounter strategy, became pastor of the Batan Church in 1985. His arrival added depth of experience to the widening enthusiasm of Quito's evangelism efforts.

Growing bigger and stronger, the cap-

ital's Alliance churches addressed a major weakness: the lack of skilled and ordained pastoral leadership. The solution lay in training city people, in a city setting, to pastor city churches.

The Quito Training Center opened in 1983 to provide this solution. Using classroom facilities of the Alliance Academy, a school for missionary children, the center offered a four-year, four-weeknight curriculum. The program balanced theological studies with practical courses in urban evangelism and church growth. Thirty adults immediately enrolled, and the student body grew with the school.

Widening Response

Guayaquil, traditionally more open to change than Quito, took immediately to the Encounter strategy. Evangelism was an ongoing part of church life for *Templo Alianza*. Now this large central church united with the seventeen other city congregations for greater impact.

Together they rented a sports stadium and mounted annual evangelistic campaigns that amazed even the worldly port city, and it responded. When, for example, Dr. Lecaro, pastor of *Templo Alianza*, preached in a series of meetings during 1984, over 340 people stepped forward in commitment to Christ.

Individual churches conducted their own special meetings between citywide campaigns and made sure the converts were immediately welcomed into their fellowship. Throughout the 1980s, all eighteen churches had the enviable problem of wondering where to put all the people who came to worship.

Even among the jungle and mountain Indians, a spiritual movement finally emerged. Work among the Otavalos had

(Top) *Children look over a literature display;* (above) *the Batan congregation meets in worship.*

begun in 1916, but converts never numbered more than thirty until 1968. The EID beginning that year, plus radio programs in their language, marked an unprecedented awakening.

Over 500 Indian believers witnessed the dedication of the Otavalo Training Center in 1982. One year later, 300 Otavalos entered the waters of baptism. Membership surpassed 1,800 by 1985. One-week seminars tried to insure that at least 10 percent of the believers were in training and study at any given time.

Evangelizing the Indians seemed especially to draw fire from unsympathetic quarters. Government agencies and anthropologists accused evangelicals of causing the disintegration of Indian cultures, which they termed a national heritage. They succeeded in ousting Wycliffe translators in 1982 and posed a problem to those who continued working in tribal areas.

Continental Impact

Despite Ecuador's small size and the church's initially slow progress, the country hosts institutions whose ministries reach far beyond its borders.

The Alliance Academy commands respect throughout Latin America. Its campus in Quito houses a full academic institution, from kindergarten to grade twelve, for over 475 students in a typical year. The C&MA manages the school with its staff of eighty people, half of them C&MA teachers and dorm parents.[10]

Most of the students come from missionary families working for thirty evangelical groups. The academy also accepts children from the diplomatic and foreign business communities in Quito. Altogether, students represent over thirty na-

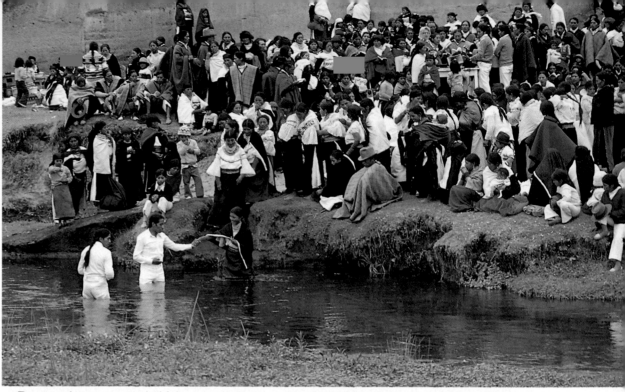

Baptismal services are held frequently for the many Otavalo Indians who receive Christ.

tionalities, and their interaction is a unique education in itself.

Reflecting their parents' background, 85 percent of the students score in the top third in college entrance examinations. Most go on to higher education.

Again reflecting their parents' influence, students in witness teams fan out for activities such as conducting services and street meetings. Their basketball and soccer athletes compete seriously with top Ecuadorian school teams.

Begun in 1929 with just eight students and two staff members, the school has grown to one of the continent's outstanding private schools for expatriates.

The Alliance Bible Seminary in Guayaquil has earned an international reputation, as well. Students come from places like Puerto Rico, Dominican Republic, Guatemala, Colombia, Peru and Chile to join the Ecuadorian young people. The

117 students in 1986 marked the highest enrollment ever.

The school actually has two identities: seminary during the day and Bible institute in the evening. This enables the school to have an immediate impact on leadership in the church, as well as training future pastors and church workers.

The tireless *Templo Alianza* and about 140 other evangelical congregations in Guayaquil give students an example to follow and plenty of churches to work in.

Radio HCJB, with headquarters in Quito, not only holds a commanding view high in the Andes; it has a signal that literally reaches around the world.

Alliance missionary Ruben E. Larson, already stationed in Ecuador, joined with Chicagoan Clarence Jones to erect a radio station in Quito. Radio engineers warned that mineral deposits in the mountains would distort the signal, but the two persisted. Technicians later conceded sheepishly that HCJB's location is perhaps one of the finest anywhere.[11]

HCJB first went on the air with a 250-watt transmitter on Christmas Day, 1931. Only six radio receivers could be found in all of Ecuador that day, but the radio revolution spread fast. By 1984, HCJB was broadcasting in fourteen languages for a total 1,300 hours. Its 500-kilowatt transmitter was twice as powerful as anything used by Voice of America, and could often be heard more clearly than Radio Moscow.

HCJB's local AM and FM radio stations in Ecuador have cooperated closely with the Alliance's Encounter campaigns and often carry local church programs. Its powerful shortwave transmitters carry *Alianza en Marcha* messages around the world.

Shadows

The future of Alliance ministry in Ecuador appears as bright as a sunrise over the Andes, but there are shadows, as well. The jungle Indians, scattered and isolated, have not yet joined the upbeat advance of the church. And the most unresponsive areas at present seem to be those provinces, like Manabi, where the Alliance first established churches at the turn of the century.

Political unrest ignited by communist elements, and the more restrained but unmistakable opposition of Roman Catholicism, serve notice that future gains for the Gospel will not go uncontested.

But having begun slowly, paying for every step forward with sacrifice and suffering, the Alliance in Ecuador has every intention of remaining a church on the grow. ☐

CHURCH AND MISSION

OFFICIAL NAME OF CHURCH:	The Ecuadorian Evangelical Church of The Christian and Missionary Alliance
ENTRY BY MISSIONARIES:	1897
NUMBER OF MISSIONARIES:	42
ORGANIZED CHURCHES:	85
UNORGANIZED CHURCHES AND PREACHING POINTS:	125
BAPTIZED CHURCH MEMBERS:	11,305
INCLUSIVE MEMBERSHIP:	15,781
EDUCATION:	Alliance Bible Seminary (Guayaquil) Seminary Extension-(Quito)
PAGES PRINTED:	230,000

COUNTRY

OFFICIAL NAME:	Republic of Ecuador
FORM OF GOVERNMENT:	Republic
OFFICIAL LANGUAGE(S):	Spanish
AREA:	109,483 sq. mi.
POPULATION:	10,490,000
CAPITAL:	Quito
PER CAPITA INCOME:	$1,299.00
LITERACY:	84%
RELIGIOUS AFFILIATION:	Roman Catholic 91%, Protestant 3.4%

GUATEMALA

The Door Music Opened

THE METHODS GOD USES to open doors for missions are as limitless as His imagination.

But who would have thought of a hymnal?

A search team arrived in New York from Guatemala in 1968, to find an international evangelical mission willing to affiliate with their churches and help them grow. Upon entering the First Spanish Alliance Church in the Bronx, they were astonished to see the Spanish-language version of *Hymns of the Christian Life*. It was the same hymnal their churches used!

The search team met with the pastor and then with leaders at the International Headquarters of the Alliance. They recounted a remarkable story.

When Stella Zimmerman graduated from Moody Bible Institute, she felt led of the Lord to Guatemala. Affiliated at first with a faith mission, she started her own mission in 1913 because of disagreements concerning money. Miss Zimmerman was independently wealthy, enabling her to finance both the *Mision Evangelica Interdenominacional* she founded and the churches she started.

She accomplished remarkable results. Strong in leadership, sound in doctrine and rich in resources, she singlehandedly established a cluster of churches in a hostile, Roman Catholic-dominated country. She chose the Alliance hymnal, *Himnos de la Vida Cristiana*, for use in her churches because it best reflected her own understanding of the Bible.[1]

By the time Miss Zimmerman died in 1958, she had organized over forty churches and firmly established them in evangelical precepts.

The churches tried to carry on alone, as their founder had done. But as time passed, they realized they had some serious shortcomings. The Christians knew little about self-support, because Miss Zimmerman had paid many of the bills and supported the pastors. The churches knew little about self-governing, because she had made most of the decisions.

One group of twenty-two churches recognized their need of counsel and training if they were to continue growing and effectively serve the Lord. They dispatched a search committee to the United States in 1968. The group's mandate: Seek assistance from a mission faithful to the same beliefs Miss Zimmerman had taught them.

Thanks to a hymnal, the Guatemalan representatives and Alliance leaders got together. They explored a wide range of topics during that eventful visit to New York. Discussions left both parties confident they could be mutually helpful.

The Guatemalan churches represented by the group would receive assistance in leadership training and growth strategy from a mission with years of proven success in Latin America. The Alliance would receive another open door in fulfillment of its global mandate to preach the Gospel and make disciples in all nations.

The Christian and Missionary Alliance formally entered Guatemala in June of 1969 and affiliated with twenty-one churches of the Evangelical Interdenominational Mission.

Protestant Prosperity

Protestantism entered Central America's third largest and most populous nation in an even more remarkable fashion than the Alliance: by presidential invitation.

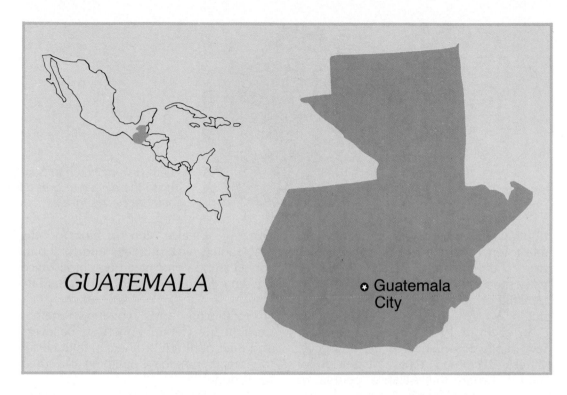

GUATEMALA

Guatemala City

Justo Rufino Barrios, a liberal Catholic president popularly called the Great Reformer of his country, invited the Presbyterian Church, U.S.A., to provide missionaries in 1882. He believed that Protestants could help his country develop.[2]

In earlier years, such an act or idea would have been considered heresy and roundly censured. The papacy considered Guatemala, like the rest of Latin America, the exclusive domain of the church.

Catholic domination of Guatemala began in 1523, when Spanish conquistadores, accompanied by emissaries of the church, defeated tribes related to the Mayan civilization. Priests forced the Indians into settlements and made them converts to Catholicism, willing or not.

The Indians conformed to the religion of their conquerors, but it was merely an overlay on their stubbornly held Mayan beliefs. Four centuries of Catholicism did little to change that attitude. For reasons of their own, the *Ladinos* (mestizos), who form half of the population, have a similar disinterest in the church.

Although the Vatican still considers Guatemala a Catholic country, less than one in ten citizens is a practicing Catholic. Support for the church is indicative of the prevailing attitude: only one priest for every 25,000 people.[3]

Some church observers may be right in asserting there are more active Protestants than Catholics in the country. Protestants claim as much as 25 percent of the population, half of them baptized church members. Whether this claim is accurate or not, Guatemala is certainly one of the most evangelized countries in Latin America.

Why, then, did the Alliance accept the Evangelical Interdenominational Mission's invitation to enter the country? Because its three areas of strength in missions—encouraging church auton-

omy, training pastoral leadership, promoting church growth—fit precisely the needs expressed by the Guatemalan churches.

Support in Suffering

Rev. and Mrs. William Paul transferred to Guatemala in 1972 to work with the churches. They had previously served in Colombia, and then with Specialized Ministries in Texas. Their primary task was to provide leadership training and biblical studies for the pastors.

Using Theological Education by Extension (TEE) methods seemed altogether natural—the whole system of TEE originated in a Guatemalan-based Presbyterian seminary.

The Pauls organized short-term training courses, retreats, seminars, literature dis-

(Left) *Belen Church in San Raimundo;*
(right) *the market in Solela is typical of
many cities and towns.*

tribution and whatever other means available to encourage a higher level of ministry. They encountered slow going at first, especially among some pastors who had little or no training and saw no need of it.

An event in 1976 not only brought a new depth of urgency to the churches' witness, it created a new dimension of unity between the Alliance people of Guatemala and North America. In the early morning darkness of February 4, a massive earthquake snaked through the nation. It killed over 23,000 people, injured 100,000 others and rendered 1 million homeless.[4]

The Alliance in North America, along with others, immediately responded with money, food, clothing and tents. Relief funds paid for twenty-five building-block machines and their shipment from Colombia. At a later date, Alliance Men showed their support of the Guatemalan churches by an unforgettably personal touch: They came themselves to help rebuild the nation.

Over 200 men—carpenters, electricians, plumbers, painters, self-styled handymen and others who just wanted to help—flew to Guatemala in teams organized by Alliance Men. In nine months they rebuilt nine churches and four parsonages and constructed a central office building for the church in Guatemala City.

Worshiping and working together brought the Central American believers and their northern brothers in faith closer together than perhaps anything else could have done.

The earthquake shook many Guatemalans from their spiritual indifference. They could no longer be sure of the ground underfoot. The altered spiritual landscape provided a special opening for witness.

The C&MA's Guatemalan Relief Fund helped the churches respond to this openness by providing a 500-seat tent and public-address system. Thus, while the nation was still shaken by its staggering losses, gifted evangelists toured the country with a message of hope and comfort. Response from the crowds gave the churches new appreciation for what the Gospel could accomplish.

Cause to Celebrate

The year 1982 proved unforgettable in a way more pleasant than an earthquake.

Guatemalan Protestants celebrated their first centennial by giving the capital city a demonstration of just how far they had come in one hundred years.

Thousands of people gathered at eight locations in Guatemala City in late November. Two local radio stations broadcast directives and music, to coordinate movement of the marchers. Carrying transistor radios at full blast, roaring gospel songs in unison and brandishing banners, eight massive columns of ecstatic Christians converged on the rally site, a military parade area.

The columns were so well organized that each participating church had assigned its own litter sweeper for the parade. The sweepers formed a rear guard, to clean up any debris dropped by the marchers, leaving the streets cleaner than before the celebration.

An estimated 750,000 people gathered at the climactic rally, to hear evangelist Luis Palau. President Efrain Rios Montt, the nation's first Protestant head of state, spoke first. He told the huge gathering, "The King of kings is the head of government in Guatemala."[5]

(President Montt's evangelical stance offended too many interest groups. He

was deposed within a year by a bloodless coup.)

The eight Alliance churches in Guatemala City prefaced the huge centennial observance with their own campaign in early November. Evangelist Rolando Pichardo preached nightly to crowds averaging 900 in attendance. Over 185 people publicly committed their lives to Christ.

Throughout Guatemala, Alliance people had reason to rejoice in the centennial year of 1982. Since 1969, their numbers had increased from twenty-one to forty churches, all self-supporting. Their inclusive membership had doubled, to over 3,400.

Transfer of the Guatemalan Alliance from Specialized Ministries to the Division of Overseas Ministries brought the churches into closer contact with sister churches in South America and increased their potential for growth.

Some congregations had registered strong gains in recent years. The Tecpan church, for example, had been rebuilt by Alliance Men after the earthquake and was now seeing from 400 to 500 worshipers every Sunday. The Chiquimulilla congregation conducted a Lima-type Encounter campaign (*see* Peru) with average attendance of over 1,000 every night for two weeks. Some 100 people came forward for prayer during the campaign.

The Quiche-language congregation in Agua Escondida had even more to celebrate. Communist-instigated guerrilla activity in 1981 had forced the entire community to flee. The church was disbanded as its members scattered. They returned a year and a half later, after government troops had secured the area,

Refugee Christians who lost everything in flight from guerrillas tend gardens made possible with seeds donated by Alliance churches.

only to find their houses plundered and burned by the rebels.

With help from North America, they rebuilt their homes and started planting crops. For them, 1982 was the Year of the Return, but their rejoicing was tinged with apprehension when attacks took place within a mile of the church.

Quickened Tempo

The centennial year may have been something of a turning point for the Alliance, because the tempo of growth and outreach quickened in succeeding years.

In 1984, the denomination joined with other evangelicals in a nationwide evangelism program called DAWN, "Discipling a Whole Nation." Campaign leaders estimated that, if the churches could increase their growth rate to 17 percent annually, evangelicals could form 50 percent of the population by 1990.[6]

Alliance leaders committed themselves to a demanding objective of winning and baptizing 15,000 new believers by 1990. Regardless of eventual results, the act of setting the goal evidenced a new spirit among the churches.

The TEE program shared in the increased tempo of advance. It had shrunk to two centers and four students in 1982. Three years later, quickened by goals for growth, TEE centers increased to ten, each supervised by a trained tutor.

As guerrillas were pushed back to the borders by government troops, churches in the rural areas and small cities increased their outreach. The San Jose Pinula congregation was especially significant: Only three years old itself, the church established three preaching points served by the pastor and several laymen.

To achieve the kind of growth it set for its goal, the denomination will need to concentrate on Guatemala City.

Some of the capital's evangelical churches are large and growing, but most—including Alliance ones—are small and hard to find. An Encounter-type program of nonstop evangelism by a large and active central church could have an impact not only on Guatemala City, but the nation as well—and perhaps beyond.

An Alliance pastor moved from Guatemala City to San Salvadore, capital of neighboring El Salvadore, in July of 1986. While the Guatemalan Alliance still debated whether to undertake the missionary venture, the pastor was already ministering to a congregation of 200. The procedure may seem a bit unusual, but that's the way it goes in Guatemala.

Protestantism entered Guatemala in an unusual manner: by presidential invitation. The Alliance entered in another unexpected manner: by a hymnal.

Considering this kind of pattern, Guatemala may hold yet another surprise: a nation evangelized from within. □

CHURCH AND MISSION

OFFICIAL NAME OF CHURCH:	The Christian and Missionary Alliance of Guatemala
ENTRY BY MISSIONARIES:	1969
NUMBER OF MISSIONARIES:	8
ORGANIZED CHURCHES:	37
UNORGANIZED CHURCHES AND PREACHING POINTS:	47
BAPTIZED CHURCH MEMBERS:	2,329
INCLUSIVE MEMBERSHIP:	4,433
EDUCATION:	5 TEE Centers
RADIO BROADCASTS:	2

COUNTRY

OFFICIAL NAME:	Republic of Guatemala
FORM OF GOVERNMENT:	Republic
OFFICIAL LANGUAGE(S):	Spanish, Indian dialects
AREA:	42,042 sq. mi.
POPULATION:	9,412,000
CAPITAL:	Guatemala City
PER CAPITA INCOME:	$1,000.00
LITERACY:	48%
RELIGIOUS AFFILIATION:	Roman Catholic 66%, Protestant 20.4%

MEXICO

Too Close to Home?

ALLIANCE PEOPLE in North America generally have a curious logic about mission fields. They seem to reason that the spiritual needs of foreign nations increase in direct ratio to their distance from North America. Countries farther away are thought to need the Gospel more than those closer to home.

Exhibit A of this faulty logic is the United Mexican States. Mexico has all the dramatic elements of a first-class mission field, except for one drawback: It borders the United States.

Consider numbers.

In Latin America, Mexico ranks second in population only to Brazil. It has more people than any other Spanish-language nation. Its capital, Mexico City, with a massive population of 18 million in the mid-1980s, was the largest city in the world.[1]

Consider culture.

Mexico is built on a multilayered foundation that by 1500 had reached the highest development of indigenous civilization in the Western Hemisphere. Spanish conquistadores stood dazzled when they first saw Tenochtitlan, capital of the Aztec Empire. It rivaled anything they had known in Europe.

Consider people.

Some nations in Latin America have only small Indian minorities, while the majority take pride in their European roots. Six of every ten Mexicans have some Indian background, while three of every ten trace their sole heritage to Olmec, Mayan, Toltec or Aztec culture.

Consider religion.

An estimated 97 percent of Mexicans call themselves Roman Catholic, yet many of their beliefs relate directly to pagan religions. Perhaps unconsciously, they follow the way of their ancestors who were forced by weight of the sword to bow before an upraised crucifix, all the while guarding ancient beliefs in their hearts.

Even today, good Catholics pray to the Virgin of Guadalupe, patron saint of Mexico, so similar to the Indian goddess Tonantzin ("our revered mother"), that many Indians still call her by that name.[2]

Belated Entry

Had Mexico been located in South America instead of next door to the United States, it may have been targeted along with other countries by Alliance missionaries in the 1890s. However, it did not see Alliance missionaries until 1947, and then only temporarily.

Two home missionaries left their work among Hispanics in Texas's Rio Grande valley to attempt opening a church in Mexico City. Opposition and obstacles ended their courageous venture within a year.

Not until 1954 did the Alliance establish a permanent witness in Mexico—by an indirect and undirected manner. A young Mexican, Ricardo Salvador, was converted through the witness of some translation missionaries. He returned to Mexico City and began witnessing to his countrymen.

Rev. H. E. Nelson, C&MA home secretary, heard about Salvador and his thirteen converts. Through Nelson's encouragement, the small congregation affiliated with the home department, and Mexico joined other Latin American nations for whom the North American Alliance recognized a spiritual responsibility. At last.[3]

The entry of still another Protestant

group in Roman Catholic Mexico aroused hardly a ripple. The nation already counted forty-one Protestant missions and over 2,450 missionaries, both foreign and national. Their combined efforts by 1960 amounted to 2,420 churches and 645,000 adherents.[4]

Evangelical witness entered Mexico in 1824, when John C. Brigham began his first of three years in distributing Bibles. The remarkable James Thompson, of the British and Foreign Bible Society, came to Mexico City in 1827 with twenty-four mules loaded with Bibles and Gospels.

Helped by Catholic clergy, he distributed his stock in the capital—and then saw his work undone by higher church authorities who forbade people to read the Scriptures. Thompson remained until 1830 and then returned in 1842 for a brief stay.[5]

A few independent missionaries worked in Mexico before American Baptists, the first denominational mission, arrived in 1870. Their ministry, and that of other missions that followed, aroused intense opposition. On one occasion, a Catholic priest incited a mob in Guadalajara to such a frenzy they murdered an

MEXICO

Monterrey •

Mexico City ◉

American missionary and his Mexican assistant.

Inherent Stumbling Blocks

By 1982, opposition to evangelical witness had generally assumed more subtle but no less formidable tactics. In that year also, the Mexican Alliance churches were transferred from oversight by the Office of Specialized Ministries to cooperation with the Division of Overseas Ministries.

Over a period of two decades, the work had developed into clusters of churches stretching across Mexico—churches as diverse in character as they were separated in distance. The churches fell into three areas: the federal district, including the capital; the southern border next to Gua-

temala; and the northern border facing the United States.

In 1962, the first Alliance church in Mexico City had matured enough that the pastor turned it over to his assistant. He began a second church in Puebla, a large city southeast of the capital. The federal district contained two churches by 1982, including one in Neza, a suburb of 3 million people known as the world's largest slum.

A number of small, unorganized churches in the mountainous area bordering Guatelama considered themselves Alliance. They received visits from time to time from Alliance pastors of churches across the border. When the organizational transfer took place in 1982, representatives of the south traveled 700 miles to the three-hour session in Mexico City.

The most progressive and numerous churches ranged along Mexico's northern border. Over a ten-year period ending in 1982, Alliance churches grew from nine to nineteen, membership from 245 to 664. Rev. and Mrs. Ramon Esparza were largely responsible for this growth. During an earlier period, the Carl Mollings also played a significant role.

While Esparza pastored a C&MA Spanish-language church in Brownsville, Texas, he crossed the border frequently to preach in a rural area of Matamoros. A small congregation organized, and in 1962 they built a chapel.

Meanwhile, Esparza started a Bible study in Matamoros proper and eventually devoted his full time to pastoring the growing congregation. He started four churches in the Noreste District by 1982, including one in the large industrial city of Monterrey.

He was equally concerned about training laymen for ministry and enrolled forty students in Theological Education by Extension courses by 1983. Meanwhile, Kay, his wife, organized youth groups and prayer fellowships for the women.

Youth work in Mexico, like other Latin American countries, plays a crucial role in church life. Since more than half the population of Mexico is under age seventeen, young people form an important part of the church's evangelistic efforts.

In 1982, for example, Mrs. Esparza organized a two-day training seminar and then dispatched ninety-six young people to ten churches for summer ministries. In

one location, a group conducted Vacation Bible School (VBS) for 300 children.

All told, the summer youth corps conducted VBS classes for 2,000 children and helped over 570 children to trust in Jesus.

Carl Molling was working for the German embassy in Mexico City prior to World War II when he was hospitalized with serious illness. He later married one of the hospital nurses who had cared for him. She proved an even greater blessing by leading him to the Lord.

The Mollings moved to Tucson, Arizona, where they attended an Alliance church. He became greatly concerned for villagers in the Mexican state of Chihuahua. Through periodic visits in the early 1950s, he succeeded in organizing six churches, which became part of the Alliance in 1967.

National Identity

These diverse churches, in widely scattered areas ranging from the northern to the southern border, lacked a sense of national identity. Churches in the north of Mexico had developed a strong sense of unity, but a lack of strong, full-time lead-

(Far left) The main cathedral in Mexico City contrasts sharply with the Monterrey Alliance Church (left).

ership in the south left the churches scattered and weak.

Encouraging them to become a unified national church became a major priority of the regional director. Two spiritual retreats in 1984 brought the people closer together, and they began thinking about a national identity. The first national church conference convened two years later, setting the stage for a stronger, unified ministry.

The Alliance mission and national church face an awesome task. Mexico looms as one of the most spiritually needy nations in Latin America. Mexico City alone represents a major challenge to missions.

Calling it "an alarming giant," sociologists speak of the nation's capital in near-apocalyptic terms. Studies project that by the year 2000, still the world's largest city, it will have over 31 million people. One writer pointed out that in 1985 there were more young people under the age of fifteen in Mexico City than all the people in Los Angeles.[6]

Despite its proximity to the United States, Mexico is a first-rate mission field the Alliance needs to take seriously. ☐

CHURCH AND MISSION

OFFICIAL NAME OF CHURCH:	The Christian and Missionary Alliance of Mexico
ENTRY BY MISSIONARIES:	1954
NUMBER OF MISSIONARIES:	16
ORGANIZED CHURCHES:	19
UNORGANIZED CHURCHES AND PREACHING POINTS:	23
BAPTIZED CHURCH MEMBERS:	2,263
INCLUSIVE MEMBERSHIP:	3,183
EDUCATION:	Bible Institute-(Reynosa) 4 TEE Centers

COUNTRY

OFFICIAL NAME:	United Mexican States
FORM OF GOVERNMENT:	Federal Republic
OFFICIAL LANGUAGE(S):	Spanish
AREA:	761,604 sq. mi.
POPULATION:	88,087,000
CAPITAL:	Mexico
PER CAPITA INCOME:	$2,082.00
LITERACY:	80%
RELIGIOUS AFFILIATION:	Roman Catholic 88%, Protestant 4%

PERU

A City Set Upon a Hill

GOD HAS A WAY of permitting unprincipled men to set the stage for His marvelous acts. Lima is one such stage. Although founded in treachery, greed and violence, the city has become a model of God's power and grace in urban evangelism.

Renowned as the "City of Kings," it stood front stage and center for three centuries as capital of Spain's empire in the New World. Lima had the greatest concentration of wealth and power in Latin America, but it was a troubled city from the start.

The conquistador Francisco Pizarro founded Lima in 1535 after crushing the Inca Empire, the continent's oldest and most highly developed civilization.

By laying treachery on top of deceit, he had captured Atahualpa, the Inca ruler, who offered him a room full of gold and gems in exchange for his freedom. Pizarro agreed to the swap—and then had Atahualpa strangled after the ransom was paid.

The trail of blood had only begun. Pizarro quarreled with his coleader, had him executed and was himself later assassinated in revenge. Intrigue, treachery and murder continued in Lima until a strong governor wrested control in 1555. Thus began three centuries of Spanish rule enforced by sword and pike.[1]

Over 400 years later, in 1958, God began to do something marvelous in Lima. And, as often happens, He used a most unlikely beginning: a foreign missionary and a small group of believers that included Indians and mountain people—the kind of folk the proud city dwellers looked down on. They overlooked the slurs and threats, the opposition and suspicion, and started an Alliance church with twenty-eight members.

Another missionary arrived to pastor the congregation the following year. With a vision of reaching the middle class of Lima, he got the mission to purchase a strategic property in the Lince District. Perhaps without realizing the full significance of that step, missionary Kenn Opperman set in motion an internationally effective program of urban evangelism.

Realizing that *Limenos* (Lima residents) refused to take rural church workers seriously, he convinced an Argentinian Alliance pastor to lead the congregation.

They conducted twelve two-week campaigns during 1960 and 1961, and saw the congregation grow to seventy people. Converts included twenty-three members of a prominent Chinese family, who became key people in the church.[2]

Evangelism-in-Depth came to Lima in 1967, and for one year mobilized Protestants for door-to-door evangelism and public rallies. The growing Lince congregation, impressed by the results, continued their efforts for another six months after the citywide campaign ended. Their hearts reached out to embrace all of Lima as they prayed for a citywide witness.

The shattered myth of urban indifference, the reality of middle-class Limenos coming to Christ, the enthusiasm of a church that envisioned great possibilities for evangelism, all came together in 1972, as a new era dawned for the Lince Church.[3]

Discussions, plans and preparation materialized into the most intensive evangelistic effort to reach middle-class people ever undertaken by the Alliance.[4] A highly qualified Argentinian pastor, Dr. Alfredo Smith, developed as the pacesetter for the team.

PERU

Iquitos

Piura

Chimbote

Huanuco

Lima

Cuzco

Arequipa

The stage was set for an exciting pioneer project in urban evangelism.

Phase One: Lince

The year 1973 saw the beginning of *Lima al Encuentro con Dios*. The mission provided funds, one-half grant and one-half loan, to build an attractive church center; the congregation organized prayer cells; individuals witnessed to their friends and invited them to church.

An Encounter coordinating committee, composed of missionaries and Peruvian pastors, agreed to use only the best speakers and musicians for the public campaign. Furthermore, they determined to make all of Lima aware of the meetings through extensive use of radio and print media.

Encounter's ultimate goal at that time was to establish twelve churches with 1,000-seat sanctuaries throughout the city.

Church growth on this scale could never be realized on a financial base of local-church giving or the mission's annual budget. The Encounter program needed an outside organization that could help finance its vision, while local believ-

ers took care of their internal church expenses.

The American-based LeTourneau Foundation, founded by an Alliance layman, loaned money to the North American C&MA to finance the Lince Church facilities. The same funding group also provided money for extensive advertising

in Lima and for travel expenses to bring outside evangelists to Peru.

Other organizations, such as Bible Literature International, helped as well. But without the LeTourneau Foundation, the Encounter program would never have flourished as it did.[5]

Campaign strategy was simple and ex-

The Pueblo Libre Alliance Church in Lima is the largest C&MA church in Peru.

hausting. The church would hold a fifteen-day campaign every month for fifteen months, alternating with Bible classes for the converts until the start of the next campaign.

From October of 1973 to December of 1974, church lights burned twenty-seven nights out of every month for one meeting or another. Over 2,000 people declared their faith in Christ.

The remodeled old structure was used for all activities until construction crews completed a four-story Christian education unit. Encounter meetings then moved to the new unit until a 1,000-seat sanctuary was built. Campaign attendees filled the new church after only four months, and regular attendance jumped to 700.

The campaign proved conclusively, as Dr. Arnold Cook put it, "that the middle class was not so much rejecting Christ as they were rejecting Protestantism with its humble church buildings, inadequately trained pastors, and the lower class, which comprised its congregations."[6]

Phase Two: Pueblo Libre

The original plan included a second congregation. After an evangelist finished a series in the Lince Church, he was to open a campaign with the Jesus Maria congregation. This second project, however, encountered legal snags, and the congregation did not seem ready for such a big step, so arrangements were postponed.

Nevertheless, the Encounter coordinating committee secured a large property in a choice location of the Pueblo Libre District during 1975. They renovated the existing building to accommodate 230 people, and at the same time worked with the Jesus Maria congregation, preparing them for an evangelistic witness.

During a series of meetings in October, the Spirit of God moved across the congregation in a cleansing and refreshing wave. The growth that followed in the church was such that only God could have done it.

By mid-1977, the congregation numbered 360 members—an increase of 1,000 percent in less than two years. The Pueblo Libre Church dedicated its 2,000-seat auditorium one year later, while 3,800 people looked on or looked in from the outside. That very evening of the first day in their new building, the church launched a fifteen-day campaign with 2,000 people attending.

Phase Three: Miraflores

A core group of fifty dedicated people branched off from the Lince congregation in 1977 to form a third church, in the Miraflores District, an upper-middle-class area of Lima. By 1986, membership had grown to nearly 600, and the congregation needed three Sunday morning services to handle the many people who attended. The church began construc-

Pueblo Libre's seating capacity of 2,000 is often crowded.

The Lince church has sponsored over ten new congregrations.

tion of its 1,100-seat sanctuary in 1987.

During the same period, the Alliance received an unusual request from a German mission working among Lima children. The mission's nearly empty El Agustino Church contrasted sharply with the bustling activity of its adjoining preschool day-care center, grade school and secondary school.

Kinderwerk Lima, sponsoring mission of the El Agustino school-church complex, watched the growing Alliance churches with admiration. In 1978, mission leaders requested Alliance personnel to provide leadership for their church and help it grow.

An Encounter program of evangelism produced 390 conversion decisions and fifty-six baptisms. Membership rose to 102 and average attendance grew to 150. In less than two years, the El Agustino Church faced the necessity of either a second Sunday service or building an addition.

Phase Four: Proliferate and Consolidate

Seven years of campaigns by *Lima Al Encuentro con Dios* brought dramatic changes to the Alliance community in Peru.

The four Encounter churches reported a total of 3,005 members—more than half the C&MA Peruvian membership in 1980. During the previous year, the four had given 80 percent of the national church's total budget. Together they employed twenty-three pastors and two Christian-education workers.

Fifteen Alliance churches throughout Lima pointed people to Christ in a variety of locations, such as storefront chapels, a former bar, a soccer club headquarters, and commodious church sanctuaries. They formed the Metropolitan Convention of Alliance Churches in order to advance their work on a united front.

Pueblo Libre seemed by 1980 to spe-

cialize in evangelism, with its record of 3,702 decisions—more than the other three churches combined. By the end of 1985, it became the largest evangelical church in Peru.

Lince, however, majored in giving: Its monthly average income of $7,342 topped the combined giving of the other three churches, even that of the mission's monthly budget. Lince also sponsored ten new churches, providing them with pastors and some of its fine church members.

Meanwhile, both Miraflores and El Agustino grew in size, filling available space in their two sanctuaries. In addition, seven new churches traced their beginnings directly to Encounter efforts.

Seven years of experience qualified the Lima churches to sponsor their first Seminar for Urban Evangelism and Leadership. During four weeks in 1980, over forty Alliance pastors and missionaries came from all parts of Latin America, to

(Above) *This Encounter sign is a familiar sight throughout Peru;* (right)
highland Indians pose a great challenge to church evanglelism.

see and learn from the Encounter program.

The seminar was designed to inspire pastors to return home and launch their own versions of mass urban evangelism, and in numerous instances this happened. The 1980 seminar was the first such annual event.

Consolidating gains gave the Encounter coordinating committee constant concern. A retention rate of 15 to 20 percent seemed high by current standards, but that still meant that eight out of ten who professed faith in Christ did not follow on to become His disciples.

The Encounter churches organized a system of training and teaching on five levels, to help both new believers and church workers. The network began with "academies" to establish new believers in God's Word. Correspondence courses, TEE classes, and Christian education material provided graduated levels of instruction, culminating in evening classes at the Alliance Bible Institute's new three-story center in Lima.

The pressing need to provide biblical instruction to the rapidly growing number of new believers forced the Encounter leadership to become innovative. Their solution: "The Bible Academy of the Air."

The half-hour program began broadcasting twice weekly in 1980 to home Bible studies throughout Lima and Peru. Trained tutors then led group discussions of the topic taught by the radio pastor. The method not only proved effective in helping new Christians, it encouraged still others to commit their lives to Christ.

Bolivia and Beyond

It was inevitable that churches committed to evangelism should eventually look beyond the borders of their own country.

The Lince Church took the initiative in sending a young Peruvian couple to La Paz, Bolivia, where a group of believers had already been established by an Ecuadorian Alliance couple and a Bible translator. The congregation consisted of thirty members and averaged sixty in attendance by 1982.[7]

The group rented classrooms in the American School at first, but later decided they had to find a more central location if they were to attract new people. Economic conditions in Bolivia precluded building a church at the time, but the congregation secured a charter from the government, in anticipation of better days to come. Their patience was rewarded in 1986, when the church was able to rent a large house on a main boulevard and begin Lima-style meetings.

Meanwhile, like sparks from a forest fire igniting other areas, the effects of *Lima al Encuentro con Dios* spread in unpredictable directions. A congregation formed in Cajamarca, about 500 kilometers north of Lima.

In Barranca, some 200 kilometers north of Lima, a small group listened to Sunday evening broadcasts from the Pueblo Libre Church. They asked for a pastoral visit and eventually formed a congregation.

Eight prayer cells in Callao, Lima's port city, discovered one another and decided to unite and start their own church. They called for a pastor and rented a union hall in April. By year's end, 300 people had been converted in meetings, attendance rose to 120 and membership stood at sixty.

Cuzco, ancient Imperial City of the Incas, took little note of a small but enthusiastic nucleus of Christians that called for the formation of an Alliance church within its walls. They had all been

converted in Lima's Encounter campaigns.

The Alliance responded with a Peruvian pastor and a missionary couple. Undaunted by the city's strong attachment to tradition, for a time the congregation rented a union hall in the central square, near Cuzco's main cathedral.

Heritage of Faith

In terms of history, the Lima churches arrived late in the religious saga of Peru. Once again, it was James Thompson, educator by profession and colporteur by calling, who first brought the evangelical message to Peru.

Thompson arrived in 1822, at the invitation of the liberator Don Jose de San Martin, to introduce a system of popular education. He secured cooperation from many Catholic priests as he founded schools and distributed Scriptures.

The next Bible colporteur was not so fortunate.

Argentine-born Francisco Penzotti entered Peru in 1888. He tried to observe the law by conducting services only behind closed doors, since Roman Catholicism was the only official religion. But he was nonetheless apprehended and thrown in jail. He was detained in filthy dungeon-like quarters for eight months, while fanatical Catholics demanded his execution.

A story published in the *New York Herald* aroused public opinion in the United States and England, causing Peruvian authorities to release Penzotti. He thus won the first important case for religious liberty in Peru.[8]

When The Christian and Missionary Alliance arrived in 1925, however, bigotry still ruled with a violent hand in many interior areas. Missionaries established a jungle base camp among the Indians, but months passed before the local people overcame their fear and suspicion enough to visit the station.

Meanwhile, other workers established a station in Huanuco, the district center for a large area. Their arrival was sharply contested. Local priests, who seemed to have more influence over women than men, incited them to riot against "devil-worshipping Protestants."

Unlike their wives, Huanuco men gen-

A highland Indian woman.

erally responded to the Gospel. In ensuing domestic quarrels, a missionary observed wryly, "many earthenware jars were broken over the heads of rebellious wives."[9]

Persecution and opposition gradually died down, and Huanuco became a very responsive area of ministry for a period. The main city congregation became a strong self-supporting church, while a hundred smaller groups sprang up in the surrounding area.

At first, the Alliance joined with two other missions to form the Evangelical Church of Peru. The arrangement worked for several years, but irreconcilable differences arose, especially in regards to church leadership. The Alliance considered trained, full-time clergy essential, while other mission leaders viewed "professional" pastors as a hindrance to church growth.

Lima-based Alliance missionaries founded the Peruvian Bible Institute in 1933 and invited other missions to cooperate in the venture. Later, recognizing that church growth could be better achieved by each mission's working in its own way, the Alliance adopted an independent course.

The Lima institute was reorganized in 1946 as an autonomous interdenominational school. The Alliance founded the Huanuco Bible Institute three years later, to train Alliance workers.

Then the mission withdrew from the church union in 1954 to concentrate on establishing churches in its given area of responsibility. The Peruvian Alliance Church was officially organized and recognized by the government one year later.

Dynamics of Change

Encuentro con Dios has had to adapt its strategy to changing conditions.

Original strategy called for twelve churches, each capable of serving a thousand people. But Lima had twenty-one churches by 1985 and several more that could begin, each with a nucleus of one hundred people. Growth had outstripped the financial means to help all these congregations erect large churches, but Encounter plans ultimately to have twenty large churches in the city. Established churches commit 20 percent of their monthly income to help daughter churches through a revolving church-growth fund.

By the mid-1980s, Lima churches used more local campaigns than citywide efforts and found that results were about the same. Even weekend meetings in homes, called Christian Growth Cells, proved effective. In one weekend during 1986, twelve of these cells reported a total of 550 commitments to faith in Christ.

Meanwhile, the concept of Encounter campaigns was impacting on the provinces.

Piura, for example, is a city of 200,000 sitting on the edge of the desert of northern Peru. Two missionary couples entered the city in 1970, without a single Christian to count on.

Door-to-door visitation graduated into house meetings. The church in Piura organized two years later with thirteen members, a national pastor and a missionary team. By 1981, Sunday morning attendance grew to 200, and the church was working on a 700-seat sanctuary in preparation for Encounter-type evangelism.

Similar accounts of response and growth characterized other towns and cities. Lima's Encounter program accomplished two great things for churches throughout Peru when it shattered the false and unattractive stereotype of Protestantism and created momentum for the Gospel.

Lima, the "City of Kings" built on a conquistador's treachery and greed, has become by God's grace an outstanding model of urban evangelism for the King of kings. □

CHURCH AND MISSION

OFFICIAL NAME OF CHURCH:	The Christian and Missionary Alliance Church of Peru
ENTRY BY MISSIONARIES:	1925
NUMBER OF MISSIONARIES:	39
ORGANIZED CHURCHES:	91
UNORGANIZED CHURCHES AND PREACHING POINTS:	112
BAPTIZED CHURCH MEMBERS:	18,534
INCLUSIVE MEMBERSHIP:	31,872
EDUCATION:	A. B. Simpson Elementary and High School Bible Institute-(Lima) 30 TEE Centers
RADIO BROADCASTS:	5
PAGES PRINTED:	237,000

COUNTRY

OFFICIAL NAME:	Republic of Peru
FORM OF GOVERNMENT:	Constitutional Republic
OFFICIAL LANGUAGE(S):	Spanish, Quechua
AREA:	496,222 sq. mi.
POPULATION:	21,792,000
CAPITAL:	Lima
PER CAPITA INCOME:	$940.00
LITERACY:	88%
RELIGIOUS AFFILIATION:	Roman Catholic 90%, Protestant 3.6%

SURINAM

To the Chinese First

SURINAM IS A NEWCOMER, both to the family of nations and to the fellowship of overseas Alliance churches.

Before independence in 1975, it carried the name of Dutch Guiana. The area was something of a consolation prize, ceded in 1667 to Holland by England after taking New Amsterdam (now New York) from the Dutch by force.

Although new to the Alliance, Surinam has a distinctive place in the religious history of the continent. British and Dutch Guianas, reflecting the religious character of their colonial masters, had the largest concentration of Protestants in both Central and South America.[1]

As late as 1917, the Protestant population of 159,600 in the Guianas totaled more than the combined Protestant communities in all the rest of Latin America.[2]

Unlike most other Latin American nations, Surinam has almost no Spanish or Indian population. Hindustanis and Javanese from the Asian Pacific constitute more than 50 percent of the population. Overseas and mainland Chinese also have a significant community in the country.

Chinese Challenge

Through contacts in Surinam, the Chinese Alliance churches of Canada became interested in establishing a church in the Chinese community of Paramaribo, the capital. A survey trip in 1978 resulted in appointment of the first missionaries to Surinam the following year.

Six years later, the congregation dedicated a church building capable of seating 400 people. In less than three years, the church was debt free. Government officials proudly pointed to the attractive sanctuary as one of the city's premier sights.

Sunday church attendance in 1986 varied from ninety-five to 125, and Sunday school attracted some seventy children. An impressive system of advance preparation enabled worshipers to follow the sermon in one of four languages. Written copies of the coming Sunday message were distributed to translators

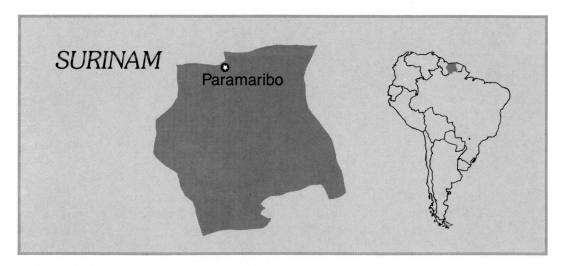

SURINAM
Paramaribo

on the previous Wednesday, so they could be well aware of the topic.

The congregation also showed concern for a sister community in neighboring French Guiana. The pastor and a visitation team went from door to door among the Chinese in Cayenne, the capital, until they had enough new believers to form a prayer cell.

The church needed these encouraging steps because, by the mid-1980s, it faced severe testing:

The missionary pastor died, abruptly ending a fruitful and growing ministry. . . .

Economic setbacks and severe government policies forced businessmen and their families to leave the country. . . .

Church attendance plateaued, as the arrival of new members was offset by the departure of others. . . .

Young people growing into their teens were losing interest, because Dutch was their first language, and nothing was available to them in special courses or training by the church. . . .

Monetary restrictions hindered efforts to establish a church in neighboring French Guiana's Chinese community.

The church, encouraged by a new pastor, has shown willingness to overcome these obstacles. One change involved greater emphasis on Dutch for youth activities. A number of young Chinese from mainland China have rejected their atheistic background and become Christians.

Surinam, the young nation of Latin America, has more to look forward to than back on. So does the youthful Alliance in Paramaribo, the capital city. They both have much to overcome, but one of the nice things about youth is that they keep growing. ☐

CHURCH AND MISSION

OFFICIAL NAME OF CHURCH:	Surinam Christian and Missionary Alliance
ENTRY BY MISSIONARIES:	1979
NUMBER OF MISSIONARIES:	0
ORGANIZED CHURCHES:	1
UNORGANIZED CHURCHES AND PREACHING POINTS:	0
BAPTIZED CHURCH MEMBERS:	112
INCLUSIVE MEMBERSHIP:	170
MEDICAL WORK:	0
EDUCATION:	0
RADIO BROADCASTS:	0
PAGES PRINTED:	0

COUNTRY

OFFICIAL NAME:	Surinam
FORM OF GOVERNMENT:	Republic
OFFICIAL LANGUAGE(S):	Dutch
AREA:	63,037 sq. mi.
POPULATION:	400,000
CAPITAL:	Paramaribo
PER CAPITA INCOME:	$2,920.00
LITERACY:	80%
RELIGIOUS AFFILIATION:	Muslim 19%, Hindu 27%, Roman Catholic 21.6%, Protestant 19.9%

VENEZUELA

The Second Time Took

VENEZUELA is commonly considered one of the last Latin American nations entered by Protestant missions. The date of entry generally cited is 1910, when the Brethren-sponsored Christian Missions in Many Lands established a permanent presence.[1]

That perception, however, needs clarifying, and the key word is "permanent."

As early as 1854, a Bible society representative distributed the Holy Scriptures in Venezuela. One self-supporting missionary made Caracas his base in 1865, as did a Brethren couple.

None of these efforts had the quality of permanence. The missionaries soon departed, leaving few traces of their work.

Initial Alliance penetration proved temporary, as well. Considering "the destitute condition of Venezuela" in 1895, the C&MA Board of Managers appointed Miss Bessie White and Miss Bessie Lanman to begin pioneer work in the capital city.[2]

Rev. and Mrs. Gerard A. Bailly came two years later, joined by still another single woman the following year. In Caracas, they erected the first Protestant chapel in the nation and eventually established four main stations.

Bailly joined the American Bible Society in 1914 and directed the activities of numerous local colporteurs. The Alliance work, lacking strong leadership, declined and disappeared.

It may appear that the investment of lives and money was wasted, but if nothing else, one conversion in 1900 brought remarkable results.

Bailly wrote an article on Angel Villamil Ortiz for the C&MA magazine. "A young priest under the pretext of a vacation," he recounted, "received a leave of absence from his parish in Barceloneta, Puerto Rico, but really threw off his official robes never to don them again.

"He went to the Island of St. Thomas, declared for Protestantism in the Moravian Church and was married. He had purposed to go to Mexico, but a steamer arriving in the port bound for Venezuela came first, and not knowing hardly whither he went, was led of God to Caracas and to our Mission. After some months he was fully saved and a little later his wife also.

"The Lord then laid upon him the burning message, 'Go home to thy friends and tell them how great things the Lord hath done for thee, and hath had compassion on thee' " (Mark 5:19).

Ortiz did return to Puerto Rico, and his obedience to the Lord had a singular effect for Alliance missions, both on that island and on the country where Christ had become his Savior.[3]

Debt Repaid

The second Alliance missionary effort in Venezuela owed its beginning to two remarkable factors: Alliance radio broadcasts and gratitude of C&MA churches in Puerto Rico.

Beginning in 1964, *Alianza en Marcha* programs carried by Trans World Radio in Bonaire touched lives all across Venezuela. People not only wrote for spiritual help, they requested that churches be formed in their areas.

A Colombian pastor and his wife agreed to pioneer work for the Alliance in Venezuela, but could not get visas. Attention then focused on a young Puerto Rican who had married a Venezuelan and was finishing seminary studies in the country.

Churches in Puerto Rico agreed to support him in recognition of Venezuela's part in bringing the Gospel and the Alliance to their island.

Jose and Nora Rivera began their ministry in Valencia in 1971. The historic city, founded in 1555, had a population of over one-half million, but no strong gospel witness throughout the southwest section.

Again *Alianza en Marcha* played a key role. Supplied with the names and addresses of respondents in the city, Rivera soon had a nucleus of Christians for a church. Dr. Miguel Lecaro, radio pastor of *Alianza,* came to Valencia in 1972 to conduct a radio rally. Over 160 people jammed into Riveras's residence, which also served as a meeting place.

The Riveras left the work and returned to Puerto Rico in 1979. The church had grown to about forty members in the care of a part-time Venezuelan pastor.

Threatening Factors

Rev. and Mrs. Herbert Garland transferred from Colombia in 1981, to a difficult situation in Valencia. It seemed as if the church, like its pastor, had become part time. Very little was happening, either in the church or its outreach.

Other aspects proved difficult, as well. Garlands' temporary residence turned into classrooms on Sunday. The adjoining chapel, with its corrugated iron roof, seemed to become a baking oven at service time.

But within a year, the congregation's deficit budget gave way to a healthy balance, and attendance doubled, to an average of ninety. Most important, the people began showing concern for other areas of the city and nation.

Growth continued more slowly over the next several years, as difficulties emerged.

The Alliance still had no full-time pastors, though Theological Education by Extension courses proved successful and

(Above) Alliance church in Caracao; (below) an Alliance layman, business manager of the International School of Caracas, hands out flyers for an evangelistic campaign to people passing the church.

a corps of trained and exceptional lay leaders was gradually emerging. The Valencia pastor resigned, rather than devote all his time to church work as requested by the congregation.

Economic conditions further hampered growth, as unemployment soared past 20 percent by 1984. Lowering prices for oil, which constituted 95 percent of Venezuela's national income, pushed inflation to dizzying heights. Over 80 percent of the population lived in towns and cities, not on farms, which meant that for many people, life was reduced to a struggle for survival.[4]

When the veteran missionary couple went on furlough in 1984, the remaining six first-term missionaries represented a combined total of three years' experience. It must have seemed at times as if history would repeat itself and the Alliance would again leave only memories in the country.

Permanence Achieved

Yet by the mid-1980s, the Alliance was firmly established in Venezuela. The church and mission achieved that permanence that had eluded the first attempt in the late 1890s.

The central church in Valencia now

CHURCH AND MISSION

OFFICIAL NAME OF CHURCH:	The Christian and Missionary Alliance of Venezuela
ENTRY BY MISSIONARIES:	1972
NUMBER OF MISSIONARIES:	19
ORGANIZED CHURCHES:	2
UNORGANIZED CHURCHES AND PREACHING POINTS:	4
BAPTIZED CHURCH MEMBERS:	171
INCLUSIVE MEMBERSHIP:	487
MEDICAL WORK:	0
EDUCATION:	3 TEE Centers
RADIO BROADCASTS:	0
PAGES PRINTED:	0

COUNTRY

OFFICIAL NAME:	Republic of Venezuela
FORM OF GOVERNMENT:	Federal Republic
OFFICIAL LANGUAGE(S):	Spanish
AREA:	352,143 sq. mi.
POPULATION:	19,246,000
CAPITAL:	Caracas
PER CAPITA INCOME:	$2,629.00
LITERACY:	86%
RELIGIOUS AFFILIATION:	Roman Catholic 90%, Protestant 2.6%

owned both the property it had previously rented and an adjoining house formerly occupied by a family stridently opposed to the church.

La Esperanza Church, in another part of the city, secured property and was attracting middle-class professional people. Bible studies and preaching points reached out to other areas of Valencia.

After two years of dogged door-to-door visitation in the San Diego Valley area of the city, a missionary couple saw church attendance rise to an average 100 people on Sunday. When fully developed, this new middle-class district of the city would contain nearly 100,000 people.

The church and mission drafted a strategy that would result in a string of churches advancing from Valencia and the capital city to other states by the year 2000. With less than 1 percent of population attending evangelical churches, Caracas stood as one of the least evangelized cities in Latin America.

A century ago, the Alliance had entered Venezuela through its capital city and gave the nation its first Protestant chapel. Before the close of another century, it had returned to reclaim that heritage and build on it. ☐

MIDDLE EAST/
EUROPE

ISRAEL   214

ARAB LANDS   222

EUROPE   240

MIDDLE EAST/EUROPE

The Macedonian Call—Again

CHURCHES of the Middle East and Europe share at least one similarity in their respective religious heritages: the need to recover biblical truths their spiritual forefathers believed so fervently that they redirected the course of humanity.

Each in its own era and region embraced the Gospel and grew strong in faith.

Each obeyed the Great Commission and dispatched missionaries to the outer reaches of its known world.

Each allowed love to cool and faith to fragment to the point that the Macedonian Call once heard from Europe and answered from the Middle East has become their common cry: "Come over and help us."

Decline of Jerusalem

Jerusalem was the starting point of the original Christian missionary movement. The Book of Acts records that many Jewish pilgrims heard the Gospel for the first time in the Holy City at Pentecost. They carried the Good News back home to their communities and synagogues.

Tradition claims that the eleven apostles got together in Jerusalem after Pentecost and partitioned the known world into areas of individual responsibility. Their intention was to fulfill the Great Commission mandate, "Go into all the world and preach the Gospel."

Eusebius Pamphilus (260-339), one of the Early Church fathers and a church historian, listed the missionary activities of several apostles.

"But the holy apostles and disciples of our Saviour, being scattered over the whole world," he wrote, "Thomas, according to tradition, received Parthia as his allotted region; Andrew received Scythia, and John, Asia, where, after continuing for some time, he died at Ephesus. Peter appears to have preached through Pontus, Galatia, Bithynia, Cappadocia and Asia, to the Jews that were scattered abroad."[1]

Those who remained in the Holy City wanted it to become the religious capital for Jesus' followers, as it already was for Judaism.

"Jerusalem was to them the centre of the world; this was where the Lord had died and risen; this was where he would shortly descend again from heaven to proclaim his sovereignty and to accomplish what was still unfulfilled in the purposes of God."[2]

These Jewish believers would have continued in Jerusalem, keeping the Mosaic Law, attending temple prayers and services, formalizing a message distinctly Jewish and proclaiming a suffering Messiah. They did not foresee the danger that "Jerusalem might have become the Mecca of the Christian world; and the Jordan River might have become to Christians what the Ganges River is to Hindus."[3]

A series of events—and nonevents—freed the infant movement from Jerusalem's confining boundaries. Christ did not quickly return to set up His kingdom. Movement of the new religion was outward from Jerusalem, not inward toward it.

Three individuals played a key role in the decline of Jerusalem as the center of Christianity: Stephen, Paul and Peter.

Stephen was martyred, igniting a persecution that scattered most of the believers. Saul of Tarsus, converted on the road to

Damascus, became Paul, Apostle to the Gentiles. Peter, senior member of the Jerusalem church, was the recipient of a vision that undeniably opened the door of salvation to Gentiles on an equal basis with Jews.

The destruction of Jerusalem in A.D. 70 by Roman legions ended the city's future as a geographical center for the followers of Christ. The congregation disbanded and its members scattered before Roman legions surrounded the city. Christendom was set free "to become what its Founder intended it to be—spiritual and not temporal, universal and not provincial."[4]

Rise of Antioch

As would happen repeatedly throughout church history, the center of Christianity moved closer to the area of most response. In the first century, that meant moving northward from Jerusalem to Antioch.

Founded in 300 B.C., by the time of Christ Antioch had become one of the three most important cities of the Roman Empire. Only twenty miles from the Mediterranean Sea on a fertile plain of what is now Syria, Antioch served as a crossroads for some of the main trade routes between east and west, north and south.

The domination of Greek culture and stability of Roman administration made Antioch a safe place for the fledgling movement to grow rapidly. The Gospel naturally flowed along the caravan routes radiating from the city.

The Apostle Paul started on his three epochal missionary tours from Antioch. His travels lasted less than fifteen years but covered the four most populous provinces under Roman rule.

His work laid the foundation for the spiritual conquest of history's most enduring empire.

Paul, however, was not alone in achieving this. Although he is considered the greatest missionary in church history, his efforts were supported, and in sheer numbers even surpassed, by a host of unnamed laypeople. They knew nothing of missionary organization or strategy, but they freely shared the experience of their faith.

Historian Will Durant notes, "Nearly every convert, with the ardor of a revolutionary, made himself an office of propaganda."[5] Stephen Neill adds: "The church of the first Christian generation was a genuinely missionary church . . . . The church could count on the anonymous and unchronicled witness of all the faithful."[6]

Contested Expansion

The total number of Christians rose to approximately one million by A.D. 100,[7] with churches located as far west as Rome and Spain. A century later, Christian communities were still small and scattered, but they had spread throughout the empire a universality remarkable for the times.[8]

J. Herbert Kane estimates that by A.D. 250, the believers in Rome numbered 50,000, supported 100 clergy and cared for 1,500 poor people. Fifty years later, Antioch's population of one-half million was between 20 and 50 percent Christian.[9]

About the same time, perhaps as many as five million of the Roman Empire's fifty million people called themselves Christians, though the distribution was uneven. Up to one-half the population in some parts of Asia Minor were considered followers of Christ, while in Greece the born-again population was almost nil.[10]

Pliny the Younger (61-113), ruler of Bithynia, complained to Emperor Trajan, "The contagion of this superstition has spread not only in the cities but in villages and rural districts . . . . The temples have been almost deserted and the social rites neglected."[11]

The missionary zeal of the church aroused alarm and resentment among Roman rulers who normally exercised a religious policy of "live and let live." They viewed this new religion as a threat to the empire as it spread everywhere and taught that people should worship only God, not Caesar. Christianity therefore became the only religion in the Roman Empire to suffer violent opposition as an official policy over a long period of time.[12]

The church suffered numerous periods of persecution, beginning with Nero in A.D. 64. Like the last convulsive thrashings of a mortally wounded beast, the final ten-year tribulation mounted by Diocletian was the most sustained and cruel. When it ended in A.D. 303, over 1,500 Christians had been martyred, thousands had lost their homes and possessions and many churches had either been destroyed or confiscated.

Persecution, however, only served to strengthen the church and give it added visibility.

"It was severe enough to serve as at least a partial deterrent to light-hearted adoption of the faith," according to historian Kenneth Scott Latourette. "It gave tone to the morale of the church and strengthened the sense of solidarity against paganism. Yet it was not severe enough seriously to threaten the existence of Christianity or even greatly to weaken the Christian community."[13]

Hollow Triumph

When Constantine fought his way to the throne in A.D. 306, the role of Christianity in the Roman Empire suddenly and drastically changed. Believing he had been aided by the Christian's God in his struggle for power, the emperor ended persecution of the church.

More secure on his throne by the year 313, Constantine issued the Edict of Milan, granting toleration of religions in general and restitution in particular for Christians who had suffered losses under Diocletian. The edict began an unaccustomed era of peace, prosperity and popularity for the church.

Constantine himself converted to Christianity ten years later, thus making it the preferred religion of Rome. The whole realm opened to missionary work, pagans stampeded into the church, and becoming Christian was fashionable, even profitable. Christian clergy, for example, were exempted from paying taxes. The Christian Sunday became a legal holiday. Constantine erected and enlarged churches, authorizing bishops to call upon civil authorities for help in building churches.

"It seems likely," believes Neill, "that the number of Christians in the empire at least quadrupled itself in the century that followed the Edict of Milan."[14]

Constantine's generous policy, unfortunately, did as much harm as the ten preceding periods of persecution.

John Caldwell Thiessen points out that once Christianity became popular, it declined in vitality. Great numbers of

unconverted pagans brought their practices into the church. Simplicity of worship gave way to elaborate ceremonies. True missionary activity declined, while conquered peoples were forcibly converted.[15]

The group that seemed most resistant to the Gospel was the Jewish community. Though lay missionaries persisted in witness to the Jews over a long period of time, they encountered the same frustrations experienced by the Apostle Paul, who was rebuffed when he went to the synagogues first in his missionary travels. Even the shrinking number of Jewish believers failed to win a following among their own people, and the Jewish Christian church eventually disappeared.

"Jewish Christendom waned and dwindled and finally died away in heresy."[16] Centuries would pass before the Jewish church would be reborn in the land of its birth through the witness of Gentile believers.

Judaism suffered a fate no less tragic, though not terminal. As the Jews continued to reject the Gospel, the impatience of Christians soured into frustration, then to anger and finally hatred. The church that had so recently paid dearly for its faith under the Caesars now instituted persecution as an accepted weapon of coercion in an attempt to convert the followers of Judaism.

"Such an injustice as that done by the Gentile church to Judaism is almost unprecedented in the annals of history," judged Adolf Harnack. "The daughter first robbed her mother and then repudiated her."[17]

Everything considered—the lowered level of spirituality in the church and its heightened aggressiveness against those of differing persuasions—the Edict of Milan became something of a hollow triumph for Christendom.

Vocational Shift

For the first several hundred years, missionary work in both the East and the West surged forward on the shoulders and in the hearts of lay Christians who took the Gospel wherever they went. They did a remarkable job, says Latourette: "Never in the history of the race had so complete a religious revolution been wrought in so short a time among so large a proportion of the population."[18]

From about A.D. 500, however, the initiative in missions shifted from laypeople to career workers.

Latourette notes that between the fifth and nineteenth centuries, "a practically continuous flow of missionaries poured into non-Christian regions . . . . The professional missionary seems to have been much more prominent in these ten centuries than in the first few hundred years of the expansion of the faith."[19]

Celtic Catalyst

Ireland was the last major area to be evangelized during the first five hundred years of the church. But, like the Apostle Paul, it "labored more abundantly than they all," and quickly forged to the fore.

The most important event in Irish Christianity actually began when a sparsely educated but warmhearted boy named Patrick was snatched from his home in Scotland and carried off to Ireland as a slave. During the next six years of herding sheep, he learned to live close to the Great Shepherd. After escaping from captivity in Ireland, he received a vision similar to the Apostle Paul's Macedonian Call and returned to Ireland to evangelize his former masters.

During Patrick's thirty-five years of ministry in the fifth century, he baptized thousands of converts, established hundreds of churches and ordained clergy to lead them. Contrary to widely publicized claims, Patrick was not a Roman Catholic missionary sent to Ireland by the pope.

He was, in the words of V. Raymond Edman, "a Bible-reading, Bible-believing, and Bible-preaching missionary"[20] who formed Irish Christianity into a powerful force for the Lord.

Kane calls the Irish church of the sixth and seventh centuries "one of the greatest missionary churches of all time."[21] From its well-ordered monasteries monks spread out to evangelize not only the Celts of Ireland but also the Picts of Scotland, the Angles and Saxons of England, the Frisians of Holland. They pressed on to Germany, Switzerland and even northern Italy.

Other dedicated men covered astonishing distances in their missionary crusades. Columba (521-597), an Irishman, tramped through Scotland. Columbanus (543-615) and twelve other Irishmen penetrated Switzerland. Boniface (680-755), an Englishman, did remarkable work in Germany, while a compatriot, Willibrord (657-739), took on Holland and Denmark.

Missions by Force

Some missionary methods, however, might seem strange to a twentieth-century supporter of missions. Hungary was "christianized" by German colonists, Poland through the pious wives of some rulers.

Russia was won through pageantry. An old Russian account, part truth and part legend, records how Vladimir sent representatives to investigate the religions of neighboring countries in order to adopt the religion most sublime. His ambassadors scrutinized Judaism, Islam and Western Christianity and found them all wanting.

When the delegation reached Constantinople and observed the rites of the Eastern Orthodox church, they were ecstatic. They wrote to the czar in glowing terms: "We do not know whether we were in heaven or on earth. It would be impossible to find on earth any splendour greater, and it is vain that we attempt to describe it . . . . Never shall we be able to forget so great a beauty."[22]

Vladimir sent for Orthodox missionaries to convert his people, a task requiring the better part of 500 years and done mostly by Greek clergy.

One of the common methods used to expand the church during the Dark Ages was to convert people en masse by force of arms. Baptism was then imposed as a sign of surrender. In fact, Olaf Tryggvason used the war cry "baptism or battle" in his efforts to bring Norway into Christendom. Those who refused to join the church were either killed or exiled.

The ugliest of these militant methods of expanding the church found expression in the Crusades of the Middle Ages.

The primary aim of the four large and several smaller Crusades between 1095 and 1272 was territorial, not spiritual. The knights of Europe vowed to regain the Holy Sepulchre and all lands occupied by Muslim armies.

These crusaders of the Prince of Peace considered Muslims as

simply "unbelievers who had no right to exist, with whom no faith need be kept, and who might be slaughtered without ruth or pity to the glory of the Christian God."[23]

The Jewish population of Palestine fared no better. When the crusaders liberated Jerusalem in 1099, they were not content with killing the entire Muslim garrison. They massacred some seventy thousand Muslim civilians, herded the city's surviving Jews into a synagogue, and then burned them alive.

The crusaders then filed into the Church of the Holy Sepulchre and had a thanksgiving service, praising God for His help in achieving victory.

For Western Christians, the Crusades happened long ago, only to be remembered and romanticized in novels about noble knights. But "to every Muslim in the Mediterranean lands," writes Neill, "the Crusades are an event of yesterday, and the wounds are ready at any moment to break out afresh."[24]

Similar deep resentments run through the Orthodox communities. "Even today," noted one missionary in 1984, "the Eastern hierarchies, far from applauding either Roman Catholic or Protestant missionary efforts, are more inclined to regard them as comparable to the Crusades of earlier centuries."[25]

Monks and Friars

Rulers who decreed the mass conversion of their subjects in the Middle Ages left the task of baptism and instruction to the church. The ones charged with the responsibility of christianizing the masses were not the pioneering full-time missionaries of an earlier era. Those had been replaced by monks who, for about five hundred years, provided the church with its foreign workers.

The idea of monastic missions contradicts the usual perception of monasteries as cloistered havens for introverts fleeing society in search of salvation through solitude and meditation.

"Some monks almost inevitably became missionaries," explains Latourette. "The monastic movement attracted those who were not content with the superficial religion which went by the name of Christianity, but were resolved to give themselves entirely to the faith."

"What more natural than that some of them should be caught by that desire to propagate the faith?" he reasons.[26]

The initiative of missions passed from monasteries to religious orders in the early 1200s. For the next two centuries, two great orders of friars, the Franciscans and the Dominicans, carried the banner of Rome to the outer perimeters of civilization. Their emergence as missionary societies coincided with—and depended upon—the two maritime powers of the Iberian Peninsula: Spain and Portugal.

Franciscan and Dominican priests marched with Spanish conquistadores in the New World, sailed with Portuguese explorers down the coastline of Africa, accompanied Italian merchants to the Far East.

A declaration by Ferdinand and Isabella of Spain expressed the close ties between mission and monarchy: "Nothing do we desire more than the publication and the amplification of the Evangelic Law, and the conversion of the Indians to our Holy Catholic Faith."[27]

When the Reformation dawned over Europe in 1517, Roman Catholic missionaries were already operating worldwide, while the Reformers were otherwise preoccupied.

Several factors contributed to the lack of missionary vision during the early Reformation years. One reason was survival itself: Luther, Calvin and other such leaders were too busy fighting for their lives and the survival of their movements to give much thought to faraway places. Unfortunately, they were also too busy fighting among themselves.

Another factor contributing to missions myopia was theology. Many Protestant leaders actually believed the Great Commission was intended only for the original apostles.

Calvin himself wrote, "We are taught that the kingdom of Christ is neither to be advanced nor maintained by the industry of men, but this is the work of God alone."[28]

So while Protestants dug their foxholes deeper and consolidated their position in Europe, papal emissaries spread out to conquer the rest of the world. Kane and others estimate that during this period, Rome won more converts worldwide than it lost to European Protestantism.[29]

Missionary vision among Protestants did not become a major factor until England and Holland emerged as great maritime powers and vigorously expanded their trade routes. This fact may also help explain the glaring unconcern in early years of the Reformation. Luther's Germany was land oriented and Calvin's Switzerland landlocked, while Catholic Spain and Portugal dominated the high seas.

Early Protestant Pioneers

Though early Protestant missions paralleled national developments, their dynamics grew out of biblical teaching and spiritual experience.

These qualities were rooted in the Pietist Movement sparked by Philip Spener, a German Lutheran pastor in the latter 1600s. He maintained that "there can be no missionary vision without evangelistic zeal . . . no evangelistic zeal without personal piety . . . no personal piety without a genuine conversion experience."[30]

Spener helped develop Halle University in Prussia as the great educational center of Pietism and missionary enterprise. His successor at Halle, August Franke, became one of the outstanding missionary statesman of the eighteenth century.

Danish King Frederick IV, who sensed a spiritual responsibility for the colonists and native peoples of a crown colony on the east coast of India, visited Franke at Halle. Out of their discussions grew the Danish-Halle Mission in 1705, a cooperative effort in which Halle provided the personnel and Denmark the funds, at least initially.

Pietism also launched one of the most remarkable missionary movements in church history: the Moravian Brethren. Count Nicolaus Ludwig Zinzendorf (1700-1760), godson to Spener and student under Franke at Halle, early became an ardent Pietist. He declared when still a youth: "I have one passion; it is He and He alone."[31]

Zinzendorf gave shelter on his Saxony estate to some Waldensian and Moravian refugees, survivors of a religious brotherhood nearly wiped out by Jesuits during the Counter Revolution. Taking the name *Herrnhut* (The Lord's Watch), the Moravian Church grew to a worldwide missionary movement under Zinzendorf's leadership.

Though despised as ignorant people by the cultured society

of their day, the Moravians set for themselves a high standard of commitment to Christ. When one man was asked if he would go to Labrador, for example, he promptly responded: "Yes, tomorrow, if I am only given a pair of shoes."

"Within twenty years of the commencement of their missionary work in 1732, the Moravian Brethren had started more missions than Anglicans and Protestants had started during the two preceding centuries."[32]

Thiessen makes the astonishing observation that "a survey of the fields entered by the Moravians shows there is scarcely a country where they have not at least attempted to gain a foothold."[33] Even as recently as 1930, the proportion of missionaries to communicant members was one in twelve![34]

Buildup and Breakthrough

The real breakthrough in Protestant missionary endeavor, however, was yet to come. Various factors were lining up to provide a catapult for a remarkable century of missionary activity originating in Europe.

Scientists and inventors harnessed power through the steam engine and brought the world closer to home through steamships. Businessmen and financiers founded trading companies that made insular Europeans world conscious. Entrepreneurs sparked an industrial revolution that demanded raw materials from faraway places. Explorers sailed the seven seas in search of new resources and untapped markets. Politicians and statesmen spearheaded the expansionist mood under national colors.

The inquisitive mood of Europe, including England, quickly turned acquisitive. "Exploration was followed by exploitation,"

wryly comments Neill. "The white man came to trade, but he stayed to rule."[35]

The Christian community, as often happens, reflected the national mood of expansion and began singing Isaac Watts' great hymn, "Jesus Shall Reign Where'er the Sun." The Pietist Movement in Germany and the Evangelical Awakening in England aroused Protestants from their cramped, self-centered world.

An often overlooked catalyst of the eighteenth-century surge of missionary activity was a widespread prayer movement. It began with the publication in 1723 of a treatise on missions by Robert Millar. In his book he promoted intercessory prayer as a powerful means of converting the heathen world. The idea caught on, and within twenty years prayer groups were meeting throughout the British Isles.

Christians in the American colonies were invited to join in a seven-year "Concert of Prayer" beginning in 1746. America's most famous preacher, Jonathan Edwards, wrote a pamphlet to promote the movement. Forty years passed before Edwards' powerful call to prayer reached England, but when it did, the Baptists were moved to set aside every Monday for missionary intercession.

"The Great Century"

William Carey is known as "the father of modern missions" and rightly so, even though he built on the work of earlier pioneers like Philip Spener, August Franke and Nicolaus Zinzendorf.

A British cobbler by trade and Baptist preacher by calling,

Carey was obsessed with the spiritual need of unevangelized peoples. He prepared himself for a missionary career by educating himself with books while he mended and made shoes. He was also a linguist, teaching himself Latin, Greek, Hebrew, Italian, French and Dutch. He denied being brilliant, just a plodder. Some plodder!

Carey's ministerial colleagues rebuked him for his missionary aspirations, but being a plodder, he persisted. In 1792, he published an eighty-seven-page book that some consider the most convincing missionary appeal ever written.[36]

But Carey did more than merely read and write about missions. He packed his reluctant wife and four excited children on board ship in 1793 and sailed for India, where he spent the next forty years in continuous ministry.

Carey's book and subsequent reports from India helped stir into existence a whole series of missionary societies in both the Old and New Worlds. The list reads like an honor roll: London Missionary Society (1795), Scottish and Glasgow Missionary Societies (1796), Netherlands Missionary Society (1797), Church Missionary Society (1799), British and Foreign Bible Society (1804), American Board of Commissioners for Foreign Missions (1810), American Baptist Missionary Union (1814), and American Bible Society (1816).

Neill evaluates Carey's work as "a turning point; it marks the entry of the English-speaking world on a large scale into the missionary enterprise—and it has been the English-speaking world which has provided four-fifths of the non-Roman missionaries from the days of Carey until the present time."[37]

To a lesser extent, parallel events were taking place on the continent. The first Swiss mission, the Basel Evangelical Mission Society of Switzerland, organized in 1815 and supplied personnel to the Anglican Church Missionary Society before initiating its own work in 1834, the year Carey died.

During the nineteenth century, at least fourteen other European missionary societies organized in Germany, France, Holland, and the three Scandinavian countries of Denmark, Sweden and Norway.

By the end of "The Great Century," as Latourette terms the period between 1815 and 1914, every Christian nation in the world was represented on the mission field.[38] He described the period in terms similar to the days of the Early Church: "Never before in a period of equal length had Christianity or any other religion penetrated for the first time as large an area as it had in the nineteenth century."[39]

Even Palestine felt the embrace of "The Great Century." One of the early nineteenth-century missions indirectly inspired by Carey was the London Jews' Society, founded in 1820 by Anglicans. Their missionary to Palestine, a Jewish Christian named Joseph Wolff, began the first permanent Protestant witness in Jerusalem since the Crusades.

A second Anglican mission supported by the Church Missionary Society directed its ministry primarily to the Arab population, while a third Anglican group sponsored work throughout the Holy Land. These and later missions concentrated their efforts on reaching the people through hospitals and schools.

The few Palestinians who responded to the Gospel were mostly Arabs. Jewish believers were extremely rare, considered traitors by their own people, and treated as if they were dead.

Agencies, Women and Rome

The expansion of Protestant missions in the 1800s assumes even greater significance because it was volunteer agencies, not denominations, that spearheaded the movement.

Ecclesiastical structure has seldom been enthusiastic about missions. Neill observes, "In many cases the Protestant churches as such were unable or unwilling themselves to take up the cause of missions. This was left to the voluntary societies, dependent on the initiation of consecrated individuals, and relying for financial support on the voluntary gifts of interested Christians."[40]

Ralph D. Winter points out that for almost three hundred years after Luther, the Protestant movement had no effective missions program. "Speaking specifically, then, it is notorious . . . that the churches as churches have never in history cut a very impressive prophetic role, either at home or abroad."[41]

Individuals organized the English Baptist Missionary Society that supported Carey in India, not the denomination. The church's attitude was reflected in one minister's rebuke directed at Carey: "When God pleases to convert the heathen, He will do it without your aid or mine."[42]

The structure and attitude surrounding that first English mission became a long-term pattern in mission/denomination relations.

The rebuke aimed at Carey seems also to have reflected the historical attitude of most missions with regard to single women missionaries. A few great missionary leaders such as Willibrord enlisted women in their cause, but not until the mid-1800s did either Protestant or Roman Catholic agencies begin to send unmarried women overseas on a permanent and continuing basis.

When the first proposal was made, strong opposition arose from every direction. Anglican Bishop Daniel Wilson of Calcutta voiced the pessimism of many when he remarked that such young women "would be married off within the year and would be the source of endless troubles."[43]

This expected result did not materialize, but a totally different one did: Single women contributed greatly to missionary successes of "The Great Century." By the twentieth century, single and married women would greatly outnumber men on the mission field.

Even Adoniram Judson, America's first foreign missionary, showed lukewarm support for single women missionaries. When he learned that Mrs. Charlotte H. White, a widow being sent to India, was married in 1816 while still en route, he sighed with relief.

"Mrs. White very fortunately disposed of herself in Bengal," he confided in private correspondence. "Fortunately, I say; for I know not how we would have disposed of her in this place. We do not apprehend that the mission of single females to such a country as Burmah, is at all advisable."[44]

The first single woman sent overseas from America was Mrs. Betsey Stockton. *The Annual Report, 1824* of the American Board of Commissioners for Foreign Missions referred to her as, "Betsey Stockton, colored woman, *Domestic Assistant.*"

Although born a slave in Princeton, New Jersey, about 1798, she had for many years worked in the household of the president of Princeton College. While there, she read avidly and widely with the help of his library. Described as "qualified to teach school and take charge of domestic concerns,"she conducted a "well run school" in Hawaii.[45]

By 1815, when Protestants began their century of expansion, the Roman Catholic Church was just beginning to recover from rough times. The Society of Jesus, with its 2,000 Jesuit missionaries, had been disbanded because of its excessive political activities. The papacy itself had been battered by Napoleon. French Catholicism, one of Rome's prime supporters of missions, had been virtually paralyzed by the French Revolution.

Rome gradually recovered from these wounds and moved slowly toward a more centralized church. As often happens after a period of suffering, the church also experienced a renewal of inner vitality that expressed itself this time in the emergence of new ministry groups.

The hundred years after 1815 saw more new orders and congregations organize than in any previous century of the Catholic Church's history.[46] Among the new orders were missionary societies such as the Salesians of Dom Bosco, the Scheut Fathers and the White Fathers—as well as over one hundred new congregations of celibate women whose rise to prominence paralleled that of Protestant single women missionaries.[47]

Twentieth Century Wounds

Events in the first half of the twentieth century inflicted crippling wounds from which Protestant missions in Europe have never fully recovered.

The most serious wound was theological. The first World Missionary Conference, held in Edinburgh in 1910, spent little time discussing theology because nearly all the participants agreed on fundamentals concerning Christ, the Bible and the church's role in missions. But by the second conference, held in Jerusalem just eighteen years later, theological liberalism had so completely permeated mainstream Protestant missions that Christ and His Word were demoted to the rank of partners in dialogue with other world religions.

Missionary activities of major European denominations drastically decreased as uncertainty increased over the credibility of the Gospel. Churches unsure of their beliefs were not inclined to pay the high costs of promoting those uncertain beliefs overseas.

The second major blow to European-based Protestant missions was inflicted by two global conflicts in three decades. Virtually any vision and support that survived the First World War succumbed during the Second. More than 3,000 church buildings were completely destroyed or heavily damaged. Countless hospitals, orphanages, schools and other church-related institutions disappeared, never to be rebuilt.

With its churches prostrated, its Christian message discredited and its economy ruined, the continent was left "economically impoverished and without a shred of virtue."[48]

Missions—indeed, Christianity itself—retreated to a minor role as the shattered nations of Europe struggled to renew their societies and rebuild their economies. Then the short-term push for material recovery became the unending obsession of materialism and its contempt for religion.

David B. Barrett estimates that the self-professed Christian population of Europe dropped from 90 percent in 1900 to 66 percent in 1986.[49] But such statistics hardly represent the true

spiritual decline of a continent even European church leaders concede is no longer Christian.

Post-Christian Europe

Bishop Hans Lilje, of the Evangelical Church of Germany, says outright: "The era when Europe was a Christian continent lies behind us."[50] Swiss theologian Dr. Rene Pache acknowledges that "Europe needs missionaries."[51]

Only 13 percent of France's population attends mass on Sunday. In Scandinavia, a mere 3 to 4 percent attends Sunday morning worship. In Italy's large cities, the ratio is down to two in a hundred. Britain's overall church attendance declines 2 percent annually, standing at 11 percent of the people in the mid-1980s.[52]

Lesslie Newbigin explains why the church is declining: It has lost the distinctive message of the Gospel.

"It would be hard to deny that contemporary British (and most of western) Christianity is an advanced case of syncretism," he reasons. "The church has lived so long as a permitted and even privileged minority, accepting relegation to the private sphere in a culture whose public life is controlled by a totally different vision of reality, that it has almost lost the power to address a radical challenge to that vision and therefore to modern civilization as a whole."[53]

Barrett estimates that the defection of Europeans and North Americans to other religions or nonreligion reaches 2,774,000 persons annually. Churches are losing an average of 6,000 members and 7,600 attendees per day. At this rate, he concludes, the massive gains of Third World churches are offset by greater losses in Europe and North America.[54]

"Inexorably," Barrett observes, "the center of gravity of committed Christianity continues its century-long shift from the Western world's capitals . . . to Third World cities."[55]

Some European countries, however, remain a significant source of missionary activity. In the United Kingdom, 5,319 Protestants and 1,158 Roman Catholic missionaries served overseas in 1984. Most Roman Catholic overseas personnel, and approximately 10 percent of Protestant missionaries, are sent and supported by European churches.[56]

In fact, European nations still lead the United States on a ratio basis in reference to missionaries. The United States sending ratio in 1970 was one missionary to every 4,800 people. Switzerland did twice as much (1 to 2,400). Even Sweden, with only 5 or 6 percent of the population attending church weekly, did better (1 to 4,600). Ireland, with one missionary for every 328 Irishmen, had the best record.[57]

Statistics, however, cannot dispel the acute spiritual need of Europe. Alan Walker, director of evangelism for the Methodist World Council, states the need clearly: "World evangelism must grapple with the spiritual crisis of the West. The Western world is now the toughest mission field on earth. . . . If churches which have been declining for years were to find answers within themselves, they would surely by now have appeared.

"Now the West needs to experience by cross-cultural interchange the vitality and joy of Christians from Developing Countries. Now the missionary age is moving in reverse, and the rest of the world must reach out to help the West."[58]

For European Christians, no less than for their beleaguered brothers and sisters in nations of the Middle East, the cry is clear: "Come over and help us!" □

ISRAEL

Connecting the Incompatibles

THE *1990 Prayer Directory* lists one organized Alliance church and forty-one baptized members in Israel, all of them Arab Christians. There is not one Jewish congregation, not one Hebrew believer on an Alliance church membership list.

Some Israeli Jews have been won to Christ by Alliance missionaries, but they belong to messianic assemblies that studiously avoid affiliation with any foreign mission.

This is the visible response after nearly continuous missionary work by the Alliance in the Holy Land since 1890.

Why the dismal record, especially among the Jewish population?

The most obvious answer concerning the Jews lies in rejection of a religion that almost from its inception has seemed intent on changing or annihilating them. The children of Abraham have suffered more cruelly over a longer length of time at the hands of so-called Christian nations than they have under any other religious or political system—including Islam.

But rejecting the Lord of their tormentors only partially explains Jewish intransigence.

The root cause lies in a war against assimilation that began about 2,000 B.C. Yahweh spoke to the children of Israel concerning a special relationship they must always safeguard: "For you are a people holy to the Lord your God. The Lord your God has chosen you out of all the peoples on the face of the earth to be his people, his treasured possession" (Deuteronomy 7:6).

Thus, for centuries predating the birth of Christ, the children of Abraham have resisted countless attempts by neighboring peoples, conquering armies and ruling powers to assimilate them into an alien religion or culture. Their worldview has steadfastly recognized only two kinds of people: Jews and everyone else.

The Impossible Wall

Israel's special relationship to Yahweh was based on the requirement they worship Him only. But from the days of Moses, Israel was plagued with the sin of idolatry. Wholesale deportations around 600 B.C. and cruel years of slavery forever cured the Jews of running after other gods.

The Hebrew people became fiercely antagonistic to any form of idolatry. "Hear, O Israel, the Lord our God is one Lord," rang daily through their temple and synagogues.

Ironically this divine mandate to worship Yahweh alone became a stumbling block when Jesus Christ lived among them. Nothing infuriated the Jews more than His assertion, "I and the Father are one."

When Christ stood before the Sanhedrin and reasserted His divine origin, His fate was sealed—and rightly so, in their eyes. His claim was the supreme blasphemy, they argued, not only an affront to their one God, but an attack on the very foundation of their identity as a people.

After destruction of the temple in A.D. 70, a high-level rabbinical council met to settle the matter in Yavneh, near the salted and furrowed fields that were once the Holy City. Learned spiritual leaders made a clear-cut decision that Judaism and Christianity were incompatible. Any Jew who declared for Christ was henceforth to be considered an apostate, a non-Jew.

The rabbinical council issued a circular

letter in A.D. 80 to all Jewish communities scattered throughout the civilized world. It called on them to excommunicate and ostracize all Jewish Christians. They were to be severed not only from the religious life of the community but from its social and economic activities as well. Compatibility with Christianity was impossible, rejection had to be total.[1]

The leaders of Judaism made sure the traitorous followers of Jesus withdrew from the synagogue: they added a nineteenth article to the "Eighteen Benedictions" recited in synagogue services. The new benediction was a curse on all apostates from the faith, something no Hebrew Christian could recite without bringing a curse upon himself.

Thus, while in Christ the wall of separation between Jew and Gentile had been dismantled, in Judaism the wall was raised to a new and impossible height. For almost two millennia, the rabbinical council decision of the first century has shaped Jewish thought and action toward Christ and Christianity.

Byron Spradlin, board chairman of Jews for Jesus at the time of writing, sums up both the historical and contemporary

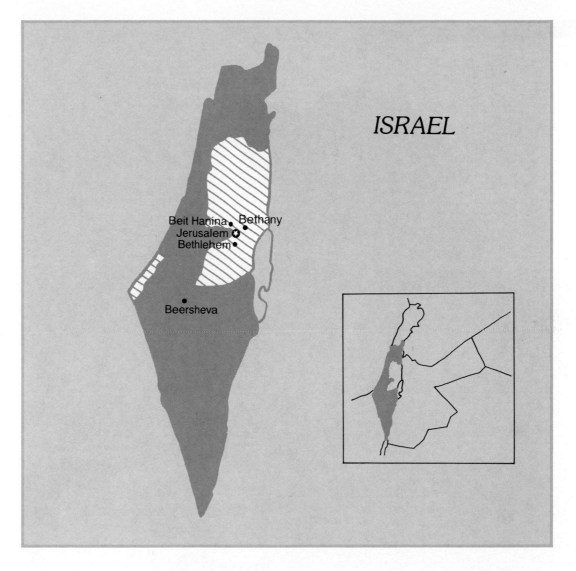

ISRAEL

Beit Hanina
Bethany
Jerusalem
Bethlehem
Beersheva

Jewish position: "The Jewish community continues to wage a 4,000-year-old battle against assimilation. It has assumed for at least 1,800 years that believing in Jesus means 'assimilation.' Therefore the Jew who declares allegiance to Jesus is declared a 'traitor' and a 'non-Jew.' "[2]

It is then not surprising to hear a member of Israel's Knesset (parliament) call missionaries "a cancer in the body of the nation," a hated disease to be removed.[3]

It is understandable how an orthodox rabbi can raise his voice in a world gathering of Jewish leaders: "Every Jewish child baptized into the Christian faith is stolen from the Jewish people. He becomes a

(Left) *An Orthodox Jew in Jerusalem
prays at the Wailing Wall,*
(right) *which is
all that remains of the temple in
Jerusalem dating back to the time of Christ.*

Christian missionary and often an enemy of the Jew."[4]

It becomes apparent why, after Protestant missions in Israel since 1820, total estimates of Hebrew evangelical believers run as low as 500 to 1,000,[5] though a more recent figure suggested is 2,000.

"Anti-Missionary Law"

The prevailing Jewish antagonism against the Gospel and its bearers took one form in 1977, when the Knesset passed the so-called "Anti-Missionary Law."

A member of the United Christian Council in Israel explains that "this bill was intended as the beginning of a series of bills to stop all missionary activity in Israel and eventually to eliminate any visible Christian presence in the Israeli-Jewish milieus."[6]

The small radical party that authored the bill recognized it could not outlaw all missionary work in Israel because of an inevitable storm of protest from churches in Western nations. The politicians therefore decided to move against "enticements to change of religion," basing their action on "the Middle East assumption

that material, social, or educational benefit is the pressing motive for religious conversion."[7]

Accusing Christian missions of buying converts has some historical validity, though the practice may have diminished or stopped in recent years.

Rev. George S. Constance, a former regional director of the Alliance, observed as recently as 1955: "Numerous societies and missions are waiting around to support any Hebrew who will make a profession of faith. Many individuals approach our missionaries weekly to ask what they can get if they profess Christianity.

"Most of the Jewish missionary societies working in the country operate on the premise that should a Hebrew make a decision to embrace Christianity he immediately becomes the financial respon-

sibility of the evangelical community."[8]

Passage of the "Anti-Missionary Law" had the opposite effect than its intended purpose to rid the country of Christians. Arab, Jewish and non-Israeli Christians closed ranks to oppose the law. Christian young people and formerly lukewarm adults vowed to witness publicly even if it meant prison.

"It is a matter of record," reports one observer, "that there have been three times as many Jews and Arabs won to Christ in Israel in the six years since the passage of the law as in the previous ten years."[9]

When a test case of the new law came before the attorney general in 1978, he dismissed the charges and apologized to the missionary community. No investigation involving the law, he promised,

would be permitted without his authorization.

The nation's president supported this position, noting that Israel had signed the Universal Declaration of Human Rights. Being a signatory "obligates the Israeli government to recognize the right of any citizen to freedom of religion, including the right to change that religion."[10]

Good as it sounds, however, the principle of religious freedom usually gets lost somewhere between promise and practice.

As Dr. William F. Smalley observed, "It is not illegal to be a Hebrew Christian, but it is very inconvenient. They are considered to be apostates. They are not worthy of being allowed to earn a living. They should not be tolerated socially. Everything should be done to make it so uncomfortable for them that they will either return to the fold of Judaism, or else leave the country."[11]

Messianic Assemblies

Human rights or not, the Israeli government and people in general have made manifestly clear that they want missionaries to stop evangelizing Jews and they want Jews to stop becoming Christians. The Hebrew mind-set on this matter has not wavered in almost two thousand years.

The Alliance in Israel can therefore claim no organized Jewish church, no list of baptized members. Missionaries work quietly on a personal basis with Jewish people in Jerusalem and Beersheva.

They do participate in the activities of messianic assemblies in both cities. These nondenominational groups comprised of Hebrew Christians are self-governing under lay leadership. Spiritual oversight resides with elders rather than paid clergy. The assemblies are a studied effort by Jewish evangelical believers to develop their own form of worship, evangelism and spiritual development independent of Western influence.

A more visible form of missionary activity takes place in Beersheva. The Bible House carries stocks of hymnals, Sunday school materials and general Christian literature, in addition to Bibles and Testaments. In the highly literate society of Israel, one given to much reading, the bookstore assumes a greater importance than similar operations in other countries.

The Bible House serves both Jewish and Arab publics throughout the Negev area. The government tourist office in Beersheva considers the store something of a showpiece of religious freedom, calling it "the unofficial Christian Information Center" of the city and region. Coming days may hold an even larger ministry for the Bible House, as people in Israel display a more open interest in Jesus Christ.

Dr. Pinchas Lapide, an Israeli religious scholar, evaluated Israel's elementary and secondary textbooks and found an increasing amount of material regarding the controversial Man of Galilee. Dr. Lapide concludes, "School books in Israel today, without a doubt, contain the most sympathetic picture of Jesus that any generation of Jewish children was ever offered by its elders."[12]

While conditions turn more favorable for a relaxed discussion of Jesus Christ, who He was and what He did, Hebrew Christians are at the same time showing more initiative in speaking openly of their faith in Him.

These changes encourage evangelical friends of Israel, but they do not promise a dramatic breakthrough in the near future. It will take a miracle by Messiah Himself to overcome the mind-set against the Gospel that has prevailed over the past two thousand years.

Arabs First

In startling contrast to their opposition against evangelizing Jews, Israeli govern-

Jewish boys and young men examine the sacred scrolls of Jewish Scripture.

At an open market in Jerusalem, goods are displayed and business is conducted much as it has been for many centuries.

ment officials and Jewish people in general seem quite willing for missionaries to attempt the conversion of Arabs to Christianity.

The one organized Alliance church of twenty baptized members and ninety inclusive members (1986) is the Old City Church in Jerusalem's ancient quarters. The congregation, which is totally Arab, was forced to relocate in the predominately Muslim Old City after the State of Israel was established in 1948. The partition of Jerusalem left the beautiful church built by Thompson in the Israeli sector inaccessible to Arab Christians.

Sunday service attendance in the Old City Church reached 120 by the mid-1980s. A baptismal service in the Jordan River for five new believers drew a congregation of seventy. Bible studies in the church and private homes reach out to Arabs in the city and into a suburb called Beit Hanina. Missionaries participate fully in the life of the church.

Response, however, does not come easy. Ministry among city and town Arabs and countryside Bedouins meets with resistence and rejection fully as determined as that among the Jews.

It has always been so.

When Miss Lucy Dunn and Miss Eliza J. Robertson went to Palestine in 1890, they found a situation that has not changed appreciably over the intervening years.

"People did not want to rent houses to them," recounts Dr. Smalley. "It was difficult to get interpreters. They found a population divided into three distinct classes: Muslims, Jews, and Christians of the Eastern Orthodox and Roman Catholic churches almost totally separate in culture and living standards, and with

The narrow streets of Jerusalem seem impervious to the passage of generations and empires.

religions which were mutually antagonistic, but united in their opposition to the Gospel."[13]

The two ladies began to quietly visit villages surrounding Jerusalem, hold services in their home and conduct meetings for women and children. As more missionaries arrived, the work spread in 1892 to the fanatical Muslim center of Hebron, and later to Jaffa and Beersheva.

Given the male-dominant cultures of Palestine, the mission needed a man to take charge. God answered prayer in the person of Rev. A. E. Thompson. Dr. Smalley wrote of him, "There can be no question as to who was the person most greatly used of God in the eighty years at time of writing of Alliance missions in the Near or Middle East."[14]

Thompson was Canadian by birth, Scottish by descent and Presbyterian by choice. Over a twenty-year period he provided leadership for the Palestine mis-

sion. During one furlough he wrote the official biography of his mentor and contemporary, Dr. A. B. Simpson.

In 1904, a year after Thompson and his family arrived in Jerusalem, he engineered construction of the "Tin Tabernacle," a wood-frame building covered with corrugated iron sheets. He later built a beautiful stone structure that served as mission headquarters and home for the International Evangelical Church in its witness to the city's large international community.

Still called "Mr. Thompson's church," the property plays an important role in the Alliance work in Israel and, because of its rich past, has been designated in the official tourist guidebook of Jerusalem as a historical site.

Highways and Byways

Alliance missionaries carry on a third type of ministry in addition to participating in messianic assemblies and Arab church activities. Bedouins who roam the countryside and skirt the highways can be met no other way than by taking to the road and tramping hills in search of their elusive camps.

One missionary couple, dedicated to evangelizing Bedouin nomads, writes of an average day's work off the beaten track: "On our way again we met Bedouin women who asked for food and medicine. We shared what we had with them, and later with an old woman shaking from fever. We told her of the Great Physician and how he can heal hearts as well as bodies.

"Thirsty shepherds cupped their hands to drink as we poured water for them from our supply. Young goatherds came dashing across the sand and stones to have their jugs or canteens filled. We gave them Gospels telling of the Living Water.

"Farther along we met young women gathering sticks into bundles for firewood. They carry the loads on their heads, their babies slung on their backs. Their burdens challenge us to tell them of Jesus who promises rest from the heavy load of sin."[15]

Missionaries in Israel must surely have a heightened appreciation for the Apostle Paul, who described his missionary method as essentially becoming "all things to all men so that by all possible means I might save some."

This flexibility is needed wherever Christians witness to nonbelievers, but it seems especially crucial in Israel, where missionaries try to bring Christ into contact with Jews and Muslims whose religious convictions are utterly incompatible with the Gospel. ☐

CHURCH AND MISSION

OFFICIAL NAME OF CHURCH:	not organized
ENTRY BY MISSIONARIES:	1890
NUMBER OF MISSIONARIES:	9
ORGANIZED CHURCHES:	0
UNORGANIZED CHURCHES AND PREACHING POINTS:	1
BAPTIZED CHURCH MEMBERS:	14
INCLUSIVE MEMBERSHIP:	40
MEDICAL WORK:	0
EDUCATION:	0
RADIO BROADCASTS:	0
PAGES PRINTED:	0

COUNTRY

OFFICIAL NAME:	State of Israel
FORM OF GOVERNMENT:	Parliamentary Democracy
OFFICIAL LANGUAGE(S):	Hebrew, Arabic
AREA:	7,847 sq. mi.
POPULATION:	(1989) 4,477,000
CAPITAL:	Jerusalem
PER CAPITA INCOME:	(1986) $5,995.00
LITERACY:	88% (Jewish), 70% (Arab)
RELIGIOUS AFFILIATION	Jewish 83%, Muslim 13%

ARAB LANDS

Fortress Islam

THE SAGA of Alliance missions in the Arab Middle East is best told in terms of resolve, not results. The first C&MA missionaries entered Palestine in 1890, prepared to work among both Arabs and Jews. The results, by the mid-1980s, after almost continuous missionary work among Arab peoples from 1890 onward, show only a total of nineteen churches and 2,871 inclusive members in Jordan, Syria and Lebanon.

Results are obviously not the primary story of Alliance missions in the region, though the presence of an Alliance church is of great significance.

Despite a long history of threats, imprisonment and harassment, curses to their faces and behind their backs, campaigns of intimidation against would-be converts, C&MA missionaries still occupy a beachhead in areas closest to the heartland of Islam.

That is the story of the Alliance in the Middle East.

Almost all the congregations in the three Arab countries consist of believers with non-Muslim background. The consensus among some church groups is to avoid direct attempts to convert Muslims—which is forbidden by law—lest the ensuing storm by the authorities sweep away the limited freedom and tolerance they do have. There is no indication that this public stance of implacable Muslim resistance to the Gospel will change any time soon, but privately expressed interest is on the rise.

Strengths of Islam

Why has the religion of Muhammed proven so hard to penetrate and its followers so hostile to Christ? Why, in fact, has Islam proven more successful than any other world religion in winning Christians to its own faith?

Some credit the advance of Islam to its generous use of the sword as a persuader. Others point to its simplicity, saying that it offers much and demands little. But such generalities do not adequately explain how a relatively new religion can now claim over 817 million adherents worldwide, including vast areas once staunchly Christian.

One strength of Islam has been its success in emphasizing its difference from other religions. Islam is the youngest and last major world religion, dating its genesis some six hundred years after Christianity.

Yet instead of suffering from an inferiority complex the followers of Muhammed claim that last is best.

Kenneth Cragg, a recognized authority on Islam in the Middle East, says, "The assurance that their faith was no innovation, but the essence of all true religion before God, gave Muslims a confidence over against the older systems and precluded the inferiority that lateness might have otherwise occasioned."[1]

Any prior claims or teachings that conflict with Muslim beliefs are therefore considered distortions that have been corrected in Islam's ultimate body of truth. This is especially true of Judeo-Christianity, with which Islam has more in common than other world religions.

Cragg illustrates: "They claimed Moses and Jesus in Islamic terms and rejected as distortions of their teaching many of the characteristic convictions within Judaism and Christianity. In this way the new faith was able to assert . . . a correction and displacement of them."[2]

Clashes of Conviction

Nowhere is this clash of conviction more evident than in the relative roles of Muhammed and Christ. Dr. Samuel

Zwemer, one of history's greatest missionaries to Muslims, points out: "Muhammed is always in the foreground. Jesus Christ, in spite of his lofty titles and the honor given him in the Koran, is in the background.

"There is not a single biography of Jesus Christ alone and unique, as a great prophet of God, to be found in the literature of Islam. Christ is grouped with the other prophets: with Lot, Alexander the Great, Ishmael, Moses, Abraham, Adam."[3]

Dr. Zwemer concludes, "Christ to them occupies no supreme place in heaven, nor does he in history. He has been at once succeeded and superceded by Muhammed in this respect."[4]

Islam's denial of Christ as the unique Son of God brings every other Muslim teaching into conflict with everything that is essential to Christian faith. This denial is as central to Islamic faith and teaching as its assertion is critical to the Gospel.

Nothing stirs Muslim opposition more vehemently than the claim of Christ's deity, because it runs counter to Islam's most cherished belief: There is only one God, and his name is Allah.

Muhammed was a crusader against the hundreds of local gods he encountered among his fellow Arabs. His followers consider their religion the ultimate expression of monotheism and its defense their supreme destiny in a world of many false gods.

"To associate Jesus Christ with God," says Cragg, "is to commit the supreme sin against the basic assertion of the Muslim Shahadah, or Creed, that there is no god except God."[5]

Sheikh Abdul-Haqq some years ago expressed the depth of Islamic enmity toward the Christian belief concerning Christ. "For us in the world there are only believers and unbelievers," he wrote.

"Love, charity, fraternity toward believers; contempt, disgust, hatred and war against unbelievers. Amongst unbelievers the most hateful and criminal are those who, while recognizing God, attribute to Him earthly relationships, give Him a son, a mother."[6]

Another major clash of conviction between Muslims and Christians centers on their sacred books. Cragg writes that, according to Islam, "The Quran (Koran) is the infallible Book. All other true Scriptures agree with it. The Biblical Scriptures, as they are, do not agree. Therefore these are corrupted. But their corruption is offset by the Quranic embodiment of what they ought to be."[7]

Muslims consider their low esteem of the Bible altogether reasonable. After all, the Quran was written by only one inspired man in just twenty-three years in two places, Mecca and Medina. The gospels, however were written over scores of years by four men scattered in different places.

They infer from this that the original gospel written by Christ was lost, so "several leaders set themselves to making up the deficiency with the result that they all differed and they are all wrong."[8]

Some Muslims encourage reading the gospels, but dismiss accuracy of the biblical record. The Quran states formally concerning Christ: "They did not kill him, they did not crucify him, it was made to appear so to them" (iv. 157).

Muhammed categorically rejected the crucifixion, and later commentators explained that the likeness of Christ was put upon another, who was crucified in His place.[9] And because there was no cross, neither could Christ die for all, make atonement for their sins, rise again for

their justification and give eternal life to those who believe in Him.

Coupling such dogmatic denials with a fanatical belief in their own creed and with the sword of conquest, the armies of Islam swept out of the barren hinterland of Arabia centuries ago. Like a blinding sandstorm, they enveloped vast areas once considered Christian. Confirmed in the rightness of their cause by such conquests, the followers of Muhammed have never relaxed their hostility toward the Gospel and its believers.

Widening Circles

This was the attitude among Muslims encountered by Misses Lucy Dunn and

Jordanian citizen

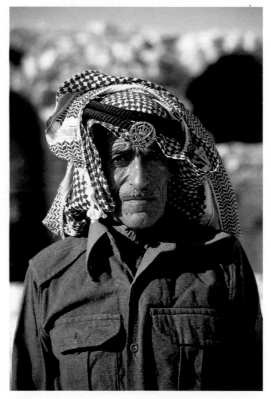

Eliza J. Robertson when they entered the Holy Land in 1890. Both had studied in Dr. A. B. Simpson's training school and then had gone separately to Palestine. Once there, they joined forces and began talking about Christ to anyone who would listen—Jew, Muslim or traditional Christian.

Whether knowingly or not, the two women and others who came later followed the widening circles of witness indicated by the risen Lord in Acts 1:8. "You will be my witnesses," He commanded, "in Jerusalem, and in all Judea and Samaria, and to the ends of the earth."

Misses Dunn and Robertson established their home base in Jerusalem. Rev. and Mrs. George A. Murray moved southward to the fanatically Muslim town of Hebron in Judea. Though he was lame and his wife blind, they served well. When the Murrays left southern Palestine in 1907, their carriage was followed by people who wept and begged them to stay.

As the circle of witness widened, Miss Mary F. Maxwell headed northward toward Samaria and Galilee. Although she had come to Palestine with denominational backing, she was drawn to the Alliance by Miss Dunn.

The circle spread even wider when Rev. and Mrs. Archibald Forder came to the Palestine C&MA Mission from an unaffiliated group. They set their sights on what could be considered "the ends of the earth"—the barren and hostile interior of Arabia, birthplace of Islam.

From December of 1900 to March of the following year, Forder traveled by animal and on foot for 1,400 miles, distributing gospel literature and preaching in Bedouin tents and Arab towns throughout north-central Arabia.

Though ill part of the time and in constant danger, he made one of the most remarkable and heroic missionary tours ever attempted in the homeland of Muhammed. His would be the first of six such forays by Alliance missionaries into Arabia.

JORDAN: Wary Hosts

During the early 1900s, Alliance missionaries concentrated their efforts within Palestine, while seeking to establish permanent work in neighboring Arab territories. World War I hampered but did not halt their work.

Rev. A. E. Thompson, longtime chairman of the Palestine C&MA Mission, reported that "ours was the only group that had been able to maintain a semblance of mission work throughout the entire war period, even though for a period of more than a year there had been no foreign missionary in residence."[10]

The year 1920 represented something of a second wave as five new missionaries arrived to expand Alliance ministry into new areas. Their appearance coincided with a decision by the Church Missionary Society to cede all its responsibility in southern Jordan to the Alliance. The Palestine C&MA Mission agreed that same year to accept oversight of the schools and small groups of believers that Miss Ford had started in Syria.

Thus, by the 1920s, the Alliance worked in three fields under three different types of government: British mandate in Palestine, largely autonomous Jordan and French-ruled Syria.

Rev. and Mrs. W. F. Smalley tried to

reopen the mission station in Karak, Jordan. It had been earlier founded by the Forders, then transferred to the Church Missionary Society, and finally ceded to the Alliance. Local officials, however, refused to allow the station to reopen.

Smalley remembers the Bedouin sheikh administrator of the area giving him a blunt warning: "If we were in Karak at the end of another night, they would know how to dispose of us."[11]

He added that the Arab chieftain could assemble 10,000 armed and mounted warriors within a few hours. That same sheikh would later come to Smalley and ask that his son be registered in the

mission school when the Karak mission was reopened.

Jordan's First Alliance

With Karak closed for the time being, the Smalleys turned to the small town of Madaba, one of the few villages east of the Jordan River that had a significant Christian population. They were able to establish both a school and a mission.

An Arab Christian taught in the school, but he became so abusive and aggressive in his manner toward Muslims that both he and Smalley were evicted from the country. Mrs. Smalley was not included in the deportation.

When Smalley returned a short while

Arena ruins, a reminder of ancient Roman rule

later, a high-ranking official told him, "We got rid of you once. If a person takes a snake out from under his clothes, does he then allow the snake to crawl back again?"[12]

Eventually, however, the government relented and allowed both Smalleys to continue their work—but not the unwise assistant.

Officials kept a close watch on the missionaries and any Arab Muslim who visited them often. On separate occasions the Smalleys became friends with a doctor, a bank manager and an army officer. All three showed an interest in the Gospel and all three were transferred to posts far from missionary contact.

Persistence and resolve finally paid off in 1929. A congregation of five Madaba believers, all from non-Muslim background, organized the first Alliance church in Jordan. The small school expanded and eventually included children of some influential Muslim families.

The congregation in Madaba experienced frustrations common to other groups of believers throughout the area. Unable to afford their own chapel, they met in small rooms of small homes. This limited the number of attendees and kept the church from growing.

One missionary observed: "Members came early to secure a seat, and when townspeople arrived they had to stand on the balcony or porch, or go home again. Many would not come at all for they knew there would be no place for them. Others arranged with their families to alternate at the meetings so that more people might have a chance to hear the Gospel."[13]

When the resident missionary was finally able to lay out the foundation for a 150-seat chapel years later, the people asked why he was building such a large building.

When the chapel was completed and crowded to capacity for the first service, they then asked why he had not made it larger.

The Hashwehs

An unusual young Palestinian, Albert Hashweh, came to Madaba in 1950 to pastor the church and teach in the mission school. Although only in his mid-thirties, he had seen enough suffering to

Guitar accompaniment to the mingled voices of men and women in praise to God marks the location of an Alliance congregation of Arab Christians.

give him a maturity beyond his years.

Beersheva was his birthplace twice over. Born there in 1912, he was born again in his hometown through the ministry of Alliance missionaries. He graduated from the C&MA Bible Training Institute in Jerusalem and joined the police force in order to have a witness among the Arabs in the Sinai Desert.

The 1948 Arab-Israeli War that won the Jewish people a homeland deprived the Hashweh family of theirs. Forced to flee the family homestead of four generations, he could have become embittered, like many thousands of other Palestinian refugees. God spared him and his family from that empty fate by leading him to the ministry at Madaba.

The mid-fifties were an unsettled time for the church as well as the region. The Palestine C&MA Mission was encouraging full autonomy for the Arab Lands churches, a move that included withdrawing subsidies from church and school programs.

Hashweh refused to join those who left the Alliance in search of continuing financial support. He determined to stay with the people who had led him to Christ and helped him surmount the tragic loss of his homeland.

God blessed his ministry, and in 1956 he was chosen president of the Jordanian Alliance national committee. He moved to the capital in 1958 as pastor of the Jebal Amman Church, the leading Alliance church in Jordan.

Hashweh's cousin also honored the Lord and was used of God in a remarkable way. Although blinded in early childhood, Jamil Hashweh completed his education in the Alliance mission school at Beersheva. He learned to type, play

CHURCH AND MISSION

OFFICIAL NAME OF CHURCH:	The Evangelical Church of the Christian Alliance
ENTRY BY MISSIONARIES:	1890
NUMBER OF MISSIONARIES:	7
ORGANIZED CHURCHES:	4
UNORGANIZED CHURCHES AND PREACHING POINTS:	1
BAPTIZED CHURCH MEMBERS:	210
INCLUSIVE MEMBERSHIP:	630

COUNTRY

OFFICIAL NAME:	Hashemite Kingdom of Jordan
FORM OF GOVERNMENT:	Constitutional Monarchy
OFFICIAL LANGUAGE(S):	Arabic
AREA:	37,737 sq. mi.
POPULATION:	(1989 est.) 3,031,000
CAPITAL:	Amman
PER CAPITA INCOME:	$552.00
LITERACY:	31%
RELIGIOUS AFFILIATION:	Sunni Muslim 93.6%, Christian 5%

the violin, and translate theological books into Arabic. He also wrote many poems and hymns.

His impact extended well beyond the church. He produced the first Arabic Braille magazine in the Arab world, devised a universal Braille in Arabic, and managed the transcribing unit of Helen Keller House. For this and other achievements, King Hussein of Jordan honored him with a gold medal.

Jamil Hashweh responded: "This has reminded me of the crown of life which I shall soon receive from the Lord when He appears as King of Kings and Lord of Lords."[14]

ARABIA: Closed Country

Alliance missionaries had been wanting to establish a permanent post in Arabia since 1900, when Forder made his first scouting trip of 1,400 miles throughout the arid desert along Arabia's northern border with Jordan. The second expedition did not come until twenty-five years later.

Little had changed in the intervening years, especially the constant threat of danger and unforeseen difficulties.

At one point, the Ford vehicle carrying the three missionaries and their guides rounded one side of a hill while thirty Bedouin horsemen passed on the opposite side with orders to shoot the foreign intruders on sight. The men learned later that 2,000 camels had been stolen and the local Bedouin sheikh thought they were the guilty ones returning on another raid.

Driving the Ford over desert terrain and caravan trails often resulted in mechanical problems. In addition to broken springs and engine failure, the men had to stop one hundred times to repair punctured tires.

Smalley and a missionary colleague, George Breaden, set out in November,

(Left) *Syria's many mosques attest to the Islamic character of the nation, providing not only a place to worship,* (right) *but also a familar landmark where people meet.*

1927, on another scouting trip along the coastal area of Arabia to see if the local people would tolerate a mission in their part of the country.

Five days by camel into their trip, they were detained at a military post and became, in Smalley's words, "guests of the Arabian government." They were taken, under arrest and armed guard, by camel and boat to Jeddah, seaport for Mecca, Islam's most holy city.

Smalley summarized their experience: "We were arrested, guarded for thirty-seven days, carried 250 miles farther than we admitted we wanted to go, granted no trial and no explanations, and then ignominiously ejected from the country.

"The parting gesture of defiance to the missionaries, and to the Gospel which they represented, was written on our passports when they were returned to us. It read, 'It is not permitted for the bearer of this passport to enter the land of Kedjaz or Nejd Saudi Arabia.' "[15]

News spread fast concerning the Arabian government's action. Some claim that the Muslim governments of the Middle East had a secret organization that circulated news of such happenings and distorted facts to inflame the masses against Christian missions.

Arrest and expulsion of the missionaries occurred about the same time an evangelism conference was being held on the Mount of Olives. Propagandists seized upon both events to inflame the Arab world against missionaries. Disturbances broke out in Palestine, Jordan and Syria following their arrest. One mission worker was severely beaten, a Danish mission was closed and crowds in several cities called for the expulsion of all missionaries.

The episode also had political repercussions. Word of their arrest reached Washington and caused considerable concern over Arab-American relations. The Jordanian government promised the Arabian monarch it would prevent missionaries' using its country to enter Arabia.

Smalley and a missionary colleague next planned to itinerate in southern Arabia, well away from the disputed area around Mecca, and then continue on to Persia on a survey trip. A series of

cables between Jerusalem and New York ended with a final word from the Board of Managers: "Survey Persian Gulf only."

That ended further attempts to enter Arabia. Though deeply disappointed at the time, Smalley conceded later, "Looking back at it from the advanced knowledge of forty years' greater experience, one can only say that doubtless the Lord's will was carried out."[16]

Although barred from Arabia, Messrs. Smalley and Paul S. Allen did survey the southern coastline of Persia (now Iran). The Allens and the R. E. Bresslers later settled in Persia and for several years carried on a very successful ministry.

SYRIA: Beginning by Adoption

The year 1920 that signaled entry into Jordan also marked the beginning of Alliance work in Syria. But unlike the Jordanian mission, which began through pioneering, the Syrian ministry began by adoption.

After joining Miss Dunn and the Palestine C&MA Mission, Miss Mary T. Maxwell concentrated her efforts in Galilee and in the Syrian Plain of Hauran, east of the Sea of Galilee. Since the area did not form part of the Alliance responsibility under mission comity, she eventually formed her own mission, while maintaining close ties to her former colleagues.

Miss Maxwell petitioned the Alliance in 1920 to take over her work, which consisted mainly of small groups of believers and small schools with local teachers funded entirely from her resources. After conferring with the established missions of the region, the C&MA accepted the Syrian part of Miss Maxwell's work.

Kharaba, site of the first Alliance mission, was one of the few Syrian Christian villages that survived the Muslim conquest centuries ago. The congregation consisted of several Greek Orthodox people, who realized that previously they had only been Christian by tradition and needed a personal faith in Christ. Ostracized and berated by their own people, the new believers banded together to form a congregation.

Spreading out from Kharaba, missionaries established a center in Dera'a among the Muslims, Eastern Orthodox and Druze (a highly secretive and syncretic Muslim sect in Syria, Lebanon and Israel.) Their first Muslim convert was a dentist, member of a prominent and influential Muslim family in Damascus.

The dentist testified openly of his faith in Christ and was baptized in a public meeting. Within weeks, he was poisoned and taken to Damascus in critical condition. When he later recovered and returned to his dental work in Dera'a, the missionaries noted a strange, distant manner about him.

"When I tried to talk to him about the Lord," reported one missionary, "he spoke in a passive, unemotional way, and said that his faith in Christ had given him joy and peace before, but the way was too hard and the price too great. He asked us to let him alone."[17]

Opposition came not only from Muslims but also from Greek Orthodox clergy. A priest burst into a village meeting near Dera'a and angrily confronted the mis-

A Syrian follower of Muhammed washes his feet before entering the mosque to pray.

sionary, ordering him out of town. When ignored, he seized several villagers and tried to expel them from the service, but only succeeded in getting himself evicted.

Financial Tensions

The Syrian work taken on by the Alliance had internal tensions as well as external. The former policy had been for the mission to finance every aspect of the work—schools, teachers, church workers —a practice prevalent throughout Middle East missionary work. A farsighted attempt was made by the Alliance not to continue this policy in regard to the Syrian believers.

Missionary Ralph Freed (whose son Paul later founded Trans World Radio) observed: "In these Arab lands it is an almost unheard-of-thing for a missionary society to attempt to work apart from mission-conducted and -paid schools, hospitals, or some form of mate-

rial assistance, to win the people to Christ.

"We are determined that if any souls were to be won to Christ in Jebait or elsewhere, it must be done by the direct operation of the Spirit without any of these means."[18]

Results elsewhere in the Middle East indicate that mission-financed institutions, no matter how humane and commendable, do not contribute significantly, either numerically or spiritually, to a vigorous national church.

An American medical missionary working in Israel estimated that he and his medical co-workers had treated about 180,000 Jewish and Arab patients over a fifteen-year period. "Yet of these thousands, he was not able to recall even one who, as a result, acknowledged Jesus Christ as Savior, although the Gospel had been faithfully presented to all of them."[19]

Missionaries and local church workers spread out from Kharaba in the 1920s and 1930s to other towns across the broad Plain of Hauran. They penetrated the Druze Mountains, home of the fanatical, reclusive Muslim sect that viewed other branches of Islam with almost the same contempt and hostility it displayed toward Christianity.

Their religion, a mixture of eastern religions brought into a pattern of belief about one thousand years ago, remains remarkably strong. The Gospel even entered the mountain stronghold of Aara, administrative center of the powerful Druze prince responsible for the mountain district.

Although begun later than either Palestine or Jordan, the Syrian Alliance community grew more rapidly. In his 1939 annual report, the chairman of the Palestine-Arab Lands Mission charted the number of conversions since the mission began in 1890. Of the total 303 baptisms in forty-nine years, the Palestine work accounted for 142 baptisms, the Jordanian mission had 18, and the Syrian Alliance numbered 143.[20]

Capital Move

The most significant advance in Syria came during 1944, when the Alliance was finally able to establish a resident ministry in Damascus, the capital.

Missionaries had long wanted to work among the people of this city with its special historical and political status. Although the capital of present-day Syria, Damascus is reportedly the oldest continuously inhabited city in the world.

Missionaries moving to Damascus during the 1940s, however, were reminded on every hand that the city was now the Muslim capital of a Muslim nation. Trying to find property for their base of ministry turned into a nine-month ordeal. They finally found a small office on the second floor of an apartment house in the Muslim part of the city.

The struggling congregation began an era of growth and stability in 1948, when Rev. Ibrahim Oueis became its pastor. He had been serving the Arab Alliance Church in Jerusalem but was forced to leave the city during the Arab-Israeli War. Numerous Arab Christian refugees who fled from Jerusalem to Damascus were drawn to the pastor, who had suffered along with them.

CHURCH AND MISSION

OFFICIAL NAME OF CHURCH:	Evangelical Church of the Christian Alliance of Syria and Lebanon
ENTRY BY MISSIONARIES:	1890
NUMBER OF MISSIONARIES:	0
ORGANIZED CHURCHES:	15
UNORGANIZED CHURCHES AND PREACHING POINTS:	5
BAPTIZED CHURCH MEMBERS:	769
INCLUSIVE MEMBERSHIP:	2,907

COUNTRY

OFFICIAL NAME:	Syria Arab Republic
FORM OF GOVERNMENT:	Socialist
OFFICIAL LANGUAGE(S):	Arabic
AREA:	71,498 sq. mi.
POPULATION:	(1989 est.) 12,210,000
CAPITAL:	Damascus
PER CAPITA INCOME:	$702.00
LITERACY:	78% males (1986)
RELIGIOUS AFFILIATION:	Sunni Muslim 74%, other Muslim 16%, Christian 10%

(Left) *The statue of a mortally wounded Lebanese fighter starkly portrays the dilemma* (right) *of Beirut, a dying city whose suffering is muted by distance.*

LEBANON: Shattered Model

Syria unintentionally influenced the founding of C&MA missionary work in Beirut, Lebanon, when on two occasions missionaries had to leave Syria.

First, the fall of France in World War II made French-dominated Syria untenable to American-born Alliance missionaries Rev. and Mrs. George W. Breaden. They moved to Beirut and started an international church among the large English-speaking community.

The Breadens continued their contacts with born-again Christians among the Druze in Syria. Later, when a severe drought forced many Druze to seek employment in Beirut, the Christians among them gravitated to the Arabic-speaking missionaries formerly in Damascus. Breaden eventually pastored one of the largest evangelical churches in Beirut, attended primarily by Syrian Christians.

When the Breadens went on furlough after the war, however, no one followed up on their work in Beirut, and both the international and Syrian congregations passed into the care of other missions.

Syria again focused Alliance attention on Lebanon by showing its hostility to Americans around 1950, when American policy seemed to tilt toward the Israelis. The regime forced all missions to leave the country. Some workers, like the Breadens, were given only twenty-four hours.

Those who transferred their work to Beirut after the stressful hostility of Damascus must have considered the Lebanese capital almost a resort city.

Almost equally divided between one million Muslims and one million Christians (mainly Maronites) for many years, Lebanon demonstrated that Muslims and Christians could get along with each other in an open, democratic society.

Christian minorities all over the Middle East viewed Lebanon as their hope for more freedom and equality in their own Muslim-dominated nations. Prospering remarkably, like a sparkling oasis in an ugly desert of hatred and fear, Lebanon seemed like a dream too good to last—and it was. Its bright future proved nothing more than a shimmering mirage.

Excited hopes that Lebanon would prove more responsive to the Gospel than Syria were quickly dashed on the rocks of the two centuries-old traditional religions, Muslim and Christian.

"Some Protestants in the West have so casual an attitude with respect to denominational loyalty that they feel quite justified in changing affiliation at will," argues one observer of Middle East Christianity.

"This is not the case in the traditional churches of Lebanon as elsewhere in the Middle East," he explains. "There one's church membership is integral to his or her identity among those whose Christian history dates back to the apostolic era, and whose struggle for survival as a Christian people is centuries old."[21]

Partly as a result of this resistant attitude by Lebanese Christians as well as Muslims, denominational missionary work primarily took the form of institutional ministry. Nearly one-half of all school-age children—Christian and Muslim alike—have been educated in mission or church-related primary and secondary schools.

The world-famous American University in Beirut has Protestant roots, just as St. Joseph University in the city was founded under Roman Catholic auspices. Likewise many hospitals, clinics, welfare projects, orphanages and

CHURCH AND MISSION

OFFICIAL NAME OF CHURCH:	Evangelical Church of the Christian Alliance of Syria and Lebanon
ENTRY BY MISSIONARIES:	1890
NUMBER OF MISSIONARIES:	0
ORGANIZED CHURCHES:	1
UNORGANIZED CHURCHES AND PREACHING POINTS:	1
BAPTIZED CHURCH MEMBERS:	157
INCLUSIVE MEMBERSHIP:	471
MEDICAL WORK:	Dental Clinic

COUNTRY

OFFICIAL NAME:	Republic of Lebanon
FORM OF GOVERNMENT:	Republic
OFFICIAL LANGUAGE(S):	Arabic
AREA:	4,015 sq. mi.
POPULATION:	(1989 est.) 2,852,000
CAPITAL:	Beirut
PER CAPITA INCOME:	$1,150.00
LITERACY:	75%
RELIGIOUS AFFILIATION:	Muslim 57%, Christian 42%

(Facing page, left to right) Alliance church for the international community in Beruit; Arabic hymnal used in services; Lebanese Christians meet for prayer.

century and follows Eastern Orthodox rites. *Sunni* is the name given to the largest branch of Islam. It represents Muslims with a puritanical and fanatical allegiance to Muhammed and the Quram. By contrast, Sh'ite Muslims revere Muhammed's son-in-law Ali; they believe the Quram is inadequate and in need of additional doctrines and traditions.)

As Middle East tensions polarized Christian and Muslim populations, many of the more educated and prosperous Christian families fled the country. At the same time, Muslim Palestinian refugees poured into Lebanon. The population ratio shifted to about sixty Muslims for every forty Christians.

As Muslims demanded a greater share of power, the confessional form of government turned from coalition to conflict. Neighboring states and world powers stepped in and took sides.

Lebanon began its decline from a model state to a burned-out shell of abandoned ideals and lost hope.

Lebanon's fall dragged down as well the dreams of others. "Christians in other countries have become less interested in working for freedom," comments one

homes for the aged were expressions of missionary commitment.

Decline to Chaos

Another disappointment soon to be shared by Alliance missionaries and all others who wished Lebanon well was the breakdown of "confessional government."

Muslims and Christians had shared the powers of government for many years on the basis that the two populations were roughly equal in size. The president, for example, was traditionally a Maronite Christian, while the prime minister was a Sunni Muslim.

(*Maronite* refers to the Syrian Christian Church, which dates back to the first

Lebanese church leader. "There is the feeling that they had better remain quiet and maintain the status quo . . . . What happens in Lebanon will affect Christians and Muslim-Christian relations throughout the Middle East."[22]

Lebanon Toward A.D. 2000

To say that history is the big story of Alliance missions in the Arab Middle East does not mean these areas have neither current growth nor a promising future. As the Alliance in Jordan, Syria and Lebanon moves toward A.D. 2000, significant developments are taking place.

Churches of numerous denominations in Lebanon are struggling for survival, trying to hold fast what they had accomplished before the havoc and ruin of civil war engulfed the nation.

The Karentina Alliance Church in Beirut, however, started during the civil war and grew stronger as the fighting swelled in intensity. Attendance grew from fifty to 400 members between 1975 and 1986. The church had to enlarge its facilities five times to accommodate the increasing attendance.

The latest renovation in 1985 doubled the sanctuary seating capacity. The church also purchased some adjacent buildings and organized a Bible school to train church workers.

Two major factors contributed to the church's growth: its pastor and its relief program.

Rev. Sami Dagher was well along in a hotel management career when the Lord called him first to be a son, and then a servant. He was copastor of the international church in Beirut for several years. Then in 1976, he started a church for his Lebanese countrymen in the Karentina sector of Beirut.

Since then he was kidnapped and shot at, he saw his home and car damaged by shell fire, and he has survived countless artillery barrages. His family as well was often under fire.

Knowing he was marked for kidnap or murder, Dagher still refused to abandon his homeland and ministry. "We are immortal till our work for Christ is completed," he believes.[23]

"Relief Into Belief"

Dagher's hotel management training may have disciplined him to look after the needs of others. Whatever the reason, when fighting erupted in 1978 between Muslim and Christian militias, he viewed the long, pathetic lines of refugees and mobilized his church to have a relief ministry.

Although the sacking of his own hometown of Ramali occurred seven years later, it illustrates the kind of relief program the Karentina church developed as the war stumbled on.

The people in Ramali were awakened at midnight by the sound of approaching tanks and supporting infantry. Behind the tanks came columns of empty trucks to be filled with loot from village homes, shops and fields. Within hours, the once-prosperous farmers and businessmen found themselves homeless and impoverished.

An Alliance missionary in nearby Nogura helped secure a small ship to take the refugees to Beirut. There they were met by Pastor Dagher.

"We noticed the sadness, the desperation, the lost look in their eyes," he recalls. "Once they had everything and now nothing. Everyone was crying and it was a heartbreaking experience."[24]

Financial assistance from Samaritan's Purse, TEAR Fund England and CAMA Services enabled the church to provide the Ramali refugees with basic food and household items. The church also gave them blankets, mattresses, furniture and clothing.

Then the church found apartments for twenty-four families and paid the rent in advance for two years. Five families crowded into the pastor's apartment until they could find housing of their own.

Out of that group in Dagher's home, six became Christians. A total of forty-five refugees openly confessed their faith in Christ before the Karentina congregation.

By June of 1986, the church had helped about 1,000 families in this manner.

Aiding others while they themselves suffer has made the Karentina congregation strong in faith. During a Sunday of especially heavy fighting in 1987, Pastor Dagher raised his voice above the explosions and gunfire to shout a question to the congregation: "Are you prepared to go to heaven from here?"

They shouted back an affirmative answer. He turned to a visitor and exclaimed, "It's a great group of people. Marvelous!"[25]

Syria Toward A.D. 2000

The imposing Alliance church building on a main street in Damascus serves as the nerve center and heartbeat of the largest evangelical denomination in Syria. It also represents one of the largest and fastest-growing Alliance national churches in the Middle East.

A big sign identifies the building as the "Jesus the Light of the World Church." Since the Damascus Alliance church acts

The historical Alliance church in Madaba, Jordan

as spiritual leader of all fourteen other organized C&MA churches in Syria—and proud parent of many—the same inscription is seen over each church door.

Both the name and growth of the church in Syria owe much to Rev. Ibrahim Oueis. When pastoring the Damascus church and wondering what to name it, Oueis noticed that all the other churches carried names of saints, like Saint Ananias, Saint Helena and Saint Barnabas.

"These titles suggest to people what these churches stood for," explains a pastoral friend of Oueis. "He wanted the Alliance churches to be known for the preaching of Jesus Christ."[26]

This attitude of exalting Christ and maintaining loyalty to the C&MA was typical of Pastor Oueis.

During the 1950s, the Syrian field was suffering the transition from mission support to autonomy and self-support. Several pastors and congregations transferred to high-subsidy missions rather than undergo the self-discipline of tithing and learn dependence on God rather than a mission paymaster.

The same problem developed in Palestine and Jordan as groups left the Alliance for the comfortable paternalism of subsidy-minded missions.

Not Pastor Oueis. He determined to trust God and continue with the mission that had brought to him the knowledge of Jesus Christ. Responding to their pastor's faith, the Damascus church took on his total support.

Revival came to the Damascus church around 1958. Through the pastor's faithful biblical preaching, the congregation became more concerned about stewardship and outreach. Evangelistic services, Sunday school, even congregational singing experienced a new vitality.

Muslim neighbors who had previously tolerated a Christian church in their apartment building now became hostile toward the rejuvenated believers. A move to better and larger facilities became necessary for several reasons.

A prosperous merchant in the congregation showed the way to accomplish this by deciding to give his full tithe to the church. Others followed his example, and soon almost the entire church was tithing. They soon had $10,000 in a building fund and eventually saved twice that amount.

With a matching grant of $20,000 from Alliance churches in North America, they purchased property and gradually built what would become an impressive complex with a sanctuary accommodating 500 people, a Sunday school unit for over 200 students, and three apartments for pastoral staff.

The church's spiritual vitality and strategic location attracted people who came from all over Syria to study in the capital. On a given Sunday, some 70 percent of

Small shops add color to the streets of Amman, Jordan

the congregation would not be city residents.

The high percentage of out-of-towners proved an asset, not a liability. One of the pastors explains: "While in the church, these people are nurtured in Christ and established in the faith. When they return to their villages they start Bible studies. As these studies grow, they then ask if they can become Alliance churches."[27]

At least three village churches started in this manner by 1986. The Damascus congregation started its own daughter church during the 1980s by choosing Aleppo, the second largest and most important city of the northern region. With a population of 1.5 million and no Arab-speaking church, Aleppo and its environs posed a major challenge to the Gospel.

The Aleppo congregation grew to 150 persons worshiping on Sundays, enabling the church to rent a 200-seat hall. The pastor, however, estimated that the hall would only be adequate for a few years.

This kind of indigenous church growth, free from all outside help, has stirred considerable opposition from traditional religions. But as long as the church does not try to convert Muslims, the government seems uninclined to interfere.

(Left) *Jordanian Christians, an unpopular minority, have had to learn the art of praying* (right) *in a nation with a long history of commitment to Islam.*

While official tolerance continues, the Alliance church in Syria will openly continue its remarkable growth in the midst of one of the world's most zealous Muslim populations.

Jordan Toward A.D. 2000

When a small group of Arab Christians gathered on New Year's Eve in a suburb of Amman for their first Bible study, they were intent on making history.

The year was 1982, and the group's goal was to establish an organized church within five years. They knew that such an achievement was foreign to the norm; the last C&MA church in Jordan had been opened in 1951. But the organizers lived in West Amman, a new suburb only ten years old and filled with middle- and upper-class business and professional people—the kind of individuals used to doing new things and getting what they wanted.

Five years later, on New Year's Eve of 1987, the Bible study had grown to thirty people and was meeting in a well-situated apartment that could accommodate 150. Taking the name of Sixth Circle Alliance Church, the congregation initiated a full schedule of services.

Thus the small group of believers kept faith with their vision and Jordan had its first new Alliance church in thirty-five years.

Much of the credit for helping the new church get started belongs to the Jebal Amman Church and pastor, Rev. Albert Hashweh, in the capital.

Although the central church of the Alliance in Jordan, the congregation's place of worship was the smallest of all three churches in Jordan. Their apartment meeting place could only hold part of the 150-member congregation at one time. The people had to divide into three groups so that everyone could worship in the apartment sanctuary.

When the Jebal Amman Church helped the new congregation in West Amman get started by providing funds and some key members, it received in return a valuable contribution from the daughter church: the realization that church planting does indeed work!

Evangelism and church planting are possibilities precious and rare in most Arab states. Yet the exercise of religious freedom is possible in Jordan, even if by an unwritten law that freedom may be directed toward only "the minority population," i.e., Arabs with a non-Muslim background.

Given the successful establishing of the Sixth Circle Church and awakened interest in church planting by the Jebal Amman congregation, it is likely Jordan will not have to wait another thirty-five years before seeing another new Alliance church.

Arab Middle East Toward A.D. 2000

Fortress Islam has for centuries withstood almost every attempt to penetrate its Middle East defenses and lead its masses to freedom in Christ. In recent years, sounds of awakening have come from within the walls, and it appears that Muhammed's faithful are once again on the move.

The amassed riches of oil-producing Arab states did not spark this resurgence of Islam in the region. Neither did the shattered myth in Lebanon of Israeli military invincibility or the helplessness of Western powers before taunting hostage-takers.

Even Iran with its holy war fanaticism cannot claim credit for the awakened movement. "The Iranian revolution may have been a catalyst," editorializes *The Economist* of London, "but it does not sound like a sufficient explanation. One which many people offer depends on the

common need among young people for some sort of ideology or goal."[28]

Arab nationalism in the 1960s failed its generation. Capitalism in the 1970s was a foreign ideology, as was Communism. Materialism in the 1980s became a goal won and discarded.

Only Islam with its local roots seemed to make any sense. Rediscovering Islam's claims to rightness and superiority gives the Muslim masses of all ages a renewed sense of direction and alignment with something bigger than their hapless existence.

Christians should not expect a massive breach in Islam's rejection of the Gospel in the Middle East. To the contrary, they can anticipate a more militant resistance, while at the same time Muslim emissaries in greater numbers will seek to turn Christians to Muhammed's Allah.

But the Arab populations of the Middle East, by their great numbers and spiritual needs, represent such suffering and lostness that no opposition dare keep the servants of Jesus Christ from reaching out to them with truth and love.

That is why The Christian and Missionary Alliance measures its commitment to the Arab Middle East not in terms of results, but of resolve. ☐

EUROPE

The Mission Connection

EUROPE may be "the world's most difficult mission field," but its first link to The Christian and Missionary Alliance was as a sending continent, not a receiving one.

Of the five European countries in which the Alliance works, three—England, France and Netherlands—provided missionaries well before they received them. Only in Germany and Spain did the Alliance begin with church-planting ministries.

Why would the North American Alliance take missionaries from Europe when the continent has greater spiritual needs and fewer Christian workers than most mission fields of the Third World? Because Europeans took the initiative, not Americans or Canadians.

French nationals volunteered for service in then-called French West Africa and French Indochina. Christians in Holland asked to work in what was known as Dutch East Indies. British citizens approached the Alliance regarding Viet Nam. All these volunteers came forward before the C&MA had work in Europe.

Eventually, however, evangelism and church planting did begin in the "Old World," though missions in Europe differs in many respects from work carried on in developing countries.

"Mission schools, which played an important role in the evangelization of Africa, are nonexistent," J. Herbert Kane writes. "The same is true of medical work.

"Bible translation is no problem, since the Bible has been available in most of the languages of Europe for many years. Indeed, many of the European countries for decades have had their own Bible societies."[1]

Yet with all these advantages, the continent challenges the power of the Gospel and the perseverance of its bearers to the utmost. The words of Christ seem most sadly appropriate: "If then the light within you is darkness, how great is that darkness!"

FRANCE: Cosmopolitan Flair

The French link to Alliance missions has a certain cosmopolitan flair: It connects a surprising variety of nations in a concerted effort.

The link began after World War II, when French Christians indicated an interest in working among Africans in France's vast colonial territories. With French as their mother tongue and their understanding of colonial administration and education, they proved a valuable asset to the Alliance missions spreading throughout Africa and Indochina.

A French couple serving with the Alliance in Viet Nam was asked to return home in 1962 and represent the C&MA in their homeland. The goal was to provide missions-minded French Christians an opportunity to work overseas with an evangelical mission.

The tie with France became more crucial two years later, when a change in government in Kampuchea (then Cambodia) meant American missionaries were no longer welcome. The C&MA of France provided a continuing relationship with the Alliance Church in Kampuchea until North American missionaries could return after a pro-Western government seized power in 1970.

Consortium of Compassion

When Indochina fell to Communism in 1975, France provided a haven for refugees from Viet Nam, Laos and Kampuchea, all of them former French colonies. Even in the early 1980s, from 1,000 to 1,500 Asians were arriving in France each month.

Among the refugees were those who had lost everything but their faith. Christians who had belonged to Alliance churches in their country of birth soon formed congregations in their adopted homeland.

Churches and agencies of various nations joined in a consortium of compassion to help these groups. The minister of a Paris-based church received support from the Alliance Church Union of Hong Kong as he worked among ethnic Chinese from Viet Nam and Kampuchea. Chinese churches in the Philippines backed the pastor among Lao and Hmong believers.

The refugee groups were quick to reach out on their own. The Lao and Hmong established nine church groups among their people in the provinces. Vietnamese in Paris started their own church in 1972, while former missionaries to Viet Nam assisted another congregation in the southern city of Toulouse. An active Cambodian Alliance church in the capital also

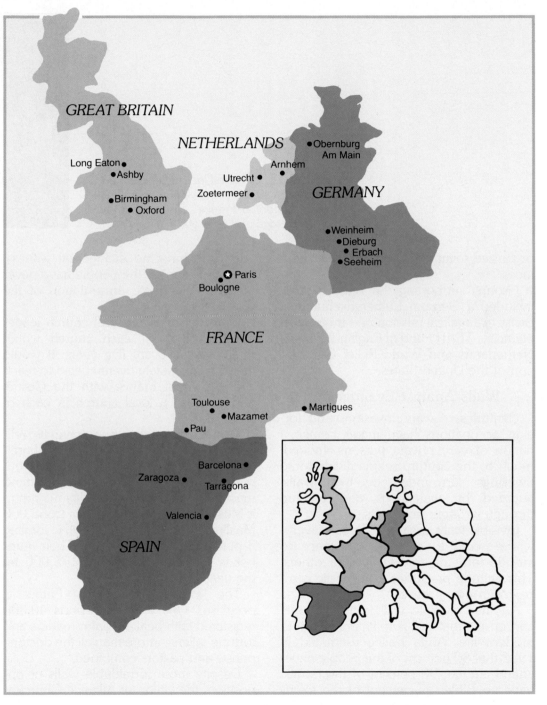

(Right) The Sacre Coeur Cathedral and (facing page) the Arc de Triomph in Paris symbolize France's Roman Catholic heritage and its proud national spirit.

organized several fellowships in the provinces.

Groups supporting the refugee work included a German Lutheran church, a Swiss evangelical mission and three relief agencies: TEAR Fund of England, ZOA of Netherlands and World Relief Corporation of the United States.

Walls Against Evangelism

Centuries of wars, invasions and foreign occupations have made France a nation of very private persons. Indeed, much of the country seems divided into dwellings surrounded by high walls, guarded by watchdogs and entered through wrought-iron gates.

Invisible walls exist, too. People everywhere seem to share a reluctance to intrude into the private lives of others. This attitude precludes evangelistic campaigns in many areas.

Another invisible wall is the national consensus that religion is irrelevant to modern life. Anita Bailey estimated in 1982 that 80 percent of the people never attend church; 90 percent of the homes have no Bible; 95 percent of the towns

and cities have no evangelical witness; and 96 percent of the people have never heard an adequate presentation of the Gospel.[2]

One French evangelical church leader estimates that "if each church would multiply itself every five years, it would take approximately twenty years to reach every town of France with the Gospel and establish a local church in each of them."[3]

France, however, does have its religions. The Roman Catholic Church claims 90 percent of the population, but only about two in every ten people attend mass. The second largest religious group is Muslim, not Protestant. Over 1,653,000 Muslims lived in France in 1984, totaling 3 percent of the population. Their number is projected to reach 2,175,000 by the year 2000.[4]

The "unseen" religion of France is occultism. One estimate reports 40,000 registered faith healers, palm readers and fortune-tellers—more than all the doctors, priests and pastors combined.[5]

Despite these formidable walls of opposition, the Union of Alliance Churches

in France registered as a church-planting denomination in 1977. It joined eighty-seven other North American missions and religious agencies at work in the nation.[6]

Each Alliance church reflects its surroundings and helps create a diverse composite of the Alliance in France.

Pau is a university town; Martigues is a Communist stronghold. Historic Mazamet was founded in A.D. 413 and long-forgotten years ago was a Huguenot Protestant stronghold.

Little by little, the French C&MA has developed in its dual role as both mission field and sending church. French Alliance churches held their first annual conference in 1981 and then began to conduct missionary conventions regularly.

Rev. Christian LeFlaec, president of the Alliance in France, found special significance in the Pau convention held in 1985: "This convention afforded us an unusual opportunity to transmit the missionary vision to the 120 Christians gathered there. This is the same number as the disciples gathered in the upper room in Acts 2—and we know well the result of their gathering."[7]

CHURCH AND MISSION

OFFICIAL NAME OF CHURCH:	Union of C&MA Churches in France
ENTRY BY MISSIONARIES:	1962
NUMBER OF MISSIONARIES:	27
ORGANIZED CHURCHES:	10
UNORGANIZED CHURCHES AND PREACHING POINTS:	20
BAPTIZED CHURCH MEMBERS:	554
INCLUSIVE MEMBERSHIP:	1,400
MEDICAL WORK:	0
EDUCATION:	0
RADIO BROADCASTS:	0
PAGES PRINTED:	0

COUNTRY

OFFICIAL NAME:	French Republic
FORM OF GOVERNMENT:	Republic
OFFICIAL LANGUAGE(S):	French
AREA:	220,668 sq. mi.
POPULATION:	(1989 est.) 55,813,000
CAPITAL:	Paris
PER CAPITA INCOME:	$13,046 (1986)
LITERACY:	99%
RELIGIOUS AFFILIATION:	Roman Catholic 74%, Muslim 4.6%, Protestant 2%, Jews 1.1%, Non-Religious 16%, Other 2.3%

GERMANY: Reevangelizing Luther's Land

The Alliance had a curious genesis in the Federal Republic of Germany.

Although the nation has a distinguished history in missionary endeavor, and although the nation itself has in this century become a mission field, Alliance beginnings in West Germany did not originate with the Division of Overseas Ministries. The story began instead through efforts of the North American-focused Division of Church Ministries.

DCM had for several years been sponsoring spiritual retreats in Germany for American and Canadian armed forces personnel serving in Europe. Rev. Leslie Pippert, vice president for the division, expanded the annual retreats into a permanent witness among the German people by recruiting a missionary already serving with another mission in Europe.

The first American Alliance couple, Rev. and Mrs. Richard J. Schaefer, began church-planting efforts in the Frankfurt area in 1972. They moved to Seeheim in response to an invitation from a group of believers in 1975. Two important organi-

A church near Seeheim serves as a reminder that, whatever its present state, the church has long been present in West Germany.

zational changes took place that same year. First, they set up headquarters for the work that became known as Missions-Allianz-Kirche. Second, the whole German effort became part of the Division of Overseas Ministries.

In 1975, the Schaefers established Germany's first Alliance church in Seeheim—a mission project some twenty-five miles from the historic site where Martin Luther had taken his courageous stand before the Diet of Worms in 1521.

Tradition Bound

The Seeheim congregation grew slowly and steadily, meeting first in the centuries-old City Hall and then moving to larger quarters in 1977. The deliberate pace of church growth is generally to be expected, according to John Caldwell Thiessen, because most Germans resist change when it concerns their traditional church ties—even when they ignore such ties for many years.

"When an individual has received his Protestant or Catholic confirmation certificate, he is considered to have finished his course and returns only on rare occa-

CHURCH AND MISSION

OFFICIAL NAME OF CHURCH: Missionary Alliance Church
                                    of Germany

ENTRY BY MISSIONARIES: 1975

NUMBER OF MISSIONARIES: 7

ORGANIZED CHURCHES: 3

UNORGANIZED CHURCHES AND
PREACHING POINTS: 2

BAPTIZED CHURCH MEMBERS: 66

INCLUSIVE MEMBERSHIP: 140

MEDICAL WORK: 0

EDUCATION: 0

RADIO BROADCASTS: 0

PAGES PRINTED: 0

COUNTRY

OFFICIAL NAME: Federal Republic of Germany

FORM OF GOVERNMENT: Federal Republic

OFFICIAL LANGUAGE(S):   German

AREA: 95,975 sq. mi.

POPULATION: 60,162,000

CAPITAL: Bonn

PER CAPITA INCOME: (1986) $10,680

LITERACY: 99%

RELIGIOUS AFFILIATION: Roman Catholic 45%, Protestant
                           44%, Non-Religious 5%, Muslim
                           3%, Other 3%

sions. Many parishes have thousands of members but attendance is considered good if 3 or 4 percent are present at any given service."[8]

Despite this widespread reluctance to accept religious change, the Seeheim congregation prospered. The church sponsored an Alliance extension work in Weinheim in 1979. Average attendance in Seeheim grew to over one hundred in 1980.

A 1982 evangelistic penetration of Erbach encountered the problem of resistance to religious change. Centuries-old family ties to established churches was a major factor why this area of Bavaria had never experienced a spiritual awakening.

A German layman backing the Alliance initiative in Erbach explains the obstacle to church growth in his city: "The German is more bound by church tradition than he is bound to Christ. He prefers to remain spiritually starved in a church that is not preaching the Gospel than to break tradition of family and friends to attend a church that is true to the New Testament."[9]

A typical street in Rothenberg an der Tauber evokes the orderliness universally associated with Germany.

Despite reluctance encountered among church traditionalists and opposition from many occultists, the Alliance was successful in establishing a church in Erbach. A nucleus of believers led by the Schaefers used various means that included evangelistic campaigns for adults and open-air meetings for children. Within two years the congregation outgrew its meeting place in a private home and rented an office building. Dedication of the renovated facilities in 1984 drew an estimated one hundred people.

The Missions-Allianz-Kirche recorded several significant events in 1985. The first German missionary candidate, a nurse on her way to the Alliance mission in Mali, did her home service in Erbach. The Seeheim congregation observed its tenth anniversary, and the German C&MA groups held their first General Assembly. By 1987, the Alliance in Germany grew to five churches.

Martin Luther, who knew enough about small beginnings, would appreciate the gains realized during the Alliance's first few years in his homeland.

Now a C&MA church, this building in Ashby was the first headquarters site for the Alliance in Great Britain.

GREAT BRITAIN: A Fresh Start

On June 9 and 10 of 1987, a study committee met in Nyack to evaluate the future of an Alliance work that had fallen on hard times.

Acting on an earlier decision by the British Missionary Alliance, representatives from England met with members of the Division of Overseas Ministries. They scrutinized the causes and conditions that had brought the once-promising work in England to the brink of failure. They then had to decide what to do next: Attempt a fresh start or withdraw from the country.

As in France, the first introduction of The Christian and Missionary Alliance to Great Britain related to missions.

A group of Christians banded together in the early 1970s with a common concern to see Viet Nam evangelized. They named their group Viet Nam Missionary Vision and chose as director a bank official and Baptist lay preacher named Raymond Smart. Since the C&MA was the principal mission in Viet Nam, the British group supported a missionary couple through the Holland-based sending agency affiliated with the Alliance.

After the fall of South Viet Nam to Communism in 1975, the English decided to transfer their couple to the Alliance work in Indonesia and at the same time seek closer ties with the North American C&MA. The group reorganized as the British Missionary Alliance in 1976, with Raymond Smart continuing as director.

The British work reached its zenith in 1981, when it counted eight congregations and planned to start one new church

each year. The goal, however, proved too ambitious.

The thriving mother church at Ashby de la Zouch sent out so many members to start daughter churches that the congregation itself began to struggle. The very next year, the Alliance withdrew from four areas and consolidated its strength in the four locations where congregations either had their own property or were soon to secure one.

Layman director Smart was transferred to another region by his bank employer, and the British Missionary Alliance continued to decline despite short-term help from North American personnel. By 1987, all that remained of the movement was the original self-supporting Ashby church with a British pastor and the small Long Eaton church pastored by an American couple. Something had to be done.

Starting Over

The process of reorganizing began with a request by the British Missionary Alliance board of directors early in 1987. The board unanimously requested the North American Division of Overseas

Ministries to appoint a director and expand Alliance ministry in England.

The study group meeting in the international headquarters at Nyack later that year drew up a plan eventually approved by both the British and North American boards in late 1987. The plan provided for the immediate appointment of a North American director and the eventual reorganization of the British Missionary Alliance with its own director and board of managers.

The plan also included additional overseas personnel to work with the British believers. If by a mutually agreed deadline sufficient progress were not achieved, the North American Alliance would then withdraw from Great Britain.

Elusive Promise

A cursory glance over the religious landscape of Great Britain might yield little encouragement for a great future ministry.

Nine percent of the population—only 4,023,000 out of 46,804,000—attend church with any regularity. Church membership from 1980 to 1985 dropped from 17 to 16 percent of the population. The

Alliance headquarters for ministry in Great Britain is now located in the famous university town of Oxford.

number of missionaries remained static at one per thousand church members. The total of British ministers decreased by 650 during the same five-year period.[10]

Yet despite widespread thinking that religion is irrelevant, crusades by Billy Graham and Luis Palau in 1986 drew over one million in attendance, and 100,000 went forward for prayer.

"The spiritual thirst is evident once it can be aroused," observes European MARC director, Peter Brierly: "The response rate has been substantially higher than at recent Graham rallies elsewhere in the world."[11]

Brierly also points out in catchy terms that many people still look upon the church as important in their lives: "There is still a demand for Christian blessing of hatching, matching and dispatching, and high attendance—roughly double the norm—at seasonal festivals."[12]

Even more significant is emergence of the House Church Movement. In 1970, there were no reported small groups of believers meeting in private homes for Bible study and worship. But by 1985, as many as 5,000 house churches counted 180,000 members and constituted a sig-

nificant "hidden church" in Great Britain.[13]

This new development in the nation's religious life should serve as a caution to those who would too readily dismiss the prospects of a widespread awakening in one of the most important nations of church history.

Should God once again move across the British Isles in a sovereign display of His mighty power, the Alliance wants to be there. In the vanguard.

CHURCH AND MISSION

OFFICIAL NAME OF CHURCH:	The Christian and Missionary Alliance of Great Britain
ENTRY BY MISSIONARIES:	
NUMBER OF MISSIONARIES:	4
ORGANIZED CHURCHES:	1
UNORGANIZED CHURCHES AND PREACHING POINTS:	2
BAPTIZED CHURCH MEMBERS:	24
INCLUSIVE MEMBERSHIP:	45
MEDICAL WORK:	0
EDUCATION:	TEE
RADIO BROADCASTS:	0
PAGES PRINTED:	0

COUNTRY

OFFICIAL NAME:	United Kingdom
FORM OF GOVERNMENT:	Constitutional Monarchy
OFFICIAL LANGUAGE(S):	English
AREA:	94,226 sq. mi.
POPULATION:	(1989 est.) 56,648,000
CAPITAL:	London
PER CAPITA INCOME:	$7,216.00
LITERACY:	99%
RELIGIOUS AFFILIATION:	Christian incl. Roman Catholic 69.4%, Non-Religious 26%, Muslim 2.7%, Hindu 1%, Other .8%

NETHERLANDS: Building Carefully

The massive dikes of Holland constantly remind the Dutch people they must build carefully and well. Most of their land, reclaimed from the sea at great cost over many years, could dissolve overnight in a froth of murky saltwater if their wall against the sea were not carefully built and tirelessly maintained.

That same willingness to work hard and well characterizes the two parallel but separate Alliance groups in the Netherlands: the missionary-sending Stichting Alliance Zendings Centrum "Parousia" and the church-planting Alliantie van Evangelische Gemeentenn "Parousia."

As in France and England, the first link between Holland and the North American Alliance came through missions. Rev. and Mrs. H. C. J. Konemann, supported by Dutch and Belgian churches, sailed to Indonesia (then the Dutch East Indies) in 1937 to work with the Alliance. Along with American and Canadian missionaries, the Konemanns were imprisoned by the Japanese during World War II, an ordeal that ruined his health.

Itinerate evangelists from many overseas Alliance churches attended the Amsterdam '86 convocation organized by Billy Graham.

Unable to resume their missionary career after the war, the Konemanns prayed that God would send ten Dutch workers overseas in their place—a request God honored threefold.

Cooperating with the North American Alliance, the Konemanns organized Alliance Zendings Centrum "Parousia" in 1953. This Dutch recruiting and sending agency established its headquarters on a beautiful estate in Wassenaar near The Hague. Ample grounds and facilities served as a Bible and mission conference center, as well as providing staff housing. The office relocated in 1977 to more modest quarters in Utrecht.

Building carefully and well, Alliance Zendings Centrum "Parousia" matched candidates from Holland with specific ministries needed on numerous Alliance fields. Coming from different denominational backgrounds, they served in a whole array of roles: teachers, doctors, nurses, evangelists, church planters and refugee workers.

By 1986, thirty-four Dutch Alliance missionaries were working in the African countries of Burkina Faso, Ivory Coast, Mali and Zaire; and in Far Eastern nations of Indonesia, Philippines and Thailand. Twenty-four received their full financial support from a fellowship of 3,200 missions-minded Dutch Christians in various denominations and also from eight C&MA Alliance churches of the Netherlands.

Spiritual Reclamation

Church-planting by the Alliance only began in recent years because this type of ministry was not previously needed. Rev. Leendert Kolle, who established the first Alliance church and became the Dutch Alliance churches' first president, says that even in the 1950s Holland was a God-fearing nation. But by the end of the 1960s, a high standard of living helped produce a lowered level of moral and spiritual life in the nation.

Eight million of Holland's eleven million people "openly rejected God," says Kolle. Both Protestant and Catholic churches began closing, while the dark powers of occultism became more active.

"So why did the Alliance start a church-planting ministry in the Netherlands?" Kolle asks. "Because during the last two decades a majority of the Dutch people have declared they want nothing to do with God or the Gospel."[14]

The Alliance of Evangelical "Parousia" Churches began in 1975 and was formally organized in 1980. Over the next

CHURCH AND MISSION

OFFICIAL NAME OF CHURCH:	Alliance of Evangelical Parousia Churches
ENTRY BY MISSIONARIES:	
NUMBER OF MISSIONARIES:	0
ORGANIZED CHURCHES:	4
UNORGANIZED CHURCHES AND PREACHING POINTS:	5
BAPTIZED CHURCH MEMBERS:	239
INCLUSIVE MEMBERSHIP:	1,186
MEDICAL WORK:	0
EDUCATION:	0
RADIO BROADCASTS:	0
PAGES PRINTED:	0

COUNTRY

OFFICIAL NAME:	Kingdom of the Netherlands
FORM OF GOVERNMENT:	Parliamentary Democracy
OFFICIAL LANGUAGE(S):	Dutch
AREA:	14,481,000 sq. mi.
POPULATION:	14,689,000
CAPITAL:	Amsterdam
PER CAPITA INCOME:	(1987) $13,065
LITERACY:	99%
RELIGIOUS AFFILIATION:	Roman Catholic 36%, Dutch Reformed 19.3%

five years, a new church was established each year. Working carefully and hard, the Dutch C&MA grew to seven congregations with an average 1983 weekly attendance of 400 adults and 200 children. Total attendance grew to nearly one thousand in 1986.

The new Alliance church in Zoetermeer indicates how church planting is done in the Netherlands.

When Anton Bol registered with the civil authorities in Zoetermeer, the clerk asked if he belonged to a church. "Yes," said Bol, "the Evangelical Church Parousia."

"There isn't any such church here," the clerk answered.

"True," Bol replied. "We intend to start one."[15]

Zoetermeer, a satellite suburb of The Hague, has been the fastest growing town in Holland—from 10,000 in 1960 to 80,000 in 1983. The Bols advertised,

visited homes, conducted Bible studies. But when they conducted their first Sunday morning service in 1977, no one came.

Acting in faith, the Bols rented some schoolrooms. People started to respond. Some were converted and baptized. Several experienced miraculous healing. The congregation grew to 125 adults and 100 children in 1981 and became self-supporting. It organized officially the following year. One year later, the young Zoetermeer church started its first daughter church in the world-famous pottery town of Delft.

Kolle, a former missionary to Peru, is enthusiastic about his country's half-century of Alliance missions, "but now our priority is also the mission field of the Netherlands itself," he says.[16]

Building carefully and well, the Dutch Alliance people want their churches to be as enduring and beneficial for their coun-

try as the massive dikes that assure its future.

SPAIN: "To the Hardest of Places"

Alliance congregations often sing during missionary conventions, "To the hardest of places He calls me to go." Translated into geographical terms, the hymn includes Spain.

In fact, Spain's entrenched resistence to evangelical witness over a period of centuries made it the obvious choice for the forty-sixth Alliance mission field. Unlike other European countries entered by the C&MA, the move into Spain followed two in-country surveys with the specific intent of starting churches.

The surveys left no doubt concerning the national attitude toward Protestant missionary initiatives. Rev. Fred Kowalchuk, a member of the survey teams in both 1976 and 1977, remembers: "Spanish church leaders had cautioned

(Above, left to right) *Holland preserves its unique links with the past with well-tended windmills and street canals, while staying competitive in the modern world by attracting conventions to its futuristic Congress Hall in Amsterdam.*

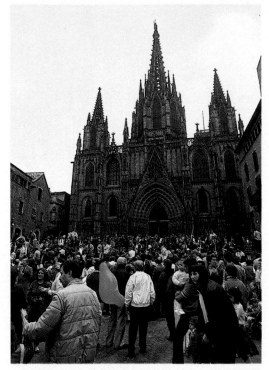

(Above) *Holiday celebration in Barcelona, Spain;* (above right) *crowd outside one of Spain's ancient cathedrals;* (facing page) *the Alliance chapel in Valencia.*

us not to expect rapid growth. We were told that if in eight years we had a congregation of twenty-five, we would have ample cause to rejoice."[17]

The church leaders' attitude reflected the experience of Spanish Protestants, who had by God's grace endured harassment, persecution and martyrdom for over four hundred years as they painfully and slowly built the church in their homeland.

History of Intolerance

Menendez y Pelayo expressed the mingled patriotic and religious fervor of Spanish Catholicism: "Spain, the evangelizer of half the globe, Spain the hammer of heretics, light of Trent, sword of Rome, cradle of St. Ignatius . . . : this is our greatness and our unity, we have no other."[18]

Some of the nation's finest citizens disputed this claim in the sixteenth century when they embraced the Reformation message. Eminent scholars, clergy and nobility promoted the gospel of faith without works even at the royal court. "Reformed churches" drew congregations in the thousands.

Illescas, a prominent Catholic author, wrote: "These people were of such quality and so numerous that had we waited but two or three months before halting the evil, the whole of Spain would have been ablaze."[19]

The remedy for such evil: the Inquisition.

With the ruthless tenacity that only misguided religion can excite, inquisitors roamed Spain for almost three centuries in search of heretics. Wherever they suspected heresy, properties were confiscated, books were burned, and so were people.

Political changes won for the few surviving Protestants a brief respite in the mid-1800s. Then the clerics resumed their crusade against those who dared to

believe other than the dogma of Rome.

Even as recently as 1953, a concordat between Spain and the Vatican enabled Roman Catholicism "to acquire more rights and advantages than it had enjoyed under the most Catholic kings."[20]

Laws concerning marriage, military service, education, health care and burial were designed to keep Roman Catholics faithful to their church from birth to death. Protestant meeting places were not even allowed to resemble church buildings in appearance or indicate in any way what they were.

The whole country, whether in legislation, institution or attitude, had no place for people who differed with the Church. Not until 1980 was the spirit of the Second Vatican Council reflected in a consti-

tution that guaranteed individual and collective rights to religious freedom.

By 1984, after four centuries of almost continuous persecution, the Protestant community had an estimated 40,000 communicant members and a community of 100,000—about three in every thousand Spaniards.[21]

No wonder Spanish Protestant leaders warned the Alliance survey team in 1976-1977 not to expect quick results—and no wonder the Alliance, viewing the spiritual need, officially entered Spain the following year.

Double Entry

Two experienced missionary couples from Peru took up residence in densely populated areas without an evangelical

witness. Rev. and Mrs. Fred Kowalchuk settled in Barcelona, while Rev. and Mrs. Bertil A. Lofsted entered Valencia.

Barcelona presented a missionary challenge typical of all Spain. An area of two hundred city blocks had no evangelical church. Although perhaps 95 percent of the people would profess themselves Roman Catholics, less than 10 percent attended mass regularly. Spiritual erosion was especially evident among the young people: 42 percent did not believe in God; 50 percent saw nothing wrong with homosexuality; and over 90 percent approved of premarital sex.[22]

Not until the fifth attempt were the missionaries able to find someone willing to rent them property for a chapel. The small, mezzanine-level office did not deter them from starting a community awareness campaign. They distributed 40,000 pieces of literature, visited from house to house, offered evening Bible studies and English classes.

The progression of meeting places marked the success of their efforts. Beginning with no core group or even prior contacts in 1978, the work moved from the cramped mezzanine-level office to a

(Clockwise from top left) *In 1985, Alliance "construction missionaries" helped renovate a building, turning it into a chapel for use by the Barcelona C&MA congregation for Bible studies and worship services.*

street-level chapel with an eighty-seat capacity in 1981. At that time, the missionary commented that he hoped the chapel would be crowded out in five years.

He was happily wrong. In less than four years attendance grew to 120 and necessitated another move. By this time, campaign that lasted thirty-five days. The the Barcelona congregation had become the first organized Alliance church in Spain.

The church next found a building that could be remodeled into a 400-seat chapel, along with eight classrooms, three offices, two lounges, a nursery and other facilities. Twenty volunteers from the Alliance Men organization in North America flew in to help put the plans into action.

Some 350 people attended the dedication service of the renovated building in September of 1985. And already the missionaries were talking about building a 1,000-seat auditorium the next time.

Church-planting in Valencia developed in similar fashion. After holding formal services for a year, the Valencia congregation joined with eighteen other evangelical groups in 1981 for a citywide tent 2,000-seat tent was filled several times, and 110 converts confessed their faith in

CHURCH AND MISSION

OFFICIAL NAME OF CHURCH:	The Evangelical Christian and Missionary Alliance of Spain
ENTRY BY MISSIONARIES:	
NUMBER OF MISSIONARIES:	15
ORGANIZED CHURCHES:	4
UNORGANIZED CHURCHES AND PREACHING POINTS:	1
BAPTIZED CHURCH MEMBERS:	85
INCLUSIVE MEMBERSHIP:	255

COUNTRY

OFFICIAL NAME:	Spain
FORM OF GOVERNMENT:	Constitutional Monarchy
OFFICIAL LANGUAGE(S):	Spanish
AREA:	194,896 sq. mi.
POPULATION:	(1989) 39,784,000
CAPITAL:	Madrid
PER CAPITA INCOME:	(1984) $4,490.00
LITERACY:	97% (1987)
RELIGIOUS AFFILIATION:	Roman Catholic 93.6%, Protestant 0.5%

Christ. The Valencia congregation became a fully organized church in 1984.

Familiar Struggle

The following year, Alliance missionaries began the familiar struggle of penetrating another populous urban area. Two experienced church-planting couples were assigned to Zaragoza, Spain's fifth largest city.

The Virgin of Pila, to whom many thousands make pilgimage, including Pope John Paul II on two occasions, has given the city a status in Spanish Catholicism it zealously guards. Protestant activity draws special resistance.

Only one evangelical church has more than 150 attendees. The others are small, struggling congregations with part-time pastors. The total Protestant population is less than 1,000 in a city of 700,000.

Invitations to an evangelistic service drew the same kinds of responses heard elsewhere in Spain: "We are already Christians; we don't need you." "Why did you come? We have enough churches." Devotion to the Virgin of Pila gave an added edge to their questions.

The two couples followed the low-key, person-to-person strategy that proved successful in Barcelona and Valencia. They settled in a densely populated area without a gospel witness. They made friends with neighbors and acquaintances wherever they found them—the park, the store, the school-bus stop. Then they offered to show films, start English classes and conduct home Bible studies.

As interest stirred, a meeting place be came essential. The staff found an excellent location on a main artery of traffic through the city and renovated it into a chapel in late 1985. A group composed of enthusiastic converts and excited missionaries shortly became Spain's third Alliance church. Other new churches soon followed.

When God leads, even in "the hardest of places" His work can prosper.   ☐

PACIFIC ISLANDS

THE REPUBLIC
OF CHINA
(TAIWAN)   274

HONG KONG   282

INDONESIA   294

JAPAN   330

PHILIPPINES   340

PACIFIC ISLANDS

Of Commerce, Creeds, and Conquest

L IKE successive ocean waves surging up coral beaches, each rank overcome by the next, world religions have swept over the Pacific island world for thousands of years.

Hindu merchants from India arrived in search of spices and precious woods during the first centuries after Christ. They also boasted of their superior gods and beliefs. Buddhist pilgrims came from India too, but their search was for souls, not spices.

Then came Muslims in the twelfth century to barter goods in exchange for the islands' exotic treasures. They stayed to teach the "infidels" about their Allah, the only true God.

The Arabs in turn were overtaken by Spanish and Portuguese Roman Catholics in the sixteenth century. They sailed in search of trade, but also to rule the islands, Christianize the "savages" and halt further advance by Muslim heretics.

A century later, Dutch and English Protestants overpowered the despised "papists" and settled down to perpetuate colonial rule on their own terms. Again, the church wrapped itself in the flag and carried on its Christianizing mission.

Not until the nineteenth century did the next religious wave arise. Following the fleet into Tokyo harbor and Manila Bay, American Protestants spread out in Japan, the Philippines and other islands of the Pacific, a missionary force more numerous and versatile than anything the region had ever seen.

Each successive wave of foreign expansion sweeping over the Pacific islands carried a mixture of commerce, creeds and conquest. Whatever their nationality—Indian, Chinese, Arab, European or American—they all left the imprint of their religion: Hindu, Buddhist, Muslim, Catholic or Protestant.

European powers, perhaps more than others, wove political, commercial and religious aims in a tightly knit trilogy.

What Ralph Tolliver observes concerning Spanish Catholics in the Philippines applies equally to Portuguese, Dutch and English of the period. He writes that "five Augustinian monks landed behind the muskets, cannon and armorplate of the conquering Spanish forces, and this relationship continued for three centuries of Spain's rule with church and state, cross and crown, cassock and cannon interlocked and interdependent."[1]

However, missionary enterprise could not be free of national associations even had it wanted to. Then, as now, sea power determined the course of events in the Pacific. If missionaries sought entry to the islands, they had to book passage on the same ships that carried merchants and soldiers.

If missionaries wanted to evangelize the indigenous people, they usually worked under the protection of their nation's flag, because hostile elements were intent on destruction of all foreigners, whether missionary or military.

FIRST WAVE:
Indian Hinduism and Buddhism

In the opening years of the Christian calendar, commerce flourished between India and Indonesia. Ships of the island princes carried cloves, peppers, precious woods and other exotic cargo to the subcontinent. Mariners returned with news of Hindu India as well as its goods. Thus informed, island rulers welcomed Brahman priests to their courts, often adopting practices and doctrines of these imposing teachers.

Unlike the high-caste Brahmans, Buddhist pilgrims came

from India specifically for the purpose of converting the islanders. "They would appear at Indonesian courts, preach the law, convert the ruler and his family, and found an order of monks."[2]

One famous Chinese Buddhist pilgrim visited Srivijaya (now Palembang), Sumatra, on his way to India in A.D. 671. He found over a thousand Buddhist monks observing the same rules and ceremonies found in India.[3]

Hinduism and Buddhism helped form Indonesian life for about a thousand years before being swamped by another world religion: Islam.

SECOND WAVE:
Arabic Islam

Malacca, a strategically placed port near the southern tip of the Malay Peninsula, attracted Muslim merchants from Mecca, Cairo and Persia. It became a vast trade fair midway between the Near and Far East. Products from China found their way to Malacca, there to be exchanged for goods from western Asia and Europe.

The Muslims' intent at first seemed only to buy and sell. But before the end of the thirteenth century, they appeared more dedicated to the cause of the Prophet than profit.[4]

A political entity as well as commercial, Malacca saw something more in Islam than just a religion spread by traders. By becoming a Muslim sultanate, Malacca could profit from the vaunted "unity of Islam," which meant political allies and military alliances. The ensuing deal benefited both parties: Malacca found powerful backing in its wars with Thailand, and

Islam obtained a strategic trading center from which to spread the teachings of Muhammad throughout the region.

Muslim trader/missionaries first penetrated Indonesia in the thirteenth century by crossing the Straits of Malacca and infiltrating the northern part of Sumatra. By the time Marco Polo passed that way, he could report that the region had been converted to "the law of Mahomet."[5]

Ironically, Islam got its biggest boost from the unwitting Roman Catholic seafaring nations of Spain and Portugal. One Dutch historian suggests, "The close coherence of the Muslim powers . . . found expression in their annual meeting at Mecca, and through the medium rumours of the Christian struggle against Islam in the Iberian Peninsula reached Indonesia ahead of the Portuguese."[6]

Alarmed at the prospects of an invasion by Europeans, many people previously indifferent to Islam were driven into its arms for protection. Movement toward the Allah of Islam became even more pronounced once the Portuguese landed in Indonesia and the Spanish in the Philippines.

Notes one historian concerning the region: "The alliance of priest and soldier in [Catholic Christianity] often proved an advantage for Islam, for the reluctant people frequently sought help and protection of neighboring kingdoms which had already turned to Islam."[7]

Even so, the Pacific islanders did not mindlessly accept Islam without alterations. Indonesians especially were proud of their religious heritage, a mixture of Hinduism, Buddhism and traditional spirit worship. "Arabic influences were slow to gain ground in Indonesia," writes Frank Snow; "when Islam was accepted it was in a compromised form rather than its exclusive purity."[8]

To this day, Indonesia does not have a uniform religion of Islam, but rather an Islamic community of varying beliefs and practices ranging from folk religion to rigid fundamentalism demanding adherence to the Qur'an (or Koran), Islam's holy book.

THE THIRD WAVE:
Portuguese and Spanish Roman Catholicism

Spain and Portugal, both Roman Catholic countries, led the rest of Europe in exploration and contact with non-Christian peoples in the three centuries after A.D. 1500. Enriched by colonies in the New World and emboldened by successes elsewhere, the two sea powers looked eastward to attain more triumphs, treasures and territories.

Religious fervor paralleled commercial and political ambitions in the neighboring nations on the Iberian Peninsula. Neither country had been unsettled by the Protestant Reformation, yet each had been revitalized by the Roman Catholic Counter-Reformation—and both had a score to settle with Islam for trying to overrun their Iberian homeland.

Though acting at times more like foes than friends, the two sea powers divided the two major island groupings between them: Portugal targeted Indonesia, and Spain settled for the Philippines.

Bound by a pledge to the Holy See to fight Islam, Portugal made the conquest of Malacca, by now a major center of Islamic expansion, one of the first steps of its strategy. The forces of Don Alfonse de Albuquerque stormed the Malaysian stronghold in 1511, ending its domination of the seaways and its role as a Muslim stronghold.

Under the watchful eyes and open cannon ports of Portuguese warships, colonies and factories multiplied in Sumatra, Java and the lesser islands of Indonesia. The Muslim sultans, however, had stolen a march on the European infidels by seizing control of large areas. Portuguese settlements were consequently limited to fortified areas on the coast, and so were missionary efforts of the church.

Thus, when Portuguese armed might prevailed, the mission made converts. When the military faltered and faded, so did the church. "In practice, the fortunes of Christianity depended almost entirely upon the military strength of the Portuguese."[9]

For nine months in 1546, Francis Xavier, famed founder of the Society of Jesus (Jesuits) and missionary pioneer, counseled and encouraged the missionaries in the Molucca islands. An estimated two hundred priests established a church that totaled approximately 160,000 communicants in various islands by 1580. "However, the work was without plan or order, and frequently the recipients of mass baptism were unable to receive any further attention."[10]

Rival Muslim groups made life miserable for the Roman Catholics, inflicting martyrdom on thousands of converts and even some European priests. But fellow countrymen of the missionaries harmed the church's cause far more than the Muslims.

An English historian described Portuguese settlers as having a crusading zeal that intensified rather than restrained their cruel

treatment of islanders: "Although priests and monks multiplied in their dominions, they were ineffectual missionaries because of the misdeeds of traders and freebooters."[11]

Even Francis Xavier noted with disgust "that the knowledge of the Portuguese in the Moluccas was restricted to the conjugation of the verb *rapio,* in which they showed 'an amazing capacity for inventing new tenses and participles.' "[12]

The colonists' vicious conduct drove the Indonesians to violent revolt. This weakened Portuguese missionary work, which was based on the promise of government protection from hostile neighbors. For this reason, when the Portuguese were forced out of Indonesia at the end of the sixteenth century, almost all vestiges of the Roman Catholic Church disappeared with them.[13]

Philippines: Facade of Faith

Ferdinand Magellan's fleet landed in the Philippines about 1521. He claimed its islands and islets for Spain and paid for the honor with his life. Magellan's fate was something of a harbinger of the bloody wars Spain would unsuccessfully wage to subjugate the islands before losing them to the United States in 1898 after one final war.

Spain's agenda for the colony was threefold: to carve out a share of the spice trade; to use the islands as stepping-stones to China and Japan; and to Christianize the masses. Only the third goal gave Spain a limited measure of success—and that was more often superficial than real.

Spain also intended that its missionary efforts would halt Islam's island-hopping advance northward from Indonesia through the Philippines. The king's fleets and forces arrived just in time: Islam had already seized control of Mindanao, Sulu and other islands of the southern archipelago.

Attempts to push back the Muslim Moros not only failed but stirred fierce counterattacks. The badly stung Spanish forces probably wondered why they ever bothered to kick the hornets' nest. Rebellious Moros have continued their resistance to the "Christian" government in Manila ever since.

Spanish clergy viewed their mandate in the 1600s quite differently than did the military and therefore fared somewhat better. An Augustinian friar, Andres de Urdaneta, "and his fellow missionaries, believing that Spanish dominion over the peoples of the newly acquired territories should be guided rather by the papal injunction to convert them to Christianity than by the crusading notion of subjugating infidels, showed themselves more effectual than the military in the work of conquest, and zealous in protecting their flocks from exploitation from the colonists."[14]

This progressive policy won the support of Spain's King Philip II, who made the spread of Christian faith a priority of his colonial policy. He encouraged the organizing of hospitals and schools as well as churches, and the training of indigenous clergy.

Within forty-five years of Urdaneta's arrival, Spain claimed that the island colony was Christianized. Even in the early nineteenth century, when Napoleonic wars in Europe forced the church to curtail activities, Catholic membership in the Philippines—including babies—continued to flourish, growing from four million to seven million.

Spain's boast that the Philippines was Asia's first Christian nation, however, had a hollow ring. From an evangelical perspective, the Filipino Roman Catholic Church was seriously deficient.

The Bible, for example, was withheld from the people and vernacular translations forbidden. The average communicant, lacking understanding of even basic church doctrine, continued animistic, spirit-worshiping practices. Filipino clergy were not advanced to leadership roles. Religious liberty was nonexistent in that proclamation of any other faith was forbidden and punishable by imprisonment.[15]

Internal Strife

Even between the power-sharing institutions of church and state, tensions and frictions constantly flared like quarrels between incompatible Siamese twins.

Historian Hall notes that from the very beginning, "Church and State remained entirely interdependent, with the State supporting the Church and ecclesiastical advance aiding the consolidation of political control."[16]

The organic union was not one of equals. Priests wielded more influence in Madrid and more power in Manila than did civil authorities. If church officials disagreed with local policy, they complained directly to the king, and changes followed. The church held the real reins of power.

"In examining the political administration of the Philippines," write historians Blair and Robertson with a touch of humor, "we must be prepared to find a sort of outer garment under which the living body is ecclesiastical."[17]

Local government officials, however, refused to concede that their territory was more mission than colony. They complained constantly to Spain that the clergy were usurping civil authority. So "the struggle for power went on without abate throughout the whole Spanish period."[18]

Clergy within the church hierarchy also rubbed one another the wrong way, to the point of intolerance with racist overtones. Spanish "regulars" (priests of European nationality and training) held tightly to the reins of leadership. They looked down on Filipino "seculars" (indigenous clerics with local training) as ignorant, immoral and unfit to lead. Discrimination became blatantly obvious by 1870: Out of 792 parishes, Filipino priests had charge of only 181.[19]

Friction flared into open conflagration during the 1890s, when dissident Filipino priests appointed one of their number, Gregorio Aglipay y Labayan, as "Supreme Bishop of the Independent Church of the Philippines." Numerous priests and an estimated three million Catholics eventually joined the schismatic church.[20]

The massive exodus was partly in protest against many of the Spanish friars. Their abuses were numerous, such as charging exorbitant fees to say mass, but the most serious offense against the people was the friars' mismanagement of the church's vast land holdings.

This greed for power and money cost the church heavily, because the dispute over land "was one of the provocations that led to a revolt against Spain in 1896, a revolt which eventually involved the United States and led to independence and the opening up of the Philippines to the gospel message."[21]

Meteoric Mission

The flood tide of Spanish and Portuguese expansion across the Pacific coincided with a period of disarray in Japanese cultural and political life during the sixteenth century.[22]

The reigning shogunate suffered from old age; civil wars weakened traditional ties; and native sons returning home from abroad brought new and revolutionary ideas. In addition, many Japanese truly hungered for a spiritual alternative to Buddhism, which had grown politically corrupt and ethically immoral.

With resistance to foreign influence at its lowest ebb, Japan proved vulnerable to the advances of European politics and religion, as both the Portuguese and Spanish discovered.

First to arrive in 1542, the Portuguese were more interested in commerce than religion. One of their returning ships stopped at Malacca just when the Jesuit commander Francis Xavier was heading home to Europe from the Moluccas.

Intrigued by the traders' tales about Japan, Xavier made a momentous decision: He reversed his direction to eastward, leading the church's first missionary band to Japan in 1549.

Key factors pointed toward success. Japan's spiritual defenses were lowered, and the Jesuits were well trained and financed. Most important, they were led by Xavier, the greatest missionary leader the Roman Catholic Church has ever known.

The mission flourished remarkably for nearly a generation. An estimated 30,000 Japanese converted to Catholicism by 1571. The total of communicants increased to 150,000 just nine years later—almost 1 percent of the whole population. The trading port of Nagasaki became headquarters for the Jesuits and led the nation in conversions.[23]

The meteoric rise of Catholicism was not to last.

A new shogun rose to power with the determination to unite his country and make it once again powerful. He was well aware that "in nearly every land into which it expanded . . . Christianity was closely associated with political conquests by European powers."[24]

The shogun and his entourage of revitalized national leadership resented any activity that might expose their country to aggression. They were especially incensed at the priests' attacks on Buddhism and the nation's other religions, which they considered a unifying force among the people.

Hostility toward Catholicism was fed from other sources as well. Dutch and English traders vilified Catholicism; Spanish and Portuguese merchants battled each other for special deals with the government; even Jesuits tried to undermine other Catholic religious orders, considering them poachers in their special domain.

"Thus the competing nations, priests and faiths of the West undermined one another's position and prestige in Japan and paved the way for the drastic proscription of the Christian faith."[25]

The shogun issued an edict in 1587 outlawing Christianity and ordering all missionaries to leave Japan within twenty days. Jesuit priests defied the edict and secretly continued their work with the help of converts. Persecution followed—even the crucifixion of some Christians—but faltered and stopped when the reigning shogun died. The anti-Christian edicts, however, remained on the books.

Catholic Christianity peaked in the early 1600s. With a

reported 70,000 baptisms between 1602 and 1607, the church claimed a following of one-half million and 250 Japanese priests and catechists by 1615.[26]

Cruel Eclipse

Persecution resumed in 1612 under a new shogun, this time in all seriousness.

Missionaries were expelled, borders closed to all trade with Roman Catholic countries, strict censorship imposed, the death sentence instituted for those who did not recant, and anti-Christian edict boards placarded across the land. "In no other country," writes Latourette, "were such persistent and thoroughgoing efforts made to stamp out the Christian faith."[27]

Thousands of Catholics experienced martyrdom in horrible ways: Some were hacked to pieces and beheaded with swords, others were roasted over slow burning fires, and many were suspended by their heels for days before they eventually died.

Missionaries trying to sneak back into Japan disguised as merchants or sailors met the fate of their followers.

When Christians in one area were goaded beyond endurance, they banded together and sought refuge in a deserted castle. Surrounded and overcome, they were slaughtered one by one. Over 37,000 adults and children died in a bloody massacre that became known as the Shimabara Rebellion.[28]

Nagasaki, the Jesuit headquarters city, suffered a more prolonged fate. As late as the last half of the eighteenth century, every inhabitant of the city had to take an anti-Christian oath and trample a cross underfoot every year.[29]

Some Catholics in the hills behind Nagasaki and in some outlying islands secretly persisted in their faith, handing down their beliefs from generation to generation. Too weak and fearful to initiate any new spiritual movement, they nonetheless remained loyal to what the missionaries had taught them, even though cut off from all outside Christian contact for centuries.

So fearful and respectful of Christianity were the shoguns that for over two hundred years they hermetically sealed the kingdom against all influences from Europe. Only the Dutch had a tightly controlled permit to occupy a small trading port.

All literature from abroad was confiscated and destroyed. Japanese were forbidden to travel overseas. Shipwrecked fishermen rescued by foreigners and delivered safely home were executed on the beaches. Foreigners trying to infiltrate the closed kingdom were tortured and killed.

Summing up the history of Christianity in Japan through the eighteenth century, Latourette concludes: "Its course was more meteoric and more marked by the blood of martyrs than in any other region in Southern or Eastern Asia."[30]

FOURTH WAVE:
Dutch and British Protestantism

The five centuries from A.D. 1400 to A.D. 1900 witnessed Catholic and Protestant sea powers divide the years almost equally among themselves as they rolled across the Pacific like one tidal wave after another.

Catholic Spain and Portugal roamed the high seas at will during the fifteenth and sixteenth centuries. The next century marked their decline, even as Protestant England and Holland were on the rise. The eighteenth and nineteenth centuries belonged to the Protestants, the latter often called the "Great Evangelical Century," partly due to successes in the East.

As with the Roman Catholics in the heyday of Spanish and Portuguese imperialism, the church in Protestant nations matched the national expansionist mood with a missionary spirit.

Latourette believes that "the general spirit of expansion which was abroad among Western peoples helped to prepare the way for the birth and growth of enterprise for the propagation of Christianity.

"When merchants were dreaming in terms of new markets and enlarging foreign trade, and when statesmen were planning fresh colonial adventures, it was natural for the more earnest among the Christians to seek to parallel these movements with others for the world-wide extension of their faith."[31]

Except for some territorial claims on scattered islands and a brief occupation of Indonesia during one of the European wars, Britannia contented herself with colonial enterprises on the mainland. Even Hong Kong, described contemptuously by one Englishman as "a piece of useless granite with no water and nothing to commend it," came under British control as a stepping-stone to the continent.[32]

In the vast, watery reaches of the Pacific, it was Holland and later the United States who brought Protestant Christianity to the island world.

Dutch Crusade

The Dutch sailed into Indonesian waters during the late 1500s to rout the Catholics with something of the same zeal the Portuguese exercised against the Muslims. In a series of sharp encounters, the Dutch drove the Portuguese from almost all their settlements and territorial claims to Indonesia.

The Declaration of November 21, 1599, opened the islands to Dutch pastoral and missionary work. The document included a statement "that Christians traveling to and from the Indies should not be left without Christian instruction and that it was hoped to get an opportunity to teach the people there in darkness the true Christian religion."[33]

"Sick visitors" or "comforters" sailed with the Dutch fleets for the purpose of ministering to sailors and colonists. Their spiritual ministry soon enlarged to embrace Indonesians found in the settlements.

The various Dutch commercial concerns were organized by the government into the United East India Company. It assumed absolute rights and authority over the whole Indonesian venture. Unlike its English counterpart in India, this trading company recorded as one of its primary functions the promotion of Christianity among the natives.

Until it was abolished almost two hundred years later, the company hired, supported and supervised its own clergy in the islands. Civil authorities appointed by the company determined which territories should have missionaries, what languages were to be spoken in what religious services, what schools and hospitals were to be opened.

Company Converts

The colonial administration made what it no doubt considered another great contribution to religious advancement among the indigenous peoples. Adopting the Roman Catholic practice of *cuius wegio euis religio* ("who reigns, his religion"), the civil authorities enacted a law coercing Roman Catholics to become Protestants.[34]

Although scattered Roman Catholic groups refused, some 80,000 switched their allegiance overnight from Rome to the Reformed Church. Authorities also forced the general population to embrace the Christian faith, "with the result that hundreds of thousands of persons 'requested' baptism without undergoing a corresponding change of heart."[35]

Village chiefs in some areas were ordered to have a quota of candidates ready for baptism every time a clergyman appeared, and "the latter was paid a specified sum for each person baptized."[36]

Those who submitted to baptism generally believed the ceremony was some kind of naturalization process that entitled them to some of the privileges enjoyed by the ruling Dutch.[37]

The United East India Company's priority, however, focused on trade, not converts. Not surprisingly, commercial concerns flourished more than religious ones. Only twenty-two ministers were on the company payroll by 1776. The total dropped to seven by the time the company was abolished in 1799.

Out of 500,000 recorded members, only 15,000 were active enough to be called communicants. The 240 congregations had only four Dutch ministers.[38] Protestant missionary work in Indonesia was at its nadir. Only hard work by Indonesian catechists kept the church going and saved the mission from total failure.

Serious Evangelism

The Reformed Church of the Netherlands knew little of what was happening in Indonesia for many years. It had no part in the selection of clergy or supervision of their work. Earnest Christians began gradually to have serious doubts about the policy of allowing a commercial company to oversee the spiritual welfare of a population.

This concern materialized in formation of the Netherlands Missionary Society in 1797 along the lines pioneered by several British missions. Although independent of the state church, it drew many of its workers from Reformed ranks.

Evangelism of the islands now began in earnest. The mission was blessed in having a spiritual giant for its first missionary to Indonesia. Joseph Kam was appointed to Ambon but spent six months in Java on his way to the field.

Kam profoundly influenced several members of the state church to consider their spiritual debt toward the Javanese. They formed a witness group—derisively called the "Surabaja pietists" by critics—and spread out to evangelize east Java.

Kam's impact on sincere Christians in Java presaged the ministry he was to have for many years. Arriving in Ambon, he found 20,000 communicants who had been visited only twice by a minister in seven years. Again he stirred the churches to spiritual renewal and a vision for the unevangelized.

He ranged widely for the next seventeen years and "wherever he went, the reviving effects of his ministry were to continue throughout the rest of the century."[39]

Two other missions soon joined the Dutch. The Rhenish Missionary Society, an 1828 union of four German missions, pioneered work in Kalimantan. The Mennonite Missionary Union, founded in 1847, sent workers to Sumatra and Java.

These and other missions uniformly found their greatest response among animist peoples in areas yet untouched by Islam. But even witness among the Muslims proved more fruitful than in any other Muslim area of the world.

Taiwan Exchange

Having rid Indonesia of Portuguese commercial and religious enterprises, the Dutch turned their attention to Taiwan. The island, which in the course of its history has seen a bewildering exchange of conquerors and settlers, was occupied in the seventeenth century by Portugal and Spain in their strategy to reach China.

Dutch forces ended those plans by force of arms. They in turn built Fort Zeelandia and proceeded to extend their influence across the island. Along with traders and settlers came at least twenty-nine clergymen. They itinerated in the villages, destroying idols, building schools and organizing churches.

Though most of the converts were aborigines easily persuaded, the missionaries still needed military protection when entering new areas. This identifying the church with the crown had short-lived benefits. Dutch occupation of Taiwan lasted only forty years and then ended under pressure by the Chinese, leaving a weak church behind.

"As far as we know, the congregations did not long survive the collapse of Dutch rule," writes Latourette. "Presumably the Christianity which was so dependent upon Dutch prestige disappeared with the regime under whose aegis it had been initiated."[40]

FIFTH WAVE:
American Protestantism

The appearance of American missions in the Pacific island world was significant enough in size and far enough removed in time from the Dutch era of expansion—and so different in approach—as to represent a totally new wave of missionary effort.

When Commodore Matthew Perry, U.S.N., and his fleet of black warships forced Japan to reopen its doors in 1853, he was championing the cause of trade, not religion. Yet the treaties that followed in 1858 and 1859 allowed missionaries to edge their way back into a land that for 219 years had been closed to missions like a vacuum-sealed safe.

The first American consul, Townsend Harris, was a devout Christian who made sure the commercial treaties contained provision for the exercise of religious beliefs. Foreigners residing in the three treaty ports were allowed to worship and build their own places of worship. Harris reinforced this right by hosting religious services in his own home and attending church services in a temple supplied by the imperial government.

Authorities even agreed to abolish traditional anti-Christian practices, such as annually forcing residents of Nagasaki to trample a cross. But anti-Christian laws remained on the books, and edict boards still hung prominently throughout the realm. Conversion continued to be a crime punishable by death.

For about two decades after Japan reopened its doors to the West, the price of becoming a Christian was very high. Roman Catholic missionaries learned this the hard way.

Shortly after dedication of a church in Nagasaki in 1865, a small delegation of Japanese approached the priests and identified themselves as Christians. Their testimony led to an amazing discovery.

Isolated groups of secret believers—even whole villages—still existed in mountainous areas and on small islands around Nagasaki. Although cut off from all contact with Rome and holding some strange doctrines, these underground believers still practiced baptism, recited the Ten Commandments and observed other instructions given their ancestors by missionaries over two hundred years earlier.

The delegation of believers from the mountains quizzed the priests concerning the Virgin Mary, supremacy of the pope, celibacy of the clergy and other teachings distinctly Roman Catholic. They then concluded that the newcomers to Nagasaki were indeed the spiritual successors to their long-departed priests.

About ten thousand of these hereditary Christians rejoined the church of their ancestors. Many thousands more held to their familiar ways, which after generations of isolation had accumulated numerous non-Christian beliefs and practices.

The priests in Nagasaki tried to keep their discovery a secret as they began visiting the villages to instruct the hidden believers, but word soon reached the government. Severe persecution broke out. Hundreds were imprisoned, tortured and killed, just as their forefathers had suffered. Four thousand were taken from their homes and resettled in districts where authorities tried to break down their faith and force them to recant.

Protests from European nations finally brought an end to the pogrom in 1873. The government permitted the exiled people to return home. Roman Catholic priests continued their work, mainly among rural and working-class people, slowly enlarging their community, which numbered about 15,000 communicants in 1873.[41]

Protestant Predominance

The first Protestant missionaries, workers of outstanding ability and character, chose a different method of planting the church in Japan. They spent years carefully building bridges across cultures and earning respect from the wary Japanese. From 1859 to 1872, only ten converts were baptized.[42]

During those opening years, they distributed thousands of copies of the Scriptures in Chinese (which many Japanese could read), operated medical dispensaries and hospitals, trained Japanese doctors in western medicine, opened schools for both sexes.

Above all, they taught English—something most Catholic priests were unable to do because they were French nationals. The great demand to learn English, particularly in the middle and upper classes, grew out of a nationwide fascination with the United States and Great Britain, both great sea powers.

The pent-up hunger for western technology and training ran especially strong among the samurai, the privileged "warrior" class in Japanese society that placed great emphasis on both fighting skill and good education. The new professional class that emerged in the middle and upper economic levels consisted mainly of mission-trained children of samurai families.[43]

Thanks to the careful foundation laid by some remarkable American missionaries like Dr. James C. Hepburn (Presbyterian medical doctor), Bishop Channing M. Williams (Episcopalian educator) and Samuel R. Brown (Reformed Church of America theologian), Protestant missionary work began to mushroom.

By 1872, nearly five thousand adults worshiped in ninety-three churches; six years later, the total jumped to over 25,500 members in 249 churches led in part by 142 ordained Japanese pastors. More cities were asking for missionaries and pastors than the churches could accommodate.[44]

The church advanced boldly despite anti-Christian legislation

still on the law books. Not until 1889 was freedom of religion inserted in the revised constitution. Even then, the government was suspected of making such a move to enhance its bargaining position with western nations in negotiating new treaties.[45]

Fukuzawa Yukichi, a highly respected and influential civic leader who owned a newspaper and had founded a university, epitomized this opportunistic attitude toward Christianity.

He urged that Japan be officially declared a Christian nation, with baptism to be gradually introduced among the middle and upper classes. He reasoned that this would help Japan qualify for admission to the international club of Europe and America and thereby gain economic and technical advantages.

Fukuzawa openly admitted "he had little or no interest in religion, but he argued that regardless of what they might actually believe, Japanese should profess to be Christians and so outwardly conform to the Occident."[46]

For whatever reason, Christianity spread so rapidly between 1880 and 1914 that some missionaries called it the greatest mass movement toward Christ since Constantine. Some even predicted that Japan would be predominantly Christian by the twentieth century.[47]

Challenged Growth

Buddhists and Shintoists refused to give up the struggle for the soul of Japan. Gordon H. Chapman, long-time missionary to Japan, writes: "The renewal and rapid growth of [the church in] the eighties proved to be preparation for a period of testing and persecution. The nineties were perhaps the most crucial period of all for the development of the Christian movement during the next fifty years."[48]

When Japan failed to secure more equitable trade treaties with western nations, a strong revulsion against Christianity swept across the nation. Japanese rediscovered Buddhism, and the revitalized ancient religion attacked Christianity.

In another development, the emperor legalized Shinto as a state religion.

When Christians protested vigorously against laws requiring them to bow in worship before a portrait of the emperor, they were branded as traitors to their country and threatened with imprisonment.

Faced with strong criticism both inside and outside the nation, the government eventually backed down and made a semantic difference between "cult" Shinto and "state" Shinto, describing the latter as civil practices rather than religious. The problem of performing acts patently religious and idolatrous remained for many years a conflict of conscience for devout Christians.

Despite such adverse conditions, which prevailed up to and through World War II, the church continued to grow. In doing so, Christianity in Japan provided a distinct contrast to the church in India and China. Unlike response on the mainland, the Gospel in Japan had its best response in the middle and upper classes, not the lower classes; and the majority of these believers were Protestant, not Catholic.[49]

Philippine Opening

Just as Japan's isolation ended when an American fleet pried open the door in Tokyo harbor, Spanish domination in the Philippines sank under bombardment from American ships in Manila harbor.

Commodore Dewey's naval victory did more than initiate

political change. It made possible the entry of Protestant missions—an impossibility during the 330 years of Spanish Roman Catholic rule.

When word of Spain's defeat reached New York, representatives of several denominational mission boards met and agreed on two matters. First, missionary work must commence immediately in the Philippines; second, it should be based on comity, not competition. Their decision matched a widespread enthusiasm among the churches to make up for lost time in evangelizing an area long denied the Gospel.

Except for some initial work by the British and Foreign Bible Society, missionary work was carried on exclusively by American boards. "The Philippines appealed to American idealism as both an opportunity and an obligation," notes Latourette.[50]

Once again, history repeated itself as the church followed the flag. Just as Catholic priests sailed to the islands with Spanish armadas, Protestant missionaries rode to their work on supply wagons of the U. S. Army.

First came Presbyterians in 1899, then Methodists and Baptists one year later. United Brethren and Disciples of Christ arrived in 1902, followed by The Christian and Missionary Alliance within a year.

Episcopalians arrived in 1899 but limited their ministry at first to the military, maintaining that "the Roman Catholic church was a sister communion among whom they would not proselyte."[51] Instead, they courageously pioneered work among the unevangelized Igorots and Muslim Moros.

An ecumenical spirit among the mainline denominations prevailed from the start. The Ministerial Alliance organized in 1900, and the Evangelical Union of six denominations began the following year. In 1907, Presbyterians and Methodists founded Union Theological Seminary in Manila; three other denominations later joined.

Although the Filipinos quickly adapted to American ways, missionaries found them a complex people to evangelize. One church worker noted humorously that during the working day a Filipino functioned like an American, went to mass like a Spaniard and ruled his home in a traditional manner with Malayan-Indonesian roots.[52]

Missionaries also faced a Roman Catholic population whose Spanish hierarchy opposed them on political as well as religious grounds and yielded ground grudgingly at best. The problem of cemeteries, for example, became a real live issue between Protestants and Catholics.

Before 1898, the only cemeteries belonged to the Roman Catholic Church. Only by great effort and insistence did American civil authorities get a law that required every town and village to have public, nonsectarian burial grounds. Even then, many rural communities refused.

Local priests often used the burial issue as an effective threat to discourage people from becoming Protestants. "If you join the Protestants, you will have no one to bury you!" was a threat heard from the pulpit and in the street.[53]

Despite such obstacles, Protestant missions and churches made rapid progress. Starting from point zero in 1898, the missionary force grew steadily. In just twelve years, 167 missionaries claimed a Protestant community of 36,500 believers.[54]

Grounds for Schism

Roman Catholicism in the Philippines had to face a problem

even greater than that of Protestant inroads: schism within its own ranks resulting from its own policies.

Conflicts between Spanish "regular" priests and Filipino "secular" priests, intensified by disputes between landlord friars and the general population, had flared openly in the closing decade of Spanish rule.

The resulting Philippine Independent Church, led by "Supreme Bishop" Aglipay, grew rapidly after Spanish restraints were abolished. Catholics stampeded out of the European-dominated church and into the schismatic church until an estimated one out of every four Filipinos was following Aglipay.

Worse yet, in many areas the departing congregations tried to take the church properties with them. Roman Catholic officials sued for return of the church's properties, and in 1909 the Supreme Court ruled that no matter how many priests and parishioners defected from a parish, the property still belonged to the church in whose name it was built.

The court order delivered a stunning but not fatal setback to the independent church movement. Rather than give up the disputed properties, "many of the clergy and a large percentage went back to Rome, unable to give up forever the beautiful parish churches which their forefathers had built with blood, sweat and tears under the Spanish system of forced labor."[55]

The nationalistic spirit soon made itself felt in Protestantism as well, causing what one historian called diametrically opposed forces among Protestants: "a drive toward unity and a drift toward division."[56]

Beginning first among Methodists and then Presbyterians, divisions and schisms spread among the churches. Combined with indigenous churches and sects, these breakaway groups numbered in the hundreds. Many groups could be called neither Catholic nor Protestant for they incorporated such widely divergent beliefs as spiritism and nationalism, Masonic principles and Unitarian doctrine, humanism and animism.

Bona fide Protestant churches exhibited their own ability for dynamic growth, surging from 36,500 communicants in 1910 to over 193,600 just twenty-six years later.[57]

Taking advantage of the switch from Spanish to American administration in the Philippines, Rome gradually replaced the often quarrelsome Spanish priests and friars with Americans and other nationalities. The change in leadership and policies helped Roman Catholicism retain its dominance.

Latourette estimates that by 1939 nine-tenths of the population preferred association with Catholicism, Protestantism or independent churches such as the one known commonly as the Aglipay Church. "The Philippines continued to contain more Christians than all the rest of the Far East and, indeed, constituted a larger Christian enclave than was found in any one country in Asia."[58]

* * *

The successive waves of Hindus, Buddhists, Muslims, Catholics and Protestants drastically influenced the religious character of the Pacific islands. But they did not have the last word in the spiritual destiny of the region. Still another wave was yet to come: nationalism.

A modern mixture of religion and politics, economics and philosophies, tradition and innovation, the new wave sweeping over the Pacific brought changes that are still becoming evident in the islands of the ocean. □

THE REPUBLIC OF CHINA (TAIWAN)

Earning Respect the Hard Way

DWARFED by the massive size of mainland China, overshadowed by the economic prowess of Japan, and even upstaged by frenetic Hong Kong. Deprived of member status in the United Nations, divested of diplomatic relations with the United States, and denied recognition as a sovereign state in the eyes of most governments.

Nevertheless, the Republic of China, situated on Taiwan, shrugs off these sleights to its stature and earns respect the hard way: by skill-and-sweat successes that draw sidelong glances of envy all around.

The island republic has the fastest growing economy in the Far East, bar none. Its paltry per capita income of $110 in 1952 has now soared to $5,000 per person—twenty times that of Red China.[1] Fully one-half of its citizens consider themselves in the economic middle class.

Taiwan deserves respect for other reasons as well.

Its 20 million people form the largest concentration of Chinese in the Free World. An average of 1,181 persons per square mile crowd into an area about the combined size of Massachusetts, Connecticut and Rhode Island.

Moreover, of the 4,000 Chinese Protestant churches worldwide, apart from mainland China, one-half are in Taiwan.[2] This does not make the Republic of China a Christian nation. Far from it. At present, only 2.5 percent of the people profess either Protestant or Roman Catholic Christianity. Even that percentage is declining as the general population increases faster than the Christian community.[3]

Material well-being accounts in part for Taiwanese disinterest in the Gospel. Many islanders are too prosperous to feel interest in spiritual matters. Of even more serious consequence are the traditional religions, which have been experiencing a revival of their own.

An outsider, however, might have difficulty distinguishing which religion an individual Taiwanese prefers. "Most Chinese profess Taoism and Buddhism, follow Confucian ethics, while practicing ancestor worship at home," writes one observer.[4] Over 13,000 temples of traditional religions cover the island.

Like the island republic ignored in the family of nations, the Christian community on Taiwan is outnumbered and outflanked by revived Eastern religions and a surging economy. Christians too must gain a hearing in the nation by earning it the hard way: by following a life-style consistent with the testimony of God's Word.

Stepchild Status

In a somewhat parallel pattern to Taiwan's being upstaged by surrounding larger nations, the island went largely unnoticed by Alliance mission leaders, who saw more of a challenge in the larger, more populous areas such as the Philippines, Indonesia and Japan. Even when missionaries were forced out of China by the Communists in the late 1940s, they were reassigned to other Asian areas, not Taiwan.

One former Alliance missionary, however, refused to bypass Taiwan. Coming out of retirement after years of ministry in China, Miss Margaret Oppelt began working independently on the island in 1952. She was joined by an associate five years later and together they organized two small churches.

The Alliance formally entered Taiwan

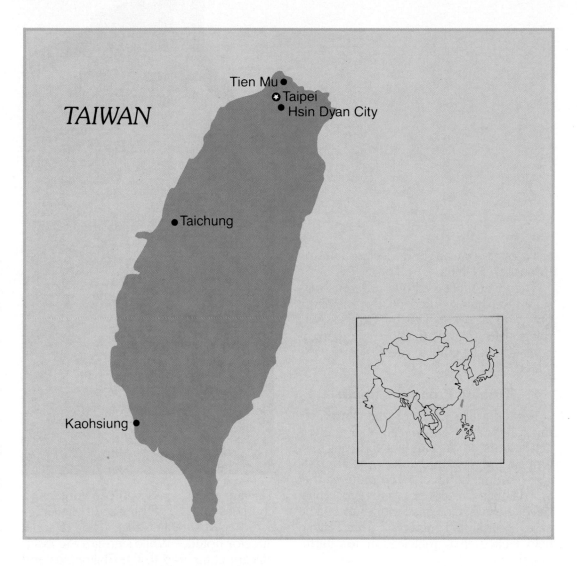

TAIWAN

Tien Mu •
✪ Taipei
• Hsin Dyan City

• Taichung

Kaohsiung •

in 1963, but for years the work seemed like an ignored stepchild. Some say Taiwan was considered merely as a stepping-stone for activities back on the mainland at a later date.

During the many years prior to the fall of China to Communism, the Alliance was not alone in ignoring Taiwan. Presbyterian missionaries from England and Canada were virtually the only Protestants working among the Taiwanese from 1865 to 1950. They established churches, medical and educational facilities that gained respect among the islanders.[5]

A remarkable spiritual awakening swept through the island's ten original tribes during World War II. The "Pentecost in the Hills" was led by a Presbyterian-trained Taiyal tribeswoman, Chioang, who preached from village to village—often one step ahead of her Japanese pursuers.

All ten tribes embraced the Christian faith in a people movement "that is without precedent in that part of the world," writes historian J. Herbert Kane.[6] About one-half the converts joined the Roman Catholic Church and 40 percent became Presbyterians.

The five Presbyterian missions from the West united their work to become the Presbyterian Church of Taiwan, the largest Protestant denomination on the island. Approximately one-half of Taiwan's 2,000 churches belong to this confession and about one-half of its members are from the tribal groups.[7]

The Presbyterians' unplanned monop-oly of Protestant missionary work on Taiwan ended when Generalissimo Chiang Kai-shek and his Nationalist Party, or Kuomintang, were defeated by the Red Chinese in 1949.

Some 1.8 million bedraggled military and civilian refugees of the defeated regime staged a Dunkirk-like retreat to the island from the mainland. They literally took over Taiwan and declared it the Republic of China.

They were followed by numerous missions that had worked on the mainland but were also expelled by China's new rulers. The total of missionary organizations gradually grew to nearly sixty by the late 1980s.[8]

Turning Point in Growth

Paradoxically, one of the "newest" missions is the Alliance. Although it unofficially entered Taiwan in 1952 with Miss Oppelt, the mission did not organize until 1987. Administrative policy requires that an Alliance missionary endeavor must have twelve senior missionaries to qualify as a "constituted mission." The Taiwan field lacked that qualification for thirty-five years.

The small, struggling staff of foreign workers was matched by an equally inadequate force of Chinese pastors. Not surprisingly, the total Alliance community by 1976 numbered just four organized churches and 611 baptized believers.[9]

Then the work accelerated dramatically. In the next decade, the Christian and Missionary Alliance Church Union of

Taiwan grew to seventeen organized churches and 1,178 baptized believers— a 93 percent increase. The regional director noted, "While statistics are insignificant compared to the Philippines and Indonesia, the Taiwan Alliance church has clearly begun to establish itself as a growing denomination."[10]

The sudden spurt in growth could be explained in part by an influx of Alliance Christians from the Chinese congregations in Viet Nam. Taking refuge in Taiwan after Communism triumphed in Indochina, the "refugees brought new life

(Left) The Alliance Literature Center stakes its claim in a busy business district. (Facing page) City life on Taiwan goes neither by the sun nor the clock.

to churches through their testimonies of God's goodness in times of suffering."[11]

Breakthrough in Leadership

The most significant turning point for Alliance work on Taiwan came when mission and church began to prepare their own young people for ministry.

The Alliance had operated for many years on the basis that Taiwan already had enough theological schools; every major denomination or group had its own program. Why should the Alliance duplicate the good educational resources available through other evangelical groups?

The principle was fine, the result was not. Dedicated, capable Alliance young people went off to study in other theological schools, and then went off to serve in other churches. This "youth drain," combined with problems within their home churches and the mission, deprived the Alliance of a whole generation of young leaders.

The Alliance was forced to recognize that the only way to produce a viable, growing denomination was to prepare the churches' own youth for ministry in a school specifically suited to their needs.

Taiwan Theological College is a "most significant breakthrough."

The school must specialize in preparing young men and women to plant and nourish Alliance churches.

The Taiwan Alliance Theological College (TATC) opened in 1982. It used borrowed facilities of the Taipei Central Church, the most influential of Alliance churches on the island. The missionaries had prayed for fifteen students in the first-year class, but they got twenty—an indication that the school would repeatedly surpass their expectations.

Dr. Philip Teng termed the founding of the school a "most significant breakthrough for the church."[12]

True to the school's commitment to preparing church leaders, for several years the curriculum followed an innovative 2-2-1 plan. Each student was to have daytime secular employment and attend evening classes for the first two years. Then those who evidenced a call to ministry spent the next two years as full-time students. The final year consisted of seminars while the student engaged in ministry.

Throughout the student's five years of study, he or she was expected to attend and serve in a local church. This not only brought more workers into the church but tied the school closely to the real life of the church, so that both had a sense of belonging to the other.

The seminary still retains the 2-2-1 plan as an option for students. It has, however, also adopted a more formal four-year curriculum. As an added service, TATC videotapes special lectures and seminars and then distributes them to local pastors and workers.

When the college transferred to Chinese leadership in 1984, the third and fourth years of study had been added and student enrollment reached forty. With four more years, the school grew to approximately forty part-time and twenty-one fulltime students. An extension program enrolled another thirty-nine.

While students anticipating pastoral ministry go on to fulltime study, other students have a role to fill also. Some are lay leaders attending TATC in order to move into unchurched areas and team up with pastors to start churches.

These "Gospel immigrants," as they call themselves, are businessmen, teachers, doctors and others. "They have status in the community and often find doors open to hundreds of homes normally closed to a pastor."[13]

The first graduating class of the Taiwan Alliance Theological College in 1986 represented a major milestone in the churches' development. Noting that eight of the nine graduates, each with a Bachelor of Theology degree, entered Alliance ministry, regional director Peter Nanfelt said,

The theological college specializes in preparing young people for work in Alliance churches.

"Never in its history has the church received such an infusion of manpower."[14]

Injecting new leadership into the life blood of the church should help one of the Taiwan Alliance's most serious ailments: its youth drain. During the years of stagnation or minimal church growth, energetic young pastors opted for more promising pastorates in North America and among concentrations of overseas Chinese elsewhere.

Equally significant, the steady flow of well-prepared young people into the ministry will relieve a concern caused by the uncertainty of a continuing missionary presence in Taiwan.

The central government in Taipei announced a freeze at the May, 1984, level

of all mission staffs. The Alliance would therefore be limited to eight family units, hardly enough to promote an aggressive church-planting campaign.

The freeze was not consistently followed in later years, but the precedent remains as a constant reminder that missions operate in Taiwan only through the sufferance of civil authorities.

The arrival of TATC graduates in Alliance churches coincided with and contributed to an awakening by the congregations to the opportunities of growth and witness all around them. Though the concentration of Alliance congregations has been in Taipei, growth-conscious pastors and "Gospel immigrants" are moving to other parts of the island and among native Taiwanese, as

well as among former mainlanders and their children.

The regional director calls the 90-plus percent growth in recent years "a notable achievement in a country where the Christian community has traditionally grown very slowly."[15]

Mainland Prospects

After the United States "normalized" relations with the Beijing regime in 1979 at the expense of its ties with the Taiwan government, some future accommodation between the two Chinas became inevitable. That process has now begun.

Taiwan has lifted the nearly forty-year state of martial law—the longest in recent times—and is allowing its citizens aged fifty-five or older to legally visit relatives on the mainland. Small businesses are also permitted to have commercial contacts across the Taiwan Straits.

Meanwhile, the Beijing regime has committed itself to using peaceful rather than military means to bring Taiwan under the sovereignty of the mainland government. It has repeatedly promised Taiwan that "the island will be allowed to find its own means of government."[16]

Both Chinas consider Hong Kong a test case of the "one country, two systems" policy, Beijing being concerned with the application of principle and Taiwan with results.

The Crown Colony of Hong Kong, now under British rule, is to revert to mainland control in 1997. The Communists have already publicly assured Hong Kong that it may continue its freewheeling capitalistic system without change well into the twenty-first century.

(Top) Sunday school teacher and students; (right) young adults worshiping in song; (above) handcraft challenge

Taiwan will probably scrutinize how the Communists carry out that pledge in Hong Kong before making serious moves toward closer ties with the mainland government. The 1989 Tiananmen Square massacre and subsequent crackdown on dissidents by the Beijing regime have made the Taiwanese even more cautious.

The death of Taiwan's President Chiang Ching-kuo in 1988 brought a change in government that could ease the process. Both Chiang and his father, Generalissimo Chiang Kai-shek, had ruled Taiwan for thirty-nine years based on a policy of armed confrontation with Red China.

President Chiang's successor could also have implications for Taiwanese churches in relation to the mainland. Lee Teng-hui was described by one journalist as "a tall, sportive, broadly-educated, 65-year-old Taiwanese."[17] He failed to mention that the new president was also an outspoken evangelical Christian.

Should the two Chinas someday lower their barriers like a drawbridge across the dividing waters, Taiwan could still become—for the Gospel and the Alliance—a stepping-stone back to the mainland. □

CHURCH AND MISSION

OFFICIAL NAME OF CHURCH:	C&MA Church Union of Taiwan
ENTRY BY MISSIONARIES:	1952
NUMBER OF MISSIONARIES:	25
ORGANIZED CHURCHES:	18
UNORGANIZED CHURCHES AND PREACHING POINTS:	14
BAPTIZED CHURCH MEMBERS:	1,296
INCLUSIVE MEMBERSHIP:	1,944
MEDICAL WORK:	0
EDUCATION:	1 Preschool Kindergarten 1 TEE Course 1 Theological College
RADIO BROADCASTS:	0
PAGES PRINTED:	0

COUNTRY

OFFICIAL NAME:	Republic of China (Taiwan)
FORM OF GOVERNMENT:	One Party System
OFFICIAL LANGUAGE(S):	Mandarin, Taiwan, Hakka
AREA:	13,885 sq. mi.
POPULATION:	(1989 est.) 20,283,000
CAPITAL:	Taipei
PER CAPITA INCOME:	(1984) $3,000.00
LITERACY:	90%
RELIGIOUS AFFILIATION:	Buddhism, Taoism, Confucianism- 60–70%, Protestant 3.5%

HONG KONG

The Many Faces of Fragrant Harbor

A GRUMPY Englishman called it "a piece of useless granite with no water and nothing to commend it."[1] Chinese looked more kindly on the mountainous island. Noting its forested stretches and almost landlocked harbor, they called it Hong Kong, meaning "Fragrant Harbor."

The British too must have seen more to the island than they admitted. They wrested control of the "useless granite" in 1841 from a weak Chinese government.

Within decades, they transformed its barren beaches and unpeopled slopes into a bustling hub of the British Empire due east. The stark, natural beauty of Hong Kong succumbed to a complex assortment of faces that even today allows the territory to appear as whatever the onlooker wants to see.

The economist looks at Hong Kong and sees an economic miracle. Hardworking residents pushed their living standard upward over 400 percent in one generation.[2] Frugality and shrewdness by the tiny 5.7 million population turned their "piece of useless granite" into the world's third largest financial center.[3]

Not even a frightening stock market meltdown on New York's Wall Street in October of 1987 could damage Hang Seng, the colony's stock exchange.[4]

The sociologist looks at Hong Kong and sees something resembling a teeming anthill. An average of 9,000 people cram into each acre of living space, and everyone seems to be going somewhere at the same time. Ferries shuttle 100,000 people daily across the harbor, a tunnel under the bay serves 120,000 vehicles, and mass transit trains carry over 2 million passengers.

Unable to spread outward, housing stretches skyward in huge apartment complexes called estates. Over 100 highrises, the largest containing 144,000 residents, give shelter to 2.8 million Hong Kongese.[5] Public and private developers in 1988 built nearly 90,000 apartments, yet the hunger for housing seems never to slacken.

Lacking space, builders gouge earth from the island's flanks to fill the bay. As one writer remarked, "The government creates land for housing literally by removing mountains and casting them into the sea."[6]

Hong Kong wears yet another face for entrepreneurs. In just twenty years, an empty seabed became the world's second largest container port.[7] Dock facilities handle 24,000 vessels a year, giving Hong Kong "the reputation of moving freight faster than any other port in the Orient."[8]

To refugees, however, Hong Kong represents a different kind of port—a harbor of safety. One-half of the colony's 5.7 million residents are Chinese immigrants who fled from violence and repression by mainland Communists in the 1950s and 1960s.[9]

After the war in Indochina, thousands of Vietnamese headed for Hong Kong on anything that would float. The first 3,700 arrivals in 1975 were followed by 66,000 the following year. Despite relocation and repatriation efforts, the overcrowded colony still had to feed and house 43,000 boat people in 1989, with some estimates going as high as 70,000.[10]

Masking Uncertainty

Hong Kong's variety of faces, however, serves only to mask a deep sense of foreboding. "Fragrant Harbor" now seems more filled with fear than fra-

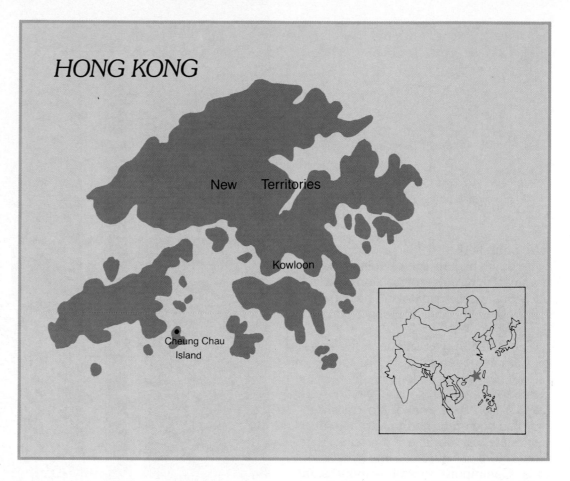

HONG KONG

New   Territories

Kowloon

Cheung Chau Island

grance. The focal point of this apprehension is 1997, the year mainland China regains control of the lively colony.

The root cause of this uneasiness goes back many decades. After a humiliating defeat in the First Opium War, China was forced to cede Hong Kong island to the victorious British. The 1842 Treaty of Nanking granted England port facilities to refit ships and store supplies, but in effect it was a certificate of occupation.

Hong Kong Island and later Kowloon Peninsula on the mainland were given to Britain in perpetuity. New Territories followed on a lease in 1898 for ninety-nine years.

For over a century, Hong Kong may have been viewed by the British as a monument of empire building. To the Chinese it was a galling blemish on their history, a goading reminder of past weakness.[11] With Oriental patience, they waited for the right time to settle accounts.

That opportunity came in the early 1980s when representatives of England and the People's Republic of China met to discuss the crown colony's future after the ninety-nine-year lease expired.

Many residents of Hong Kong hoped the lease would be renewed without fuss. After all, they reasoned, the colony served as the mainland's primary source of western currency. Any disruption of Hong Kong's sensitive financial market would adversely affect China's economy.

Beijing representatives at the Sino-British conference brushed aside that hope with a clear statement that China's sovereignty was of more consequence than Hong Kong's stability.[12] They would only discuss how the crown colony would once again become part of China.

The Sino-British Joint Declaration signed in December, 1984, stipulated that Hong Kong would revert to mainland rule in 1997. In return, the Beijing government promised to administer the territory as a Special Administrative Region, permitting the former colony to continue its economic and political structure without serious change for another fifty years.

The Joint Declaration promised, in effect, a one-country, two-system solution: Communism on the mainland and capitalism in Hong Kong, both under the rule of Beijing.

From the moment the Joint Declaration

was published in 1984, a slow, painful countdown began. The singular issue that dominated business transactions, political decisions, public debate and personal decisions was the fate of Hong Kong after June 30, 1997.

The situation was unique in the annals of human government. "No colony in history has known so long in advance the precise date of its demise. Hong Kong knew 5,000 days ahead. No British colony has been returned to another sovereign state, let alone a Communist one. No territory has ever become subservient to a Communist master without some kind of revolutionary struggle."[13]

Flawed Law

Hong Kong's continued identity as a capitalist enclave in a socialist system is in principle assured by a legal code called Basic Law. Residents of the colony even had five months in 1988 when they could discuss and suggest changes in the document that would govern their affairs for the first fifty years of mainland rule.

Not surprisingly, opinion is divided concerning the document. "After more than two years of drafting, substantial details of

(Left) Most of Hong Kong's 5.7 million people live in huge apartment complexes called estates. (Right) A cross signals the location of a chapel in a high-rise building.

the Basic Law have emerged and they do not appear conducive to fostering the high degree of economy promised in the Sino-British Joint Declaration on the future of Hong Kong.

"Many are doubtful whether Hong Kong will be able to retain its freedoms, rule of law and current lifestyle after 1997. Many do not believe the 'one-country-two systems' policy that China will impose on Hong Kong is a workable one."[14]

An analyst, writing in the *Far Eastern Economic Review,* explains why the prevailing mood is one of uncertainty. "Not even the proposed Basic Law provides any real safeguard for Hong Kong's future integrity," he believes. "Article Five of the Chinese constitution stipulates that no law shall contravene the constitution.

"In other words, only those Hong Kong laws which are in line with China's constitution will be valid after 1997. This also means that China can at any time end its capitalistic experiments in her Special Economic Zones by authority of Article One of the same constitution that stipulates China's political system is a Socialist one."[15]

As often happens in times of political uncertainty, people vote with their feet. One report on the colony's brain drain observed, "Many of Hong Kong's brightest young professionals are among the thousands lining up at immigration offices in anticipation of the British colony's return to communist Chinese control in 1997."[16] The report noted that of the 200,000 who emigrated from Hong Kong over the past ten years, most were university-educated young adults in their thirties.[17]

Others, however, are not so pessimistic about the colony's future under socialism. Dame Lydia Dunn, perhaps the most visible and powerful woman in Hong Kong during the 1980s, wrote, "Of course the handover will have an effect, but it will be a good one, in all senses.

Certainly confidence can be sustained and it will indeed grow."[18] (Subsequent events, notably the Tiananmen Square massacre, may have changed this assessment.)

Acknowledging that some 45,000 people, mostly professionals, are leaving annually, she insisted, "We can weather it." Dame Lydia, who in 1989 was the senior member of the Hong Kong government's inner cabinet, entertained no thought of leaving. "No other place has the sheer power of Hong Kong—and the Chinese know that well, and I believe them implicitly when they say they won't change a thing."[19]

Striking a Balance

The evangelical community of Hong Kong strikes a balance between the defeatism of emigrants and the optimism of mainland supporters.

On the one hand, few church leaders believe the colony's present and future rulers will be as concerned about religious freedom as they are about economic rights. One writer noted, "Those sets of freedoms which have come to be known as human rights are, in China's opinion,

gifts of the state; they are extended by the state and, if necessary, can be withdrawn by the state."[20]

Belief in the lordship of Christ over all nations enables evangelical leaders to take the high road to the coming reunification of Hong Kong to the mainland. Approximately 3,000 pastors and key laymen of various church groups met in 1984 under the banner theme, "Jesus Is the Lord of History."

The convocation marked the first time Hong Kong evangelicals spoke out concerning 1997, and they did so through a statement that outlined ten enduring biblical convictions held by evangelicals in the context of social and political change. Keynote speaker of the historic meeting was Dr. Philip Teng, president of the Christian and Missionary Alliance Church Union of Hong Kong.[21]

Not content with merely stating principles, evangelicals and other Protestants among the colony's fifty denominations and groups began preparing in practical ways for 1997 and beyond. The Alliance mission director reported in 1988: "The church looks upon encroachment of the

future not with a simplistic view of its role, but not with great fear either. . . .

"Even now there is a trend among our churches to change the rigid style practiced in Hong Kong among all denominations to a format that is going to be operable and meaningful in the challenging years ahead."[22]

Flexible Format

The 1988 field director's report indicated just how flexible that format had already become. Applications that year had been presented to the government for approval of a new kindergarten in conjunction with a church-planting project, a church-sponsored senior citizen center, and five other social centers combined with plans for starting new churches.

Meanwhile, the report continued, individual churches presented their own requests to sponsor an adult education center, a family service center and a senior citizens center—all in connection with planting new churches.[23]

Two factors combine to make the Hong Kong format for evangelism and church

planting unlike any other situation in the Orient.

First, Chinese Christians do not look upon a church building as an utter necessity for worship. Although the C&MA Church Union has some large and very attractive sanctuaries for worship, space is so scarce and often prohibitively expensive that Alliance people are content to worship anywhere.

The second factor is the government's search for specialized or volunteer agencies to provide social services to a population that has outstripped public resources.

The administration's need for help and the churches' need for space found a solution worthy of British pragmatism and Chinese ingenuity: The government pays for the basic construction of a social center while the church furnishes the interior and provides program and personnel. On Sundays and weekday evenings, the center becomes a place of worship.

For instance, some Alliance church planters spotted a spacious ground-floor area being used to store garbage cans for an apartment complex. They secured per-

(From far left) Study center activities: serious studies interrupted; classroom exercises; reading room for older students

Chinese Alliance churches sponsor a large Christian academy.

mission to turn the area into a beautiful facility to serve the spiritual and social needs of the community. It was thus the Shui Pin Wai study center church was born.[24]

Temporary Housing Areas (THA) proved especially promising for this format of social service and spiritual witness. The government official in charge of this housing in 1984 told a mission representative that, being a Christian himself, he was greatly burdened that churches be established in these developments. He offered to open many THAs, provide facilities for church-run centers and allow religious services any time they wished.[25]

Temporary Housing Areas are so called because of the type of buildings used: one-story barracks of cramped units put up wherever flat terrain permits. A housing area may hold as few as 100 or as many as 10,000.

Most of the residents are either refugee Chinese from the mainland and Indochina in search of work, middle-aged unskilled workers who cannot afford better quarters, or elderly people who have nowhere else to go. Social-center churches sponsored by Alliance congregations often provide the only bright spot of hope or variety in the crowded and drab Temporary Housing Areas.

Priority One

This flexibility in ministry has earned the Hong Kong Alliance a reputation for aggressive growth. One missionary commented, "We are known as the church planters. Colleagues of mine who are in other missions sometimes ask, 'What is your secret? How are you able to do it?' We have no special formula. It's just that this is our number-one priority."[26]

Chinese church leaders share this sense of priority. A ten-year plan adopted in 1987 reflects this determination: baptized membership from 14,000 to 30,000 and established churches from 60 to 120.[27]

The specter of 1997 helped spur the churches to adopt these special goals. But equally significant has been youthful leadership among the churches. According to one missionary, "Probably the average age of [Alliance] church leaders in Hong Kong is the youngest in all of Asia."[28]

How did this happen? By the mid-1980s, pastors who had come to Hong

Dr. Philip Teng

Kong with the great influx of refugees after World War II and the fall of Nationalist China had either died or retired. Many middle-aged ministers emigrated to other countries during the social unrest in 1966-1967. So the majority of church leaders by the late 1980s were young men in their twenties and thirties.

The churches' concern to multiply themselves stretches far beyond the crown colony. The Foreign Missionary Society had already fielded twenty-five missionaries in South America, Africa, the Pacific islands and mainland Asia by 1988. Hong Kong ranked first in the number of missionaries among Third World sending churches of The Alliance World Fellowship.

But this was not enough. Part of the C&MA Church Union's ten-year plan was to send and support 100 missionaries by 1997.

The one person used of God more than others to arouse a missionary vision among the Hong Kong churches was Dr. Philip Teng. He believes this initiative among Chinese churches is long overdue. In 1981 he commented, "It is not easy to pinpoint [the rising interest in missions], but it is safe to say the Lord's time has come for the Chinese churches to be engaged in missionary outreach. He has been long waiting for the Chinese churches to respond."[29]

Dr. Teng's own involvement in missions began when he attended the Third Asia (C&MA) Conference in 1961. "I was impressed by the fact that the Alliance churches in Japan had already sent out their first missionary to Brazil," he recalled.[30]

He returned to his pastorate of the North Point Alliance Church and began pushing missions. The initial response was small—a missions budget of only US $2,000—but he and others persisted. By 1980, the Hong Kong Alliance Church Union was supporting numerous missionaries and his own church's missions budget reached US $120,000.

The Lord, however, had something even more personal for Dr. Teng's involvement in missions. "We had never

(Top) Seminary students at lunch break (above) before returning to class lecture

thought of going out as missionaries," Dr. Teng said, "but one day the Lord seemed to be saying to me, 'You think that you are a promoter of missions; are you yourself willing to be a missionary?'

"I didn't pay too much attention at the time, but the thought kept coming back to me again and again. Then I began to pray about it and I asked my wife if she were willing to go to Kalimantan with me as a missionary. She said, 'Yes, wherever the Lord leads you to go, I'll go with you gladly.' "[31]

Taking a sabbatical from North Point Alliance for one year, they worked among Chinese settled along the coastline of Kalimantan, Indonesia. He also helped to start a church among Dayak Christians, mainly university students in the capital city of Pontianak.

Refugee Missions

Alliance believers found enough overseas people crowded into their little colony to start a foreign mission just across the fence. The first Vietnamese refugees arrived in 1975 and kept coming despite strenuous efforts by Hong Kong authorities to discourage them.

Finally, in 1989, the government adopted a hard-nosed policy of distinguishing between political refugees (those whose lives were endangered for political reasons) and economic migrants (those who simply came in search of a better life). Of the 18,000 boat people who arrived from Vietnam in 1989, only fifty-four were deemed political refugees. The rest were herded into detention centers to await repatriation.[32]

In addition to island prisons for deportees, Hong Kong maintains two other types of refugee centers. "Open camps"

A bookstore run by the Alliance Press, one of four major Christian publishers in Hong Kong

house refugees who are free to move around the city and hold small jobs. "Closed camps" hold newcomers who have no access to the outside world. At first, all boat people were put together, but after fighting erupted between North and South Vietnamese, they were segregated into separate camps.

As missionaries and Chinese church workers ministered in the camps, a distinct response pattern emerged among the refugees: North Vietnamese were far more responsive to the Gospel than those from the South.[33] Relief workers estimated in 1988 that approximately 1,000 believers were scattered among the various camps.[34]

Alliance Bible Seminary

Among the specialized institutions of the Hong Kong Alliance, none goes back farther in history than the Alliance Bible Seminary. Founded in 1899 in Wuchow, South China, by Dr. Robert Glover, it was the first Bible school opened anywhere overseas by Alliance missionaries.

Forced to flee after the Communist sweep of the mainland, the school's entire staff and senior class of eighteen students moved into Dr. Jaffray's home on Cheung Chau Island, Hong Kong.

The move did nothing to hurt the school's growth. It developed into one of the major evangelical seminaries of the colony. One important stage of development was the transfer of administration from mission to church in 1975.

Faced with the prospects of once again coming under Communist rule, school leaders decided on a course completely different from the 1950 flight from the mainland. The seminary announced plans to intensify its academic program. The goal: to prepare more students for ministry from 1986 to 1997 than it had in the previous eighty-seven years of its history.[35]

The seminary embarked on an ambi-tious campus expansion that resulted in an enlarged four-level library and new dormitories for both men and women. Some outsiders questioned the wisdom of investing so much money on a property that in a few years might be taken over by the new government.

The mission director responded, "Some people say we are foolish to spend money on development at the school, but we believe it is money well spent. To what better use could we put money than to train young people for service in the church that will be another part of China after 1997?"[36]

Media Missions

Two media ministries have enabled the Hong Kong C&MA churches to extend

Alliance radio, production center for programs, targets listening audience beyond Hong Kong.

their witness far beyond the cramped confines of the colony.

China Alliance Press ranks as one of the four major Chinese evangelical publishers in Hong Kong. Together they form the primary source of Christian literature for widely scattered communities of overseas Chinese believers. Recognizing this need, the Alliance publishers established branch offices in Taiwan and Canada.

C&MA publishing activities in Hong Kong operate from a strong base. The press and six bookstores generated over $880,000 in sales revenue during one recent year. The editorial staff produced eighteen new and reprint book titles with a combined total of 31,600,000 pages.[37]

This report would gratify but not sur-prise Dr. Jaffray, founder of China Alliance Press. Son of an influential and wealthy newspaper publisher in Toronto, he early acquired a deep respect and high expectations for the printed page.

The publishing house, however, suffered some serious setbacks before reaching its present level of operations. A fire in 1930 destroyed the original printing plant in Wuchow. Transferred to Shanghai, the work had to be suspended again during Japanese occupation in World War II.

Presses started to roll again after the war—only to face a new obstacle in the civil war that erupted. Press personnel arrived in Hong Kong in 1949 with nothing but an address list, a typewriter and an adding machine.[38]

Careful management nursed press op-erations back to robust health. Transfer to total Chinese administration in 1980 further enhanced its growth. Cosponsoring two Christian Cultural Festivals made the publishing house known to a wider public.

The second festival, held in late 1987, featured nearly one hundred different types of activities, ranging from a blood donor appeal and relief help for Vietnamese to a film festival and book exhibit that attracted 20,000 visitors to the city hall display.

The ministry of Alliance Radio differs from the press operation in that its outreach is focused on audiences outside Hong Kong, especially listeners on the mainland.

One mission broadcaster defines the potential audience in China that drew the Alliance into using airwaves as an avenue of witness. He reported, "Radio in China today is what radio was in North America forty or fifty years ago: the single most important means of information and entertainment—especially to the outside world."[39]

Alliance mission and church leaders began planning a radio ministry in 1977

Suen Douh Camp: (left) small group Bible study; (right) soccer match

and aired the first daily fifteen-minute broadcast the following year on Trans World Radio. Within ten years, Alliance Radio was producing sixty-three program hours per month and receiving over 6,400 response letters annually.[40]

Trans World Radio facilities in Guam were joined by Far East Broadcasting Company transmitters in the Philippines and South Korea. Programs aired on both short and medium wave bands covered all twenty-six provinces of China and also reached into other Asian nations.

Evangelism is only one goal of Alliance Radio. The studio's heavy emphasis on Bible study and teaching helps fill a vast void for many believers. They are totally dependent on the broadcasts because they have been without trained leaders and literature since the Cultural Revolution swept across China from 1965 to 1968.

One elderly Christian's experience was common: "During the years of persecution, all the books, notes and Bibles were burned. In the battle against Satan I could only use verses I had memorized."[41]

Alliance Radio will continue its ministry

to the mainland after 1997, but not from Hong Kong. Beijing looks with disfavor on religious broadcasting because it breaks the law confining all religious activities within the four walls of an officially recognized church.[42]

Nonstop Camp

Approximately two million young people live in Hong Kong, hemmed in by cement walls, sidewalks and streets. Few have access to nonpolluted fresh air and nature's greens, just as they have little contact with a gospel message directed to their needs.

These were reason enough for Alliance missionaries and church leaders to embark on an innovative camp program that by any standards is hugely successful. Suen Douh ("Proclaim the Truth") Camp was secured in 1969 through the generosity of Christian Children's Fund. Camp-of-the-Woods, a Christian camp in upstate New York, has maintained a special supportive Big Brother relationship ever since. Other groups and individuals also contribute to the camp's ministry.

By the mid-1980s, the 250-occupant

camp was in such demand it had to turn down 80 percent of groups applying for reservations. In 1985 alone, some 2,600 groups received a regretful "no vacancy" response.

Along with churches, such diverse organizations as youth centers, welfare agencies, factories and government-sponsored groups used camp facilities.

Special programs are held for senior citizens, refugees and handicapped people.

By the camp's nineteenth year, the staff of thirty was running a 356-day-per-year schedule. In two three-day camps per week, they served 578 groups for a total of 89,744 camper days. Of the 12,098 who attended the church-sponsored, gospel-oriented program, over 7,000 became followers of Christ.[43]

Suen Douh is in fact more of an evangelistic camp than a church vacationland. Priority often goes to non-Christian groups, including Muslims and Hindus. As part of the church's flexible format of ministries, the camp presents a clear gospel message in a place where people often do not expect to hear it.

Behind the Faces

Both colony and church of Hong Kong wear many faces. To the onlooker, the colony appears a financial whiz, a social phenomenon, an economic miracle, a refugee haven. Despite these masks of success and stability, the real face of Hong Kong has a look of uncertainty, even fear.

What will happen when the incredible little enclave of capitalism reverts to the Communist mainland in 1997? No one knows for sure. The 1989 massacre of students in Beijing's Tiananmen Square and subsequent campaign of suppression did nothing to reassure the colony.

One consulting firm reported, "The [Tiananmen Square] events in China have confirmed the very worst fears of many Hong Kong people, and if they were even thinking of leaving or sending their money out, their decision is now definite."[44]

According to another observer at the time, even the more optimistic "residents are losing faith that officials in Beijing will abide by their pledges to leave the colony's economic and political freedoms intact."[45]

Behind the many forms of ministry by the church there is an altogether different attitude: Fear not, expect not. They neither fear for the future of the Lord's work, nor expect Christians to have an easy life under the new rulers.

Even the flexible format of ministries undertaken by the Alliance —from social centers to Suen Douh Camp—indicates they will not be content merely to get by; they must grow.

The Hong Kong C&MA has no clearer idea than anyone else what lies beyond 1997. However, they do know God will be there. ☐

CHURCH AND MISSION

OFFICIAL NAME OF CHURCH:	C&MA Church Union Hong Kong Ltd.
ENTRY BY MISSIONARIES:	1933
NUMBER OF MISSIONARIES:	27
ORGANIZED CHURCHES:	50
UNORGANIZED CHURCHES AND PREACHING POINTS:	20
BAPTIZED CHURCH MEMBERS:	17,241
INCLUSIVE MEMBERSHIP:	34,482
MEDICAL WORK:	0
EDUCATION:	1 Theological School
RADIO BROADCASTS:	10–15 minutes daily to ½ hour weekly
PAGES PRINTED:	31,612,196

COUNTRY

OFFICIAL NAME:	Crown Colony of Hong Kong
FORM OF GOVERNMENT:	Constitutional Monarchy (U.K.)
OFFICIAL LANGUAGE(S):	English
AREA:	409 sq. mi.
POPULATION:	(1988 est.) 5,700,000
CAPITAL:	Victoria
PER CAPITA INCOME:	$6,000
LITERACY:	82%
RELIGIOUS AFFILIATION:	Non-religious 14.5%, Chinese religion 62%, Christian 18.9%

INDONESIA

From Diversity to Unity

WATER IS a dubious bond when it comes to holding a nation together. Such is the experience of Indonesia.

The Pacific Ocean serves not only to unite but also to divide the 13,000-plus islands of the Asian republic strung out over 3,000 miles—the distance between New York and Los Angeles. Many specks of land protruding from the ocean lack human life, while the 3,000 populated land areas surrounded by water include some of the world's largest islands and one of its most densely populated.

The people on those thousands of islands separated by ocean-sized moats lived in an isolation that over the centuries intensified the differences among them. Between 600 and 800 languages and dialects reflect an almost equal number of variant cultures. For example, while some interior peoples in Kalimantan revel in wild pig feasts, Balinese dancers raise temple rituals to a near perfection of graceful movements.

Aided in part by their ocean moats, Indonesian religions have also developed along distinctive and differing paths.

The term "Javanese Islam" refers to a folk form of Islam heavily infiltrated by ancient animistic beliefs and influenced by major religious tenets of Buddhism and Hinduism. Balinese Hindu Dharma, entrenched in a mental fortress of culture and tradition, embraces a curious mixture of orthodox Hindu tenets and aboriginal practices of spirit worship. Traditional Dutch Protestantism, infused with heavy doses of local beliefs and European liberal theology, often regards evangelical missions with somewhat the same suspicion shown to non-Christians.

The Indonesian government wages a constant campaign to turn the nation's many forms of diversity into a stronger sense of national identity. Adopting the stance of a neutral secular state, the government has for years pursued a policy that at least in principle treats all citizens alike.

This policy of *Pancasila* has been in effect since independence from Holland in 1949. It promotes five cardinal principles: belief in a supreme Being; a just and civilized humanity; the unity of Indonesia; democracy led by deliberations among representatives; and social justice for all the peoples of Indonesia.[1]

Unity in Diversity

The Gospel Tabernacle Church of Indonesia (GKII, or *Gereja Kemah Injil Indonesia,* in the vernacular) faces a problem similar to that of the government. It must forge a sense of unity among seven regional groups of churches whose diversity is both their richness and their weakness.

That is not to say that some unity does not even now exist in the church resulting from Alliance missions in Indonesia since 1929. A Presbyterian author and former missionary in Java referred to the Alliance-sponsored church as "the oldest and best established among denominations not affiliated with the Indonesian Council of Churches."[2]

He further recognized that "the C&MA has established a widely spread national movement which appears to have solid roots in both national leadership and financial support"—a considerable achievement in a nation where most of the missions and churches usually work

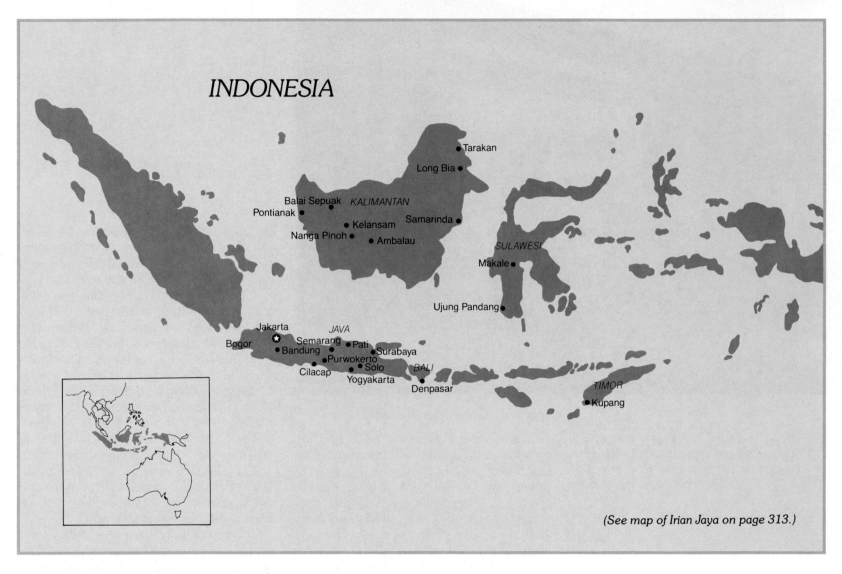

INDONESIA

Tarakan

Long Bia

Balai Sepuak

KALIMANTAN

Pontianak

Kelansam

Samarinda

Nanga Pinoh

Ambalau

SULAWESI

Makale

Ujung Pandang

Jakarta

JAVA

Bogor

Semarang

Pati

Bandung

Surabaya

Purwokerto

Cilacap

Solo

BALI

Yogyakarta

Denpasar

TIMOR

Kupang

(See map of Irian Jaya on page 313.)

with just one ethnic group in one area.[3]

The Alliance mission and national church minister to a broad cross section of the nation. The two regional GKII churches in East and West Kalimantan are composed primarily of Dayaks, an ethnic group that lives in villages and towns surrounded by dense rain forests.

Another regional GKII church works with the more advanced populations of Java and Sumatra, which have a concentration of commercial development and governmental power. The three regional churches in Sulawesi and East Indonesia range in social and economic order somewhere between Kalimantan and Java.

(The Gospel Tabernacle Church of Indonesia in Irian Jaya is significantly different in character and will be featured separately.)

Still another church region, the KIBAID church in Sulawesi, has many informal ties with GKII and works in close cooperation with the mission.

(Above) Jaffray Theological School is a "finishing school" for students headed for the ministry; (right) official name of the school introduces the campus.

Common Heritage

The Gospel Tabernacle Church owes its wide-ranging national character to the panoramic vision of a great missionary statesman, Dr. Robert A. Jaffray.

He had already pioneered Alliance missionary work in interior China and then had spearheaded the opening of Indochina to the Gospel. At age fifty-seven he could well have retired back home in Canada as the honored son of a highly respected and powerful family in the newspaper industry.

But God had other plans.

Dr. Jaffray sensed an inner leading toward Indonesia, then called the Netherlands East Indies. After a survey trip on an island-hopping steamer in early 1928,

he knew why. In port after port he asked the question, "Is there anyone here who believes in Jesus Christ?" He met with only blank stares and indifferent shrugs.[4]

Alliance headquarters officials in New York gave him their permission and blessing, but no personnel or funds. Undaunted, Dr. Jaffray made funds available from his personal resources. Then with two Chinese associates he organized the Chinese Foreign Missionary Union (CFMU) and recruited former students of the Alliance Bible Seminary in Wuchow.

The CFMU was the original—and may still be the only—foreign missionary-sending agency ever organized in mainland China. It eventually supported twenty-one workers and achieved some remarkable results in Indonesia.

The first church in Ujung Pandang was organized by the Chinese mission. The second was Kemah Injil (Gospel Tabernacle), a name later included by the Indonesian Alliance church in its official title.

Dr. Jaffray chose Ujung Pandang as his base of operations for a definite reason: It suited his vision for a broad-based national church.

Looking back on the first days, he

wrote in 1937: "In the very beginning of the work we were definitely directed of the Lord to make Makassar [Ujung Pandang] our headquarters. To the east and to the west, our workers have gone forth till we will soon be covering an area larger than that of Europe, wider than the width of the U.S.A."[5]

His vision moved quickly into action. Within ten years, North American and Chinese missionaries and their Indonesian co-workers were operating on every major island of Indonesia.

This rapid expansion was made possible largely through another key element in Dr. Jaffray's strategy: the founding of a Bible school to train Indonesian pastors and evangelists as rapidly as possible with a combined program of classroom studies and practical field experience.

Dr. Jaffray pulled David Clench into Ujung Pandang from his pioneer work in East Kalimantan and told him to start a Bible school. Fifty young people enrolled in the Makassar Bible School's first class in 1932.

Clench died suddenly the following year, but not before laying a good foundation for the institution known today as Jaffray School of Theology, "finishing school" for Gereja Kemah Injil's church leaders.

Each student was required to spend an extended period of ministry before returning to school for the final year of study. Sometimes with missionaries, sometimes only in twos, teams of student evangelists radiated out from Ujung Pandang like spokes from the hub of a wheel to start churches and penetrate unevangelized areas. East and West Kalimantan, Sulawesi, Sumatra and Alor—these and other areas felt the impact of student teams.

Results at first were meager. In Lombok, for example, the first American and Chinese missionaries arrived in 1929, but did not baptize the first converts until 1933. Even after ten years, they could only count 130 local Christians.[6]

"The walls are not tumbling or falling," admitted Dr. Jaffray in his annual report for 1930. "Our enemies are still jeering at us, but by His grace, like the Israelites of old, we are going round and round, apparently in silent weakness, but inspired by faith in His promise that the hour will come when we shall shout, and the wall of opposition, the wall of heathenism, the wall of Mohammedanism, will fall before us. Hallelujah!"[7]

As soon as they set foot in Indonesia, the first missionaries arriving from North America in 1929 realized they had stepped into a spiritual war already heated up. There would be no time for coddling or leisurely paced orientation.

"All five had to seek their own rented quarters, hire a language tutor and in general make all the necessary contacts themselves while they spoke only English. . . . Clearly, Jaffray did not pamper his young missionary force. Nor did they need it."[8]

Some of the earliest and most encouraging responses came from Dayaks of East Kalimantan. Hundreds of miles upriver from the coast, past roaring rapids and falls that discouraged Muslims from penetrating the interior, whole Dayak villages appeared waiting and ready for the Gospel.

Jalong Ipoy, for example, was king of the Pujungan district when he first heard about Jesus Christ and immediately trusted in Him. His conversion in 1931 initiated the first people movement in Kalimantan as 270 people turned to Christ within a year and their numbers grew rapidly.[9]

In one fast-moving decade, writes a

mission administrator, "missionaries and national workers were able to: open stations on every major island of the archipelago; build a Bible school with an enrollment of 300 students; baptize over ten thousand new believers; and bring the Gospel to major geographical areas where the name of Christ had never been heard before."[10]

Oneness in Evangelism

Out of the common heritage that binds together the diverse GKII church regions, one factor prominently evident was Dr. Jaffray's insistence on always claiming more territory and reaching more people for the Lord. His example influenced fellow missionaries and national colleagues to make evangelism the top priority of their agendas.

Christians in the Toraja region of central Sulawesi have special reason to thank God for Dr. Jaffray's unflagging drive to evangelize.

A young man named Bokko saw an advertisement about the Bible school in Ujung Pandang and sensed a call to prepare for ministry. He completed several years of study and student ministry before World War II broke out.

Returning to Toraja, he ministered extensively to many churches whose pastors had fled in fear from the Japanese occupiers. Bokko seemed to travel with a safe-conduct pass issued from headquarters in the heavens, because not once was he hindered or harmed by the Japanese as he openly itinerated among the churches.

He returned to Ujung Pandang after the war to finish his schooling. Then, knowing the Alliance was barred from Toraja through the influence of Dutch state-sponsored churches in the region, Bokko returned to evangelize his people.

A strong indigenous church developed among the Toraja people, aided by a Bible school that provided 90 percent of the trained workers for more than 100 churches by 1988. All this was accomplished without mission funds, personnel or supervision.

A Toraja church stands not far from the pig farm used by the Japanese to intern hundreds of prisoners during the war. Dr. Jaffray was one of the many who did not survive the filthy conditions of the makeshift camp.

Thinking of the strong indigenous church and Dr. Jaffray's imprisonment in their area, one Toraja pastor mused, "You know, we wonder sometimes if during his internment Dr. Jaffray did not spend a lot of time praying for the Toraja people. The church may be the result of those prayers."[11]

Growth continued to characterize the Gospel Tabernacle Church as evangelism and prayer headed its agenda. By 1940, the missionary staff had increased to thirty-nine, the number of national workers to 141, and total membership to almost 13,100.

GKII gained only 2,000 members during the next decade, due mainly to the war. But an enlarged staff of forty-nine missionaries helped the church regain its momentum. Church membership jumped to over 50,300 baptized believers in 410 churches by 1965.

During the next three decades, church membership increased 300 percent and inclusive membership approached the half-million mark. This record made GKII the largest overseas Alliance church in the 1980s.

(Top) Rev. B. Bokko, outstanding Toraja church leader; (middle left, right) Toraja man and woman in traditional dress; (bottom) traditional Toraja house

(Top) Dayaks in East Kalimantan welcome Dr. Nathan Bailey and Rev. Potu, former church president, who spent many years as missionary to the Dayaks; (bottom) students graduate from the Bible school at Long Bia, East Kalimantan.

Precursors of the Message

Although advance through programmed evangelism works well for the Gospel Tabernacle Church, the sovereign working of God's Spirit through unusual circumstances meant much in the early days.

Missionaries on a reconnaissance trip in East Kalimantan in 1932 met Dayaks of the Tanah Tidung area. They listened in amazement as the villagers told of dreams urging them to accept the message brought by white men.

Word spread of the missionaries' arrival and Dayaks came in from eighty to one hundred miles around. Others waited at appointed places for three or four days. Services sometimes lasted from eight to ten hours and when ended, drew a response by hundreds of people. Nearly a thousand Dayaks were converted and baptized by 1936 and many more thousands of inquirers lined up to accept the Lord.[12]

Villagers in the Ketungau district of West Kalimantan had a reputation as the most wicked of the Dayaks. When the leader of one rebellion received a fifteen-year jail sentence, he prophesied: "Someone will be coming from the east. He will bring news that will change the Dayak people. He will have light that isn't hot and fire that doesn't smoke."[13]

An Alliance missionary from East Kalimantan arrived shortly after. The Dayaks noted among his possessions a "light that isn't hot [flashlight]," and a "fire that doesn't smoke [kerosene pump stove]." Some 1,700 Dayaks became followers of Christ in the first two years.

Later surges in conversions due to spiritual awakenings or political developments would dwarf the initial movements toward God among the Dayaks. One of the most famous events, however, would have little direct impact on GKII. The much publicized "Indonesian Revival" in the 1960s referred more accurately to the island of Timor and had its greatest impact on mainline denominational churches whose members were heavily involved in spirit worship and fetishes.

Timorese church leaders themselves acknowledged that "before the revival an estimated 90 percent of their members used fetishes and sought the services of the local shaman [similar to the African witch doctor]. Following the revival, this estimate dropped to 65 percent of total church membership in Timor."[14]

Strategies for Advance

Without ruling out the sovereign intervention of God through revivals and awakenings, the Gospel Tabernacle Church has become increasingly committed to deliberate strategies for growth.

Several factors have influenced this emphasis on goal-oriented advance. In more recent years the annual total of new believers has steadily declined, with an increasing number of second-generation Christians relating to the church through family ties, not necessarily through spiritual rebirth.

In addition, political developments are making significant changes in the demographic profile of the country. For example, several hundred thousand families are being resettled at government expense from overpopulated Java to sparsely inhabited surrounding islands such as Kalimantan and Irian Jaya.

GKII regional presidents met in early 1982 to assess the spiritual needs of both the church and the nation. Each region

set new church-planting goals that projected a combined total of 1,500 new churches by 1990.[15]

A significant portion of the overall target related to JAVA 500, an ambitious plan drafted in 1978 to open 500 new churches in Java by 1990. It would later be modified to JAVA 5.5.2, meaning 500 churches, of which five would be in major urban centers, by the year 2,000.

Java, with its overcrowded population of 100 million, its concentration of 10 million people in Jakarta alone, its strategic importance as the center of political and economic power, and other factors,

would seem an obvious choice for Alliance missions.

Dr. Jaffray and his early associates, however, determined to take the Gospel into hitherto unreached areas. Parts of Indonesia already entered by other missions and churches did not have priority status with these pioneer-minded people.

This fifty-year policy ended in 1978, when the Alliance mission and Gospel Tabernacle Church adopted JAVA 5.5.2. By that time it had become clear that evangelical groups already working on the island could not cope with the large and rapidly expanding population.

One missionary drove across the southwest section of Java and then observed: "After six hours of driving through one of the most densely populated regions of the world, I had not seen one Christian church. By contrast, in west Java alone (about one third of the island) there are over 60,000 mosques and Muslim houses of worship."[16]

In support of JAVA 5.5.2, North American C&MA churches designated Jakarta a special target for funding and prayer. The church and mission in Indonesia appointed personnel to Jakarta, Surabaya (the island's second largest city) and

(Far left) Women express their Christian joy in song; (left) one of nation's universities targeted for evangelism in JAVA 5.5.2; (right) theological students combine JAVA 5.5.2 outreach with their seminary studies.

other areas. East Kalimantan set the example for other regional churches by sending and supporting eleven missionary couples in Java by 1987.

The Muslim-dominated island did not welcome the attention of still another group of evangelizing Christians. Hostility took different forms.

Unsympathetic local officials raised obstacles where none needed to exist. One new church had to negotiate with authorities for ten years before receiving permission to purchase property and build. Church planters realized that in some areas of anti-Christian feeling, believers had best settle for low-profile, small-group congregations meeting in private homes.

Such low-key policies did not always succeed. Clashes erupted between radical Muslims and police in the harbor area of Jakarta in 1984. Before the riot was over, violence spilled over into the city, and church buildings became special targets. One Gospel Tabernacle church in the troubled area escaped damage but two other congregations in the city suspended construction of their churches because of unrest.

Lack of trained church workers posed another serious problem for JAVA 5.5.2. Regional Bible schools and the central Jaffray School of Theology could not keep pace with the need for new workers. The logical solution seemed to be the creation of a Bible school right in Java to train workers for the island's churches.

The resulting Simpson Theological Seminary took form on a six-acre campus in Ungaran, near Samarang, Central Java. Fully operational by 1987, the school projects a student body of 200 by the year 2000.

Unity through Education

Education and leadership training claim much of the mission's resources.

GKII has a constant need for trained church workers, and the government's policy of eventual "Indonesianization" of all institutions and activities requires the training of nationals to take over positions held by foreigners.

Missionaries view formation of church leaders as one of their most rewarding ministries in the nation. Equally important, the church's educational network serves to bring the diverse regions into closer harmony of beliefs and ministries.

All told in 1987, the Gospel Tabernacle Church reported 1,705 students in twenty regional four-year theological schools and Bible schools and one central school with a graduate division. Another 850 students were enrolled in theological education by extension (TEE) courses administered by various schools.

Jaffray School of Theology, like its namesake, the great missionary statesman, looms large in GKII history. The school has never been content with just educating young people. As a wise headmaster prepares his students for the real world and then pushes them out the door to face it, the Ujung Pandang-based school has for many years required students to suspend their studies in order to engage in actual ministry before completing classroom requirements for graduation.

The practice not only added realism to academics, it multiplied new churches for GKII and gave them a sense of unity. In one recent year, the school decided to concentrate its efforts in helping JAVA 5.5.2. A team of fourteen student evangelists conducted services in cities across Java. In three weeks they reached 10,000 people and recorded 500 decisions for Christ.[17]

Another year the students raised $20,000 to cover expenses of student evangelists going to Kalimantan, and then secured another $12,000 to purchase musical instruments for the team. Jaffray students made history in 1986 by sending an evangelistic team into Malaysia, the first time a group from the school ministered outside its own country.[18]

The Jaffray School achieved national stature in 1975, when the government authorized the training of teachers for religion classes in state-run schools.

In announcing the decision, the American-educated coordinator for higher education, although a Muslim, encouraged the students to develop their minds because of the "great need for strong Christian leaders in Indonesia."[19]

The school itself modeled the importance of national leadership when direction of the school passed from missionary to Indonesian leadership in the mid-1960s.

Later, patient and persistent upgrading of the faculty enabled the school to obtain an Indonesian director with an earned doctorate from Fuller Seminary in California and several professors with graduate degrees from the Alliance Biblical Seminary in Manila. This helped the Jaffray School win government recognition as a degree-granting institution.

Improving the educational standards of both Jaffray and twenty regional schools grew out of a combined sense of vision and realism.

The determination of Indonesia to take its place among the leading nations of the world stirred escalating demands for better and higher education among young people. Even church-sponsored schools realized they must upgrade or die. Just as serious, lagging behind accepted standards of education would leave the church with students of limited potential. Brighter and more aggressive youth would go to secular schools, where education would prepare them for almost any occupation except serving the Lord.

The Gospel Tabernacle Church therefore raised the academic level of its regional schools. The institutions in Java, West and East Kalimantan and Irian Jaya now award bachelor degrees.

In addition to these regional schools, the church has organized through Jaffray School of Theology a number of extension programs in different areas of the country. The academic center in Jakarta, opened in 1984, actually serves as Jaffray School's second campus, with a special focus on preparing urban church leaders.

A partial solution to Indonesia's unending need for trained church workers may be found in missionaries supplied by other Asian Alliance churches. The Gospel Tabernacle Church has a historical precedent for receiving help from this quarter. Chinese missionaries associated with Dr. Jaffray were the first to bring the Gospel to areas of Indonesia where the church now exists.

Rev. and Mrs. Carlos Cristobal, missionaries from the Alliance church in the Philippines, arrived in Palembang, Sumatra, in 1968 to begin their ministry as the first Asian C&MA missionaries in recent times to work in Indonesia. When a congregation was organized through their work, Alliance churches in Hong Kong provided money to help construct a sanctuary.[20]

The Cristobals eventually returned

(Above) Dr. Peter Anggu, director of Jaffray Theological School; (below) class in session at the school; (right) school library

home after their visas were not renewed in 1988.

Learning at Home

Even with twenty schools and help from abroad, GKII could not hope to have an adequate supply of trained workers for all its churches. A way had to be found to train layworkers and to help pastors already active in ministry who needed further schooling.

TEE (Theological Education by Extension) provided an obvious solution: learning while working. When missionaries first proposed TEE courses, church leaders agreed without much enthusiasm. How could anyone prepare for ministry without going away to school, as they had done?

But once the idea of TEE caught on, church leaders backed it wholeheartedly. They recognized, for example, that JAVA 5.5.2 would never have enough formally trained pastors. About one-half the workers for Java may come through TEE courses administered by Simpson Theological Seminary.

Several GKII regions have a network of TEE training centers supervised by the regional church and school. East and West Kalimantan had the largest enrollment in 1987: a total of 275 students in twenty-one centers.

Bonding Ink and Paper

Ink on paper is a proven way to hold people and organizations together. When

an organization gathers infrequently and its people are widely scattered, publications take on even greater importance as the cement that holds them together.

Kalam Hidup, the Bandung-based publishing house of the Gospel Tabernacle Church, fulfills that necessary function. Through its publications, services and other media activities, GKII churches strung across the islands have a sense of unity that would otherwise be impossible.

Kalam Hidup did not gradually become an influential part of the work over a number of years. It began strong. Dr. Jaffray, raised in the tradition of newspaper publishing in Canada, knew the power of the printed page, and he knew how to use it.

As early as 1930, he began publishing Kalam Hidup ("Word of Life"), a Bible magazine for pastors and committed layworkers in the church. He distributed 30,000 copies of two free introductory issues and then began charging for subscriptions. The monthly magazine gradually attracted an average of 3,000 to 4,000 subscribers in numerous church groups throughout the archipelago.

When the publishing house was organized in 1930, it assumed the name and publication of the widely read periodical and began to print other materials as well.

Kalam Hidup benefited from the government's decision in the 1960s to require that all printing be done within the country. The demand for locally produced literature rose sharply. Placing the publishing house under Indonesian management in 1965 also enhanced Kalam Hidup as a truly indigenous venture.

It received another big boost when an aborted Communist coup led to the burning of tons of Marxist literature. Left with

(Left) East Kalimantan girls join villagers (right) in building an airstrip by hand; they will wait for air drops of tea, sugar and rice for refreshment.

little to read, Indonesians grasped for any available reading matter. The publishing house did its best to fill the vacuum.

One missionary reported seeing two policemen in a precinct station scuffling over some papers. When he discovered they were quarreling over a copy of the Bible magazine, he ended the dispute by promising each one his own copy.[21]

By 1987, the publishing house was providing indispensable services to both GKII and numerous other church and mission groups. Seventeen new book titles appeared on bookshelves that year, and another fifty-seven reprinted books were also put on the market. Sales from literature and other church supplies topped $534,000.

Kalam Hidup distributes its material through a chain of nine bookstores that serve many religious groups. The most recent literature center is a modern and attractive facility close to the Institute of Technology, two colleges and two high schools in Bandung.

The publishing house turns out more than just books and magazines. It produced an Indonesian version of the Living New Testament prepared by a team of five Indonesian and two missionary translators. They then turned their attention to the Old Testament and completed that project in 1988. Another group of writers worked with Gospel Light International in the preparation of graded Sunday school lessons in the vernacular.

Kalam Hidup devised a generous and practical way to help GKII churches. The "Pastor's Library Project" is a long-term commitment to provide all 2,000 pastors and evangelists with a set of basic study books cased in a protective container.

"Operation Wedge"

Although Kalam Hidup produces a great deal of literature to nurture the church, it also has a heart for evangelism.

"Operation Wedge" was conceived to produce and distribute easy-reading evangelistic material for non-Christians. The idea turned into a major operation. A series of tracts were printed, sorted and wrapped in small packets. The 300,000 individual sets, weighing a combined total of twelve tons, were delivered to numerous church groups for evangelistic outreach.[22]

The publishing house supervises the use of another communication medium as an evangelistic wedge. "Dawn of Hope" has been aired twice daily, nationwide over shortwave radio since 1977.

A sister program called "Fountain of Love" reaches into major cities across the country through local radio. The programs have proven quite popular, averaging over 1,000 letters a month from listeners. Keeping track of all the correspondence became a much easier procedure when the work was connected to Kalam Hidup's computer system.

Winged Evangelism

While the spiritual awakening on Timor had limited impact on other areas of Alliance work, God demonstrated that He was not bound to one method in stirring people to seek His face.

In recent years, amazing people movements in Kalimantan, Irian Jaya and other islands were made possible through mechanical means: God's message rode the wings of Mission Aviation Fellowship. MAF began operations in Kalimantan in 1969, twelve years after beginning service to Alliance missionaries in Irian Jaya.

Telescoping into hours the distance

that would normally take arduous weeks of land and water travel, MAF put even the remotest areas within easy reach of ministry. Evangelistic teams could penetrate hitherto unevangelized regions; TEE instructors could maintain regular contact with widely scattered training centers; district superintendents could tour their churches—the list could go on and on.

It may fairly be said that the stationing of one MAF plane in a church or mission center had the immediate effect of multiplying the staff's capabilities by four to five times.

In 1948, for example, missionaries in East Kalimantan received a most unusual telegram from a Dutch territorial official: "At the meeting of the village chiefs it was decided that after the next rice harvest, fetish worship would be abolished in all the Apo Kayan. Therefore, a great turning to Christianity can be expected. We request you to place preachers in every village and missionaries in Long Nawang."[23]

The missionaries responded to the remarkable invitation and a large church with thousands of Dayak believers eventually developed in the Long Nawang area.

But getting to that remote area of the Apo Kayan district required six to eight weeks of dangerous travel upriver by

canoe and a three-day trek over mountains. By MAF plane, the trip now takes less than two hours.

Winged evangelism in Indonesia had an early enthusiast: the visionary Dr. Jaffray, of course. In 1936 he requested funds from New York to purchase a plane but Depression years left no cushion in the budget for luxuries such as an airplane to ferry missionaries to their work.

Dr. Jaffray refused to be put off. A few years later, he came into a sizable family inheritance that enabled him, with the help of other donors, to purchase the Alliance its first missionary aircraft, a single-engine Beechcraft biplane with floats.[24]

The plane provided outstanding service for the mission from 1939 until 1942, when war came to Indonesia and brought a tragic end to the Alliance's airborne ministry: Japanese troops destroyed the plane and executed its pilot. Not until 1948 and the return of Alliance aviators would missionaries and church workers be freed once again from the rivers, rapids and ranges.

Unity through Adversity

Historical roots, common goals and

specialized ministries are not alone in bringing unity to the diverse regions of the Gospel Tabernacle Church. Adversity has also played an unwelcome but effective role in bringing believers closer together.

The most active agent in this painful process has been militant Islam.

Indonesia theoretically basks under the benevolent sun of *Pancasila,* the official policy that encourages all Indonesians to believe in God by whatever name they may call Him. But paradoxically, the island nation also claims a population 87 percent Muslim—a religion not known for its tolerance of other faiths.

That the government has been able to call Indonesia a secular state with no official religion may be explained in part by the "folk nature" of Islamic beliefs held by many of its citizens. The tenets of

(Top) Dayak villagers crowd around an arriving MAF plane, an event of major importance, (bottom) as is also its departure.

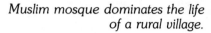

Muslim mosque dominates the life of a rural village.

Muhammad coexist with ancestral beliefs in spirit worship and traditional practices in a manner that has diluted orthodox Islam's well-known hostility toward other religions.

But a growing number of Indonesians believe that this overwhelming Muslim majority of the population constitutes a mandate for transforming the secular state into an Islamic republic. They believe it is their historical right dating back to 1912, when *Sarekat Islam* (Islamic Association) became the first religiously and politically based nationalist organization.

Militant Muslims fought hard for national independence and many died believing their sacrifice advanced the cause of Islam in Indonesia. When the new nation emerged a secular state embracing all religions equally and endorsing none, the Islamic Association felt betrayed. Radical elements began agitating by every means to secure what they believed to be their rightful reward, an Islamic republic.

GKII believers inevitably felt the heat of their anger. Through hardships ranging from religious riots to harassment in local government offices, they were made to feel like second-class citizens with dim prospects for the future.

Followers of folk Islam present a group more potentially responsive to the Gospel, yet even among them nothing may be taken for granted. Although large numbers turned to Christ after political upheavals in the 1960s, one missionary cautioned against unbridled optimism.

"The same climate . . . that gave Christians unprecedented opportunities for evangelism," he wrote, "brought to Indonesian Muslims a revival of interest and militant strategy." Success of the Gospel would not go unchallenged, he warned. "Where there has been a movement toward Christianity, a Muslim reaction is almost certain to follow."[25]

Balinese Uniqueness

Bali is an island fortress of Hinduism in a sea of Islam. That reality helps explain its fierce rejection of attempts by the Alliance to plant churches on its soil.

Denpasar, the capital, is home to the largest GKII church in Bali. When the church celebrated its twenty-fifth anniversary in 1987, over 400 people attended the observance. That same year, the Christian Children's Home in Klungkung reported construction of a three-story dormitory for girls among its nearly 200 orphan and homeless children.

Such positive statistics, however, are rare for Bali. Deeply entrenched resistance to the Gospel has severely limited church growth. Sometimes the hostility turns violent, even to burning homes of newly converted Balinese Christians.

Closed ranks against evangelism has both historical and cultural causes on the island. Back in the fifteenth century, a defeated Hindu king in East Java fled to Bali after a successful Muslim uprising.

Bali is a Hindu enclave in a predominantly Muslim nation.

From that time on, the island has fought off every attempt by Muslims and Christians alike to establish a strong presence among its people.

Balinese Hinduism proved more vulnerable to forces native to the island. The *Indonesia Handbook* notes, "Bali-Hindu religion is much closer to the earth and more animist than Hinduism proper. The two sects are as different from each other as Ethiopian Christianity is from Episcopalian Christianity or from the Catholicism practiced by the Irish and the Catholicism practiced by American Indians."[26]

Resistance to the Gospel also grows out of cultural factors and their economic implications. Hindu beliefs dominate Balinese art, music and drama so completely that religious competition with Hinduism is viewed as an attack on the existence of the Balinese mystique: its famous cultural life (and its lucrative tourist trade).

Alliance attempts to evangelize the island met determined resistance from the start. Dutch authorities refused the mission permission to work in Bali but reluctantly agreed to Dr. Jaffray's argument that at least the Chinese inhabitants could

be approached, since they were not Balinese.

A missionary of the Chinese Foreign Missionary Union arrived in 1932 and soon proved too successful. Balinese wives of Chinese converts became Christians and began witnessing to their own people.

The Gospel spread through the local population, causing an uproar not only

from Hindus, but also from an international hodge-podge of artists, anthropologists and travel agents who called upon the government to maintain Bali as something of an island-sized museum and art gallery quarantined from a changing world.

The Christian community continued to grow, even after the expulsion of missionaries in 1935 and a temporary ban on

Balinese students' attending Jaffray School of Theology. Churches are now established not only in Denpasar and Klungkung but in scattered villages on the island.

Tragedy and Glory

Despite the aggressive nature of radical Muslims and the intense hostility of Balinese Hindus, no Alliance missionary has as yet suffered martyrdom at the hands of Indonesians.

It took the passions of war and the deliberate policy of Japanese military commanders to give the Alliance one of its most glorious and tragic chapters in Indonesia.

Some missionaries were able to leave the islands ahead of Japanese invasion forces in 1941; others were caught and imprisoned. Dr. Jaffray and his family could have escaped on a ship in Ujung Pandang harbor, but he refused to leave while some of his colleagues could not.

Rev. Fred C. Jackson, pilot of the mission plane, was another who willingly gave himself up rather than abandon his friends and fly to freedom. For him and the Andrew Sande family, with their little

child, internment was brutally short. Within a year, they and about 120 other foreigners were murdered by the Japanese—first men, then women and children.

Rev. John Willfinger was deep in Kalimantan when the island fell. Dayak Christians urged him to remain hidden in their care. After pondering the dilemma and much prayer, he wrote to a local Dayak official who had befriended him: "In this letter I inform you of my decision, which is the most difficult one of all my life," he wrote. "If I hide, naturally the saints will be forced to lie and disobey orders if they shelter me. I would be forced to drag them into sin."

He then explained why such a situation was unbearable: "My intention upon leaving my country and family was only

Dr. Jaffray's grave is located on the outskirts of Ujung Pandang.

to make mankind righteous and not to bring them into sin, even though I pay for it with my life. In short, sir, because of Jesus Christ and His sheep, before I will do anything whatsoever that is not right, I will surely surrender myself."[27]

He gave himself up to the Japanese soldiers in early December, 1942, and on Christmas Eve they used him for bayonet practice.

Before returning to Indonesia in 1938 for the last time, Dr. Jaffray had surveyed the gathering war clouds and said prophetically, "If I do not go back now, there is little likelihood that I can ever go back at all. I must return to the Far East. I want to die out there where my life has been."[28]

His wish became reality just two weeks before the war ended. Confined to a prison cot on a pig farm turned into an internment camp, Dr. Jaffray succumbed to disease and starvation on July 5, 1945. He joined seven other Alliance missionary adults and one child who died, either directly or indirectly, as a result of the war.

Someone has well said, "Tyrants die and their power ends; martyrs die and

their power begins." The missionaries and their manner of dying will always be a powerful example for the Indonesian church.

Marxist Miscalculation

Indonesia's relations with Alliance missionaries came close to being stained with blood in 1965.

The widely popular *Partai Komunis Indonesia* (PKI) had long chafed under its inability to bring the nation into the Communist bloc. The PKI had already mounted two unsuccessful uprisings in 1926 and 1948, both of which were quickly put down.

The second attempt put the party in disfavor with the majority of people, who considered it "an act of treason against the government and it took a long time for the PKI to overcome this shattering defeat," according to Dr. William W. Conley.[29]

For the next seventeen years they made major adjustments in their Marxist-Leninist doctrines. Nonalignment in international politics and domestic capitalism would be acceptable—as long as the people combated international imperialism.

(Top) The Indonesian national flag; (bottom) a war monument in honor of the nation's fallen defenders

Even belief in God would be tolerable, provided believers did not try to spread their religion to others.

By 1965, the PKI again thought it had won the people over to its side. Furthermore, they believed that President Sukarno backed their plan to take over the country.

They miscalculated on both counts. The masses did not believe Communism could embrace Pancasila's first principle of belief in God and they therefore refused to support the uprising. The president, faced with a choice between soldiers and rebels, sided with the few generals who had escaped the Communist slaughter of six top generals and their aides on the eve of their revolt.

One who survived the assassination sweep was General Suharto, who later succeeded Sukarno as president. He rallied the troops and quickly put down the attempted coup. The penalty for failure began a month later.

Furious over the brutal murder and mutilation of their top generals, army units in central Java teamed up with Muslim youth gangs and began the most bloody purge in the nation's short and turbulent history. The hunt for Communists then spread to other major islands of the archipelago, but the violence on Java was almost beyond description.

"Over the following months, all of Java ran amok, resulting finally in the mass political murdering of perhaps one million people shot, knived, strangled, hacked to death."[30] (Subsequent investigators reduced the total number of deaths to an estimated 400,000.)

The monumental tragedy did have one positive effect: an unprecedented openness to the Gospel. Some of the response came from Indonesians who had been secretly convinced the Bible was right but were afraid to confess their faith openly due to Communist pressure. The government's victory encouraged these spiritual children of Nicodemus to go public.[31]

A government "suggestion" that every Indonesian should "have a religion" also had a part in bringing people into the church. The ominous underlying logic suggested that those who did not have a belief in God must obviously be Communists.[32]

In the Apo Kayan district of Kalimantan, an energetic army officer decided to take the "suggestion" a step further. He "ordered all the pagans to accept either the Catholic religion, join the Protestant church or KINGMI [now called GKII]. In some villages he sent a Bible and a bullet for them to choose which they wanted. They were scared to death, and most of them joined KINGMI."[33]

These human prods to church growth eventually faded, and fortunately so, since they brought into the church people who did not believe deeply and later caused problems.

The majority of conversions, however, were sincere decisions on the part of people who turned to the Lord and joined the Gospel Tabernacle Church because of their disillusionment with every other way of life. They were especially offended by the brutality of Muslim and even Roman Catholic groups during the purge.

After the aborted coup, the missionar-

CHURCH AND MISSION

OFFICIAL NAME OF CHURCH:	Gospel Tabernacle Church of Indonesia
ENTRY BY MISSIONARIES:	1929
NUMBER OF MISSIONARIES:	140
ORGANIZED CHURCHES:	1,622
UNORGANIZED CHURCHES AND PREACHING POINTS:	417
BAPTIZED CHURCH MEMBERS:	173,179
INCLUSIVE MEMBERSHIP:	466,084
MEDICAL WORK:	78 Clinics
EDUCATION:	73 Secular Schools 23 Theological Schools 39 TEE Centers
RADIO BROADCASTS:	48 per week
PAGES PRINTED:	32,212,305

COUNTRY

OFFICIAL NAME:	Republic of Indonesia
FORM OF GOVERNMENT:	Independent Republic
OFFICIAL LANGUAGE(S):	Bahasa Indonesia (Malay), Javanese, other Austronesia
AREA:	735,268 sq. mi.
POPULATION:	(1989 est.) 187,726,000
CAPITAL:	Jakarta
PER CAPITA INCOME:	$560.00
LITERACY:	72%
RELIGIOUS AFFILIATION:	88% Muslim

ies learned how close they had all come to being wiped out. One report read, "In Bali the nephew of a Protestant pastor was captured. He had been leader of a Communist cell. Among his papers was found a list of Balinese pastors who were to have been killed.

"In Karubaga, West Irian [Irian Jaya], a Javanese government official told a group of RBMU missionaries, 'If the coup had succeeded, their plans were to exterminate 250,000, present company included.' One of our Alliance missionaries in West Kalimantan was told of the grave that had been dug for him and his family in the woods near their home."[34]

Virtually every Alliance missionary's name could be found on one Communist death list or another, and the graves of some had already been dug. One missionary observed: "The words of Psalm 57:67 were fulfilled literally right before our eyes: 'They have digged a pit before me, into the midst whereof they are fallen themselves.' "[35]

The irony of Communists' filling graves they had dug for others joined a long list of similar happenings in history dating back to Old Testament times, when Ha-man himself was hanged on the gallows he had intended for the Jew Mordecai.

The fate of such people should serve to remind other tormentors and would-be exterminators of the church that they are more likely to end up the victims of destruction rather than its agents.

And all the while, through common heritage, special ministries and adversity, God continues to draw His people in the Gospel Tabernacle Church of Indonesia closer together in a singular harmony that safeguards the rich diversity of its regions, cultures and peoples.

ADVANCE INTO IRIAN JAYA

"Good for One, Good for All"

"During the month of May, the Uhunduni [Damal] leaders continued their long conferences dealing with minute implications of becoming Christians. In their tight-knit cultural pattern, it never occurred to them that this was a message they could accept or reject as individuals. They had always done things together. It was not likely that they would start a new trend at this important juncture.

"If the message was good for one, it was good for all."[36]

Several weeks later, on May 25, 1957, twenty leading men of one Damal (formerly called Uhunduni) clan in the Ilaga Valley approached a missionary to discuss "declaring their faith in Christ and burning their fetishes."[37] They returned next day with another 110 men and boys, ninety women and girls, carrying nets and armlets, miniature bows and arrows and other objects dedicated to appeasing evil spirits.

Holding aloft each object in turn, they called out the name of the spirit they had formerly worshiped and then threw the object into the fire. Then, with eyes fixed intently on the burning pyre of paraphernalia that had once been their trusted shield against misfortune, they sang hymns of praise to their newfound Savior.

Another clan of about sixty Damals came to the Ilaga Valley station in August and lit a bonfire of charms and fetishes as evidence of their collective acceptance of Christ. The courageous decision of these initial groups reverberated in widening circles among their kinsmen.

The following year, 1958, opened with

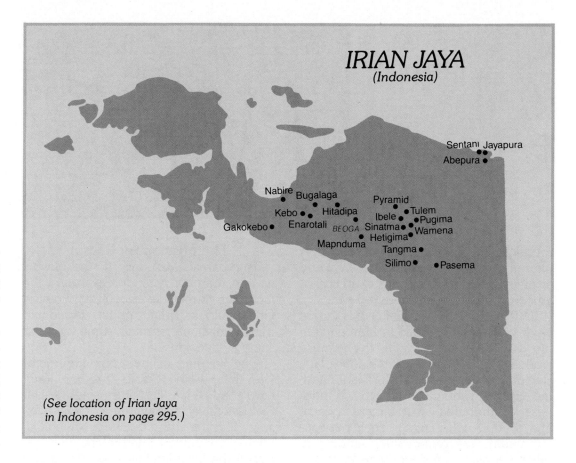

IRIAN JAYA
(Indonesia)

Sentani Jayapura
Abepura

Nabire Bugalaga
Pyramid
Kebo Hitadipa Tulem
Ibele Pugima
Gakokebo Enarotali BEOGA Sinatma Wamena
Hetigima
Mapnduma Tangma
Silimo Pasema

*(See location of Irian Jaya
in Indonesia on page 295.)*

an awesome spectacle. In the Beoga Valley, some three to four walking days distant, four groups of Damals, about 1,000 in each, joined their Ilaga Valley relatives in declaring for Christ.

Other groups and villages responded to the Gospel in a deliberate, collective fashion until almost all the Damals—about 1,400 persons—in the Ilaga Valley had become Christians by 1963. Almost the entire Damal population in Beoga Valley likewise trusted in Christ over the next few years. One missionary called the two valleys "good examples of 'clean sweeps' in people movements."[38]

This multi-individual decision to accept Christ characterized the spread of the Gospel throughout interior Irian Jaya after World War II. Although virtually unknown in the splintered society of western nations, people movements are effective means of evangelism. Dr. Donald McGavran, noted church growth authority, estimated that "at least two-thirds of all converts in Africa, Asia and Oceania" have come to the Christian faith through people movements.[39]

Fortunately, over a period of time, most of the missionaries in Irian Jaya came to understand and accept multi-individual decisions as one method of God's working. "The period of decision for a communal group may be a long road," explains one missiologist. "It may spread over years of village or family discussion, as individuals, one by one, come to the position where they can at last say that they are of one mind, and when they can burn their fetishes as a total group."[40]

Dr. McGavran classifies people movements such as that seen in Irian Jaya into a larger context of evangelism: "Mankind is not one vast homogeneous mass; it is made up of many societies, classes, castes and tribes." Each receives or resists the Gospel in its own time and in its own way.

"If we are to see humanity correctly we must see it as a great mosaic, each piece of which, though it is in contact with the others, has its own color and texture. That many pieces are today responsive is of paramount importance to the Church as it engages in mission."[41]

In the years that followed that first people movement in the Ilaga Valley, Damal Christians silenced critics who contended that such conversions were shallow and short-lived. Using the Damals as

(Left) MAF plays a key role in ferrying evangelists to targeted areas for evangelism; (right) people movements in response to the Gospel become congregations of committed believers.

a bridge, the Spirit of God crossed over into other tribes of interior Irian Jaya and awakened tens of thousands to an acceptance of Jesus Christ.

In 1961, fifteen years after missionary work had recommenced in Irian Jaya at the close of World War II, the Alliance work became known as the Irian Jaya Region of Gereja Kemah Injil Indonesia, the Gospel Tabernacle Church of Indonesia. It numbered 7,700 baptized people and 29,000 adherents.[42] Their missionary vision was remarkable, sending to other people groups an average of one cross-cultural missionary for every eighty members.[43] By 1988, the church in the region had grown to 59,392 baptized believers, 738 organized and unorganized churches, and over 1,200 ordained and lay workers.

This kind of church growth prompted the regional director for Alliance work in the Pacific islands to conclude, "Irian Jaya could be one of the few areas of the world where the Christian community has reached the point where it can successfully evangelize the rest of the population without assistance from outside groups."[44]

The Missionary Factor

The Damals' response to the Gospel was so dramatic it tends to obscure the fact that the whole movement toward God would never have gotten started had not the missionaries made some wise and strategic decisions.

One key part of the missionary factor was their willingness to take the long, hard road of learning and using the Damal language to convey the gospel message. Instead of the quick-fix solution of relying on untried interpreters, they reduced the local language to writing and taught the people to read from the very inception of their work in Irian Jaya. Then they made certain their message was contextualized in the culture of the people.

Furthermore, Alliance missionaries focused their major effort on winning adults, traditional decision makers of the clan. Then, despite their own cultural background, wherein faith and conversion were individual choices, they accepted group decisions among the Damals as an authentic conversion experience.

They worked within the people's social network rather than forcing converts to

reach the Cross by a path familiar to western Christians but alien to the Irianese. They were careful even to the point of not obligating converts to don western clothing in lieu of their traditional grass skirts and gourds.

Equally significant in the missionary factor, Damal converts were immediately taught the necessity of witnessing to others concerning their spiritual rebirth in Christ. They faced no long-term incubation period before being "ready" to speak of their faith.

Freed from the fear of evil spirits, emancipated from the deadly cycle of war and revenge, awakened to a wonderful new life with an eternal future, the Damals had every reason to tell their kinsmen about the Gospel.

Early Attraction

Although Irian Jaya represents one of the more dramatic and successful Alliance missionary efforts in recent years, its attraction as a mission field began many decades ago.

Dutch missionaries initiated work on the coast around 1860. Limiting their efforts to the fringes of the island, they

won only a handful of converts at first. When a people movement to Christ swept through the coastal region, the Dutch mission regrouped and concentrated its work along the north coast, leaving the south coast to the Catholics. Gradually developed through the years, the Dutch-founded church became the largest Protestant community on the island.

Dr. Albert B. Simpson, founder of the C&MA, singled out the island as an area of great spiritual need in 1887, the very first year of the new movement.[45] Another fifty years would pass, however, before Irian Jaya received serious consideration as a mission field.

A Dutch aviator, F. J. Wissel, was doing aerial surveys for an oil company in December of 1936 when he spotted a network of lakes, villages and neatly plotted gardens in the western highlands. Named after its discoverer, the Wissel Lakes stirred the pioneer spirit of Dr. Robert A. Jaffray, the renowned Alliance missionary strategist. At the time, he was directing mission activities in Indonesia from his base in Ujung Pandang.

The interior tribes "could be among the very last people of earth to be discovered," he exclaimed![46] Would Irian Jaya hold the last people groups to be reached before Christ's return?

To those who protested that the Alliance already had its hands full without adding another island of trackless jungles and impassable mountains, Dr. Jaffray replied, "How do we reach them? We do not know, but we are sure that we will never find out by sitting here in Makassar [Ujung Pandang].

"We feel an urge to go and see what can be done. These people are included in the 'every creature' of my commission.

If men after gold and oil may go, why not the missionary seeking precious souls, even though he may have to fly to them?"[47]

When Dr. Jaffray approached the Dutch government administrator of Irian Jaya concerning missionary work, he received a most encouraging answer. "I

(Above) Wreckage of Al Lewis's plane; (right) warrior equipped for battle stands guard.

want to give these people the best that civilization has to offer," said Mr. Jensen. "I want you to take the Gospel to them."[48]

First Move

Equipped with government maps and even the status of a government expedition, Alliance missionaries C. Russell Deibler and Walter M. Post left Ujung Pandang in early December, 1938, for an exploratory trip to Irian Jaya. A shortage of carriers and supplies—the hiking boots fit only Deibler's feet—forced Post to turn back.

Deibler and his retinue started inland the day after Christmas. Two days of

travel by canoe brought them to what could hardly be called a trail.

"At times it was almost a perpendicular climb, and often we had to resort to the use of a crude ladder," he later wrote. "There were sharp stones on the trail which cut one's boots to shreds; boulders which if set in motion would destroy everything in their path; and precipices which made one shudder to look over them."[49]

After nineteen days of trekking and a midnight boat ride that almost ended in disaster on Lake Paniai, Deibler arrived at the newly established Dutch government post at Enarotali.

After gathering the information he had come for, Deibler found his return trip delightfully easy. The Dutch official at the lake post had become severely ill and had to be evacuated by plane. Deibler was permitted to fly out with him, a trip that took a few hours instead of nearly three weeks.

Age Gap

The second missionary expedition arrived at Enarotali two months later to establish a permanent base in central Irian Jaya. The missionary and Indonesian workers encountered the Ekari (formerly called Kapauku) people and also their first major problem: an age gap. The difference could not be computed in years, but in ages and generations. The difference stretched between the local Stone Age culture and the missionary's own Industrial Age background.

The Ekaris' primitive way of life had been a necessary price to pay for their very survival. According to one missionary, the interior peoples had once lived along the coast. They chose to flee inland from the larger, stronger Papuan invaders

rather than face slavery. "Jungle soon covered the trails they had followed," he wrote. "In the interior they set up a way of life that needed nothing from the outside."[50]

One student of the inland cultures believes that the flight en masse from the coast happened long ago: "Archaeological finds lead us to believe that people were already inhabiting these interior valleys when Christ was born."[51]

The various peoples hidden behind the ranges have strikingly similar legends about their origins. Ekaris in the Wissel Lakes area, for example, recount the legend of a tall white woman coming to them in a canoe and bearing sweet potatoes, pigs and shell money. Her canoe drifted away and was lost. A young man offered to help her find the canoe, but when they were alone in the woods he raped her.

Enraged by such treatment, the woman put a curse on the people: "I give you flies, death and darkness." Then she left with a tall white man and the legend ends with, "We do not know where they went. The people say they went to the sun and moon. In the distant future they may return."[52]

Other legends and myths concern the interior peoples' belief about heaven. The Damals believe there is a place in the sky where death does not exist, but women and pigs do in abundance. *Hai* was lost through the greed of men, and "never again have earthly people been able to climb to the place of *hai*."[53]

Such oral accounts, handed down from generation to generation, were more than yarn-spinning diversions. Tall white people coming from the "outside" . . . suggestions of a long-lost Eden and a future

The deadly game of war adds color and excitement to the highland tribes, but perpetuates costly feuds from generation to generation.

Paradise . . . hints of a message that would bridge the abyss from mortality to a golden age of immortality. These and other folk tales helped prepare the Stone Age Irianese for the people movements that would eventually write a new chapter in the annals of Alliance missions.

First Post

The missionaries busied themselves with establishing a post at Enarotali, learning the language and trying to make friends with the people. Their attempts at evangelism, however, seemed to get nowhere. The village chief explained that the Ekaris could not accept the Gospel because they were real people and the strangers were spirits.

When the missionaries protested that they too were human, the old chief countered: "It just can't be. You two mission-aries are men; the student workers are men; the government officials are men and all the field police are men. Not one of you has a wife and none of you has children. If you aren't spirits, just how did you come into existence in the first place?"[54]

Arrival of the first missionary wives in 1940 clarified the misconception, but time was running out. World War II began, the Netherlands fell to Germany and the Japanese invaded Indonesia. Three months after the women arrived, the entire staff of missionaries and Indonesian workers was ordered out of the Wissel Lakes.

Later that year the colonial government reversed its decision and even encouraged the Alliance to resume its work in the lakes region. The mountains seemed to swallow the returning workers, and for the next two years they lived in almost total isolation from the outside world, cut off from communication and from supplies.[19]

The first reported conversions among the interior people were sixteen Ekaris in August, 1942. By the end of that year, approximately one thousand Ekaris were regularly attending services in eight or nine churches which they themselves had helped build. Mission work had been established among the neighboring Moni people as well.

Once again the war intervened, this time undeniably closer. Japanese planes made frequent passes over the lakes region, and word filtered through that Japanese soldiers were only forty miles away. A Catalina flying boat arrived in May of 1943 to evacuate the missionaries and others. On its way to the coast, the Dutch plane slipped from one cloud bank to

another, dodging the pursuing Japanese fighters.

The dangers of war and years of isolation must have seemed worthwhile to the missionaries as they looked down on the fast-receding Wissel Lakes. They left behind something of an indigenous church with nine centers, "each manned by an Indonesian national and a total of approximately 2,000 adherents."[55]

Contested Return

Following the defeat of Japan, Mickelson and six Dayak and Ambonese Christians returned to Irian Jaya in October, 1946, eager to resume their work in the Wissel Lakes.

It some respects, however, it was like starting over. The mission station, ransacked and destroyed by the Japanese, had to be rebuilt. Many friends among

the Ekaris had moved away, and converts had fallen back into traditional religious practices.

Only four days after their return, the missionary party learned that about 1,000 warriors had assembled and were being incited by some chiefs to kill them. Their harangue seemed logical: "The white man was here before the war. Because he was here the Japanese came. We were badly treated by them. We had to kill forty of them before they left us. This white man has come back. The Japanese will surely follow. Let us kill the white man, then the Japanese will not come."[56]

The threatened attack failed to materialize, as did several other death threats against Mickelson. Opposition then took the form of boycotts as hostile villagers refused to sell food to the strangers and tried to kill their livestock.

The first baptisms and a communion service for fourteen new believers in August, 1947, set off a new round of threats and opposition. By now, however, several chiefs had allied themselves with the missionaries, and the work was firmly established.

Several events stood out in 1948 as milestones that would have a significant bearing on the future work in Irian Jaya:

• The Dutch colonial government delegated to missions the responsibility of educating Irianese children. It pledged that costs would be "underwritten by the government if minimum standards were maintained."[57]

• The international Alliance headquarters in New York directed the mission to secure an import license for an airplane.

• The Dutch colonial government granted

permission for church work in the Moni and Damal areas.

Though each event was important in its own way, the matter of an import license had special significance. It would spare the missionaries debilitating weeks on the trail, double or even triple their capacity for work, and enable them to launch one of the most dramatic and widely publicized exploits of missions in recent times.

Shangri-La

The Baliem River Valley, high in the central highlands, first came to public notice in 1938. Richard Archbold, an American explorer and naturalist, discovered it when on assignment for the American Museum of Natural History.

During World War II, American cargo planes provided high-flying sightseeing tours of the valley for off-duty servicemen. When one of the huge planes crashed and survivors had to be airlifted out of the valley, the Baliem Valley gained further notoriety as the mysterious and dangerous Shangri-La.

The valley hidden behind the ranges did have an uncommon beauty. One airborne observer noted, "Below lay the beautiful Baliem Valley, a vast carpet of green stretching out toward the west as far as we could see, surrounded by an expansive network of ragged mountains, some of them with snowcapped peaks. . . .

"The river winds serpentine through the valley, passing villages and making its way through the well cultivated and well drained gardens of sweet potatoes and taro. Practically the whole valley is under cultivation. Side valleys branching out from the Baliem also have gardens and villages. All along we could see well defined trails, indicating there must be considerable travel in the area."[58]

Alliance missionaries had wanted for years to enter the Baliem, but two critical factors held them back: lack of air transport—the only way to maintain work in the valley—and lack of government permission. Both problems were solved in 1952.

Knowing the Baliem could not be kept isolated much longer, Dutch government officials permitted the Alliance to enter, but only if a two-engine plane were used. And they added, "Understand, you are on your own." Hearing of this changed position, the Board of Managers in New York authorized the purchase of an amphibian twin-engine Sealand, costing about $100,000 at the aircraft plant in Ireland.

The actual penetration of the Grand Valley of the Baliem had all the earmarks of a meticulously planned and executed military maneuver. Two missionaries and an Ekari pastor with his wife and daughter (the latter two to assure the Danis of their peaceful intentions) were airlifted to the plateau valley on April 20, 1954.

A second flight the following morning brought reinforcements to the beachhead: a third missionary and two more Indonesian workers. Meanwhile, across the world, Alliance people were praying for their safe arrival and peaceful encounter with the fierce Danis.

Initial contacts with the Danis were friendly, but the newcomers knew it would not continue so, and they were right. Among the highland peoples, the Danis were reputed to be the most violent, cruel and treacherous of all.

One of their notorious tactics was to take the body of a fallen enemy, roast

(Below) The Baliem Valley, mysterious Shangri-La, (right) is flanked by almost impenetrable ranges.

and eat it in derision and in full view of distraught relatives, who could only stand on a distant hill and wail in helpless rage. Nicknaming the Baliem "Cannibal Valley" was no exaggeration.

On numerous occasions, as missionaries tried to explore the Baliem Valley, they were accosted by war-painted warriors brandishing their spears and bows. More than once the men saw arrows whiz over their heads. On one trip, a missionary and the Ekari pastor were thrown to the ground and spears pricked their throats. Dani warriors ambushed another missionary, wounding him in the leg with an arrow.

The most serious incident took place in April, 1955. Three missionaries were giving injections to villagers with yaws, when an old man incited the people to attack the foreigners with spears and arrows. After one of the group was hit by an arrow, a colleague drew his revolver and attempted to fire over the heads of the attackers, but a warrior was shot and later died.

From then on, a mission directive ordered personnel not to carry firearms and not to defend themselves with weapons.

That same tragic day, the Sealand aircraft was carrying supplies to the Baliem when it crashed into one of the ranges. Pilot Al Lewis was killed. The Baliem exacted its price in blood from those who would change its ways.

Ukumhearik, a powerful chief of the lower Baliem, symbolized by his response the progress of the Gospel in the valley. He met the church planters in friendly fashion at first, but when he perceived that the foreigners and their message might threaten his authority, he turned against them. He confronted missionaries

who wanted to evangelize in his area and threatened to kill them.

Later, as some of his villagers embraced the gospel message, Ukumhearik showed a bit of interest. He even allowed two of his wives and several sons to become Christians. He eventually attended a service and listened carefully. In front of all present, he said, "I want to pray, but I don't understand it. I want to learn more."[59]

As life ebbed from his body years later, he allowed missionaries to come and pray for him. "As we would pray, we would hear Ukumhearik repeating our words and praying along with us," remembered one who visited him.[60]

Before the old chief died, he gathered together his considerable family and told them "to follow the Gospel, to stay inside its 'good fence.' "[61]

Cultural Bridge

Once the pioneers, both western and Indonesian, did the initial work of evangelism in the highlands, the transforming truth of God moved across the bridge of culture from one group to another.

Damals in the Ilaga Valley witnessed to neighboring Dani villages. Then a chain reaction of small group conversions spread among the Ilaga Danis until about 2,000 burned their fetishes and charms.

A group of the Danis decided to tell their kinsmen in the Baliem Valley what God had done for them. Accompanied by their wives, carriers and a missionary— plus a hundred warriors to insure safe passage through hostile areas—the ten witness men made the eighty-mile round trip to visit the Baliem Danis living around the Alliance station at Pyramid.

The results exceeded highest hopes. Having already heard the Gospel from missionaries and, in some cases, deciding to follow Jesus, the Baliem Danis responded in droves to the testimony of their kinsmen. About 5,000 attended the first meeting and burned their pagan talismans. The following day another 3,000 took the same decisive step of faith.

(Left) Footpaths provide the only way to most highland villages, (right) but evangelists follow them in an effort to make sure everyone has a chance to hear the Gospel.

The Ilaga witness band visited other areas of the Baliem, including the stations of other missions, before returning home. What an impact they left behind!

Out of a population of at least 100,000 Danis, about 25,000 had heard the preaching of the Gospel. Perhaps 15,000 had taken part in the fetish burnings. Four adult witness schools immediately began preparing converts for evangelistic work.

As was true concerning the Damal people movements, not all the missionaries agreed with the group conversions. "With concern for the future of the Gospel and a desire to follow what they felt were more tried and true methods, some of the Alliance missionaries had sincere doubts about the spiritual quality of the movement which began with such wholesale burning of charms. They feared the impetuous response of the people might actually block the advance of the true faith."[62]

As one put it, "God never intended . . . to use widegate evangelism to win narrowway Christians."[63]

But as Dr. McGavran pointed out, "People movements in themselves do not encourage the production of nominal Christians."[64] And, it must be admitted, superficial conversions and shallow living are not problems unique to the church in Irian Jaya.

Later events, not only among the Damals and Danis, but also among the Monis, Ekaris, Ndugas and others, would demonstrate that group converts hold fast to their faith even with death the consequence.

Peace and War

After the initial years in the Baliem had passed without serious disruptions, "the Dutch government came to regard missionary occupation of the Baliem Valley as an exceptional instance of gaining respect for law and order without the use of force."[65]

Dutch officials at the time could not foresee the fiery ordeal two decades later that would test the interior churches to the limit. Roots of the conflict were embedded in faith and religion as well as politics and nationalism.

Following a protracted and bitter struggle between Dutch and Indonesian forces at the end of World War II, Indonesia gained its independence. All the islands formerly under Dutch colonial rule came under its sovereignty—except the Dutch half of New Guinea. The Europeans held on to that territory for another twelve years, "the one last pearl of their former island empire."[66]

During that conflict of political and military forces, the Irian Jaya work of the Alliance was separated from the Gospel Tabernacle Church (C&MA) of Indonesia and organized as a distinct field. Once the island came under Indonesian rule in May of 1963, the Irian Jaya mission and church were welcomed back into the Indonesian Alliance fellowship.

Political integration of the island into the Jakarta government, however, did

not proceed as smoothly. Irianese hostility flared toward the Jakarta government, and a period of unrest began.

The years 1976 and 1977 brought severe testing to Irian Jaya. Mission stations and churches were destroyed in political uprisings. Many Christians lost their lives during intertribal warfare. Dissensions flared in the church, misunderstandings arose between mission and church. Mission-church-government relations soured as the Indonesian government restricted visas, banned activities outside of church buildings and closed down teacher training schools.

No sooner would one area be subdued, than uprisings would surface elsewhere. More intense persecution followed, more churches closed.

Christians were killed not only by rebels, but also by pagans wanting to stop the spread of Christianity. In one especially tragic incident, eighteen Ibele believers were bound and herded into their church. They were then led out one by one and hacked to death.

The Pyramid area of the Baliem was overrun, 4,000 houses destroyed, the mission station ravaged. By December,

1977, the situation seemed stabilized enough for Dani Christians to return home, only to have 150 of their number massacred by rebels. Thirty of the thirty-six Pyramid churches were closed by the end of that year.

Indonesian forces gradually reasserted control over the contested areas, the crisis passed and the churches regrouped and continued to grow in numbers and spirit.

Evangel in Writing

The initial movement of people groups toward the Lord emphasized the utter necessity of giving new believers the Scriptures in their own language and of training individuals to lead them in spiritual matters.

Uninformed people might assume that so-called primitive cultures would have equally crude and simple languages. Nothing could be more untrue—perhaps because without all the pressures and distractions of "civilized" cultures, they had time to develop their language to a high degree of expression and make it a source of pride.

"Because there was little contact between villages even in close proximity," writes Anita Bailey, "there are enormous variations in the language of different districts. Fifteen miles may make a difference, not only in vocabulary, but also in grammatical construction."[67]

Dani mythology took this diversity of languages into account while explaining

(Left) A Bible woman gathers other women for a lesson from the Word, (right) while men at a witness school prepare messages to take back home.

the origin of man: When people first came out of a hole in the ground and traveled across the high plateaus, a bad storm came down on them and the intense cold caused them to stammer and stutter, each in his own way.[68]

The Dani family of languages, for example, has features not shared by adjacent linguistic groups. Their sound system has seven vowels, two more than nearby groups. To one linguist, "the inflectional system [the way words are modified with different endings and prefixes] seemed very different."[69]

A single verb could contain all the information expressed by a whole sentence in English. The verb *angginggiraagin* is one such word, meaning "I will teach it all to you." A single verb may have as many as 2,000 different forms.[70]

The Alliance eventually became involved in seven major languages and six smaller but distinct linguistic groups. In each case, missionary linguists reduced the language to writing, prepared literacy materials and translated the Scriptures.

After literally decades of painstaking, determined effort, by 1988 translators had seen the entire New Testament printed in three major languages. They

had also completed translations in five more languages and prepared them for printing. In all, fourteen translation projects in the New and Old Testaments were in progress, all of which were to be completed in a few years.[71]

Leadership Priority

Preparing leaders ranked equal to translating Scripture since the earliest days of church planting on the island. The first witness schools anticipated by decades the now-familiar Theological Education by Extension (TEE) programs that have multiplied worldwide.

Without the aid of textbooks or

Scripture—or even a written language at first—the witness schools were elementary to the extreme.

"Classes" consisted of men and women fresh out of paganism; the "lecture" was an often-repeated Bible story or passage that had to be memorized word for word by students who could neither read nor write. "Homework" required taking the carefully rehearsed message back to the village and repeating it to a gathering of equally unlettered, newly converted kinsmen.

Basic though the witness schools may have been, they spearheaded the advance of the Gospel from village to village and across bridges of culture to neighboring areas. The schools eventually matured into more recognizable centers of learning.

As elsewhere in Indonesia, the Irian Jaya region pays the salaries of most Bible School teachers. The church supports five Indonesian-language schools and four using a vernacular language.

Some of these schools may not survive the pace of change. Even in Irian Jaya, the growing awareness of a larger world increases pressure for a higher level of theological studies. One mission adminis-

(Left) Though handicapped by limited budgets and inadequate numbers, missionaries place great emphasis on providing learning centers, where Irian Jayans can study, (above) and also participate in the training of their own people.

trator observes, "It is generally felt that some of the vernacular schools may eventually be closed, while those institutions using the Indonesian language will be strengthened and developed.

"A pressing goal of church leadership is to begin a college-level program. This will be difficult to do in many parts of Indonesia, but perhaps more difficult in Irian Jaya, where qualified personnel is most limited. Times of transitions are never easy but usually necessary."[72] The Walter Post Theological School was opened in 1987 in the university town of Abepura to meet this need.

In the mission's overall church-planting strategy for Irian Jaya, emphasis on individual witness and the witness schools and their development into Bible schools played an early major role in achieving success. An outside observer of Alliance work cites three other key factors.

First, missionaries seized the opportunity to evangelize responsive peoples such as the Danis, whose legends prepared them for the Gospel. Secondly, the mission decided to win adults and accept—even seek—group conversions. Thirdly, they emphasized learning and using the local languages as quickly as possible.[73]

Struggling and Coping

A specialist in Irianese church matters characterized the changing religious scene in terms of decade:

- 1950s: decade of pioneering in key locations
- 1960s: decade of church planting in hundreds of valleys
- 1970s: decade of discipling thousands of new believers.[74]

The decade of the 1980s and beyond could well be labeled "Struggling and Coping." In some respects the problems now facing the church in Irian Jaya present more subtle and complicated challenges than those faced by pioneer workers.

In the "good old days," the problems were straightforward: opposition from the local witch doctor or hardship on nearly impassable foot trails. But solutions, however hotly resisted, were recognizable and attainable.

The new pattern of conflict may have no end and few immediate evidences of success. To name a few:

Growing secularism and materialism: As Irianese Christians have more contact with the outside world, their life becomes more complicated and in need of skillful pastoral care.

Increasing leadership gap: The increase in membership is outpacing the church's ability to produce workers adequately prepared for more demanding congregations and a more complicated church organization.

Shrinking mission staff: The general government policy of reducing the presence of foreigners in Indonesian institutions extends to Irian Jaya, forcing a gradual but relentless reduction of mission personnel.

Evangelizing second-generation Christians: Already a second generation is growing up in the church, comprised of children who know nothing of the sheer paganism their parents threw off to follow Christ. Some are even dabbling in spirit worship and use of charms and fetishes to see what they are like.

Continuing rebel activity: Although the danger of violence from the indepen-

Once considered on a par with pigs, women of Irian Jaya now conduct their own retreats—while the men care for the children and prepare their meals.

dence movement is generally in check, some pockets of resistance remain.

Worsening school problem: Neither the mission nor the church can continue to underwrite the burgeoning expense of its primary school system, but if the government takes over the schools, it would likely replace the present teaching staff with Muslims to teach the children of Christian families.

Transmigrant Opportunity

Over against these inner struggles looms an extraordinary opportunity represented by tens of thousands of transmigrants from Java. They should be evangelized by the numerous Dutch founded churches in the area, some of which date back to the late 1800s. The sheer number of transmigrants, however, overwhelms the churches' resources for evangelism, and perhaps even their missionary vision.

Most of the newcomers are Muslims, yet they are now far from the watchful scrutiny of their former religious leaders and thrust into totally new and difficult surroundings. They are more open to the Gospel than they could ever have been in Java.

These facts prompted the regional director to report in a 1986 survey: "The primary challenge to the church and mission over the next fifteen years will continue to be the evangelization of transmigrants."[75]

But can the Irian Jaya GKII, a church still emerging from the Stone Age, win a hearing from the more sophisticated Muslims from progressive Java? The answer is a qualified yes, but one that awaits confirmation.

A Long Way

Considering the obstacles that face the Gospel Tabernacle Church in Irian Jaya, some may wonder if the church can continue its startling growth in numbers and maturity. Part of the answer lies in how far the Irianese Christians have already progressed from a cultural past where even kindness was cruel by civilized standards.

A 1982 women's retreat in the Pyramid district of the Baliem Valley indicates the church has already come a long way. "The grace of God was evidenced over and over in the lives of redeemed men who formerly would have shown disdain and contempt for service to women," writes a missionary observer, who attended the conference.

"But during the retreat the men of the church gathered happily each morning to cook a big rice, vegetable and pork dinner for the [277] ladies.

"They daily gathered the baby sitters and organized a day-care service so the ladies could sit undisturbed throughout each service and seminar. . . . Again in the evenings when the ladies sat in the services, the men ran the nursery to care for all babies and small children."[76]

Baby-sitting, day-care service, cooking meals and serving women—this was the remarkable conduct of men who, only a

CHURCH AND MISSION

OFFICIAL NAME OF CHURCH:	Gospel Tabernacle Church of Indonesia
ENTRY BY MISSIONARIES:	1929
NUMBER OF MISSIONARIES:	140
ORGANIZED CHURCHES:	1,622
UNORGANIZED CHURCHES AND PREACHING POINTS:	417
BAPTIZED CHURCH MEMBERS:	173,179
INCLUSIVE MEMBERSHIP:	466,084
MEDICAL WORK:	78 Clinics
EDUCATION:	73 Secular Schools 23 Theological Schools 39 TEE Centers
RADIO BROADCASTS:	48 per week
PAGES PRINTED:	32,212,305

COUNTRY

OFFICIAL NAME:	Republic of Indonesia
FORM OF GOVERNMENT:	Independent Republic
OFFICIAL LANGUAGE(S):	Bahasa Indonesia (Malay), Javanese, other Austronesia
AREA:	735,268 sq. mi.
POPULATION:	(1989 est.) 187,726,000
CAPITAL:	Jakarta
PER CAPITA INCOME:	$560.00
LITERACY:	72%
RELIGIOUS AFFILIATION:	88% Muslim

few years ago, considered women on a par with pigs.

Don Richardson, director of the Institute of Tribal Studies, did not exaggerate when he wrote, "Future historians will remember the advance of the Gospel into central Irian Jaya as one of the greatest breakthroughs in the saga of faith."[77]

But bringing together Indonesia's enormous diversity of peoples into the unity of faith also ranks as a monumental breakthrough of God's grace.

From the cosmopolitan cities of Java and the cultural centerpieces of Bali to the recessed highland villages of Irian Jaya or Kalimantan, Indonesians of vastly varying backgrounds are finding they have much in common—in Christ.

Alliance missionaries and leaders of The Gospel Tabernacle Church of Indonesia have begun a good work. It will never be perfected, never completed until Jesus comes. Yet what has been accomplished stands as both reward and goad. Much has been done; much more remains to do.

Perhaps that is why the Apostle Paul speaks of the gifts of ministry as dedicated to a yet-unattained goal: "Until we all reach unity in the faith." ☐

JAPAN

Still Unreached

SOME MISSION STRATEGISTS consider a recognizable people group, whether defined by linguistic or social distinctives, evangelized when at least 20 percent of the group are Christians capable of reaching their own group with the Gospel.

Japan, with its tightly compacted population bound together by both language and culture, is therefore an unreached people group of national proportions.

After more than a century of missionary activity, less than 1 percent of the total 120 million population is Christian. In the few thousand Protestant churches scattered sparsely across the land, Sunday service attendance averages only between fifteen and forty people.[2]

"For whatever reason," writes missiologist Peter Wagner, "our missionary investment in Japan has perhaps produced the lowest return of any nation. In spite of our many strategy conferences, our theses and dissertations, and even our many prayer meetings for Japan, still fewer than one percent of Japanese are practicing Christians."[3]

How is it possible that an entire nation can ignore the Gospel after more than 100 years of witness?

No one factor gives the total answer. Several causes can be noted, however, explaining why a whole country like Japan or a smaller people group elsewhere can resist the Good News from one generation to another.

Uniqueness Mentality

Japanese in general hold to a certain sense of uniqueness, says Edwin O. Reischauer, a former U.S. ambassador to Japan and highly respected for his understanding of its people. He writes, "The Japanese do seem to view the rest of the world, including even their close cultural and racial relatives in Korea and China, with an especially strong 'we' and 'they' dichotomy. Throughout history they have displayed almost a mania for distinguishing between 'foreign' borrowings and elements regarded as natively 'Japanese.' "[4]

"Not only do Japanese see themselves as different, a growing number also are convinced that they alone know how to do things right," according to a newsman with five years of experience in Tokyo. "To many Japanese, their ample gross national product proves the superiority of their culture. They have reason to swagger. Their country works."[5]

This sense of superiority gives rise to a strong code of uniformity intolerant of change or deviation from a highly successful system. "Regardless of personal cost, everyone is expected to conform in habits, attitudes and spirit to what is accepted as 'Japanese.' As the ancient Japanese proverb says, 'The nail which stands up will be pounded.' "[6]

Nail-and-hammer uniformity is evident throughout politics, business and government. The Tokyo-based newsman observed in 1988, "In the special brand of democracy that distinguishes postwar Japan, where the same party has governed for thirty-three years and may well govern for another thirty-three, the range of opinions on any subject is extremely narrow.

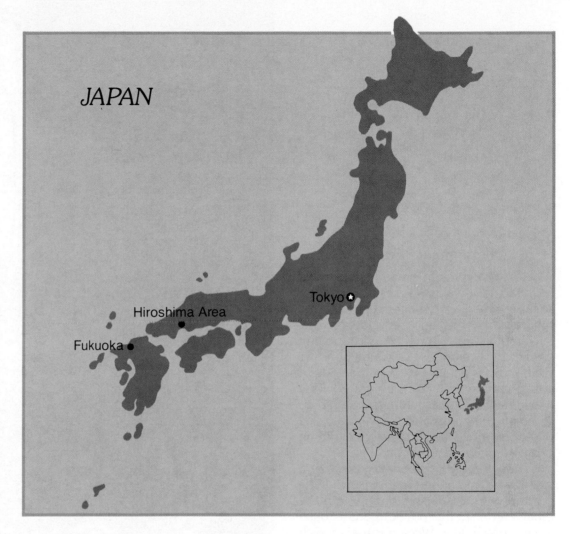

JAPAN

Tokyo

Hiroshima Area

Fukuoka

"When it comes to national direction, an elusive consensus somehow develops among big business, government bureaucrats, ruling party politicians and, to a lesser extent, the national newspapers. This led long ago to the concept of Japan, Inc."[7]

Japan's distinctiveness, worn like a coat of armor, is buttressed by another line of defense uniquely homemade: language. Former Ambassador Reischauer writes: "A major reason for Japan's continuing great cultural distinctiveness is the language and writing system which cut her off sharply from the rest of the world."[8]

St. Francis Xavier, renowned missionary who brought Roman Catholicism to the island kingdom centuries ago, had another way of describing the language. He called it "a contrivance of Satan."[9]

Fiercely proud and protective of their language as the custodian of heritage, the Japanese people raise a wall against outsiders who speak their language poorly or not at all. For the few who have breached this linguistic barrier by mastering its intricacies, they reserve considerable respect.

Justly proud of economic achievements, convinced of cultural uniqueness

and further distanced from the outside world by a complex language, many Japanese have shackled themselves to an inability to change. As one observer put it, "The belief in their uniqueness is so powerful that it can paralyze the Japanese when they come to grips with the outside world."[10]

How is it the Japanese can so heartily embrace western technology, learning

and methods—and yet retain so exclusively their national character?

One young Japanese student in the United States explains the dichotomy this way: "Someone has mentioned that Japanese live in a two-story house. On the first floor they feel like Japanese. On the second floor they have neatly lined up learning from Europe. No stairs connect the two, however."[11]

Foreignness Factor

The high premium on all things 'made in Japan' renders the Gospel an outsider. Japanese media have been all too happy to dramatize this apparent foreignness.

Describing the church as a "stranger in the land," Robert Lee explains how the media reinforce this view: "In the popular image, as communicated by much of the mass media, Christianity is portrayed as something extraordinary and unnatural or uncommon. It is depicted either in exotic terms or as unsavory.

"Thus, the public hears the news of a well-known movie star holding a wedding ceremony in a Christian church. On the other extreme, the public reads a best-selling novel like *Black Gospel,* which details gory 'facts' about a priest who murders an airplane hostess."[12]

All things considered, it is small wonder that despite a century-plus of missionary work, Japan remains an unreached nation. Some converts to Christianity despair that it will ever change.

Shusaku Endo, a Roman Catholic author, has the main character in his novel, *Silence,* saying: "This country of Japan is not suited for Christianity. It is a swamp,

(Left) Japan holds to its ancient religions despite attempts by missionaries to evangelize the nation; (right) western materialism has much more success, as evidenced by Tokyo at night.

and Christianity cannot put down its roots here."[13]

Spiritual Barricades

In addition to cultural and linguistic barriers, the Gospel has encountered stiff opposition from two major religions already firmly entrenched in Japanese life.

Mahayana Buddhism, which has over 106,600 temples across the nation, conveniently forgets it too is a foreign religion, being imported from China in the sixth century. It opposes the Gospel mainly on familial grounds. Having thoroughly penetrated family ties and social customs, Buddhism claims that anyone who converts to Christianity dishonors the family and should be treated as an outcast.[14] When Tomeoka Kosuke, founder of the social welfare system in Japan, became a Christian, he encountered family opposition that might have been humorous were it not indicative of an actual mood.

"When he became a Christian, his father became deeply perturbed and tried repeatedly to dissuade him. Finally the father asked the chief of police to help, but he too was unable to turn him away from Christianity."

The police chief then told the father, "I can't do anything with your son, but since he is your son, you can either boil or fry him and eat him."[15]

Although the event supposedly happened in 1900 and no Japanese law officer would offer such advice today, deep feelings of hostility still surface within the family against anyone converting to Christ.

Numerous religions have sprung up in Japan within the past century, and especially since World War II. Of these new cults, the most successful and powerful is Buddhist-rooted Soka Gakkai. It has an estimated five to eight million followers, mostly from the lower classes.[16]

Like other "new" religions, Soka Gakkai is actually rooted in traditional values and ancient religion. Its claims date back to tenth-century Buddhism, yet its militant, politics-oriented program on a religious base obviously meets a need among many Japanese today.

Shinto, the second major religion opposing the Gospel, is both the oldest and newest religion in the Land of the Rising Sun. It opposes the church on political grounds, claiming that conversion to Christianity is an act of treason against the state.

This ancient religion was not born waving a patriotic flag. Rather, it was "based on a simple feeling of awe in the presence of any surprising or awesome phenomenon of nature," according to former ambassador Reischauer. Only later did this nameless religion call itself Shinto, "the way of the gods," to distinguish itself from Buddhism.

"The underlying stream of Shinto today remains little changed since prehistoric times," he believes. "Much has been done during the past 1,500 years to make an organized religion of this simple nature worship. And, more recently, by emphasizing the early mythology connected with Shinto, to employ it as a force for natural solidarity and an inspiration for fanatical patriotism."

But Reischauer believes that "despite these imposed superstructures, the true basis of Shinto remains unchanged, a simple and naive nature worship."[17]

Allied with these ancient and modern religions opposing the Gospel is a sinister power about which even now little is known.

Timothy Warner, a former missionary and later professor of missions, writes: "I have come to believe that Satan does indeed assign a demon or corps of demons to every geopolitical unit in the world, and that they are among the principalities and powers against whom we wrestle."[18]

Dr. Peter Wagner believes that their major assignment is to prevent God from being glorified in their territory, which they do by directing the activities of lower-ranking demons.[19]

Cultural inflexibility, self-perceived uniqueness and enforced uniformity, long-entrenched religions and vicious persecution of Christians—for these and perhaps other reasons, Japan remains an unresponsive and unreached nation despite more than a century of missionary effort.

Momentary Openness

In spite of Japan's apparently impregnable defenses against the Gospel, history records periods of openness to the "foreign" religion.

The *Roman Catholic Century* (1549–1639) was spearheaded by St. Francis Xavier, Catholicism's greatest missionary. This era came to an abrupt end when the ruling dynasty suspected the church of plotting with European powers to subjugate Japan. Two hundred years of self-imposed isolation followed.

The *Golden Days of Protestantism* (1882–1889) began with the arrival of Commodore Perry's black squadron in Tokyo harbor. For a brief period, Japan was open to everything western, including religion. An unfavorable treaty on trade, however, quickly shifted public opinion against Christianity. Protestant missions

continued, but not with the same degree of success.

The third era of openness began after World War II. Japan was prostrate in defeat, and her emperor abdicated any claim to being divine. General Douglas MacArthur, commander of American occupation forces, recognized that the nation was plunged into a religious vacuum.

He called upon American churches to send 10,000 missionaries immediately. Only about 2,500 came, and most were supported by evangelical mission boards. Thus the period earned the title, *Evangelical Opportunity* (1945–1952).[20]

While the two opportunities of extraordinary openness in the 1800s and 1900s were cut short by shifts in public opinion, Protestant missions hastened the reversal by some serious strategical errors.

Missionaries imported western-style services and music. Even church buildings looked western. Church government centered on the pastor instead of involving the laity.

Methods of evangelism caused even more harm. Specialized missionaries concentrated efforts on women's work and child evangelism—activities that aroused anger and alienation among husbands and fathers in the rigidly male-oriented society. Furthermore, evangelistic appeals insisted on individual commitments in a society where major decisions are usually reached through a collective process binding on the whole family or group.

Blessing and Bane

One social class in Japan surprisingly overlooked these errors and led the way in acceptance of the Gospel. The *samurai*, well educated and ambitious, had been ousted from their special status by a

(Below) Japan's prosperity raises an added wall of resistance to the Gospel, (bottom) building on its traditional heritage and (right) deep rooted worship of nature symbolized in sacred Mt. Fiji.

change in government. For them, the arrival of missionaries from the West could not have been better timed.

Why the *samurai,* of all people? "They saw in Christianity not only a means of reclaiming status but also a new dynamic for transforming Japanese society," explains Robert Lee.

"In search of a new role, and challenged by the missionary's teachings, they responded with a fervent loyalty to God and the Church that was reminiscent of the loyalty previously pledged to their feudal lord."[21]

Even today, their successors in the educated middle class are often more accepting of Christianity than either the higher or lower social classes. This middle-class, intellectual response to the Gospel has produced mixed results.

"Through them, the ethics and ideals of Christianity had a much more pro-found influence on Japanese thought and life than one may assume from the fact that less than one percent of the population became professing Christians."[22]

However, the educated approach to the message of salvation has diminished the importance of a personal spiritual experience. A veteran missionary observes, "In contrast to the 'immediate conversion' concept, many churches now appear to practice a 'conversion by learn-

(Below) Japan Alliance School of Theology provides (below right) opportunity for young people to study God's Word.

ing' process. The church is thought of as a school where the person attends, learns about God, and in time 'graduates,' that is, receives baptism." He adds, significantly, "The word 'church' in Japanese, *kyokai,* means 'learning society.'"[23]

Such internal church problems, combined with elements in Japanese society, indicate why the Gospel has attracted so little response.

As mentors of the church and bearers of the message, missionaries share responsibility for the current state of Christianity in Japan. The nation as a whole may be militated against the church's advance, but it also appears that Protestant missions unnecessarily complicated the situation.

Alliance Entry

The first contact with Japan by the Alliance was both tragic and heroic. A missionary en route to China died of smallpox in 1888 and was buried in Kobe.

A three-member Alliance contingent arrived soon afterward to begin a permanent work in Kobe, but their focus of ministry soon changed. Dr. and Mrs. James Ludlow encountered difficulty with the language and shifted to mission work among the mostly foreign seamen docking at Kobe.

Miss Helen Kinney also met with frustration because of problems posed by fast-rising nationalism. She moved to Yokohama and founded an orphanage. All three were furloughed home in 1892 due to sickness.[24]

The C&MA mission began officially in Japan in 1891, when it assumed support of the original trio of workers, who were initially supported from private sources. Three years later, Dr. Simpson visited the field and established two principles that would thereafter guide development of Alliance work in Japan.

First, "the advanced state of the Christian Church in Japan, as compared with the greater need of many fields, made it unnecessary that the Alliance should ever place or maintain a large missionary force in that land."[25]

Second, the missionaries should "concentrate on training and using Japanese workers in the evangelization of neglected areas."[26]

Dr. Simpson rightly recognized Japanese strengths in organization and initiative. But limiting the number of missionaries to train national workers hobbled the church's ability to grow and

expand. From 1913 to 1925, for example, the total of baptized believers only edged upwards from 214 to 249.

The missionary staff peaked at sixteen in 1925 and then declined as responsibility increasingly shifted to the church. The Japan Alliance Church formally organized in 1931, followed by the withdrawal of mission personnel in 1934. Foreign subsidy of national workers ended in 1936.

The mission withdrew completely from Japan in 1937. It gave two reasons for this decision: the church was prospering under Japanese leadership, and missionaries were needed elsewhere to open unevangelized areas.[27]

Two missionaries, Mabel Francis and her sister Anne Dievendorf, disagreed with the rosy rationale and elected to continue working with the church despite loss of support. They were still in Japan when war broke out between their homeland and adopted country.

Subjected first to house arrest and then to imprisonment, the two women suffered added afflictions of malnutrition and verbal abuse. They also shared with their

captors the horrors and dangers of massive Allied air raids. When the war ended, they still refused repatriation, recognizing that their sufferings earned for them an unusual hearing among the dispirited and defeated Japanese people.

Miss Francis said later, "It was worth going through the war here in Japan to be able to be here at the end of it and to minister to these spiritually hungry people."[28]

At the same time, she echoed General MacArthur's call for 10,000 missionaries to come work among a people whose gods had miserably failed them. Too few came too late, and the golden opportunity was lost.

Looking back upon the inadequate response of evangelicals, Miss Francis said in 1967, "That's where America failed Japan. Our churches didn't grasp the

opportunity. During the first ten years after the war, the Japanese people were really very open and seeking. Now their financial situation is so much better. They are on easy street, and it's harder to reach them."[29]

Japanese officials took note of Miss Francis's tireless efforts to rally the demoralized population. Emperor Hirohito himself later awarded her membership in the exclusive Fifth Order of the Sacred Treasure. She was the first person in Japanese history to receive this highest civilian honor while still living.

Durable Faith

The Japan Alliance was scattered and shattered by the end of World War II.

Whole churches and congregations had disappeared in the holocaust of Hiroshima. Pastors had often borne the

brunt of official displeasure for their association with a foreign religion. They had been conscripted into the army, assigned to factory jobs or even imprisoned by the authorities.

Alliance teaching on the Second Coming especially angered government officials. They termed the doctrine treasonous, since it appeared to disparage the emperor, whom they upheld as a god.

Lay believers also suffered for their faith. The Japan Alliance, along with twenty-two other denominations, had been forced into *Nihon Kirisuto Kyodan,* the United Church of Christ in Japan, which was supervised by the Bureau of Education.

The government insisted that each church service begin with a pledge of allegiance that bordered on idolatry because of the emperor's alleged divinity. A crisis of conscience thrust many Alliance believers into conflict with their own government. They suffered for years at the hands of their own countrymen as well as from the havoc sown by Allied bombs.

After the war, a doubly battered church slowly regrouped with encouragement by the two little American missionary women who had elected to suffer with them through the war years. In 1950, Miss Francis opened a Bible school for four students. Their campus was an abandoned construction shack.

One year later, Japan Alliance withdrew from *Kyodan,* the wartime United Church. And in 1952, after years of petitions by Japanese believers, the North American C&MA resumed missionary work in conjunction with the national church.

Enduring Grace

Given the built-in opposition and obstacles of Japanese society against the Gospel, the continuing presence of Japan Alliance people and North American missionaries is evidence in itself of the enduring grace of God.

Some areas of church life, however, excite more concern than confidence. During the Alliance global drive of Centennial Advance during the 1980s, Japanese church membership actually declined.[30]

One cause of this nongrowth situation arises from a legitimate concern for doctrinal purity as liberalism takes over churches once strong in biblical belief. As a result, requirements for Alliance church membership in the 1980s became more strict than they were in 1975.[31]

At the same time, some local churches are notable exceptions, stepping out as pacemakers in growth.

The Alliance church in Kure led the denomination in membership during the 1980s and registered steady growth. Average attendance of 150 demonstrated that Alliance churches need not settle for the fifteen or so people that typify most congregations in the nation.[32]

The Kure church's pastor was a would-

be kamikaze pilot whose life was spared when the war ended two weeks before his scheduled suicide mission. Dedicating to God the years restored to him, the pastor chose the right methods—evangelism, Bible study cells, systematic teaching—that showed how church growth can be achieved even in Japan.[33]

The nation's villages are noted for lack of openness to the Gospel, but Alliance churches in the relatively rural areas of Shikoku Island prove otherwise. Part of the reason lies in willingness to learn from non-Japanese believers. "Some of the pastors travel to Korea annually for prayer conferences and seminars on church growth. Those who have come back inspired and renewed have seen their churches grow."[34]

The Japanese Christian community considers the Shibuya Church in downtown Tokyo one of the fastest-growing congregations in the country.[35] Begun in 1983 by a Korean-born Alliance missionary, the initial intent was to minister among the capital's Korean population. But within three years, Japanese as well as Koreans belonged to the church.

Attendance topped three hundred by 1989, and the congregation reached out to start several preaching points. To insure a resource group of trained workers, the church supported thirteen seminarians from its fellowship.

"Shibuya Harvest" showed the church's alertness to local opportunity. Noticing that young people crowded into the area on weekends, the congregation initiated a service designed to reach youth. Christian singing groups, low-keyed messages and trained lay people made the Shibuya Church an "in" spot for Tokyo's youth.[36]

(Above) Japanese Christians view their church as a place (below) of worship and focus of efforts to safeguard the purity of biblical beliefs.

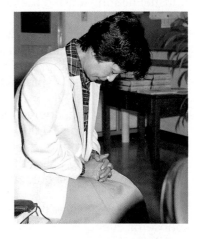

Hints of Change

The inching progress of the church need not shackle the church's future to more of the same. Some trends appear to favor a larger place for the Gospel in coming years.

Sociologist Kiyomi Morioka believes that the "population movement ought to favor the churches."[37]

Urbanization has meant an irreversible flow from the countryside to the city. By 1980, an estimated one person in every three lived in high-rise apartment complexes, severed from traditional family ties and lost in lonely, crowded cities.[38] Rural-based Shintoism and class-oriented Buddhism find their grip on such urban families weakening.

Another study in 1980 indicated that a surprising 30 percent of the population had visited a church and 30 percent actually owned a Bible. James Montgomery says that missiologist Hisanori Suzuki considered these statistics so significant that he thought the Christian church should aim its outreach at three, not two, groups of people: Christians, non-Christians and "peripheral Christians."[39]

These factors could lead to new openness in Japan, removing the nation from its unreached status. It would be a fitting reward for a beleaguered Christian community that by the grace of God has endured almost overwhelming odds.

But before that can happen, the evangelical community—including Japan Alliance—must experience spiritual renewal. "Old prejudices and outmoded patterns of church life must be swept away by the wind of the Spirit in order to allow the life of the body of Christ to express itself fully and creatively in modern Japan."[40] □

CHURCH AND MISSION

OFFICIAL NAME OF CHURCH:	Japan Alliance Church
ENTRY BY MISSIONARIES:	1891
NUMBER OF MISSIONARIES:	20
ORGANIZED CHURCHES:	29
UNORGANIZED CHURCHES AND PREACHING POINTS:	51
BAPTIZED CHURCH MEMBERS:	3,350
INCLUSIVE MEMBERSHIP:	10,050
MEDICAL WORK:	0
EDUCATION:	1 Theological School
RADIO BROADCASTS:	0
PAGES PRINTED:	825,000

COUNTRY

OFFICIAL NAME:	Nippon
FORM OF GOVERNMENT:	Parlimentary Democracy
OFFICIAL LANGUAGE(S):	Japanese
AREA:	145,856 sq. mi.
POPULATION:	(1989 est.) 123,231,000
CAPITAL:	Tokyo
PER CAPITA INCOME:	(1984) $10,266.00
LITERACY:	99%
RELIGIOUS AFFILIATION:	Buddhism, Shintoism

PHILIPPINES

From Slow Starter to Pacesetter

THE SCRIPTURAL injunction, "Despise not the day of small beginnings," has the initials CAMACOP stamped all over it.

No other phrase more accurately describes the initial missionary efforts by the Alliance that eventually led to a church with one of the most striking success records of church growth on the Pacific rim. That church of small beginnings and startling results is the Christian and Missionary Alliance Churches of the Philippines (CAMACOP).

The first Alliance missionary, a single woman named Elizabeth White, arrived in 1900 so poorly supported she could not venture beyond Manila due to the "enormous expense" of travel.[1] Perhaps this curtailed travel helped her get to know a bachelor missionary with another group. After a few months, they were married and she joined his mission.

The second Alliance missionary to the Philippines, J. A. McKee, got off to a promising start on Mindanao in 1902— only to die of cholera the following year. Not until 1908 did the mission actually have personnel with a permanent ministry, but even their association was more

of convenience than conviction, since their own mission had disbanded and they were left stranded.[2]

The Philippine Mission of the C&MA consisted of only two families until 1923. Thereafter, the most significant increases in staff came after Alliance missionaries were forced out of China and Indochina and then reassigned to the islands.[3]

Target Thinking

It is difficult to equate the painful, halting start of Alliance missions in the Philippines with the present-day church making such rapid and remarkable strides in growth. CAMACOP ranks second in size only to its pacific neighbor, the Gospel Tabernacle Church of Indonesia, among member churches of The Alliance World Fellowship.[4]

Targets have come to symbolize and measure the dramatic growth of the church. Target 400, Target 100,000 and Target 2.2.2. galvanized the churches into action and gave them goals that began in 1975 and run through to the end of the century.

CAMACOP's Target 400 grew out of interdenominational efforts in the early

1970s. The All-Philippine Congress on Evangelism in 1970 brought together evangelical missions and churches in the first united church growth campaign in the nation's history. Then a church growth seminar in 1974 encouraged Alliance leaders to develop their own campaign.[5]

Setting a goal for 400 new churches and 40,000 baptized members in four years seemed an impossible task. In the previous forty-six years, CAMACOP averaged less than nine new churches and 750 new members annually.[6]

However, everyone set to work— congregations, collegiate and youth groups, evangelistic teams—and in four years CAMACOP had 415 new churches. The increase of 32,000 new members by 1979 did not quite reach the Target 400 goal of 40,000, but considering previous annual averages, no one could complain.

Target 100,000 followed hard on the heels of Target 400, shifting the emphasis from new churches to a goal of 100,000 members by 1983. Again the four-year effort fell short, but the addition of 20,000 new members, raising total membership to nearly 90,000, still proved remarkable.

PHILIPPINES

Lubuagan

Luzon

Angeles City

Manila

Bulanao

Iloilo · Bacolod City
· Cebu City
· Tagbilaran City

· Butuan

Sindangan · · Cagayan de Oro City

Lapuyan · **Mindanao**

Zamboanga City

Timanan · · Bulatukan
Cotabato · · Davao City
City   Kidapawan · · Mt. Apo
Sinolon · · Malagupos
Lemdelag · · General Santos City

Further convinced of the value of targeted growth, Filipino Alliance leaders next settled on an ambitious sixteen-year growth campaign. Target 2.2.2 represents a goal of 2 million believers and 20,000 churches by A.D. 2000. Whatever the bottom line by the end of this century, CAMACOP will certainly reinforce its reputation as an aggressive, growth-minded church that increased from 34,700 baptized members in 1976 to over 118,000 in eleven years.

Metro Manila Mission

"Good News Metro Manila" exemplifies the can-do attitude of Filipino Alliance churches.

Metro Manila has a near monopoly on distinctions for the nation: capital city of the 7,000-island nation; home to over 8 million people spread out in 245 square miles, four cities and thirteen municipalities; site of the country's oldest university and other academic institutions that in some way relate to one of every four city residents.

Manila encompasses the nation's largest concentration of population, productivity, power and politics. Yet for many

years the city did not have even one Alliance church.

Historically, the reason is plausible: Alliance work focused on Mindanao and the Sulu Archipelago through a mutual agreement with other missions known as comity. These areas were chosen because they had not yet received the Gospel and were considered extremely difficult areas to evangelize. Even though Manila was declared "an open city" in which all

missions could work, the Alliance chose to concentrate on interior areas.[7]

Not until the aftermath of World War II did mission and church turn their attention to Manila—and then primarily because thousands of youth from Alliance churches were converging on the city to attend school.

A missionary couple and single woman were assigned to work with the students. The couple opened their home for Sun-

Capital City Alliance Church is a prolific church planter in Metro Manila.

day services, but the congregation quickly outgrew the living room and carport, just as its outreach rapidly expanded beyond the student population. The group organized and developed into the influential Capital City Alliance Church in Quezon City.[8] Over a period of years, this remarkable congregation started over forty new churches.

Good News Metro Manila became CAMACOP's centerpiece for urban evangelism. The Canadian Alliance backed the 1983 campaign with a fund drive to raise $1,250,000. Plans called for multimedia promotion, large and sustained rallies, and the development of strong central churches that in turn would sponsor daughter churches.

About half the Alliance churches in Manila joined hands in cooperation and witnessed unusual blessing. In six years, the number of churches resulting from Good News Metro Manila and other efforts grew from twelve to twenty-one.[9]

A CAMACOP news release in late 1983 reported, "As the Good News Metro Manila program gains momentum, an amazing pattern is emerging. Not only are groups of believers being formed faster than church buildings being built, but there is a question as to how long the new structures will be able to accommodate their growing congregations."[10]

The Pasay City Alliance Church fit the communique's description. Its congregation had averaged about 170 attenders on Sunday mornings before the Metro Manila campaign, but it had the potential to become a strong central church called for in campaign strategy.

The believers pledged themselves to an intense and sustained evangelistic outreach. Meanwhile, Canadian Alliance churches supplied $750,000 to build a mini-cathedral seating 800 people in the

Pasay City Alliance Church, Manila, grew from 170 to 1200 inclusive members in four years.

main sanctuary and space for another 300 to 400 in the adjoining educational wing.

The sanctuary was completed in 1984 while the church conducted four evangelistic campaigns. The seventy-voice choir gave a concert that drew 700 people. In less than a year, the congregation doubled in size.[11] Within four years, attendance surged from an average 170 to over 1,200 worshipers.

The Alliance Fellowship Church, though smaller, grew even faster. Using dozens of home Bible studies to fuel their advance, the congregation swelled from fifty to 450 in four years and launched its own major building program.

Quality Education

CAMACOP's target of 2 million believers and 20,000 churches by A.D. 2000 raised the need of yet another goal: an additional 15,000 to 20,000 pastors and workers to serve the increased church community.

While this need seems enormous, the Philippine Alliance has a remarkable network of schools and programs for the preparation of church leaders.

Student enrollment reached 1,200 students in 1985, an all-time high. Preparing them for ministry was one seminary, two Bible colleges, four Bible schools and two extension branches.[12]

The schools provided quality education as well as flexible programs. The Ebenezer Bible College led all other such undergraduate schools in the nation to be accredited by the Asia Theological Association. Likewise, the Alliance Biblical Seminary was the first such institution in the Philippines to receive similar recognition.

The seminary started in conjunction with the Ebenezer Bible College in Zam-

*Three-quarters of all Ebenezer Bible
College graduates move into
Alliance ministries.*

boanga, but moved to Metro Manila in 1982 because of the more strategic location. It struggled at first, having to depend on rented space in Quezon City, but by 1984 the seminary had its own facility. Enrollment increased to 124 students in 1988, and the school was recognized as one of the most important evangelical institutions in Asia.[13]

Graduates of the Alliance Biblical Seminary can continue their studies on a doctoral level and still be associated with the school because of its part in a five-seminary cooperative that forms the Hong Kong based Asia Graduate School of Theology.

The seminary's president acts as area dean of the graduate school for the Philippines. The five seminaries share their facilities in this unusual consortium that answers to the highest level of need for theological education among the churches of Asia.

Ebenezer Bible College holds the rank of dean among the undergraduate schools of CAMACOP. Founded in 1928 in Zamboanga City specifically as a center to prepare church leaders, the school has never deviated from that role through the years of mounting educational standards. Nearly 78 percent of all Ebenezer graduates move into Alliance church ministries.

Part of the school's success lies in its pragmatic and demanding four-year curriculum. Before students can enter their senior year and qualify for graduation, they must spend twelve months of internship in church ministry.

As academic standards at Ebenezer moved higher, entrance requirements grew stricter. This trend prompted the formation of another level of education for church workers: regional Bible schools.

The churches of East Mindanao, for example, found that fewer of their young people were being accepted by the Bible college in Zamboanga City. This was happening at the very time more skilled workers were needed for new and growing churches.

The region therefore organized its own school in 1959 to prepare workers specifically for its own needs. Within five years, the Mt. Apo Alliance Bible Institute had a student enrollment larger than Ebenezer's—and they did it all on a self-supporting basis.[14]

The B'laan and Manobo people of southeastern Mindanao followed the same route in 1965, opening the Tribal Bible School, later renamed the Mickelson Alliance Bible School, to prepare pastors for the tribal churches.

The Subanon Christians in West Mindanao founded the Lommasson Memorial Alliance Bible School at Lapuyan two

Enthusiasm and hard work contributed significantly to CAMACOP's rapid church growth record.

years later for the same purpose. Later, the Alliance churches of Davao Province bought the campus of a former high school and turned it into the Davao Alliance Bible School.

Equipping Lay Workers

Even if all the campuses of formal education were overflowing with ministerial students, CAMACOP still would not have enough workers to meet the churches' staff needs. This realization forced the missionaries and church leaders years ago to devise a basic level in the system of theological education: Lay Preachers Institutes.

Whether it was done knowingly or not, the decision to use lay workers followed a highly successful strategy already in use by the Seventh Day Adventists. Their missionary work had gotten off to a slow start—only five converts from 1905 to 1911—and did not accelerate until the missionaries gave laymen an active role.

"Eighty percent of our converts are the work of laymen," reports an Adventist leader. He has no doubts about who gets the credit for rapid expansion of their work: "Laymen who do the work of

ministers are undoubtedly the greatest factor in Seventh Day Adventist success."[15]

Dr. David L. Rambo, former missionary to the Philippines, made a similar observation about Alliance church growth on the islands: "The widespread use of lay preachers was a *sine qua non* for Alliance expansion. Their spontaneous witness and zeal to establish congregations in the next village was one of the monumental realities of this period in Cotabato and elsewhere."[16]

CAMACOP training sessions for lay preachers claim four to five days each quarter. At first, the institutes were little more than memorization marathons, somewhat akin to practices already used to preserve oral traditions in nonliterate

cultures. Lay preachers committed whole sermons to memory and then went back to their towns and villages to repeat them. In time, however, the lesson material expanded to include systematic study courses.

Lay Preachers Institutes grew in importance and size. An estimated 40 percent of all leaders and workers in CAMACOP churches study these continuing education courses.[17]

In some areas, women attend institutes as well. Workers among the T'boli people, for example, prevailed on seminar organizers to set up a special two-day retreat for their wives. They even cooked meals and baby-sat the children so the women could attend all the classes.[18]

Deaconesses can fill the role of lay

Deaconesses fill the role of lay leader in local churches to an extent not possible in most other Asian nations.

preachers and church leaders to an extent not possible in other Asian countries. This equality in ministry is partly due to a significantly higher role for women in Filipino society, compared to the place of women in some other Asian cultures. The lack of men leaders also contributes to this practice.[19]

Lay preachers prove especially effective in tribal areas where churches cannot support full-time pastors. Rev. R. M. Chrisman, regional director in the 1950s, noted, "What impressed me most was the number and size of the churches which have been started by lay workers and are being cared for by them. There is nothing comparable to this in any of our other fields in the Far East."[20]

TEE and Literacy

The basic level of CAMACOP's multi-layered educational system offers Theological Education by Extension (TEE) courses. Still largely under missionary supervision, the study program has yet to come into its own as a significant means of schooling for church workers. The field director reported in 1988 that only twenty-eight centers were in operation with 370 enrollees.[21]

With the formal schools and informal institutes unable to provide enough trained leaders, the benefits TEE offer will probably become more evident.

CAMACOP's literacy courses form an evangelistic outreach rather than serve as preparation for leadership. Over 700 people enrolled in literacy courses led by 57 teachers in the mid-1980s. Of this number, eighty-one professed faith in Christ and helped to start eight churches.

Reviewing CAMACOP's strong theological education program, Dr. Rambo concluded, "Whether by circumstance or design, the church has arrived at an imaginative approach to training for the ministry that fits comfortably into the educationally diverse society. . . .

"Willingness to accept the vast ethnic and educational difference of its constituency and making that the basis of pastoral training has provided the kind of light needed throughout the missionary world. . . .

"A good case may be made for the contention that CAMACOP has developed a more realistic and comprehensive program for training ministers than its North American counterpart."[22]

Print Support

In its wide-ranging variety of activities, CAMACOP has an indispensable support team called Alliance Publishers, Inc. The publishing house gives the church an essential service by first determining what

literature is needed and then getting the material written, published and distributed.

If Metro Manila church planting needs evangelistic tracts, Alliance Publishers provides them. If TEE needs a series of study books, the publishing house takes care of it. If the seminary or a Bible school needs foreign textbooks, the business office tries to order them.

Alliance Publishers is a fairly recent newcomer to the church team. It began in 1978 in an old rented building in Manila and quickly expanded to a staff of twenty workers producing two magazines and a variety of other materials. The purchase of an expensive phototypesetting machine and other equipment underscored

the need for an improved, permanent office location.

The staff was directed to a new three-story office building just a few minutes walk from a key hub of transportation in Manila. The missionary adviser was amazed to learn that the building's floor plan met her estimates of needed layout and space almost perfectly.

"The actual measurement was only about six inches short of what I had designed six weeks previously," she marveled.[23]

The building owner had only wanted to rent the structure, but as discussions developed, she agreed to sell with very favorable conditions for the church. While the publishing house board looked for

financing, other interested parties came to her with cash in hand.

She, being a devout Roman Catholic, refused to consider any other buyer and held the property until the publishing house was ready to buy. "I think God will be good to me if I do," she said.[24]

Alliance Publishers, Inc. quickly expanded operations in its new central location. In addition to other printed materials in 1987, the publishing house printed twelve books and a total of 5.4 million pages.[25]

Campus Evangelism

Filipino Alliance churches have a keen interest in students and schools from a totally different perspective. The Philippine Student Alliance Lay Movement (PSALM) is another name for successful campus evangelism.

PSALM chapters witnessed for Christ on ninety-six campuses in sixteen cities and sixteen towns in one recent year. The thirty-seven full-time workers were joined by a volunteer staff of 350.

Over a ten-year period, PSALM members witnessed to 70,000 students, prayed with 40,000 young people seeking salvation, taught 25,000 students in Bible study groups and congratulated 9,000 of their peers who completed the initial course of study.[26]

The campus evangelism effort originated in Zamboanga City in 1970, based on the simple principle of each one win one. "Every convert is taught to tell others about Christ," writes one missionary reporter. "Perhaps more than anything else, this factor has contributed to the growth of PSALM."[27]

The Walled City ministry, for instance, follows the basic pattern of establishing an evangelical witness in an academic community. PSALM organizers targeted the old walled city of Manila because of its concentration of four colleges and fifty student boarding houses.

They started by offering Christian films and Bible studies. When interested students progressed from spectators to converts to members, they were recruited into a rigorous four-level training program. They first studied basic Christian doctrine, then learned how to evangelize their peers. Finally, they became proficient in conducting Bible studies and engaged in community improvement projects.

Meanwhile, the PSALM chapter strengthened its presence in the old walled city by opening a small bookstore, a reading room and lending library stocked with current college textbooks. Bolstered by volunteer staff, the center developed a variety of activities during the week: choir practice, seminars, prayer services, child evangelism and distribution of food and clothing to needy people.

One of PSALM's strengths is a studied effort to integrate students into local churches. This has a double reward: Not only are the young people established in their faith, some of them return home and, not finding a church, start one.

When one young student went home from school, she angered her family by her testimony of conversion. But she persevered and eventually led most of her family to the Lord. Her parents helped start an Alliance church in their town, a source of great encouragement to her as she went to Thailand as a CAMACOP missionary.[28]

Missions Enthusiasm

The young lady was only one of several church workers sent abroad and supported by the Alliance churches of the Philippines. By 1986, CAMACOP was supporting two single women in Thailand, a couple in Micronesia, and preparing to send another couple to Africa and a single woman to Hong Kong.

Enthused by the opportunity to be a missionary-sending church, Filipino Alliance people have "responded with a high level of liberal and joyful giving."[29] Financial struggles in their own churches or personal fortunes have not dampened that enthusiasm. Despite a severe drought in 1983, for example, CAMACOP congregations increased their missions giving by 39 percent.[30]

A Womens Missionary Prayer Fellowship retreat attracted 659 women instead of the expected 400. They arose each morning at 5:00 to pray for missions. Then throughout the day they listened to Filipina speakers representing Indonesia and Guatemala, supplemented by recorded messages from Thailand. At the close of the retreat, the women presented a check for over $1,200 to the CAMACOP missions department.

(Above) PSALM youth groups are active on many university campuses; (top right) well organized missions conferences promote the church's outreach to other countries; (bottom right) Filipino Alliance believers have been supporting missions for many years.

Supporting a foreign missions program in the 1980s was not something new. As early as 1946, the churches had begun directing workers toward the unreached peoples of their own country. When the Third Asian Conference convened in 1961 in Zamboanga City, about 60 percent of CAMACOP churches were financially supporting their home missions program.

The Zamboanga conference, organized to "study how each national church could send out its own missionaries," broadened the Filipino Alliance's vision to evangelism beyond their borders. The first missionary couple sailed for Indonesia in 1967, followed by a second couple three years later.

By 1989, second only to the Hong Kong Alliance churches, CAMACOP had the most aggressive missionary program of all non-Western Alliance churches.[31] Its eleven missionaries and three tentmakers served in Latin America, Africa and Australia as well as Asia.

Opposition and Obstacles

CAMACOP's record of growth and achievements would be respectable even under ideal conditions. That they are done in the face of opposition and obstacles makes them all the more significant.

The church does not operate in a religious vacuum. Over 360 religious groups are registered with the government. Nearly 200 are indigenous movements started since World War II. Many are syncretestic in nature—a confused assortment of nationalism, Catholicism, Pentecostalism and Unitarianism.

Iglesia ni Cristo is one of the two largest and most popular of these indigenous groups. The church was founded by Felix

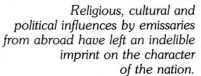

Religious, cultural and political influences by emissaries from abroad have left an indelible imprint on the character of the nation.

Manalo, a Catholic who associated with several churches before starting his own. It has about 1.5 million followers, 3,000 congregations and over thirty elaborate cathedrals.

Organized like an army, with some ministers carrying guns, the highly aggressive and authoritarian movement claims there can be no salvation outside its membership. Evangelicals, however, consider the church to be an heretical sect.

The Filipino Independent Church, also known as Aglipayan, was founded in the waning years of Spanish rule. Its ritual is considered "Catholic, but not Roman," since it does not acknowledge the authority of the Pope. Priests, many of whom are married, conduct services in local languages.

Since the church affiliated with the American Episcopal Church in 1948, it has achieved a nominal Protestant status. It is therefore known as the largest "Protestant" denomination, claiming between one and two million followers.[32]

Of Rome and Mecca

The Roman Catholic Church has changed its position radically in comparison to the era of Spanish domination, when Protestant missionaries were forbidden and the Bible not allowed. Now the church displays a more tolerant attitude toward Protestants and in some areas permits faithful Catholics to attend Bible studies.[33]

Catholicism, however, remains a curious mixture of old and new. One missionary comments on the church: "It is the most progressive of churches and the most backward, the most modern and the most medieval.

"Here, for instance, is a Jesuit priest, a Ph.D. in anthropology from an American university, dressed in sport shirt and slacks, on his way to give a lecture on family planning. And here is an Austrian priest dressed in black cassock down to his ankles, pausing before a well-dressed lady as she presses the back of his hand to her forehead and mumbles the traditional *Manu-po,* 'Your right hand, sir.' "[34]

The nation has the highest percentage (84 percent) of Roman Catholics of all Asian nations, but traditional beliefs give the practice of Catholicism the character of a folk religion.[35]

Even in that diluted state, the church has a difficult time. On an average Sunday, only two men and five women out of every 100 Filipinos attend mass. Part of this indifferent devotion results from a lack of pastoral care. On average, one priest cares for the spiritual needs of 6,500 adherents, but since half the clergy are assigned to seminaries and other institutions, the church in reality averages one parish priest for every 12,500 members.[36]

Resistance to evangelical witness, however, continues strong in some areas. Cebu City, the nation's second largest city, is one of the most unresponsive of all urban populations. Roman Catholic heritage runs so deeply among its one million inhabitants that only fifty evangelical churches manage to function. In compar-

ison, Davao City, similar in size, numbers over 500 evangelical churches.[37]

While Catholicism moves slowly to a more tolerant stance toward evangelicals, Islam intensifies its adversarial attitude. Islamic nations of the Middle East invest large sums of money in the Philippines to deepen the division between the faithful and the infidels.

Alliance people in Zamboanga City have especially felt the brunt of this hostility as Muslim missionaries fight to keep their followers grounded in Islam and out of reach of the Gospel. One incident in 1988 involved Muslim zealots' going beyond words and demolishing a CAMA-COP chapel in the city.[38]

Despite this well-funded militancy, Alliance missionaries and Filipino church workers find an openness among Muslims. One indication of this took place in the Sulu Archipelago, with its 97 percent Muslim population.

Although the Alliance had worked for years among the people with very limited success, a district superintendent determined to try again. Accompanied by a group of believers, he made an evangelistic foray in Manubel, one of the 300 islands of the island string.

Nearly 2,000 people, some with auto-matic weapons, watched impassively as a film was shown and an evangelistic appeal was given in the town plaza. The speaker sensed they were moved but afraid to show it. So he invited them to bring people in need of healing.

Nothing happened at first. Then someone brought a totally deaf person, another came with a boy having deformed feet. A third man came complaining of a backache. One by one, all three were visibly and immediately healed.

The amazed crowd broke and ran to get ailing friends and relatives. One who experienced healing from a severe asthmatic condition was a prominent imam, a Muslim priest. A hunchback man suddenly stood straight and walked normally. Thirty-two people received healing during

Pacific Islands   351

(left and right) The park-like Ebenezer campus was protected during World War II largely through the efforts of a Japanese lady and Japanese army officer who were Christians.

that evangelistic rally and four large family groups requested regular services.

Such openness almost invariably leads to persecution. When thirty Muslims in another area responded to the Gospel, ostracism was immediately imposed by the entire community. One pregnant young woman in the group of new believers went into labor, but the Muslim midwife refused to deliver the baby and caused the infant's death. More determined than ever, the grieving family requested a Christian burial.[38]

The pattern of response and retaliation, of increased outreach and intensified opposition, has little chance of changing. CAMACOP's commitment to evangelism is bound to bring the church into more frequent conflict with Islam as the latter grows in strength through foreign funding and local sentiment.

Rebel Menace

Competing religious systems are not the only hindrance to the church's advance. Politics poses an even more deadly threat.

The New People's Army (NPA) openly espouses Marxist doctrine, wages guerrilla warfare and aims to topple the government in Manila and replace it with a Communist regime.[39] Rebel strategy generally follows three steps: secure military dominance of the mountainous areas through terrorist tactics; from the mountain bases launch attacks on the countryside, causing economic and political disruption; then overthrow local governments and replace them with Marxist cadres.[40]

As outlying tribal areas come under Communist control, Christians come increasingly under pressure and even attack. Churches are closed, believers forced to flee and their leaders threatened.

CAMACOP reported eleven pastors kidnapped by rebels in 1985; some were released, others killed.[41] The 1987 regional report listed fifty churches closed, dozens of congregations threatened and several church leaders slain.[42]

Manuel Impit had nearly completed his Bible school education when he went to a village in Barrio Tamugan, Mindanao, to pastor a small CAMACOP congregation. Representatives of the rebel army came one day to demand the tin-roofed chapel for an indoctrination center. They intended to herd all villagers into the church and teach them Communist doctrine.

Pastor Impit refused and they left. Shortly after, rumors began circulating that the pastor was "an informer" and "against the NPA." A little while later, he and a deacon were shot.[43]

Another pastor went to a rural area in Davao, where a church had lost 250 of its 300 people. Communists—including some church young people—controlled the area and tried to pressure the pastor into joining them. When he refused, unsuccessful attempts were made on his life.

As a countermeasure, the pastor called the people to prayer and Bible study five nights a week. Revival quickened the congregation and brought back many who had left the church. Even some of the rebels attended Bible studies and were won to Christ. The NPA backed off and left the church in peace.[44]

CAMACOP leaders know there will be more martyred pastors as the insurgency spreads. They do not shrink from entering NPA-controlled territory to encourage the Christians. The church also works with

relief agencies to provide help to believers and others displaced by the fighting or cut off from normal supplies.

It is a sign of the times that ministerial students at the Alliance Bible Seminary and in other CAMACOP-supported schools study measures the church can take in rebel-held areas.

The curriculum includes a course on Marxist theory and biblical responses. Professors lead studies on how some churches cope with totalitarian regimes, including the Early Church under Rome, the evangelical churches in Eastern Europe and Protestants in Nazi Germany.

In one seminary class, students discussed options for the church under totalitarian rule: (1) refuse to cooperate, (2) submit to the state, (3) go underground, (4) or flee. Such discussions are conducted with a seriousness born of reality, not academic pursuit.

As one professor put it: "Ultimately there will be no substitute for costly grace in the Philippines."[46]

Historical Conflict

In retrospect, struggle and suffering had confronted the Gospel years before Prot-

estant missionaries were able to enter the Philippines under United States administration in 1898.

Conflict began when a British and Foreign Bible Society colporteur landed in Manila in 1838 with only one purpose in mind: to distribute the Word of God. He did not get very far.

The Roman Catholic Church waged a relentless campaign to keep the Bible out of the hands of the Filipinos. Priests circulated a tract entitled "The Protestant Farce." The cover drawing depicted Martin Luther translating the Bible. Across from him sat the Devil, telling him what to write.[47]

The church's opposition took more direct and forceful measures as well. In Zamboanga, Filipinos found with Bibles were forced to burn them. Right up until the end of Spanish domination, people caught with the Scriptures were imprisoned.[48]

The Word of God, however, is sometimes as elusive as it is enduring. After the end of Spanish rule and the departure of Spanish priests, an old Bible was found in a convent in Zamboanga. Local Catholics compared the church's official version

with one banned by the hierarchy. The results convinced "many of the genuineness of the Protestant Bible."[49]

Initial Attempts

Despite the Catholic ban on Bible distribution and Protestant missions, the Alliance attempted to enter the Philippines. Rev. D. W. LeLecheur, sent by Dr. Simpson to probe unevangelized areas for openings to start missionary work, arrived in Manila in 1893. He was not even permitted by Spanish port authorities to leave the ship.

The Spanish-American War several years later was looked upon by the Alliance as God's way of opening the Philippine Islands to the Gospel. "It is a war in which the providence of God seems destined to have an important place in the fulfillment of prophecy, inasmuch as it is to be, we trust, God's instrumentality for striking another blow at that system of antiquity."[50]

Once the islands were wrested from Spain, C&MA officials in New York sent a representative to Washington "to impress upon the Administration . . . the importance of securing an open door for missions in the Philippine Islands and holding the advantage which God has given to the American government in the interests of religious liberty and Christian evangelization in this important region." [51]

Such bold statements, unfortunately, did not square with actions. Although LeLecheur started back to the Philippines in 1899 with a group of missionaries, they were redirected to China "for the time being" and never got to their original destination.[52]

It was then that Miss Elizabeth White attempted to be the standard bearer of the Alliance, but within months of her arrival in Manila, she met and married a Presbyterian missionary.

Mr. J. A. McKee, a former U.S. soldier stationed in the Philippines, returned in 1902 to establish a self-supporting industrial mission in Mindanao. He ignored the treaty banning evangelistic work among Muslim Moros.

"God has laughed at such diplomacy," he said, "for He has most blessedly flung wide open the doors of opportunity to these Mohammedan hearts."[53]

Such was his zeal that at one point he

toured the area on foot, traveling 300 miles along the coastline, where roads or trails did not often exist. His promising ministry abruptly ended after fourteen months. He died of cholera probably contracted from an ailing American stranger to whom he gave shelter.

When D. O. Lund and his wife came to the Alliance from another mission in 1908, they brought the first semblance of permanence to the mission. They also brought a new direction in ministry that diverted efforts from the previous emphasis on evangelism and establishing the church.

Mrs. Lund was concerned for the "many children of American military who need attention. These were children of mixed marriages, some whose fathers remained in Mindanao and others whose fathers were deserters to the U.S."[54]

The Lunds named their grade school Ebenezer and later started one for boys in the nearby town of Mercedes. The initiative started "a discernible trend . . . toward an institutional form of missionary work."[55]

Schools began to proliferate: a school

Ethnic groups guard closely their cultural distinctions.

for Muslims on Basilan Island, a night school for Chinese in Zamboanga City, another for the Subanos, agricultural instruction for Subanens.

"It must be concluded that the Alliance did not reach its potential in achieving its avowed goals of winning adults to the faith and establishing churches. After nearly a quarter-century, seven congregations were founded with less than three hundred members."[56]

Apparently not content with such mea-

Early Alliance missionary work concentrated on Mindanao and the Sulu Archipelago.

Dr. Jaffray took direct aim at the mission's foremost activity: the schools. Though education in general was a humane and worthy vocation, it did not start churches. He further recommended that a new mission chairman, strong in administration and Bible teaching skills, be appointed directly from New York.

Closing the schools for boys and girls proved painful, especially for parents more concerned that their children be educated than churches started. The Ebenezer school facilities were redirected to prepare Filipino pastors for Filipino congregations. This reorganization paved the way for a new era when Ebenezer Bible Institute students and graduates would take the lead in church planting and church growth.

The second shock to the Alliance work was swift and tragic. A combined team of missionaries and Filipinos left Zamboanga in late 1929 to do evangelistic work in Cotabato. As the boat pulled away from the dock, Miss Mabel Christensen called back to her students from the Bible institute, "Boys! Let your lives burn out for Jesus!"[59]

ger results, the Lord seemed to subject Alliance work in the Philippines to at least three distinct shocks in order to revive it: a visit by Dr. Robert A. Jaffray, a fatal accident and, most traumatic of all, a war.

Turning Points

Dr. Jaffray, the dynamic missionary statesman in China, was asked by mission leaders in New York to inspect the Alliance mission and church on the islands. The missionaries had become so discour-

aged they had decided to close the work and go elsewhere![57] Dr. Jaffray was to suggest how the work could break out of its holding pattern.

After touring Mindanao and Sulu in 1925, Dr. Jaffray concluded what others had suspected: "The Philippines should not be one of the Alliance's small fields, but . . . should become one of the largest fields."[58] It would take another four to five decades for this assessment to become reality.

Relics of history (left) and ruins of war (right) remind the nation of past colonial conquests and suffering.

The following morning, while some of the team went ashore, one of the women tried to light a fire on the boat to cook breakfast. An explosion ripped through the launch, claiming Miss Christensen's life and that of a Filipina companion and completely destroying the craft.

Five of Miss Christensen's students at Ebenezer mounted an all-night vigil by her coffin in a chapel near the school. During the quiet night hours, they gave themselves to serious thought and prayer. Next morning, one of the students told the institute director: "We'll never stop until the pagan tribes have been evangelized."[60]

Following graduation, they spread out to five major unreached areas of Mindanao and Sulu. Their pioneering efforts opened large new areas responsive to the Gospel. Linking this new era of growth to the tragic deaths of a missionary and her companion, some strongly believed "this was the price to be paid to mobilize the developing church."[61]

From 1928 to 1940, the church multiplied more than twenty-four times, from 224 to 5,414 baptized members. Most of the growth took place among tribal peo-

ple in Cotabato and Davao, including a people movement in the Mindanao town of Baguio that involved 400 people in a multi-individual decision.

War Interlude

The third great shock that propelled the church toward full stature was World War II, in which missionaries and Filipino Christians suffered alike.

Alliance mission staff arrived in the Philippines from China and Indochina in hopes that they had outrun the invading Japanese forces in 1941. Some of them found a prison instead of a haven, as did missionaries already stationed in the islands.

Some of the local missionaries tried in their own way to evade the Japanese. A group of seventeen adults and fourteen children fled Zamboanga in a moonlit convoy to the interior in January, 1942. Abandoning the vehicles, they pushed deeper into the jungle on foot and with the help of Filipino Christians established a camp. They remained undisturbed by the Japanese for a full year before being rounded up and hauled off to internment camp.[62]

Seven missionaries in Cotabato fled to the interior in September of 1942, but threats of violence forced them back to the city and from there to prison in Davao. The local pastor and congregation did what they could to help the missionaries even at the risk of punishment to themselves. The pastor was arrested and charged with crimes against the Japanese. Only the providential intervention of a Christian Japanese officer saved his life.[63]

Japanese believers proved very helpful in another way as well by arranging for care of the Bible institute campus in Zamboanga throughout the war. A Japanese lady gathered all the library books and had them sent to another town, where a Japanese army captain, also a Christian, stored them.[64]

Eventually most of the captured missionaries were brought to Manila's University of Santo Tomas, founded by Spanish Dominicans in 1611. None of the Alliance internees or their children died during the years of internment in these camps, but they all suffered through malnutrition.

Only the Lommassons managed to elude capture throughout the war. Suba-

New Beginning

non Christians in Mindanao hid and cared for them until American forces retook the island.[65]

Filipino Christians as well felt the heavy-handed disfavor of the invaders. Approximately one-half of all CAMACOP church buildings were destroyed. Numerous pastors and church members experienced intense suffering, none more so than Florentino de Jesus.

De Jesus and some members of his congregation were accused of spying for the enemy. He was subjected to almost continuous interrogation, beatings and death threats for forty-six days. He later learned the identity of his accuser, met her publicly and forgave her for the great wrong and suffering she had inflicted on him by her false charges.[66]

Until World War II, explains a former missionary, only lip service by both missionaries and nationals had been given to the indigenous policy of the Alliance. Principles promoting church maturity had been the stated objectives of Alliance overseas missions since 1927. These were not implemented in the Philippines until 1947.

"It is doubtful if Filipinos would have been prepared for the idea of a self-supporting, self-governing and self-propagating church had not the war freed them into an unsought independence from the mission."[67]

The end of World War II presented the Alliance church of the Philippines an opportunity for a new beginning. Scarred by suffering under Japanese occupation and matured by forced separation from foreign missionaries, there could be no return to prewar ways. But just how different would be the new beginning? What form and direction would it take?

At this critical juncture of CAMACOP's development, two veteran missionaries from Viet Nam came to help the church regroup. Meanwhile, the released missionary internees, exhausted and emaciated from years in the Santo Tomas prison camp, were returned to North America to recuperate.

Rev. Herbert Jackson and Rev. Harold Dutton stayed for only a few years, but during that time their inspiration and encouragement set the church firmly on the road to full autonomy.

Emerging from the war, Filipino church leaders had already faced the realization they could not always count on missionary presence and help. To this the interim missionary administrators added another argument: The nation was gaining its independence; why not the church?

The veteran missionaries knew church autonomy worked because they had seen it happen. "If indigenous principles worked for the Vietnamese, they could work in the Philippines as well," they reasoned, and the church listened.

Most of the missionaries returning to the Philippines also had autonomy on their minds. Refreshed and ready to work, they sought a new partnership with the local believers who had risked and suffered so much in their behalf.

The mission's initiative in encouraging autonomy before the church had to ask for it created an atmosphere of goodwill and cooperation in which God could greatly bless the work.[68]

Augmented by missionaries forced out of China, the C&MA mission in the Philippines doubled its prewar size by 1950. The church —its work reorganized and its churches rebuilt — was in a strong position to advance. Together "they witnessed the greatest period of geographical and numerical expansion the church had ever known,"[69] at least until the target-setting church-growth campaigns that later developed.

During a twelve-year period after the war, as the mission redirected its role from leader to adviser and the church

developed increasing confidence in taking the lead, CAMACOP tripled in size. Growth was qualitative as well as quantitative. Blessed with leaders who believed in the indigenous principle of self-support, the church moved toward financial independence.

However, over the next twelve-year period from 1958 to 1970, the church expanded at a slower annual rate of 3.1 percent, slightly less than the national population growth.

Much of the problem lay with the local church's inability to solidify its gains. "A high attrition rate suggests that the back-door of the church was nearly as large as the front door."[70]

The dozen years would be better characterized as a time of consolidation rather

When CAMACOP churches focused their resources on church planting in Metro Manila, they experienced an explosion of growth.

than of expansion. The number of self-supporting churches rose by 300 to a total 655; Filipinos in leadership roles increased to 474; the transfer of control from mission to church was completed.

The stage was now set for an explosion of growth that would dwarf previous records and catapult CAMACOP into one of the fastest patterns of expansion in The Alliance World Fellowship.

In that same year of 1970, the All-Philippine Congress on Evangelism united evangelical churches and missions in the nation's first broadly based evangelistic effort. A seed thought took root and flourished among CAMACOP and other denominational leaders: Why not set targets for our own church and see what God can do?

Like the biblical seed that fell on good ground, the idea of target-thinking produced a harvest—first 32,000 new believers, then total membership of nearly 90,000. And for the future, why not 2 million believers in 20,000 churches by A.D. 2000?

"Despise not the day of small beginnings"—small as a seed thought capable of producing a harvest. □

CHURCH AND MISSION

OFFICIAL NAME OF CHURCH:	Christian and Missionary Alliance Churches of the Philippines (CAMACOP)
ENTRY BY MISSIONARIES:	1902
NUMBER OF MISSIONARIES:	83
ORGANIZED CHURCHES:	1,457
UNORGANIZED CHURCHES AND PREACHING POINTS:	476
BAPTIZED CHURCH MEMBERS:	82,574
INCLUSIVE MEMBERSHIP:	206,435
MEDICAL WORK:	0
EDUCATION:	24 TEE Courses 8 Theological Schools
RADIO BROADCASTS:	1 per week
PAGES PRINTED:	5,438,800

COUNTRY

OFFICIAL NAME:	Republic of the Philippines
FORM OF GOVERNMENT:	Republic
OFFICIAL LANGUAGE(S):	Filipino (Tagalog), English
AREA:	115,831 sq. mi.
POPULATION:	(1989 est.) 61,971,000
CAPITAL:	Quezon City (Manila defacto)
PER CAPITA INCOME:	(1985) $598.00
LITERACY:	88%
RELIGIOUS AFFILIATION:	Roman Catholic 83%, Protestant 9%, Muslim 5%

THE
SUPPORT
NETWORK

THE SUPPORT NETWORK

Alliance missions has resulted in an overseas fellowship of believers and churches more than five times larger than the combined total of all C&MA work in the United States and Canada.

Statistics make the point. The Alliance in North America numbered nearly 325,000 inclusive members attending over 2,000 churches in 1989.[1] The records for overseas work one year earlier (due to delay caused by distance) showed more than 1,820,000 inclusive members and almost 10,500 churches.[2]

Credit for this remarkable five-to-one ratio goes to a network of people who not only give money but also involve themselves in the work of missions. They believe that response to the Great Commission involves every believer, not just a small corps of specialized paid church workers.

This strong sense of partnership in missions is reflected in an unusual working relationship between the two autonomous Alliance denominations in Canada and the United States.

For nearly ninety years, the Alliance movement in both nations developed with little consideration of nationality. A free exchange of pastors flowed across the longest unfortified border in the world. Missionaries toured churches of both nations, finding a unity of purpose free of chauvinistic rivalries.

The inevitable moment arrived, however, when political and economic realities forced the Canadian Alliance to recognize that autonomy was essential to continued growth. The Canadian C&MA therefore became an independent entity in 1981, incorporated by the national government in Ottawa.

Even then, separation of the two national churches was achieved in harmony. Canadian and American church leaders found many reasons for continuing their

Melvin Sylvester (center), president of the Canadian C&MA, and Arnold Cook (right), Canadian director of personnel and missions, discuss strategy with Argentine church leaders, Walter Perez and Guillermo Gitz.

joint efforts in overseas missions.[3] A cooperative agreement with the Division of Overseas Ministries of the American denomination went immediately into effect.

The articles of agreement, which formalized some practices already in effect and added new ones, were simple and comprehensive. The C&MA of Canada would:

- Assume financial support of all its missionaries.
- Be represented on the advisory council and administrative committee of the Division of Overseas Ministries.
- Cooperate with its American counterpart in determining policies and regulations governing overseas work.
- Share costs of administrative and support services related to overseas work.

In 1988, for example, the Canadian Alliance devoted nearly $7 million to missions from its total giving of $9,880,000 (Canadian) to the Global Advance Fund. From this income came the complete support of 219 overseas missionaries. The year also climaxed an "Above and Beyond" fund drive that

Annual missionary conference in the local church keeps lay people informed concerning the overseas work they support.

netted $1,452,000 (Canadian) for evangelism and church planting in Buenos Aires.[4]

During that same year, the Great Commission Fund of U.S. based Alliance churches received $23,400,000. The fund supported 909 missionaries and their work. In addition, a year-end "Opportunity Sunday" appeal netted another $611,775 to finance new initiatives in evangelism overseas and in local communities.[5]

Alliance missionaries do not have to raise their own support. They are financed from the Great Commission or Global Advance Funds. Furloughing missionaries, however, are assigned to fall and spring speaking tours to represent their work to the churches.

One distinguishing feature of an Alliance church is its practice of conducting a missions conference every year. The special series of meetings keeps the lay people informed concerning progress of the

overseas work they support. A great deal depends on these tours, because from missions conferences and rallies flow the offerings and pledges that fuel the Alliance's multimillion-dollar work overseas. Local church and district-level missionary committees contribute to the success of these semiannual tours.

Inclusive Calling

Support for missions involves more than just a central fund. In one way or other, to one degree or another, every organization or office related to Alliance administration contributes time and energy to the call of missions.

Stewardship Ministries, for example, accounted for over one-half million dollars designated to the Great Commission Fund from bequest income in 1988. Over half of all its completed agreements relate to missions.[6]

Alliance higher education also contributes directly to the overseas enterprise.

Canadian Bible College and Canadian Theological Seminary are the principal source for Canada's Alliance workers.

In addition to preparing students at Nyack, Alliance Theological Seminary supervises several extension programs.

Each of the five Alliance-related colleges carries courses in missions and prepares young people for service abroad or advanced schooling for ministry.

Alliance Theological Seminary and Canadian Theological Seminary offer graduate degrees in missions. They send from their halls each year a new wave of graduates that spread out to worldwide ministries.

Local church-related organizations put their emphases on activities rather than academics. They recruit women, men and young people in programs involved with missions.

Womens Missionary Prayer Fellowships in the United States and Alliance Women in Canada form the largest and oldest organizations of lay people involved in missions. The first groups began in 1914, but "not until 1929 did the Board of Managers get around to granting formal approval, and then only after they found many prayer groups already active in local churches."[7]

By 1989, the American organization claimed 18,432 members and the Canadian sister group had grown to over 5,500 women.

Although prayer ranks as the primary purpose of meeting, the two groups have for years sponsored local and district projects such as helping new missionaries with their outfits. The local women's groups also unite in funding a national project and almost invariably surpass their goal.

American prayer fellowships set a 1989 goal of $270,000 to build a seminary in Africa. Instead, they raised more than $321,000. Their total giving for the year exceeded $1,371,000. Canada's Alliance Women chose for their national project "Voices of Promises" for Alliance Radio ministries and raised nearly $111,800.

Alliance Men in both countries trace their origin to three friends on a fishing trip on Lake Erie in 1951.[8] After an animated discussion, the trio concluded that men in the churches should take a more active role in witnessing for Christ. The Board of Managers officially recognized the laymen's organization a year later.

The disastrous 1976 earthquake in Guatemala prompted Alliance Men to expand their activities from local church evangelism to international projects. Calling themselves "construction missionaries," skilled and unskilled volunteers bought their own airline tickets and brought their own tools to help Guatemalan Christians rebuild their homes and churches.

Volunteers gradually extended their assistance to include Alliance missions and national churches in Europe, Africa and elsewhere in Latin America. Their projects include building churches, drilling wells,

One national WMPF project was to fund overseas women's retreats and leadership training.

Alliance Men assist the Barcelona (Spain) congregation in readying a new place of worship.

renovating properties damaged by natural disasters and improving school campuses.

Young people take their place alongside Alliance laymen and women in getting personally involved in missions. *Alliance Youth Corps* sends college-age youth overseas at their own expense during school-free summer months. From its inception in 1967 to 1988, the youth corps office assigned over 1,500 Canadian and American students to short-term service in forty countries. During the same two decades, nearly 200 youth corps members returned overseas as career missionaries. Another 175 qualified as candidates.[9]

Auxiliary Professionals

Two organizations related directly to the C&MA recruit full-time personnel.

CAMA Services conducts relief operations openly and in full cooperation with host countries. The *International Fellowship of Alliance Professionals* relies on professionally qualified adults who use their vocational skills and quietly witness for Christ in countries with restricted access to professional missionaries.

CAMA Services was a war baby. It was brought into the world by the violence of war in Indochina and the compassion of Alliance missionaries who could not look the other way when meeting orphans, displaced families, the wounded and sick. Organized in 1972, the relief agency put together and distributed thousands of "survival kits" to provide Vietnamese, Cambodian and Laotian war victims with at least minimal means to survive.

When all of Indochina came under Communist rule in 1975, CAMA Services moved its operations to refugee camps strung along Thailand's borders. Alliance medical teams and relief administrators joined other agencies in keeping alive the tens of thousands of sick, weary and malnourished refugees.

Activities in Thailand then shifted to combating one of the worst enemies of refugee settlements: boredom. Young volunteers from North America opened schools to teach basic literacy. Other CAMA workers concentrated on job skills, securing sewing machines and other tools so that enterprising refugees could start small businesses.

CAMA Services extended its mission of compassion into Lebanon in 1978 to help the battered population survive the madness of war. Other relief personnel moved into Mali and Burkina Faso to battle the crushing juggernaut of drought and famine.

With each new crisis came new forms of help. Relief workers helped Lebanese rebuild their homes and find new ways to make a living. In Africa they distributed thousands of tons of grain, clothing, medicine and tools. When the threat of starvation subsided, they moved to the next stage: prevention of famine by deepening wells or digging new ones, reclaiming farmland and replenishing livestock.

CAMA Services follows a basic strategy in its operations. It works only in areas where Alliance missions are present and national churches established. This reduces drastically the high costs of administration and staffing. And it provides an instant network of local leaders and people who can make the system of distribution function economically, honestly and effectively.

This policy greatly helps CAMA Services reach a basic goal of ministry: "Turning Relief into Belief." Agency directors believe that the ultimate goal of bona fide aid in the name of Christ is to bring suffering people to the inexhaustible resources of hope and strength in Christ. The next step is to see them become part of a local church.

Although closely allied with Alliance missions and overseas churches, CAMA Services *receives no direct assistance from the Great Commission Fund or the Global Advance Fund.* Individual Alliance

members, however, do support CAMA Services. Their giving in 1988 totaled *a half-million dollars.*

From the beginning, the major part of operating funds has come from outside agencies, including ZOA (Christian businessmen in Holland) and TEAR (The Evangelical Alliance Relief) Funds in Holland and England. In more recent years, agencies in the United States such as World Relief/USA and Samaritan's Purse have provided important aid.

Canadian agencies have given substantial aid in goods as well as money. The Canadian Food Grains Bank, of which the Canadian C&MA is a member, has sent hundreds of tons of grain to Africa; World Relief of Canada is also a major supporter.

The International Fellowship of Alliance Professionals (IFAP), unlike the refugee relief agency, works best in quiet

(Top) CAMA Services enables Indochinese refugees in Thai camps to set up a cottage-style sewing industry and (above) the manufacture of prostheses for war casualities.

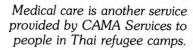

Medical care is another service provided by CAMA Services to people in Thai refugee camps.

anonymity. Publicity and excessive exposure would cause it to wither. Even in a religious publication of limited circulation, one careless word or reference could quickly end a personal ministry painstakingly pieced together over a course of cautious years.

An anonymous Alliance professional writes, "Another friend was notified that he had ten days to leave the country because his residence permit was being revoked. This was totally shocking, because he is a tentmaker like us. In fact, he teaches at another school and has been doing such for eleven years! He only had another month to finish the school year.

"There are no charges, because no law was broken. The British embassy has received official *unwritten* word that he was ousted because of Christian propaganda. This worker was very humble and quite low key. He was independent like us, so I know him pretty well. . . . And now this. We think it came from an informer. All sorts of lies can be said, and if there are no formal accusations then one cannot prove his innocence. He has been asked to leave and has not been told why."[10]

What is this tight-lipped association, and who are its members?

The International Fellowship of Alliance Professionals was organized in 1985 by the Division of Overseas Ministries. Its role is to answer the challenge of nations closed to traditional missionary work.

The plan follows a strategy originally used by the Apostle Paul twenty centuries ago. He used his profession as a tentmaker to support himself on his missionary travels. At the same time, it gave him a legitimate reason—or cover—to reside in cities or areas hostile to the Gospel.

Modern day "tentmakers" even bear some personal resemblance to the Apostle Paul. The director describes them: "All are highly trained professionals, many with theological degrees, gifted in sharing their faith effectively. They are not Christian people who 'just happen to live

overseas.' They are men and women who have sensed a call from God to minister cross-culturally in a limited access country, and they have meticulously prepared themselves for these ministries."[11]

While the fellowship does not hire or pay these individuals, it backs them in various ways. Initially, the organization provides guidance and counselling during their preparatory period, then fellowship and pastoral care while they serve overseas. In some cases, help also extends to language studies and medical coverage.

IFAP originally helped Alliance professionals find jobs and ministries in the People's Republic of China, then gradually expanded its support to tentmakers in Turkey, Saudi Arabia and Malaysia. By 1989, the fellowship included thirty-one associates; the director believed it could easily surge to one hundred members.

"It is clearly evident that huge sections of the world are no longer reachable by traditional career missionaries," he explained. "In the Far East we talk about the 'Asian box,' an area bordered by India on the west, China on the north, Japan and the Philippines on the east and Indonesia on the south.

"Over half the world's people already live in this 'box,' and by the end of the century two-thirds of the world will reside in this people-packed area of earth.

"A closer look at this cluster of countries reveals that the two largest nations in the world, China and India, are closing or already closed to missionaries and most of the other countries are either closed or partially closed. Unless God chooses to arrange things otherwise, a very large percentage of unreached peoples will be beyond the influence of regular mission-

ary activity by the end of this century."[12]

The International Fellowship of Alliance Professionals will never replace regular missionary work, but it obviously has great potential as an alternative means of fulfilling the Great Commission. The growth of IFAP and its converging activities with CAMA Services resulted in a merger of the two offices under a single director in 1990.

Serving Servants

In some organizations, people in the field serve the home office. In the Division of Overseas Ministries, office staff support personnel working overseas in order to maximize their efforts.

For many years, the division vice president has been aided by four regional directors. They maintain constant contact with missionaries and national church

leaders in Africa, Asia, Latin America and Middle East/Europe.

Adding several Central American nations to the division in the 1980s made imperative a fifth regional director. This proposed post would be responsible for six nations of Central America and the Caribbean rim: Mexico, Guatemala, Costa Rica, Dominican Republic, Venezuela and Surinam.

The overseas division's main responsibility, however, is not to geographical regions—or even to national churches in those countries.

Primary and personal concern focuses on missionaries and their families who, after all, are very human. They live in totally strange surroundings, and are often associated with minority religious groups that attract hostility from majority populations and their governments.

(Left) Famine victims in Burkina Faso line up for grain distribution supervised by CAMA Services and made possible by Canadian and American churches; (right) an opium addict in a Thai refugee camp seeks help from CAMA Services medical personnel.

Missionaries need encouragement, guidance, a supportive network of peers and superiors, as well as believers in the host country. Above all, they need pastoral care. This latter need prompted the overseas division to organize pastoral team ministries. An experimental program in 1984 developed into a permanent plan.

Husband-wife teams carefully selected from successful pastorates in North America minister every two years in the same assigned overseas areas. They conduct four-day retreats that feature Bible studies, prayer and discussion groups, time for personal counselling—but no mission business.

The pastor and his wife, supported by their local churches, serve outside the authority structure. Overseas division staff honor complete confidentiality of any counselling sessions between the pastoral couple and missionaries seeking help.

The husband/wife teams increased to three from the United States and three from Canada by 1989. They often return home believing they received more than they gave.

Writes one pastor's wife: "Without a doubt, Paul and I have been the ones who have profited the most from this investment of our lives. We strongly desire to be in tune with God's larger purposes in the world and not be content to settle back and enjoy creature comforts. These trips help keep us focused to be models before our own family and congregation concerning true values of the Christian life."[13]

The overseas division's care for its own extends with deep concern to missionary children, commonly known as "MKs." Schooling is provided for school-age children of all families residing abroad. Wherever possible, Alliance personnel serve as dormitory parents to look after MKs from their mission.

In recent years, extensive and continuing studies were conducted to determine how best to help MKs adjust to an increasingly complex world once they return home to North America. Known by a strange combination of abbreviations, MK-CART/CORE involves educators, psychologists, counselors and administrators from over a dozen missions and graduate schools.

The Alliance operates two twelve-grade schools and three grammar schools for missionary children. The Alliance Academy in Quito, Ecuador, serves not only C&MA children but also those from thirty-four other missions. Some children are accepted from families in embassy and foreign business communities in Latin America. The smaller Dalat School in Panang, Malaysia, fulfills a similar function for Alliance missionary families in the Far East.

Missionary children in Africa attend the International Christian Academy in Bouake, Cote d'Ivoire. Another mission administers the school, but several missions including the Alliance assign teachers and dormitory parents to the academy. As an alternative arrangement in Africa and elsewhere, some parents are permitted to place their children in local public or private schools.

Unreached Peoples

If caring for its own summarizes the overseas division's "family" responsibilities, then its "work at the office" is cross-cultural communication of the Gospel, especially among unreached people groups.

Going where others have never taken the Gospel is as essentially Alliance as the founder's hymns and the Four-fold Gospel. From the very beginning, Dr. Simpson urged, "We must mobilize the neglected forces of the church at home to reach the neglected peoples of earth."

But, as the work grew and time passed, a subtle change of direction overtook Alliance missionary work. "As national churches organized and developed, missionaries increasingly found themselves serving the church in training roles and support ministries such as literature, medical work and schools. Fewer and fewer overseas personnel engaged in frontline evangelism among nonbelievers."[14]

Centennial Council in 1987 called attention to this problem and termed it serious: "We realize there is a great unfinished task in many areas of Alliance responsibility. Some people groups in our areas have never heard the Gospel. In other groups only a few have had this privilege. Such unreached peoples often exist outside the boundaries of already established Alliance national churches, yet within the areas of our responsibility."[15]

Canadian General Assembly delegates joined with their American colleagues in mandating a renewed effort to identify and evangelize these unreached people groups.

Responding to this directive, the overseas division called in a missions research consultant and set up a network of field researchers. Their assignment: Identify unreached peoples and draft a strategy for evangelizing them. The impact of this finetuning process will profoundly affect Alliance missions for years to come.

Dr. Arnold L. Cook, Canadian director of personnel and missions, said the renewed emphasis would require some "hard-nosed decisions." "We do not command enough resources to mount a

(Facing page top) Teen-age missionary children overseas are no different than their stateside peers; (lower left) dining in M.K. hostels is family style; (left) M.K. school curricula follow North American programs.

totally new effort in a different direction," he said. "We should continue multiplying churches and do it well, and at the same time redeploy some of our personnel and resources to open new frontiers of evangelism overseas."[16]

Pakistani Punjabis

The Alliance support network, ranging from the local church to denominational offices, works to lengthen boundaries of ministry, not to maintain the status quo. Being constantly on the stretch is consistent with the very nature of the C&MA.

Dr. Louis L. King, former president of the denomination, describes it this way: "The Alliance through the years has been called a movement. At its inception the Master breathed into its wheels the word 'GO'. It was never constituted to stand still. Its equilibrium depends upon forward movement. It wobbles only when speed is slackened. It will topple over into the ecclesiastical scrap pile if it stops. Therefore, it must not stop. It must never be satisfied with what it has done."[17]

It is therefore not surprising that the list of nations with Alliance-related work grows constantly. As the decade of the 1980s drew to a close, two new countries joined the family of forty-seven served by Alliance missions either directly or indirectly: Pakistan and Burma.

Although Alliance missionaries entered Pakistan for the first time in 1986, the C&MA was already a registered mission due to its ownership of property prior to the partition of India and Pakistan. To the amazement of the first two young Canadian couples, their applications for resident visas were granted in a single day on the basis of their being Alliance missionaries. This in a nation under Islamic rule!

The mission's intention to do adult literacy education played a major part in the rapid granting of visas. Pakistani officials look with special favor on literacy work. Only 23.3 percent of the population knows how to read and write. This compares unfavorably with the 36 percent literacy rate in India, its arch rival and potential aggressor.[18]

Christian churches and agencies enjoy unusual freedom of action. Public evangelistic services from three to seven days have been traditionally held for many years in major cities. A Christian study center openly operates as an evangelical witness. Campus Crusade and other evangelical student movements pursue on-campus ministries.

The Punjab Religious Book Society offers Bible correspondence courses, and the Pakistan Bible Society publishes the Scriptures in several major languages. Four small seminaries and four Bible schools provide theological training for ministerial candidates.

All of this takes place in a nation governed by Islamic law and among a 100 million population, in which nine of every ten are Muslims.

Pakistan's tolerance of Christians does have its limits. The nation's constitution grants freedom of religion, including the right to propagate faith and seek converts. Yet regular religious broadcasts are not permitted and other activities are coming under increasing government control.

Although the country has one of the largest Christian populations in the Arab world, the total only accounts for 1.4 percent of the populace. Most of the nominal believers belong to a minority Hindu caste of untouchables despised by Muslims, quarantined from the mainstream of national life, and tolerated because they do menial work others will not touch.

After surveying the nation's spiritual needs and work being done by other missions, the two young Alliance couples settled in Rawalpindi in 1988. The city is both modern and ancient. Its population of 2 million people ranks third largest in the nation; its trade and commerce predate the days of Cyrus the Great.

Rawalpindi has a large number of Punjabis, who, making up 60 percent of the population nationwide, form Pakistan's largest unreached people group. However, the missionaries realized that evangelizing the Punjabis in the city was an objective too general, since there are numerous distinct sects such as Sunnis, Shias and Ahmadias.

Furthermore, literacy and ministry efforts increase in effectiveness as they are more narrowly focused on specific social and economic groups. Research showed, for example, that Punjabi Muslim drivers and mechanics of Suzuki cars form a distinct community of their own.

The missionaries therefore determined that through adult literacy classes they would concentrate their efforts on the nominal Christian community within the Punjabi population of Rawalpindi and elsewhere. This ministry would respond to a social need in the nation and enable them to focus their witness on a specific group within the larger ethnic group.

Fluctuation of regional politics and Islamic fundamentalism cast a shadow on the future of ministry in Pakistan, but the same may be said of numerous other regions where Alliance missionaries work and consider the risk worth taking.

As one missionary in Rawalpindi observed, "Muslims are the second largest unreached people in the world—over 800 million. Almost 100 million live in Pakistan. How many Muslim countries are there in the world where Alliance missionaries can work this openly?"[19]

Myanmar's Millions

Dr. Kawl T. Vuta could have stayed where he was, a high-ranking official and member of the governing board of a denomination in Myanmar (formerly Burma). But he could not forget the unevangelized hill villages and plains people.

Born in 1942 to Christian parents and a committed believer since his midteens, Mr. Vuta lived with deep concern for the vast numbers of people without knowledge of Christ. When he first heard of the C&MA in 1977, what excited him most was its pioneering spirit of evangelism.

He wrote to a missionary in Saigon and requested more information. Back came the cryptic reply, "You should join us first."[20]

At Fuller School of World Mission, where he studied for five years and earned a doctorate in missions, he admitted: "I did not really understand what he meant at that time, but now I understand. I have come and seen the life, the work and beliefs of the C&MA. Now I know that this church is very evangelical and missionary minded."[21]

Mr. Vuta returned home after graduation and pressed his associates in the denomination's hierarchy to reach out to Myanmar's unevangelized millions. Instead, he met a preoccupation with internal church politics and a liberal shift in theology that rendered his denomination incapable of evangelistic concern.

After prolonged reflection and deep emotional struggle, Mr. Vuta wrote to the Division of Overseas Ministries, declaring his intention to join the Alliance and start a church in Myanmar.

Stressing the autonomous nature of the new church and its missionary character, he concluded with an impassioned plea: "Let The Christian and Missionary Alliance come to existence [in Burma] and reach the unreached people, rich and poor, urban and rural, not only Chan and Naga, but also Burmese and Chinese and Shan, Mon and Kaya—for whom Christ once died, shedding His precious blood. Let Burma hear His voice!"[22]

Although the Myanmar Alliance needs funds to help its church growth and building efforts, an even greater need exists for adequately trained church leaders. Going into the 1990s, the church's only formally prepared pastor was Mr. Vuta.

Some funds from North America go to church extension projects. However, the most serious mission-supplied aid for years to come will be short-term theological education courses for church leaders already in ministry. In the long term, study abroad will be offered to carefully selected church leaders.

Unreached people groups not only encompass (above) populations identified by language and culture, but also (left) city dwellers grouped together by common economic or social interests.

THE ALLIANCE WORLD FELLOWSHIP MEMBERS

Argentina	The Argentine Christian and Missionary Alliance
Australia	The Christian and Missionary Alliance of Australia
Brazil	The Brazilian Christian and Missionary Alliance
Burkina Faso	The Christian Alliance Church of Burkina Faso
Canada	The Christian and Missionary Alliance Church of Canada
Chile	The Christian and Missionary Alliance of Chile
Colombia	Colombian Christian and Missionary Alliance
Cote d'Ivoire	Evangelical Protestant Church (CMA) of the Cote d'Ivoire
Dominican Republic	The Christian and Missionary Alliance of Dominican Republic
Ecuador	The Ecuadorian Evangelical Church of the Christian and Missionary Alliance
France	Union of Christian and Missionary Alliance Churches in France
Gabon	The Christian Alliance Church of Gabon
Germany	Missions—Allianz-Kirche in Deutschland
Great Britain	British Missionary Alliance
Guatemala	The Christian and Missionary Alliance of Guatemala
Guinea	The Evangelical Protestant Church (C&MA) in the Republic of Guinea
Hong Kong	The Christian and Missionary Alliance Church Union Hong Kong, Ltd.
India	The Christian and Missionary Alliance of India
Indonesia	Gospel Tabernacle Church of Indonesia
Japan	Japan Alliance Church
Jordan	The Evangelical Christian Alliance of Jordan
Kampuchea	Khmer Evangelical Church
Korea	Korea Alliance Holiness Church (C&MA)
Laos	Laos Evangelical Church
Lebanon	The Evangelical Church of the Christian Alliance of Lebanon
Mali	The Evangelical Church of Mali
Myanmar (Burma)	The Christian and Missionary Alliance Church of Burma
Netherlands	Alliance of Evangelical "PAROUSIA" Churches
New Zealand	The Christian and Missionary Alliance of New Zealand
Nigeria	The Saviour's Evangelical Church of Nigeria
Peru	The Christian and Missionary Alliance of Peru
Philippines	The Christian and Missionary Alliance Churches of the Philippines, Inc.
Spain	Evangelical Christian and Missionary Alliance of Spain
Syria	The Evangelical Church of the Christian Alliance of Syria
Taiwan	Christian and Missionary Alliance Church Union of Taiwan
Thailand	The Gospel Church of Thailand
United States of America	The Christian and Missionary Alliance of U.S.A.
Uruguay	The Christian and Missionary Alliance of Uruguay
Vanuatu	Vanuatu Christian Church
Vietnam	Evangelical Church of Vietnam
Zaire	Evangelical Community of the Alliance in Zaire

Of One Faith

The Burmese Alliance was barely organized before it sought membership in The Alliance World Fellowship, an action reflecting the importance overseas Alliance-related churches attach to it.

The thirty-nine-member organization, a consultative body, exists for the sole purpose of strengthening its churches through mutual encouragement and advice to fulfill the Great Commission.

This does not mean it is a group where everyone gathers to talk, then returns home unchanged. Far from it. The fellowship functions like a team that spurs one another around the track until they all cross the finish line as winners.

Although the idea for such a fellowship originated in North America, its existence grew out of a natural process, not a forced birth. American and Canadian Alliance leaders favored such a nonlegislative group as early as 1952, but its time had not yet come.

Instead, the Division of Overseas Ministries, under the leadership of Dr. Louis L. King, began with regional fellowships. The First Asian Conference convened in Bangkok in 1955. Another ten regional

Alliance World Fellowship leaders during the 1980s included (left to right): Jose Plaza, Ecuador; Melvin Sylvester, Canada; Philip Teng, Hong Kong; Louis King, United States; Benjamin de Jesus, Philippines; John Pocock, Australia; Sami Dagher, Lebanon.

conferences and twenty years passed before conditions encouraged formation of a global grouping.

Dr. Nathan Bailey, president of the C&MA in North America and an enthusiastic supporter of a worldwide fellowship, cited some of the conditions compelling its formation.

He noted, "Autonomy of overseas churches has left them open to the overtures of continent wide and world associations such as the East Asia Christian Council and the World Council of Churches. These organizations often accompany their subversive appeals with assurances of financial aid and sometimes personal gain in the form of salaries and scholarships. In some cases these overtures have been very persuasive."[23]

Dedication of a new headquarters building in Nyack, New York, in June of 1975 provided an impressive backdrop for the meeting of seventy-four represen-

tatives of Alliance churches from thirty-four nations. Within a week, they drafted and approved a seven-page document that laid the formal foundation of The Alliance World Fellowship. Dr. Bailey was unanimously chosen as the first president. A seven-member executive committee was formed at the same time to represent national churches in six geographical areas of the world.

First Among Equals

The newly formed group was a family of equals, not a pair of North American parents with a flock of siblings doing their bidding. Many of the member churches resulting from Alliance missions already had by 1975 or would soon have a church-mission agreement recognizing that equality with the North American C&MA.

These formal documents, generally in effect for five years, pioneered a method

of cooperation between sending and receiving churches. "[They] operated on a basic premise that both parties were full and equal partners in the ministry of the Gospel. Each had separate, defined responsibilities, while together they shared other activities."[24]

First among equals are overseas churches with foreign missionary programs of their own. Many Alliance denominations in developing countries support their own home missions work, placing workers among other people groups within their national borders. But several churches go beyond that by sending their own missionaries abroad.

Seven of these C&MA churches in 1988 were supporting overseas missions. The two Hong Kong Alliance sending agencies, Chinese Foreign Missionary Society and Hebron Evangelical Association, topped the list with twenty-nine workers. The C&MA Church of the Philippines accounted for eleven missionaries and three tentmakers.[25]

Australia and New Zealand

The Australian Alliance supported nine workers under supervision of the Division

FOREIGN MISSIONARY ACTIVITIES (1989)

Overseas Churches of
The Alliance World Fellowship

COUNTRY	SENDING CHURCH	MISSIONARIES
Argentina	The Argentine Christian and Missionary Alliance	4
Australia	The Christian and Missionary Alliance of Australia	7
Germany	Missions-Allianz-Kirche in Deutschland	2
Hong Kong	Chinese Foreign Missionary Society of the C&MA Church Union Hong Kong Ltd.	16
	Hebron Evangelical Association of the C&MA	15
Japan	Japan Alliance Foreign Missions Board	1
Netherlands	Alliance Zendings Centrum "Parousia" (nine additional missionaries supported by North American C&MA churches)	19
Philippines	C&MA Churches of the Philippines Foreign Missions Department	15

of Overseas Ministries in 1989. Its active role as a sending church seems only natural, because missions played a prominent part in the church "down under" from the very beginning just twenty years earlier.

Dr. Bailey, one of the fact-finding team that visited the country in 1969, underscored the link between Australia and Alliance missions. "One of the factors which influenced The Christian and Missionary Alliance in deciding to establish in Australia," he said, only half-joking, "was that we liked the quality of the Australians already serving as Alliance missionaries and we would very much like to have more."[26]

Rev. Robert T. Henry and his family were recuperating in the country at the time. They had narrowly escaped death in the Tet offensive that had claimed the lives of six missionary colleagues in Viet Nam. He set up an itinerary that took the fact-finding delegation from Brisbane in the north to Melbourne in the south. After the group left, he stayed to start the first Alliance church in the home of an interested layman in Sydney.

The officials from New York had laid down some clear guidelines for establishing an Alliance work in Australia:

• To start churches through evangelism, not proselytizing from other denominations.

• To supply North American pastors at first, but encourage the churches to be self-supporting and start sending missionaries as quickly as possible.

• To have the entire work supervised by an Australian committee from the beginning.[27]

This was an ambitious plan in a nation officially listed by the United Nations as a non-Christian nation, and where all the mainline denominations were declining in numbers. Yet it worked.

By 1987, most North American pastors had been "phased out," leaving most of the churches and their inclusive membership of over 2,000 to be pastored by Australians. The Alliance College of Theology in Canberra installed its first full-time president, who was not only an Australian but also an alumnus of the college.

Another significant event occurred in 1987 when the Baulkham Hills Church in Sydney was completed. The half-million-dollar sanctuary with seating for 200 people was only the first of several major buildings envisioned by SCOPE, the Strategic Cities Outreach Plan for Evangelism.

This plan had taken shape initially in the heart of John Pocock, the first and deeply loved full-time president of the Australian Alliance. He had noted that 85 percent of the population lived in eight major cities. Furthermore, one-half of all Australians lived in or around two of the cities: Sydney and Melbourne.

If the Alliance wanted to impact on the nation, Mr. Pocock reasoned, it must establish large, visible churches in the key eight cities. Baulkham Hills Church in Sydney was the first of those projects.

Growth of the C&MA in Australia attracted an unexpected response in the neighboring island nation of New Zealand. Rev. Maru Check, a Congregational minister and former missionary, had met some Alliance missionaries during a Singapore conference in 1968 and was favorably impressed. The following year he came upon a copy of *The Alliance Witness* and the conviction grew that this was a church group New Zealand needed.

Contacts with the Alliance in Australia led to a visit by a fact-finding team from North America in 1971. Before leaving, the group announced that within a year the first Alliance church would be planted in Auckland. Although work progressed slowly, by 1988 seven Alliance churches dotted the beautiful north island.

In a manner similar to Canadian-American cooperation in missions, the Alliance churches of the two neighboring island states pooled their resources to carry on overseas work. They were thus able by 1987 to jointly support seven missionaries working with the North American Alliance in Spain, Chile, Philippines and Indonesia.

They were also invited to send missionaries to the nearby island nation of Vanuatu (formerly New Hebrides). The Vanuatu Alliance Church was accepted into The Alliance World Fellowship gathered in St. Paul before the Centennial Council.

A Shared Calling

During that fourth quadrennial session in 1987, representatives from thirty-six national churches attended The Alliance World Fellowship. In just twelve years, the total of organized congregations had grown from 5,845 to over 10,000.

As the 1980s ended and the fellowship grew to forty-one member churches, the need for a new role became apparent.

"It was a growing conviction that The Alliance World Fellowship must assume a more active role among the overseas churches," David H. Moore, vice president for Overseas Ministries, later recalled. "Alliance World Fellowship leadership is becoming more Third World. There is an increasing level of maturity among church leaders. . . . Overseas churches are becoming more aware of the responsibility within and beyond their national borders."[28]

Dr. Ben de Jesus, former president of the Alliance Church in the Philippines, was appointed by the executive committee to head the fellowship on a full-time, nonsalaried interim basis until the 1991 meeting of the full membership in Cote d'Ivoire.

Inner structure of The Alliance World Fellowship will continue to change, perhaps in unexpected ways, as it grows in size and stature. But this much is clear: Overseas Alliance churches will play an increasing role in missions until, as Christ foretold, "This gospel of the kingdom will be preached in the whole world as a testimony to all nations, and then shall the end come."[29]

This shared calling between North American and overseas Alliance people is the crowning achievement of Alliance missionaries and the churches that support them. Equals in fellowship and partners in ministry, they pursue the singular goal of making Christ known to all peoples. □

EPILOGUE

Twenty-First Century Missions

DR. DAVID L. RAMBO, PRESIDENT

THIS WORLD BOOK spans over a century of truly heroic accomplishments by Alliance missionaries and their supporting churches. Seldom, if ever, in church history has one small movement been responsible for establishing so many churches in such a multiplicity of languages, cultures and countries.

All of this was accomplished during a century convulsed by two global wars and hundreds of regional conflicts. Economies fluctuated wildly and social upheavals left few traditional landmarks intact. Yet difficult and complex though the work appeared at times, we may soon look back on the twentieth century as the easy years.

Unchecked and Uncharted

I do not have in mind the apparently unchecked forces of destruction that sweep us down uncharted courses: the transcontinental plagues of AIDS and drug abuse, cosmic disaster in the ozone, national debts and regional conflicts.

I refer to other forces that bear more directly on the church and its primary calling to world evangelization, such as rampant materialism, resurgent world religions, hardening political attitudes toward the Gospel. Only in the passage of time will we be able to measure their impact on the missionary enterprise.

However, this we can count on: Obeying the Great Commission will be harder, costlier and riskier in the twenty-first century.

Harder because by some estimates over 80 percent of the world's unreached peoples at the turn of the century will live in areas that restrict traditional missionary work.[1] "Tentmakers,"

witnessing Christian laymen, will have an increasing role in world evangelization.

Costlier because world inflation and crumbling economies will require more financial support for overseas missions. Alliance churches in North America have proven they can do their part, but they will have to buck a disturbing trend.

Some statistics indicate that American Christians possess 80 percent of all Christian wealth to fulfill the Great Commission. But most of the money raised for church budgets stays at home. Only "an estimated 4 percent goes overseas to help reach 94 percent of the world's population with the Gospel."[2]

David L. Rambo

Riskier because forces opposed to the Gospel will intensify their hostility in more open, violent ways. David B. Barrett writes, "I would expect to find by A.D. 2000 something like 500,000 Christians a year becoming martyrs, that is, losing their lives for Christ in a situation of witness as a result of human hostility. Already today the rate is as high as 300,000 a year."[3]

Over against these grim projections stands a thrilling certainty as Alliance missions enters the twenty-first century: God's Truth will always have its seekers.

Assets and Allies

Communist regimes in Russia and mainland China learned to their chagrin in 1989 that encouraging economic progress cannot be separated from freedom of the spirit. Mikhail Gorbachev's policy of openness unleashed an avalanche of requests for the Bible in Eastern Europe and in Russia itself.

Metropolitan Vladimir, chief administrator of the Moscow Patriarchate, said: "I never had any doubt about the need of Scriptures among believers. But this new era of glasnost has stimulated an interest in the secular population for the Scriptures. I have not met a nonbeliever in this country who did not want a Bible."[4]

Deng Xiaping's modernization of China's economy led to the tragic massacre of students in Tiananmen Square and to renewed interest in unofficial house churches, those courageous gatherings of Christians all across mainland China, numbering between one hundred and three hundred thousand a few years ago.[5]

Viewing church growth in Africa, Ralph W. Winter quotes David Barrett's projection that not only will Christianity be the major religion in Africa by A.D. 2000, it will win a steadily larger part of the total population (3 percent in 1900, 28 percent in 1970, 46 percent in 2000).[6]

The Alliance has been a part of this encouraging growth of the church worldwide. During the 1980s, the North American C&MA achieved a level of missionary commitment probably unequaled by any other Protestant denomination, according to figures compiled by Asbury Theological Seminary.[7] During that same decade of time, over 818,000 inclusive members were added to Alliance churches overseas—an 81 percent increase.[8]

God's Spirit, like a sweeping wind, will see to it that there will always be nations and peoples open to the Gospel. In the new century, as in the twentieth, Alliance missions will have more than enough to do.

Allied with us in obeying the Great Commission will be multiplying numbers of missionaries sent and supported by overseas churches.

Surveying cross-cultural witness by the so-called "younger churches," one newsletter reports: "As of the end of 1988 our survey indicates there were an estimated 35,924 non-Western missionaries serving in 118 countries among 2,425 people groups. This represents almost 30 percent of the total Protestant missionaries in the world!"[9]

Our sister Alliance churches in other lands are part of this burgeoning missionary force. The Alliance World Fellowship will doubtless become a greater force for the Gospel. They will place their people in nations where western missionaries can no longer work, all the while serving and encouraging one another in the work of the Gospel.

Overseas Alliance churches will also supply pastors and evangelists to work among their own people who have emigrated to Canada and the United States. We anticipate with joy a growing cooperation and interdependence in reaching the ethnic communities in North America.

Neighbors and Strangers

The only biblical way to enter the twenty-first century with a strong commitment to missions is to begin by witnessing to our neighbors. This is the New Testament strategy expressed in Acts 1:8.

But some may ask: Why bother with the United States or Canada? Aren't they blanketed with religious broadcasts and overpopulated with churches to the point of competition?

Perhaps we should take a new look at North America. A Gallup poll indicated that 57 million evangelical Christians live in the United States, but sheer numbers have not brought the nation to God.

A *Wall Street Journal* editorial makes the point uncomfortably clear: "Where are all those Christians? How can one explain the presence of so many Christians in the light of an epidemic of crime, drug addiction, divorce, pornography, teenage pregnancies and abortions? Are not Christians supposed to be the 'salt of the earth' and 'the light of their world'?"[10]

The re-evangelization of Canada is no less critical. Ninety percent of Canadians claimed in the 1980s to be Christians, yet only one in three attended church on Sunday. One Canadian researcher put the evangelical population at no more than one in ten.[11]

Yet, however compelling these spiritual needs at home and our sacred calling to address them, an even larger challenge faces us: the staggering number of unreached peoples forgotten or ignored by the church. Some *two billion* people are total strangers to the love of God in Christ Jesus, and their numbers are growing.

Were someone to challenge me as to why the Alliance must multiply churches, add missionaries and intensify giving, I must reply that there are two billion reasons why.

Missions is what we are called to do. Missions is what we do best. Missions is what we are. Missions is what we must excel in doing in the twenty-first century.

Let our churches exist for this; let our ministers preach for this; let our seminaries and colleges be on fire for this one theme; let our laborers toil for this; let our businessmen carry on their business for this; let our consecrated women sacrifice for this; let our homes be furnished and our wardrobes be purchased with reference to this; and let a whole army of true hearts prove to the world around and the heavens above that they understand the meaning of the cross of Calvary, the cry of dying souls, and the glory of the coming Kingdom.

— Albert B. Simpson

APPENDICES

ACKNOWLEDGEMENTS

A BOOK EMBRACING forty-five nations and a hundred-plus years of missionary service requires cooperation from many sides. Moreover, as an official overview of overseas work by The Christian and Missionary Alliance, such a book must be subjected to close scrutiny by many eyes because it becomes a basic reference source on which writers, speakers, students and others will depend.

It is therefore fitting to recognize individuals who have had a part in this comprehensive and attractive worldbook of Alliance missions. Not only have many of them offered their help freely and gladly, the listing of their names—albeit incomplete—indicates how seriously has been the attempt to insure accuracy of information.

In addition to submitting the material to two different review committees, an attempt was made to submit the material to at least one missionary and, if possible, a local church leader of each country profiled in the book.

The Christian and Missionary Alliance owes a singular debt of gratitude to Robert L. Niklaus for his work on this book. On him fell the responsibility of researching, writing, verifying and guiding the material through the publication process. Oftentimes he had to put aside this project to carry out other writing assignments smaller in size but more immediate in nature.

He brought to this publication milestone of Alliance missions not only the technical skills of writer and editor, the academic background of a graduate degree in journalism, but also fifteen years of experience as a missionary in Africa and over ten years as a columnist for *Evangelical Missions Quarterly.*

Mr. Niklaus's coauthoring *All For Jesus,* an official history of

the Alliance in North America, provided valuable insights of the interlocking development of the Alliance at home and overseas. He presently serves the denomination as assistant to the president for publications.

Anne Stebbins Moore, born in Viet Nam to missionary parents and she herself a missionary to Indonesia, designed the book cover and page layouts. In addition, she prepared the maps locating Alliance work in each of the countries featured.

The striking collection of pictures that illuminate and expand on the text represent her final selection from many hundreds of slides and prints drawn from all parts of the world. Only another graphic designer can appreciate the enormous amount of time necessary to assemble such a significant collection of illustrations.

Anita M. Bailey, retiring after thirty-four distinguished years on the editorial staff of *Alliance Life,* devoted another two years, from 1981 to 1983, to update information published in the *Missionary Atlas,* predecessor to the present volume. When Mr. Niklaus took up the study of each country in this worldbook, the first material he consulted was that of Miss Bailey.

The list of individuals who reviewed *To All Peoples* in manuscript form literally spans the globe. The permanent in-house editorial committee was composed of: David L. Rambo, David H. Moore, Anne S. Moore, James A. Davey, Arni Shareski. G. Linwood Barney, for many years a professor and administrator in Alliance Theological Seminary, was also a member of this permanent committee.

Louis L. King, who provided the original inspiration and support for this project when he was C&MA president, and

Jewel Hall, secretary to several vice presidents, Division of Overseas Ministries, worked with the permanent review committee from beginning to end.

Toni Sortor, free-lance copy editor, subjected all the material to close scrutiny. She also did the tedious but necessary work of compiling the index and bibliography.

Missionaries and national church leaders who critiqued the sections pertaining to their countries were:

AFRICA—David L. Kennedy, regional director; Tite Tienou, faculty member of Alliance Theological Seminary; David R. Shady, Burkina Faso; David W. Arnold, Cote d'Ivoire; R. E. Cook, Sr., Gabon; Arlene Miller, Paul Ellenberger, Guinea; Robert Fetherlin, Mali; David P. Harvey, Nigeria; Paul Keidel, Joseph Nicholson, Dean F. Kroh, Zaire.

ASIA MAINLAND—Robert W. Reed, regional director; Peter N. Nanfelt, regional director (Korea); Edgar H. Lewellen, India; Clement R. Dreger, Korea; Wayne Persons, Randolph R. Brock, Thailand; James Bollback, Le Hoang Phu, Countries under Communism.

LATIN AMERICA—David K. Volstad, regional director; Vernon Caston, Craig Bundy, Jack Shannon, Argentina; James W. Hemminger, David P. Jones, Brazil; Thomas J. Sawyer, Costa Rica; Kenn W. Opperman, Dominican Republic; John and Mary Bucher, Dorothy Bucher, Barbara Volstad, Chile; Laurence Cardoza, Arlene Westmeier, Colombia; Bruce A. Jackson, Ecuador; William A. Paul, Guatemala; Ramon Esparza, Mexico; Richard J. Abrams, Peru; Johnny Li, Surinam; Herbert L. Garland, Venezuela.

MIDDLE EAST/EUROPE—Robert W. Reed, regional director; G. Louis Zeigler, Israel; Yousef Hashweh, Andrew R. Kerr, Ray Whitman, Arab Lands; Donald I. Dirks, France; Richard J. Schaefer, Germany; John A. Harvey, Great Britain; Fred Kowalchuk, Spain; Frank Ferrell, Harold Shelly, Europe.

PACIFIC ISLANDS—Peter N. Nanfelt, regional director; Andrew B. Pigott, China (Taiwan); Charles W. Fowler, Philip Teng, Clifford Westergren, Hong Kong; Marion Doble, John and Helen Ellenberger, Irian Jaya; Vonnie Morscheck, Yakob Tomatala, Indonesia; Rogelio D. Dubrico, David L. Rambo, Jacob and Louis Bouw, Philippines; Jack Davidson, Japan.

Keyboard operators who prepared the computer-stored material for ascii files compatible with typesetting equipment were: Cindy Jennings and Dinita Feather. In addition to keyboarding, Teri Burgo also efficiently and cheerfully pulled together all the final front and back matter and seemingly endless details necessary in this type of publication.

To all of the above-mentioned individuals, almost seventy in number—and probably others whose names have been inadvertently overlooked—I express not only my appreciation but that of the entire Alliance family in North America and overseas for this remarkable publication of which we can all be proud.

David L. Rambo, President

PHOTO CREDITS

Thomas H. White: pages vii, 2, 14, 15, 16, 36, 37, 44, 45, 46, 47, 48, 52, 57, 58, 59, 62, 76, 78, 79, 80, 81, 82, 83, 84, 110, 111, 112, 132, 133, 134, 135 (top), 146, 147, 148, 149, 150, 159 (below), 171, 172 (top), 174, 188, 189, 190, 191, 192, 200, 216, 217, 218, 219, 220, 224, 225, 226, 228, 229, 230, 232, 233, 235, 236, 237, 238, 239, 243, 258, 276, 277, 278, 279, 280, 284, 285, 286, 287, 288, 289, 290, 291, 292, 332, 333, 334, 335, 336, 337, 338, 342, 343, 345, 346, 347, 349, 350, 351, 352, 353, 354, 355, 356, 357, 358, 362, 363, 365 (left), 375.

David C. Ritchie: pages ii, iii, viii, 28, 29, 30, 31, 32, 56, 60, 94, 95, 96, 97, 98, 99, 100, 101, 102, 120, 154, 155, 156, 157, 158, 159 (top), 160, 173, 296, 297, 300, 301, 302, 303, 306 (below), 307, 309, 310, 314, 315, 317, 318, 319, 320, 321, 322, 323, 324, 325, 326, 327, 328, 366 (below), 367, 368, 369, 370, 371, 373 (below).

Marty Allen: pages 254, 255, 256, 365 (right).
Joe Arthur: page 348.
Nathan Bailey: pages 89, 106, 107, 108, 109, 117, 299, 304, 305, 306 (top), 316, 344.
Bill Carlson: page 115.
Gordon Chapman: page 298 (center, below).
Paul Collord: pages 248, 249, 253 (center).
Helen Evans: page 298 (top).
Gene Hall: page 113.
Brad Hess: page 378.
Dean Kroh: pages 20, 21.
Anne Moore: pages 38 (lower), 396.
Jack W. Morin: pages 363, 373 (top).
Walter Neale: page v.
Randy Newburn: page 172 (below).
Robert L. Niklaus: pages 251, 253, (left, right), 364.
William A. Paul: page 178.
Tim Ratzloff: page 366 (top).
Harold Shelly: page 245, 247.
Roy G. Solvig: page 40.
Tom Stebbins: page 116.
Debbie Storlie: pages 140, 141, 170 (left), 184 (left), 198.
Canadian Theological Seminary: page 364 (left).
Clarence Wulf: pages 11, 22, 23, 24, 38 (top), 39, 172 (top), 308.
David K. Volstad: pages 135 (below), 136, 142, 162, 166, 170 (right), 179, 180, 184 (right).

Commercial: Courtesy Weldon Trannies (Sydney, Australia) page 360.
Courtesy "La Goelette" (Paris, France) page 242.

NOTES

INTRODUCTION: Why Take on the World?

1. Albert B. Simpson, "Editorial," *The Christian Alliance* (August 7, 1891): 93,94.
2. Louis L. King, "He Has It All Together," *Open Line* (May-June, 1982): 6.
3. Alfred C. Snead, *Missionary Atlas* (Harrisburg: Christian Publications, Inc., 1936), 5.
4. Albert B. Simpson, *The Challenge of Missions* (New York: The Christian Alliance Publishing Co., 1926), 57,58.
5. Ibid., 59.

AFRICA: A Christian Continent?

1. Adrian Hastings, *African Christianity* (New York: Seabury Press, 1976), 2.
2. David B. Barrett, ed., *World Christian Encyclopedia* (New York: Oxford University Press, 1982), 151.
3. David B. Barrett, "Annual Statistical Table on Global Mission: 1985," *International Bulletin of Missionary Research* (January, 1985): 31.
4. Tokumbah Adeyemo, "An African Leader Looks at the Churches' Crises," *Evangelical Missions Quarterly* (July, 1978): 151.
5. Samuel Wilson, *Mission Handbook* (Monrovia, Calif.: Missions Advanced Research and Communications Center, 12 ed., 1979), 35.
6. John S. Mbiti, "Encounter of Christian Faith and African Religion," *Christian Century* (August 27, 1980): 818.
7. Charles R. Taber, ed., *The Church in Africa 1977* (Pasadena, Calif.: William Carey Library, 1977), 146.
8. Peter Falk, *The Growth of the Church in Africa* (Grand Rapids: Zondervan Publishing House, 1979), 75.
9. Stephen Neill, *Christian Missions* (Grand Rapids: Wm. B. Eerdmans Publishing Company, 1964), 138.
10. Ibid., 199.
11. Ibid.
12. Ibid., 200.
13. Taber, *The Church in Africa*, 149.
14. Hastings, *African Christianity*, 14.
15. Falk, *The Growth of the Church in Africa*, 72, 73.
16. Ruth A. Tucker, *From Jerusalem to Irian Jaya* (Grand Rapids: Zondervan Publishing House, 1983), 148.
17. Taber, *The Church in Africa*, 150.
18. Ibid., 151.
19. Ibid., 152.
20. Falk, *The Growth of the Church in Africa*, 439.
21. Ibid., 449.
22. Taber, *The Church in Africa*, 155.
23. David B. Barrett, *Schism and Renewal in Africa* (Nairobi, Kenya: Oxford University Press, 1968), xv.
24. Ibid., 3, 4.
25. Ibid., 278.
26. Tite Tienou, "Christians in Africa." N.p., n.d., 12.

ASIA MAINLAND: Still the Greatest Challenge

1. Donald E. Hoke, ed., *The Church in Asia* (Chicago: Moody Press, 1975), p. 19.
2. Ibid., p. 17.
3. Ibid., p. 20.
4. "Work to Begin on $6.7 Million Press," *Missionary News Service* (June 1, 1986): p. 1.
5. David B. Barrett, "Annual Statistical Table on Global Missions: 1987," *International Bulletin of Missionary Research* (January, 1987): p. 24.
6. David B. Barrett, ed., *World Christian Encyclopedia* (New York: Oxford University Press, 1982), p. 441.
7. "Asian Leader Sees Vital Link," *Missionary News Service* (September 15, 1985): p. 2.
8. Barrett, *World Christian Encyclopedia,* p. 441.
9. "Christian Gains Offset by Population Gains," *Missionary News Service* (February 15, 1986): p. 1.
10. Barrett, *World Christian Encyclopedia,* pp. 370, 664, 447, 430.
11. Gordon H. Chapman, "Christianity Comes to Asia," in *The Church in Asia,* Donald E. Hoke, ed. (Chicago: Moody Press, 1975), p. 181.

12. Acts 2:5–11.
13. Gordon H. Chapman, "Christianity Comes to Asia," in *The Church in Asia,* Donald E.Hoke, ed. (Chicago: Moody Press, 1975), p. 182.
14. Ibid.
15. Ibid., p. 185.
16. Ibid.
17. Ibid., p. 188.
18. Ibid., p. 50.
19. Kenneth Scott Latourette, *A History of the Expansion of Christianity,* vol. 1, *The First Five Centuries* (Grand Rapids: Zondervan Publishing House, 1974), p. 108.
20. Hoke, *The Church in Asia,* p. 190.
21. Ibid., p. 194.
22. Kenneth Scott Latourette, *A History of the Expansion of Christianity,* vol. 2, *The Thousand Years of Uncertainty* (Grand Rapids: Zondervan Publishing House, 1974), p. 264.
23. Hoke, *The Church in Asia,* p. 183.
24. John B. Noss, *Man's Religions,* sixth edition (New York: Macmillan Publishing Co., Inc., 1980), p. 73.
25. Gordon H. Chapman, "Important Religions of Asia," in *The Church in Asia,* Donald F. Hoke, ed. (Chicago: Moody Press, 1975), p. 668.
26. Ibid., p. 672.
27. Latourette, *The Thousand Years of Uncertainty,* p. 2.
28. Hoke, *The Church in Asia,* p. 196.
29. Ibid., pp. 196, 197.
30. Ibid., p. 199.
31. Ibid., p. 200.
32. Kenneth Scott Latourette, *A History of the Expansion of Christianity,* vol. 3, *Three Centuries of Advance* (Grand Rapids: Zondervan Publishing House, 1974), p. 253.
33. Hoke, *The Church in Asia,* p. 53.
34. Latourette, *Three Centuries of Advance,* p. 358.
35. Ibid., p. 273.
36. Ibid., p. 298.
37. Kenneth Scott Latourette, *A History of the Expansion of Christianity,* vol. 6, *The Great Century* (Grand Rapids: Zondervan Publishing House, 1974), p. 435.
38. Ibid., p. 436.
39. Ibid., p. 438.
40. Hoke, *The Church in Asia,* p. 50.
41. Ibid., p. 51.
42. Sharon E. Mumper, "Emerging Missions: A Vast New Force," *Evangelical Missions Quarterly* (April, 1986): p. 213.
43. Hoke, *The Church in Asia,* p. 23.
44. Mumper, "Emerging Missions," p. 214.
45. Sharon E. Mumper, "Asia Perspective," *Pulse* (September 19, 1986): p. 8.
46. Hoke, *The Church in Asia,* p. 26.

INDIA: A Conclusion Ordered and Orderly

1. Louis L. King, "A Presentation of the Indigenous Church Policy of The Christian and Missionary Alliance" (Unpublished policy paper, Office of the President, International Headquarters, Colorado Springs, Colo., August 29, 1960): p. 13.
2. Theodore Williams, "India, a Seething Subcontinent," in *The Church in Asia,* Donald E. Hoke, ed. (Chicago: Moody Press, 1975), p. 218.
3. Samuel Wilson and John Siewert, eds., *Mission Handbook,* Thirteenth Edition (Monrovia, California: Missions Advanced Research and Communication Center, 1986), p. 22.
4. Wilson, *Mission Handbook,* p. 588.
5. Hoke, *The Church in Asia,* p. 218.
6. Ibid., p. 221.
7. Ibid.
8. Ibid., p. 228.
9. John Caldwell Thiessen, *A Survey of World Missions* (Chicago: Moody Press, 1970), p. 25.
10. "Report Concerning Mukti Mission" (Unpublished annual field report, c. 1922).

SOUTH KOREA: A Boost Toward Maturity

1. Samuel Hugh Moffett, "Korea," in *The Church in Asia,* Donald E. Hoke, ed. (Chicago: Moody Press, 1975), p. 369.
2. Samuel Wilson and John Siewert, eds., *Mission Handbook,* Thirteenth Edition (Monrovia, California: Missions Advanced Research and Communications Center, 1986), p. 22.
3. Hoke, *The Church in Asia,* p. 370.
4. Ibid., p. 374.
5. Ibid., p. 375.
6. John Caldwell Thiessen, *A Survey of World Missions* (Chicago: Moody Press, 1961), p. 118.
7. Ibid.
8. Hoke, *The Church in Asia,* p. 379.
9. "Holiness Seminary," unpublished report (Seoul, Korea: Jesus Korea Alliance Holiness Church): p. 6.
10. Clement R. Dreger, "Evaluation Report," unpublished report (Colorado Springs, Colo.: Division of Overseas Ministries, 1981): p. 3.

THAILAND: Hairline Cracks in the Wall

1. William D. Carlsen, "Do Not Put Away All Your Decorations," *The Alliance Witness* (January 2, 1985): p. 17.
2. David B. Barrett, ed., *World Christian Encyclopedia* (New York: Oxford University Press, 1982), p. 664.
3. John Caldwell Thiessen, *A Survey of World Missions* (Chicago: Moody Press, 1961), p. 625.
4. Ibid., p. 636.
5. Donald E. Hoke, ed., *The Church in Asia* (Chicago: Moody Press, 1975), p. 33.
6. Norman Ford, Timothy Jeng, "Bangkok: Thailand's Strategic City," *The Alliance Witness* (March 17, 1982): p. 19.
7. Ibid.

8. Leon B. Gold, "Thailand," in *The Church in Asia,* Donald E. Hoke, ed. (Chicago: Moody Press, 1975), p. 637.
9. Ibid., p. 625.
10. Ibid., p. 626.
11. Elmer J. Sahlberg, "Overcrowded Thailand Needs More Asians?" *The Alliance Witness* (September 14, 1983): p. 17.
12. Harvey Boese, "Missions Comes Full Circle," *The Alliance Witness* (May 11, 1983): p. 20.

CHURCHES UNDER COMMUNISM

1. Phu Hoang Le, *A Short History of The Evangelical Church of Viet Nam,* vol. 2 (unpublished doctoral dissertation), pp. 480–481.
2. Samuel Wilson and John Siewert, eds., *Mission Handbook,* Thirteenth Edition (Monrovia, California: Missions Advanced Research and Communications Center, 1986), p. 23.
3. Arthur F. Glasser, "China," in *The Church in Asia,* Donald E. Hoke, ed. (Chicago: Moody Press, 1975), p. 171.
4. Ibid., p. 172.
5. Ibid., p. 174.
6. Ibid., p. 172.
7. Tom Goosmann, Edward E. Plowman, "Visitors See Signs of Strong Evangelical Faith in China," *China and the Church Today* (February, 1986): p. 6.
8. Ibid.
9. Sharon E. Mumper, "Global Report," *Evangelical Missions Quarterly* (July, 1986): p. 323.
10. Robert L. Niklaus, "Global Report," *Evangelical Missions Quarterly* (April, 1985): p. 172.
11. Sharon E. Mumper, "Global Report," *Evangelical Missions Quarterly* (January, 1986): p. 84.
12. "Church Structures in China Today," *China and the Church Today* (October, 1986): p. 9.
13. Louis L. King, ed., *Missionary Atlas* (Harrisburg, Penna.: Christian Publications, Inc., 1964), p. 135.
14. James A. Bollback, "China Trip Journal Notes," unpublished notes (June, 1985), p. 10.
15. Mumper, "Global Report" (July, 1986): p. 323.
16. Niklaus, "Global Report" (April, 1985): p. 172.
17. Ibid.
18. Edward A. Cline and Billy Brag, "The Khmer Republic," in *The Church in Asia,* Donald E. Hoke, ed. (Chicago, 1975), p. 366.
19. David P. Chandler, *A History of Cambodia* (Boulder, Colorado: Westview Press, 1983), p. 192.
20. Hoke, *The Church in Asia,* p. 358.
21. Unpublished confidential report.
22. Reg Reimer, "Summary Report on Religious Freedom," unpublished report (World Relief of Canada, May 15, 1986), p. 16.
23. Nguyen Ngoc Huy and Stephen B. Young, *Understanding Vietnam* (Bussum, Netherlands: The DPC Information Service, 1982), p. 237.
24. Reimer, "Summary Report," appendix 4.

LATIN AMERICA: Primacy of Politics

1. Kenneth Scott Latourette, *Christianity in a Revolutionary Age,* vol. 3, *The Nineteenth Century Outside Europe* (Grand Rapids: Zondervan Publishing House, 1969), 295.
2. William R. Read, Victor M. Monterroso, Harmon A. Johnson, *Latin American Church Growth* (Grand Rapids: William B. Eerdmans Publishing Co., 1969), 35.
3. Ibid.
4. German Arciniegas, *Latin America: A Cultural History* (New York: Alfred A. Knopf, 1967), 147.
5. Victor Alba, *The Latin Americans* (New York: Frederick A. Praeger, 1969), 52.
6. Ibid., 77.
7. Ibid.
8. Simon Collier, *From Cortez to Castro* (New York: Macmillan Publishing Co. Inc., 1974), 164.
9. Alba, *The Latin Americans,* 79.
10. Ibid., 80.
11. Collier, *From Cortez to Castro,* 190.
12. Ibid.
13. Ibid., 189.
14. Read, *Latin American Church Growth,* 36.
15. Ibid., 37.
16. Ibid.
17. Ibid., 38.
18. Ibid.
19. Ibid., 39.
20. Ibid.
21. Latourette, *The Nineteenth Century Outside Europe,* 302.
22. Read, *Latin American Church Growth,* 40.
23. Ibid.
24. Kenneth Scott Latourette, *A History of the Expansion of Christianity,* vol. 7, *Advance Through Storm* (Grand Rapids: Zondervan Publishing House, 1970), 172.
25. Read, *Latin American Church Growth,* 36.
26. Ibid., 43.
27. Ibid., 45.
28. Ibid., 46.
29. Ibid., 47.
30. Samuel Wilson, ed., *Mission Handbook* (Monrovia, Calif.: Missions Advanced Research and Communication Center, 1980), 36.
31. Daniel H. Levine, ed., *Churches and Politics in Latin America* (Beverly Hills, Calif.: Sage Publications, 1980), 16.
32. Kenneth Scott Latourette, *Christianity in a Revolutionary Age,* vol. 5, *The Twentieth Century Outside Europe* (Grand Rapids: Zondervan Publishing House, 1969), 162.
33. Dayton Roberts, "Never the Same Again," *Latin American Evangelist* (April–June, 1987): 11.
34. Ibid.

35. Samuel Escobar, "Future Trends," *Latin American Evangelist* (April–June, 1987): 8
36. Marlise Simons, "Latin America's New Gospel," *The New York Times Magazine* (November 7, 1982): 47.

ARGENTINA: The Lean Years First

1. Thomas H. White, "And Now What?" *The Alliance Witness* (July 20, 1983): 6.
2. Anita M. Bailey, "Argentina" (Colorado Springs, Colo.: C&MA Division of Overseas Ministries, 1982): 7.
3. White, "And Now What?" 9.
4. Jack Shannon, "Annual Report/1981" (Colorado Springs, Colo.: C&MA Division of Overseas Ministries): 1.
5. Myrna McCombs, "Canadians Challenged to Go the 'Second Mile,'" *The Alliance Witness* (December 4, 1985): 20.
6. Vernon Caston, "Annual Report/1979" (Colorado Springs, Colo.: C&MA Division of Overseas Ministries): 3.
7. Shannon, "Annual Report/1981," 1.
8. George S. Constance, "The Church Is Alive," *The Alliance Witness* (December 4, 1968): 14.
9. "Paraguay," *Background Notes* (Washington: United States Department of State, 1982): 2.

BRAZIL: Spiritism—The Majority Choice

1. Warren Hoge, "Macumba," *The New York Times Magazine* (August 21, 1983): 30.
2. Ibid., 33.
3. Reinhard Fischbach, "Spiritism in Brazil," unpublished study #746 (Nyack, N.Y.: Alliance Theological Seminary, 1967): 4.
4. Anita M. Bailey, "Brazil" (Colorado Springs, Colo.: C&MA Division of Overseas Ministries, 1982): 7.
5. Arnold Cook, chairman, "Brazil Study Team Report" (Colorado Springs, Colo.: C&MA Division of Overseas Ministries, 1983): 10.
6. Ibid., 11.
7. David K. Volstad, "Regional Report/1984" (Colorado Springs, Colo.: C&MA Division of Overseas Ministries): 2.
8. James G. Medin, "Narrative Report/1984" (Colorado Springs, Colo.: C&MA Division of Overseas Ministries): 1.

CHILE: Supernatural Among the Surprises

1. Anita M. Bailey, "Chile" (Colorado Springs, Colo.: C&MA Division of Overseas Ministries, 1980): 2.
2. Ibid., 9.
3. Ibid., 15.
4. David K. Volstad, "Regional Report/1986" (Nyack, N.Y.: C&MA Division of Overseas Ministries): 21.
5. Stephen L. Bishop, "The History of The Christian and Missionary Alliance in Chile" (Nyack, N.Y.: Alliance Theological Seminary, 1985): 13, 14.

COLOMBIA: Evil Worked for Good

1. Anita M. Bailey, "Colombia" (Colorado Springs, Colo.: C&MA Division of Overseas Ministries, 1982): 8.
2. William R. Read, Victor M. Monterroso, Harmon A. Johnson, *Latin American Church Growth* (Grand Rapids: William B. Eerdmans Publishing Co., 1969), 124.
3. Karl Wilhelm Westmeier, "Evangelical Churches in the Colombian State" (Nyack N.Y.: Alliance Theological Seminary, 1978): 4, 5.
4. Ibid., chapters 12, 13.
5. Read, *Latin American Church Growth*, 125.
6. Ibid.
7. Bailey, "Colombia," 16.
8. David J. Peters, "Chairman's Report/1982" (Colorado Springs, Colo.: C&MA Division of Overseas Ministries): 1.

COSTA RICA: Follow the Spirit's Working

1. John Caldwell Thiessen, *A Survey of World Missions* (Chicago: Moody Press, 1970), 376.
2. Anita M. Bailey, "Costa Rica" (Colorado Springs, Colo.: C&MA Division of Overseas Ministries, 1982): 3.
3. William R. Read, Victor M. Monterroso, Harmon A. Johnson, *Latin American Church Growth* (Grand Rapids: William B. Eerdmans Publishing Co., 1969), 143.

DOMINICAN REPUBLIC: Bypassed but not Abandoned

1. Guiseppe Sormani, chief editor, *The Caribbean Region and Central America, The World and Its Peoples* (New York: Greystone Press, 1965), 59, 60.
2. Anita M. Bailey, "Dominican Republic" (Colorado Springs, Colo.: C&MA Division of Overseas Ministries, 1982): 2.
3. William R. Read, Victor M. Monterroso, Harmon A. Johnson, *Latin American Church Growth* (Grand Rapids: William B. Eerdmans Publishing Co., 1969), 440.

ECUADOR: Church on the Grow

1. William R. Read, Victor M. Monterroso, Harmon A. Johnson, *Latin American Church Growth* (Grand Rapids: William B. Eerdmans Publishing Co., 1969), 118.
2. John Caldwell Thiessen, *A Survey of World Missions* (Chicago: Moody Press, 1970), 391.
3. Anita M. Bailey, "Ecuador" (Colorado Springs, Colo.: C&MA Division of Overseas Ministries, 1982): 6.
4. Thiessen, *A Survey of World Missions*, 392.
5. Mark Searing, "H. G. Crisman: Forever a Missionary" (Nyack, N.Y.: Alliance Theological Seminary, 1977): 2.

6. Nancy Ernst and Ken Schultz, "Church Growth Analysis," pamphlet #1315 (Nyack, N.Y.: Alliance Theological Seminary, 1977), 3.
7. Read, *Latin American Church Growth*, 119.
8. Michael C. Otto, "Protestant Missions in Ecuador" (Nyack, N.Y.: Alliance Theological Seminary, 1985): 10.
9. David K. Volstad, "Ecuador: Fifteen-Year Report" (Colorado Springs, Colo.: C&MA Division of Overseas Ministries, 1972): 17.
10. Anita M. Bailey, "Alliance Academy" (Colorado Springs, Colo.: C&MA Division of Overseas Ministries, 1982): 1.
11. "The Gospel Work in Ecuador" (Colorado Springs, Colo.: C&MA Division of Overseas Ministries, n.d.): 1.

GUATEMALA: The Door Music Opened

1. Anita M. Bailey, "Guatemala" (Colorado Springs, Colo.: C&MA Division of Overseas Ministries, 1982): 2.
2. John Caldwell Thiessen, *A Survey of World Missions* (Chicago: Moody Press, 1970), 365.
3. Ibid., 364.
4. Patricia Reilly, "Guatemala: Past, Present, and Future" (Nyack, N.Y.: Alliance Theological Seminary, 1985): 7.
5. "Guatemala" (Colorado Springs, Colo.: C&MA Division of Overseas Ministries, 1983): 1.
6. David K. Volstad, "Regional Report/1985" (Colorado Springs, Colo.: C&MA Division of Overseas Ministries): 22.

MEXICO: Too Close to Home?

1. "Mexico," *Background Notes* (Washington: United States Department of State, 1983): 2.
2. John Caldwell Thiessen, *A Survey of World Missions* (Chicago: Moody Press, 1970), 357.
3. Kay Esparza, "Mexico" (Colorado Springs, Colo.: C&MA Division of Overseas Ministries, 1984): 1.
4. William A. Read, Victor M. Monterroso, Harmon A. Johnson, *Latin American Church Growth* (Grand Rapids: William B. Eerdmans Publishing Co., 1969), 164.
5. Anita M. Bailey, "United Mexican States" (Colorado Springs, Colo.: C&MA Division of Overseas Ministries, 1982): 3.
6. Robert L. Niklaus, "Global Report," *Evangelical Missions Quarterly* (April, 1985): 173.

PERU: A City Set Upon a Hill

1. John Caldwell Thiessen, *A Survey of World Missions* (Chicago: Moody Press, 1970), 395.
2. David L. Rambo, "Reaching the Professional and Middle Classes in Lima," *Latin American Pulse* (January, 1980): 2.
3. Ibid., 2, 3.
4. Anita M. Bailey, "Peru" (Colorado Springs, Colo.: C&MA Division of Overseas Ministries, 1981): 10.

5. Miguel Angel Palomino, *Lima al Encuentro con Dios* (Lima, Peru: Lince C&MA Church, 1983), 10.
6. Rambo, "Reaching the Professional and Middle Classes in Lima," 4.
7. David K. Volstad, "Bolivia" (Colorado Springs, Colo.: C&MA Division of Overseas Ministries, 1983): 1.
8. Thiessen, *A Survey of World Missions*, 396.
9. Thomas Froehlich, "An Overview of the Birth and Growth of The Christian and Missionary Alliance Church," pamphlet #1528 (Nyack, N.Y.: Alliance Theological Seminary, n.d.): 6.

SURINAM: To the Chinese First

1. William R. Read, Victor M. Monterroso, Harmon A. Johnson, *Latin American Church Growth* (Grand Rapids: William B. Eerdmans Publishing Co., 1969), 36.
2. Ibid., 41.

VENEZUELA: The Second Time Took

1. William R. Read, Victor M. Monterroso, Harmon A. Johnson, *Latin American Church Growth* (Grand Rapids: William B. Eerdmans Publishing Co., 1969), 131.
2. Anita M. Bailey, "Venezuela" (Colorado Springs, Colo.: C&MA Division of Overseas Ministries, 1981): 3.
3. Gerard A. Bailly, "Porto Rico and Spanish Evangelization," *The Alliance Witness* (February 16, 1901): 85, 86.
4. "Venezuela," *Background Notes* (Washington: United States Department of State, 1984): 6.

MIDDLE EAST/EUROPE: The Macedonian Call—Again

1. Eusebius Pamphilus, *Ecclesiastical History* (Grand Rapids: Baker Book House, 1974), p. 82.
2. Stephen Neill, *A History of Christian Missions* (Grand Rapids: Wm. B. Eerdmans Publishing Company, 1965), p. 21.
3. J. Herbert Kane, *A Global View of Christian Missions* (Grand Rapids: Baker Book House, 1971), p. 8.
4. Ibid.
5. Will Durant, *Caesar and Christ* (New York: Simon and Schuster, 1944), p. 662.
6. Neill, *A History of Christian Missions*, pp. 23, 24.
7. David B. Barrett, *World Christian Encyclopedia* (New York: Oxford University Press, 1982), p. 3.
8. Kenneth Scott Latourette, *A History of the Expansion of Christianity*, v. 1, *The First Five Centuries* (Grand Rapids: Zondervan Publishing House, 1974), p. 85.
9. J. Herbert Kane, *A Concise History of the Christian World Mission* (Grand Rapids: Baker Book House, 1985), p. 17.
10. Neill, *A History of Christian Missions*, p. 44.

11. John Caldwell Thiessen, *A Survey of World Missions* (Chicago: Moody Press,1970), p. 9.
12. Latourette, *The First Five Centuries*, pp. 128, 129.
13. Ibid., p. 170.
14. Neill, *A History of Christian Missions*, p. 46.
15. Thiessen, *A Survey of World Missions*, p. 11.
16. Neill, *A History of Christian Missions*, p. 32.
17. Adolf Harnack, *The Mission and Expansion of the Christian World Since 1938* (New York: Harper and Row, 1962), p. 69.
18. Latourette, *The First Five Centuries*, p. 369.
19. Kenneth Scott Latourette, *A History of the Expansion of Christianity*, v. 2, *The Thousand Years of Uncertainty* (Grand Rapids: Zondervan Publishing House, 1974), pp. 8, 9.
20. Thiessen, *A Survey of World Missions*, p. 12.
21. Kane, *A Global View of Christian Missions*, p. 37.
22. Neill, *A History of Christian Missions*, p. 89.
23. Ibid., p. 113.
24. Ibid., p. 115.
25. Norman A. Horner, "The Future of Christian Missions in Lebanon," *International Bulletin of Missionary Research* (October, 1984): p. 147.
26. Latourette, *The Thousand Years of Uncertainty*, p. 17.
27. Kane, *A Concise History of the Christian World Mission*, p. 57.
28. Ibid., p. 74.
29. Ibid., p. 73.
30. Ibid., p. 77.
31. Ibid., p. 79.
32. Ibid.
33. Thiessen, *A Survey of World Missions*, p. 21.
34. Kane, *A Concise History of the Christian World Mission*, p. 79.
35. Neill, *A History of Christian Missions*, p. 247.
36. Kane, *A Concise History of the Christian World Mission*, p. 85.
37. Neill, *A History of Christian Missions*, p. 261.
38. Ibid., p. 252.
39. Kane, *A Concise History of the Christian World Mission*, p. 100.
40. Neill, *A History of Christian Missions*, p. 252.
41. Ralph D. Winter and R. Pierce Beaver, *The Warp and Woof* (South Pasadena, Calif.: William Carey Library, 1970), p. 60.
42. Kane, *A Concise History of the Christian World Mission*, p. 85.
43. Neill, *A History of Christian Missions*, p. 256.
44. R. Pierce Beaver, *All Loves Excelling* (Grand Rapids: William B. Eerdmans Publishing Company, 1968), p. 66.
45. Ibid., p. 67.
46. Kenneth Scott Latourette, *A History of the Expansion of Christianity*, v. 4, *The Great Century* (Grand Rapids: Zondervan Publishing House, 1974), p. 26.
47. Ibid.
48. Neill, *A History of Christian Missions*, p. 452.
49. Samuel Wilson, John Siewert, eds., *Mission Handbook*, Thirteenth Edition (Monrovia, Calif.: 1986), p. 18.
50. Robert P. Evans, "The Missionary Situation in Europe," *Christianity Today* (July 20, 1962): p. 15.
51. Ibid.
52. Wilson, *Mission Handbook*, p. 26.
53. Lesslie Newbigin, *The Other Side of 1984* (Geneva: World Council of Churches, 1983), p. 23.
54. Barrett, *World Christian Encyclopedia*, p. 7.
55. Ibid., p. 9.
56. Wilson, *Mission Handbook*, p. 26.
57. Ibid., p. 43.
58. Ibid., p. 57.

ISRAEL: Connecting the Incompatibles

1. Jakob Jocz, "Primitive Hebrew Christianity," *The Jewish People and Jesus Christ* (Grand Rapids: Baker Book House, 1979), pp. 146ff.
2. Bryon Spradlin, "Sapping the Strength of Witness in Israel," *Evangelical Missions Quarterly* (January 1985): p. 24.
3. Robert Niklaus, "Global Report," *Evangelical Missions Quarterly* (April 1978): p. 70.
4. J. Herbert Kane, *A Global View of Christian Missions* (Grand Rapids: Baker Book House, 1971), p. 302.
5. Spradlin, "Sapping the Strength of Witness in Israel," p. 28.
6. Ray G. Register, Jr., "Christian Witness in the State of Israel Today," *International Bulletin of Missionary Research* (January 1983): p. 16.
7. Ibid.
8. William F. Smalley, comp., *Alliance Missions in Palestine, Arab Lands, Israel*, unpublished collections (Colorado Springs, Colo.: Simpson Historical Library, 1971): p. 517.
9. Register, "Christian Witness in the State of Israel Today," p. 17.
10. Robert L. Niklaus, "Global Report," *Evangelical Missions Quarterly* (October 1978): p. 198.
11. Smalley, *Alliance Missions in Palestine, Arab Lands, Israel*, p. 520.
12. Niklaus, "Global Report," (April 1978): p. 74
13. Smalley, *Alliance Missions in Palestine, Arab Lands, Israel*, p. 9.
14. Ibid., p. 20.
15. Virginia L. Jacober, "As Quickly as Possible," *The Alliance Witness* (August 5, 1981): p. 17.

ARAB LANDS: Fortress Islam

1. Kenneth Cragg, *Christianity in World Perspective* (New York: Oxford University Press, 1968), p. 124.
2. Ibid.
3. Samuel M. Zwemer, *The Disintegration of Islam* (New York: Fleming H. Revell, 1916), p. 182.
4. Ibid., p. 185.
5. Kenneth Cragg, *The Call of the Minaret* (New York: Oxford University Press, 1956), p. 286.
6. Zwemer, *The Disintegration of Islam*, p. 190.
7. Cragg, *The Call of the Minaret*, p. 282.
8. Ibid., p. 276.

9. H. A. R. Gibb and J. H. Kramers, *Shorter Encyclopaedia of Islam* (London: Luzac & Company, 1961), p. 173.
10. William F. Smalley, *Alliance Missions in Palestine, Arab Lands, Israel*, unpublished collection (Colorado Springs, Colo. : A. B. Simpson Memorial Library, 1971), p. 51.
11. Ibid., p. 53.
12. Ibid., p. 64.
13. Donald O. Ward, "A New Church in Jordan," *The Alliance Witness* (May 16, 1931): p. 299.
14. S. Virginia Jacober, "Jamil Hashweh," *The Alliance Witness* (October 13, 1982): p.21.
15. William F. Smalley, "Guests of the Arabian Government," *The Alliance Weekly* (May 12, 1928): pp. 298, 299.
16. Smalley, *Alliance Missions in Palestine, Arab Lands, Israel*, p. 271.
17. Ibid., p. 354.
18. Ralph Freed, "Harvest Time in Jebaib," *The Alliance Weekly* (August 23, 1930): p. 551.
19. John Caldwell Thiessen, *A Survey of World Missions* (Chicago: Moody Press, 1970), p. 158.
20. Smalley, *Alliance Missions in Palestine, Arab Lands, Israel*, p. 350.
21. Norman A. Horner, "The Future of Christian Missions in Lebanon," *International Bulletin of Missionary Review* (October 1984): p. 148.
22. Sharon Mumper, "Lebanese Conflict Dashes Hope of All Middle East Christians," *Pulse* (Wheaton, Il.: Evangelical Missions Information Service, January 24, 1986): p. 2.
23. Harry Taylor, "The Only Happy Man in the Crowd," *The Alliance Witness* (January 30, 1985): p. 12.
24. Andrew Kerr, "Suddenly Made Refugees," *The Alliance Witness* (September 4, 1985): p. 18.
25. Robert Reed, "Narrative Report, 1987," unpublished (Colorado Springs, Colo. : Division of Overseas Ministries): p. 5.
26. "A Growing Witness in Syria," *The Alliance Witness* (April 9, 1986): p. 20.
27. Ibid.
28. "A Matter of Faith," *Pulse* (Wheaton, Il.: Evangelical Missions Information Service, January 23, 1987): pp. 7, 8.

EUROPE: The Mission Connection

1. J. Herbert Kane, *A Concise History of the Christian World Mission* (Grand Rapids: Baker Book House, 1985), p. 156.

France

2. Anita M. Bailey, "France" (Colorado Springs, Colo. : Division of Overseas Ministries, 1982): p. 7.
3. Gail Bennett, "French Protestant Leaders Reveal Churches' Needs," *Pulse* (Wheaton, Il.: Evangelical Missions Information Service, April 18, 1986): p. 2.
4. "Muslim Evangelism Planned for Europe," *Europe Report* (Wheaton, Il.: Greater Europe Mission, November-December, 1984): p. 1.
5. Bailey, "France," p. 5.
6. Samuel Wilson and John Siewert, eds., *Mission Handbook*, 13th ed. (Monrovia, Calif.: Missions Advanced Research and Communication Center, 1986), pp. 386, 525.
7. Christian LeFlaec, "A Springtime First in France," *The Alliance Witness* (November 6, 1985): p. 19.

Germany

8. John Caldwell Thiessen, *A Survey of World Missions* (Chicago: Moody Press,1970), p. 481.
9. Catherine Wulf, "A Critical Week in Erbach, West Germany," *The Alliance Witness* (September 15, 1982): p. 19.

Great Britain

10. Peter Brierly, ed., *United Kingdom Christian Handbook* (Kent, England: MARC Europe, 1987): p. 5.
11. Ibid., p. 6.
12. Ibid.
13. Ibid., p. 7.

Netherlands

14. Leendert Kolle, "New Life in an Ancient Land," *The Alliance Witness* (November 23, 1983): p. 16.
15. Anton Bol, "The Touch of God in Zoetermeer," *The Alliance Witness* (October 10, 1984): p. 19.
16. Kolle, "New Life in an Ancient Land," p. 17.

Spain

17. Fred Kowalchuk, "God-Given Growth in Spain," *The Alliance Witness* (November 6, 1985): p. 16.
18. *The Churches in Spain* (Geneva: World Council of Churches, 1984): p. 11.
19. Ibid., p. 13.
20. Thiessen, *A Survey of World Missions*, p. 467.
21. *The Churches in Spain*, p. 15.
22. Fred Kowalchuk, "Narrative Report" (Colorado Springs, Colo. : Division of Overseas Ministries, 1984): p. 3.

PACIFIC ISLANDS: Of Commerce, Creeds and Conflict

1. Ralph Tolliver, "Philippines," in *The Church in Asia*, Donald E. Hoke, ed. (Chicago: Moody Press, 1975), p. 541.
2. D. G. E. Hall, *A History of South-East Asia*, 2nd ed. (London: Macmillan and Company, Ltd., 1964), p. 20.
3. Ibid., p. 42.
4. Ibid., p. 69.
5. Ibid., p. 62.

6. Ibid., p. 200.
7. Frank Snow, "Indonesia," in *The Church in Asia*, Donald E. Hoke, ed. (Chicago: Moody Press, 1975), p. 281.
8. Ibid., p. 278.
9. Hall, *A History of South-East Asia*, p. 223.
10. Hoke, *The Church in Asia*, p. 283.
11. Hall, *A History of South-East Asia*, p. 225.
12. Ibid., p. 222.
13. Hoke, *The Church in Asia*, p. 284.
14. Hall, *A History of South-East Asia*, p. 226.
15. Hoke, *The Church in Asia*, p. 542.
16. Hall, *A History of South-East Asia*, p. 227.
17. Hoke, *The Church in Asia*, p. 542.
18. Hall, *A History of South-East Asia*, p. 672.
19. Kenneth Scott Latourette, *A History of the Expansion of Christianity*, vol. 5, *The Great Century* (Grand Rapids: Zondervan Publishing House, 1974), p. 267.
20. John Caldwell Thiessen, *A Survey of World Missions*, rev. ed. (Chicago: Moody Press, 1961), p. 326.
21. Hoke, *The Church in Asia*, p. 542.
22. Kenneth Scott Latourette, *A History of the Expansion of Christianity*, vol. 3, *Three Centuries of Advance* (Grand Rapids, Mich.: Zondervan Publishing House, 1974), p. 322.
23. Ibid., p. 325.
24. Ibid., p. 323.
25. Gordon H. Chapman, "Japan," in *The Church in Asia*, Donald E. Hoke, ed. (Chicago: Moody Press, 1975), p. 306.
26. Ibid., p. 305.
27. Latourette, *Three Centuries of Advance*, p. 330.
28. Hoke, *The Church in Asia*, p. 306.
29. Latourette, *Three Centuries of Advance*, p. 333.
30. Ibid., p. 322.
31. Latourette, *The Great Century*, p. 20.
32. David Woodward, "Hong Kong," in *The Church in Asia*, Donald E. Hoke, ed. (Chicago: Moody Press, 1975), p. 211.
33. Thiessen, *A Survey of World Missions*, p. 311.
34. Hoke, *The Church in Asia*, p. 284.
35. J. Herbert Kane, *A Global View of Missions* (Grand Rapids, Mich.: Baker Book House, 1971), p. 180.
36. Latourette, *Three Centuries of Advance*, p. 305.
37. Ibid., p. 303.
38. Hoke, *The Church in Asia*, p. 285.
39. Ibid., p. 287.
40. Latourette, *Three Centuries of Advance*, p. 360.
41. Ibid., p. 377.
42. Hoke, *The Church in Asia*, p. 308.
43. Latourette, *The Great Century*, p. 372.
44. Ibid., p. 391.
45. Ibid., p. 390.
46. Ibid.
47. Ibid., p. 392.
48. Hoke, *The Church in Asia*, p. 313.
49. Latourette, *The Great Century*, p. 409.
50. Ibid., p. 269.
51. Hoke, *The Church in Asia*, p. 544.
52. Ibid., p. 526.
53. Latourette, *The Great Century*, p. 269.
54. Kenneth Scott Latourette, *A History of the Expansion of Christianity*, vol. 7, *Advance Through the Storm* (Grand Rapids, Mich.: Zondervan Publishing House, 1974), p. 212.
55. Gerald H. Anderson and Peter G. Gowing, "Four Centuries of Christianity in the Philippines: An Interpretation," *Encounter*, vol. 25, no. 3, p. 358.
56. Hoke, *The Church in Asia*, p. 547.
57. Latourette, *Advance Through the Storm*, p. 212.
58. Ibid., 211.

CHINA (TAIWAN): Earning Respect the Hard Way

1. Paula Chin, "An Opening to Peking?" *Newsweek* (September 14, 1987): p. 10.
2. Philip Teng, interview (December, 1988).
3. Dennis McKeever, "Narrative Report" (Colorado Springs, Colo.: Division of Overseas Ministries, 1983): p. 1.
4. Anita M. Bailey, "Taiwan," unpublished report (Colorado Springs, Colo.: C&MA Division of Overseas Ministries, 1971): p. 3.
5. J. Herbert Kane, *A Global View of Christian Missions* (Grand Rapids, Mich.: Baker Book House, 1971), p. 232.
6. Ibid.
7. Ibid.
8. Samuel Wilson, John Siewent, eds., *Mission Handbook* (Monrovia, Calif.: Missions Advanced Research and Communications Center, 1986), p. 449.
9. Peter Nanfelt, "State of the Region" (Colorado Springs, Colo.: C&MA Division of Overseas Ministries, 1987): p. 9.
10. Ibid.
11. Teyet Moy, "Who Cares? Taiwan's Youth Do!" *The Alliance Witness* (October 26, 1983): p. 8.
12. Philip Teng, private interview (December, 1988).
13. Doyle Carlblom, "Steps of Faith," *The Alliance Witness* (April 24, 1985): p. 17.
14. Peter Nanfelt, "State of the Region" (Colorado Springs, Colo.: C&MA Division of Overseas Ministries, September 1986): p. 38.
15. Ibid.
16. Paula Chin, "An Opening to Peking?", p. 15.
17. David Thurston, "Taiwan After the Chiangs," *Asia Magazine* (March 6, 1988): p. 8.

HONG KONG: The Many Faces of Fragrant Harbor

1. David Woodward, "Hong Kong," in *The Church in Asia*, David E. Hoke, ed. (Chicago: Moody Press, 1975), p. 211.

2. Aladin Ismail, ed., *Hong Kong 1988* (Hong Kong: Government Information Service, 1988), p. 1.
3. David Thurston, "The Trick Is Confidence," *Asia Magazine* (June 28, 1987): p. 8.
4. Charles W. Fowler, "Annual Field Report 1988" (Colorado Springs, Colo.: C&MA Division of Overseas Ministries, 1988), p. 1.
5. Anita M. Bailey, "Hong Kong" (Colorado Springs, Colo.: C&MA Division of Overseas Ministries, 1982), p. 2.
6. Hoke, *The Church in Asia*, p. 208.
7. Ismail, *Hong Kong 1988*, p. 1.
8. Hoke, *The Church in Asia*, p. 210.
9. Barbara Basler, "Capital Flees an Edgy Hong Kong," *The New York Times* (June 15, 1989): p. D1.
10. Henry Kamm, "Britain and Vietnam Still at Odds on Refugees," *The New York Times* (June 15, 1989): p. A19.
11. Thurston, "The Trick Is Confidence," p. 13.
12. Peter Nanfelt, "State of the Region 1982" (Colorado Springs, Colo.: C&MA Division of Overseas Ministries, 1982), p. 10.
13. Thurston, "The Trick Is Confidence," p. 8.
14. Charles W. Fowler, "Annual Field Report 1988," p. 26.
15. Charles W. Fowler, "Annual Field Report 1987" (Colorado Springs, Colo.: C&MA Division of Overseas Ministries, 1987), p. 3.
16. "Hong Kong Brain Drain Is Call for Christians to Return," *Pulse* (October 14, 1988): p. 4.
17. Ibid.
18. Dame Lydia Dunn, "Hong Kong," *Vis-a-Vis* (May, 1989): p. 51.
19. Ibid., p. 54.
20. Charles W. Fowler, "Annual Field Report 1986" (Colorado Springs, Colo.: C&MA Division of Overseas Ministries, 1986), p. 2.
21. Timothy D. Wolfe, "Hong Kong Christians Encounter the Lord of History," *The Alliance Witness* (September 26, 1984), p. 19.
22. Fowler, "Annual Field Report 1988," p. 26.
23. Ibid., p. 6.
24. "Good News for Hong Kong," "Foreign Field Flashes" (November, 1982): p. 1.
25. Cliff M. Westergren, personal letter (June, 1984), p. 1.
26. Don Bubna, "Uncertainty Breeds Opportunity," *The Alliance Witness* (September 26, 1984): p. 17.
27. Fowler, "Annual Field Report 1987," p. 6.
28. Cliff M. Westergren, "What's Hong Kong All About?" personal papers, p. 7.
29. "An Interview with Dr. Philip Teng," *The Alliance Witness* (January 7, 1981): p. 19.
30. Ibid.
31. Ibid., p. 20.
32. Kamm, "Britain and Vietnam Still at Odds on Refugees," p. A19.
33. Tot van Truong, "Open Hearts in Closed Camps," *The Alliance Witness* (September 26, 1984): p. 21.
34. Fowler, "Annual Field Report 1988," p. 19.
35. Peter Nanfelt, "State of the Region 1986" (Colorado Springs, Colo.: C&MA Division of Overseas Ministries, 1986), p. 9.
36. Bubna, "Uncertainty Breeds Opportunity," p. 18.
37. "Annual Report" (Hong Kong: China Alliance Press, 1988).
38. Fowler, "Annual Field Report 1986," p. 4.
39. Cliff M. Westergren, "Alliance Radio Three-Year Plan" (Hong Kong: C&MA Mission, 1989), p. 2.
40. Fowler, "Annual Field Report 1988," p. 22.
41. Douglas Weibe, "A Bible School for China," *The Alliance Witness* (July 8, 1981): p. 19.
42. Bubna, "Uncertainty Breeds Opportunity," p. 18.
43. Fowler, "Annual Field Report 1988," p. 16.
44. Basler, "Capital Flees an Edgy Hong Kong," p. D5.
45. Ibid., p. D1.

INDONESIA: From Diversity to Unity

1. Robert L. Niklaus, "Global Report," *Evangelical Missions Quarterly* (January, 1985): p. 88.
2. Frank L. Cooley, *Indonesia: Church and Society* (New York: Friendship Press, 1968), p. 46.
3. Ibid., p. 47.
4. Robert L. Niklaus, John R. Sawin, Samuel J. Stoesz, *All for Jesus* (Camp Hill, Penna.: Christian Publications, 1986), p. 178.
5. Peter N. Nanfelt, "The Christian and Missionary Alliance in Indonesia," unpublished study (Colorado Springs, Colo.: C&MA Division of Overseas Ministries, May, 1972): p. 24.
6. Ibid., p. 7.
7. Ibid., p. 6.
8. William Conley, *The Kalimantan Kenyah, a Study of Tribal Conversion* (Nutley, N.J.: Presbyterian and Reformed Publishing Company, 1976), p. 283.
9. Anita M. Bailey, "Indonesia" (Colorado Springs, Colo.: C&MA Division of Overseas Ministries, 1982): p. 21.
10. Nanfelt, "The C&MA in Indonesia," p. 1.
11. Walter M. Post, "God Builds a Church Among the Torajas," *The Alliance Witness* (August 20, 1969): p. 10.
12. Bailey, "Indonesia," p. 23.
13. Janet Kuhns, "If the Gospel Had Ever Come to Us," *The Alliance Witness* (March 27, 1985): p. 16.
14. Peter N. Nanfelt, "Indonesian Awakening: Revival or Ruse?" *The Alliance Witness* (April 11, 1973): p. 18.
15. Gunther Kamphausen, "Indonesia Field Annual Report," unpublished report (Colorado Springs, Colo.: C&MA Division of Overseas Ministries, 1982): p. 1.
16. Peter N. Nanfelt, "Java Cities," unpublished report (Colorado Springs, Colo.: C&MA Division of Overseas Ministries, 1981): p. 1.
17. David Heath, "Narrative Field Report," unpublished report (Colorado Springs, Colo.: C&MA Division of Overseas Ministries, 1985): p. 2.
18. Gunther Kamphausen, "Annual Field Report," unpublished report (Colorado Springs, Colo.: C&MA Division of Overseas Ministries, 1986): p. 8.
19. "Lately," *The Alliance Witness* (July 30, 1975): p. 11.
20. F. L. Kamasi, "Missions and the Receiving Church," *Report of the Fifth*

Asia Conference (Colorado Springs, Colo.: C&MA Division of Overseas Ministries, 1969): p. 115.

21. "Christian Books for Indonesia," *The Alliance Witness* (February 1, 1967): p. 24.
22. Gunther Kamphausen, "Annual Field Report," unpublished report (Colorado Springs, Colo.: C&MA Division of Overseas Ministries, 1973): p. 6.
23. Bailey, "Indonesia," p. 22.
24. Niklaus, *All for Jesus*, p. 204.
25. Ebbie C. Smith, *God's Miracles: Indonesian Church Growth* (South Pasadena, Calif.: William Carey Library, 1970), p. 65.
26. Bill Dalton, *Indonesia Handbook*, 2nd ed. (Rutland, Vt.: Moon Publications, 1978), p. 182.
27. Niklaus, *All for Jesus*, p. 193.
28. Ibid., p. 190.
29. William W. Conley, "The Rise and Fall of the Indonesian Communist Party," unpublished paper (Colorado Springs, Colo.: C&MA Division of Overseas Ministries, 1969): p. 9.
30. Dalton, *Indonesia Handbook*, p. 11.
31. Smith, *God's Miracles: Indonesian Church Growth*, p. 27.
32. Ibid.
33. Gunther Kamphausen, "Apo Kayan Report," unpublished report (Colorado Springs, Colo.: C&MA Division of Overseas Ministries, May, 1968): "Conclusion."
34. A. Rodger Lewis, "The Opportune Moment in Indonesia," *The Alliance Witness* (October 26, 1966): p. 11.
35. Ibid.
36. Russell T. Hitt, *Cannibal Valley* (Grand Rapids, Mich.: Zondervan Publishing House, 1962), p. 169.
37. Smith, *God's Miracles: Indonesian Church Growth*, p. 114.
38. James Sunda, *Church Growth in the Central Highlands of West New Guinea* (Lucknow, India: Lucknow Publishing House, 1963), pp. 17, 18.
39. Donald A. McGavran, *Understanding Church Growth* (Grand Rapids, Mich.: William B. Eerdmans, 1970), p. 298.
40. A. R. Tippett, *Religious Group Conversion in Non-Western Society*, Research-in-Progress, No. 11 (Pasadena, Calif.: School of World Mission, 1967): p. 4.
41. Donald A. McGavran, "Why Neglect Gospel Ready Masses?" *Christianity Today* (October, 1966): p. 769.
42. Sunda, *Church Growth in the Central Highlands of West New Guinea*, p. 11.
43. Alice Gibbons, *The People Time Forgot* (Chicago: Moody Press, 1961), p. 16.
44. Peter N. Nanfelt, "State of the Region," unpublished report (Colorado Springs, Colo.: C&MA Division of Overseas Ministries, Sept. 7, 1988): p. 4.
45. Robert Stanley Wick, *The Alliance Mission in Irian Jaya*, unpublished dissertation, California Graduate School of Theology (Colorado Springs, Colo.: Simpson Historical Library, 1985): p. 53.
46. Robert A. Jaffray, "Until He Find It," *The Pioneer* (July, 1938): p. 18.
47. Hitt, *Cannibal Valley*, p. 37.
48. Einar H. Mickelson, *God Can* (Manila: Far East Broadcasting Company, 1966), p. 22.
49. William F. Smalley, "Alliance Missions in Indonesia," vol. 1, unpublished study (Colorado Springs, Colo.: C&MA Division of Overseas Ministries, 1976): p. 523.
50. Mickelson, *God Can*, pp. 33, 34.
51. John E. Ellenberger, "The Battle for the Baliem," *Behind the Ranges* (November, 1951): pp. 1, 2.
52. Leopold Pospisil, *Kapauku Papuans and Their Law* (New Haven, Conn.: Yale University Publications, 1958), p. 16.
53. Gibbons, *The People Time Forgot*, p. 77.
54. Darlene Deibler Rose, "The Stone Age Speaks Again," unpublished report (Colorado Springs, Colo.: C&MA Division of Overseas Ministries, 1948): pp. 8, 9.
55. Walter Post, "The Bible School and the Establishment of the Church," *Behind the Ranges* (March, 1965): p. 11.
56. Mickelson, *God Can*, pp. 100, 101.
57. Ibid., p. 165.
58. Hitt, *Cannibal Valley*, pp. 79, 80.
59. Ibid., p. 201.
60. Wick, *The Alliance Mission to Irian Jaya*, p. 385.
61. Ibid., p. 386.
62. Hitt, *Cannibal Valley*, p. 231.
63. Ibid.
64. Smith, *God's Miracles*, p. 115.
65. "Transformations in the Baliem Valley," *The Alliance Witness* (November 30, 1960): p. 20.
66. Dalton, *Indonesia Handbook*, p. 419.
67. Anita M. Bailey, "Irian Jaya" (Colorado Springs, Colo.: C&MA Division of Overseas Ministries, 1982): p. 5.
68. Mary Owen, "Literacy—Opening the Door to the Scriptures," *Behind the Ranges* (May, 1970): p. 12.
69. Gordon Larson, "The Meat Tastes Honey-Sweet," *The Alliance Witness* (August 31, 1983): p. 7.
70. Hitt, *Cannibal Valley*, p. 115.
71. Peter N. Nanfelt, "State of the Region," unpublished report (Colorado Springs, Colo.: C&MA Division of Overseas Ministries, September 7, 1988): p. 4.
72. Peter N. Nanfelt, "State of the Region" (Colorado Springs, Colo.: C&MA Division of Overseas Ministries, August 4, 1987): p. 4.
73. Smith, *God's Miracles*, p. 115.
74. John D. Ellenberger, "Chairman Report to Conference," unpublished report (Colorado Springs, Colo.: C&MA Division of Overseas Ministries, 1971): p. 2.
75. Peter N. Nanfelt, "State of the Region" (Colorado Springs, Colo.: Division of Overseas Ministries, September 3, 1986): p. 3.
76. Harold W. Catto, "Field Director's Report" (Colorado Springs, Colo.: Division of Overseas Ministries, 1982): p. 4.
77. Gibbons, *The People Time Forgot*, p. 16.

JAPAN: Still Unreached

1. Harley Schreck and David Barrett, eds., *Clarifying the Task* (Monrovia, Calif.: MARC 1987), p. 7.

2. Jack Davidson, "God 'Needs' Harvesters," *The Alliance Witness* (August 3, 1983): p. 17.
3. C. Peter Wagner, "Territorial Spirits and World Missions," *Evangelical Missions Quarterly*, vol. 25, no. 3 (July 1989): p. 287.
4. Edwin O. Reischauer, *The Japanese* (Cambridge, Mass.: Harvard University Press, 1977), p. 33.
5. Clyde Haberman, "The Presumed Uniqueness of Japan," *The New York Times Magazine* (August 28, 1988): p. 48.
6. Kenneth W. Young, "The 'Jungle' of Japan," *The Alliance Witness* (September 10, 1986): p. 18.
7. Haberman, "The Presumed Uniqueness of Japan," p. 44.
8. Edwin O. Reischauer, *Japan, Past and Present*, 3rd ed. (New York: Alfred A. Knopf, 1965), p. 294.
9. Evangeline Davidson, "Strategy Seminar J4," *The Alliance Witness* (January 6, 1988): p. 20.
10. Haberman, "The Presumed Uniqueness of Japan," p. 46.
11. Hiroko Imamura, "Japan," unpublished paper (Redding, Calif.: Simpson College, March 21, 1989): part 3.
12. Robert Lee, *Stranger in the Land*, (New York: Friendship Press, 1967), p. 156.
13. Shusaku Endo, *Silence* (Tokyo: Sophia University, 1969), p. 292.
14. Anita M. Bailey, "Japan" (Colorado Springs, Colo.: C&MA Division of Overseas Ministries, 1982): p. 9.
15. Imamura, "Japan," part 3.
16. Reischauer, *Japan, Past and Present*, p. 290.
17. Ibid., p. 13.
18. Wagner, "Territorial Spirits and World Missions," p. 278.
19. Ibid., p. 279.
20. Alvin D. Hammond, "Japan's Postwar Renaissance," in *The Church in Asia*, Donald E. Hoke, ed. (Chicago: Moody Press, 1975), p. 330.
21. Lee, *Stranger in the Land*, p. 37.
22. Reischauer, *Japan, Past and Present*, p. 143.
23. Jack Davidson, "Combatting Nominalism in the C&MA Church in Japan," unpublished paper (Redding, Calif., Simpson College, August 17, 1987): p. 8.
24. Robert B. Eckvall, ed., *After Fifty Years* (Harrisburg, Penna.: CPI, Inc., 1939), p. 196.
25. Ibid.
26. Ibid.
27. *Annual Report* (Colorado Springs, Colo.: C&MA Simpson Memorial Library, 1937), p. 47.
28. Davidson, "God 'Needs' Harvesters," p. 18.
29. Mabel Francis, *One Shall Chase a Thousand* (Harrisburg, Penna.: CPI Inc., 1968): p. 22, 25.
30. Davidson, "Combatting Nominalism in the C&MA Church in Japan," p. 8.
31. Peter Nanfelt, "State of the Region" (Colorado Springs, Colo.: C&MA Division of Overseas Ministries, 1982): p. 4.
32. Davidson, "Combatting Nominalism in the C&MA Church in Japan," p. 34.
33. Ibid.
34. Peter Nanfelt, "State of the Region" (Colorado Springs, Colo.: C&MA Division of Overseas Ministries, 1986): p. 5.
35. Peter Nanfelt, "State of the Region" (Colorado Springs, Colo.: C&MA Division of Overseas Ministries, 1988): p. 6.
36. Jack Davidson, "An Accurate Picture of the Shibuya Gospel Church," unpublished report (Pasadena, Calif.: Fuller Seminary World School of Mission, 1986): p. 7.
37. Kiyomi Morioka, *Religion in Changing Japanese Society* (Tokyo: University of Tokyo Press, 1975), p. 164.
38. Hoke, *The Church in Asia*, p. 346.
39. James Montgomery, *The Discipling of a Nation* (Santa Clara, Calif.: Global Church Growth Bulletin, 1980): p. 131.
40. Hoke, *The Church in Asia*, p. 346.

PHILIPPINES: From Slow Starter to Pacesetter

1. David L. Rambo, "The Christian Missionary Alliance in the Philippines, 1901–1970," Ph.D. dissertation, New York University (Colorado Springs, Colo.: Simpson Historical Library, 1974): p. 43.
2. Ibid., p. 61.
3. Anita M. Bailey, "The Philippines" (Colorado Springs, Colo.: C&MA Division of Overseas Ministries, 1982): p. 11.
4. *Annual Report of the President to General Council 1989* (Colorado Springs, Colo.: C&MA International Headquarters, May 1989): p. 71.
5. Don Bubna, "CAMACOP: Fastest Growing Church in the Philippines," *The Alliance Witness* (August 29, 1984): p. 16.
6. Bailey, "The Philippines," p. 22.
7. Ibid., p. 18.
8. Ibid.
9. Peter N. Nanfelt, "State of the Region" (Colorado Springs, Colo.: C&MA Division of Overseas Ministries, 1987): p. 8.
10. "Good News Metro Manila Key-Cities Project," CAMACOP news release (Manila, Philippines, September 1983): p. 1.
11. Peter N. Nanfelt, "State of the Region" (Colorado Springs, Colo.: C&MA Division of Overseas Ministries, September 1988): p. 7.
12. D. Franklin Irwin, "Annual Field Report" (Colorado Springs, Colo.: C&MA Division of Overseas Ministries, 1985): p. 2.
13. Peter N. Nanfelt, "State of the Region" (Colorado Springs, Colo.: C&MA Division of Overseas Ministries, October 1982): p. 8.
14. Rambo, "The C&MA in the Philippines, 1901–1970," p. 245.
15. Ralph Tolliver, "The Philippines," in *The Church in Asia*, Donald E. Hoke, ed. (Chicago: Moody Press, 1975), p. 529.
16. Rambo, "The C&MA in the Philippines, 1901–1970," p. 195.
17. Lee A. Peters, "Annual Field Report" (Colorado Springs, Colo.: C&MA Division of Overseas Ministries, 1988): p. 10.
18. Eldora Huffman, "Can't Our Wives Come Too?" *The Alliance Witness* (July 30, 1986): p. 19.
19. Rambo, "The C&MA in the Philippines, 1901–1970," p. 262.
20. R. M. Chrisman, area secretary's report on itinerary, May 27–August 12, 1959 (Colorado Springs, Colo.: Division of Overseas Ministries).

21. Lee A. Peters, "Annual Field Report" (Colorado Springs, Colo.: C&MA Division of Overseas Ministries, 1988): p. 10.
22. Ibid., p. 291.
23. Willy D. Marquez, "A New Home for Alliance Publishers," *The Alliance Witness* (December 9, 1987): p. 18.
24. Ibid.
25. David L. Rambo, *Annual Report of the President to General Council 1989* (Colorado Springs, Colo.: C&MA International Headquarters, 1989): p. 74.
26. Peters, "Annual Field Report 1988," p. 8.
27. Debbie Cowles, "Reaching Students in the Philippines," *The Alliance Witness* (April 23, 1986): p. 19.
28. Ibid.
29. Nanfelt, "State of the Region, 1988," p. 7.
30. Gerald E. Otis, "Annual Field Report" (Colorado Springs, Colo.: C&MA Division of Overseas Ministries, 1983): p. 6.
31. Nanfelt, "State of the Region, 1988," p. 7.
32. Hoke, *The Church in Asia*, p. 532.
33. Ibid., p. 527.
34. Ibid., p. 534.
35. David B. Barrett, ed., *World Christian Encyclopedia* (New York: Oxford University Press, 1982), p. 561.
36. Hoke, *The Church in Asia*, p. 534.
37. Lee A. Peters, "Annual Field Report, 1986" (Colorado Springs, Colo.: C&MA Division of Overseas Ministries, 1986): p. 10.
38. Peters, "Annual Field Report, 1988," p. 7.
39. Otis, "Annual Field Report, 1983," p. 4.
40. Peters, "Annual Field Report 1986," p. 1.
41. Thomas N. Wisley, "Costly Grace in the Philippines," *The Alliance Witness* (April 24, 1985): p. 18.
42. Ibid.
43. Nanfelt, "State of the Region, 1987" (Colorado Springs, Colo.: C&MA Division of Overseas Ministries, 1987): p. 8.
44. Wisley, "Costly Grace in the Philippines," p. 18.
45. Romy B. Bangayan, "Saved from the Rebels," *The Alliance Witness* (August 29, 1984): p. 21.
46. Wisley, "Costly Grace in the Philippines," p. 19.
47. Bayani Mendoza, "The C&MA in the Philippines," Ph.D. thesis, California Graduate School of Theology (Colorado Springs, Colo.: Simpson Historical Library, 1979): p. 44.
48. Ibid.
49. Ibid.
50. *The Christian and Missionary Alliance*, XX, 20 (May 18, 1988): p. 468.
51. *The Christian and Missionary Alliance*, XX (March, 1988): pp. 291–292.
52. Bailey, "The Philippines," p. 10.
53. J. A. Mckee, "Alliance Missions," *The Christian and Missionary Alliance*, XXX, 22 (October 31, 1903): p. 303.
54. Rambo, "The C&MA in the Philippines," p. 65.
55. Ibid., p. 76.
56. Ibid., p. 84.
57. "The Philippines," *The Alliance Weekly*, LX, 26 (June 27, 1925): p. 444.
58. A. W. Tozer, *Let My People Go* (Harrisburg, Penna.: CPI, Inc., 1947), p. 104.
59. Rambo, "The C&MA in the Philippines, 1901–1970," p. 102.
60. Ibid., p. 104.
61. Ibid., p. 105.
62. Ibid., p. 149.
63. Ibid., p. 159.
64. Ibid., p. 172.
65. Bailey, "The Philippines," p. 11.
66. Rambo, "The C&MA in the Philippines," p. 171.
67. Ibid., p. 175.
68. Bubna, "CAMACOP: Fastest Growing Evangelical Group in the Philippines," p. 16.
69. Rambo, "The C&MA in the Philippines, 1901–1970," p. 189.
70. Ibid., p. 286.

THE SUPPORT NETWORK

1. "Minutes of General Council 1989 and Annual Report 1988" (Colorado Springs, Colo.: Office of the President): p. 18, and "World Report Highlights" (Willowdale, Ont.: Office of the President, 1989): p. 6.
2. "Annual Report of the President to General Council, 1989" (Colorado Springs, Colo.: Office of the President, 1989): p. 29.
3. Robert L. Niklaus, John Sawin, Samuel Stoez, *All for Jesus* (Camp Hill, Pa.: Christian Publications, Inc., 1987), p, 245 ff.
4. "World Report Highlights," p. 10.
5. "Annual Report of the President," p. 53.
6. Ibid., p. 46.
7. Niklaus, *All for Jesus*, p. 127.
8. Ibid.
9. Dawn Stanard, " 'Hands On' Missionary Experience," *Alliance Life* (January 4, 1989): p. 16.
10. Peter Nanfelt, Interoffice Memo (Colorado Springs, Colo.: C&MA Division of Overseas Ministries), July 13, 1989.
11. Ibid.
12. Ibid.
13. "Africa Is Their Parish," *The Banner* (May 27, 1989): p. 7.
14. Robert L. Niklaus, "Fine-tuning the Focus of Missions," *Alliance Life* (May 25, 1988): p. 8.
15. "Minutes of General Council 1987 and Annual Report 1986" (Colorado Springs, Colo.: Office of the President): p. 324.
16. Niklaus, "Fine-tuning the Focus of Missions," p. 9.
17. Louis L. King, "Pastoral Letter to the Church" (Colorado Springs, Colo.: Office of the President, May 28, 1983).
18. Ibid., p. 4.
19. Ibid., p. 27.
20. Personal correspondence by Dr. Vuta, April 26, 1982.
21. Ibid.
22. Ibid.

23. Nathan Bailey, "Toward an Alliance World Fellowship," *The Alliance Witness* (February 26, 1975): p. 16.
24. Niklaus, *All for Jesus*, p. 236.
25. *Prayer Directory* (Colorado Springs, Colo.: The Christian and Missionary Alliance, 1989), p. 145.
26. "Alliance Under the Cross" (Baulkham Hills, Australia: The Christian and Missionary Alliance in Australia, 1970): p. 6.
27. William K. Kerr, "Administrative Trip, January 1–March 4, 1969," unpublished report (Colorado Springs, Colo.: C&MA Division of Overseas Ministries): p. 2.
28. David H. Moore, "World Overview," unpublished report (Colorado Springs, Colo.: C&MA Division of Overseas Ministries, 1989): p. 4.
29. Matthew 24:14.

EPILOGUE: Twenty-First Century Missions

1. J. Christy Wilson, Jr., "Tentmakers Task Force," *World Evangelization* (November–December, 1988): p. 21.
2. William R. Bright, "Re-Evangelization of the United States," *World Evangelization* (July–August, 1989): p. 10.
3. David B. Barrett, "Living in the World of A.D. 2000," *World Evangelization* (November–December, 1988): p. 12.
4. Robert L. Niklaus, "Glasnost Reaches for the Bible," *Pulse* (May 20, 1989): p. 4.
5. "Church Structures in China Today," *China and the Church Today* (October, 1986): p. 9.
6. Ralph W. Winter, *The 25 Unbelievable Years 1945–1969* (Pasadena, Calif.: William Carey Library, 1970), p. 41.
7. George Hunter, "Two Questions for Church Growth: Lessons from United Methodism," *The Asbury Herald* (Spring, 1988): p. 2.
8. David L. Rambo, "Annual Report of the President to General Council, 1989" (Colorado Springs, Colo.: Office of the President), p. 29.
9. Larry R. Pate, "The Dramatic Growth of Two-Thirds World Missions," *Bridging Peoples*, vol. 8, no. 3 (July 1989): p. 1.
10. William Bright, "Re-evangelization of the United States," p. 9.
11. Brian C. Stiller, "A New Day for Evangelizing in Canada," *World Evangelization* (July–August, 1989): pp. 12, 13.

National office of The Christian and Missionary Alliance in the United States, Colorado Springs, Colorado

BIBLIOGRAPHY

Adeyemo, Tokumbah. "An African Leader Looks at the Churches' Crises." *Evangelical Missions Quarterly* (July 1978).

"Africa Is Their Parish." *The Banner* (27 May 1989).

Alba, Victor. *The Latin Americans.* New York: Frederick A. Praeger, 1969.

"Alliance Under the Cross." Baulkham Hills, Australia: The Christian and Missionary Alliance in Australia, 1970.

Anderson, Gerald H., and Peter G. Gowing. "Four Centuries of Christianity in the Philippines: An Interpretation." *Encounter* 25:3.

Annual Report. Colorado Springs, Colo.: Simpson Memorial Library, 1937.

"Annual Report." Hong Kong: China Alliance Press, 1988.

Annual Report of the President to General Council. Colorado Springs, Colo.: C&MA International Headquarters, 1989.

Arciniegas, German. *Latin America: A Cultural History.* New York: Alfred A. Knopf, 1967.

Bailey, Anita M. "Alliance Academy." Colorado Springs, Colo.: C&MA Division of Overseas Ministries, 1982.

———. "Argentina." Colorado Springs, Colo.: C&MA Division of Overseas Ministries, 1982.

———. "Brazil." Colorado Springs, Colo.: C&MA Division of Overseas Ministries, 1982.

———. "Chile." Colorado Springs, Colo.: C&MA Division of Overseas Ministries, 1980.

———. "Colombia." Colorado Springs, Colo.: C&MA Division of Overseas Ministries, 1982.

———. "Costa Rica." Colorado Springs, Colo.: C&MA Division of Overseas Ministries, 1982.

———. "Dominican Republic." Colorado Springs, Colo.: C&MA Division of Overseas Ministries, 1982.

———. "Ecuador." Colorado Springs, Colo.: C&MA Division of Overseas Ministries, 1982.

———. "France." Colorado Springs, Colo.: C&MA Division of Overseas Ministries, 1982.

———. "Guatemala." Colorado Springs, Colo.: C&MA Division of Overseas Ministries, 1982.

———. "Hong Kong." Colorado Springs, Colo.: C&MA Division of Overseas Ministries, 1982.

———. "Indonesia." Colorado Springs, Colo.: C&MA Division of Overseas Ministries, 1982.

———. "Irian Jaya." Colorado Springs, Colo.: C&MA Division of Overseas Ministries, 1982.

———. "Japan." Colorado Springs, Colo.: C&MA Division of Overseas Ministries, 1982.

———. "Peru." Colorado Springs, Colo.: C&MA Division of Overseas Ministries, 1981.

———. "The Philippines." Colorado Springs, Colo.: C&MA Division of Overseas Ministries, 1982.

———. "Taiwan." Colorado Springs, Colo.: C&MA Division of Overseas Ministries, 1971.

———. "United Mexican States." Colorado Springs, Colo.: C&MA Division of Overseas Ministries, 1982.

———. "Venezuela." Colorado Springs, Colo.: C&MA Division of Overseas Ministries, 1981.

Bailey, Nathan. "Toward an Alliance World Fellowship." *The Alliance Witness* (26 February 1975).

Bailly, Gerard A. "Porto Rico and Spanish Evangelization." *The Alliance Witness* (16 February 1901).

Bangayan, Romy B. "Saved From the Rebels." *The Alliance Witness* (29 August 1984).

Barrett, David B. "Annual Statistical Table on Global Mission: 1985." *International Bulletin of Missionary Research* (January 1985).

———. "Living in the World of A.D. 2000." *World Evangelization* (November–December 1988).

———. *Schism and Renewal in Africa.* Nairobi, Kenya: Oxford University Press, 1968.

———. *World Christian Encyclopedia.* New York: Oxford University Press, 1982.

Basler, Barbara. "Capital Flees an Edgy Hong Kong." *The New York Times* (15 June 1989).

Beaver, R. Pierce. *All Loves Excelling.* Grand Rapids, Mich.: William B. Eerdmans Publishing Company, 1968.

Bennett, Gail. "French Protestant Leaders Reveal Churches' Needs." *Pulse* (18 April 1986).

Bishop, Stephen L. "The History of The Christian and Missionary Alliance in Chile." Nyack, N.Y.: Alliance Theological Seminary, 1985.

Bol, Anton. "The Touch of God in Zoetermeer." *The Alliance Witness* (10 October 1984).

Brierly, Peter, ed. *United Kingdom Christian Handbook*. Kent, England: MARC Europe, 1987.

Bright, William R. "Re-Evangelization of the United States." *World Evangelization* (July–August 1989).

Bubna, Don. "CAMACOP: Fastest Growing Church in the Philippines." *The Alliance Witness* (29 August 1984).

———. "Uncertainty Breeds Opportunity." *The Alliance Witness* (26 September 1984).

Carlblom, Doyle. "Steps of Faith." *The Alliance Witness* (24 April 1985).

Caston, Vernon. "Annual Report." Colorado Springs, Colo.: C&MA Division of Overseas Ministries, 1979.

Catto, Harold W. "Field Director's Report." Colorado Springs, Colo.: C&MA Division of Overseas Ministries, 1982.

Chapman, Gordon H. "Japan." In *The Church in Asia*. Edited by Donald E. Hoke. Chicago: Moody Press, 1975.

Chin, Paula. "An Opening to Peking?" *Newsweek* (14 September 1987).

Chrisman, R. M. "Area Secretary's Report on Itinerary, May 27– August 12." Colorado Springs, Colo.: C&MA Division of Overseas Ministries, 1959.

The Christian and Missionary Alliance xx: (March 1898).

The Christian and Missionary Alliance xx:20 (18 May 1898).

"Christian Books for Indonesia." *The Alliance Witness* (1 February 1967).

The Churches in Spain. Geneva: World Council of Churches, 1984.

"Church Structures in China Today." *China and the Church Today* (October 1986).

Collier, Simon. *From Cortez to Castro*. New York: Macmillan Publishing Co., Inc., 1974.

Conley, William. *The Kalimantan Kenyah: A Study of Tribal Conversion*. Nutley, N.J.: Presbyterian and Reformed Publishing Co., 1976.

———. "The Rise and Fall of the Indonesian Communist Party." Colorado Springs, Colo.: C&MA Division of Overseas Ministries, 1969.

Constance, George S. "The Church Is Alive." *The Alliance Witness* (4 December 1968).

Cook, Arnold, chairman. "Brazil Study Team Report." Colorado Springs, Colo.: C&MA Division of Overseas Ministries, 1983.

Cooley, Frank L. *Indonesia: Church and Society*. New York: Friendship Press, 1968.

Cowles, Debbie. "Reaching Students in the Philippines." *The Alliance Witness* (23 April 1986).

Cragg, Kenneth. *The Call of the Minaret*. New York: Oxford University Press, 1956.

———. *Christianity in World Perspective*. New York: Oxford University Press, 1968.

Dalton, William. *Indonesia Handbook*. 2d ed. Rutland, Vt.: Moon Publications, 1978.

Davidson, Evangeline. "Strategy Seminar J4." *The Alliance Witness* (6 January 1988).

Davidson, Jack. "An Accurate Picture of the Shibuya Gospel Church." Pasadena, Calif.: Fuller Seminary World School of Mission, 1986.

———. "Combatting Nominalism in the C&MA Church in Japan." Redding, Calif.: Simpson College, 1987.

———. "God 'Needs' Harvesters." *The Alliance Witness* (3 August 1983).

Dunn, Dame Lydia. "Hong Kong." *Vis-a-Vis* (May 1989).

Durant, Will. *Caesar and Christ*. New York: Simon and Schuster, 1944.

Eckvall, Robert B., ed. *After Fifty Years*. Harrisburg, Penna.: Christian Publications, Inc., 1939.

Ellenberger, John E. "The Battle for the Baliem." *Behind the Ranges* (November 1951).

———. "Chairman's Report to Conference." Colorado Springs, Colo.: C&MA Division of Overseas Ministries, 1971.

Endo, Shusaku. *Silence*. Tokyo: Sophia University, 1969.

Ernst, Nancy, and Ken Schultz. "Church Growth Analysis." Pamphlet no. 1315. Nyack, N.Y.: Alliance Theological Seminary, 1977.

Escobar, Samuel. "Future Trends." *Latin American Evangelist* (April–June 1987).

Esparza, Kay. "Mexico." Colorado Springs, Colo.: C&MA Division of Overseas Ministries, 1984.

Evans, Robert P. "The Missionary Situation in Europe." *Christianity Today* (20 July 1962).

Falk, Peter. *The Growth of the Church in Africa*. Grand Rapids, Mich.: Zondervan Publishing House, 1979.

Fischbach, Reinhard. "Spiritism in Brazil." Unpublished study no. 746. Nyack, N.Y.: Alliance Theological Seminary, 1967.

Fowler, Charles W. "Annual Field Report." Colorado Springs, Colo.: C&MA Division of Overseas Ministries, 1986, 1987, 1988.

Francis, Mabel. *One Shall Chase a Thousand*. Harrisburg, Penna.: Christian Publications, Inc., 1968.

Fried, Ralph. "Harvest Time in Jebaib." *The Alliance Weekly* (23 August 1930).

Froehlich, Thomas. "An Overview of the Birth and Growth of The Christian and Missionary Alliance Church." Pamphlet no. 1528. Nyack, N.Y.: Alliance Theological Seminary, n.d.

Gibb, H. A. R., and J. H. Kramers. *Shorter Encyclopedia of Islam*. London: Luzac & Company, 1961.

Gibbons, Alice. *The People Time Forgot*. Chicago: Moody Press, 1961.

"Good News for Hong Kong." *Foreign Field Flashes* (November 1982).

"Good News Metro Manila Key-Cities Project." CAMACOP news release (September 1983).

"The Gospel Work in Ecuador." Colorado Springs, Colo.: C&MA Division of Overseas Ministries, n.d.

"A Growing Witness in Syria." *The Alliance Witness* (9 April 1986).

"Guatemala." Colorado Springs, Colo.: C&MA Division of Overseas Ministries, 1983.

Haberman, Clyde. "The Presumed Uniqueness of Japan." The New York *Times Magazine* (28 August 1988).

Hall, D. G. E. *A History of South-East Asia*. 2d ed. London: Macmillan and Company, Ltd., 1964.

Hammond, Alvin D. "Japan's Postwar Renaissance." In *The Church in Asia*. Edited by Donald E. Hoke. Chicago: Moody Press, 1975.

Harnack, Adolf. *The Mission and Expansion of the Christian World Since 1938*. New York: Harper and Row, 1962.

Hastings, Adrian. *African Christianity.* New York: Seabury Press, 1976.

Heath, David. "Narrative Field Report." Colorado Springs, Colo.: C&MA Division of Overseas Ministries, 1985.

Hitt, Russell T. *Cannibal Valley.* Grand Rapids, Mich.: Zondervan Publishing House, 1962.

Hoge, Warren. "Macumba." *The New York Times Magazine* (21 August 1983).

"Hong Kong Brain Drain Is Call for Christians to Return." *Pulse* (14 October 1988).

Horner, Norman A. "The Future of Christian Missions in Lebanon." *International Bulletin of Missionary Research* (October 1984).

Huffman, Eldora. "Can't Our Wives Come Too?" *The Alliance Witness* (30 July 1986).

Hunter, George. "Two Questions for Church Growth: Lessons from United Methodism." *The Asbury Herald* (Spring 1988).

Imamura, Hiroko. "Japan." Redding, Calif.: Simpson College, 1989.

"An Interview with Dr. Philip Teng." *The Alliance Witness* (7 January 1981).

Irwin, D. Franklin. "Annual Field Report." Colorado Springs, Colo.: C&MA Division of Overseas Ministries, 1985.

Ismail, Aladin, ed. *Hong Kong 1988.* Hong Kong: Government Information Service, 1988.

Jacober, Virginia. "As Quickly as Possible." *The Alliance Witness* (5 August 1981).

———. "Jamil Hashweh." *The Alliance Witness* (13 October 1982).

Jaffray, Robert A. "Until He Find It." *The Pioneer* (July 1938).

Jocz, Jakob. "Primitive Hebrew Christianity." In *The Jewish People and Jesus Christ.* Grand Rapids, Mich.: Baker Book House, 1979.

Kamasi, F. L. "Missions and the Receiving Church." *Report of the Fifth Asian Conference.* Colorado Springs, Colo.: C&MA Division of Overseas Ministries, 1969.

Kamm, Henry. "Britain and Vietnam Still at Odds on Refugees." *The New York Times* (15 June 1989).

Kamphausen, Gunther. "Annual Field Report." Colorado Springs, Colo.: C&MA Division of Overseas Ministries, 1973, 1968.

———. "Apo Kayan Report." Colorado Springs, Colo.: C&MA Division of Overseas Ministries, 1968.

———. "Indonesian Field Annual Report." Colorado Springs, Colo.: C&MA Division of Overseas Ministries, 1982.

Kane, J. Herbert. *A Concise History of the Christian World Mission.* Grand Rapids, Mich.: Baker Book House, 1985.

———. *A Global View of Christian Missions.* Grand Rapids, Mich.: Baker Book House, 1971.

Kerr, Andrew. "Suddenly Made Refugees." *The Alliance Witness* (4 September 1985).

Kerr, William K. "Administrative Trip, January 1–March 4, 1969." Colorado Springs, Colo.: C&MA Division of Overseas Ministries.

King, Louis L. "He Has It All Together." *Open Line* (May–June 1982).

———. "Pastoral Letter to the Church." Colorado Springs, Colo.: Office of the President (28 May 1983).

Kolle, Leendert. "New Life in an Ancient Land." *The Alliance Witness* (23 November 1983).

Kowalchuk, Fred. "God-Given Growth in Spain." *The Alliance Witness* (6 November 1985).

———. "Narrative Report." Colorado Springs, Colo.: C&MA Division of Overseas Ministries, 1984.

Kuhns, Janet. "If the Gospel Had Ever Come to Us." *The Alliance Witness* (27 March 1985).

Larson, Gordon. "The Meat Tastes Honey-Sweet." *The Alliance Witness* (31 August 1983).

"Lately." *The Alliance Witness* (30 July 1975).

Latourette, Kenneth Scott. *Christianity in a Revolutionary Age* 3. Grand Rapids, Mich.: Zondervan Publishing House, 1969.

———. *A History of the Expansion of Christianity.* Grand Rapids, Mich.: Zondervan Publishing House, 1974.

Lee, Robert. *Stranger in the Land.* New York: Friendship Press, 1967.

LeFlaec, Christian. "A Springtime First in France." *The Alliance Witness* (6 November 1985).

Levine, Daniel H., ed. *Churches and Politics in Latin America.* Beverly Hills, Calif.: Sage Publications, 1980.

Lewis, Rodger. "The Opportune Moment in Indonesia." *The Alliance Witness* (26 October 1966).

McCombs, Myrna. "Canadians Challenged to Go the 'Second Mile.'" *The Alliance Witness* (4 December 1985).

McGavran, Donald A. *Understanding Church Growth.* Grand Rapids, Mich.: William B. Eerdmans, 1970.

———. "Why Neglect Gospel Ready Masses?" *Christianity Today* (October 1966).

McKee, J. A. "Alliance Missions." *The Christian and Missionary Alliance* xxx:22 (31 October 1903).

McKeever, Dennis. "Narrative Report." Colorado Springs, Colo.: C&MA Division of Overseas Ministries, 1983.

Marquez, Willy D. "A New Home for Alliance Publishers." *The Alliance Witness* (9 December 1987).

"A Matter of Faith." Pulse (23 January 1987).

Mbiti, John S. "Encounter of Christian Faith and African Religion." *Christian Century* (27 August 1980).

Medin, James G. "Narrative Report." Colorado Springs, Colo.: C&MA Division of Overseas Ministries, 1984.

Mendoza, Bayani. "The C&MA in the Philippines." Colorado Springs, Colo.: Simpson Historical Library, 1979.

"Mexico." *Background Notes.* Washington, D.C.: United States Department of State, 1983.

Mickelson, Einar H. *God Can.* Manila: Far East Broadcasting Company, 1966.

"Minutes of General Council 1989 and Annual Report 1988." Colorado Springs, Colo.: Office of the President.

Montgomery, James. *The Discipling of a Nation.* Santa Clara, Calif.: Global Church Bulletin, 1980.

Moore, David H. "World Overview." Colorado Springs, Colo.: C&MA Division of Overseas Ministries, 1989.

Morioka, Kiyomi. *Religion in Changing Japanese Society.* Tokyo: University of Tokyo Press, 1975.

Moy, Teyet. "Who Cares? Taiwan's Youth Do!" *The Alliance Witness* (26 October 1983).

Mumper, Sharon. "Lebanese Conflict Dashes Hope of All Middle East Christians." *Pulse* (24 January 1986).

"Muslim Evangelism Planned for Europe." *Europe Report* (November–December 1984).

Nanfelt, Peter N. "The Christian and Missionary Alliance in Indonesia." Colorado Springs, Colo.: C&MA Division of Overseas Ministries, 1972.

———. "Indonesian Awakening: Revival or Ruse?" *The Alliance Witness* (11 April 1973).

———. Interoffice memo. Colorado Springs, Colo.: C&MA Division of Overseas Ministries (13 July 1989).

———. "Java Cities." Colorado Springs, Colo.: C&MA Division of Overseas Ministries, 1981.

———. "State of the Region." Colorado Springs, Colo.: C&MA Division of Overseas Ministries, 1982, 1986, 1987, 1988.

Neill, Stephen. *Christian Missions*. Grand Rapids, Mich.: Wm. B. Eerdmans Publishing Company, 1964.

———. *A History of Christian Missions*. Grand Rapids, Mich.: Wm. B. Eerdmans Publishing Company, 1965.

Newbigin, Lesslie. *The Other Side of 1984*. Geneva: World Council of Churches, 1983.

Niklaus, Robert L. "Fine-tuning the Focus of Missions." *Alliance Life* (25 May 1988).

———. "Glasnost Reaches for the Bible." *Pulse* (20 May 1989).

———. "Global Report." *Evangelical Missions Quarterly* (April 1978).

———. "Global Report." *Evangelical Missions Quarterly* (October 1978).

———. "Global Report." Colorado Springs, Colo.: C&MA Division of Overseas Ministries, 1982.

———. "Global Report." *Evangelical Missions Quarterly* (January 1985).

Niklaus, Robert L., John R. Sawin, and Samuel J. Stoesz. *All for Jesus*. Camp Hill, Penna.: Christian Publications, Inc., 1986.

Otis, Gerald E. "Annual Field Report." Colorado Springs, Colo.: C&MA Division of Overseas Ministries, 1983.

Otto, Michael C. "Protestant Missions in Ecuador." Nyack, N.Y.: Alliance Theological Seminary, 1985.

Owen, Mary. "Literacy—Opening the Door to the Scriptures." *Behind the Ranges* (May 1970).

Palomino, Miguel Angel. *Lima al Encuentro con Dios*. Lima, Peru: Lince C&MA Church, 1983.

Pamphilus, Eusebius. *Ecclesiastical History*. Grand Rapids, Mich.: Baker Book House, 1974.

"Paraguay." *Background Notes*. Washington, D.C.: United States Department of State, 1982.

Pate, Larry R. "The Dramatic Growth of Two-Thirds World Missions." *Bridging Peoples* 8:3 (July 1989).

Peters, David J. "Chairman's Report." Colorado Springs, Colo.: C&MA Division of Overseas Ministries, 1982.

Peters, Lee A. "Annual Field Report." Colorado Springs, Colo.: C&MA Division of Overseas Ministries, 1986, 1988.

"The Philippines." *The Alliance Weekly* LX:26 (27 June 1925).

Pospisil, Leopold. *Kapauku Papuans and Their Law*. New Haven, Conn.: Yale University Publications, 1958.

Post, Walter. "The Bible School and the Establishment of the Church." *Behind the Ranges* (March 1965).

———. "God Builds a Church Among the Torajas." *The Alliance Witness* (20 August 1969).

Prayer Directory. Colorado Springs, Colo.: The Christian and Missionary Alliance, 1989.

Rambo, David L. *Annual Report of the President to General Council*. Colorado Springs, Colo.: C&MA International Headquarters, 1989.

———. "The Christian and Missionary Alliance in the Philippines, 1901–1970." Colorado Springs, Colo.: Simpson Historical Library, 1974.

———. "Reaching the Professional and Middle Classes in Lima." *Latin American Pulse* (January 1980).

Read, William R., Victor M. Monterrosa, and Harmon A. Johnson. *Latin American Church Growth*. Grand Rapids, Mich.: William B. Eerdmans Publishing Co., 1969.

Reed, Robert. "Narrative Report." Colorado Springs, Colo.: C&MA Division of Overseas Ministries, 1987.

Register, Ray G., Jr. "Christian Witness in the State of Israel Today." *International Bulletin of Missionary Research* (January 1983).

Reilly, Patricia. "Guatemala: Past, Present, and Future." Nyack, N.Y.: Alliance Theological Seminary, 1985.

Reischauer, Edwin O. *Japan, Past and Present*. 3d ed. New York: Alfred A. Knopf, 1965.

———. *The Japanese*. Cambridge, Mass.: Harvard University Press, 1977.

Roberts, Dayton. "Never the Same Again." *Latin American Evangelist* (April–June 1987).

Rose, Darlene Deibler. "The Stone Age Speaks Again." Colorado Springs, Colo.: C&MA Division of Overseas Ministries, 1948.

Schreck, Harley, and David Barrett, ed. *Clarifying the Task*. Monrovia, Calif.: MARC, 1987.

Searing, Mark. "H. G. Crisman: Forever a Missionary." Nyack, N.Y.: Alliance Theological Seminary, 1977.

Shannon, Jack. "Annual Report." Colorado Springs, Colo.: C&MA Division of Overseas Ministries, 1981.

Simons, Marlise. "Latin America's New Gospel." The New York *Times Magazine* (7 November 1982).

Simpson, Albert B. *The Challenge of Missions*. New York: The Christian Alliance Publishing Co., 1926.

———. "Editorial." *The Christian Alliance* (7 August 1891).

Smalley, William F. "Alliance Missions in Indonesia." Vol. 1. Colorado Springs, Colo.: C&MA Division of Overseas Ministries, 1976.

———. "Guests of the Arabian Government." *The Alliance Weekly* (12 May 1928).

Smalley, William F., comp. *Alliance Missions in Palestine, Arab Lands, Israel*. Colorado Springs, Colo.: Simpson Historical Library, 1971.

Smith, Ebbie C. *God's Miracles*. South Pasadena, Calif.: William Carey Library, 1970.

Snead, Alfred C. *Missionary Atlas*. Harrisburg, Penna.: Christian Publications, Inc., 1936.

Snow, Frank. "Indonesia." In *The Church in Asia*. Edited by Donald E. Hoke. Chicago: Moody Press, 1975.

Sormani, Guiseppe, ed. *The Caribbean Region and Central America*. In *The World and Its Peoples*. New York: Greystone Press, 1965.

Spradlin, Bryon. "Sapping the Strength of Witness in Israel." *Evangelical Missions Quarterly* (January 1985).

Stanard, Dawn. " 'Hands On' Missionary Experience." *Alliance Life* (4 January 1989).

Stiller, Brian C. "A New Day for Evangelizing in Canada." *World Evangelization* (July–August 1989).

Sunda, James. *Church Growth in the Central Highlands of West New Guinea*. Lucknow, India: Lucknow Publishing House, 1963.

Taber, Charles R., ed. *The Church in Africa 1977*. Pasadena, Calif.: William Carey Library, 1977.

Taylor, Harry. "The Only Happy Man in the Crowd." *The Alliance Witness* (30 January 1985).

Thiessen, John Caldwell. *A Survey of World Missions*. Rev. ed. Chicago: Moody Press, 1961.

————. *A Survey of World Missions*. Chicago: Moody Press, 1970.

Thurston, David. "Taiwan After the Chiangs." *Asia Magazine* (6 March 1988).

————. "The Trick Is Confidence." *Asia Magazine* (28 June 1987).

Tienou, Tite. "Christians in Africa." n.p., n.d.

Tippett, A. R. *Religious Group Conversion in Non-Western Society*. Research-in-Progress, no. 11. Pasadena, Calif.: School of World Mission, 1967.

Tolliver, Ralph. "The Philippines." In *The Church in Asia*. Edited by Donald E. Hoke. Chicago: Moody Press, 1975.

Tozer, A. W. *Let My People Go*. Harrisburg, Penna.: Christian Publications, Inc., 1947.

"Transformations in the Baliem Valley." *The Alliance Witness* (30 November 1960).

Tucker, Ruth A. *From Jerusalem to Irian Jaya*. Grand Rapids, Mich.: Zondervan Publishing House, 1983.

van Truong, Tot. "Open Hearts in Closed Camps." *The Alliance Witness* (26 September 1984).

"Venezuela." *Background Notes*. Washington, D.C.: United States Department of State, 1984.

Volstad, David K. "Bolivia." Colorado Springs, Colo.: C&MA Division of Overseas Ministries, 1983.

————. "Ecuador: Fifteen-Year Report." Colorado Springs, Colo.: C&MA Division of Overseas Ministries, 1972.

————. "Regional Report." Colorado Springs, Colo.: C&MA Division of Overseas Ministries, 1984, 1985, 1986.

Wagner, C. Peter. "Territorial Spirits and World Missions." *Evangelical Missions Quarterly* 25:3 (July 1989).

Ward, Donald O. "A New Church in Jordan." *The Alliance Witness* (16 May 1931).

Weibe, Douglas. "A Bible School for China." *The Alliance Witness* (8 July 1981).

Westergren, Cliff M. "Alliance Radio Three-Year Plan." Hong Kong: C&MA Mission, 1989.

————. Personal letter (June 1984).

————. "What's Hong Kong All About?" Personal papers.

Westmeier, Karl Wilhelm. "Evangelical Churches in the Colombian State." Nyack, N.Y.: Alliance Theological Seminary, 1978.

White, Thomas H. "And Now What?" *The Alliance Witness* (20 July 1983).

Wick, Robert Stanley. *The Alliance Mission in Irian Jaya*. Colorado Springs, Colo.: Simpson Historical Library, 1985.

Wilson, J. Christy, Jr. "Tentmakers Task Force." *World Evangelization* (November–December 1988).

Wilson, Samuel. *Mission Handbook*. 12th ed. Monrovia, Calif.: Missions Advanced Research and Communications Center, 1979.

Wilson, Samuel, and John Siewert, ed. *Mission Handbook*. 13th ed. Monrovia, Calif.: Missions Advanced Research and Communication Center, 1986.

Winter, Ralph. *The 25 Unbelievable Years: 1945-1969*. Pasadena, Calif.: William Carey Library, 1970.

Winter, Ralph, and R. Pierce Beaver. *The Warp and Woof*. South Pasadena, Calif.: William Carey Library, 1970.

Wisley, Thomas N. "Costly Grace in the Philippines." *The Alliance Witness* (24 April 1985).

Wolfe, Timothy D. "Hong Kong Christians Encounter the Lord of History." *The Alliance Witness* (26 September 1984).

Woodward, David. "Hong Kong." In *The Church in Asia*. Edited by David E. Hoke. Chicago: Moody Press, 1975.

"World Report Highlights." Willowdale, Ontario: Office of the President, 1989.

Wulf, Catherine. "A Critical Week in Erbach, West Germany." *The Alliance Witness* (15 September 1982).

Young, Kenneth W. "The 'Jungle' of Japan." *The Alliance Witness* (10 September 1986).

Zwemer, Samuel M. *The Disintegration of Islam*. New York: Fleming H. Revell, 1916.

INDEX

A

Abdul-Hagg, Sheikh, 223-24
Abidjan, Ivory Coast, 34, 38-39
Africa, 4-62
African Inland Mission, the, 7
Africanization, of Guinea, 26, 33
African religiosity, 4
Aglipayan, 350
Aglipay y Labayan, Gregorio, 264, 273
Agreement, Alliance: Argentina, 132; Brazil, 142; Burkina Faso, 16; Korea, 90
Alba, Victor, 123, 124
Aleppo, Syria, 237
Alianza en Marcha, 159-60, 166, 175, 196
All Africa Council of Churches, the, 10
Allah, 42, 69, 260
All Asia Missions Consultation, the, 73
Allen, Horace N., 87
Allen, Paul S., 229
Alliance: Academy, the, 173, 174; Academy, Quito, 369; Bible Institute, the, 190; Bible Seminary, 91, 99, 159, 171, 174; Bible Seminary, Hong Kong, 290; Bible Seminary, Wuchow, 296; Biblical Seminary, 343, 344; Canadian, 362; Canadian, in Manila, 342; Church Association, the, 84; Church Union of Hong Kong, 241; College of Theology, Canberra, 376; Men, 148, 178, 180, 256, 364; ministries in India, 74; of Evangelical "Parousia" Churches, the, 251-53; Publishers, 346-47; Publishing House, Chile, 149, 150; Theological Seminary, 364; women, Canada, 364; World Fellowship, the, 50, 52, 91, 99, 137, 288, 340, 359, 374-77, 379; Youth Corps, 365; Zendings Centrum "Parousia," 251
Alliantie van Evangelische Gemeentenn "Parousia," 250
American Bible Society, the, 163, 169, 196
American Board of Commissioners for Foreign Missions, the, 126
American Methodist Church, in Costa Rica, 163
American University, the, Beirut, 232
Amity Foundation, the, 111
Amman, Jordan, 238
Animism, 42; in Burkina Faso, 12; in Gabon, 18; in Mali, 48; missionaries and, 9; in Thailand, 92

"Anti-Missionary Law," the, 216-18
Antioch, 203
Arabia, 228-29
Arab Lands, 222-39
Araucanian people, the, 144
Arciniegas, German, 123
Argentina, 130-37; Argentina Alliance, 132, 133, 135-36, 137; Argentine Alliance Mission, 131
Asia Graduate School of Theology, 344
Asia mainland, 63-119
Asian Conference: First, 374; Third, 288, 349
Assemblies of God, the, 86
Asuncion, Paraguay, 136-37
Auchland, New Zealand, 377
Australian Alliance, the, 375-76
Autonomy, church: Burma, 372; Canada, 362; Guinea, 32, 33; the Philippines, 358

B

Bailey, Anita, 242, 324
Bailey, Nathan, 375, 376
Bailly, Gerard A., 196
Bali, 307-10
Baliem River Valley, Irian Jaya, 320-24
Bamako, Mali, 47-48
Banfora, Burkina Faso, 14
Bangkok, 102
Bangkok Bible College, 98, 99, 101
Baoule people, the, 36
Baptist Missionary Society, the, 7, 211
Baptists, American, 183
Barcelona, Spain, 255-56
Barnes, Samuel G., 130, 139
Barranca, Peru, 190
Barrett, David B.: on Africa, 9; on Asia, 64; on Europe, 212-13; on martyrs, 378; on Thailand, 92; *The World Christian Encyclopedia,* 4, 64

Barrios, Justo Rufino, 177
Bartholomew the apostle, 65
Basel Evangelical Missionary Society, the, 7
Basic Law, Hong Kong, 284-85
Batan Church, Quito, 173
Bateke Country, Zaire, 54, 58, 59
Bates, Carrie, 83
Baulkham Hills Church, Sydney, 376
Bedouin peoples, the, 221
Beersheva, Israel, 218
Beijing, Taiwan and, 279-81
Beirut, Lebanon, 232
Bible: House, The, 218; Institute, Brazil, 140; Literature International, 187; school movement, the, 127; schools, African, 13
"The Bible Academy of the Air," 190
Bobo Dioulasso, 12
Bogota, Colombia, 156
Bogota al Encuentro con Cristo, 157
Bokko, 298
Bol, Anton, 252-53
Bolivar, Simon, 125
Bongolo, Gabon, 19-21
Bouake, Ivory Coast, 34-35
Brahmanism, Indian, 77
Brahmans, 260
Brasilia, 139
Braudy, Alfredo S., 166
Brazil, 138-43
Breaden, George W., 228, 232
Bressler, R. E., 229
Brierly, Peter, 249
Brigham, John C., 183
British and Foreign Bible Society, the, 152, 183, 272, 353
British Missionary Alliance, the, 248
Brown, Samuel R., 270
Bucaramanga, Colombia, 160
Buddhism, 66, 265; in China, 110; the Early Church and, 67-68; in India, 77; in Japan, 271, 333, 339; in Korea, 86; in Laos, 115; nineteenth century, 72; in the Pacific islands, 260-61; in Thailand, 92-93; in Viet Nam, 119
Buenos Aires, 132-33; Bible Institute, the, 132, 133, 134; "Buenos Aires Encounter with God," 133
Burkina Faso, 12-17
Burma, 372-74

C

Cajamarca, Peru, 190
Cali, Colombia, 156
Callao, Peru, 190
Calvin, John, 208
CAMACOP, 340, 345, 346, 348, 351, 352, 357, 358, 359; in India, 84
CAMA Services, 365, 366, 368: in Lebanon, 236; relief aid and, 44

Cambodia. See Kampuchea
Camp-of-the-Woods, 292
Canadian: Food Grains Bank, the, 366; general assembly, 370; theological seminary, 364
Cannibal Valley, 321
Capao da Imbuia, Brazil, 140
Capital City Alliance Church, the, Quezon City, 342
Caracas, Venezuela, 196
Carey, William, 72, 209-10, 211
Caste system, the, 67
Catholic Church, Roman: in Abidjan, 39; African exploration and, 5; in Argentina, 130; in Asia, 71-72; in Brazil, 138; in Chile, 144, 145; in China, 109; in Colombia, 153, 154; in Costa Rica, 163; in the Dominican Republic, 166; in France, 242; in Guatemala, 177; in Japan, 265, 334; in Korea, 87; in Latin America, 122-23 ; missionary societies of, 212; in the Pacific islands, 260, 262-65; in the Philippines, 350, 353; in Viet Nam, 119
Cebu City, Philippines, 350
Centennial Council, 370
Central American Mission, the, 163
Chapman, Gordon H., 65, 66, 271
Charismatic movement, Latin American, 129
Check, Maru, 377
Chiang Ching-kuo, 281
Chiang Kai-shek, 275, 281
Chile, 144-51; Chile Alliance Mission, 144; Chilean Alliance, 144
China, 104
China Alliance Press, 291
China Inland Mission, the, 7
Chinese Foreign Missionary Union, the, 296, 308
Chioang, 275
Chou En-lai, 109
Chrisman, R. M., 346
Christensen, Mabel, 355-56
Christian and Missionary Alliance, the: Bible Training Institute, Jerusalem, 227; in Brazil, 139; of Canada, 133; of Chile, 150-51; in China, 112; in Colombia, 155-60; Church Union of Hong Kong, 99, 286; of India, 74, 78, 83; of Taiwan, 276; in Kampuchea, 113-15; in Korea, 89-91; in Lebanon, 235-36; in Mexico, 183-85; in Peru, 192
Christian and Missionary Alliance Churches of the Philippines, the. See CAMACOP
Christian Growth Cells, 193
Christianity: in Asia, 64-73; colonialism and, 8; in the Dark Ages, 206-208; expansion of, 204-205; Irish, 205-206; Islam and, 222-24; Judaism and, 214-16; Maronite, 234; in Russia, 206
"Christian Manifesto," the, 109
Christian Missions in Many Lands, 196
Christians: Japanese, 356; Jewish, 205
Church: movements, African independent, 9; organization, in Mali, 47-48; planting, in Nigeria, 52
Church and state: Hong Kong, 286-88; Philippines, 264

Churches: house, Chinese, 112; self-supporting, Filipino, 359; Three-Self, Chinese, 111; under Communism, 104-19
Church Growth: in Argentina, 134-35; in India, 75-77; in Kinshasa, Zaire, 56-58; in Mali, 46-48; seminars on, 148
Church Missionary Society, the: in Jordan, 225; in Sierra Leone, 6, 7
Cities, open, 39, 341
Civil war, Colombia, 153-55
Clench, David, 297
Clergy, Spanish, 263
Colombia, 152-61
Colombo, Brazil, 140
Colonialism, 8, 72
Colportage, 125-26, 196, 353
Columba, 206
Columbanus, 206
Columbian Alliance, the, 156
Comity, 54, 272, 341
Communism: Chinese, 104; and the Church, 109-12, Colombian, 160-61; in Indonesia, 310-12
Conakry, Guinea, 29-32
Confucianism, 66; in China, 110; the Early Church and, 68-69; in Korea, 86
Confucius, 68, 69
Congregacao Crista, the, 127
Conley, William W., 310
Conquistadors, the, 122-24, 177
Constance, George S., 217
Constantine, Emperor, 66, 204
Contag, Manuel, 173
Conversions, forced, 267-68
Cook, Arnold L., 188, 370
Correspondence courses: in Chile, 149; in India, 78, 80; in Peru, 190; in Thailand, 98
Cortes, Hernan, 122, 123
Costa Rica, 162-64
Costa Rican Christian and Missionary Alliance, the, 163
Counter-Reformation, the, 262
Cowman, Charles E., 89
Cragg, Kenneth, 222, 224
Crisman, Homer and Leticia, 170
Cristobal, Carlos, 302
Crowther, Samuel Ajayi, 6
Crusader mentality, 5
Crusades, the, 206-207
Cultural Revolution, the, 110
Curitiba, Brazil, 140
Cuzco, Peru, 190-91

D

Dadazou, Guinea, 27
Dagher, Sami, 235, 236
Dalat School, Panang, 369

Damal peoples, the, 312, 313, 314, 317, 320, 322, 323
Damascus, Syria, 231, 236
Dani peoples, the, 320, 321, 322, 324
Danish-Halle Mission, the, 208
Davao Alliance Bible School, 345
Davao City, Philippines, 351
Dawley, Helen, 83
Dawson, Albert E., 150
Dayak peoples, the, 295, 297-98, 299, 305, 309
de Albuquerque, Alfonse, 262
Dedougou district, Burkina Faso, 13
Deibler, C. Russell, 316
de Jesus, Benjamin, 84, 377
deJesus, Florentino, 357
Deng Xiaoping, 110
Denpasar, Bali, 307
Desaparecidos, the, 131
Desertification, West African, 43
deUrdaneta, Andres, 263
deValdivia, Pedro, 144
Dewey, Commodore, 271-72
Diaz, Ricardo, 156
Diaz del Castillo, Bernal, 123
Didache, The, 65-66
Dien Bien Phu, 107
Dievendorf, Anne, 336
Diocletian, Emperor, 204
Disasters, natural, in Burkino Faso, 12
Division of Church Ministries, the, 244
Division of Overseas Ministries, the, 363, 368, 372
Dogon district, Mali, 48
Dominican Alliance, the, 166, 167
Dominican Republic, the, 165-67
Dominicans, the, 207
Dreger, Clement, 91
Drought and famine, in Mali, 43-46
Druze peoples, the, 230, 231, 232
Dunn, Dame Lydia, 285
Dunn, Lucy, 220, 224, 229
Durant, Will, 203
Dutch Guiana. See Surinam
Dutton, Harold, 357

E

Early Church, the, 202-205; Buddhism and, 67-68; in China, 70-71; Confucianism and, 68-69; Islam and, 69-70; Hinduism and, 67
Eastern Church, the, 64-65, 71
Eastern Orthodox Church, the, 206
East Kalimantan, 297, 299, 301
Ebenezer Bible College, 343, 344
Ebenezer Bible Institute, 355

The Economist, on Arab nationalism, 238-39
Ecuador, 168-75
Ecuadorian Alliance, the, 168
Ecuadorian Evangelical Church, the, 171
Eddy, Sherwood, 77
Edessa, Mesopotamia, 65
Edict of Milan, the, 66, 204, 205
Edman, V. Raymond, 206
Education, Christian: Argentina, 133-34, 137; Brazil, 143; Burkina Faso, 17; Chile, 149, 151; Colombia, 155, 161; Costa Rica, 164; Dominican Republic, 167; Ecuador, 175; Gabon, 25; Guatemala, 181; Guinea, 32, 33; India, 85; Indonesia, 301-303; Irian Jaya, 325, 327; Ivory Coast, 34-35, 41; Korea, 90-91; Lebanon, 232; Mali, 49; Mexico, 185; Nigeria, 53; Peru, 190, 193; Philippines, 343-45; Taiwan, 276-79; Thailand, 103; Venezuela, 199; Zaire, 57-58, 59, 61
Edward, Jonathan, 209
Ekari peoples, the, 316-321
El Agustino Church, the, 189
El Salvadore, 181
Emigration, from Hong Kong, 285
Encounter: campaign, Guatemalan, 180; Church, the, 157; program, 181; with Christ, Colombia, 156-58; with God, 133, 155, 187-92
Encuentro con Dios, 148, 173, 192-93
Erbach, Germany, 246-47
Escobar, Samuel, 129
Esparza, Ramon, 184
Europe, 213, 240-57
Eusebius Pamphilus, 65, 202
Evangelical Alliance Community of Zaire, the, 58
Evangelical awakening, European, 209
Evangelical Church of: Bangkok, 102; Laos, 116; North Viet Nam, 119; Peru, 192; Viet Nam, 106, 117
Evangelical Foreign Missions Association, the, 128
Evangelical Interdenominational Mission, the, 176, 177
Evangelism: French, 242; mass, 133; Nigerian, 52; pioneer, 54-55; urban, 187
Evangelism Explosion, 133, 148
Evangelism-In-Depth, 172, 186
Expansionism, European, 209

F

Famine: evangelism and, 46-47; Indian, 83
Far East Broadcasting Company, the, 96, 292
Far Eastern Economic Review, The, on Hong Kong, 285
Ferdinand and Isabella, 207
Fertile Crescent, the, 69
Fetishes: in Guinea, 27; in Indonesia, 312; in Mali, 48; in Zaire, 54
Filipino Alliance Church, the, 84
Filipino Independent Church, the, 350
First Spanish Alliance Church, the, 176
"Five Classics," the, 69

Forder, Archibald, 224-25, 228
Foreign Missionary Society, the, 288
Four-fold Gospel, the, 89, 370
"Four Noble Truths," the, 68
France, 240-44
Francescon, Luis, 127
Franceville, Gabon, 22-23
Francis, Mabel, 336-38
Franciscans, the, 207
Franke, August, 208
Frederick IV, 208
Freed, Ralph, 230
Freeman, Thomas Birch, 6
French Guiana, 195
French Huguenots, 124, 139
French West Africa Federations, the, 13, 16
Fritz, W. G., 169
Fukuzawa Yukichi, 271
Fulani peoples, the, 48-49
Fuller, Jennie, 82, 83
Fuller, M. B., 83
Fuller School of World Mission, 99, 372
Fulton, C. Darby, 88

G

Gabon, 18-25, 59
Gardiner, Allen Francis, 126
Garland, Herbert, 197
Gautama, 68
Genghis Khan, 70
Gerber, Vergil, 148
Germany, 244-47
Ghana, 6
Glasser, Arthur F., 109
Global Advance Fund, the, 363
Glover, Robert, 290
Goiania, Brazil, 139-40
"Golden age of early missions," the, 66
Good News Bookstore, Guinea, 32
"Good News for Great Cities," 79, 102
"Good News Metro Manila," 341
Gorbachev, Mikhail, 379
Gospel, the, Colombian resistance to, 152; hostility toward, 378
Gospel: Church of Thailand, the, 96, 99, 102; Missionary Union, the, 7, 169, 170, 171; response, in Burkina Faso, 16-17
"Gospel Immigrants," Taiwan, 278
Graham, Billy, 249
Great Britain, 248-49
"The Great Century," 72, 209-12, 266
Great Commission, the, 362
Great Commission Fund, the, 363

Greek Orthodox Church, the, 230
Group decisions, 314
Guatemala, 176-81
Guatemalan Alliance, the, 181
Guatemalan Relief Fund, the, 178
Guayaquil, Ecuador, 168-73
Guerrillas: Colombian, 156, 161-62; Guatemalan, 180, 181; Filipino, 352-53
Guevede, Gabon, 21
Guinea, 26-33
Gundaphorus, 65
Gunther, Paul, 94
Gutzlaff, Carl F. A., 94

H

Halle University, 208
Harnack, Adolf, 205
Harris, Townsend, 269
Hashweh, Albert, 226-27, 238
Hashweh, Jamil, 227
Henry, Robert T., 376
Henry the Navigator, 5
Hepburn, James C., 270
"Here's Life," Ivory Coast, 34
Herrnhut, the, 208
Hinduism, 66: in Bali, 307-308; Early Church and, 67; Indian, 77; nineteenth century, 72; in the Pacific islands, 260
Hisanori Suzuki, 339
Hispaniola, 165
Hmong peoples , the, 116, 241
Ho Chi Minh, 105, 107, 108, 117
Ho Hien Ha, 118-19
Hoke, Donald E., 66; on Asia, 64, 93; on colonialism, 72
Holland, in Irian Jaya, 314, 316
Hong Kong, 282-93
Houphouet-Boigny, Felix, 34, 41
House Church Movement, the, 249
Huanuco, Peru, 192
Hymns of the Christian Life, 176

I

Iglesia ni Cristo, 349-50
Ileka, Gabon, 21
Illescas, 254
Impit, Manuel, 352
India, 74-85
Indians: Colombian, 160-61; of Ecuador, 168; Igbo, 50, 52, 53; Inca, 186; Mayan, 127; Mexican, 182; Otavalos, 170, 173-74; Peruvian, 186; Quechua, 170
Indigenous church, the, 50; in Asia, 66-67; in Guinea, 26; in Korea, 87-88; Nehru on, 74; in the Philippines, 349-50, 357
Indonesia, 294-329

Indonesian Communist Party, the, 105
Inflation, Argentinean, 131
Inquisition. *See* Spanish Inquisition
International Christian Academy, Bouake, 369
International Evangelical Church, Jerusalem, 220
International Fellowship of Alliance Professionals, 365, 366, 367, 368
International Foreign Mission Association, the, 128
International Missionary Alliance, the, 83
Internment, Philippine, 356
Ipiales, Columbia, 152
Ipoy, Jalong, 297
Iran, 229, 238-39
Irian Jaya, 312-29
Irish Church, the, 205-206
Islam, 66, 239; in Abidjan, 39; in Africa, 6; in Burkina Faso, 12; in China, 110; Christianity and, 222-24; Early Church and, 69-70; in Guinea, 26-27; in India, 77; in Indonesia, 306-307; in Mali, 42-43, 48; militant, 69-70, 307; in the Pacific islands, 261-62; in Pakistan, 372; in the Philippines, 351-52; strengths of, 222
Israel, 214-21
Ivory Coast, the, 34-41

J

Jackson, Fred C., 309
Jackson, Herbert, 357
Jainism, Indian, 77
Jaffray, Robert, 72, 296-98, 303, 306, 309, 316, 355
Jaffray School of Theology, 297, 301-302, 309
Jakarta, Indonesia, 300
Japan, 265-66, 330-39
Japanese Alliance, the, 139, 336, 337
Java, 300
JAVA 5.5.2, 300, 301, 303
Jebal Amman Church, Jordan, 227, 238
Jehovah, Brahman and, 67
Jeng, Timothy, 93
Jerusalem, 202-203
Jesuits. *See* Society of Jesus
"Jesus grain," 44 , 46
Jesus Korea Alliance Holiness Church, the, 89, 90
Jews for Jesus, 215
Jiang Kaishek, 104
Johnson, Paul and Priscilla, 97
Jones, Clarence, 174
Jones, Howard, 34, 38
Jordan, 225-27, 229, 238
Judaism, 205, 214-16
Judson, Adoniram, 7, 72, 211
Judson, Anne, 94

K

Kalam Hidup, 303, 304

Kalimantan, 289
Kam, Joseph, 268
Kampuchea, 108, 113-15, 240
Kane, J. Herbert, 26, 203, 206, 240, 275
Karak, Jordan, 225
Kardec, Allan, 138
Kardecism, 138
Karentina Alliance Church, Beirut, 235, 236
Karma, 67, 68
Kato, Byang H., 9
Kharaba, 230, 231
Khmer, Red, 108
Kikongo language, the, 59
King, Louis L., 34, 374
Kinney, Helen, 336
Kinshasa, Zaire, 54, 55-56
Kinshasa Alliance churches, the, 58
Kissidougou district, Guinea, 27
Kiyomi Morioka, 339
Knesset, the, 215
Kolle, Leendert, 251, 253
Konemann, H. C. J., 250-51
Kongo, kingdom of, 5
Koran. See Quran
Korea, 104-105
Korean Christian Church of Japanese Christianity, the, 88
Koula Moutou, Gabon, 21
Kowalchuk, Fred, 253-54, 255
Kowloon Peninsula, 283
Kublai Khan, 70, 71

L

Ladinos, 177
Language: Dani, 325; Japanese, 331
Lanman, Bessie, 196
Lao peoples, in France, 241
Lao People's Democratic Republic, the, 115
Laos, 108-109, 115-16, 118
La Paz, Bolivia, 190
Lapide, Pinchas, 218
Larson, Ruben E., 174
Latin America, 121-99
Latin American Mission, the, 163
Latourette, Kenneth Scott, 66, 72, 112; on the Early Church, 205; on expansionism, 267; on Francis Xavier, 71; on Japan, 266; on militant Islam, 69; on monastic missions, 207; on persecution, 204, on the Philippines, 272; on Taiwan, 269
La Violencia, Colombia, 153-55
Lay Preachers Institutes, 345
Lay witness, Indian, 77
Lebanon, 232-35

Lecaro, Manuel, 160, 171, 173
Lecaro, Miguel, 197
Lee, Robert, 332, 335
Lee Teng-jui, 281
LeFlaec, Christian, 242
LeLecheur, D. W., 353, 354
Leopoldville. See Kinshasa
LeTourneau Foundation, the, 187
Levine, Daniel H., 129
Lewis, Al, 321
Liberation Theology, 128-29
Libreville, Gabon, 22
"Light of Life," 80
Lilje, Hans, 213
Lima, Peru, 173, 186, 192, 193
Lima al Encuentro con Dios, 187, 189, 190-91
Lince Church, the, 186, 189, 190
Linguists, missionary, 325
Literacy, Indian, 80
Literacy courses: Pakistan, 371; Philippines, 346
Literature: religious, 78; Roman Catholic, 87
Livingstone, David, 6-8
Lofsted, Bertil A., 255
Lommasson Memorial Alliance Bible School, 344
London Jew's Society, the, 210
London Missionary Society, the, 94
Lon Nol, 108, 114
Lopez, Alfred, 153
Ludlow, James, 336
"Luminous Religion," the, 70
Lund, D. O., 354
Luther, Martin, 208, 245, 247, 353
Lutheran Church, German, 242
Lyall, Leslie, 110

M

MacArthur, Douglas, 334, 337
Macedonian call, the, 202
McGavran, Donald, 56, 313, 323
McKee, J. A., 340, 354
Macumba, 138-39
Madaba, Jordan, 225, 226, 227
Magellan, Ferdinand, 263
Maharashtra Bible College, 84
Mahayana, 68
Makassar Bible School, 297
Malacca, 261, 262
Mali, 42-49
Manalo, Felix, 350
Manila, the Philippines, 340, 341, 348
Mao Zedong, 104, 110

Maranatha Bible School, 96
Maranatha Institute, 13
Marathi Bible College, 79
MARC, *The Mission Handbook,* 4
Mar del Plata Trio, the, 133
Maronites, 232
Mar Thoma Church, 65, 75
Martigues, France, 242
Martyn, Henry, 72
Martyrdom, 262, 266
Marxism, 27, 29
Maxwell, Mary, 224, 229-30
Mayombe peoples, the, 57, 58
Mazamet, France, 242
Mbiti, John S., 4
Medellin, Colombia, 155
Media programs, mass, 79-81, 290-92
Medical work, Alliance, 8; in Burkina Faso, 17; in Gabon, 25; in Guinea, 33; in the Ivory Coast , 41; in Lebanon, 234; in Mali, 49; in Nigeria, 53; in Zaire, 61
Mennonite Missionary Union, the, 268
Messianic assemblies, Israel, 218
Mestizos, 137, 169
Methodist Church, the, 6, 86, 88, 139
Mexico, 182-85
Mexico City, 182, 184, 185
Mickelson Alliance Bible School, 344
Middle East/Europe, 201-39
Migration, urban, Ivory Coast, 36-37
Millar, Robert, 209
Mindanao, the Philippines, 340, 341
Ministry to women, Nigeria, 52
Miraflores, Peru, 188-89
Missionaries: early Protestant, 208-209; female, 211-12; Congregational, 125; Kongo, 5; Methodist, 125; Moravian, 125; non-Western, 379; Roman Catholic, 93-94
Missionary freeze, Taiwan, 279
Missionary-sending church, a, 348
Missionary work, Alliance: African, 5-8; Arab, 224-27; Bobo Dioulasso, 12; Brazil, 139-40; Burkina Faso, 13-14; Chile, 144-45; Colombia, 152; Guatemala, 176-77; India, 77-85; Irian Jaya, 314-19; Japan, 336-37; moratorium on, 10; Nigeria, 52-53; Peru, 192; Port Gentile, 18-19; Taiwan, 274-76; Thailand, 93-103; Venezuela, 196; World War II and, 13; Zaire, 58-59
Missionary work, American Protestant, 270-72
Missionary work, Dutch, Philippines, 267
Mission Aviation Fellowship, the, 304-306
Mission Handbook, The (MARC), 4, 74
Missions: Argentina, 130-31; Africa, 9; monastic, 207; twentieth century, 212-13; twenty-first century, 378-80
Missions-Allianz-Kirche, the, 247

Mission schools, Latin American, 127-28
Missions conferences, 363
Mitsogo peoples, Gabon, 21
MK-CART/CORE, 369
Modernization, Ivory Coast, 34
Moffatt, Robert, 7
Moffett, Samuel Hugh, 86
Molling, Carl, 184
Monotheism, 223
Montgomery, James, 339
Montt, Efrain Rios, 178
Moore, David H., 377
Moran, Dr., 171
Moravian Brethren, the, 196, 208-209
Moro peoples, the, 263
Morrison, Robert, 72
Mothers of Plaza de Mayo, the, 131
Mouila, Gabon, 21-22
Mt. Apo Alliance Bible Institute, the, 344
Mouyanama Falls, Gabon, 21
Mozambique, 5
Mueller, George, 83
Muhammed, 6, 69, 222, 223, 224, 225, 234, 261
Murray, George A., 224
Muslims: in France, 242; missions and, 222; in the Pacific islands, 260; Sh'ite, 234; Sunni, 234
Mwela, Kuvuna ku Konde, 61
Mythology, Dani, 324-25

N

Nagasaki, Japan, 265, 266, 269-70
Nanfelt, Peter, 278
National Bible Society of Colombia, the, 126
National Council of Churches, the, 89
Nationalism: Arab, 238-39; Hindu, 74-75, 85; Filipino, 273
Nationalists, Chinese, 104
Nehru, Prime Minister, 74
Neill, Stephen, 9; on Catholic African missions, 5-6; on the Crusades, 207; on the Early Church, 203; on the Edict of Milan, 204; on exploration, 209; on missions, 211; on William Carey, 210
Nelson, H. E., 182
Nero, 204
Nestorian Church, the, 65
Nestorian Monument, the, 70
Netherlands, The, 250-53
Netherlands Missionary Society, the, 94, 268
Newbigin, Lesslie, 213
New Bombay Church, the, 78-79
New People's Army, Philippines, 352
New Territories, Hong Kong, 283
New York Herald, the, on Francisco Penzotti, 192

New York Times, the, 34, 113
New Zealand, 377
Nigeria, 50-53
Niger River, the, 42, 48
Ninomiya, Mutsuko, 139
Nirvana, 68
"Noah's Ark" puppet show, 142-43
"Noble Eightfold Path," the, 68
Nominalism: African, 9; Indian, 77
North Berar Faith Mission, the, 83
North German Missionary Society, the, 7
North Korea, 104
Ntorosso Bible School, 47
Nubia, 16
Nyack College, 61

O

Occultism, French, 242
Old City Church, the, 220
Onokalah, Ronald O., 51-52, 58
"Operation Wedge," Indonesia, 304
Oppelt, Margaret, 274, 276
Opperman, Kenn, 167, 186
"Opportunity Sunday," 363
Oriental Missionary Society, the, 89
Ortiz, Angel Villamil, 196
Otavalo Training Center, the, 174
Ouagadougou, Burkina Faso, 14
Oueis, Ibrahim, 231, 236

P

Pache, Rene, 213
Pacific islands, the, 260-357
Pakistan, 371
Palau, Luis, 178, 249
Palestine, 222, 224, 225
Panama Congress, the, 128
Pancasila, 294, 306, 310
Paraguay, 136-37
Paramaribo, Surinam, 194, 195
Paris Evangelical Mission, the, 19
Paris Foreign Missionary Society, the, 94
Partai Komunis Indonesia, 310
Partition, African, 9
Pasay City Alliance Church, Manila, 342
Pastoral care, missionary, 369
Pastoral training, 151, 158-59
Pastor's Library Project, Indonesia, 304
Pathet Lao, 108-109, 115, 116
Pau, France, 242
Paul, William, 177-78

Paul the apostle, 64, 202-203, 221
Pelayo, Menendez y, 254
Pentecost, 65, 202
Pentecostal movement, the, 127
Penzotti, Francisco G., 163, 169, 192
People movements, 312, 313, 323
People's Republic of China, Hong Kong and, 283-84
People's Republic of Congo, the, 59
Perry, Matthew, 269, 334
Persecution: Early Christian, 66; in Japan, 265-66; in Korea, 88-89; in the Philippines, 352-53; of Protestants, 152-55; Roman Empire and, 203-204
Peru, 186-93
Peruvian Alliance Church, the, 192
Peruvian Bible Institute, the, 192
Peter the apostle, 65, 203
Philip II, 263
Philippine Independent Church, 273
Philippines, the, 271-73, 340-57
Philippine Student Alliance Lay Movement, the, 347-48
Phnom Penh, 114
Pichardo, Rolando, 180
Pietist Movement, the, 208, 209
Pioneer evangelism, 54-55, 58
Pippert, Leslie, 244
Piura, Peru, 193
Pizarro, Francisco, 122, 186
Pliny the Younger, 204
Pobee, John S., 9
Pocock, John, 376
Politics, religion and, 154
Polo, Marco, 261
Pol Pot, 108, 114
Pope John Paul II, 129
Pope Paul III, 8
Port Gentil, Gabon, 18, 25
Port Harcourt, Nigeria, 50-51
Porto Alegre, Brazil, 142, 143
Portugal, 5, 122, 139
Post, Walter M., 316
Prayer Directory, The, 214
Presbyterian Church, the, 86; in Brazil, 139; in Colombia, 152; in Guatemala, 177; in Korea, 88; in Taiwan, 275
Protestants: in Argentina, 130; in Asia, 72-73; in Brazil, 138; in China, 109, 274; in Japan, 334; early Latin American, 124-27; in the Guianas, 194; in the Pacific islands, 260
PSALM. See Philippine Student Alliance Lay Movement
Publishing, Alliance: Argentina, 137; Brazil, 143; Burkina Faso, 17; Chile, 151; Colombia, 161; Ecuador, 175; Gabon, 25; Guinea, 33; Hong Kong, 291; India, 85; Indonesia, 303-304; Ivory Coast, 41; Mali, 49; Nigeria, 53; Peru, 193; Philippines, 346-47; Thailand, 103; Zaire, 61

Pueblo Libre Church, 188, 189
Punjabi peoples, the, 372
Punta Arenas, Chile, 145

Q

Quezon City, the Philippines, 342
Quiroz, Nidia, 162
Quito, Ecuador, 168-73
Quito Training Center, the, 173
Quran, the, 69, 224, 234, 262

R

Radio, Alliance: Argentina, 137; Burkina Faso, 17; Chile, 146, 148, 151;
    Colombia, 159-60, 161 ; Gabon, 25; Guatemala, 181; Guinea, 33; Hong
    Kong, 291-92 ; India, 78, 80, 85; Indonesia, 304; Ivory Coast, 34, 35-36,
    41; Laos, 118; Mali, 49; Nigeria, 53; Peru, 190, 193; Thailand, 103;
    Vietnam, 119; Zaire, 61
Radio Esperanza, Chile, 146
Radio HCJB, Quito, 171, 174, 175
Ramabai, Pandita, 81-82
Ramabai Mukti Mission, India, 81-82
Ramali, Lebanon, 235
Rambo, David L., 52, 345, 346
Rangoon, Burma, 372
Rawalpindi, Pakistan, 372
Reed, W. E., 171
Reeducation camps, 115, 117-18
Reformation, the, 122, 207-208, 254, 262
Reformed Church of the Netherlands, the, 268
Refugees, Viet Nam, 276, 282, 289
Refugee work, France, 240-41
Reincarnation, 68, 138
Reischauer, Edwin O., 330, 331, 333
Relief aid, 44, 178
Religions, traditional: in Taiwan, 274; West African, 4-5, 6
Religiosity, African, 4
Religious: change, Ecuador, 168-69; competition, Asian, 66-70; liberty, Peru,
    192; toleration, Guinea, 33
Republic of China, the. See Taiwan
Retention, Chile, 149
Revival, Korean, 88
Rhenish Missionary Society, the, 268
Richardson, Don, 329
Rifflart Alliance Church, 57-58
Rio de Janeiro, Brazil, 138
Rivera, Jose and Nora, 197
Roberts, W. Dayton, 129
Robertson, Eliza J., 220, 224
Roman Catholic Church. See Catholic Church; Roman Empire, the, 66,
    203-204
Russians, 32

S

Sahel, the, 43-44
St. Joseph University, Beirut, 232
Saint Patrick, 205-206
Salesians of Dom Bosco, the, 212
Salvador, Brazil, 138
Salvador, Ricardo, 182
Samaritan's Purse, 236, 366
Samurai, the, 270, 334-35
Sande, Andrew, 309
San Martin, Jose de, 125, 192
San Salvadore, 181
Santiago, Chile, 146-47
Santiago, Dominican Republic, 166
Santidougou station, Burkina Faso, 13
Santo Domingo, Dominican Republic, 166
Sao Paulo, Brazil, 138, 142, 143
Saviour's Evangelical Church, Mali, 50, 52, 53
Schaefer, Richard J., 244
Scheut Fathers, the, 212
Schism, Roman Catholic, Philippines, 273
Scranton, George, 163
Seeheim, Germany, 244-45, 247
Seleucia, 65
Seminar for Urban Evangelism and Leadership, 189
Seminario Biblico Latinoamericano, 162
Seoul, Korea, 86
Seventh Day Adventists, 345
Shamanism, Korean, 86
Shangri-La, 320
Shibuya Church, Tokyo, 338
Shimabara Rebellion, the, 266
Shintoism, 271, 333, 339
Shusaku Endo, *Silence,* 332-33
Sierra Leone, 7
Sihanouk, Norodom, 108, 114, 115
Sikhism, Indian, 77
Silence (Shusaku Endo), 332-33
Simpson, A. B., 89, 90, 220, 224, 380; African missions and, 7; Chile and,
    146, 150; India and, 83; Irian Jaya and, 316; Japan and, 336; the
    Philippines and, 353; Timbuktu and, 42; on unreached peoples, 370;
    Zaire and, 58
Simpson Theological Seminary, Java, 301
Sino-British Joint Declaration, Hong Kong, 283-85
Sixth Circle Alliance Church, Jordan, 238
Slave trade, the, 8
Smalley, William F., 228, 229-30; on A. E. Thompson, 220; on Jewish con-
    verts, 217-18; in Jordan, 225-26
Smart, Raymond, 248
Smith, Alfredo, 148, 173, 186
Snow, Frank, 261-62

Society of Jesus, the, 212, 262, 265
Soka Gakkai, 333
Sonson, Colombia, 159-60
Sorcerers, Shamanist, Korean, 86
Sorcery, 138
So Sang Yun, 87
South Korea, 86-91
Souvanna Phouma, 109
Spain, 122, 253-57
Spanish-American War, the, 353
Spanish Inquisition, the, 122, 124, 125, 254-55
Special Economic Zones, Hong Kong, 283, 285
Specialized ministries, Guinea, 26
Spener, Philip, 208
Spiritism: in Brazil, 138, 139, 143; in Mali, 48
Spradlin, Byron, 215
Stephen the apostle, 202
Stewardship Ministries, 363
Stichting Alliance Zendings Centrum "Parousia," 250
Stockton, Betsey, 211-212
Straits of Magellan, the, 145
Sudan Interior Mission, the, 7
Suen Douh Camp, Hong Kong, 292, 293
Sulawesi, 298
Sulu Archipelago, the, 341, 351
Surabaja pietists, the, 268
Surinam, 194-95
Suwatchalapinum, Vaneda, 99, 100
Suzanne, 31
Syncretism, European, 213
Syria, 229-31, 236-38

T

Taipei, 279
Taiwan, 104, 269, 274-81
Taiwan Alliance Theological College, 278
Tamerlane, 70
T'ang dynasty, the, 70
Taoism, Chinese, 110
Tarbox, Edward T., 169
Target 400, 340
Target 100,000, 340
Target 2.2.2, 340
Taylor, Hudson, 7, 72
TEAR Fund of England, 236, 242, 366
Teke peoples, Zaire, 54
Telekoro Bible Institute, Guinea, 32
Templo Alianza, 171, 173, 174
Temporary Housing Areas, Hong Kong, 287
Temuco, Chile, 145-46
Teng, Philip, 278, 286, 288, 289

Tentmakers, 367, 378
Terranova, Carmelo, 136, 137
Thai Congress on Evangelism, the, 97-98
Thailand, 92-103
Theological Education by Extension, 25; Argentina, 132; Chile, 149; Costa Rica, 164; Dominican Republic, 167; Guatemala, 177, 181; Indonesia, 301, 303; Irian Jaya, 325; Mexico, 184; Peru, 190; the Philippines, 346; Venezuela, 197
Theological institute, Santiago, 149
Theravada, 68, 92
Tianamen Square massacre, the, 281, 285, 293, 379
Thiessen, John Caldwell, 204-205; on German Christianity, 245-46; on the Korean Church, 88; on the Moravian Brethren, 209; on Thailand, 92
Third World missions, Asian, 73
Thomas the apostle, 65, 75; in China, 70; in India, 65-66; martyrdom of, 66
Thompson, A . E., 220, 225
Thompson, James, 126, 152, 169, 183, 192
"Three-Self Patriotic Movement," China, 109-110
Tienou, Tite, 10
Timbuktu, Mali, 42, 49
Timor, 299
Tin Lanh, 117-19
Tolliver, Ralph, 260
Tomeoka Kosuke, 333
Tomlin, Jacob, 94
Toure, Sekou, 26, 33
Tozer, A. W., 80
Traditional religions. See Religions, traditional
Transmigrants, in Irian Jaya, 328
Trans World Radio, 80, 160, 196, 197, 292
Treaty of Nanking, the, 283
Tribal Bible School, Mindanao, 344
Trumbell, David, 144
Tryggvason, Olaf, 206

U

Ujung Pandang, 296, 298, 301
Ukumbearik, 321, 322
Unemployment, Zaire, 56
Union Biblical Seminary, 79, 84
Union Church, Chile, 144
Union of Alliance Churches in France, 242
Union Theological Seminary, 272
United Christian Council, the, 216
United Church of Christ in Japan, 337
United East India Company, 267, 268
United Nations, the, 43
Universal Declaration of Human Rights, the, 217
University of Conakry, Guinea, 31
University of St. Thomas Aquinas, the, 124
University of Santo Tomas, Manila, 356, 357

Unreached peoples, 369-72, 378, 380
Urbanization, Japanese, 339
Uruguay, 135-36
Uruguay Alliance, the, 136

V

Valdivia, Chile, 145, 150
Valdivia Alliance Church, the, 145
Valencia, Spain, 256-57
Valencia, Venezuela, 197, 199
Valparaiso, 144
Vatican II, 129, 155, 255
Venezuela, 196-99
Viet Nam, 105-108, 116-19
Vietnamese peoples, in France, 241
Viet Nam Missionary Vision, 248
Vina del Mar, Chile, 144
Violence, Colombian, 152
"Voix de la Bible," 12-13
Vo Nguyen Giap, 107
Voodoo, 138
Voth, Myron, 136
Voth, Peter A., 94
Vuta, Kawl T., 372

W

Wagner, Peter, 330, 334
Walker, Alan, 213
Wall Street Journal, The, on Christianity, 380
Warfare, spiritual, Brazil, 143
Warner, Timothy, 334
Watts, Isaac, 209
Weiss, Henry, 145, 149-50
Westernization, Ivory Coast, 34
West Kalimantan, 299
Westmeier, Karl-Wilhelm, 153, 154
White, Bessie, 196
White, Charlotte H., 211
White, Elizabeth, 340, 354
White Fathers, the, 212
Willfinger, John, 309
Williams, Channing M., 270
Williams, Theodore, 74, 77
Willibrord, 206, 211
Wilson, Daniel, 211
Winter, Ralph D., 211, 379
Wissel, F. J., 316
Wissel Lakes, Irian Jaya, 317, 319
Witness schools, Irian Jaya, 325
Wolff, Joseph, 210
Womens' Missionary Prayer Fellowship, the, 348, 364

World Christian Encyclopedia, The (Barrett), 4, 64
World Council of Churches, the, 10, 89
World Missionary Conference, the, 127-28, 212
World Radio Missionary Fellowship, the, 171
World Relief Corporation of the U. S., 242, 366
World Relief of Canada, 366
World War II, missionaries and: in Bali, 309-310; in Irian Jaya, 318-19; in Japan, 337-38; in the Philippines, 356-57
Wu, Empress Dowager, 70
Wu Tsung, Emperor, 70
Wycliffe translators, Ecuador, 174

X

Xavier, Francis, 71, 262, 263, 265, 331, 334

Y

Yamoussoukro, Ivory Coast, 13
"The Year of the Protestants," Mali, 44
Youth: camps, Alliance, 103; complex, Ivory Coast, 35; drain, Taiwan, 279; work, Mexico, 184
Yuan dynasty, China, 70

Z

Zacharias, Ravi, 78
Zaire, 7, 8, 54-61
Zamboanga City, the Philippines, 344, 348, 349 , 351, 353
Zaragoza, Spain, 257
Zimmerman, Stella, 176
Zinzendorf, Nicolaus Ludwig, 208
ZOA of Netherlands, the, 242, 366
Zwemer, Samuel, 71, 223

The Christian and Missionary Alliance